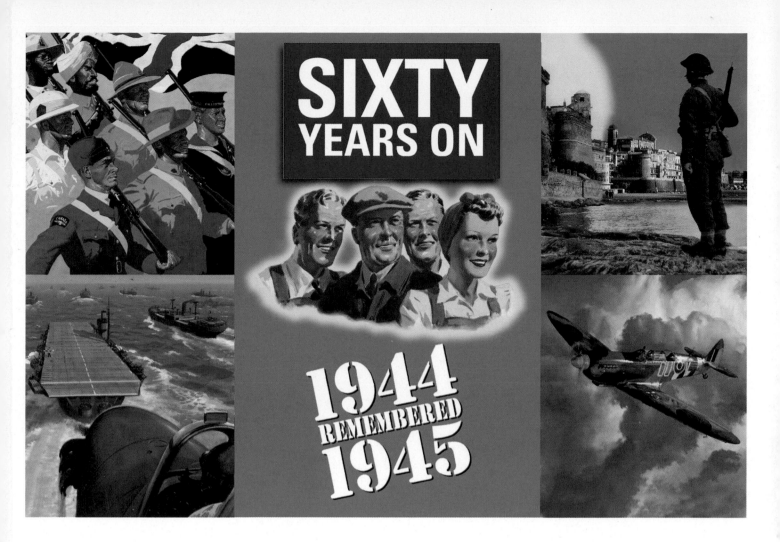

"I see the world being slowly transformed into a wilderness, I hear the approaching thunder that, one day, will destroy us too, I feel the suffering of millions. And yet, when I look up at the sky, I somehow feel that everything will change for the better, that this cruelty too shall end, that peace and tranquility will return once more."

ANNE FRANK

Born 1929.
Betrayed to the Nazis in August 1944.
Died in Auschwitz – Birkenau Concentration Camp, March 1945.

SIXTY YEARS ON

'Souvenir' - this evocative photograph was in fact taken on 5 June 1954 - the day before the 10th anniversary of D-Day. The young boy is chipping off the plaster '1944' on a remant of Hitler's Atlantic Wall at Courseulles-sur-Mer, the first port in France to be liberated.

The United Nations was founded in 1945. As the World War was coming to an end, the organisation symbolised hope for the future and as the original artwork for this poster states: 'Freedom from Fear'.

Contents

SIXTY YEARS ON

FOREWORD

By DAME VERA LYNN

Time passes so quickly, is it really more than six decades since the nation rejoiced at the end of the Second World War?

The stories and the images of the heroism, the pain, and the compassion still linger in the memory. Most of all I remember the spirit that held us all together. I do believe that much of the essence of that spirit is to be found in this book that contains so many stories of the lives of ordinary people - servicemen and women, civilians and children - all caught up in those extraordinary times.

I went out to entertain the troops in Burma in 1944, and it was there that I realised just what our boys were undergoing every day; constantly in danger and existing in the severest of conditions, yet they never lost their tenacity.

One of my greatest regrets is that I was unable to keep a diary as it was forbidden in case of capture. When I arrived home, I did record a lot of what had happened, but that is not the same as a day-by-day account. I wish I could remember all the names and faces but at least now through this book *Sixty Years On*, the story of the two final years of the war is recorded in fascinating detail. I have been especially enthralled at the many contributions written by individuals who experienced great sorrow and loss and sometimes joy. Some of the stories are being told for the very first time, perhaps because only now with the passage of the years has an author's memory permitted the telling of a traumatic tale that otherwise might have been lost to the world.

I still receive letters and cards from around the world. The troops and the people I met during this time were all so friendly and kind. I shall never forget them.

Sincerely Yours,

Vera Lynn

Dame Vera Lynn DBE, LLD

SIXTY YEARS ON

Original artwork for Ministry of Information wartime posters reproduced in Sixty Years On *by kind permission of the National Archives – Art of War.*

Introduction

When we began the series *Sixty Years On* in the **csma** magazine *Motoring & Leisure* in January 2004, I had an inkling it would prove of interest to quite a number of people. But I did not imagine just how many folk would respond to it. At times I was simply overwhelmed.

The concept was simple. To unfold in print, almost day by day, the story of the years 1944 and 1945 and invite ordinary people to add tales of their own experiences or that of family or friends who lived through those turbulent times. There was, of course, a lot to unfold.

Let me set the scene. As the year 1944 opened, Hitler's legions still held sway over most of the Continent with nations under Nazi thrall from the Arctic Circle to the Greek islands; from the Black Sea to the Pyrenees. At sea the deadly U-Boats continued to menace Britain's maritime lifeline and there was talk of sinister new 'Vengeance' weapons being developed in secret by German scientists.

In the Far East, Allied forces were locked in battle with the Japanese whose militarist creed made them a fanatical and cruel opponent.

Yet by the late spring of 1945 the 'Great Crusade' against the Fascist beast had prevailed and the Allies occupied a shattered Fatherland of smashed cities peopled by crushed and broken spirits. Japan fought on, determined to exact a staggering price in Allied lives should their enemies dare invade the Home Islands. Yet within a few months of the demise of Hitler and Nazism, Japan too was forced to admit defeat in the face of the most terrible weapons ever used in anger - the atom bombs dropped on the cities of Hiroshima and Nagasaki.

Here was history on an awesome scale and within living memory for many.

So it was that the *Sixty Years On* series began 'in time' in January 1944 with a major development in the Italian Campaign. The amphibious landings at Anzio and Nettuno within striking distance of Rome that month were intended to bypass the impasse at Cassino. The plan didn't succeed. For the rest of the war, the fighting in Italy was hard and bloody and very costly to friend, foe and civilians alike. But there were many survivors and lots of them submitted their stories together with photographs and wartime mementos.

It was a pattern to be repeated again and again as *Sixty Years On* moved in time and place through 1944. Memories of preparations for the invasion of Europe and D-Day itself; the terrible Battle of Normandy and the euphoria of the Breakout that took the Allies in a matter of days from the Seine almost to the borders of the Reich.

We heard from people who were children at the time; their recollections of vast armadas on the sea and in the air and of Doodlebugs and fearsome V2 rockets. Hundreds of stories, long and short, some very funny and others unbelievably sad, came in each month following another instalment of *Sixty Years On*. Soon I noticed that many people were asking the same question. Would we consider publishing the series in an omnibus book? The answer was an emphatic 'yes' but, of course, we had to first finish the series. And so the 60th anniversary of *Operation Market Garden* came and was duly commemorated. Then the Ardennes Offensive, better known to many as the Battle of the Bulge and, later, the crossing of the Rhine and the end of the war in Europe. In the Far East there was fighting in the jungle in Burma and across the islands of the vast Pacific Ocean. This was truly a World War.

Next I had to consider how best to present an omnibus book. The series had taken on a momentum of its own; stories were published that were not necessarily in chronological order. Nor were we absolutely rigid

The book *Sixty Years On* was first published in Great Britain in 2005 by Motoring & Leisure Services Ltd, Britannia House, 21 Station Street, Brighton BN1 4DE. Tel: 01273 744721.

Printed by Stones the Printers. Print managed by Communisis UK Ltd.
Repro and Origination by Oliver & Graimes Design Associates Ltd.

about only publishing contributions that related solely to 1944 or 1945; servicemen and women and civilians in those years had already lived through half a decade of conflict that was in itself packed with incident and action. In the book I have tried to maintain a chronology to the timeline from January 1944 to November 1945. Reading the book from start to finish will hopefully present a seamless story of the years in question. However, there are plenty of excursions and detours along the way that I very much hope give added interest.

A *Sixty Years On* book, it seemed to me, also needed to have a 'top and tail', something to set the scene prior to '44 and place the formal Japanese surrender on 3 September 1945 in context. To fulfill these aims I've included a summary of the period 1918 to 1939 and the war years up until the end of 1943. I have also taken the day-by-day diary of events up until 11 November 1945. It was the date of the very first Remembrance Day dedicated to the fallen of two World Wars and as such seems wholly appropriate.

I have been extraordinarily fortunate in that two writers of consummate skill who both lived through 1944 and 1945 have made significant contributions to *Sixty Years On*. The astonishing experiences of D-Day veteran Christopher Portway make gripping reading while the tales of former Telegram delivery boy Ron McGill are by turns humourous, always evocative and often intensely moving.

Luck was with me as well in that the National Archives took the opportunity in 2005 to catalogue for the first time their collection of the original artwork for hundreds of wartime illustrations and paintings produced for the Ministry of Information. They kindly gave me access to this 'Art of War' collection and many unique works from it are published for the very first time in this book. More good fortune came when Dame Vera Lynn most graciously gave her support to the concept of *Sixty Years On*.

So here is the book. It's an irony that though the subject matter is six decades and more in the past it has been very, very hard work to put it all together in a very short period of time.

I have tried to smooth out any rough edges but I hope I'll be forgiven if the printer's devil has been up to mischief on any of the pages. We can put the record straight in the Second Edition! The hardest task of all, though, has been deciding on what goes in and what doesn't, especially as so many people took so much trouble to write their stories. Every submission was appreciated and valued; in the end, however, I had to look for as balanced and varied a content as possible, reflecting the myriad aspects and elements of those extraordinary times. I very much hope I've achieved these aspirations but in the final analysis it is you, the readers, who will be the judges.

A corner of a Foreign Field...

Royal Scots Fusilier George 'Geordie' Kane was killed at Anzio on 18 April 1944. At 28 years of age, Geordie was a veteran who had survived the Dunkirk evacuation and another four years of soldiering before taking part in the Italian Campaign. At the time of the Anzio landings in January he was with the British forces along the Garigliano river, some 80 miles south of the beach-head. The Second Battalion of the Royals Scots Fusiliers were withdrawn from the Minturno area in late February 1944, reformed and then sent by sea to reinforce the Allied forces who had suffered many casualties. By 9 March the whole Battalion had disembarked at Peter Beach, north of the port of Anzio, and were in position along the left flank of the beach-head.

The exact circumstances of Geordie's death are unknown to his family, shellfire being the most likely cause. He is buried in the Beach-Head War Cemetery at Anzio, as are many fellow servicemen. Geordie left a widow in Ayr, Scotland, together with three children, the youngest of whom he was never to see for the soldier was posted before the birth of his last daughter.

For over 45 years no member of Geordie's family had ever been to Anzio to visit his grave. Not at all an unusual thing in the aftermath of a war in which so many died. But then in 1988, Geordie's older sister Elizabeth Huxley of High Hurstwood in East Sussex began to talk more and more of Geordie. His picture had been on display in her house for decades past. In the spring of that same year, Mrs Huxley's daughter Barbara was able to take a weekend break in Rome. She and her husband hired a car and drove out of the city for an hour or so until they came to Anzio. There they located the Beach-Head Cemetery and found the grave of Fusilier Kane, maintained wonderfully well as if Geordie had died just weeks before and not four and half decades ago. Barbara was able to bring home photographs for her mum showing the headstone and cemetery, together with the story of how Geordie's memory is preserved in such a pristine setting in that far-off corner of a foreign land. Geordie's sister Elizabeth herself died just a few months later.

However, that journey to Anzio achieved more than serve to revive the memory of Geordie and bring some comfort to his sister Lizzie's last days. For out of that poignant visit came also the ultimate inspiration for *Sixty Years On*. You see, Geordie's niece, Barbara, is my wife.

David Arnold, Editor, *Sixty Years On*

Epitaph to the Great War 1914 -1918. Nearly 10,000,000 soldiers, sailors and airmen from all the countries involved were killed in battle and some 6,000,000 crippled or invalided for life. Countless thousands of civilians also died. When it was over the League of Nations vowed 'never again'. Twenty one years later the world went once more to war. How did it happen?

The Path To WAR

The origins of World War Two are to be found in the aftermath of the 1914-1918 Great War. Germany felt aggrieved at the peace terms imposed by the French and British victors and their allies. The punitive Treaty of Versailles, signed on 28 June 1919, limited the size of the German army to 100,000 men and restricted the navy to 36 warships. At the same time it imposed territorial penalties with France regaining Alsace-Lorraine, which the Prussians had taken from her in 1871. Poland was also granted a strip of German land; the 'Polish Corridor' gave the Poles access to the Baltic at Danzig, which was made a League of Nations trust territory. Germany was also required to pay massive war reparations.

This humbling of the Fatherland was deeply resented by the German army generals. Many of them took the view that they had, in fact, not actually been defeated by the French, British and United States armies. The war had ended with an armistice, a poorly negotiated one in the German military view, and not an unconditional surrender.

Even so, Germany remained the biggest economic power in Central Europe, a position reinforced by the post-war disbanding of the Hapsburg's defeated Austro-Hungarian Empire. A new country, Czechoslovakia, was sanctioned as a direct result and part of its territory, the Sudetenland, was dominated by a population of German origin.

Germany's continuing importance was also reinforced through the effects of the Treaty of Brest-Litovsk. Signed in March 1918, this document saw the Bolsheviks withdrew from the war. Even though the Treaty was repudiated within eight months, territorial concessions prevailed and these included independence for Poland and Finland. The latent might of Russia was marginalized.

Versailles also led to the foundation of the League of Nations, an international forum where nations could settle their problems by mutual agreement rather than war.

Adolf Hitler is the man most responsible for provoking World War II. Here he is reviewing a parade of his infamous 'Brownshirts' at a Nazi rally in Nuremberg in 1927. The name Nazi was derived from letters contained in Nationalsa Zlatstiche Deutsche Arbeiter Parteir (National Socialist German Workers Party). The Swastika is a very old, sacred symbol with links to the Hindu and Buddhist cultures. In his book Mein Kampf, Hitler wrote of the device, 'In the red we see the social idea of the Nazi movement, in the white the Nationalist idea and in the Swastika the vision of the struggle for the victory of the Aryan man.'

Unfortunately, the League lacked the will and the power to influence world affairs right from the start, a situation not improved by the failure of the USA to join. Instead, the most powerful country on earth withdrew into isolationism, leaving Europe and the rest of the world to fend for itself.

Economic disaster

In the early Twenties, economic disaster struck Germany. The fastest and most disastrous monetary inflation ever known destroyed the value of the German currency and plunged millions of citizens into poverty almost overnight. It required millions of Marks simply to purchase a loaf of bread.

Germany's Weimar Republic of the time was a coalition government that had replaced the autocratic rule of the Kaiser. It proved ineffective and its unpopularity was not helped when a League of Nations-imposed plebiscite resulted in part of Upper Silesia

being given to Poland. Political weakness coupled with a dire economic climate created the conditions where a strong character with a simple message of national ambition would be sure of an eager audience.

Adolf Hitler strode onto Germany's political stage in 1923. With a group of right wing, thuggish supporters he made a first attempt to seize power in 1923 in what became known as the Beer Hall Putsch. It failed and Hitler was sent to gaol for nine months. In prison he wrote *Mein Kampf* (My Struggle), his blueprint for the future of Germany and its place in the world. Anti-Semitism and the policy of *Lebensraum* - Germany's right to take 'living space' by force from its eastern neighbours - were enshrined in the book.

For the next 10 years Hitler slowly but surely gathered support for his National Socialist Party - the Nazis. The Great Depression that hit the world's stock markets in October 1929 gave him a big boost; Hitler's promises to bring full employment and make Germany militarily strong again found broad appeal in a country where a third of working men were without jobs.

By 1932 the Nazis had won 230 seats in the Reichstag parliament. On 30 January 1933 the respected but ageing President Hindenburg felt obliged to offer the Chancellorship of Germany to Hitler. Though he had achieved power via the ballot box he was determined that he would never lose it through the same process. When Hindenburg died in 1934, Hitler declared himself President as well as Chancellor, assumed command of Germany's military and called himself 'Fuhrer', leader of the Third Reich and its people.

Hitler was not the first dictator to emerge in Europe in the years following the Great War. Benito Mussolini had led the Italian Fascist party to power in 1922 after marching on Rome and demanding that the king appoint them to govern the country. Mussolini did indeed embark on a major public works programme and famously made 'the trains run on time'. But he too harboured ambitions of empire and in 1935 he sent an army across the border from Italian Somaliland into independent Ethiopia.

Militarist Japan

Meanwhile, on the other side of the world, the Empire of Japan was on the rise. Lacking in natural resources on their home islands, a militarist creed held sway with influential politicians and senior officers. Japan invaded Manchuria in 1931 and in 1932 changed the country's name to Manchukuo; it had become a Japanese colony. A Chinese boycott of trade with Japan resulted in an attack on Shanghai. Incidents and annexations of parts of China continued in the following years until, in July 1937, the Japanese decided they must overthrow the Chinese Nationalist leader, Chiang Kai-shek, and conquer the whole of China.

In the previous year, 1936, it came as no surprise to some observers - including Winston Churchill - when Germany and Italy first established the Rome - Berlin Axis of Fascist States. A few months later, Hitler concluded a treaty - the Anti-Comintern Pact - with Japan. The three most militarily aggressive countries in the world were thus in alliance and bent on pursuing their individual territorial aims at any cost.

Hitler was now pushing his luck and testing the resolve of the French and British. In 1935 he had reintroduced conscription and brought in extensive rearmament programmes. All German soldiers, sailors and airmen had to swear an oath of personal loyalty to him as their Fuhrer. In 1936 the *Wehrmacht* marched into the Rhineland, de-militarised under the Treaty of Versailles. France and Britain took no steps to punish

Hitler's action. But both countries were now looking at their own armaments situation and discovering serious shortcomings.

Civil War broke out in Spain in 1936 when General Franco led a Fascist revolt against the newly democratically elected Government. The latter did not cave in and a bitter conflict ensued that polarised the divisions between right and left. Hitler and Mussolini sent troops and aircraft to aid Franco and took advantage of the opportunity for a dress rehearsal of the far, far bigger war to come. The Soviet leader Stalin sent aid for the Republican side who were also bolstered by the arrival of volunteers from all over Europe, especially Britain. Unfortunately, part of the cost of Stalin's help was political infighting between the different Communist factions and left-wing bodies that resulted in many deaths. The war ended with a Franco victory early in 1939 but so war-wracked and exhausted was Spain by then that the Generalissimo wisely adopted a neutral stance as the war clouds gathered elsewhere in Europe.

For his part, Stalin had already hamstrung his own armed forces in Russia with a deadly purge of the most senior generals and officers. He was paranoid of plots, real or imagined, against his total control of the Soviet Union.

On 12 March 1938 Hitler ordered *Anschluss*, the annexation of Austria, a mission accomplished in two days. He next turned his attention to Czechoslovakia where the Sudetenland border area was already an issue, being populated in the main by ethnic Germans; its transfer to Germany had been imposed only in 1918.

The British attempted to negotiate the problem but Hitler held firm. At a crucial

meeting in Munich, British Premier Neville Chamberlain felt he had extracted the best deal possible with Hitler. He returned to Croydon Airport with that infamous piece of paper and the words, 'Peace in our Time'.

Sudetenland occupied

There was no peace for the Czechs. The Germans marched into the Sudetenland. Within a short time, Poland and Hungary took the opportunity to occupy smaller parts of Czechoslovakia where a majority of Poles and Magyrs were resident.

Hitler next demanded German control of the rest of the country. In March 1939 he made his move. German and Hungarian forces took control of the remaining Czechoslovakian land. On 16 March Hitler himself went to Prague to proclaim Bohemia and Moravia as German Protectorates.

Now it was Poland's turn to take centre stage. Britain and France tried to enlist Russia's aid in guaranteeing military assistance for Poland in the event of a German attack. When Russia asked for a similar pact for themselves, they were astonished when Chamberlain refused. Put simply it meant that Britain and France wanted Russia's help if an attack on Poland led to Germany being at war with them but the two western countries were not prepared to side with the Soviet Union in the event of a German attack on Russia. The problem was that Britain and France were suspicious of Stalin and believed that the long term aim of the Soviets was to spread Communism and revolution.

Next occurred one of the great *volte faces* in history. Unable to reach an agreement with Hitler's adversaries, the Russians concluded a pact with the Nazis. Signed on 23 August 1939, the deal effectively sealed Poland's fate; both Hitler and Stalin had agreed on the partition of that country following an imminent invasion by the Germans that was to be followed up by a Soviet move into the eastern part.

On 25 August the British Government signed a Treaty of Mutual Assistance with Poland. Hitler paused for a week during which he demanded that the Poles give up territory or face war. The Poles refused. The Luftwaffe commenced the bombing of Warsaw on 1 September. Britain's latest ally was under attack. The House of Commons demanded that Chamberlain send an ultimatum to Hitler. It was duly despatched as was a similar one by the French. The British ultimatum expired at 9am on 3 September. The furious German assault on Poland continued unabated. That same day Britain and France found themselves at war in Europe, just 21 years after the end of the Great War, the war that was supposed to end all wars.

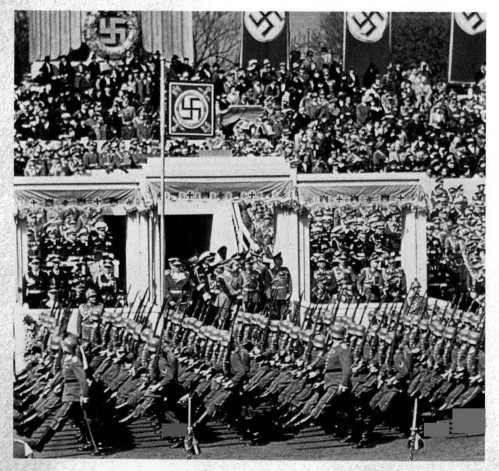

Hitler paid no heed to the restrictions on Germany's armed forces imposed by the Treaty of Versailles and quickly built up a powerful modern army, air force and navy. The parade here was held in Berlin on 20 April 1939 in celebration of the Fuhrer's 50th birthday.

THE DAILY MAIL, Monday, September 4, 1939

Daily Mail

FOR KING AND EMPIRE

NO. 13,529   MONDAY, SEPTEMBER 4, 1939   ONE PENNY

BRITAIN & FRANCE AT WAR WITH GERMANY

We meet a challenge which would be fatal to civilised order —THE KING

OUR NEW WAR CABINET

GREAT BRITAIN AND FRANCE ARE AT WAR WITH GERMANY.

At nine o'clock yesterday morning Germany was informed that unless Britain received satisfactory assurance by 11 a.m. that Germany had stopped aggressive action in Poland "a state of war would exist as from that hour."

At 11.15 Mr. Chamberlain announced to the nation that "no such undertaking has been received and this country is at war with Germany."

France delivered a similar ultimatum to Germany at noon, to exp— at 5 p.m. At that hour she considered—
declaration of—

Churchill as First

The King's Message

BROADCASTING to the Empire last night, the King said: "In this grave hour, perhaps the most fateful in our history, I send to every household of my people both at home and overseas this message, spoken with the same depth of feeling for each one of you as if I were able to cross your threshold and speak to you myself.

"For the second time in the lives of most of us we are at war.

"Over and over again we have tried to find a peaceful way out of the differences between ourselves and those who are now our enemies. But it has been in vain.

"We have been forced into a conflict. For we are called with our allies to meet the challenge of a principle which, if it were to prevail, would be fatal to any civilised order in the world.

Pursuit of Power

"It is the principle which permits a State in the selfish pursuit of power to disregard its treaties and its solemn pledges; which sanctions the use of force or threat of force against the sovereignty and independence of other States.

"Such a principle stripped —

Poles Launch Counter-attack

POLAND yesterday launched her counter-attack. She struck at East Prussia in the Deutsch Eglan sector. After violent fighting the town of Zbaszyn, taken by the Germans on Saturday, was recaptured.

The Polish attack suggests that a German claim on Saturday that their forces driving east and west across the neck of the Corridor had made contact was unfounded.

In the south violent fighting was reported around Czestochowa, the Lourdes of Poland. The Germans claimed that the town had fallen, and the Poles admitted that it was in flames.

North of Czestochowa, the Germans claimed to have captured the —— Wielun, after crossing t—— Warthe. Polish sources —— town's municipal h—— during the attack, —— miles from the G—— Eastern front.

Polish radio —— night that W—— camp in D—— resisting Ge——

The camp —— times, was —— cruiser——

GE——

POLES SMASH WAY INTO EAST PRUSSIA

Warsaw, Sunday.

Officials in Warsaw to-night state that the Polish Army has smashed a way across the northern border into East Prussia, after driving the Germans from several Polish towns in bitter fighting.

On the northern front the Poles are reported to have defeated the German effort to drive a barrier across the upper part of the Corridor by driving the Germans back across the border.

The Poles say they have broken through the German fortifications as far as the railway terminus of Deutsch Eylau. One of the most important towns recaptured is stated to be Zbaszyn.—British United Press.

CONVOY AGAIN

THE STORM BREAKS

Below: Map from News Review, 21 September 1939

The War 1939 - 43

Poland fought hard for three weeks before her poorly-equipped army and obsolete air force were finally overwhelmed. At this point the Russians moved into eastern Poland, largely unopposed. They took into captivity some 200,000 Polish servicemen. A number of these would live to fight another day either with the Red Army or with the Western Allies, where their bitterness at the fate of their country and knowledge of the privations visited upon their families would turn them into dauntless airmen and soldiers of the highest calibre.

In Britain the period following the subjugation of Poland became known as the 'Phoney War'. Anticipated German air attacks spreading bombs and lethal gas amidst British cities did not materialise. Children were evacuated, a black-out was imposed and rationing entered the lives of everyone.

It was different at sea. German submarines began sinking British warships and merchant vessels. In October 1939 a U-Boat penetrated the defences of Scapa Flow in the Orkneys and sank the battleship *HMS Royal Oak* with tremendous loss of life. Two months later the Royal Navy hit back and chased the German pocket battleship *Graf Spee* into Montevideo harbour in neutral Uruguay where her captain scuttled the ship rather than risk a fight.

Outside of Britain and France, for much of Europe the war became very real indeed. Despite his unlikely pact with the Nazis, Stalin knew he could not trust Hitler. Consequently he sought to strengthen the Soviet borders by taking back into the Kremlin's fold, by force if necessary, those countries that had been given their independence and freedom some two decades earlier by the Treaty of Brest-Litovsk, ironically a peace arrangement concluded with Germany.

The Baltic States of Estonia, Latvia and Lithuania were pressured into granting rights of occupation to the Red Army. Then, on 30 November 1939, the Russians attacked Finland after the Finns had turned down the former's demands for territory and strategic bases that they considered vital for the protection of the city of Leningrad.

Hitler strikes north

In the course of the 'Winter War' the Finns, outnumbered by more than two to one, nevertheless gave the Russians a bloody nose before being finally forced to give in to Russian demands on 13 March 1940. British

Left: 'Looking for Trouble' by the celebrated aviation artist Frank Wootton. It depicts a trio of Spitfires flying in a formation that was employed by RAF fighter pilots at the outbreak of war until some months into 1940 when it was dropped in favour of the 'finger-four' formation.

public opinion had been firmly on the side of the gallant Finns. Germany gave more tangible support to the Finnish commander, General Mannerheim, in the form of arms and war materiel. Ironically, the Red Army learnt a lot of lessons about the right way to fight in the snow and frozen mud, lessons that would prove invaluable in the years ahead.

TO THE BRITISH TROOPS

"**I want to know where your unit is stationed —so that I can bomb you and drop parachute troops to machine-gun you. This information I will get from you and your friends—please continue to give your friends military details. I shall hear.**" *Lieutenant-General Schultz* GERMAN INTELLIGENCE.

A poster warning of the consequences of loose talk (National Archives - Art of War).

Less than a month after the end of the Winter War, Hitler struck north and invaded Denmark and Norway. Denmark had no chance of offering serious resistance and reluctantly gave in without a fight. German troops landed at Oslo on 9 April 1940 and, despite counter-landings by the British Army and Navy and a serious naval reverse to the *Kriegsmarine* at Narvik, were able to occupy the country.

By early May the mood of the House of Commons was very much against the Conservative Neville Chamberlain continuing as Prime Minister. A coalition government was required in the face of tribulation. Though Winston Churchill was also a Conservative it was the Labour Party that sealed the appointment of him as Prime Minister on 9 May.

The last British units withdrew from the north of Norway on 8 June but by then momentous things had occurred in mainland Europe. Hitler had ordered a simultaneous Blitzkrieg attack against France, Belgium and Holland. The defenders included the relatively small but powerful British Expeditionary Force (BEF) who were equipped with a significant proportion of Britain's operational tanks, artillery and transport. The RAF were present in force as well.

The German assault in the West began in

the early hours of 10 May 1940 with parachute troops capturing key objectives in Holland and Belgium. Then the German panzer armies erupted out of the Ardennes, a region that the vaunted French Maginot Line of 'impregnable' fortifications did not extend to. One of the panzer commanders was Erwin Rommel, demonstrating the audacity and panache that would later make him such a dangerous adversary in North Africa.

Miracle of Dunkirk

The speed and fury of the German attack threw the French and British into confusion. Holland and Belgium quit the fight in the early stages. The huge French army found itself split by the German columns and unable to function as a cohesive force. Just one French commander, Charles de Gaulle, who had long warned of the German menace, was able to put in a serious counter-attack. It failed.

The BEF at first rushed north into Belgium, according to pre-arranged plans. When the Germans reached the English Channel at Abbeville on 20 May the British turned around and headed for the Pas de Calais region. With the French in disarray and much of their army isolated from the battlefield, the BEF commander Lord Gort realised the British were trapped with their backs to the coast. Evacuation by sea offered the only escape if things continued to go badly.

Now came the 'Miracle of Dunkirk'. On 26 May Lord Gort was given permission to evacuate the BEF from France to England. Next day a perimeter was formed around Dunkirk and evacuations also commenced out of Calais and Boulogne. For some reason, three days earlier Hitler had ordered his panzers not to press home the assault and although the infantry and Luftwaffe remained very active, *Operation Dynamo* saw 338,226 British and French troops saved to fight another day.

As France went down under the German onslaught there was one remarkable lifeline thrown by Churchill; the serious proposal of an act of union between Paris and London that would bind the two countries as tightly together as that which bound England, Scotland, Wales and Northern Ireland. But it was too late for gestures, however well-intentioned.

Hitler danced a jig of delight in Paris to celebrate his crushing victory in mainland Europe. Now in the summer of 1940 Britain faced the very real prospect of a German invasion. The majority of the BEF may have escaped capture but most of their tanks, artillery and heavy weapons were destroyed or left behind. The Navy had sustained heavy losses in the course of the evacuation and

FRANCE 1940

The drawings on this page were the work of a German artist who accompanied the *Wehrmacht* on their lightning conquest of France in May and June 1940. They were published in a book that was, ironically, printed in Occupied Paris during the following year. What is noticeable in the book are the large number of horses that feature and the fact that there is just one sketch of a panzer. This reflects the fact that the German Army at this early stage of the war was still very reliant on horses for moving artillery, ammunition, food supplies and baggage. The French and British outnumbered the Germans in the numbers of tanks they possessed but it was the German generals who had developed the concept of Blitzkrieg - concentrating their armour on a narrow front to achieve a local breakthrough that could quickly be exploited, regardless of any danger to their flanks. It was a concept perfect for rendering impotent the powerful fixed defences of the Maginot Line.

The wrecked bridge below is close by Chateau Amboise in the Loire Valley. It was blown up by the French themselves.

anyway the narrow confines of the English Channel, across which the German troopships must come, would put the bigger British warships at great risk from air attack. Only the RAF remained largely intact.

Battle of Britain
In the face of the debacle in France, the Head of RAF Fighter Command, Air Marshal Sir Hugh Dowding, had insisted on keeping a significant pool of squadrons in reserve in Britain. His foresight gave the RAF the chance to deny air superiority to Luftwaffe; without this an invasion was unlikely to succeed. Fortunately the RAF had excellent aircraft in the shape of the Spitfire and Hurricane. Coupled with an efficient chain of radar stations and the closer proximity of their airfields, the RAF had just enough advantages to weather the aerial storm that opened in earnest early in August. They would win the Battle of Britain.

The turning point came on 7 September when Hitler ordered his bombers to hit London in reprisal for an earlier RAF night raid on Berlin. In consequence, attacks on RAF fighter stations lessened. London and other British cities bore the brunt of the subsequent Blitz and thousands of civilians died. But Hitler's invasion never came.

The new peril for Britain was the U-Boat. Ranging out into the Atlantic and Caribbean, they exacted a growing toll of merchant shipping. The Battle of the Atlantic would last for years and the casualty rate for the civilian crews of both the ships and the U-Boats were pro rata the highest in any theatre of war. Through improved submarine detection techniques on warships and aircraft and the cracking of the German Enigma code, the Allies would eventually overcome the U-Boat threat.

A consequence of the Fall of France was the entry of Italy into the war. In the summer of 1940, Britain and Italy squared up in the Mediterranean and on the North African shore. The British held Egypt while Italian forces were based in their colonies next door in Libya and farther west. The Royal Navy got in the first decisive blow with a devastating air attack on the Italian fleet at anchor at Taranto on 11 November. Half of Italy's fleet was sunk at a cost of two Swordfish aircraft.

Within months the triumph at sea was mirrored by a brilliant victory for General Wavell's 30,000 British and Australian troops who captured 130,000 prisoners and around 400 tanks for the loss of 500 men. The Italians would have been pushed right out of Africa but for ominous German movement in the Balkans where Mussolini's men invading from Albania were being bested by the Greek army.

Greece and Crete
Hitler was not prepared to see his Axis partner humiliated. He sent his army into Yugoslavia and also set out to conquer Greece. Wavell sent a large force to the aid of the Greeks but it was not enough to stem the German advance and an evacuation became inevitable. A stand by Greek, British and New

Zealand troops on the island of Crete was ended by an audacious German airborne assault in May. The Royal Navy also lost nine ships. To add to the British troubles, a new foe now appeared in North Africa as General Erwin Rommel's Afrika Korps took to the offensive and immediately made major gains in territory recovered from the weakened British and Commonwealth forces. The desert war would now see saw backwards and forwards for the next 18 months.

Unknown at the time, but of immense importance to the outcome of the war, was the fact that Hitler's excursion into the Balkans had cost him a delay in the launching of his next massive military gamble; *Operation Barbarossa*, the invasion of the Soviet Union. This began on 22 June 1941 when three million Germans, supported by numerous satellite armies including those of the Finns and Rumanians, launched a surprise attack on a vast front. The Germans met with dizzying early success and rounded up huge numbers of prisoners caught in a series of encircling movements. Vast tracts of land were conquered and Hitler's panzers seemed unstoppable as they moved up as far as Leningrad in the north, close to the gates of Moscow itself in the centre and beyond the city of Kharkov in the south. Stalin's greatest ally now came to the rescue as the harsh Russian winter set in to cripple the German Army's ability to wage war. The Red Army, on the other hand, was equipped for the conditions and received substantial reinforcements from Siberia. The Germans were forced to retreat and the prize of Moscow slipped through their grasp. If Hitler had been able to attack in May instead of June, those extra weeks of summer campaigning could have damaged the Russian colossus beyond recovery.

National Archives (Art of War).

Stalin's decision to bring soldiers from Siberia was made possible because of the actions of one man. Richard Sorge was a German newspaper correspondent in Tokyo who was familiar with both the German and Russian ambassadors to Japan. He was also a Russian spy. Late in 1941 the Kremlin received information from Sorge to the effect that the

Japanese had decided to go to war with the United States and Britain in the Pacific and Far East. The Soviet Union would not be a target.

War with Japan
'The Day of Infamy' came on 7 December 1941 with a surprise air attack on the US Pacific Fleet at Pearl Harbour in the Hawaiian Islands followed by attacks on US bases in the Philippine Islands and the invasion of European colonies and possessions in South East Asia. For good measure, within days Hitler declared war on America. Now it was truly a World War.

Pearl Harbour was a devastating blow to the US Navy. However, by good luck, on the day of the attack no US aircraft carriers were in the port and they were spared destruction. The Japanese and the Americans both knew that air power was going to be the key to winning a war in the Pacific; whichever side could sink more of the enemy's ships must have a winning hand.

Ironically, it was the Japanese who demonstrated this point most graphically at an early stage. Two days after Pearl Harbour, the battleship *HMS Prince of Wales* and battle cruiser *HMS Repulse* were bombed and sunk when they were caught without air cover off the coast of Malaya. The British had failed to learn their own lesson from Taranto, an operation that had been studied in depth by the Japanese commander of the Pearl Harbour attack, Admiral Yamamoto.

In the opening months of 1942, the Japanese tide of conquest seemed unstoppable. Hong Kong, Malaya, Singapore, the Philippines and most of Burma were quickly occupied and the British, Australians and Americans were in retreat everywhere and thousands of Allied servicemen and women became prisoners of the Japanese. The latter's military creed did not recognise the notion of surrender and horrendous cruelty and hardship was meted out on their unfortunate captives. Darwin in Australia was bombed and Japanese submarines raided Sydney.

However, it quickly became clear that the Japanese had vastly underestimated the resources of their enemies and over-stretched their own ability to sustain and supply their armed forces who were now spread out in battlefields ranging from the Chinese mainland to thousands of miles away in far-flung South Pacific archipelagos. They were also fighting the British army in Burma, close to the frontier with India from which country upwards of a million volunteers were coming forward to join the Allied fight. On the giant islands of New Guinea and Borneo, tough Australian troops were proving more than a match for the Japanese in jungle fighting.

In early April five Japanese aircraft carriers ventured into the Indian Ocean, threatening the British naval and air bases in Ceylon. Though the Royal Navy lost two cruisers and the aircraft carrier *Hermes* it was an inconclusive engagement that eventually saw the Japanese withdraw never to return to the area in strength. The turning point in the Pacific war came in early June 1942. Thanks to good intelligence of Japanese intentions,

TOGETHER

the Americans destroyed all the carriers in an enemy fleet that sought to capture the island of Midway. The Imperial Navy's power was broken for good in a battle fought exclusively by aircraft and where the opposing ships never got within sight of each other. The war against Japan in the Pacific now became a process of slowly grinding down the stubborn and fanatical enemy and retaking one by one the islands they'd occupied and fortified.

Afrika Korps retreats

The last quarter of 1942 saw a significant reverse for the Germans in North Africa. The Afrika Korps was in Egypt, facing the British Eighth Army near the little town of El Alamein, a halt on the rail line that hugged the North African coast from east to west. A new British commander, General Bernard Law Montgomery, had instilled enormous confidence in his men. They had received copious new armaments and were backed by

a powerful air force. In October, Montgomery's 'Desert Rats' struck. Even though Rommel was absent on sick leave in Germany, his Afrika Korps and their Italian comrades fought back hard but in the end were forced to retreat. All the way to Tunisia.

On 8 November 1942 *Operation Torch* began with a combined Anglo-American landing on the Atlantic and Mediterranean shores of French North Africa. The Germans were caught by Allied advances from east and west but instead of escaping back to Europe, Hitler sent reinforcements, even switching 400 precious aircraft from the Russian Front to Tunisia. The fighting in North Africa continued until 13 May 1943. The war in the desert had cost the Germans and Italians almost one million killed, maimed or captured.

After the extreme rigours of the Russian Winter and the Red Army's resurgence, Germany regained the initiative in the spring and summer of 1942. The siege of Leningrad continued. In the south the *Wehrmacht* scored some spectacular victories of encirclement and spilled across the vast Russian plains until it approached the banks of the Volga river at Stalingrad and threatened the Caucasus and the vital oil towns of Baku, Tiflis and Maikop. The Germans didn't have the strength to both take Stalingrad and seize the oilfields. Hitler had to choose one or the other. He chose to take Stalingrad and in doing so committed a major strategic blunder.

Battle for Stalingrad

Like a deadly magnet, the long thin city on the west bank of the Volga drew the German Sixth Army into what became an urban death trap for the *Wehrmacht*. The Russians had their backs to the river and nowhere to go. Accordingly they defended with a ferocity and intensity that shocked their enemy. More and more German units were brought up and Stalingrad was reduced to a mass of broken buildings and rubble in which the Russians clung on.

Meanwhile, the Red Army had been massing new forces on the flanks of the Sixth Army where they faced mainly Rumanian and Hungarian troops. On 19 November 1942 the Russians attacked in massive strength. Within days the lines of the Axis allies were broken and it was the turn of the Red Army to win a battle of encirclement; the entire Sixth Army of a quarter of a million men became surrounded in Stalingrad.

The Germans held out until 2 February 1943 when Field Marshal von Paulus was forced to surrender his remaining 91,000 soldiers. Hitler's hopes of defeating Stalin died along with so many of his best soldiers in and around the city on the Volga.

Invasion of Italy

Stalin had been urging the US and British armies to open a Second Front in northern Europe at the earliest opportunity to relieve pressure on the Red Army. At this stage of the

'Winter of '43 - Somewhere in England' by David Shepherd. By this stage in the war the Allied bombing offensive against Germany and military targets in Occupied Europe was gaining huge momentum. The painting depicts a Lancaster being made ready for another mission.

war, the Western Allies were simply not strong enough for such an undertaking. However, from their positions along the North African shore, it was but a small step to take the war to the land of Germany's prime Axis partner. On 10 July 1943 *Operation Husky*, the invasion of Sicily, began. Within a few weeks it led to the downfall of Mussolini who was deposed by his own Fascist Grand Council and arrested. Even without their dictator, the Italians stayed in the war but looked to secure advantageous peace terms with the Allies.

The new Prime Minister Marshal Badoglio signed a secret act of surrender on 3 September, the same day that the Allies crossed the Straits of Messina to land on the mainland of Italy. Five days later when news of the surrender was broadcast, the Germans reacted quickly to occupy Rome and pour troops into the south of the country. The Germans knew that the long 'boot and heel' of mountainous Italy favoured a defensive war and that's exactly what they proposed to fight. An Allied outflanking landing at Salerno on 9 September came close to being pushed back into the sea and was saved only by the intervention of naval gunfire and massive air support. The able German General Kesselring was charged with making the Allies pay dearly for any advance up the Italian peninsula. He withdrew just to the north of Naples and set up the Gustav Line, a defensive position defined by fast-flowing rivers, high, steep mountains and valleys where attackers could be easily detected and fired upon. The line hinged around the town of Cassino which was dominated by an ancient Benedictine monastery set high above on the top of a mountain. The mountain was Monte Cassino.

Fighting in Burma

In Burma the British had not had a good start to the year 1943 with the failure of their first real offensive against the Japanese. This took place on the stretch of coast beside the Bay of Bengal known as the Arakan. A military disaster was averted when Lieutenant-General William Slim rushed in to take command of the defeated British and Indian troops; he conducted an efficient withdrawal to the India - Burma border. Slim was later appointed commander of the newly-created Fourteenth Army, under Admiral Lord Louis Mountbatten's South-East

This portrait of General Bernard Law Montgomery featured in a 'British Heroes' poster series at the end of 1943. At the beginning of 1944, Monty's new challenge was to command the Allied ground forces gathering for the invasion of Occupied Europe. Ironically, his opponent in France would again be Rommel, whose Afrika Korp was defeated at El Alamein in November 1942 and finally chased out of North Africa by Montgomery's triumphant Eighth Army in the spring of '43.

Asia Command (SEAC). Even with this reorganisation of the command structure, there would be no major British offensives in the region for the rest of the year, although the RAF remained active and Chinese forces - backed by some American units - probed with little real effect into Northern Burma late in 1943.

After the massive defeat at Stalingrad, the Germans were forced to retreat along most of the length of the Russian Front, until better weather in the spring enabled his generals to stabilise the situation. Hitler also managed to maintain the siege of Leningrad throughout the whole of 1943. In July he was able to mass one more army, equipped with new and more heavily armoured tanks, and mount a major offensive to erase a Russian salient at Kursk in the centre of the front. Kursk turned into the greatest tank battle in history. It was another disaster for the Germans as they failed to make any substantial advance and exhausted themselves battering in vain against vast belts of minefields and Russian artillery concentrations. Tank for tank, the Germans found that the Russians too had new machines, the equivalent or better of their own.

As 1943 closed, it was estimated that close to 20,000,000 Russians had died since the war began in 1941. Hitler and his Nazi henchmen now knew they could not beat the Red Army. Their only hope was to contain the Allies in Italy and defeat the Western Allies when the inevitable invasion of Northern Europe occurred. This would free troops to be sent to reinforce the Eastern Front and stem the Russian advance. Meanwhile, German scientists were feverishly working on secret weapons that ranged from revolutionary jet fighter aircraft to devastating rocket bombs. The Nazis hoped that at least one or more of their projects would prove to be a war-winning invention.

JANUARY

The Italian Campaign

New Year 1944 opened with the Allied armies firmly established in the bottom third of the enormous boot shape thrust deep into the Mediterranean that is Italy.

In the previous summer on 10 July, *Operation Husky* had seen British and American forces successfully invade Sicily. This move was made possible through the defeat of the Axis army in Tunisia, prompting General Sir Harold Alexander to signal Churchill on 11 May: 'We are masters of the North African shore.'

Sicily is divided from the Italian mainland by the narrow Straits of Messina and a crossing was the next logical step for the Allies. In the meantime, many Italians had lost confidence in their fascist leader Mussolini - Il Duce. On 25 July he was deposed and a new government under Marshal Badoglio was formed. Badoglio insisted that Italy would remain in the Axis alliance but German suspicions were aroused; they began moving more troops into the country and made plans for the disarming of the Italians should a separate peace be struck with the Allies.

Montgomery's famous Eighth Army crossed the Straits of Messina on 3 September and six days later American General Mark Clark's Fifth Army carried out a major amphibious landing in the Gulf of Salerno where German opposition was stiff from the outset. This was in part due to an official broadcast announcing the Italian surrender being made even as the Allied invasion fleet closed in on the beaches.

On 10 September the Germans occupied Rome. In the following month they evacuated Sardinia and Corsica whilst their forces on the mainland under the command of Field Marshal Albert Kesselring conducted a skilful withdrawal northwards. Naples was liberated on 1 October. In the last month of 1943, the Germans pulled back to a strong defensive position called the Gustav Line, close to the banks of the Garigliano and Rapido rivers.

The Allies closed up with the First Canadian Division taking Ortona at the northern end of the line on 27 December. Montgomery then bid farewell to the Eighth Army and left for England to take command of the 21st Army Group preparing for the invasion of Northern Europe. Monty's successor in Italy, Lt-General Sir Oliver Leese, took over on 30 December.

This Daily Telegraph *map depicted the Allied landings on the Italian mainland in the autumn of 1943.*

Setbacks at Cassino

Winter in Italy, even south of Rome, can be a wet, miserable time, especially in the mountains. As 1944 dawned with the Allies facing the Gustav Line running across the Italian peninsula from the Adriatic to the Tyrrhenian Sea, the poor weather favoured the defenders rather than the attackers.

Montgomery succinctly summed up the situation before he left for the UK: 'Caesar used to go into winter quarters about this time, when he commanded an army in these parts. And very wise too..' But politics and ambition would not permit such a course in 1944. Churchill, for one, sought decisive action in what he termed 'the soft underbelly of Europe' whilst US General Mark Clark vowed he would soon head '..the first conquering army to enter Rome from the south in 2000 years'.

With the Eighth Army stalled on the River Sangro in the east, the attention of the planners shifted west. The Liri Valley, dominated by the mountains around the town of Cassino, was the key to any advance on Rome. The mouth of the valley was bisected by the connecting rivers Garigliano and Rapido which in turn are joined by the Liri as it flows south down the valley.

Clark wanted the British 10th Corps to undertake three diversionary assault crossings of the Garigliano near where it met the sea. Then the US 36th Division was to attack across the Rapido and erupt into the Liri Valley, forcing the Germans to abandon the line at Cassino or risk being outflanked and surrounded.

The British 'sideshow' began on 17 January and met with encouraging success. Indeed, if the success had been reinforced

British infantry cross a pontoon bridge over the Garigliano river on 19 January 1944.

without delay it may well have forced a full German retreat all by itself. But time was wasted and the chance was lost. Later some blamed Clark for dallying, claiming he did not want to see the British taking the lead over the Americans.

On the night of 20 January the US 36th Division attempted to cross the Rapido. The river alone was a formidable obstacle, 12ft deep, 50ft wide, fast-running and freezing. Add the seasoned German Panzer Grenadiers manning strong defensive positions on the north bank and able to pour a withering fire on the attackers and the result was disaster. The Americans suffered 1681 casualties and over 500 men were captured.

After the war the Veterans Association of the 36th Division pressured the US Congress into an inquiry about 'the fiasco of the Rapido'. Congress concluded that General Clark's order to make the attack was a necessary one.

The reversal on the Rapido led to a lull in the Gustav Line fighting as both sides drew breath. Allied soldiers around Cassino found their attention drawn more and more to the historic Benedictine monastery set high above the town at the top of Monte Cassino. Senior commanders became convinced that here was the key to the German defensive system that wound its way along the heights. Soldiers and ordnance were surely sheltered within those massive walls; artillery spotters must be following the every movement of Allied troops and vehicles on the valley floor far below.

Something would have to be done. Unless, that is, the Allies could successfully land an amphibious force far to the rear of the German lines and close enough to Rome to liberate the Eternal City in a single bold stroke...

Anzio

'Instead of hurling a wildcat on to the shore... all we got was a stranded whale.' **Winston Churchill**

The British Premier's bitter words are in dramatic contrast to the high hopes he held for the success of this audacious plan where a powerful Anglo-American task force was to storm ashore at Anzio and Nettuno and at once drive on Rome, just 40 miles away.

'*Operation Shingle* should decide the Battle of Rome', said Churchill, as the landing got underway: '...Anzio will astonish the world.'

What turned into a 125-day siege and one of the bloodiest European campaigns of the Second World War opened on 22 January 1944 when 36,000 Allied troops and 3000 vehicles disembarked in the face of minor resistance. The Anzio beach-head was some 80 miles north of the stalemated frontline at Cassino. Just 13 dead and 97 wounded were reported on the first day.

Perhaps the landings went too well. Instead of pushing out to find an enemy to fight, all the Allied efforts went into creating a defensible area. Yet it was nearly six hours after the landings began before the Germans in Rome were alerted. In this time armoured columns could have made it to Rome and, crucially, occupied the high ground of the Alban Hills south of the city.

By midnight, however, the initiative was already shifting in favour of the Germans as Field Marshal Kesselring could now call on some 20,000 fighting men to block any break out. Within a day the Germans had makeshift lines of defence in place just five miles from the Allied perimeter. Major General John P Lucas remained loathe to go on the offensive; he felt that his three divisions were a force insufficient to risk against a proven campaigner like Kesselring who always reacted to threats with skill and vigour. Lucas also knew that staying put allowed his men the continued protection of the navy's big guns, while riding shotgun over the beach-head skies were the numerically far superior Allied air forces.

British forces were tasked with holding the left flank of the beach-head on a five-mile front. Troops and fighting vehicles from many units had landed; Royal Tank Regiment, Grenadiers and Sherwood Foresters among them. The Irish Guards recorded: '...a sickening feeling of anti-climax. There were no Germans so what was stopping us? The 23rd was a completely wasted day.'

On 25 January came movement at last. Two

Commonwealth soldiers prepare to embark from the southern Italian port of Castellaware bound for the landing beaches at Anzio-Nettuno.

Main image: German artillery zeros in on the Nettuno beaches as amphibious DUKWs land supplies. This is a rare colour action photograph.

Above: The Anzio-Nettuno coastline as it is today.

Anzio

CAMPO DI CARNE
ON THIS SITE THOUSANDS OF MEN
FOUGHT AND DIED
AN DIESEM ORT TAUSENDE VON MENSCHEN
KÄMPFTEN UND FIELEN
IN QUESTO LUOGO MIGLIAIA DI UOMINI
COMBATTERONO E MORIRONO
"BATTAGLIA DI ANZIO-APRILIA-CISTERNA 1944" 1979

Nettuno

This astonishing aerial composite photograph of the Anzio -
Nettuno beach-head was taken early in 1944. The invasion
fleet and landing craft can clearly be seen below Nettuno
where the Americans came ashore. The British beaches
were to the north of the port of Anzio.

A view of Anzio today is inset along with a sign
commemorating the fierce fighting that took place at
Campo di Carne in the vicinity of 'The Flyover'.

Anzio

RTR troops of Sherman tanks began moving up the Via Anziate, spearheading an advance of the 24th Guards Brigade. Italian farmers waved them on as they lumbered under an overpass, known as The Flyover. By mid-morning the fighting started in earnest around a tower in Aprilia that earnt the town the nickname of The Factory. Ominously, one of the 100 or so German prisoners taken early on remarked casually upon seeing a Sherman tank: 'If we were you and we had those, we'd have been in Rome by now.'

At dawn next day the Germans counter-attacked with the support of Tiger tanks, infiltrating the numerous creek beds, or *fossos*, that dotted the Anzio plain.

At 0800 hours the British front line was engulfed in a massive artillery barrage fired off from the Alban Hills where the Germans were gathering an arsenal of guns which included captured pieces from France, Yugoslavia, Russia and Czechoslovakia. As the history of the Guards puts it: 'The heavens opened and the air was full of iron dug from every mine in Europe; the shell fragments were marked in every known language west of the Urals.'

The Factory was to change hands many times in the coming months of deadly struggle. The last day of January saw the Americans suffer a major blow. Two Ranger battalions under Colonel William Darby advanced on Cisterna by way of a half-dry irrigation channel. Slowed by enemy strongpoints, the men found themselves caught on open ground half a mile from their objective as dawn broke. In the ensuing fierce close quarter battle, despite knocking out 15 assorted enemy vehicles, the Rangers were overwhelmed. Of 767 men who set out, just six returned to the US lines.

War Correspondence

As individual instalments of Sixty Years On *were published we received numerous letters and contributions from readers. To help with the chronological flow of this omnibus book, we have, so far as possible, put the letters as close to the time they allude to.*

Anzio from the air

I was stationed at Foggia aerodrome in early 1944 and was the bomb aimer in a crew of five flying a Wellington bomber. Our boys had landed at Anzio but had not advanced because of German pressure.

In mid-February we were briefed to cross the coast and fly over the beach-head dead on midnight – no stragglers as the Navy were lying off the coast and would open up on any aircraft in the vicinity. We had to fly in to a lit-up 'T', then do an 11 second timed run before letting our bombs go (18 x 250lb) in a cluster.

Suddenly in the run-up to the 'T' another 'T' appeared. German Intelligence had gained news of our 'T' and put one of their own up to confuse. Pathfinder Force called up and told us to bomb the 'T' which was being illuminated by the Army boys with various coloured verey lights but by this time we had all gone too far!

We turned to do another run and came in to line up on the correct 'T' whereupon the Royal Navy opened up, making it quite hectic up there. I heard later that several of our aircraft were hit by what we nowadays call 'friendly fire'. We returned to base, had a snack, 'bombed up' again and then set off back to Anzio.

I was very pleased to receive a very nice 60th anniversary citation from the 'Municipal de Anzio' thanking all those who were involved on land, sea and air in the 1944 operation. I have had it framed as a piece of history!
Fred Clarke, New Romney, Kent

..and on the ground

My husband was in the thick of the Anzio fighting and got a bullet wound to the head. Although he didn't much like to talk about it, I can remember tales of The Factory and how he was caught out on open ground and bullets rained down on him and the lads so that they didn't stand much of a chance. Once he was out of the army in 1946 he used to have mood swings which you can understand, given what he'd gone through.

Malcolm Philip Williams was a young farm worker before he joined the London Irish Rifles in 1943. He was one of a family of six boys and two girls born and bred in the village of Loppington, Wem, Shropshire. They spent many happy days at Yew Tree Cottage, Brown Heath, near Ellesmere. Sadly now passed on, Malcolm was a wonderful husband and good father to our three children.
Mrs Winifred Williams, Shropshire

Early casualty

Please allow me to congratulate you on the *Sixty Years On* series which I am finding very interesting. I hope it will help younger readers realise what we had to endure in days gone by.

I was a gunner in the Royal Artillery in 10 Corps at Anzio. I paid a visit to the town and the area in April 2002. The British Forces Cemetery is in immaculate condition. There is a register at the entrance which gives details of all the personnel interred there and the grave numbers. I also visited the Beach-Head Museum. Upon learning of my participation in 1944, the Museum President gave me a scroll depicting the landings. The Italian people are still very appreciative of what we did to rid them of the Nazis.

I did not progress very far on the beach-head as I was wounded and returned to Britain via Naples, Tunis and Algiers.
N Hamilton, Fife

That's my ship!

I was delighted to find on in *Sixty Years On* a picture of the ship on which I spent almost three and half years of the war – LST368 – as it prepared to embark troops bound for the Anzio beaches. Memories!

Could I also make the point that the Fifth Army of the American General Mark Clark also included British Forces. My LST also took part in the Salerno operation and we carried British troops. I know we couldn't have won the war without America, but don't let them take all the glory.
F E Weeks, Melksham, Wilts
LST 368 is pictured on page 19 of this book.

Bridge across time

I have just been reading the fascinating January *Sixty Years On* feature. Imagine my surprise on looking at the photograph on page 18 captioned 'British infantry cross a pontoon bridge over the Garigliano river on 19 January 1944,' for it was here and on that very day that my Uncle was killed in action.

He was my mother's youngest brother - Trooper Seymour Fletcher, 10601829 46th Regiment Recce Corps, RAC. He is buried in the Minturno War Cemetery. Clearly I never knew him but remember my Grandmother talking about him when I was a child after I had found a cap badge in a button box at Grandma's house.

I was very moved to see this as it really drives home the sacrifices that were made by so many in order to ensure our freedom. I am now even more determined to visit Minturno to pay my respects.
Jim Pybus, Yorkshire

Ocean Odyssey

Jack Cooper was presumed dead after his ship was sunk by a German surface raider in the South Atlantic. In fact he ended up as a slave labourer in Yokohama, Japan. Bev Cooper recounts his father's amazing wartime experience.

On 3 January 1944 my mother receives a postcard from my father, just as many thousands of other wives have from their husbands who are overseas. But there's something very different about this communication. Firstly, the postcard was dated 4 June 1943 and had taken a long time to arrive. Secondly, on 30 April 1942 my mother had received a letter from Royal Naval Barracks Portsmouth informing her that her husband's ship was overdue and presumed lost with all hands. By 7 July 1942 this was confirmed and my mum received a letter from King George and Queen Elizabeth offering their sympathy in mum's great sorrow.

Clearly my dad was alive. What had happened to him makes for a very unusual story of wartime loss and eventual happiness. He first told his tale publicly in a Radio Norfolk interview a couple of decades ago. What follows is a synopsis of that recording.

Let me take you back to 1917 when a boy is born in Tottenham, North London. He often visits relatives in Caston and Great Ellingham, Norfolk, and grows to love the county, spending as much time there with his cousins as he can. Schooldays over, he moves to Norfolk on a permanent basis, finding whatever work he can – it is all rural jobs or forestry pit propping. One day his landlady's niece has a wedding to which this now tall and handsome young man is invited. The bride's sister is unattached but she sure is soon enough and that leads to another wedding between my mum and dad.

Bound for Middle East

The war comes along and dad is called up. His father had been a seaman in the Merchant Navy so dad goes for the Royal Navy. He went to *HMS Collinwood* for his basic training and then was sent to *HMS Nelson*, followed by three weeks Gunnery School. After this it was onto the DEMS (Defensively Equipped Merchant Ships). All merchant ships were equipped with guns manned by navy personnel. My dad ended

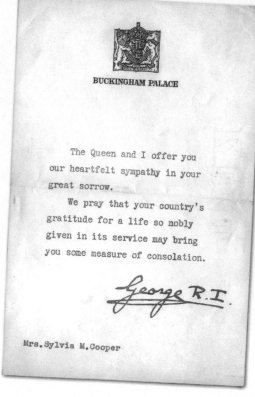

The letter of sympathy Mrs Sylvia Cooper received from King George when it was believed her husband Jack has perished at sea.

up in Middlesborough where he was posted to *SS Wellpark*, a Scottish-owned ship. He was on the Atlantic run and made two successful trips, one to Norfolk, Virginia, and the other to Canada even though this was during the height of U-Boat activity.

The third trip (early 1942) was again to America but this time to pick up cargo for the Middle East. The voyage took him to the South Atlantic to round the Cape, as the Mediterranean was too dangerous. Whilst on board they heard that Singapore had fallen (15 February). When they sailed from New York they'd been warned that German surface raiders were in the Atlantic but due to the shortage of ships they could not go in a convoy but had to risk it and go on their own.

'Abandon ship'

The journey was uneventful until they were three days out of Cape Town. Dad was on watch at the time and looking forward to some time off in South Africa when the alarm bell went off. The Chief Officer ordered the AA gun to be manned. Dad was more than perplexed at this as they were way out in mid-ocean. They had seen a smoke haze on the horizon but it was dismissed as a friendly ship. Suddenly dad saw an aircraft diving down out of the sky straight at him. He saw a splash and thought the 'b****r' had launched an aerial torpedo. He braced himself waiting for the bang but all he heard was a loud 'ping'. The aircraft had dropped a hook and as it flew over the ship it lifted the hook and pulled away the aerials leaving the ship without any means of communication to the outside world.

The aircraft returned and this time dropped a bomb that caused some damage. The next thing was the arrival of the German raider equipped with

The illustration below is derived from a poor quality photograph of the British ship Kirkpool, sinking after being attacked by the German surface raider Thor. This incident occurred during the same operation that saw the sinking of SS Wellpark and the capture of Jack Cooper.

6-inch guns. The 4-inch guns on *SS Wellpark* were not much use against such an adversary. The German shells straddled the merchant ship whilst the replies from dad's ship were falling far short of their target. At this point the captain ordered 'abandon ship'. The two remaining lifeboats were launched and all 50 crew were safely evacuated. They expected to be left to their fate but the German vessel came round and picked them all up. The next round it fired sunk dad's ship. He always believed that the Germans could have sunk their ship with all hands lost, but they did not and he was treated very well all the time he was in German hands.

The German ship was the *Thor*. It had been made to look like a merchant ship but as it went into action the sides fell away to reveal the guns. It had two aeroplanes – the one that attacked dad had USA markings on it. Dad spent three weeks on board the German raider during which time it sank another four ships. When it went into action all the prisoners were locked in the hold below the water line so if anything had happened they had no chance of escape.

Across the Pacific

From the German raider he was transferred to the German prison ship *Regensburg* whilst still in the Atlantic. This ship took them round the Cape of Good Hope (not much Good Hope for those on board) across the Pacific to end up at Yokohama in Japan in August. They had to stay on a ship – the *Ramses* - as no prison camps had yet been built. It's ironic that dad can boast that he and his comrades were the first British prisoners in Japan. Not only that, he had the 'pleasure' of watching a Red Cross ship sail full of departing British and German diplomats.

The POW camp was in Kawasaki where dad remained for some considerable time. After about six weeks there was a further influx of prisoners. These were Middlesex Regiment and Royal Scots men plus some engineers and medics, all captured in Hong Kong. The prisoners found Japanese food unpalatable but after a short time every scrap was eaten. Work commenced on unloading railway trucks, hard and unrelenting toil seven days a week.

Life in the POW camp is a story in its own right, perhaps one day I will put that part of dad's story into print. Suffice to say here that dad survived the harsh conditions and came home alive and well. There is another story – that of my mother and how she coped in such dreadful circumstances before learning of my dad's survival but unfortunately she is no longer here to tell me.

THE THOR STORY

SS Wellpark was one of 10 ships sunk by *Thor* in the course the German surface raider's second South Atlantic sortie. *Thor* sailed from Kiel in January 1942. It's interesting that Jack Cooper says the ship had two aircraft; official records show it carried one Arado 196 but perhaps they didn't want to let the world know they had a second aircraft with US insignia. A favoured aerial attack technique was to dive down out of the sun with the engine switched off. This tactic made a surprise approach possible. At the last minute the pilot would switch the engine on, deploy the hook and skilfully whisk away the victim's radio mast.

Ironically, *Thor* met her own end in Yokohama harbour on 30 November 1942. She was tied alongside a German tanker called the *Uckermark*. This vessel was previously named the *Altmark*, the same ship that was stormed by sailors from *HMS Cossack* in February 1940. With the famous cry 'The Navy's here' they released 299 prisoners who had been transferred aboard the *Altmark* from the pocket battleship *Graf Spee*. A cleaning operation in the *Uckermark*'s hold resulted in a huge explosion that sank four ships in total. *Thor* was one of them; 13 of her crew were lost.

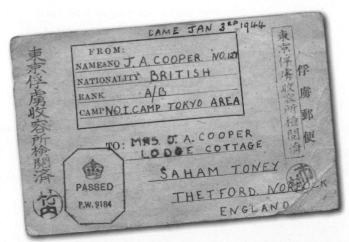

Jack sent this postcard from Japan dated 4 June 1943.
It was delivered to Sylvia in England on 3 January 1944.

1944 Dark Winter

The months of January and February 1944 were bitter days indeed for Britain and not just for the gloomy winter weeks but the daily bulletins about the Bomber Command raids on a well defended Nazi Germany. These were reaching a crescendo at this time and most of us found the rising RAF casualties more than they could bear.

As a 14-year-old at that time, I can recall one winter morning having breakfast with my mother and sister Jean and getting ready for school. The news on the radio was concluding with a list of targets attacked during the night in Germany - ending with the dramatic and dreadful postscript '..that 76 of our aircraft are missing'.

By Ron McGill

My mother looked at me with tears in her eyes. 'Does that mean we have lost 76 pilots?' she asked. 'No mum,' I replied, 'it is usually a seven man crew and 500 airmen could have been killed'. She could but say, 'It must have been awful for them last night'. Then she shook her head, quite mute with tears.

We have since learned only too well that it was indeed awful for those aircrew of 60 years ago and I think that was highlighted exactly in a small book published in the early 1950's that was called *No Moon Tonight*. It was written by Don Charlwood, a surviving bomber navigator who was one of a group of 20 Australians who enlisted for aircrew in the early 1940s. They were sent to Canada for training before becoming aircrew in Bomber Command.

The book was matter-of-fact, with no 'gung-ho' whatsoever and deservedly became a classic personal account of the air battles of that era, made all the more poignant by the fact that just five

The Little Blitz

Early in 1944, the Luftwaffe returned in force to the skies over London and Southern England in a series of attacks intended to bolster civilian morale in an increasingly bomb-battered Germany and at the same time demonstrate to the British populace that Hitler's air power remained a potent threat. *Operation Steinbock* began on 21 January with 447 sorties by various aircraft including Heinkel 177 heavy bombers. The resulting damage was slight compared to that of the 1940 –41 Blitz. Civilians were inclined to shrug off the air raid warnings and go about their business unperturbed. Because of this, deaths and injuries from 'friendly fire' greatly increased. In the course of an air raid many thousands of anti-aircraft rounds would be fired skywards only to fall back to earth in a deadly rain of shrapnel spread out for many miles around the anti-aircraft batteries. Quite a number of shells would fail to explode in the air but would detonate – effectively like a bomb - when they hit the ground. British fuses for AA shells were notoriously quirky; prior to the war efficient clockwork fuses had been imported from Switzerland, a source cut off once France fell in June 1940.

of the original 20 made it home to Australia.

There was an interesting cameo in the book when Don, off operations for a spell, discovered on a map a small village bearing his name – Charlwood – not far from Gatwick Airport. Don became close friends with the then rector of Charlwood who kindly researched the known ancestry details of Don's earlier relatives who were in fact buried in the churchyard.

In 1995 and to mark Don's 80th birthday, my sister Jean suggested that I paint in oils a picture of the ancient church, featuring the old graves in the foreground. This was completed and subsequently delivered 'down under' where it currently has pride of place in Nell and Don's home in Melbourne.

They are both now in their late 80s but continue to enjoy life... Don has said many times since that those far off days in Bomber Command are still so fresh in his mind. We can but think of the debt we owe to those young men who failed to survive in that momentous year of 1944.

Ron McGill lives near Guildford and is an accomplished artist as well as writer. This is a pen and ink study of Charlwood Church he did for Sixty Years On.

ST. NICHOLAS CHURCH CHARLWOOD, SURREY BY RON MCGILL

1 January: The year opens with Australian and US troops gaining the upper hand as they fought the Japanese on New Guinea. General MacArthur says that the capture of the whole island is likely 'within months'. It is less than 24 hours since General Montgomery had his first sight of the master plan for the Allied invasion of North West Europe, codename *Overlord*. The famous former commander of the Eighth Army has been appointed commander of ground forces for the invasion which is provisionally scheduled for May 1944. Monty's superior is the Supreme Allied Commander, US General Dwight D Eisenhower.

On **2 January** it is reported that Australian and US troops are gaining the upper hand in fighting against the Japanese on New Guinea.

On **3 January** a big RAF raid on Berlin sees some 1000 tons of bombs dropped on the German capital. The RAF lose 27 Lancasters out of the 383-strong bomber force.

The next night *Operation Carpetbagger* begins setting in motion regular supply drops to resistance forces in France, Belgium, the Netherlands and Italy. In the months ahead, fast Mosquito light bombers sometimes fulfil 'special delivery' requests within an hour or so after a coded radio message is received.

On **6 January,** Berlin Radio broadcasts a statement from the German High Command: 'We will make no effort to hold Russian territory purely for reasons of prestige.' That same day General Vatutin's First Ukrainian Front army crossed the pre-war border and entered Poland.

Next day Hollywood film star James Stewart finds himself in a real-life wartime starring role. Stewart – a major in the USAAF – led a daylight mission to bomb Ludwigshaven. On the return flight, Stewart noticed that a number of the 420 aircraft on the mission had taken a wrong bearing and were heading in the direction of German fighter stations in France. With radio contact lost, Stewart decided to follow them and lend fire support. Although eight of the strayed Liberators were shot down, Stewart's action was credited with helping prevent the downing of many more.

In Italy Allied talk of 'swanning up to Rome' evaporates in the face of strong German defensive positions around the Liri Valley in the mountains overlooking Cassino. American General Mark Clark pins his hopes on an audacious seaborne invasion at Anzio, far north of the front line, just 40 miles from Rome.

On **8 January** the RAF announced the development of a jet propelled fighter, the Gloster, to counter the threat from German inventors to produce aircraft capable of flying at 500mph. In a radio broadcast, Britain's jet propulsion pioneer, Group Captain Frank Whittle, says he finds the sudden publicity very embarrassing as a great many people besides himself had contributed to the work.

Polish leaders based in London received a message **(11 January)** from Moscow stating that the Curzon Line, the frontier proposed by the Allies in 1919, should be the basis of a post-war settlement between Poland and the USSR. Effectively it will mean the annexation of large areas of eastern Poland by the Russians.

On the same day in Verona, Count Galeazzo Ciano, Mussolini's son-in-law and former Italian Foreign Minister is executed by firing squad. The previous July, Ciano had helped oust the dictator from office. Now the resurgent German-backed fascists exact revenge.

On **12 January** Free-French leader General de Gaulle meets with the Prime Minister Winston Churchill in Marrakech to discuss Franco-British co-operation. Convoy JW-56 loaded with vital

'On 28 January the Kremlin announces that the 900 day siege of Leningrad is at an end...'

THEY'RE USING

Osram

LAMPS

Your favourite lamps are helping to bring Victory

ON BOARD

Two Wehrmacht Corps are threatened with encirclement as Field Marshal von Manstein seeks Hitler's permission to withdraw.

24 January: The hospital ship *St David* is sunk by German aircraft off Anzio. Still in Italy, to the south, the French Expeditionary Force launches an attack across the River Rapido. After initial success, German reinforcements stop them just short of Monte Cassino.

In London on **26 January** the trial by jury of 58-year-old Oswald Job, finds him guilty of spying. He is sentenced to death. British-born Job had German parents; following internment in Germany upon the outbreak of war, Job was persuaded to return to England posing as an escapee. He then sent intelligence reports back to the Reich using invisible ink to write between the lines of letters written to British POWs in German camps. It is believed that Job's activites were uncovered by a double agent.

27 January: The Argentine severs diplomatic relations with Berlin becoming the 27th republic in the Continent of North and South America to do so. President Ramirez says that German spying activity in his homeland have provoked the action. Foreign observers in neighbouring Chile believe that Ramirez is merely backing the winning side and avoiding a confrontation with the USA.

On the same day in London, D-Day planners veto any further commando raids on Occupied France or the Channel Islands. They say that to continue them will only spur the Germans to speed up work on the so-called Atlantic Wall. German engineers, soldiers and Todt Organisation slave workers are building coastal fortifications from Norway and Denmark all the way to the Bay of Biscay. Complete sections are still few and far between, one exception being the coast around the port of Dieppe, scene of an unsuccessful 'reconnaissance in force' by a mainly Canadian force on 19 August 1942. After the raid Hitler demanded that the port be made impregnable.

28 January: The people of the battered but unbowed city of Leningrad are celebrating the best they can the official end of the 900-day German siege. The event was marked last evening when 24 salvoes were fired by 324 guns and massive firework displays went off. The securing of the Leningrad - Moscow rail link marked the end of the German investment. At one time nearly three million people were trapped in Leningrad but by the end there was just under half the original population, with the rest killed by German bombs and shells or by their allies, 'Generals Hunger, Cold and Terror'.

On **29 January** the first serious attempts by the Allies to enlarge the Anzio beach-head are rebuffed in the face of tough German resistance. A deadly glider bomb sinks the cruiser *HMS Spartan* off the invasion coast.

30 January: Brunswick and Hanover are raided by day by USAAF Flying Fortresses and Liberators. That night Berlin is raided; over 5000 tons of bombs have now been dropped on German targets over the space of three days and nights.

On the last day of the month, American Marines continue an offensive on Kwajalein in the Marshall Islands. It will take another four days of fierce fighting to win the battle. US dead total 372; only 130 Japanese out of an initial garrison of 8000 survive.

Night raids by up to 200 Luftwaffe aircraft continue on London and the South East. The RAF say that the enemy never succeeds in dropping more than 32 tons of ordnance in any single night. By contrast a single 'Tallboy' bomb used to blast recently identified V-weapon sites in France weighs a whopping 12,000lbs – nearly six tons.

supplies to support Russia's war effort sets sail for Murmansk from Liverpool.

On **14 January** the Russians attacked the rear of the German forces ranged around Leningrad. Two days later the Soviets announce the capture of 37 long range guns which have been pounding the city since it was first besieged in 1941.

In Britain **(18 January)** the first 600 'Bevin Boys' begin training for work in the coalmines. The youngsters have been conscripted by ballot to replace adult miners called up by the armed forces.

On **20 January,** coastal guns at Dover engage and sink the German blockade runner *Munsterland*. On the same day in the Far East, Lt A G Harwood of the Northants Regiment becomes the first British officer to be awarded the VC in the Burma Campaign. Harwood's posthumous citation says he had displayed 'calm, resolute bravery' in several actions in the preceding days. Thirty-year-old Harwood had been taken prisoner by the Germans in France in 1940 but escaped and reached Dunkirk in time to be evacuated.

On **22 January** 50,000 British and American troops plus 3000 vehicles land unopposed on the beaches near Anzio and Nettuno, less than 40 miles from Rome. Four days later the Germans declare martial law in the Eternal City as the populace grow restless in anticipation of the imminent arrival of the Allies. US General Lucas makes no move to liberate the Italian capital but concentrates instead on building up his forces.

Relations between the London Poles and the Kremlin deteriorate. The former believe that Stalin had ordered the murder of thousands of Polish officers at Katyn Wood on Soviet territory even though the Russians blamed the Germans for the massacre. History will eventually record that it was indeed Stalin who had ordered the liquidation of the officers in a bid to wipe out this important section of the Polish middle class who would be likely to resist an imposed communist regime controlled by Russia.

23 January: More success for the Red Army is reported as another offensive tears into depleted German lines in the Ukraine.

The Bombing of Monte Cassino

FEBRUARY 1944

Bombed in error?

On 15 February 1944 Allied bombers obliterated the historic monastery at Monte Cassino, Italy, a sanctuary founded by St Benedict himself 14 centuries before.

The resulting shattered ruin made a perfect defensive position for the German paratroops who were holding off an entire Allied army. The rights and wrongs of the decision to bomb have been shrouded in controversy ever since.

Today the monastery has been completely restored to its former glory. Only the cemeteries bear silent witness to the battles.

A Flying Fortress pictured in the course of bombing Monte Cassino.

ITALY: CASSINO IMPASSE

The Abbot of the Benedictine monastery pictured with German officers assisting him into a staff car shortly before the bombing.

Early in February almost all the Allied activity on the front facing the German Gustav Line hinged around bombed and battered Cassino. The first battle for the town and surrounding heights had ended in a stalemate. In the town itself and up on the mountain peaks and ridges, the Germans took full advantage of their good fortune in facing piecemeal rather than co-ordinated assaults. The flat plains on the valley floor were easily observed from the heights and areas had also been deliberately flooded.

XIV Panzer Corps commander, Lt-General Fridolin von Senger, headed the German defence of the Liri Valley, up which ran Route 6 to Rome and the besieged Allied beach-head at Anzio. He had converted the ground around the historic monastery into a strong defensive position manned by tough paratroops. However, Senger – by coincidence a lay member of the Benedictine Order and a devout Catholic – forbade occupation of the actual building, an edifice founded in person by Saint Benedict in 529AD. But Senger sensibly recognised the danger that fighting posed to the structure and he went to great lengths in first persuading and later assisting the Abbot to evacuate the monastery's priceless artifacts to the Vatican.

Senger's fears were well-founded. After an attack by the US 34th Division failed to make progress despite the soldiers battling bravely for days on the cold, rugged and very steep terrain, the eyes of the Allied commanders could not help but be drawn to the fortress-like white walls on the mountain top.

It was Lt General Bernard Freyberg VC of the New Zealand Corps who first requested that the monastery be destroyed. His men had replaced the Americans in the line at Cassino and they quickly formed the opinion that the building must be a key part of the German defences blocking access to the Liri Valley. The American General Mark Clark and British General Sir Harold Alexander were not convinced that bombing would achieve anything of real value but at the same time they could hardly refuse a measure which Freyberg was convinced would save the lives of his men.

Leaflets warning of the impending destruction were dropped in the vicinity of the monastery on 13 February. When the Germans told the occupants that the threat was an Allied bluff the monks decided to stay and took shelter in the deep cellars along with a large number of refugees, several hundred of whom were about to lose their lives.

It was a clear, bright morning on 15 February 1944 when over 200 USAAF Flying Fortresses, Mitchell bombers and Marauder aircraft flew over the Abbey. The resulting bombing was spectacular to behold. Allied troops in the valley below had a grandstand view as massive explosions rocked the hilltop.

German paratroopers assist a wounded British soldier in Italy early in 1944.

Spurts of red flames illuminated the clouds of smoke and dust as wave after wave of aircraft delivered their lethal cargoes. For good measure, the Fifth Army artillery lobbed 314 shells of heavy and medium calibre into the ruins.

Cheering it may have been to the watching Allies and certainly deadly to any enemy soldiers in the immediate Abbey vicinity. But in terms of gaining any tactical advantage, the raid was a failure. When it was over, the Germans simply moved into the rubble to enjoy the vantage point they'd denied themselves before. Von Senger was incensed. He is recorded as saying: 'The idiots! They've done it after all. Our efforts were in vain.'

Worse followed. An attack on Monte Cassino by the 4th Indian Division on 17 February was flung back at a cost of 600 casualties. So ended the Second Battle of Cassino.

PHOENIX FROM THE RUBBLE

The 1944 air raid was not the first time that the Abbey of St Benedict had been destroyed. Down the centuries since 529AD, invading barbarians, Saracens and an earthquake (1349) have periodically brought down the mighty walls of this enduring emblem of faith. Each time the monastery has reappeared atop its mountain peak, assuming once again its role as a centre of religious, spiritual and artistic life. So it was post-war when work began on clearing the rubble and painstakingly restoring the building's glories. It was a mammoth task. American money helped fund the work. Even so, the monks refused to include any English language tourist signs. As late as 1948, an unexploded bomb was still lodged in the flooring in front of St Benedict's tomb.

Today the quiet and tranquil environs of the Abbey make it difficult to imagine the chaos, cruelty and desolation wrought by war. But in the vicinity are the cemeteries filled with the fallen of both sides. Italian writer G Spadolini penned of the Cassino dead: 'In these places the holocaust of youth coming from all over the world was consumed and the losers and the winners joined together under the sign of a common grief and heroism.'

Most visitors first sight the Abbey from their car or coach on the A2, the modern Autostrada that lances down the Liri Valley to link Rome with Naples. Follow the signs for Abbazia di Montecassino on a road which winds laboriously up the mountainside. A panoramic view unfolds, one that makes it easy to understand why it took so long for the Allies to prise open the Gustav Line.

THE PAPER WAR

In the winter and spring of 1944, the Allies and Germans fought each other to a standstill on the Gustav Line and around the beach-head of Anzio. Exploiting what they perceived to be war-weariness amongst the British and American troops, German propagandists produced vast quantities of leaflets which the Luftwaffe showered down by the ton. Lurid and often crude, the propaganda sheets had little effect on Allied morale despite the German attempts to stir up British enmity towards the Yanks.

The examples reproduced here were collected at the time by Mr T Dean of Wickford, Essex, who served with the British forces during the Italian campaign. Original material like this is today much sought-after by collectors of wartime memorabilia.

On the right we see a German attempt to upset British troops via an explicit reference to the supposed activities of American soldiers leading pampered lives over in England. The reverse side of the leaflet reads:

'The Yanks are lease-lending your women. Their pockets full of cash and no work to do, the boys from overseas are having the time of their lives.

'And what young woman, single or married, could resist such a handsome brute from the wide open spaces to have a dinner with, a cocktail at some night-club, and afterwards...

'Anyway, so numerous have become the scandals that all England is talking about them now.'

While you are away,

BEACH-HEAD

CAMPO MORTO

London BLITZED *again!*

DEATH'S HEAD!

Cassino

CASSINO
IS STILL IN GERMAN HANDS
in spite of
HUGE ALLIED LOSSES!

For weeks and weeks the Allies had been throwing all their resources into the Battle of Cassino. 800 Allied bombers dropped more than 2500 tons of H.E.'s on the small town of Cassino to blast away the German defenders.

But when the pounding from the air and the nerve-wracking barrage had ceased, the Germans rose from their foxholes and repelled in hand-to-hand fighting the massed attacks of the 2nd New Zealand and 4th Indian Divisions who were supported by numerous tanks.

Could that be the German soldier who, according to Allied press and radio reports, is war-weary?

AND NOW WHAT ABOUT THE NETTUNO FRONT?
IS THE
SLAUGHTER
TO BE REPEATED THERE?

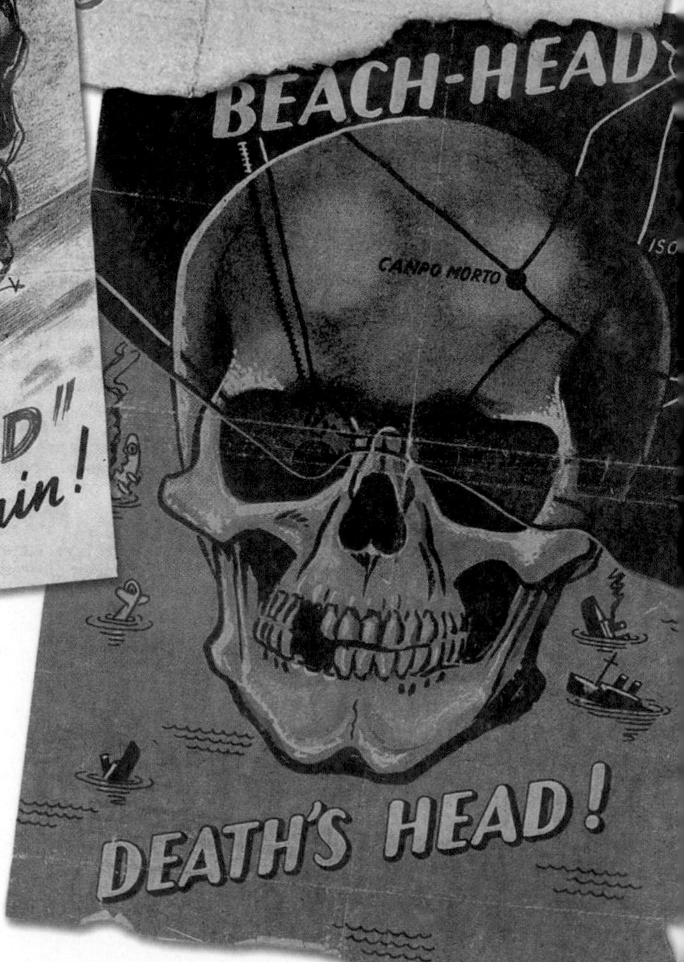

The Germans were quick to exploit any propaganda advantage. For example, in January, February and March 1944 the Luftwaffe carried out a 'Little Blitz' on the London area. Soon leaflets highlighting the raids were drifting down on the British forces fighting in Italy.

Anzio: a fire-raked cockpit

February 1944 in and around Anzio-Nettuno was a wretched time for the Allied troops as they struggled to consolidate their precarious beach-head. It was no better for the Germans as they attempted to drive the British and Americans back into the sea in the face of overwhelming air power and the big guns of the invasion fleet lying a short distance offshore. Spare a thought too for the hapless Italian civilians caught up in the vicious struggle and subjected to the grapeshot spray of deadly ordnance fired off from land, sea and air, not to mention the privations imposed by lack of provisions and access to medical help.

The War Illustrated of the time reported, '...this is the fire-raked cockpit of Anzio. The whole compact and ferocious bag of tricks is contained in an area less than that bounded by Battersea, Marble Arch, Holborn and Southwark. Every acre can be swept by enemy fire. The Fuhrer sees an immense political prize in throwing the attack back into the sea.'

Axis Sally broadcasts:

Anzio has become the largest self-supporting prisoner-of-war camp in the world

On 3 February the Germans mounted an attack on the Campoleone sector as they attempted to cut off an Allied salient known as 'The Thumb' along the line of Carroceto and The Factory. Supported by heavy artillery, they made slow but steady progress but sustained heavy losses in the process. Tiger tanks entered the fray and ground down entire companies of the Gordon Highlanders in the gullies and ridges around Campoleone.

At one point some Guardsmen were marching a group of captured Germans towards the unhappily-named Dung Farm when they in turn were surrounded by some 30 more Germans. Erstwhile POWs, they were being prodded towards the German lines when Captain Simon Lane led a revolt in which the captives turned the tables and overpowered their captors. The British then made it back to Carroceto with their wounded and nine prisoners.

On the night of 7 February, war correspondent Wynford Vaughan-Thomas recounted: '... one of those rare incidents where the fighting seemed for a few brief minutes to

HMS 'PEPPERPOT' IS SUNK

There were serious Naval casualties in the course of the Anzio operation. On 18 February *HMS Penelope* was torpedoed by U-Boat 410 off Nettuno and sunk with the loss of 417 of her crew including Captain D G Belben. *HMS Penelope* had already earned fame for her Malta role when she was nicknamed *HMS Pepperpot* due to the extensive damage she sustained whilst protecting the vital convoys to the island. Today 'The Penelope Association' is made up of survivors and friends and family of former crew members. The Association also encompasses the crew of the frigate *HMS Penelope* (F127) which was commissioned in 1963.

concentrate on one place and one man. That man was Major W P Sidney of the Grenadier Guards, defending a crucial point on the Via Anziate. If the Germans were to cut the road then the defenders of Carroceto and The Factory would be surrounded. In the action that night, Sidney and his men held fast, earning him a Victoria Cross in the process.'

But German confidence was growing. One cocky captive asked his British guard in which direction the sea was. When told he responded, 'Thank you very much. I needed to know, for very soon you will be in it.' In mid-February, Kesselring ordered *Operation Fischfang* to begin and his troops attempted to smash their way down the Via Anziate towards The Flyover.

The battle swayed back and forth, with thousands killed or wounded on both sides. By the end of it, the future for the beach-head was clear. To quote author Carlo D'Este in his enthralling account of the whole Anzio operation, *Fatal Decision*, '... what had started out a month earlier with lofty intentions ... had now turned into the bloodiest stalemate on the Western Front in the whole of World War II.'

Major General John P Lucas was replaced as Allied commander at Anzio on 23 February 1944. His successor was Major General Lucian King Truscott.

By 29 February the German counter-offensive was running out of steam as casualties steadily mounted. But would the Allies have the strength to break out? Propaganda radio commentator 'Axis Sally' didn't think so. Nightly on air she was boasting to her listeners: '...Anzio has become the largest self-supporting prisoner-of-war camp in the world.'

Despite the danger and hardships in the Anzio beach-head, soldiers kept a sense of humour. Note the Sea View Hotel sign! We also picture a 5.5 inch gun of the Royal Artillery in action.

THE SHIP THAT WON THE WAR?

Eric Sellars served aboard *HMS Petard*, a destroyer that sank submarines from the German, Italian and Japanese navies. But the greatest achievement of the ship's crew was the recovery of a top secret Enigma machine and codes from a sinking U-Boat.

On 12 February 1944 the Royal Navy Fleet Destroyer *HMS Petard* completed an astonishing hat trick of submarine sinkings when it fired a final torpedo to send the Japanese vessel I-27 to the bottom of the Indian Ocean, 60 miles north west of Addu Atoll near the Maldives.

Just a short time earlier, I-27 had fired a torpedo of her own at the troopship *Khedive Ismael*, part of British convoy KR 8 bound for Colombo, Ceylon. The troopship broke in half and went down in just 36 seconds with the loss of some 1200 men and women.

HMS Paladin went to rescue survivors. Meanwhile, *HMS Petard* detected the submarine's location and dropped Mark 7 depth charges. While the blasts succeeded in bringing the I-27 to the surface, they also caused a number of casualties among the troopship survivors stranded in the water.

As Japanese sailors rushed to man their deck gun, machine-gun fire from *Petard* cut them down. *HMS Paladin* then rammed the enemy vessel's port hydroplane but itself sustained a serious gash in the side. It was left to *HMS Petard* to administer the knock-out blow to I-27 but stubbornly the submarine was still afloat even after six torpedoes had struck it. A seventh finally sank I-27; just one crewman out of 100 on the big submarine was picked up alive.

Some 15 months prior to the Indian Ocean action, *HMS Petard*, in the space of some six weeks, had managed to sink the German U-Boat 559 (28 October 1942) and capture an Italian submarine, *Uarsciek*, (15 December 1942). Further, crewmen from *HMS Petard* were able to board both these vessels and capture codebooks and maps of incalculable value to the Allies.

From the German craft came elusive codebooks and an actual 4-Rotor Enigma machine. With these prizes the codebreakers in Hut No 8 at Bletchley Park could decipher *Kriegsmarine* radio signals, pinpoint the positions of U-Boats and sink them. It was the turning point in the Battle of the Atlantic.

From the Italian submarine came maps detailing the locations of minefields in North Africa and in and around the Italian coast and islands. Mine-free channels into Italian harbours were also indicated, along with current codes for the German and Italian navies. This haul was invaluable to the planners of *Operation Husky*, the invasion of Sicily that was to take place in the spring of 1943. For this action alone, *HMS Petard* earned a personal 'thank you' visit from General Dwight D Eisenhower.

Eric Sellars of Rottingdean in East Sussex was serving aboard *HMS Petard* in the course of all three submarine sinkings. He was part of the ship's Submarine Warfare Team and he personally pursued and eventually made possible the capture of the U-559. It was Eric who carried the Enigma machine to a place of safety on the *Petard*. Here he recounts the story of the capture of U-559 and tells why the incident remained a secret for many decades after the end of the war.

Left: Eric Sellars aboard his ship in the Tropics.

Above: The HMS Petard *Association commissioned this painting of the Enigma incident by military artist Michael Roffe a few years ago. Eric says that in fact the night was a very dark one and the sea wasn't nearly so rough as depicted here. Painting reproduced courtesy of the Cambridge Stamp Centre Ltd.*

'The magnificent exploits of the Fleet Destroyer *HMS Petard* were kept secret for 40 years and in some cases for 50 and 60 years on the direct orders of Prime Minister Winston Churchill.

The ship started naval life as *HMS Persistant*, a name so unpopular that it was changed to *Petard*. Her first Captain was Lt Cdr Sam Beattie. Before he could even take the vessel to sea he was recalled to the Admiralty for special duty. He was the man who would ram the *Campbeltown* into the dock gates at St Nazaire, winning the Victoria Cross in the process.

HMS Petard was one of only three 'P' Class destroyers to survive the war (*Paladin* and *Penn* being the other two) and was the last 'P' to be broken up in 1967. In 1942 the shortage of guns for new destroyers was so acute that *HMS Petard* was fitted with single four-inch weapons that dated back to 1916. We were the laughing stock of the Flotilla but would come to bless the day they were fitted because while the twin turrets of other destroyers could elevate to only 60 degrees, our single weapons could elevate to 89 degrees, as the German dive bombers soon discovered. All four guns firing together could deliver 22 shells per minute.

When the ship was fully commissioned, Lt Cdr Mark Thornton was Captain. He ordered 'Clear Lower Deck' which meant that everyone who could should 'fall in' on the Upper Deck. He wanted to say a few words that went much as follows: 'I am fully aware of the humorous remarks regarding our First World War single guns fitted to this ship and would refer to you a speech made by Lord Nelson.

'Now it's generally known that Nelson was often quite ill and always seasick when he first set off on a voyage. One of his fellow Captains remarked to Nelson how sorry he was about this situation. Nelson's response was: "Pity Sir? Pity? By God you will live to envy me!"'

Thornton went on, 'so it will be with this ship'.

How right he was for *HMS Petard* was to play a key role in winning the war.

Maritime lifelines

On 1 February 1942 the German Navy introduced M4, a new version of their Enigma code machine. The effect of M4 was to immediately lock the British code breakers at Bletchley Park out of SHARK, the Atlantic and Mediterranean U-Boat communications traffic. The Allied navies were no longer able to intercept the deadly U-Boat packs that were strangling Britain's maritime lifelines.

Later that year, on 30 October off the coast of Egypt, four Royal Navy destroyers, including *HMS Petard*, obtained ASDIC contact with a U-Boat. After a sustained depth charge attack lasting about 10 hours the submarine was finally forced to the surface at about 22.40. *Petard's* searchlights stabbed through the night and picked out the U-Boat's conning tower which had a white donkey emblem and the numerals U-559 painted on it. The conning tower was soon struck by a shell from one of *Petard's* four-inch guns causing the U-Boat's crew to abandon ship. *Petard's* first officer, Lieutenant Anthony Fasson, dived into the sea followed by Able Seaman Colin Grazier and Tommy Brown, a 16-year-old civilian canteen assistant who had lied about his age to get the job. They swam to the stricken U-Boat and climbed down inside the conning tower to find the lights still on.

In the submarine, Fasson found some documents printed in water-soluble ink.

Eric Sellars pictured at Bletchley Park with the Executive Director of the Bletchley Trust.

Despite the water pouring through the shell hole, Brown succeeded in keeping them dry as he clambered up the ladder in the conning tower and passed them to others waiting in *Petard's* whaler made fast alongside. Brown twice re-entered the U-Boat, each time returning with more items.

Fasson returned to the control room to wrench a radio or radar set from its fixings, but by this time the water inside the U-Boat was knee-deep and rising. Brown, now on top of the conning tower, shouted for them to come up as the U-Boat's afterdeck was well underwater. As Grazier and Fasson started up the ladder, the U-Boat suddenly sank. Brown jumped clear, but U-559 made her last dive taking Fasson and Grazier with her.

Shipping losses halved

The material retrieved from U-559 reached Bletchley Park on 24 November. By 13 December 1942, after a blackout of 10 months, Bletchley Park called the Admiralty's Operational Intelligence Centre to report a break into SHARK. Within the next hour the first intercept chattered off the teleprinter indicating the position of more than a dozen

➤

U-Boats. A stream of intercepts followed allowing the rerouting of convoys around the waiting wolfpacks. Allied shipping losses in the Atlantic were consequently halved in January and February 1943 and, perhaps even more vitally, procedures were developed which facilitated the breaking of SHARK for much of the remainder of the war. Fasson, Grazier and Brown's action consequently saved millions of tons of Allied shipping and thousands of Allied lives.

Churchill was absolutely ecstatic.

Tony Fasson and Colin Grazier were to be awarded the highest possible medals for bravery. Tommy Brown would get the George Medal. As Head of the ship's Submarine Warfare Team who had pursued and eventually made possible the capture of the U-559, I was to receive the Distinguished Service Medal.

Churchill now intervened. No medals to be awarded at that time. No written records to be made and submitted to higher authority. Any reference to the success of the *Petard* was to be deleted lest German Intelligence became aware of the coup. The crew were told that everything was now secret and would remain so for at least 40 years.

In 1980 the records became available. Lt Tony Fasson was to be honoured with a plaque on the wall of his village church telling his story. The George Cross was presented to his family. Able Seaman Colin Grazier's family also received the George Cross. Tommy Brown was awarded the George Medal. Ironically, his medal was also posthumous as he died two years after the U-559 sinking while trying to save his sister in a house fire.

Colin Grazier came from Tamworth and when the local paper's Deputy Editor, Phil Shanahan, discovered the story he decided to honour the World War Two hero. A fund eventually raised around £20,000 and an

This statue in Tamworth commemorates the bravery of Tony Fasson, Colin Grazier and Tommy Brown in recovering the Enigma machine and codes from the U-Boat.

impressive sculpture was commissioned. It was dedicated in St Editha's Square, Tamworth, on Sunday 27 October 2002.

For the same day, the *HMS Petard* Association had hoped that the Admiralty could arrange for a wreath to be put in the sea near the spot where the U-559 went down. It wasn't possible. However, on 9 November 2002, a Type 23 Frigate, *HMS Argyll,* did visit the location. The ship's crew put on a full Guard of Honour and laid a wreath. Honour was paid.

Early days in the Navy

In 1938 I was serving aboard a battleship, *HMS Royal Oak*, flagship of the Second Battle Squadron, Home Fleet. The ship was destined to be one of the early British naval losses of the war, being sunk at Scapa Flow in the Orkneys by the German submarine U-47 on Friday 13 October 1939 in an action that cost the lives of 833 seamen.

Fortunately for me, I was no longer with the ship at the time she was sunk. At Christmas 1938-39 I had been sent on two weeks leave with instructions not to return to the *Royal Oak* but to instead report to *HMS Osprey*, a 'stone frigate' (Navy slang for a barracks). Situated on the very tip of Portland Bill in Dorset, it turned out to be a top secret establishment, devoted to anti-submarine warfare. The ASDIC system was born there. ASDIC stands for Anti Submarine Detection Investigative Committee.

I was placed on a special course and by July 1939 was considered fully qualified in all aspects of anti-submarine warfare. So secret was it all that we were not allowed to wear any badges of recognition and totally forbidden to discuss anything to do with ASDIC outside the barracks.

Following my summer leave it was becoming obvious that war with Germany was inevitable. At *HMS Osprey* I was given the task of receiving Fleet Reservists, recalled for service, kitting them out and allocating accommodation.

War was declared on 3 September 1939 and by the evening of the following day I found myself stepping aboard one of the most modern fleet destroyers ever built in the dockyard at Wallsend-on-Tyne. With the exception of a single period of three months, from this day forward right through to the end of World War Two, I was at sea. If there was fighting to be done, it seemed we were always there.

The Fighting Fifth

The destroyer was *HMS Khartoum*, one of eight identical vessels, all with names that began with the letter 'K'. The others were called *Kipling, Kelvin, Kandahar, Kashmir, Kimberley, Kingston* and *Kelly*. The latter's captain was Louis Mountbatten. Known as Captain 'D', he commanded this 5th Destroyer Flotilla which became known as the 'The Fighting Fifth'.

With the Admiralty rightly worried that the Germans would make every effort to get their capital warships out into the Atlantic, our 'working up' period of three weeks was cut to seven days and we were rushed out into the cold Arctic seas without delay. Each ship was given an overlapping patrol area. Within a week of commencing our patrol, the ASDIC system proved its worth. Despite rough seas and atrocious weather we were able to detect a submarine on the surface, charging its batteries.

After closing to the point where the U-Boat could be seen through binoculars, our Captain considered the options. We could open fire with our guns, but the chance of scoring a hit with the first salvo was unlikely in the conditions. Or we could fire a torpedo to run at a depth shallow enough to hit the submarine, again a tricky task. The Captain decided that the best course was to close quickly with the U-Boat and ram it. The destroyer was aimed, bows on, at the enemy vessel. They didn't see us coming until it was too late; we struck the sub just below the conning tower. It split wide open and sank like a stone.

With the bow of our ship left twisted and mangled we were ordered back to Newcastle. There were no enemy survivors and nor did we pick up any wreckage. In the absence of any other ships to witness the sinking the Navy refused to give *HMS Khartoum* official credit for destroying the U-Boat. Even so, we of the anti-submarine team were much congratulated.

The ship was given temporary repairs and within 48 hours was back at sea with flat plate for a bow, rendering the ASDIC useless. A proper bow was fitted later. For the next six months we were guarding Atlantic convoys and participating in the ill-fated Norway campaign (in which *HMS Kelly* was almost lost).

Then one day all eight ships were ordered into port. Their boilers were cleaned, the ammunition was stocked up, stores of all kinds – including tropical gear – came aboard and the fuel tanks were topped up to the very limit. The 'buzz men' worked overtime speculating on where we were going.

Eventually, all eight ships sailed south. To our surprise, off Land's End, four of the flotilla turned east into the English Channel, leaving *Khartoum, Kelvin, Kashmir* and *Kandahar* still heading south. The Fighting Fifth never worked together again.

Exquisite haberdashery

We sailed through the Bay of Biscay and on to Gibraltar. Compared with the furious North Atlantic and Arctic seas, the Mediterranean was paradise. The street lights were on in Gib, all the bars were open and people strolled around in summer gear.

Two days later we were on our way again, this time to Grand Harbour, Malta. Here the war did not yet exist and the Maltese poured aboard, laden with lace tablecloths, beautiful bedspreads and handmade scarves. They didn't want money for their goods, preferring to trade them for our northern clothing – long underpants and vests etc. Very soon the lockers were full of exquisite haberdashery.

Our next destination was Port Said where the statue of de Lesseps invited us to enter his creation, the Suez Canal. After traversing this we sailed down the Red Sea and into the port of Aden. It seemed to me that we'd gone from the bitter cold of the northern seas to the balmy warmth of the tropics in just a few days.

So what was our mission? The Captain explained that there were four Italian destroyers and a submarine in an Eritrean port and with Italy now in the war these warships were a threat to our command of the Suez Canal and the Red Sea. Our spies on the African coast were keeping a close eye on the Italians and one day word came that the enemy was preparing to put to sea.

We set off to meet them, lying in wait just out of their sight. As soon as they came into view we attacked them and sank all four destroyers without receiving even one hit in return. It has to be said that the Italian ships had been lying idle for a long time and their crews clearly lacked practice. All the survivors of the action were picked up and taken to Aden.

There had been no sign of the Italian submarine and consequently *HMS Khartoum* was ordered to patrol the deep water channel and watch out for it. Sure enough, next morning we made ASDIC contact with the submerged vessel as it travelled south. A full load of depth charges blew the sub to the surface and the shocked crew abandoned ship as quickly as possible a short time before it sank.

'Abandon ship'

With the five Italian warships accounted for, our Captain stopped *HMS Khartoum* and ordered all boats away to pick up survivors. Soon our ship was host to scores of prisoners. It was bright and sunny afternoon when, at just about lunchtime, a torpedo came out of nowhere and hit the *Khartoum* just above the keel, blowing out the bottom of the ship. Ten of our crew were either killed or seriously wounded. The Captain ordered us to abandon ship.

Unfortunately, at this time our own lifeboats were full of Italian seamen making their way to the small island of Perim. The crew of the main motorboat were called to the side of the sinking ship. They forced the Italians overboard and came alongside just in time to load up with our own dead and wounded. The amazing thing was that the ship was sinking on an even keel.

The rest of us had to make do with Carley Floats or swim for it. I found myself in the sea alongside my mate. We kicked off our shoes and set off in the warm sea. I consoled myself with the thought that any sharks would have been driven away by the many explosions. It must have been about four miles to Perim and we made it there ahead of the Carley Floats. A platoon of Indian soldiers commanded by a British officer were stationed on the island and they took charge of the Italians.

There had been enough time before *Khartoum* sank to radio Aden and the other ships about our plight and *HMS Kelvin* and *HMS Kashmir* set off at full speed to rescue us. Myself and the rest of the crew were spread around the other ships on a temporary

The Italian submarine that sank the Khartoum *was captured a short time later by* HMS Kelvin. *Here it flies the White Ensign as it is taken into Aden.*

basis and I was allocated to *HMS Kelvin*. We learnt that the source of the torpedo that sunk us was a second submarine in Eritrea whose presence had not been reported. It had been following the first submarine but had been some distance behind it.

Back in Aden the expected position of the second submarine was worked out by the Navigator of *HMS Kelvin*. He was Second Lt David Dunbar-Nasmith, a relation of Mountbatten and the Royal Family. He explained that if our destroyers steamed at full speed to the south of the sub's location and then reversed course, there would be a good chance of finding it using ASDIC. Dunbar-Nasmith later became an admiral.

In those days a submerged sub could only travel at between five and eight knots. To our absolute amazement we found it and *Kelvin* began her depth charge attacks which very soon blew the Italian vessel to the surface. To the credit of the enemy, they managed to reach their deck guns and open fire. But they stood no chance against our four-inch guns and after a few shells had hit their conning tower they gave up and struck their colours. After removing the crew we towed the submarine intact into Aden.

The homeless crew of the *Khartoum* were eventually put aboard a depot ship permanently docked in Aden. There were no spare uniforms so we were given money to buy clothing ashore. Gradually the crew were dispersed to other ships as required.

HMS Khartoum resting on the sea bed after being torpedoed off Perim near Aden in 1940.

Operation Jericho

How the walls came tumbling down at Amiens Prison on 18 February 1944.

The Mosquito Mark VI was particularly suitable for low-level precision attacks where accuracy was all-important. Built of plywood, the light aircraft was powered by two Merlin engines. On 18 February 1944 the opportunity came to demonstrate the Mosquito's prowess in the most dramatic fashion.

Nineteen Mosquitos – six each from No 487 Squadron RNZAF, No 464 Squadron RAAF and No 21 Squadron, plus one Photographic Reconnaissance aircraft – all under the leadership of Group Captain Charles Pickard, attacked the jail at Amiens on 18 February 1944. The object was to release some 700 prisoners, many of whom faced execution as members of the French Resistance. They included a Monsieur Vivant, a key member of the Resistance Movement in Abbeville. The prison, built in the form of a cross, was surrounded by a wall 20 feet high and three feet thick.

A model of the target constructed in Plaster of Paris (wedding cake decorators were found to be particularly skilful at this form of work!) was used for the briefing. It was designed to show the objective as it would appear four miles away to a pilot flying at 1500 feet.

The weather on 18 February was bad but it was the pilots themselves who insisted the mission went ahead. They took off from RAF Hunsdon an hour before mid-day, flying through storm and snow at close to sea level. Two waves of the attack approached the prison using the straight Amiens-Albert road as their guide.

Their bombs were so accurately placed in the prison walls and buildings that Pickard called off a third follow-up wave. A few moments later his aircraft was shot down by two Focke-Wulf 190 fighters, crashing just a few miles from the prison. Pickard and his navigator, Flight Lieutenant J A Broadley, were both killed.

The daring raid resulted in the escape of 258 prisoners including Monsieur Vivant but the bombs killed 102 others.

The German FW 190s were out of the Luftwaffe's Abbeville fighter base and sported the bright yellow nose of German air ace Adolf Galland's squadrons.

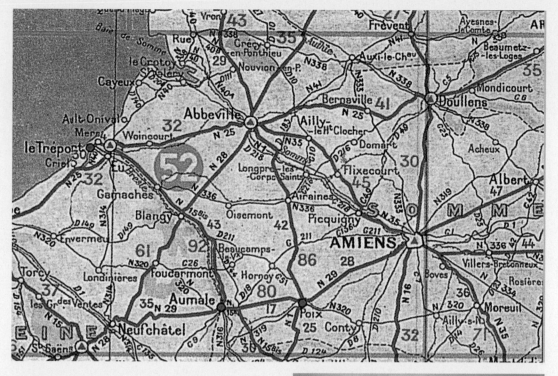

The Amiens area on a Michelin map of 1947. The road network was the same in 1944. Note the straight stretch between Amiens and Albert which the Mosquito pilots followed on their bombing approach to the prison. Abbeville – where German fighters were based – can also be seen.

International Mosquito Air and Ground Crew Memorial

The sole Memorial dedicated to the men and women who helped create, build, maintain and operate the Mosquito multi-role aircraft was unveiled in the spring of 2005 at the De Havilland Aircraft Heritage Centre in Hertfordshire.

The photograph here shows the ceremony which was conducted in the presence of members of the Mosquito Aircrew Association. From left to right are Air Vice Marshal David Walker ACAS, Eric Atkins, Chairman, MAA and Air Vice Marshal Stuart Peach.

The plaque reads: 'In Memory of all Allied Mosquito Air and Ground Crews who serviced, flight tested and flew Mosquitos on worldwide operations during and after World War II.

'Mosquitos were flown in a variety of roles, including bombing, pathfinding, unarmed photo reconnaissance, day and night intruders, night fighting, fighter/ground attack, precision

Garry Lakin

bombing attacks, interdiction, ship busting and anti U-Boat patrols, high speed courier operations, target towing and training.

'The Mosquito was the most successful multi-role combat aircraft, engineered from wood and became known as the "Wooden Wonder". The courage and dedication of both air and ground crews who flew and maintained the Mosquito was outstanding.'

Following the ceremony, the Mosquito Aircrew Association disbanded due to the advancing years of its members.

A Mosquito aircraft and the story of the 'Wooden Wonder' are to be found within the De Havilland Aircraft Heritage Centre, Salisbury Hall, London Colney, near St Albans (less than a mile from Junction 22 of the M25). The museum is open from March to October. Visit: www.dehavillandmuseum.co.uk

February 1944
WAR DIARY

The second month of 1944 opens with the repeal of a wartime austerity measure. Men can once again buy suits with as many pockets as they wish and the trousers can also sport turn-ups. Similar restrictions are lifted on pleats and buttons for women's clothing.

On **2 February** 300 Polish civilians are executed in Warsaw in reprisal for the assassination of SS Major-General Franz Kutschera the day before by resistance fighters.

In Moscow the Soviet leader Joseph Stalin finally agrees to the use of Russian air bases by American bomber planes. Aircraft hitting targets in German-occupied eastern Europe can now fly on to the nearer Soviet bases and re-fuel and re-arm for another mission before flying back to Britain. This 'Shuttle Bombing' allows for more missions and shorter flying times.

The head of Vichy France, Pierre Laval, accedes to Nazi demands for more Frenchmen to be made available for forced labour in Germany. The plan is to have 1,000,000 more men in service by June.

Red Army troops cross the border into the German-occupied Baltic republic of Estonia, capture the city of Vanakula and push back General Walther Model's Army Group North.

On **3 February** New Zealand and Indian divisions join the US Fifth Army in front of the Gustav Line in the Cassino area. Meanwhile, at Anzio the Germans begin a major offensive to reduce the beach-head. At one point along the front line a herd of 1000 or more sheep rush through the sector defended by the Irish Guards; it is thought the Germans purposely stampeded the herd in order to detonate as many mines as possible.

On the same day the Russians report the entrapment of 10 German divisions in the Dnieper River Bend, south of the Ukrainian capital, Kiev. Artillery salutes are fired in Moscow to celebrate the biggest such encirclement since Stalingrad in 1942.

On **4 February** the Japanese launch their 'Ha-Go' (operation Z) counter-offensive in Burma's Arakan region and bring the British forward movement to a standstill. Meanwhile, a brigade of Major-General Orde Wingate's famous Chindits prepare to depart Ledo in Assam on a march that will take them far behind enemy lines. The troops will be resupplied by air.

In the North Pacific, US Navy surface warships sail the closest so far to the Japanese mainland when they bombard Paramushiro, one of the Kurile Islands. Down in the South Pacific, mopping-up ends on Kwajalein atoll as the Americans close in on their next Marshall Islands objective, Eniwetok.

British Intelligence receive news from Paris of the arrest of Michel Hollard (**5 February**). Hollard is an agent who has been feeding back valuable information about the progress of Germany's secret V-weapons programme.

Newspapers report the recent sinking of three German blockade runners in the Atlantic by the US cruiser *Omaha* and two destroyers.

On the night of **6 February** a big German shell crashes through the roof of Major-General John P Lucas's command post at Anzio but fails to explode. Artillery fire is the major cause of casualties on both sides. For the Allies one statistic makes particularly ominous reading; on average 900 men are killed or wounded every day while just 500 reinforcements arrive.

Next day sees a Red air force raid on the Finnish capital Helsinki apply more pressure on the Finns to make peace now that the German armies have been forced away from Leningrad. Finland only entered the war against Russia in order to regain the territory ceded to the Soviets at the end of the 1939 'Winter War'. In that conflict Stalin was the aggressor; the Red Army initially received a bloody nose from the tiny Finnish forces but eventually their overwhelming superiority in numbers forced the Finns into a humiliating peace agreement.

On **8 February** the Japanese continue their attack in the Arakan, infiltrating the British and Indian troops of XV Corps and attempting to encircle them. The subsequent fighting mainly centres on the Corps forward administration area in the village of Sinzweya, an area that will go down in military history as 'The Admin Box'.

Next night a dozen Lancasters of 617 'Dambusters' Squadron led by Wing Commander Leonard Cheshire make a night raid on an important aero-engine factory at Limoges, dropping 12,000lb 'Tallboy' bombs to devastating effect. In the House of Lords earlier

俘 虜 郵 便
Service des Prisonniers de Guerre

WILLIAM ANDERSON,
CIVILIAN INTERNMENT CAMP,
CHANGI,
SINGAPORE.

檢閲濟
敵性人抑留所檢閲濟

FEBRUARY 2. 1944. FROM MRS HODDER
MIDLAND BANK
STAFFORD.
I HAVE BOUGHT A NICE SMALL MODERN
HOUSE. TWO RECEPTION, FIVE BEDROOMS.
LOGGIA. GARAGE. LARGE WELL KEPT
GARDEN. GOOD FRUIT TREES
FAMILY WELL
CAPTAIN BARBERS

INTERNMENT

Postcards were the only means of communication between Prisoners of War and internees and their folks back home. Martin Barton-Smith of Haywards Heath, Sussex, had an uncle, William Anderson, held in Singapore's Changi Camp. The postcard on the top left was sent to him by his wife who was in the Women's Internment Camp at Palembang. On the reverse side (not reproduced) she wrote reassuring words about being well treated. Mrs Anderson subsequently died in Japanese custody. The second postcard was sent by Mr Anderson's mother-in-law to him in February 1944. The card was censored by the British authorities before being forwarded on. Martin does not know what information on such an innocent document was considered of potential value to the enemy.

WAR DIARY
February 1944

that day, the Bishop of Chichester, Dr George Bell, questioned the morality of the RAF area bombing of cities and civilians. He quoted a figure of 74,000 persons killed in Berlin alone where 'our policy appears to be one of obliteration'. In reply, a Government spokesman denies that the RAF actions amount to terror raids, adding that the British will continue bombing 'with ever more crushing effect until final victory is ours'. Ironically, despite the weight of explosives falling on the Fatherland, production of tanks and aircraft within the borders of the Reich is rising at this time.

On **10 February** the Japanese decide to abandon the Pacific island of Truk. Holding it is untenable in the face of increasing US navy and air action following their invasion of the Marshall Islands to the east. On New Guinea, Australian forces link up with the Americans to further strengthen their grip on this immense island.

With a world war raging, Parliament still finds time for political conflict. Anthony Eden. Foreign Secretary, denies allegations by Welsh Labour MP Aneurin Bevan that the Government has been illegally putting many MPs on the State payroll with jobs outside the House of Commons (11 February). Under wartime legislation the Prime Minister can exempt MPs from having to give up their seats in the House if they accept 'offices of profit under the Crown'. Bevan says such jobs have been given out 'like confetti' to ensure Parliamentary support. The appointments are alleged to range from ambassadorships to seats on various tribunals.

12 February: Channel Islands. In the only part of the British Isles under the Nazi heel, Gestapo agents capture the author of Guernsey's clandestine newsheet (G.U.N.S.) and the duplicating machine that prints it in St Peter Port. Charles Machon and four accomplices face trial and likely death sentences. Other Channel Islanders have already suffered harsh retribution for 'crimes' such as the possession of radio sets or painting anti-German slogans on walls. One offender, cinema projectionist Stanley Green, has ended up in Buchenwald Concentration Camp. The Germans have heavily fortified the Channel Islands through the efforts of slave labour; all sorts of nationalities including Poles, Russians and even Mongolians, now live in appalling conditions in various camps.

This day also saw the sinking of the British troopship *Khedive* and the loss of 2000 lives when the ship is torpedoed by a Japanese submarine in the Indian Ocean. British destroyers later sink the submarine.

In Berlin suspicions of a plot against Hitler lead to the merging of the Abwehr military intelligence organisation with the Gestapo and Himmler's own SD security service.

On **14 February** the Germans inform the Vichy Government that they are taking direct control of the entire Mediterranean coast of France from the Spanish border all the way to Monte Carlo. Martial law will be imposed in the area, reflecting German fears of an Allied invasion and the prospect that Vichy might emulate Italy and change sides overnight.

In the Malacca Straits near Malaysia, the British submarine *HMS Tally Ho* sinks an enemy sub. Subsequently the crew is found to be German whilst the vessel itself was formerly in the Italian navy.

Pro-Nazi Argentinian army officers attempted a coup against the South American country's government on **15 February.** This is the same day that the Polish Government-in-Exile in London rejects Soviet proposals making the Curzon Line the eastern border for a post-war Poland.

On **16 February** the German III Panzer Corps leads the Korsun Pocket break-out west of Cherkassy. Soviet claims of some 52,000 Wehrmacht troops killed or captured are denied by the German High Command who say that over 30,000 men have already made their way back. Nevertheless, German losses in tanks and aircraft are severe; 45 Ju52 transport planes are known to be destroyed.

In neutral Stockholm a meeting is brokered between Finnish and Soviet representatives to discuss armistice terms. The Russian delegation hold all the aces and the Finns know they must make painful territorial and political concessions to win peace.

This example of Soviet poster art graphically depicts the Nazi beast being put to the bayonet. In the early spring of 1944, the Germans were in retreat all along the Russian Front.

The night sky over Berlin is filled with 891 British bombers returning to batter the city for the first time in a fortnight. Losses total 43 aircraft and it is apparent that the city's defences have been considerably stiffened with additional anti-aircraft guns and night-fighters.

On **17 February** American marines storm ashore on Eniwetok atoll, last bastion of the Japanese in the Marshall Islands. Fierce fighting lies ahead. Though the Japanese have already decided not to defend Truk in the Caroline Islands, they fail to evacuate their air and naval forces in time. In an intensive attack from the air, American fliers destroy 275 Japanese warplanes and sink around 40 ships gathered in and around the coral island's lagoon.

In London, plans for post-war Britain are revealed which include the introduction of a free health service for all citizens.

Off Anzio on **18 February,** the light cruiser *HMS Penelope* – a ship already nicknamed *HMS Pepperpot* on account of the number of hits it has sustained in various actions - is torpedoed and sunk by the German submarine U410 after it manages to penetrate the defensive naval screen. The Luftwaffe find success when they sink the cruiser *HMS Spartan* not far off the port. Losses of ships and landing craft are rising.

Even though the war had long since moved to the Italian mainland, Egypt remained an important staging post for the British not least because the Suez Canal was a vital link to the Indian Ocean and Far East. Here a Hudson bomber of RAF Coastal Command is shown flying over the pyramids.

WAR DIARY
February 1944

This night also sees the biggest German raid on London since the time of the 1940-41 Blitz. News is received next day of a vicious battle around the 'Admin Box' in the Arakan. Dependent on supplies brought in by air, the fighting saw rear echelon clerks, cooks and pay staff drafted into the front line in a successful bid to blunt the Japanese 'Ha-Go' offensive.

On **20 February** there is action in Norway where British Special Operations Executive (SOE) agents, aided by the Norwegian Resistance, sink a ferry taking a consignment of heavy water across Lake Tinnsjo en route to Germany. Heavy water is needed for the embryonic Nazi nuclear weapons research programme. (This incident formed the basis for the 60's Hollywood film, *The Heroes of Telemark*, starring Kirk Douglas.)

The Caribbean island of Trinidad is recognised as the British Empire's biggest source of oil with nearly 2500 wells yielding 20 million gallons a year.

American officials in Dublin pressure the Irish Government to expel German, Japanese and 'puppet' Italian diplomats. Whilst many Irishmen serve in the Allied armed forces, Dublin, as an 'anti-British' statement, continues to maintain full diplomatic relations with all the Axis powers.

On **22 February** Greek partisans blow up a German troop train on the main Athens – Salonika railway line. Over 400 soldiers die when the crowded carriages plunge into a flooded river. British SOE agents are believed to be to be assisting the Greek 'Andarte' partisan movement.

'Big Week' is well underway by 23 February. It's the codename for a joint RAF – USAAF campaign to blitz Germany's vital fighter and ball-bearing production centres. A secondary purpose of the concentrated air offensive is to draw out the enemy's fighter strength and destroy it in the air. Bomber formations pack an increasingly heavy defensive punch with machine guns covering approaches from all directions. In addition, long range Mustang fighter aircraft can now accompany the bombers all the way to their target and back all the way home.

Meanwhile London continues to receive the attention of the Luftwaffe as German planes bomb the capital for the fourth night in a row. The city's anti-aircraft defences take a heavy toll of the attackers. Press commentator Captain Norman MacMillan says that the raids are happening because the Germans are bringing aircraft to Western Europe in anticipation of the Allied invasion: 'The attacks are a combination of reprisal, exercise and employment of waiting forces … it is one of the penalties that Britain has to pay for being an advanced base.'

In the South Pacific aircraft from US carriers mount raids on the islands of Saipan, Tinian and Guam. At Anzio the besieged beach-head commander General Lucas is replaced by Major-General Lucien Trustcott.

On **24 February** the situation swings in favour of General Slim's 'Forgotten' 14th Army in Burma as they eject the Japanese from the important Ngakyedauk Pass in the Arakan. American-built Grant tanks of the 25th Dragoons blast the enemy positions in advance of the infantry going in.

In Helsinki the Finnish Prime Minister publicly announces a willingness to sign an immediate peace agreement with the Russians but subject to certain conditions. Moscow's angry response the next night comes in the form of a massive 600 bomber air attack on the Finnish capital.

That same night there's a huge 'Big Week' RAF raid by 594 bombers directed at the Augsburg aircraft plant. Success is limited as only 22 RAF planes find the target; 33 others were shot down. Nevertheless, 'Big Week' overall achieved its aims; immense damage was inflicted on Germany's industrial capabilities and 517 enemy fighters were destroyed. In pilot attrition, Germany will not be able to long stand losses of this magnitude.

On **26 February** the Japanese Premier, General Hideki Tojo, fires a number of top-ranking officers in a search for scapegoats to blame for his country's continuing reverses in the Pacific. Tojo appoints himself Chief of the Army General Staff, adding this title to his other ones of Premier, Minister for War, Controller of Munitions, Minister of Commerce and Industry and Minister of Education.

INSIGNIA OF VARIOUS ANTI-AIRCRAFT UNITS

6TH ANTI-AIRCRAFT DIVISION   **8TH ANTI-AIRCRAFT DIVISION**   **H.Q. ANTI-AIRCRAFT COMMAND**

News is released this day that Captain Randolph Churchill, the Premier's son, has parachuted into partisan-controlled Yugoslavia. A day later the BBC report German pressure on Tito's Yugoslav partisan forces south of Mostar. However, this is a minor offensive and it is becoming clear that the Germans will settle for containing the partisans rather than risking a large-scale engagement that would stretch their troop resources.

On **28 February** a big Allied convoy comprising 42 ships and a tanker arrive safely at the Russian port of Murmansk. Two U-boats were detected and sunk in the course of the voyage for the loss of the Royal Navy destroyer *HMS Mahratta*.

This being a leap year, on **29 February** the 1st US Cavalry Division lands on Los Negros in the Admiralty Islands and seizes the airfield at Momote. Debate now centres on where the US force will strike next. General Douglas McArthur says he is morally obliged to liberate the Philippines rather than by-pass the huge island chain and threaten an assault on Formosa and then Japan itself. In 1942 he had famously vowed, 'I shall return' when forced to quit the doomed fortress of Correggidor in Manila Bay.

On this day also the Finnish Parliament (The Diet) is urgently discussing the peace terms with the threat of more Russian bombing hanging over them. The bitterest pill for the Finns to swallow is the Russian insistence on occupying the Finnish naval base of Hango, key to control of the Gulf of Finland.

SHINE YOUR TORCH DOWNWARDS WHEN CROSSING THE ROAD

Government advice on how to cross the road during the black-out.

Desperate days in Italy

MARCH 1944

Anzio under siege

As March 1944 approached it was clear to the soldiers on the ground on both sides of the Anzio beach-head that neither adversary had the strength to defeat or dislodge the other. The most recent German offensive, *Fischfang*, had come close to a decisive breakthrough. But desperate Allied resistance, especially in an area known as 'The Caves' where men of the Queen's Royal Regiment at one stage found themselves holding off an estimated five enemy battalions, blunted the onslaught.

Yet still Hitler demanded one more effort from his men. On 29 February three German divisions of the LXXVI Panzer Corps attacked the American-held perimeter in the south of the beach-head, between Cisterna and Nettuno. But by 6.30pm on 1 March Field Marshal Kesselring had abandoned the attack. German losses included hundreds killed and more than 30 tanks, some of them flame-throwing types, destroyed. With some six weeks having elapsed since *Operation Shingle* began, the Germans admitted to casualties numbering 16,000 dead, wounded and missing, though the true figure was believed to be much higher. The Allies had sustained nearly 21,000 casualties, including many crew members of ships sunk or damaged.

Clear blue skies on 2 March invited Allied air action. Nearly 600 aircraft flew over the beach-head and dropped 350 tons of bombs on the surrounding German positions and troop assembly areas. BBC correspondent Wynford Vaughan-Thomas described the great flight of aircraft as '...looking strangely beautiful, remote and efficient as they came in from the south in an endless stream, jettisoned their load of death with a clinical detachment and swung back for more'.

Also watching was the beach-head's new commander, Major General Lucian Truscott. At one point an aide turned to him to exclaim, 'Christ General, that's hitting a guy when he's down!' But his mood quickly changed when he observed a B-26 bomber in flames following a direct hit by the German ack-ack.

A German gun on tracks prepares to fire on the beach-head.

THE FORTRESS

On the British side of the beach-head, fierce fighting continued well into March. Northwest of The Flyover and the main Via Anziate (the road to Rome) were a number of positions with names like 'The Boot' and 'Lobster Claws'. These were part of an area of deep gullies or wadis and large tracts of dense vegetation. For the infantry, fighting in this terrain was particularly difficult with visibility being restricted and infiltration after dark a constant threat. Close-quarter combat was common.

On 4 March the Sherwood Foresters in The Boot were relieved by the arrival of 660 men of the Royal Marine Commandos. The Foresters had suffered severe losses from nightly incursions by the men of the German Fourth Parachute Division who would lob grenades from the edges of the gullies into the British trenches – by day mortar 'stonks' and artillery barrages were plentiful. Following an ambush near a location called Pantoni, several hundred yards west of The Boot, there were only around 100 Foresters remaining who were able to stagger back to relative safety.

The fresh Commandos however, soon established their own regime of harassment and raids, giving back to the Germans more than a little of what they'd been dishing out for several weeks.

W J Campbell of Heswall, Wirral, was a Lieutenant and Intelligence Officer with the 2nd Battalion Cameronians (Scottish Rifles), part of the 5th British Division in Italy in 1944. After the fall of Rome he returned to Anzio and took the photographs reproduced above which depict the landscape of The Fortress, the most advanced and dangerous area in the British sector of the beach-head.

Anzio Annie opens fire

Raleigh Trevelyan came ashore with the Green Howards on 2 March. He remembers how, '...within 10 minutes I was almost killed by a shell from Anzio Annie, the railway gun. Within three days I was at a spot in the gullies called The Fortress... upon my arrival in the dark I was greeted with the warning, "Quiet, yer bloody fool – Jerry's only 70 yards away!"

'By day around our position it could be fairly quiet. But at night shells whirred and sighed continually overhead and there were airbursts. Machine-guns spattered, Jerry mortars coughed, ack-ack crackled and bombs crumped.

'Often we heard German voices. At one time we spotted a Spandau post on a ridge too far away to snipe at the men walking so obviously on the skyline but too near for our mortars and anyway we

didn't want to attract fire on our own positions. On another occasion two Germans, who turned out to be Danes, wandered into our lines carrying a dixie of greasy stew.'

Trevelyan also remembers the frogs in the springtime at Anzio. When they stopped croaking it was a sure sign of the approach of possibly unfriendly humans. 'On a number of occasions they warned us of the approach of Jerry marauders,' he recalls.

The young Green Howard officer had his diaries published in 1956 in a book called *The Fortress*. Following this he established contact with a number of Germans who had fought opposite him at Anzio a dozen years earlier. Trevelyan went on to write another excellent book about the Italian Campaign. *Rome '44 – The Battle for the Eternal City* was first published by Secker and Warburg in 1981.

The Goliath effect

On the ground in front of the Allied lines, a small remote-controlled tracked vehicle made its appearance. Trundling into minefields and against fortified positions its toy-like appearance belied a sinister intent. The Gerat 67 – 'Goliath' – was attached to a 2000 metre cable fed from a drum at the rear of the vehicle. Powered by petrol or batteries, Goliaths were used to move explosive charges as close to the Allies as possible before they were detonated. Over 5000 had been built before the Germans halted manufacture in late 1944. It seemed a good idea, but in practice the Goliath was slow and cumbersome and made an easy target.

An American swings a baseball bat for the camera in front of an anti-aircraft gun.

A convoy at sea laden with trucks and supplies heads for the Anzio beach-head.

Inside the beach-head a network of new roads were constructed under the most testing conditions. Any movement in the rear areas in daylight was likely to be spotted by German observers up in the Alban Hills and a rain of artillery shells could be expected. Fortunately, in the early months of 1944 the wet weather kept tell-tale dustclouds to a minimum. The US 36th Engineer Combat Regiment were especially accomplished road-builders. They also laid out the surfaces and storage facilities required for the many ammunition dumps. And when necessary these men took their place in the front line.

One unit that won itself a legendary name at Anzio was Brigadier General Robert T Frederick's colourful Canadian American First Special Service Force which has gone into the military history books under the name of 'The Devil's Brigade'. With 2500 men, one third of them Canadians, this elite force was created to 'perform impossible missions no other unit was trained to carry out.'

Frederick said that he only needed men who were 'rough, tough and unafraid of anybody or anything' and whilst the Brigade's ranks held a fair share of misfits and even criminals, the vast majority were

volunteers. They wore red berets and carried razor-sharp sheathknives. When Anzio settled down into a stalemate Frederick's 'Forcemen' continued to carry the fight to the enemy in sorties out of their positions on the extreme right flank of the beach-head. Just how effective these men were in unnerving their opponents can be gauged from a diary entry of a dead German officer: 'These devils are all around us every time we come into the line and we never hear them approach.'

The little village of Borgo Sabotini, around a quarter mile outside the 'official' beach-head front line, was taken over by the Forcemen and re-named 'Gusville' after a favourite Special Service Force Officer. They also gave new names to the village roads. The main thoroughfare became 'Tank Street', for the many German Panzer rounds that whizzed down its length. Another became 'Prostitute Avenue' after a war correspondent wrote that 'A man walking down it a little ways will soon find himself without visible means of support'. Gusville's 'mayor', Lieutenant Gus Heilman, proclaimed that his town had 'no strikes, unemployment or black market'. It also ran a well-stocked bar!

Audie Murphy's War

Audie Murphy was already a soldier with experience of fighting in North Africa and Sicily before coming ashore at Anzio on 22 January 1944 as a Staff Sergeant in the US 3rd Division. It was in the cauldron of the beach-head that this small in stature, baby-faced 19-year-old displayed the kind of coolness and courage under fire that marked him out to become one of America's most decorated war heroes.

Murphy's 'first blood' came at Cisterna. Following the disaster that befell the American Rangers on 30 January, his unit was sent in to reinforce the line. Later he was involved in dangerous night patrols, probing for German weak spots and hoping to pick up prisoners. A report from a Lt-Colonel said of Murphy, 'He could not stay out of a scrap at a Peace Convention!'. On one occasion he was awarded a Bronze Star for destroying an enemy tank with molotov cocktails and rifle grenades whilst under fire.

Audie Murphy went on to become a Hollywood film star, his biggest movie being the *The Red Badge of Courage,* in which he played a rookie Union soldier in the Civil War. In 1957 Murphy went to Rome to film scenes for *The Quiet American.* Whilst there he paid a return visit to Anzio and recorded his impressions: 'To look around it didn't seem like there had ever been a war there. But there was one thing that

makes you stop and remember ... the cemetery. Seeing those rows and rows of white crosses and knowing what they stand for surely takes away the holiday spirit.'

Audie Murphy died in a plane crash in 1970.

CASSINO - Heights of despair

One month after the formidable walls of the monastery atop Monte Cassino had been blasted into rubble by Allied bombs and shell-fire, it was the turn of Cassino town below to feel the full terrible force of Allied airpower.

'Between breakfast and lunch today', reported Christopher Buckley, Special Correspondent of Britain's *Daily Telegraph* on 15 March 1944, 'in brilliant weather, I saw Cassino flattened from the air by persistent almost ceaseless bombing over a space of four hours. The bombing, intended to reduce the German strongpoints to rubble, was followed by a terrific artillery barrage from massed Allied guns, after which the infantry went forward to the assault.'

There can have been but few occasions before or since - atomic devices apart – when a bigger load of bombs have been dropped on to so small a target. To observers watching from a hillside some two miles away, nearly all the bombing seemed to be remarkably accurate. Yet later it was discovered that less than half of the ordnance had fallen within the target area – and this in bright sunshine with practically no opposition – and the artillery bombardment also proved ineffective in crushing German resistance. As soon as the guns ceased and the troops moved forward, 'From the rubble,' reported Buckley, 'machine-gunners sprang to life. From caves and tunnels on the hillside, many of them prepared or enlarged during the previous week's lull caused by the weather preventing air operations, the enemy emerged.

Storm of explosions

'They came from the cellars of houses in front of and behind our advancing infantry. Three-quarters of Cassino was cleared and then, with the impetus of our attack partly lost, the enemy began to counter attack.'

Once more the Allies were thwarted. The combined explosive loads of 500 bomber aircraft and countless shells from 748 guns failed to subdue the tenacious German Third Parachute Regiment. Their losses had been severe: half of one battalion alone had been killed, wounded or simply buried alive in the storm of explosions. But in and around

In this propaganda leaflet the Germans cleverly illustrate the problem facing the Allies on the Gustav Line – whoever controls the mountain tops also has control of the roads in the valleys. In March 1944 the German grip on the top of Monte Cassino and in the ruins of the town below seemed as strong as it had ever been.

some hotel ruins in the heart of town, Major General Richard Heidrich had set up a strong central position surrounded by pockets of his men able to give mutually supportive fire in the face of assault from any direction. Many German snipers as well as some heavy weapons survived the air and artillery bombardment and these were soon back in action and taking a toll of the advance.

The biggest problem for the Allies though, was one they had created for themselves. The craters and vast heaps of rubble resulting from the

The ruins of the town of Cassino photographed after the massive Allied aerial bombing assault of 15 March 1944. The Germans retreated to the cellars during the attack and many later emerged unscathed to pour a withering fire on advancing New Zealand troops.

German observers survey the countryside from their vantage point on the heights at Cassino. It's easy to see what a tough task the Allies faced in trying to scale the mountains in the face of determined opposition from highly experienced paratroops.

bombs and shell-fire proved a major handicap for the attacking Second New Zealand Division. Their tanks were unable to negotiate a way through the sea of wreckage.

The Allied assault's ultimate goal was the bombed and blasted monastery at the top of Monte Cassino. But first a number of key points needed to be captured on the way up. Castle Hill was one that the New Zealanders secured by nightfall on 15 March. A prominent height nicknamed Hangman's Hill because of a gibbet-like structure visible on it from the plain below, was then the target of Gurkha soldiers of the Fifth Indian Brigade.

A company-strong group fought their way up to their objective but then found themselves cut off when the Germans counter-attacked furiously. Throughout the first night, mortar bombs, shells and small arms fire rained down on the Gurkhas. The Germans were so close at times that hand-grenades were lobbed by both sides. When daylight came the Gurkhas were forced to dig in as deep as the rocky mountainside would allow and keep their heads down. Many found themselves in hopelessly exposed positions and were picked off one by one.

For the next week these men endured a siege of their precarious mountainside position which turned into one of the most epic sagas of the whole Italian Campaign. Raleigh Trevelyan in his book *Rome '44* paid tribute thus: 'It seemed impossible that these small brave brown men, from a remote land thousands of miles from Europe, could exist up there, without enough cover from enemy fire, let alone the weather, and without enough to eat or drink.'

Gurkhas and Maoris

Soon the only means of supply for the isolated men was by air. Inevitably, most of the parachutes fell out of reach or straight into German hands. Wounded Gurkha Bihm Bahadur, a section leader, recalled after the battle: 'I can hardly remember the first supplies dropped by planes – just the sight of coloured parachutes fluttering to earth. I saw one of the cases land a few yards away, but I couldn't leave my trench because I would have been a "sitter" for the ever-alert Jerry snipers.'

Men of the Essex Regiment made a brave attempt to reinforce the Gurkhas but only 70 soldiers got through. Meanwhile, around Castle Hill and down in the town, the Allies had other problems. On the hill, other Essex soldiers, along with men of the Rajputana Rifles, found themselves under ferocious attacks by German parachutists reinforced by a Pioneer battalion. In the town, Maori troops took over 100 prisoners but were hard hit by rifle, machine-gun and mortar fire. A panzer half buried in the lobby of the Continental Hotel sprayed deadly rounds at the Maori positions.

New Zealand General Freyberg next pinned hopes on a surprise attack into the German rear via a mountain track known as the Cavendish Road. Sappers had worked on this trail in secret to make it negotiable for tanks. In Fred Majdalany's definitive account *The Battle of Cassino* the author says: 'The effect of the attack was likely to create similar consternation amongst the Germans as that experienced by the Romans when greeting Hannibal's elephants after their Alpine crossing.'

General Sir Harold Alexander, Commander of the British Forces.

Twenty two tanks destroyed

Unfortunately, things didn't work out according to plan. German surprise at the sudden appearance of American and Indian-crewed Sherman and Stuart tanks was short-lived. Panzerfaust – German bazookas – blew up the lead tanks and proceeded to decimate the rest of the column: 22 tanks were destroyed.

Within days the Third Battle of Cassino was effectively over when General Sir Harold Alexander called a halt to further offensive operations. By then Freyberg had already called off the frontal assault on the Monastery and had recalled the valiant Gurkha and Essex soldiers from Hangman's Hill.

On the night of 25 March the difficult withdrawal by 257 men began. The Monastery was bombed again to provide a diversion and fighting patrols of the Royal West Kents – who'd earlier relieved the New Zealanders in The Castle – went out to engage German attention. A heavy fall of snow settled on the mountain. Eventually all the men got safely down with the exception of several severely wounded soldiers who had to be left for the Germans to tend to. Despite the ferocity of the fighting, the Cassino battles were notable for various acts of chivalry. Red Cross flags and truces to enable the wounded to be evacuated or treated were usually respected by the fighting men on both sides.

The Colonel of the Gurkhas reported that when told they were leaving their desperate and untenable position, his men were only concerned as to which unit would they be handing the safekeeping of Hangman's Hill. Imagine their sorrow when – next morning – the German flag once more flew over their former position, so hard won.

The surviving Germans on the Gustav Line at Cassino counted the Third Battle as a victory. But the Allies hadn't so much been driven back as denied an advance. Time could only favour one side and the certainty of better weather and better visibility gave an impetus to Allied preparations for re-newed attacks with fresh forces in the springtime.

Roman relics

In one of the strange ironies of war, even as the Allies and Germans battered the town of Cassino into a vast heap of rubble, there were parts of the place that had already lain in ruins for some 1500 years past. 'Casinum' had been an important town in Roman times, famous for the thermal properties of its waters. Visitors today can view the amphitheatre (pictured right) and other examples of Roman architecture whilst in the town's National Archaelogical Museum there is a fascinating collection of exhibits ranging from the prehistoric period through to the age of Rome.

NORTH SEA RENDEZVOUS

Cold nights and deadly fast boat encounters remembered.

Early in 1944 I returned to MTB 241 at Felixstowe after three weeks in an RAF hospital with pneumonia. Not surprising really – the North Sea gets extremely cold in winter and being soaked with it nightly is not to be recommended.

MTB 241 was part of the 21st MTB Flotilla. The late Peter Dickens* (great grandson of the author, Charles) had departed a few months previously and his role of Senior Officer had been taken over by our skipper Jim McDonald, the youngest ever at 21.

I had done my Light Coastal Forces training at Fort William in the summer of '43 where we were told that crews were in the main aged under 25. Imagine my surprise on joining 241 to find Ginger Harry, a 47-year-old 'three badge' gunner – and what a character. He was much liked and knew all the wrinkles - how to get in and out of the base without going through the regulating office and how to get rabbits ashore without troubling Customs etc.

Our tasks were mainly to attack German convoys off the Dutch coast but also on moonless nights to lay mines in and around their harbours. Also there was the much detested Z patrol which entailed laying silent in the water about 40 miles off the East Coast waiting for the return of E-Boats which had attacked our coastal convoys. Their convoys were almost the exact opposite of ours in that while we generally had 20 or 30 merchantmen protected by two or three destroyers, they would have two or three merchantmen protected by 30 or more armed vessels of varying types. We would quit the enemy coast an hour before dawn.

On 19 February 1944 whilst on night patrol we encountered a convoy and after spending some 90 minutes making unsuccessful attempts to infiltrate we broke off with dawn about to break. Mac called for air cover and very soon two Beaufighters appeared and exchanged signals, circling us several times before disappearing. Ginger Harry manned the twin Vickers .5 gun turret just aft of the bridge and I was his re-loader. Sudden gunfire alerted us. One of the two Beaufighters had returned but peeled off and was strafing MTB 223 on our starboard quarter. Then he started to dive on us; Ginger didn't wait for any order from the bridge – he opened up. The plane pulled out of its dive and flew off.

All five boats stopped. Half the crew of 223 were dead or dying. Two of the badly wounded were transferred to the fastest boat with instructions to proceed full speed to Felixstowe, but they died before arrival – six of the 12 crew were lost.

We received an apology next day. With most so-called 'friendly fire' incidents some reasonable excuse can be found but try as I might I can make none for this. Visibility at the time was 12 miles with no other surface craft to be seen and our five boats were in an area the size of a football pitch, flying white ensigns and heading towards our East Coast.

A couple of weeks later we had just begun a patrol between the Hook of Holland and Ijmuiden when we sighted a large convoy protecting two big merchant ships. Torpedoes were primed and we went to infiltrate. Maybe our concentration was too much on the target as suddenly an E-Boat appeared about 100 yards off our port bow and a shower of tracer crossed our bridge. We accelerated to our maximum speed of about 38 knots and by this time were being attacked from several directions. The tracer seemed mostly aimed at the following four boats but suddenly there was a load crack and our speed dropped dramatically. The ERA emerged from the engine room to report that there was three feet of water down

Anti-Aircraft gunner on alert aboard a British Motor-Torpedo-Boat (MTB) in the North Sea.

there resulting from a below water line explosion, probably an 88mm shell.

At this point one boat came alongside to take us in tow and Mac left with the remaining three boats to continue the fruitless attack. In the meantime while ropes were being passed we came under attack again apparently from some straggling defenders of the convoy. Fortunately for us they did not press home their advantage. We were towed for 10 hours by which time the after third of 241 was completely submerged. The crew dismantled guns and took all useful items (including the rum jar!) on to the towing boat. 241 was then sunk by gunfire. On return to base Mac was very upset that we'd lost the boat.

We were sent on seven days survivors' leave and were due to return to pick up MTB 234. At 1200 a week later there was one absentee – Ginger Harry. Mac came aboard mid afternoon and noticed his absence. He did eventually arrive at 1630 and the following day he was up before the skipper to receive two days stoppage of pay and leave. I had never seen Ginger so upset; all day he kept chuntering on that he wasn't working two days for nothing, but by evening he had found his solution. 'I've had this hernia for years – it doesn't trouble me but tomorrow I shall be at the Sick Bay'. And sure enough he was – but we never saw him again. Apparently it was decided that he needed an operation but he did not survive the anaesthetic.

About mid-March again on patrol we encountered another German convoy about an hour before dawn. It was decided that two of our five boats should separate and create a diversion from the inshore side while we attacked from the seaward side. A rendezvous was pre-arranged. Once again our clever ploy was doomed to failure and we had to break off.

We'd been proceeding to the rendezvous for about 20 minutes when six ships were spotted on the horizon. We simply continued on our course and as the gap closed we came under some fairly inaccurate fire. At about 1500 yards we turned hard to port and then hard to starboard so that we had the targets - 2000-ton coasters - broadside on. Our three boats each sank one ship with one torpedo and then a coaster was selected for a concentrated gun attack. Within 10 minutes the coaster was well ablaze and the other two enemy vessels disappeared in seconds. No survivors could be observed. Our other two boats had also encountered two armed minesweepers apparently intended as escorts for the six coasters, and sank one of them.

Years later it did occur to me that Mac's determination not to ask for air cover again was a good move. If our arrival near the enemy coasters had coincided with that of the Beaufighters we would probably have been taken to be their escorts and suffered the same fate.

Bernard Hagger, Gosport, Hants

*Peter Dickens wrote Night Action, *a book about the small boat battles in the Channel and North Sea in World War II.*

THE GREAT ESCAPE

24-25 March 1944

Today the place is called Zagan and is part of Poland. But in 1944 it was known as Sagan and was in the German territory of Upper Silesia, around 100 miles south east of Berlin. Two years earlier, the Luftwaffe had chosen the area's bleak and wooded terrain as the site for a new POW camp when it became evident that extra accommodation would be needed for captured Allied aircrew officers. An isolated clearing in a pine forest with a harsh and cold climate through the long months of winter became Stalag Luft III, ideally suited in the eyes of the Luftwaffe planners for discouraging escapes.

Persistent escapees purged from other camps found on arrival six bare barrack huts ringed by a nine-foot double barbed wire fence. Just outside, 100 yards apart, on 15-ft stilts, stood sentry towers or 'goon-boxes', equipped with searchlights and machine guns. Ten yards inside the fence ran a warning wire; any POW seen crossing the wire risked being shot without warning by the guards.

From the very first day escape schemes, some opportunist, some long-term, were put in hand. By one means or another a few prisoners succeeded in getting out but evaded capture only for hours, or a day or two at most. Solitary confinement in the 'cooler' – the camp prison – was the usual consequence.

In spring 1943 the inhabitants moved to a new, larger, compound containing 15 huts. Eventually it grew to hold 10,000 prisoners contained in 59 acres encircled by five miles of perimeter fencing. By that time Stalag Luft III, under the leadership of Squadron Leader Roger Bushell, a South African-born London barrister, had become one large escape factory divided into a variety of 'trades'. There were specialists in the forgery of documents, passes and tickets, map copying, metal work, carpentry, rail and air pump manufacture, compass making, tailoring, German language tuition and counter-spying on the camp's 'ferrets' who were on constant look-out for tell-tale signs of unusual activity by the prisoners.

TOM, DICK and HARRY

While individual escape attempts continued, work began on three major projects – the digging of tunnels code-named 'Tom', 'Dick' and 'Harry'.

John Sturges' 1963 movie The Great Escape *took a lot of liberties with the facts, but made for an exciting adventure film. Whilst many incidents seen in the film were based on what actually happened, the famous scene where Steve McQueen comes agonisingly close to successfully leaping over the barbed wire border fence on a motorcycle into neutral Switzerland is totally fictional.*

Each tunnel was to be around 30-feet deep to thwart the German sound detectors. To preserve secrecy only a few dozen men knew the whereabouts of the tunnels and most inmates were even unaware of what huts the trap doors were in. Elaborate effort went into diverting the attentions of prowling 'ferrets'.

In the summer when 'Tom' was well advanced there was a slip up. One of the 'penguins' – the sand disposal team – was spotted emptying the contents of his trouser bag. A prolonged German search led to the discovery of the tunnel's trap door in one of the huts.

For a while tunnelling was suspended. Then tunnel 'Dick' was abandoned when it was seen that the area where it was due to surface had been cleared of covering vegetation. But 'Dick' did prove useful for storing much of the sand extracted from the third tunnel, 'Harry'. Another useful depository for the tons of yellow sand was under the stage of the camp theatre. The Germans encouraged the POWs to make their own entertainment (believing that prisoners kept busy and entertained would be less likely to escape) and had even lent the tools 'on parole' for the prisoners to build the theatre. Preserved theatre programmes from Stalag Luft III feature names such as George Cole, Peter Butterworth (of later *Carry On* fame) and Rupert 'Maigret' Davies.

Work on 'Harry', which had its entrance in Hut 104, went on through the winter when the Germans least expected such activity. Thanks to a long length of 'liberated' electric cable, 'Harry' even had light to aid the diggers. By March 1944 the tunnel was deemed ready. The bitter weather was far from ideal for escaping but delay was considered too risky.

On the night of the 24 – 25 March the chosen 220 assumed their varied 'civilian' clothing (although one man was dressed in a 'home-made German army uniform), checked counterfeit papers and tickets, pocketed food rations and made their way to the escape hut, which rapidly became very crowded..

Complications set in. Men lying horizontal on trolleys became wedged. Wheels came off the wooden rails. Digging up to the surface took much longer than planned. Then, horror of horrors, it was found that the exit had emerged in the open, 10 foot short of the line of trees. Nevertheless, over a period of seven hours, 76 men had scrambled up through the hole in the ground at the end of 'Harry' and made off into the darkness.

At this point, by sheer bad luck, an armed guard wandered within a few feet of the tunnel and spotted an emerging escapee. He raised the alarm and captured a couple of men on the spot. Many others in the tunnel had to wriggle around and crawl back to the hut where they were soon discovered by the alerted Germans.

HITLER ORDERS EXECUTIONS

The break-out sparked a nationwide hue and cry. German radio broadcast the news. Gestapo and police worked through trains checking papers. Vehicles were stopped and searched. In his Berchtesgarden mountain retreat, an enraged Hitler ordered that all recaptured escapees be shot. He later amended this instruction, demanding instead the execution of at least half of those rounded up.

Most of the escapees were quickly caught. In fact just three eventually reached safe havens. Per Bergsland and Jens Muller (Norwegians serving in the RAF) made it to neutral Sweden while another foreign volunteer pilot, Bran 'Bob' van der Stok, finally reached Gibraltar via a long journey through Holland, Belgium, France and Spain.

'Great Escape' organiser Roger Bushell and companion Bernard Scheidhauer caught a train from Sagan Station and made it as far as Saarbrucken before two security policemen questioned them. Their forged passes stood up to scrutiny but they fell victims to a simple trick when a parting question was fired at them which Bushell's companion answered in English. The pair were arrested and handed over to the Gestapo.

Fifty recaptured escapees were executed. Bushell and his companion were amongst the victims. On the evening of 29 March 1944 two Gestapo agents – Dr Leopold Spann and Emil Schulz - escorted the pair by car down the autobahn to Kaiserlautern. At a point along the road, the car stopped, the two airmen were ordered out and then shot. The bodies of both were cremated at Saarbrucken.

MAXIMUM CONFUSION

Bushell had always known that few escapees would get home to freedom. He was more interested in creating maximum chaos and confusion inside the Reich and forcing the Germans to divert precious troop resources in time-consuming manhunts. But he couldn't have expected such vicious retaliation that totally contravened the Geneva Convention. The Germans themselves issued identity discs to Allied POWs with which they could prove they were not spies should they effect an escape in civilian clothes and later be recaptured.

In mid-July 1944, Foreign Secretary Anthony Eden reported the killings to the House of Commons and promised that the perpetrators would one day be brought to justice. At the war's end, teams of Allied investigators launched intensive searches for the guilty Gestapo men; in the resulting trials many received the death sentence or lengthy imprisonment.

Roger Bushell's killer Dr Spann died in an air raid on Linz in the closing days of the war. His accomplice Emil Schulz was hunted down, tried and found guilty of murder. He was hanged at Hamelin on 27 February 1948.

The best-known book about the Stalag Luft III break-out is **The Great Escape** *by Paul Brickhill, first published in 1951. Since then there have been plenty of other books. An informative website dedicated to the story and detailing what happened to the participants can be found via the Google Advanced search engine. Simply key in: The Great Escape – Rob Davies.*

Squadron Leader Roger Bushell (left) pictured in captivity not long before organising the mass break-out from Stalag Luft III in March 1944. Spitfire pilot Bushell had been shot down on 23 May 1940. He effected several escapes during his time in various POW camps which included a spell in Colditz Castle. Right: A German soldier examines the tunnel the day after the break-out.

Home Front

Some jottings from newspaper gossip columns

'The town near which I live received a consignment of oranges and all the children seemed to be sucking them and throwing away the peel. I really should have liked to see a collection of it made. Now that candied peel of the sort that was so good in puddings and cakes is unprocurable, orange peel makes a very fair substitute. And although these oranges were not of the kind used for marmalade of the best quality, their peel could have been used to stiffen and flavour. It went to my heart (or should I say, to my stomach?) to see this waste. The Ministry of Food advocates the use of the peel on the grounds that there is twice as much Vitamin C in the peel of an orange as in the flesh or juice.'

*　　*　　*

'What fresh torments to railway travel has been added by the station announcers whose voices rumble overhead and for the most part, in my experience, give no help at all. Their accents, sometimes hoarse and unpleasing, sometimes ladylike and mincing but often quite agreeable or amusing, have on many passengers a merely disturbing effect. The novelty was introduced to save the station staff from being too much interrogated by passengers about their trains. But just as many flustered men and women – especially men, I think – seem to be asking questions of the harassed porters, guards and ticket-inspectors.

'Nevertheless, the good order and absence of agitation and excitement at the London termini and those in other big cities is very remarkable. People wait patiently, they move about methodically, they most of them take the trouble to look at indicator boards or posters to find out about their trains. I would have children taught to do that at school.'

*　　*　　*

'What has happened to our dog population during the war? What with meat rationing and the consequent shortage of dog food one would have expected a drastic reduction in numbers of our four-footed friends. In fact the decrease has been remarkably small. In 1939, the official estimate was of 2,800,000 dogs kept as pets or working animals in the UK. At the start of 1944 the estimate is 2,400,000 amounting to approximately one dog to every 16 human beings.'

Spring 1944 in Italy. Around Monte Cassino and the beleaguered beach-head at Anzio, the Allies and Germans remain locked in deadly struggle. Rome is the prize.

Naples to the south is a popular rest and recreation centre for the men of the Fifth and Eighth Armies. Then on 18 March, ancient Vesuvius awakes. The volcano's spectacular eruption threatens to bury Pompeii once again just as it did nearly 2000 years before.

The enormous plume of smoke can be seen by the fighting men at Cassino and by Allied sailors far out at sea. Aircraft make wide detours while hundreds of others are destroyed by a rain of ash on their airfields. Mother Nature puts war into perspective.

In the next 10 days Vesuvius will unleash explosive power equivalent and more to that contained in all the bombs, shells and mines in all the arsenals of Europe, those of friend and foe alike.

Having vented her anger, Vesuvius returns to the sleep of ages. She still slumbers today. But for how long?

VESUVIUS ERUPTS

March 1944. War Correspondent William Connor files a report from Naples.

'This country has got everything. Within an area less than that of an average English county, you can be bombed, shelled, machine-gunned, mortared and volcanoed.

And it's free.

Best, safest and most spectacular is being volcanoed.

I took time off, to see Vesuvius proving the truth of that hoary old gag about the unwisdom of living on the side of a volcano. Since a real volcanic eruption is far more rare than war, I think I should describe to you just what happens.

Away on the top all hell is a-blowing. From out of the crater comes smoke, steam, ashes and a vast, red-hot primeval sludge called lava. This stuff, billions of tons of it, is oozing down the sides of the volcano. It is a vast, crawling slag-heap about 40 foot high. It is the original black guts of the earth. Time has slipped a million years and here, slithering across a Naples vineyard in the bright sunlight, is the stuff this globe was made of when it was just a pup of a world. When it cools you have the stuff the moon is made of – black, cold clinker.

I watched it digest an Italian village for tea. The dark, smoking cliff pushed a wall down and edged into a fresh dewy garden where broad beans were in flower. The heat withered the plants within about 10 feet. On it came.

The tide crept forward and tumbled round a tree that suddenly burst into flame. Then on to the front of a house. Up the walls and round the side. The house caught fire inside and half an hour later vanished without a trace. Nearby a church was being engulfed. The sea of molten clinker came up to the roof. The old building stood it well. All around, houses had fallen, but the church held out. It collapsed suddenly with a roar and a last wild despairing jangle from the bell in the tower.

There is something rather fearsome about a town being destroyed by lava. War leaves some trace – gutted houses, bomb-pitted streets. Vesuvius leaves none.

You can go into a room and see the last few pitiful possessions that the owner could not take away – an old cot, an iron ladle, a faded photograph. Within an hour or so, all will be vanished – a handful of ashes entombed 40 foot below the sunlight. No stone will mark the place where there was once a town. Only a memory.

Vesuvius has 40 winks, and a century is gone. When he awakes he yawns, stretches his arms, and a hundred thousand people start looking for new homes. The big boy seems to be half out of his bed now and looking for a fight.'

Top: A 17th century painting depicting Pompeii during the 79AD eruption.
Below: A revealing fresco discovered in the excavation of the buried city.

The dark cone of Vesuvius silhouetted against a bright blue Mediterranean sky is the most striking sight in the Gulf of Naples, perhaps even the whole of Southern Italy. Over 4000 feet high, the volcano is composed of lava spit forth in the course of eruptions of various intensity (some 70 since the most famous one which buried Pompeii and Herculaneum). The most recent began on 18 March 1944 and continued till the end of the month. For a while the fury and fireworks of Vesuvius convinced many Neapolitans and Allied troops that another cataclysm of the kind that swallowed Pompeii and Herculaneum was imminent. It wasn't to be. Even so the energy released by the volcano in those couple of weeks was reckoned by vulcanologists to have added up to more explosive power than all the conventional bombs and shells used up in the entire Italian Campaign. It was as if Mother Nature herself was demonstrating the futility of man waging war.

A few years ago the editor of *Sixty Years On* walked to the summit of Vesuvius and enjoyed a splendid panorama of the Bay of Naples whilst observing ominous fumirole smoke wisps still emerging from within the cone. Visitors can drive quite a way up the volcano's side but the last half mile must be hiked. A funicular used to run up one side of the mountain but it's been out of action in recent years – this is still Italy, after all!

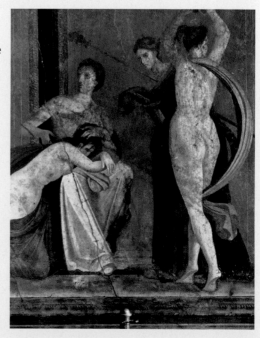

Above: Vesuvius from space! This is a NASA image of the volcano taken from a satellite. The cone of Vesuvius can clearly be seen in the centre.

LOST
ON AN AFRICAN SHORE

The poignant story of an astonishing air and sea coincidence in the midst of war, remembered by Ron Holton.

The Wellington bomber 'K for King' photographed in the position where Ron crash-landed it on the Atlantic coast of North Africa in 1942. Notice the kit of the crew in front. The photo alongside shows the aircraft going up in smoke to prevent it falling into enemy hands.

In 1942 I found myself as second pilot of a Wellington bomber and ordered to fly to India. Because Germany at that time occupied most of North Africa, and Vichy-France had gone over to the enemy, fighters operating out of Casablanca were a threat to our aircraft. Furthermore, Franco's Spain was hostile to our cause. Accordingly, it was decided that the safest route for our aircraft bound for Egypt and points east was to travel far down the Atlantic before turning left and flying across Africa. The route comprised: Gibraltar - Bathurst - Kano - Khartoum - Wadi Halfa - Cairo.

Our troubles began when we were about half-way down the long leg between Gibraltar and Bathurst and flying at about 4000 feet when, on switching over to our over-load tank, both engines stopped dead. Rapidly switching back to main tanks got both engines re-started but they ran intermittently and were clearly losing power. At about the same time we noticed that fabric was peeling off the port wing - later we discovered that some corrosive acid had been sprayed on it. Our wireless operator immediately began sending out SOS calls but was getting no replies.

It soon became evident that we must ditch. Being flanked by the hostile Canary Islands to our right and Spanish Rio-de-Oro (territory since annexed by Morocco) to our left on the African mainland, capture or death seemed inevitable. We decided that if only we could reach Africa our chances of escape might be better. Accordingly I turned sharp left and I was faced with the prospect of a dicey forced landing. We just managed to clear the top of the cliffs before I thumped her down causing severe damage to the tail of the aircraft but fortunately no injuries to the crew.

The next three days were spent in clearing the fuel systems of the contaminated fuel and making emergency repairs to the wing. In the meantime the wireless operator kept sending distress signals with a rigged up extended aerial until the batteries were exhausted - no replies were forthcoming. We cleared a strip of stones and rocks heading towards the cliffs which were about a hundred feet high and nurtured the rather suicidal hope of being able to get airborne and not simply plunge into the sea. Our plan was to fly south in the hope of finding a friendly ship near which we could ditch before we ran out of fuel.

Back to Gibraltar

On the very morning selected for making our get-away, the attempt had to be postponed because a heavy sea-fret or haar had crept in adding to our hazards. As the mist cleared, to our astonishment we saw a British warship, *HMS Laforey*, a Lightning Class destroyer, inching her way straight towards our position. At first I thought that the sun had affected me and that it was all an illusion. But it was real enough. Cutting the story short, after destroying our aircraft we spent two days on board the *Laforey* as she sailed back to Gibraltar. Everyone on board treated us as honoured guests - even the main-brace was spliced!

At the inevitable court of enquiry we discovered that the only vessel to pick up our faint distress calls was the battleship *HMS Nelson*, then operating in the South Atlantic. She had relayed our message to the naval base of Simonstown in South Africa, which, in turn, had relayed it to the ship nearest to our position, the *Laforey*, with instructions to search the coastline for a downed Wellington.

Subsequently we were sent back to the UK on board the small troopship *Leinster* and who should escort us on our lonely way? Yes, the *Laforey*. She was going home to be refitted while our future was to pick up another aircraft and fly out east for a tour of operations in Burma.

We now move on to a date in 1944. I was in the middle of another tour but this time in the Mediterranean. My detachment of No 36 Squadron was temporarily based at a small airfield named

Lost, found and lost again! Ron Holton and the crew of his RAF Wellington bomber were miraculously rescued by the Royal Navy destroyer HMS Laforey (pictured here) in 1942. By an incredible coincidence, two years later in 1944 Ron was to witness from the air the destruction of the very same ship, sunk in the Mediterranean by a U-boat that was itself doomed to destruction.

Montecorvino near Naples and close to Mount Vesuvius, which had just started to erupt. A hail of ash and pumice put our airfield out of action and for a time day turned into night. When at last the eruption died down and the wind changed, Herculean efforts soon had a runway cleared and our aircraft serviceable again.

The crew of the Wellington - Mike, Jimmy, Del (left to right, back row) with Tommy, Frenchie and Ron Holton himself in front.

Stromboli erupts

The first task allotted to my crew was to act as cover over a joint flotilla of 11 British and American destroyers and frigates in the area north of Stromboli. It was at night, Stromboli, like Vesuvius, was in full eruption and made an awesome sight. We used it as a navigational fix. Apparently a U-Boat had made a sinking in the area, and nemesis awaited the submarine as soon as it surfaced, as inevitably it had to. We were there as an insurance policy should the U-boat break through the cordon and head for its base at Marseilles in which event we would pursue it using our radar and Leigh light and sink it with depth charges.

It was a beautifully calm and peaceful night until all hell broke out around us. There came a series of large explosions, tracer fire and more explosions, and then powerful searchlights began sweeping the water, obviously looking for survivors. Soon after this we received a signal recalling us back to base. There we learnt that the U-boat had indeed surfaced but in doing so had discharged its full complement of remaining torpedoes into the hull of the nearest ship. The vessel had immediately exploded and sank within minutes, taking almost all of the crew with it. The U-Boat, whose captain was obviously a very brave man, was also sunk. Several hundred men had died within minutes that night.

Some days later we heard that the ship that had taken the full force of the torpedoes was none other than our beloved *HMS Laforey* which had saved our lives some two years before.

We felt stunned when we heard the news. This beautiful ship and her fine crew had literally saved our lives. They had taken us to their hearts, had shared their rum and meals with us, had entertained us in Gibraltar as only the Navy can, and finally had escorted our transport all the way back to the UK.

It was difficult to believe that now probably all those friendly faces were lying in many fathoms of water. And for us, who owed them so much, it seemed incredible that we alone of all crews should have witnessed their deaths. Since our last meeting the *Laforey* had sailed over 100,000 miles, and we had flown about an equivalent amount in the Far East and the Med, only to come together at the last tragic moment.

The sinking of HMS Laforey *as reported in the Forces newspaper,* The Union Jack. *The ship sank on the night of 30 March 1944.*

Ron lives in East Lothian, Scotland. The above story is an extract from A Desire for Wings, *a book, as yet unpublished, written at the behest of his three children whilst he was awaiting a heart operation some years ago.*

THE HOT BREATH OF VESUVIUS

The 60th anniversary of the eruption of Mount Vesuvius in Italy brought back memories of 1944. I was flying from Foggia aerodrome in Wellington bombers with 104 Squadron, 205 Group. We had a rest camp at Sorrento called the Hotel Minerva, financed by Lord Nuffield (of Morris Motors). It was situated on the cliff in full view of Vesuvius, across the Bay of Naples.

We were on leave at the Minerva in March 1944 and whilst sipping our vino on our hotel balcony there was a sudden rumbling and there across the bay was Vesuvius erupting - a quite fantastic sight.

After returning to Foggia our next operation took us to a turning point off the island of Ischia and whilst heading west we experienced a terrific surge of air which pushed us up a thousand feet or more, almost to the point of stalling. No fun with nine 500lb bombs on board! Everybody talked about it at debriefing, at which point we all realised we'd flown close to Vesuvius where the heat from the angry volcano was creating powerful thermal currents. It was these superheated thermals that carried us up.

I did 39 night bombing operations in all. On one occasion at Sorrento when we arrived for a rest period, the Bay of Naples was packed with every type of naval vessel you could think of - landing craft, torpedo boats, destroyers and much more. When we awoke the following morning there wasn't even a rowing boat to be seen.

Upon our return to Foggia we were assigned the target of the port of Genoa. On our way there we witnessed an amazing sight - it was the armada of vessels which had departed the Bay of Naples. They were supporting *Operation Anvil*, the South of France landings, which began on 15 August 1944.

My wife and I have been back to Sorrento. The Hotel Minerva is still there and the staff made us very welcome when we paid a visit. After a tour of Pompeii we went up to Vesuvius to look at the crater created in the eruption I witnessed over 60 years ago. I have a beautiful framed picture looking down into the crater - a little bit of history.

Fred Clarke, New Romney, Kent

*The eruption of Vesuvius in late March 1944 caused havoc on many Allied airfields in the Naples area. Some 90 US bombers were engulfed in ash and destroyed at a single location (see picture below) a loss very much higher than that sustained by enemy action over the same period in the Italian theatre of operations.

YANKS IN EAST ANGLIA

Alan Cater of Orpington, Kent, pays tribute to the role of the US Army Air Force in helping win the war in the skies over Europe.

I was 14 years old in 1944. I received the cane for the last time at school, was buried alive by a V1 explosion in July and witnessed what was probably one of the last recording sessions by the Glenn Miller wartime band at Broadcasting House.

I started work for the BBC in October 1944 and my title was 'Boy'. I was just that - an errand boy. On one occasion I was walking along Portland Place when there was an explosion in the sky which caused a violent concussion wave. There was a huge cloud of smoke but what caused the blast I know not, most likely a V1 or V2 rocket.

When I got back to the office for my next errand my boss asked me if I was OK. 'Yes', I replied. 'Right.' he said, 'It's now time to get the evening papers'. No post-traumatic stress or counselling in those days! Getting the evening papers involved a scrum which usually took place on the steps of the church opposite Broadcasting House. I had to get the right number of copies of *The Star, Evening News* and *Evening Standard* (the latter being the only survivor today). I recall one occasion near Christmas 1944 when the headlines read, 'Germans break through in Ardennes, Allies fall back, heavy fighting', etc etc. How could this be, wasn't the war nearly won?

Another of my routine tasks was to file the previous day's news bulletins. Here's a typical

Alan Carter (centre) with Jane and Bob Lash in Tuscon, USA, in 1998. Bob was a pilot with the 95th Bomber Group in Suffolk in 1944. Bob passed away shortly after this reunion.

example: 'This is the nine-o-clock news read by (Alvar Liddell / Bruce Belfrage / Stuart Hibberd). Last night a strong force of RAF Lancaster and Halifax bombers attacked targets in Germany, 42 of our aircraft are missing.'

Several decades later my interest in those times resurfaced. One day I was tramping around the remains of an old wartime American airbase at Horham in Suffolk. This was the home of the 95th Bomb Group of the Eighth USAAF. There also happened to be some former veterans visiting and we got

talking. One story they related concerned 4 March 1944 when the 95th was part of an 800-strong force of B17s and B24s which took off to make the first American daylight raid on Berlin. On the way a recall signal was received and most of the aircraft did a 180 degree turn for home. All that is, except the 95th and 100th BGs. The 95th was led by one 'Lootenant' Alvin Brown with Lt/Col 'Grif' Mumford as his co-pilot (it was Brown's aircraft so he was the boss).

For the sake of brevity it is only necessary to say that Brown and Mumford ordered the rest of the group to press on to Berlin. They got there and bombed and were about to face the wrath of the Luftwaffe when P51 Mustang fighters appeared. As one aircrew member remembered: 'It was just like the movies.' Four aircraft were shot down. Brown and his crew returned safely.

Two days later on 6 March it was the 'Big B' again. This time it was different. No recall. So all 800 set off on a mission that saw the Americans suffer their biggest loss in a single day of the air war; 69 aircraft were shot down along with 11 fighters. This was 69 times 10 plus 11 fighter pilots. Many of the aircraft carried back dead and wounded aircrew. There is a book, *B17's Over Berlin*, by Ian Hawkins which I recommend to anyone wishing to find out more about this period of history.

Moving on - in later years I have attended several Eighth Air Force reunions as a 'Friend of the Eighth'. One in particular stands out. It was in St Louis, Missouri, where I met for the first time 'Lootenant Al Brown', a very fit 80-something. I asked him about that 'recall signal' (it had always been a bit of a mystery). To use his words, 'We were suckered.' Apparently the Germans had been able to crack the code of the day and it was they who had sent the recall signal. They too must have had a Bletchley Park.

To this day many friendships still exist between the folk of East Anglia and the American veterans with reciprocal visits taking place. The USA's involvement made it possible for the Allies to win the war. At their peak they were producing 400 aircraft a day. Their resources were such that when there were parties for the children living around the UK air bases they would think nothing of making an ice cream mix and sending up a B17 to 30,000 feet to freeze it!

This article may seem 'American intensive'. Maybe so, but it is certainly not meant to diminish what the Royal Air Force achieved. Up until early 1944 they had carried out the brunt of the bombing campaign. It was in that year that the Americans overtook the British in numbers of aircraft but never the tonnage carried. One other tragic reminder; on 30/31 March the RAF attacked Nuremburg and lost 100 aircraft.

War Correspondence

As individual instalments of Sixty Years On *were published we received numerous letters and contributions from readers. To help with the chronological flow of this omnibus book, we have, so far as possible, put the letters as close to the time they allude to.*

Warrington to Monte Cassino

At the outbreak of World War II, I was 10 years old and growing up in the Warrington area, close to the Manchester Ship Canal. During the war everything was rationed and my mother used to send me blackberry picking on the banks of the canal. There you could find the juiciest, most luscious blackberries I have ever tasted and they made the most fantastic jams and pies.

Huge American ships negotiated the canal, also many other types of military vessels and even submarines. German pilots used the waterway to plot their course to bomb Manchester and Liverpool. One Saturday afternoon I can remember a German plane flying so low that I was able to see the pilot, his hat, goggles and white scarf and also the swastika on his wings! Close by, there was a factory with a children's party in progress and that was where he dropped his bomb, killing many of the children. Understandably, this had a profound effect on me.

Although he was really too old, because of his knowledge of animals, my father joined the Veterinary Corps and during the next five years, he became involved in the Italian Campaign. Last year my husband and I spent a holiday in Italy and we visited Monte Cassino, seeing many of the places my father told me about plus the war cemetery shown in *Sixty Years On*. We were extremely moved by the whole experience; we owe a great deal to these men and I, for one, will always be grateful.
Mrs Margaret Banks, Clitheroe, Lancs

Yanks in Portland

I was seven years old in 1944 living in Wyke Regis, a village between Weymouth and Portland in Dorset. It was the time of the build up for the invasion of France and Portland had a Naval Dockyard which was full of US Navy invasion shipping for the passage of tanks, vehicles and infantry. Portland is joined to the mainland by the Chesil Beach, a large causeway of shingle that carries a road and, at that time, a rail link.

The beach had been bulldozed to form an enormous vehicle park. There was a steady stream of tanks, half-tracks, trucks and jeeps etc passing through our village on their way for embarkation. When the convoys parked up, we local kids would go along and ask 'Got any gum chum?'. The Yanks had plenty of

Errol Walling of Middlesex sent the following: 'Seeing 'Anzio Annie' mentioned in Sixty Years On *in connection with* **Operation Shingle** *reminded me that I have this photo of the gun in my possession. I haven't a clue now how I acquired it as I was with my RAF Squadron in Alghero, Sardinia, from April to September 1944 and then moved on to Foggia via Naples.'*

'Anzio Annie' was a massive railway-mounted gun that the Germans housed in a tunnel miles away from the beach-head. Once a day the 280mm gun was trundled out to fire a single 563lb high explosive shell at the Allies. Two examples of this K5(E) gun that could reach targets nearly 40 miles away survive. One is on display in an Atlantic Wall museum near Cap Gris Nez, not far from Calais. The other is the original

'Anzio Annie' (pictured in colour here below Mr Walling's photograph) which can be seen at the Aberdeen Proving Grounds Museum, Aberdeen, Maryland.

supplies and would throw sweets, chocolate and cigarettes out to us. Sometimes they even gave away their K Rations which included a fruit bar, a chocolate bar, a packet of cigarettes and a condom! I always took the chocolate home to be shared and the ciggies were for my father. God knows what the condom was used for; I could never understand why a soldier going into battle needed a balloon!

As they were leaving Britain they had no further use for our currency so they tossed their coins to us kids. In one morning I collected 10 bob, more than my Dad earned in the same time as a shipwright.

Just up the road was a big tented camp for the Americans. This was also an attraction for us kids. I remember an occasion when one lad climbed aboard a parked jeep, pressed a button and the thing started up and drove in reverse around a tree before it stalled and we all scarpered.

I clearly recall the last German air raid over the dockyard. Mum, Dad and I watched as the planes came over and the sky lit up with tracer bullets. It seemed that the gunners just pointed their guns upwards and let rip. Dad then had to rush off as he was also an air raid warden.

I remember D-Day itself, though naturally we didn't know it at the time. It began with the constant heavy drone of aircraft. We stood in the garden and saw the lights of countless aircraft flying south. They carried paratroops or else were tugs pulling gliders. The invasion of France had begun.

Soon there were casualties coming back. The Navy beached the after end of a damaged LCT (Landing Craft Tank) on one of the beaches at the harbour near our home and we had a great time playing in it until one lad fell down the engine room ladder and badly gashed his thigh.
Chris Jennings, Kent

MIXED EMOTIONS

Every schoolboy loves a hero, and one particular wartime pilot delighted Peter Champion with his death-defying swoop over Brighton Station. Trouble was, the aircraft had a swastika on its fin...

The schoolboy of 1944 was the same as the present day version: a mixture of Just William and the Artful Dodger. Brought up in wartime England, he was a scavenger of all wartime relics, from anti-aircraft shrapnel to cartridge cases and pieces of liberated enemy aircraft, and would volunteer for any activity that kept him out of school.

It was with these principles in mind that I volunteered as an ARP (Air Raid Precautions) messenger boy. The only requirement was a bicycle and a willingness to be on duty at an ARP post from 10pm until 4am. The reward? The following day off school.

Our 'post' was the basement of a government-commandeered house near Brighton Station. Most nights (once a week) were spent playing snooker on a well-worn table and making tea for the adult wardens who manned telephones which, in the event of the phone lines being clobbered by bombing raids, would have brought us into being as messenger boys carrying rescue information from one ARP Post to wherever it was needed. Such an incident never occurred!

One cold crisp night in March 1944 air raids were in progress over London and down into Surrey. The reverberating throb of the synchronised German bomber engines meant that you knew when the enemy were overhead, even on a pitch black night, and it was a relief when the noise trailed off.

Dull red glow

This was such a night, attended by the rumble of heavy anti-aircraft fire and distant bomb bursts. At about 2am things were getting extremely busy and four of us left our basement shelter of the ARP Post to cross the road which was on higher ground and looked down at a slight angle over the whole of Brighton Railway Station. This gave us a good view to the north where we saw a continual dull red glow as the raid - presumably on London - progressed.

Stabbing the sky from a dozen different points and locations were the pencil beams of searchlights, criss-crossing the sky in an effort to illuminate the enemy so that the anti-aircraft batteries could get an accurate fix. When caught in the searchlight beams by probably three beams at once, the aircraft would appear as a shiny silver dot. We always hoped to see it erupt in a ball of flame, although invariably it would manoeuvre wildly and escape the lights.

As we craned our necks over the long wall, the anti-aircraft fire increased in volume and the predatory searchlights became closer; they were at a very low angle in the sky, the German was flying very low - and south, towards us!

Explosions and flashes

The excitement mounted. Fear? No, all schoolboys knew they were bullet-proof, and that nasty things always happened to other people. The noise of the German aircraft was becoming more audible now as the twin 1750V horsepower engines bit into the night sky, lending more urgency to the German's flight.

Hearts racing, we suddenly saw the streamlined aircraft almost on the deck flying just above the London to Brighton railway line. The anti-aircraft fire was now ear-splitting - he was so low that small arms fire and machine guns were opening up. There were explosions and flashes all around us. We watched, mesmerised, as it seemed certain that the German aircraft was about to fly straight into Brighton Station. He flashed past us. The aircraft was a German Messerschmitt 410 twin engine machine with a crew of pilot and navigator. It a had a mottled camouflage finish, a large black cross outlined in white on the fuselage and a similarly marked swastika on the fin - all this noted in a fraction of a second.

We astounded ourselves as we heard our own voices shouting, 'go on, go, go, faster, faster!' We were willing the Germans, our bitter foe for years, to escape. The pilot obliged us by lifting his nose just slightly over the station roof to be swallowed by the night sky and the coast. Did he make it, was he injured or is he now resting his weary bones in retirement in some home for ex-Luftwaffe aircrew?

We returned to our ARP Post puzzled by our own reactions to the incident. Was it that every schoolboy is a sucker for any Superman, or that perhaps, just perhaps, we stopped being schoolboys for a moment in time and grew up a little that night? I like to think so.

Peter Champion is a professional artist who still lives in Brighton, some 60 years on from his wartime schooldays. His painting on this page is an impression of how he remembers the incident would have looked from the air.

WAR DIARY
March 1944

March begins with the arrival in France of Field Marshal Erwin Rommel – the legendary Desert Fox. Rommel's Afrika Corps had almost pushed the British out of North Africa before the Eighth Army under Montgomery inflicted a decisive blow at El Alamein in November 1942. Now Rommel has the job of bolstering the German forces in Northern France in preparation for the expected Allied invasion. Fate decrees that Rommel's adversary will again be Montgomery.

Figures released in Berlin on **1 March** reveal that some five million 'guest' workers are now employed in keeping the Nazi war machine functioning. In reality the workers are slaves.

German Navy chief Admiral Donitz requests priority be given to production of the 'Schnorkel' device. This enables U-Boats to stay under the surface for long periods and evade the Allied warships and aircraft. Since 1 January, 34 U-Boats have been sunk.

On **2 March** tragedy befalls a train carrying hundreds of Italian civilians crammed into freight cars near Salerno. Over 400 die from carbon monoxide poisoning after being stuck for several hours deep inside a tunnel.

On the same day in Buenos Aires a coup led by army officers sympathetic to the Nazi cause fizzles out after 48 hours of confusion. Extreme right-wingers in the Argentine armed forces are angry at the government's decision to sever relations with Germany and Japan. The Minister for War, Colonel Peron, is seen as the 'strong man' influential in resisting the rebellion.

The Argentine decision to back the Allies is in contrast to Turkey's neutral stance. Access to Turkish bases would greatly aid bombing campaigns against targets in the Balkans. However, Ankara does turn a blind eye to incursions into Turkish waters by British SBS (Special Boat Squadron) forces as they make hit and run attacks on German garrisons in the Greek islands.

In London, Sir James Grigg introduced the Army Estimates to the House of Commons and reported that the British fighting forces were '…the best we've ever had. Far too little has been said in praise of the British soldier.' Grigg added, 'Sooner or later the enemy must crack. However, Germany is fighting with the utmost resolution and, except possibly where Hitler's intuition has been at work, with consummate skill.'

By **3 March** some six million Italian workers are on strike in protest at the forced deportations of Italian menfolk to Germany where they are made to work in arms factories. For two days now no trains have left Milan.

In the South Pacific desperate attacks by the Japanese on Los Negros are beaten off by the US forces.

This Vichy poster depicts the alleged toll of French civilians killed as a result of the spring 1944 Allied bombing of strategic targets.

Next day (**4 March**) the Kremlin announces that the Red Army have advanced to the River Bug in the Ukraine and have trapped a large German force in and around the town of Uman.

On **5 March** Paris radio announces the execution of 26 men convicted of resisting the German and Vichy authorities. The victims include four in Clermont-Ferrand who are described as '..members of a gang which had murdered a militiaman and a gendarme and committed many acts of sabotage.'

In Burma three brigades of Chindits begin their airlift to a position 200 miles behind the Japanese lines at Indaw. Chinese forces in the region advance on the town of Maingkwan.

Next day a daylight raid on Berlin by 658 US aircraft results in the loss of 70 bombers and 11 escort fighters, the largest number shot down in a single day so far in the war. The Americans dropped 2000 tons of bombs in and around the city and claim to have destroyed at least 123 enemy aircraft. The RAF are in action over France with a big raid on the important railway marshalling yards at Trappes, south west of Paris.

On **7 March** *The Times* reports the appointment of three additional High Court judges to help relieve congestion in the divorce courts. One of the new judges is Alfred Thompson Denning KC.

8 March: Japan hits back in Burma with a surprise offensive in the south. *Operation U-Go* is a major attack aimed at the key communications and supply centre at Imphal, in the Indian border state of Assam.

On the home front the Government announces plans for 200,000 new houses per year after the war. Meanwhile miners at pits in Wales and around Durham have gone on strike for higher wages.

On **9 March** the Americans begin air operations out of Momote in the South Pacific Admiralty Islands.

In Belfast a hunger strike by 22 jailed IRA men enters a second week. The men seek recognition that they are political prisoners and should not be made to wear prison clothes. In Dublin, the Eire Government turn down renewed US demands that German and puppet Italian diplomats be expelled. The Americans fear that the Germans are spying on the large numbers of US troops in transit through Northern Ireland as they prepare for the invasion of Europe. However, the Irish will claim they have shut down a powerful radio transmitter inside the German legation.

On **10 March** Convoy RA-57 returns to Loch Ewe in Scotland from Northern Russia. Just one vessel was lost on the way, further proof that the U-Boat threat is greatly diminishing. On the Russian Front, the Soviets say they have captured the German airbase in the Uman pocket, east of the River Bug.

In Hungary, Nazi leader Adolf Eichmann is formulating plans for the deportation of the country's Jewish population.

Berlin: **11 March.** The Germans call for more women to come forward for community service and take over jobs vacated by men called up for military service. In Russia, German Army Group South is in retreat across a 500-mile front. Some 200 Tiger and Panther tanks are abandoned for lack of fuel.

Next day in Algiers the Free French authorities sentence Pierre Pucheu, former Vichy France Minister of the Interior, to death for treason. Members of the Vichy-backed 'African Phalange' are also on trial for treason.

Casualty figures for troops from the British Empire reveal that in four years of war it is the New Zealanders who have suffered the most in relation to their home population. Some 7100 have been killed, 7300 wounded and 801 are missing. Australian casualties number 16,600 killed, 18,000 wounded and 7000 listed as missing. Aussies known to be POWs number 30,000.

WAR DIARY
March 1944

Lancasters, workhorses of the British Bomber Command. Statistically, in Spring 1944 bomber crews had just a 50% chance of safely completing their tour of 30 operations.

13 March: The UK has acted to isolate Eire following Dublin's refusal to cut Axis ties. Around 250,000 Irish citizens working in the UK are refused permission to go home for fear of intelligence leaks to the Germans. The same measure applies to 164,000 Irish serving in the British armed forces.

On **14 March** three German rocket scientists at Peenemunde on the Baltic coast are put under temporary arrest by the Nazis. The trio includes Werhner von Braun and they are accused of failing to give enough attention to the military applications of new rocket devices dubbed 'V for Vengeance' weapons.

15 March: Reports of German forces gathering on the border of Hungary. Hitler fears Hungarian regent Admiral Horthy will defect to the allies. Tonight 863 RAF bombers target Stuttgart.

16 March: South Pacific: A US task force bombards Manus in the Admiralty Islands as marines prepare to storm ashore.

Next day in the Mediterranean the troopship *Dempo* is torpedoed and sunk by a U-Boat – 498 US soldiers are lost.

In Finland, the future of 100,000 German troops in the country is undecided. Moscow wants them to be interned whilst the Finns insist that their former allies be repatriated to Germany.

Allied aircraft attack industrial targets around Vienna. Britain and the US are undecided how to treat a post-war Austria. Germany had annexed Austria into the Reich via the 1938 *Anschluss;* even the hardline Soviets describe Austria as '...the first country to fall victim to the Nazi aggression.'

On **18 March** the Nazis arrest Admiral Horthy in Salzburg whilst German army units move to occupy key locations in Hungary. This is also the 100th day of Russia's increasingly successful Great Patriotic War against Germany. Artillery salvoes are fired off in Moscow to celebrate new victories. The Russians are nearing the border with Rumania; Dubno, an ancient fortress known to the cossack warriors of Taras Bulba, has been captured.

Next day there are reports of German troops moving into Hungary from the Yugoslavian province of Slovenia despite the fact that Tito's partisans are operating as close as 10 miles from the Austrian border.

20 March: British newspapers fill with stories of the Russian advances all along the Eastern Front. The BBC discuss the proper

'Unrest in the coalfields is settled as 60,000 British miners return to work.'

pronunciation of 'Bug', a river on the Russian – Polish border. The Poles say it as 'Boch' as in 'Loch'; the Russian pronounce it 'Book' whilst most Britons call it 'Bug' to rhyme with 'Rug'.

21 – 22 March: Japanese units cross the border from Burma and enter India, establishing a foothold in Manipur.

In Budapest, the Germans have installed Dome Sjotay as a replacement for deposed Admiral Horthy. Around 50,000 German troops have also moved into Rumania to protect vital oilfields.

23 March: War Office statistics state that more than four tons of bombs fell on Germany during every single minute of the 24 hours ended at noon today. A big RAF raid on Frankfurt leaves 120,000 civilians homeless and claims nearly 1000 lives, according to German sources. Meanwhile, in Athens, trains full of Greek Jewish families are leaving the city bound for Auschwitz in Poland.

24 March: Rome. A partisan bombing of a parade of German SS soldiers is avenged in savage fashion with the execution of 336 civilians – 10 for each soldier killed - in the city's Ardeantine Caves. Many of the victims are Jews.

Maj-Gen Orde Wingate – charismatic leader of the legendary Chindits – dies in a plane crash on the India – Burma border.

In Britain the unrest in the coalfields is settled by a four-year deal guaranteeing jobs and wage levels from now until 1948. Some 60,000 South Yorkshire miners will now return to work.

A bomb explosion at the British CID Headquarters in Haifa, Palestine, last night killed three policemen. Other bombs go off in Jaffa and Jerusalem. Zionist groups demanding a Jewish homeland state are the prime suspects.

25 March: Two Mosquito aircraft of 248 Squadron armed with six-pounder guns sink a U-Boat close to the Bay of Biscay shore of France.

Next day sees 350 US Marauder aircraft drop 600 tons of high explosive on E-Boat bases at Ijmuiden in Holland. Germany's fast motor-torpedo boats pose a threat to the Allied invasion fleet.

Turkey suspends the despatch of goods to Hungary in protest at the German take-over. The Hungarian Prime Minister, Kallay, has taken refuge in the Turkish Legation in Budapest.

27 March: Vichy authorities exhort Frenchmen to enlist in the German SS, to fight against communism. But the SS also play a major role in the genocide directed at the Jews. Today in Kovno, Lithuania, SS men round up all Jewish children under the age of 13.

29 March: The growing problem of refugees in Europe is addressed by a US Congress decision to grant $1350 million to found the United Nations Relief and Rehabilitation Agency.

In the Pacific, US carrier-borne aircraft bomb Japanese ships at anchor in the Palau Islands.

Next night sees 795 RAF bombers in a major raid on Nuremberg. RAF losses are heavy with 95 aircraft lost and 12 making crash landings back in Britain at the end of the 1500-mile round trip.

Meanwhile Arctic Convoy JW-58 has arrived wholly intact in Murmansk, Northern Russia, despite sustained Luftwaffe and submarine attacks. Four U-Boats were sunk and six aircraft shot down by the powerful escort force.

On **31 March** an invasion exercise at Slapton Sands in South Devon ends in chaos. Men of the US VII Corps use live ammunition to give realism but the results are 'unimpressive' to observers.

The Luftwaffe's 'Little Blitz' of the opening months of 1944 has faded away in past weeks; figures released by the War Office show that 279 civilians died and 633 were injured by enemy air action during the month of March.

You forget — but she REMEMBERS

CARELESS TALK COSTS LIVES

APRIL 1944

The Italian Campaign

'Italy is like a boot. You must, like Hannibal, enter it from the top...'

Napoleon's words from nearly a century and a half before would have rung true with any students of history caught up in the Italian Campaign of 1944.

The Allies in April were still stalled in front of the Gustav Line, unable to find a way past the resolute German defenders who held the high ground. Monte Cassino's position at the mouth of the Liri Valley – the route to Rome – was a textbook 'impregnable' natural fortress as taught in Italian military staff colleges for years past.

Winston Churchill posed the question to General Alexander, '..I wish you would explain to me why this passage by Cassino, Monastery Hill etc, all on a front of two or three miles, is the only place which you must keep butting at. About four or five divisions have been worn out going through these jaws... looking at it from afar, it is puzzling. Please explain why no flanking movements can be made'.

Alexander responded patiently, blaming a combination of the country's geography, bad weather and the extraordinary tenacity of the German paratroopers. He might also have pointed to the German containment of the Anzio beach-head, the ambitious 'wildcat' landing far behind the Gustav Line that had become, in Churchill's words, 'a stranded whale'.

German propaganda found innumerable ways to exploit the slow advance of the Allies in Italy. This leaflet points out that by 1 April 1944 their progress towards Rome since the invasion of the Italian mainland on 6 September of the previous year amounted to 0.80 metres a minute. A snail's pace. The geographical shape and topography of the country counted against the Allies.

British troops on the Cassino front firing a captured German 75mm Pak Gun.

Anzio Annie

The men on both sides at Cassino saw the eruption of Mount Vesuvius which had begun towards the end of March. Writing 10 years ago, J A Baynes of Knutsford, Cheshire, a Royal Signals wireless operator attached to an Royal Artillery Field Regiment equipped with 25 Pounders, recalled '..a distinct memory of the time was the eruption. The huge black clouds of ash belched out by the volcano could be seen from Cassino and earth tremors felt'.

Up at Anzio, constant bombing and shelling were the main hazards in the bridge-head with the railway gun, Anzio Annie, a particularly deadly nuisance. But the mined waters off the Anzio-Nettuno coastline could be just as dangerous as the land. Ships and landing craft were shuttling non-stop backwards and forwards bringing men and supplies and taking off casualties and units going on leave. Some 20,000 Italian refugees were evacuated to Naples.

Minesweeping was an endless task. Lt Commander G H Dormer was in charge of a British minesweeper. His diary for 13 April records: 'We started sweeping again at 0800. A few minutes later ... BANG ... the sweep just ahead of us is blown up. As we alter course sharply to stay in swept water, someone looks over the side amidships ... there is a mine just under the water, about six feet away ... phew! We had to go back again to find it to sink.'

Newsman Colin Wilson filed a beach-head report on 16 April highlighting the exploits of the 18th Light Anti-Aircraft Regiment who had set up a 'world record' by shooting down 31 German planes and 10 more 'probables' during a single week: 'Here these crack Ack-Ack marksmen have to be on the alert 24 hours a day for the chance of a few seconds' snap shooting and into the bargain are watching and waiting under almost continual shellfire.

'They sleep fully dressed, ready to man the guns against night raiders or infiltration by German infantrymen.'

Wild flowers bloom

The weather improved and wild flowers bloomed all around the Anzio beach-head. Honeysuckle, narcissi and cyclamen appeared, swiftly colonising even the most recent shell and bomb craters. Apart from the ever-present sound of artillery, naval gunfire and aircraft overhead, the days saw little front line activity. At night patrols went out to recce enemy positions and hopefully capture an unwary sentry or two.

But the warmer weather brought a new hazard as mosquitoes put in an ever more frequent appearance. Lice had never gone away and were as persistent and unwelcome a guest to the Tommies in Italy as they had been to the British soldiers in the trenches on the Western Front during the Great War.

In the town of Anzio an underground cinema had been constructed, seating 35 people at any one time. Not that the troops anywhere in Italy were particularly impressed with the films on offer. A columnist in the Eighth Army's *Crusader* newspaper of 16 April 1944 complained that the 'newsreels we see out here are so old they're already history. We like to see what's happening in England. Bring our homes a little bit closer to us. That's the greatest service they can provide.

'And why aren't there any cartoons available other than Pop-Eye? Even his staunchest fans are beginning to get tired of seeing him every time they go to a show.'

By now the port of Anzio-Nettuno was said to have become the seventh busiest in the world with up to 8000 tons of supplies landed on a single day. There were setbacks; on 3 April 150,000 gallons of petrol ignited in a spectacular explosion that claimed several lives.

This early spring period seems, with the value of hindsight, to have been one where the Allies were marking time. The destiny of the beach-head was going to be decided by events elsewhere. Senior officers realised this. Indeed, neither General Sir Harold Alexander, Allied forces supremo in Italy, nor Fifth Army commander General Mark Clark, visited the beach-head at any time during the month of April.

Relentless air attack

On Easter Sunday British troops at Anzio had powdered eggs for breakfast. Their enemies fared a little better; German front line soldiers also had eggs but theirs came hard-boiled but at least were fresh.

The Germans knew they had done a good job in containing the invading forces within the confines of the beach-head for so long but

This German propaganda leaflet highlights an alternative to the BBC for British troops in Italy.

given the air superiority of the Allies and the evident build-up of men, armour and ordnance, only the most ardent Nazi would deny that time was not on Germany's side.

Road and rail supply routes from Austria into Italy were under relentless air attack from the air and Italian partisans were becoming bolder in the mountains. Though diplomatic considerations and a wariness of upsetting the Vatican were hampering bombing operations of key transport junctions in Rome, the population of that city was severely repressed by the Germans and their Italian fascist supporters but could rise up in open revolt at any time.

Down south on the Gustav Line, the Allied commanders had been mesmerised by the heights of Cassino and Liri Valley for many months. Their hammering on this door - behind which lay the road to Rome - had been immensely costly in the lives of soldiers of both sides and the hapless Italian civilian populace. But by the end of April there were signs that the military hinges of the door were weakening. Would one final push at Cassino provide the impetus for an Allied advance here and a break-out at Anzio?

The Eternal City, Rome, is the glittering prize.

Echoes from Anzio

We reproduce below extracts from a letter sent out of the Anzio beach-head early in 1944 by Sergeant Henry Patrick King to his brother Chris who was also serving in Italy.

Mike King's father is in this picture taken by an official Allied photographer visiting the Anzio beach-head. Sergeant Henry Patrick King is the one with the woolly hat, bending over a machine gun. He is binding asbestos tape on the barrel to reduce the effects of heat. The weapon is a .303 medium machine gun weighing about 56lbs and water cooled. The rounds came in boxes of 1000 and the gun could fire 500 rounds per minute but was usually fired in five second bursts. Mike believes that his father was killed within a few hours of the photograph being taken.

Dear Christy

What ho, here I am deep down in the bowels of the earth, doing my best to rattle off a couple of letters. I've just managed to write one home to Joan letting her know I'm OK. We are living like snakes out here, as soon as a Jerry plane comes over there's not a soul to be seen, everyone goes to ground a bit lively.

The lads here are still in action but will be out in a day or so for a rest, so we were lucky not to be sent up the line right away. It may be a week or so before I go up I hope. At present I've got the job of teaching them a few things they have probably forgotten about the gun. Perkins and all the others are OK. He's on guard tonight by the way. You might tell Dick Bellinger and Tom Sanders that I am OK and will do my best to win this ******* war for them. Also tell them that Mr Wallwork has gone like a lot more. Dead. I don't know how he got it.

Captain Weatherhead and Mr Smythe got here today. Weatherhead is here in MGs and Smythe in mortars. Tell Dick Bellinger to give my regards to all the sergeants, hoping to see them all soon. Also give my best to George Turner. All his old crew up here seem to be alright, though I have only seen George Blacknell so far. Jimmy Moy is alright, tell him.

Well, Chris, I think that is about all the news I can give you at present. I'll write home as often as I can, but once I do get into action I don't suppose I shall feel much like writing. Jerry planes came over last night... he doesn't dare show himself during daylight because the sky is alive with Spitfires. Our bombers give him hell during the day too. There are tons of ack-ack guns here so tell the experts that oerlikons are a thing of the past. There's a lot of stuff flying around now, ack-ack and bombs, so it's flat on my belly, safest place.

All the best Chris, don't forget to write home now and again.

Henry

PS. Any of these lads would willingly go back and do an RSM's parade every day. They're sick of it!

Mike King of Lowestoft, Suffolk, writes:

I know all about the Anzio campaign as my father was killed in action there when I was three months old. He knew of my existence but never saw me.

I have a letter my dad wrote from Anzio to his brother Chris who was elsewhere in Italy. Dad was not with the assault troops when they first landed but was transferred there a few days later. His name was Sergeant Henry Patrick King of the Middlesex Regiment. Nine days after writing the letter, he died. A shell burst close to him, knocking him into a ditch and causing wounds that were fatal.

During the Anzio fighting, the whole of the beach-head area was the frontline. Nowhere was safe, not even the field hospital. It was only a few years ago that I found out exactly what happened when I was fortunate to speak to a fellow soldier who was injured in the same mortar blast. My dad was between the shell and his colleague and took the brunt of it.

I learnt that the colleague in question, Frank Ashton, once fired 28,000 machine gun rounds in a single engagement with the enemy. When he ran out of ammo he then engaged the enemy with his rifle! As a result a very important attack was repelled and Frank Ashton was awarded the Military Medal.

My father was killed near The Flyover when he was going (in a bren-gun carrier) to relieve another unit. This was at a time when the Jerries had pushed the Allied forces back beyond the Lateral Road and were lobbing mortar shells over. Apparently there was a German tank situated by The Flyover and nobody dared poke their heads up. What our chaps did was dig holes through the embankment and crawl through so they could 'spot' for the artillery. The Lateral Road was the last line of defence before Anzio itself. Luckily it held!

Ten years ago when we were on holiday in Sorrento, I hired a car and took my wife and youngest daughter to the war cemetery at Anzio, the first (and probably the last) family visit. This was a long drive and was quite an experience in itself. We also drove around Naples; I'm afraid I wouldn't have the nerve for it now!

Left: Sergeant King never saw his son, Michael.
Above: Mike King at his father's last resting place in Anzio.
Right: The Flyover pictured after the break-out.

BAMBINI & BOMBS

The astonishing story of two little girls who left England to escape the war and ended up in the midst of the fierce battles for Monte Cassino.

A British soldier befriends a little girl refugee in Southern Italy 1944.

In August 1939 with the threat of war with Germany my parents decided it would be better for my sister Julia and myself to leave England and go to Italy to be with our grandparents.

Their home was in Valvori, a village that looks across to Monte Cassino. Life was quiet and we lived a normal country life. Italy entered the war and it became impossible for us to go back to England. As the years went by, the war came closer. We knew the Germans had occupied the mountains around Monte Cassino but it was not until the Allies arrived in the area that the conflict had any impact on us.

Bombing raids became frequent all around and one stray bomb did actually land in the village but did not explode. We used to watch the four engined planes dropping bombs on Cassino. The noise of the aircraft was frightening but the shelling was more dangerous and most of the houses in the town were hit.

Skull and crossbones insignia

On the day the Monastery on Monte Cassino was destroyed (15 February 1944) we all left our houses to watch the repeated bombing and the clouds of dust and debris thrown up. It was after this that the German soldiers came to our village regularly to patrol it and check every house for able-bodied men. They never found any. I remember the German uniforms were black and had skull and crossbones insignia on the collars.

One day we heard they were on their way to the top of the village where we lived. My aunt took me down to the cellar (where we had our beds as it was safer). She painted both our faces with lipstick to look like spots. There was only a small window and it was very dim. The soldiers put their heads round the door but would not come in as they thought we had measles – which was just as well as we were hiding an English Captain under the bed!

After that near miss my grandfather hid the Captain in the mountains on land he owned. They made him a shelter by bending down the branches of a tree.

My sister took food to him daily but never saw him; she often passed German soldiers who believed she was taking food to workers. One day he just left. We later found out that he sent messages back to his headquarters.

Escaped prisoners-of-war

During this time our grandfather helped many escaped prisoners of war. As the Germans were getting ready to retreat they evacuated the village starting at the bottom and as we lived at the very top together with two other families we were the last to be moved.

By now it was dark and we were escorted to the bottom of the village and locked in a new stable. In the middle of the night we escaped to a higher mountain and all of us hid in woodland with a small dugout where we could sleep.

The first Allied soldiers to arrive in the village were Moroccans; they were on the front line in the mountains. After some time word reached us that it was safe to go back home. Our house had been hit and left with a big hole in the side so we stayed with friends. Women and children were not allowed out and were never left alone.

Whilst the battle for Cassino was still going on there was bombing all around us. The soldiers evacuated us in the middle of the night down the mountainside to Sant Elia in the valley where open backed lorries were waiting for us. Being inquisitive children, we did wander off to look in nearby empty houses and in one there was a German soldier, tied up. I can still see the image of him even today.

We were then loaded on the lorries and set off over the mountains in the dark to Venafro. Fortunately for us, the flats we should have stayed in were full so we were moved to an old sanitorium in Aversa. There the British soldiers (who were always lovely to the children) gave us two tins of food, one was mixed vegetables, the other sweets and biscuits. We spent the night in tents.

Deserted village, ransacked homes

In the morning after being processed we were put into rail carriages and sent to Reggio Calabria. It was very crowded in the carriages and there were no windows but luckily my grandfather managed to sit near the sliding doors and wedged something in it so we were able to get some light and fresh air.

In Reggio Calabria we were put in a school prior to being moved to surrounding towns. The men checked out the availability of accommodation and work and one night with two other families we left via the windows, leaving the others behind.

We don't recall how and when we went back home, only that it was hot and that we walked from wrecked Cassino to Valvori. The village seemed deserted and homes had been ransacked. We later learned that the flats in Venafro had been bombed, killing our Aunt, Cousin and many villagers.

Seven years in all passed before we got back to England where we found we could no longer speak or even understand English. This is our experience of the Second World War, which is still very vivid in both our minds.

Mrs Silvia Ferrari and Mrs Julia DiMascio

It was an irony of war that the home of these two children in Ottaviano near Naples should have survived the fighting only to be destroyed in the eruption of Mount Vesuvius in the spring of 1944.

OVER HERE!

By the early months of 1944, many parts of
Britain had been turned into an armed camp
containing more than three and a half million
soldiers, sailors and airmen. The men and women
of the military had gathered on these British Isles
from all corners of the world and they represented
just about every creed and colour on Earth.

Some 1.7 million were British by birthright and
quite a number of these had been training in
their military crafts for over four years. The
Americans made up the next largest contingent
with around 1.5 million. Canadians, Australians
and New Zealanders made up a sizeable
proportion of the rest of the combatants.

Britain was also host to a large number of
fighting men whose homes were in the German-
occupied countries of Europe. The Allies had
trained and armed them in preparation for the
day when they could take part in the fight to free
their homelands. These Frenchmen and women,
Poles, Belgians, Dutch, Danes, Norwegians, Czechs
and other fugitives from the Nazi yoke were
perhaps the most motivated of all the forces
awaiting the order to go.

64

COUNTDOWN TO D-DAY

'Over-paid, over-fed, over-sexed and over here!' This famous description of the American 'friendly invasion' of the British Isles has become a legend in its own right. Yet it is in large part a true reflection of the way it was in spring 1944. There was a degree of resentment that the Yanks seemed to have so many more material benefits than the British had in their own land. Added to this were pay packets that afforded a buying power three times that of their British military counterparts. Coupled with the glamour and attractiveness of being an American in a country where much of the home-grown manpower was itself abroad, at sea or even locked up in POW camps in Europe and the Far East, it was small wonder so many young British women formed relationships. Over 60,000 would become GI brides by the end of the war.

It was not only the girls who took to the Yanks. Their mums and dads found canned fruit, chocolate bars, cigarettes, nylon stockings, scented soap and other prized items coming their way, not to mention chewing gum and candy for the kids. Other compensations included razor blades and the music of Glenn Miller. To help smooth their path, the Americans were educated as to the eccentricities of the British and each serviceman was issued with a booklet to help him avoid any social transgressions that might upset this island race.

One area of surprise came with the black Americans. The US forces were still almost entirely segregated, with Negro troops mainly deployed in non-combat roles, prior to D-Day, at least. Most people in Britain had never seen black soldiers before but accepted the American practice as normal - after all, the British themselves had hundreds of thousands of men from India, Africa and the Caribbean serving in what were for all intents and purposes 'segregated' units with a white officer hierarchy; the famous Gurkhas, for example. But what the majority of the British public found hard to understand was the overt racist attitude displayed by many white Americans against their fellow black countrymen, even when they were outside the confines of the camps.

British and Canadians

The plan drawn up for the invasion of occupied Europe, *Operation Overlord*, entailed approximately 1,500,000 troops being assembled along the south coast of England. *Overlord* divided the Normandy beach-head into two sectors. British and Canadian forces were to land in the eastern sector – beaches code-named *Gold*, *Juno* and *Sword*. American troops would spearhead the invasion to the west on the beaches known as *Utah* and *Omaha*.

Reflecting that east-west Normandy split, Allied troops were assembled along the south coast with the dividing line roughly along the Dorset/Hampshire border. British and Canadian forces were grouped to the east, American troops to the west.

The whole of Dorset had a pre-war population of just 240,000. But the county played host to considerably more than half a million GI's who famously came 'Over Here'. No fewer than 518,000 embarked for France from Weymouth and Portland.

All of the principal Dorset towns as well as many smaller centres of population were involved in preparations for D-Day. For example, Blandford Forum was the site of the US Army 22nd General Hospital which opened for business in April 1944. In Bournemouth, the Ambassador Hotel became the US Officers' Club while the Marsham Court Hotel and the Miramar Hotel were turned into Red Cross Clubs. The Carlton hosted Eisenhower and Montgomery in February 1944 on a visit to observe a practice beach landing in Poole Bay.

Lovely Lulworth was a US tank gunnery practice area while Lyme Regis housed units of the 1st (US) Infantry Division – the famous

Above: The quiet little village of Burton Bradstock is located on the Dorset coast overlooking Lyme Bay and lies between Bridport and Weymouth, close to Chesil Beach. American Rangers practised beach landings and cliff climbing there. A popular meeting place for GI's and local people at the time was the village pub, The Dove. A photograph from the period shows Americans enjoying a drink with some of the locals. The building is still there but it is no longer a pub.

D-Day landing ships in England.

'Big Red One' – who had already been bloodied in action against a desperate German counter-attack led by Tiger tanks in the Kasserine Pass, Tunisia, at the end of the North African campaign.

Portland was the hub of the county's invasion activity. 'The biggest little port in the world', as the US Navy dubbed it, Portland was the major loading point for the majority of GI's involved in the D-Day assault.

On 26 April, the Allied invasion forces were sealed into their various embarkation areas whilst airmen and sailors were confined to their bases or ships. Thousands of security men watched over the Americans in the south and south-west whilst others maintained a vigil around the British and Canadians and other nationalities crowded in their own perimeters further east.

DEADLY REHEARSAL

On 28 April 1944 a flotilla of German E-boats surprised a convoy of Allied transports carrying thousands of US troops and their equipment on an invasion exercise off the

coast of South Devon. British sailor Derek Wellman was a witness to the tragic aftermath of the incident.

I served for three and a half years aboard *HMS Onslow,* leader of the 17th Destroyer Flotilla, and known to the Home Fleet as 'the VC Ship' after her Captain had been awarded the Victoria Cross for his part in the Battle of the Barents Sea. Almost exactly a year later she took part in the same waters in the sinking of the German battleship *Scharnhorst.*

In April 1944, however, she came south to prepare for D-Day. General Eisenhower was greatly concerned by the fact that most of the million US soldiers on British soil were young men with no previous experience of action. His staff therefore sought to ensure that they participated in the most realistic of exercises beforehand. Many of these took place on a single stretch of coast in Devon known as The South Hams.

On 28 April 1944, *Operation Tiger* – the second of three so-called 'dummy runs' – began. Three LSTs (Landing Ship Tanks) each carrying around 250 men, were escorted by a trawler and a corvette, all the

Royal Navy could spare. Unhappily, on leaving harbour, the corvette was fouled by one of the LSTs. Though it was still seaworthy it was ordered to return to harbour and, as a fact, was not replaced. Nine German E-boats came across from Cherbourg on a routine night patrol and, crossing Lyme Bay, were astonished to find three large targets apparently unprotected from the rear. Like jackals round an elderly prey they circled and fired their torpedoes, hitting all three ships. Two sank quickly leaving a heavy slick of diesel oil. Many men leapt overboard with their lifejackets inflated but were wearing them in the wrong position. They were the first to drown.

HMS Onslow and two of her sister ships were summoned to the spot. I had been on watch below and was only aware that after dashing at full speed we had for some hours been bumping along and then stopping, an unusual experience with E-Boats in the vicinity. After being relieved I needed a wash but found the sliding doors to the bathroom secured by a rope. Suspecting a practical joke by some prankster I forced them open. The sight was unforgettable. On the deck, gleaming like freshly caught mackerel, lay the bodies of a dozen or more American soldiers, all covered by the slime of black fuel oil. Before I slammed the doors closed again I took in the fact that some had limbs missing, presumably from when the torpedoes had struck their ship.

Events took a somewhat bizarre turn. Once the bodies, each wrapped in the US flag, had been taken ashore at Portland, the Captain cleared lower deck and told us we were never to speak of this event, not just for the war's duration, but for the rest of our lives.

The reasons for silence were obvious. One was to prevent panic among those due to land at Utah Beach six weeks later. The other was to conceal what General Bradley called a 'colossal blunder leading to a major tragedy', probably the worst in scale of dead – more than 750 – that ever occurred in sight of our own coast. A secret US naval enquiry was hindered by the fact that the Commodore in charge, Admiral Moon, shot himself just after D-Day and before the enquiry was due to take place.

The next of kin of those who died were not told of their deaths until after D-Day but the inference was that they had met their deaths at that time, not weeks earlier.

With Dieppe, the *Operation Tiger* incident remains one of the greatest blunders of the war in Europe. Some say we learned from these experiences. The evidence is pretty thin. I believe they demonstrate clearly the remorseless pity of war.

Kriegsmarine torpedo boats were called E-boats by the Allies (the 'E' stood for Enemy) and S-bootes by the Germans themselves (the 'S' stood for Schnell – fast). They had two 21 inch torpedo tubes and could carry up to eight mines. They were capable of up to 40 knots and displaced around 100 tons which made them larger than the British Motor Torpedo Boats and Motor Gun Boats (MTBs and MGBs).

ENFORCED EXILE

The civilian population was evacuated from many parts of Britain's coast to make way for the military. South Devon was particularly affected as the Allies prepared for the much anticipated invasion of occupied Europe.

One reason that news of the *Operation Tiger* disaster did not spread was the lack of a civilian population on the stretch of coast closest to the scene of the naval action. The South Hams in South Devon, a 100 square mile area lying between Kingsbridge and Dartmouth, had been completely taken over and sealed off by American forces.

The South Hams is best known for the beach at Slapton Sands (nearby Blackpool Sands too). The location had a similarity to the coastline of Normandy, especially the beach code-named Utah, which made it an ideal training ground for the US forces involved with the invasion.

On 12 November 1943, the bemused residents of the South Hams were informed that the area was to be immediately and totally vacated. They were given just 32 days – until 20 December – to get out. The operation involved six parishes, 180 farms, 750 families and 3000 people. Everything and everyone had to go: the young, the old, the sick, livestock, pets, agricultural machinery, the contents of every single church, shop and home, all household goods, furniture and personal possessions, even crops still in the ground if they could be saved.

Some people, the very sick, had to be carried off on stretchers. One committed suicide rather than leave. A few of the most elderly died within days of the move, victims of the stress and strain.

Six months was set as the period of American occupation, after which the residents would be able to return – once repairs and refurbishment had taken place. In the event, because of the damage and disruption, some of the locals were not able to come back for nearly a year. A few

Above: Ken Small pictured in 2004 beside the Sherman tank he was instrumental in retrieving from the sea. Below right: A postcard of the beach at Slapton Sands in the South Hams. Below left: The inscription on the memorial presented by the US Army to honour the sacrifices made by the people of South Devon evacuated in late 1943 to make way for the military.

never returned, having made new lives for themselves elsewhere. Decades later, bomb disposal units were still dealing with cases of unexploded mines and shells in the area, left over from the 'friendly invasion'.

A Sherman tank from one of the LSTs involved in *Operation Tiger* has been recovered from under the sea and today is on display at Slapton Sands as a reminder of what happened. It stands just above the beach, not far from an American memorial to the men who died in *Operation Tiger*.

Ken Small was the local resident responsible for the recovery of the tank. He devoted most of his adult life to uncovering the truth behind the tragedy. For many, many years he has kept an almost daily vigil at this site. His autobiographical *The Forgotten Dead*, tells the story of his struggle to discover the facts and provide a fitting memorial to the casualties.

Ken died in the spring of 2004, almost on the 60th anniversary of the tragedy.

Torcross and Slapton Sands

THIS MEMORIAL WAS PRESENTED BY THE UNITED STATES ARMY AUTHORITIES TO THE PEOPLE OF THE SOUTH HAMS WHO GENEROUSLY LEFT THEIR HOMES AND THEIR LANDS TO PROVIDE A BATTLE PRACTICE AREA FOR THE SUCCESSFUL ASSAULT IN NORMANDY IN JUNE 1944 THEIR ACTION RESULTED IN THE SAVING OF MANY HUNDREDS OF LIVES AND CONTRIBUTED IN NO SMALL MEASURE TO THE SUCCESS OF THE OPERATION THE AREA INCLUDED THE VILLAGES OF BLACKAWTON CHILLINGTON EAST ALLINGTON SHERFORD SLAPTON STOKENHAM STRETE AND TORCROSS TOGETHER WITH MANY OUTLYING FARMS HOUSES

PLENTY

DIG FOR...

GROW FOOD
IN YOUR GARDEN
OR GET AN ALLOTMENT

Whale meat again!

I was 17 in 1944, ready to leave school and begin a catering course at the College of Domestic Science in Sheffield. The city suffered many air raids because of the steelworks and I often watched the factories burning in the distance after a raid before scouring the garden for scraps of shrapnel to take to school for the daily competition to see who had the largest piece.

As a child, the war had an indirect effect on me naturally, but mostly I hated having to carry my gasmask everywhere, the dreary blackout and dearth of sweets. Food rationing was strict, but enough, with imagination, for survival. Indeed, we now know that we were much healthier on the wartime diet than with the present-day surfeit

of sugar and fat. Cholesterol? Unheard of! But, as a child, health was not my first priority – I missed my chocolates and sweets!

Posters demanded 'Dig for Victory', so we buckled to after school and dug, sowed and planted, replacing garden flowers with regimented rows of vegetables. Chickens ruled the roost in the yard and I enjoyed collecting the eggs to supplement our one-per-week ration.

We registered our ration books with a grocer and collected the same rations each week, so shopping offered little interest or challenge. Every Saturday I took our meat coupons to the same butcher who then handed me whatever meat he had that week. My Aunt did the cooking and my sister and I

ate what was put before us. On one occasion I was told we'd just eaten whale meat!

Lord Woolton broadcast regular tips and recipes on the radio – one of his most famous was for 'Woolton Pie', a concoction of potatoes, carrots, cauliflower and swedes, topped with either pastry or mashed potatoes and a sprinkling of cheese. Rabbit - unrationed - became a favourite. Spam was delicious in fritters.

Vegetables were fairly plentiful as were carrots. Sweet carrot cake, carrot fudge and even carrot drink became firm favourites. The sweet ration was 12 oz (350 gms) per month, but occasionally the lady in the shop gave me a few extra crumbs of chocolate from the bottom of the jar. We may have had a far less varied diet than nowadays, but I do not remember ever being hungry.

Teenage ingenuity

As a teenager, I wanted to look smart, and this, in a way, was more difficult. By 1944, we were allowed 20 clothing coupons a year, so, as a skirt cost six and a dress eight, I knew I would have to make my own clothes, probably out of old ones, if I wanted a change or grew out of something. Luckily, I always enjoyed sewing and women's magazines were full of helpful hints on 'Make Do and Mend'. With my Aunt's old Singer sewing machine, I tackled old curtains, bedspreads, sheets and even a blanket once to produce some different and surprising outfits. I scrounged any old woollens I could, unravelled them and re-knitted 'new' socks and jumpers. On one occasion I remember getting a length of parachute silk, a rare treasure indeed. I happily listened to the radio whilst sewing industriously away.

Stockings cost coupons, so we girls painted our legs with tea or gravy browning sometimes getting a friend to draw the 'seam' down the back with a dark pencil.

Once at college, we learned at first hand how our mothers had coped with the difficulties of keeping families healthily fed and clothed. As children we had, of course, taken everything for granted. I still have the recipe book that was our Bible from 60 years ago, with a complete 'Supplement of Economical Recipes'. It was well used and is splashed with drops of this and that as we assiduously learnt how to create masterpieces from very little.

Recipes featured dried egg, Marmite (which gave both flavour and colour to otherwise insipid looking dishes), dripping (delicious on hot toast) instead of butter; oatmeal for thickening; and so much more. Saving fuel we learnt an intriguing one-pot cooking method where vegetables boiled and meat and pudding steamed using just one pan.

Our tutors emphasised economy above all else, proving an excellent training for the future – meanwhile, most importantly, we survived and we thrived.

Audrey French

The illustration above is original 1944 poster artwork by Le Bon featuring a box of winter vegetables (National Archives - Art of War).

HOME FRONT

War Baby

Baby Anna entered a world at war on 19 April 1944. As time went by she learnt about how her parents coped on the Home Front in the midst of the momentous events unfolding.

My story begins some years before I was born. Actually it is more the story of my parents, Win and Robert Bunning, an ordinary couple who had met, fallen in love and married during extraordinary times in England.

Win and Bob met through their work at the Northmet Power Company. Win's job was cookery and appliance demonstrating in people's homes. Bob was an electrical engineer. He was blind in one eye, and that, coupled with his job, meant that Dad's war years were spent at home. Home was Harpenden, Hertfordshire, close to de Havilland's airfield and the Vauxhall plant at Luton, both tempting bombing targets. As Harpenden was only 20 or so miles from London it was also a victim of

'London – miss' bombs. Mum says that when they said goodbye each morning they were all too well aware that that was exactly what it might be. Many was the time she had to dive for cover in the nearest ditch.

Their first home was in digs, though they were lucky enough to have their own sitting room. They lived on Win's salary (under £2 a week) and saved Bob's income for a deposit for a house. Bob was on call 24 hours a day and everywhere they went contact phone numbers had to be left in case a power line went down and a crew had to be called out.

Night on the tiles

Mum spent many a night out on the tiles. Quite literally. Both she and Dad were fire watchers on the rooftops of St Albans. Whilst Dad did spend a fair amount of time on the roof (and on account of his one good eye probably needed to look around twice as often as the other fire watchers!) he was more frequently manning the phones and co-ordinating operations. Meals were taken care of by the St Albans food kitchens and very good they were too, according to Mum.

Their first home came about thanks to Danny Howe, a local builder. Houses in Harpenden were in short supply but he heard that two old ladies were fed up with the bombing and moving away. The house was in bad condition and the window frames looked as if they had been devoured by a thousand woodworms where the old ladies had tried to pin up the black-out paper at the windows. From their front doorstep Mum and Dad watched the sky turn red as London burnt and, much later, the sky turn black when gliders filled with troops were towed towards the Channel and France.

Born after bombing raid

My own arrival on the scene was two to three weeks sooner than predicted. There had been a bombing raid on de Havillands and the leap out of bed resulted in my early birth at the Red House Hospital in Harpenden, Herts. Conditions were good there, much better than in London hospitals.

Like all other babies of those days I had my own special cardboard box in case of gassing. Mum never had to put me in it, but much of my first few months were spent under a table or in the tiny understairs cupboard crammed in with Mum and Gran. They dreaded most of all the silent V-weapons, first praying that the flying bombs would continue on their deadly journey and then praying for those further down their paths. We had an Italian POW to help with the garden who evidently did all he could to spoil me. With my black hair I reminded him of his own tiny daughter back home.

My own memories begin when I was three. I can remember being pushed to the shops, children playing in the nearby playground and the treat of a banana, but by then we were at peace.

Out of curiosity Anna Hyman has looked up one or two happenings that occurred on the day of her birth. The Times of 19 April 1944 reported that a horse called Happy Landing was just beaten by Borealis at Newmarket. A four-bedroom house near Guildford was on the market for £3500. It was estimated that UK householders kept 12 million hens and 'pig clubs' had been formed where individuals bought shares in a beast and saved scraps to help feed and fatten it up. In 1939 two-thirds of the food consumed in Britain came from overseas but by 1944 only one-third was imported. All available land was turned over to food production or livestock grazing. The Royal Family's Great Park at Windsor was turned into the largest wheat field in the country. By 1944 there were over 1,400,000 allotments, growing an estimated one million tons of vegetables. In the same year the Women's Land Army numbered 80,000. 'Dig for Victory' was the Home Front battle cry and potatoes and onions were said to be munitions of war as surely as bombs and bullets.

SURPRISE ATTACK FROM THE AIR

A British Hurricane fighter attacks a Japanese troop convoy in Burma in this painting by Roy Nockolds. The date of the work is unknown but it reflects the fact that air superiority was a key element in ensuring an Allied victory in the Far East (National Archives - The Art of War).

Forgotten Front?

In the early months of 1944, news from Burma was constant but rarely prominent.

A war was being waged in the jungles, mountains and plains of Burma and Assam but it was of a nature perhaps too alien and too far away to really hold the interest of most folks on the Home Front. Unless, of course, they knew of someone serving there or who had, perhaps, been made a prisoner of war of the Japanese in the opening period of the war.

British civilians still faced the occasional air raid but what the war meant to most was the sight of the vast military build-up of men and equipment in preparation for the Allied invasion of mainland Europe. The British Fourteenth Army on the Burmese – Indian border under its commander, General William Slim, even at the time considered themselves 'forgotten', a feeling which still persists amongst surviving veterans over 60 years later.

British troops check out their location in the Burmese jungle. The key to Allied success in 1944 was air supremacy that enabled Dakota aircraft to transport enough supplies and ammunition to keep isolated and surrounded garrisons or advancing troops well fed and able to fight on.

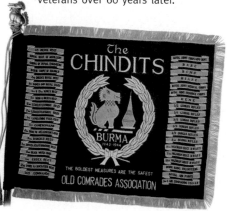

The colours of the Old Comrades Association of the famous Chindits who fought in Burma 1942 - 1944. The name 'Chindits' was derived from 'Chinthe', a mythical dragon that guards Burmese temples and which is depicted in the centre of the colours.

British, American and Chinese actions in south and north Burma in the opening months of 1944 met with considerable success. In what was called the Second Arakan Campaign, the Fourteenth Army had relieved the Seventh Indian Division and gone on to all but annihilate the Japanese forces who had encircled them. A slow advance on Akyab on Burma's Bay of Bengal coast was resumed.

Then in late February, the first American ground combat unit arrived with General 'Vinegar Joe' Stilwell in the north of Burma. This was an infantry regiment destined to go down in history as Merrill's Marauders, from the name of its commander, Frank D Merrill. His 3000 men were to be used in an encircling role, whilst their Chinese allies battered the Japanese in frontal assaults.

During March and into April the strategy worked well. Japanese General Sinichi Tanaka was forced into a series of rapid withdrawals. The American and Chinese efforts were sustained by air by US transports flying from bases in north eastern India.

Then, unexpectedly, both Stilwell's forces in the north and the Fourteenth Army in south and central Burma, found their own sources of supply – and indeed their own existence – under threat when a 100,000-strong Japanese army crossed the Chindwin River on an 80-mile front in central Burma. The Japanese goal was nothing less than the invasion of India where they hoped to find a population ready to rise up against their British rulers.

The speed of the advance surprised the British. They retreated in some disorder into the Indian state of Assam. By early April resistance was centred around Imphal – where three divisions of the British IV Corps were surrounded – and Kohima.

Up till then an unimportant little hill town, Kohima became a key position in the defence of India. Its capture would open the way to Dimapour and the cutting of the Assam railway, supply lifeline for the Allies on the Burma front. On 5 April 1944 the Japanese besieged Kohima and a bloody, close quarter, battle ensued.

In the course of April, the fight swung this way and that. Allied air power hit the Japanese supply lines and the enemy commander, over-confident of being able to capture supplies, realised he did not have sufficient material to sustain his assault. On 20 April Kohima was relieved.

But the Japanese didn't retreat. Instead it was now the turn of the British to try and dislodge their enemy from strong positions on the surrounding hilltops.

The Burma - India frontier, scene of a major Japanese offensive in March - April 1944. Kohima (not shown) is about 70 miles north of Imphal.

Men of the three-inch mortar platoon of 1st Battalion The Gambia Regiment pictured at Karvetnagar in Madras province, India, at the end of the war. They had just been provided with new uniforms and kit. Despite some of the men being away from home for more than five years, they faced a long wait for ships to take them back to West Africa.

WEST AFRICANS GO EAST

Dr Ian Morris today lives in Edinburgh. In 1944 he was a soldier fighting the Japanese on the India-Burma border. He sent us the following story of his unit, the 81st (West African) Division.

Winston Churchill decided that West Africans should be used in the war against Japan and expressed the wish that they 'make a name for themselves'. Thus began the difficult logistical task of bringing men from Gambia, Sierra Leone, Gold Coast and Nigeria to a holding area around Ibadan in Nigeria via poor roads and one railway line, before shipping them out of Lagos and on to Bombay.

At Capetown the Africans learned that not everyone saw them as potential heroes as they stretched their legs in short marches around the town. The gibe of 'White Officers with Black Privates' was heard.

From Bombay they were taken by road and rail to camps at Nasik, a Holy City that's less famous than its neighbour Doolali, the town associated from the days of Kipling with 'Doolali tap' or mental illness. There was some perfunctory training and then a journey for five days by rail to Calcutta. At the many stops bedraggled Indian men, women and children walked along the track begging. The Africans concluded that Indians were a lesser race than they were. Bengal was in the grip of a severe famine and the Australian Governor, R G Casey, used the services of pagan Africans to collect the dead bodies in trucks and transport them to the lime pits at DumDum.

The journey continued by ship to Chittagong then to railheads, road ends and on foot in the Arakan until the 81st (WA) Division could head east for the Pi Chaung and Kaladan Valley protecting the eastern flank of those in 15 Corps who had the objective of capturing Akyab. It was the first Empire Division to make contact with the Japanese. Elements of it were seen by General Christison of

15 Corps and General William Slim, later of Fourteenth Army. Christison considered them to be ill-disciplined carriers and Slim stated that the ratio of whites to Africans was too high at 72 to 1200, thus preventing African NCOs from taking initiatives. An Indian division had a higher ratio. Just as the Africans drew conclusions about Indians from an unrepresentative sample so Christison and Slim did the same with the Africans.

Harsh country

Enter Orde Wingate. He wished to have European and Gurkha troops but not Indian soldiers with his Chindits. The shortfall had to be made up with Africans and 3 Brigade from 81st Division was given to Wingate. Although it was the most experienced formation of the division with troops well able to live and move in harsh country, Wingate deployed the men as garrison troops. Wingate had charisma in spades and an unshakeable belief that he was always right. The troops under him were favoured in obtaining supplies and dedicated aircraft. They were brave men who in dark days gave people at home something to be proud of. However, Wingate was a master of PR; in time the historian revisionist will catch up with him.

The badge of the 81st (West African) Division features a spider. It was worn face down on the sleeve so that when the soldier holds a rifle to his shoulder the spider is facing the enemy. The spider is not a tarantula but represents Ananse who in Ashanti mythology can change into many guises to perform impossible feats, relying on guile rather than brute force.

Back in the Kaladan the truncated 81st Division fought their way south. They were totally dependent on supplies from the air for much longer than the Chindits. There were no battles greater than company strength but it was endless patrols and skirmishes that wore everyone down. At Kyaukta/Pagoda Hill the 1st Gambia Battalion and the East African Scouts were driven back. The division retreated to Frontier Hill, the boundary of India and Burma - a distance of about 66 crow/fly miles and 200 PBI (Poor Bloody Infantry) miles. Here a battalion of 81st Division, the 7/16 Punjabis and a State Force battalion of Tripura Rifles provided determined opposition until the Monsoon ended all movements. In fact, the entry of Japanese forces into India mattered psychologically but not at all tactically.

The respite ended when 81st Division fought its way south again eventually occupying Myohaung, which had been an objective of the first campaign. It was relieved by the 82nd (WA) Division.

Pack bullocks

Maj Gen C S Woolner, the 81st Divisional commander, had been a contemporary of Christison as young officers. He was an engineer, Christison a cavalryman. Only the engineer could have found a way into the Kaladan over hostile terrain. The cavalryman was asked for a company of medium machine gunners by the engineer; it was turned down for lack of space and 74 pack bullocks were provided instead! Now it is a court martial offence to kill a pack animal while on active service. Sadly all of them broke legs early on and the Africans being compassionate put them out of their misery. The fresh meat was welcome.

1944 was a grim year. Fast forward to 1984. I visited the Imperial War Museum. There was one postcard representing the contribution of Africans in Burma, wrongly captioned. Of the two books formally commissioned to cover the war in Burma, one, approved by Christison, was scathing about Woolner and the 81st Division. The other with about 700 pages managed a mainly inaccurate single paragraph on Africans. I attended our Divisional Reunion lunch and suggested that we should put the record straight. The result was the book *War Bush* by John Hamilton, published by Michael Russell in 2001. It took 14 years of effort. Three of us financed it and after some three years were fully reimbursed. Descendants of Slim and Woolner have copies of the book and it graces the UN library in New York. All the West African states bought copies.

If numbers matter there were 300,000 Indian, 98,000 European, 36,000 Gurkha and 82,000 African troops in Burma. Oh, by the way, survivors of the Japanese 28th Army, formed in 1944 to defend the Arakan and the Irrawaddy delta, said that Africans were the best jungle fighters the Allies had.

Ian Morris pictured in 1995 following a parade at Edinburgh Castle marking the 50th anniversary of the end of World War II. He had served as a mortar officer and later as a patrol leader. He says, 'Our job in the second Burma campaign was to maintain contact with the Japanese which made us a sort of permanent recce force. I was a lieutenant for most of the campaigns, then captain and for a short time before demob, a major. It was said to help with the final pay-off! In best Raj tradition Europeans were considered to be attached to West African forces. In the main cemetery in Rangoon all casualties are listed with their original British units. I fear racism has long roots.'

DAKOTA LIFELINE

The official history of the Royal Air Force* contains the following account of the exploits of the 81st (West African) Division in the Kaladan at the beginning of 1944. Lt Gen Sir Philip Christison's XV Corps was pressing over the Nyakyedauk Pass (called the 'Okey Doke' by the British) and to guard against any Japanese outflanking move he ordered the West Africans forward to the distant Kaladan Valley beyond the next range of hills.

'In the early stages of its march the 81st was supplied by a jeep track 73 miles long. After this, however, the Dakotas of Troop Carrier Command were to be entirely responsible for bringing the formation all it needed.

'The jungle in the Kaladan is the thickest in Burma and the flight over the hills was notable for its turbulence and the presence of the dreaded cumulo-nimbus cloud formations. Aircraft usually needed to go round about eight times to push out the entire load of supplies and the gorges made it difficult. Pilots had to get low down for the dropping and then if there was a hill in front of them it meant pretty well tearing the guts out of the engines to climb over it.

'The West Africans and the RAF were soon on terms of mutual friendship and, indeed, affection. On occasions when it was possible for a Dakota to land on a hastily devised air strip, the West Africans would flock around the aircrew with the liveliest expressions of regard.

'Admin Box' siege

'When landing was impossible and the supplies were dropped by parachute, they took the greatest care of what they received. One of them, indeed, in his zeal went so far as to try to catch one of the hundredweight bags of rice as it descended, for he had noted with regret that since these were dropped 'free', many of them burst and scattered their contents far and wide. Unfortunately, he was successful, and at once became one of the more severely injured passengers in the Dakotas detailed to fly out the sick and wounded.

'Thrice daily did the Dakotas of No 62 Squadron bring in supplies. Fortunately, the Spitfire squadrons kept any Japanese fighters well away; without the air supply the West Africans would have had to surrender within a week.

'In February a final Japanese attack of the war in the Arakan region of Burma led to our forces being besieged in what became known as the 'Admin Box' at Sinzweya, where the HQ of the administrative troops of the Seventh Indian Division was situated. The 81st (WA) Division participated in this battle and achieved success with the capture of Kyaukkwaw and Apaukwa, although a Japanese counter-attack later drove them out.

'By the beginning of April 1944 the Arakan battle was over and the Allies were the victors, having vanquished more than 5000 of the best troops the Japanese had in Burma.'

*Volume III - The Fight is Won by Hilary St George Saunders, published in 1954 by HMSO.

KILLED IN ACTION

Sgt Mervyn Hicks wrote a number of letters to his sister Doris while serving as an Air Gunner with a Canadian Squadron in RAF Bomber Command. In them he speaks of the need to fly his missions despite the fear and trepidation he felt.

In January 1944 he writes: 'Many thanks for your letter and good wishes for 1944. Yes dear I had a nice Christmas and it was good to be home for three weeks, but my how the time flew. I took the family to Wales for a week …I intended coming down to Brighton to see you but alas the RAF had other plans for us …'

In a reference to Doris taking on another evacuee, he says: 'You certainly keep yourself busy, fancy you taking on another boy. It is kind of you but I feel there were others who should be doing this. However, as you say, there are many heartless people about.'

In another letter he writes: 'Well dear on Saturday morning my name went down for Op's, gave my old tummy a turn but glad to say the flak was not too hot and all turned out OK. However, the next morning I had a shock to see my name down again and for a bigger one when we knew we were off to Essen, one of the most defended targets in Germany. Glad to say when take off came along I felt quite cool, but on the way out thought of all you dear ones and just wondered if I would see you all again. Glad to say we had cloud cover and got back safe and sound. On returning to base had an issue of rum and coffee followed by eggs and bacon, we certainly needed it. Got to bed at 4am but did not get up until 11.30 the next morning.

'The take-off was most impressive and everybody turned out to bid us bon voyage and thumbs up. I felt quite cheered. My old tummy was not too good but I did not tell the skipper as I hope to beat it and see this job through to the bitter end..

'It was an experience and sight not be forgotten in a hurry. One reads of these raids in the paper but one needs to be there to know the real thing.'

Sgt Hicks ended the last letter with a plea not to let any of this news get to '…Vic's paper or I should get into trouble'.

A snippet from another other letter reads: 'Please give Peter 3/6 out of the enclosed 10/-. Hope you can both get a little something with it. I'm afraid it is not much but now your brother is a poorly paid air gunner.'

In one letter there is a reference to the tummy problems he suffered from: 'I have been in hospital with my tummy. They would not ground me but said I could ground

myself but should get LMF (Lack of Moral Fibre). So I refused and shall try and go flying with my crew.'

In a letter from the spring of 1944, he writes of a visit to the cinema: 'This week I saw Anna Neagle in "Yellow Canary", a very good Picture.' In the same letter he confides, '..Have been on six trips now, the one yesterday, we went to Paris. It was the roughest journey we have had so far and once or twice I wondered if I should ever place my feet on ground again and was damn pleased to get back to my coffee and rum. We got back at 5am this morning and am feeling very tired. Guess you heard us return as we passed over Brighton. I thought of you below and wished I could have been with you instead of flying above.

'We then saw the London raid from above; it was hot with plenty of flak coming up … I suppose it will be as bad when we get detailed for Berlin. I have got over my attack of nerves but the old tummy turns over when I see the old name goes down for Op's.

'Well darling guess this is about all my news. Let me know if you can get to London when I get my leave. Tons of love, Mervyn.'

Earlier in this last letter the airman remarks that he has not had leave since he came to the Squadron and that leave he was due to start on 20 April had been cancelled.

Sgt Mervyn J Hicks was killed in action on 25 April 1944 when his Halifax bomber encountered severe weather and heavy icing over Karlsruhe. With the aircraft out of control, the captain ordered the crew to bale out but for some unknown reason Mervyn and another member of the crew failed to do so.

Doris was Peter Champion's mum. Peter has written two stories of his 1944 memories for Sixty Years On. *They appear on pages 56 and 101-102.*

Peter's father was Victor Champion who worked on the Brighton Evening Argus *newspaper throughout the war. Peter remembers him as having to do everything from reporting on the war through to being the sports correspondent writing under the pen name 'Crusader'. Victor and Doris both died within a month of each other in 1977.*

WAR DIARY

april 1944

April 1944 begins with the British authorities declaring a 10-mile deep strip of land from Land's End to The Wash closed to the public as a security precaution in preparation for the invasion of Northern Europe.

On **1 April** a navigational error sees 26 US aircraft drop their bombs on Schaffhausen in neutral Switzerland. First reports indicate 35 dead.

The British Red Cross are now sending 97,000 parcels each week to British prisoners of war. There are seven different kinds of parcel and 41 varieties of food which can be included in them.

Next day near Ascq in Belgium, Resistance fighters derail a German troop transport train carrying men of the 12th SS Panzer Division Hitler Jugend. In reprisal the SS murder 86 civilians.

Signal was a military magazine produced by the Germans in many different languages (including English). It gave the Nazi slant on the progress of the war. This is the cover of a mid-1944 edition and shows German troops on the Eastern Front.

In the Ukraine, the Russians have surrounded 40,000 Germans in and around the town of Skala. To the south, the Red Army crosses the River Prut and enters Rumania.

US aircraft bomb a ball-bearing factory at Steyr, 90 miles from Vienna in Austria, sparking a major air battle. Over 300 Luftwaffe planes attack the bomber formations; there are reports of the enemy dropping their own bombs from above the US aircraft in the hope of knocking them out of the sky. Long-range Lightning and Thunderbolt fighters shoot down at least 100 enemy aircraft.

Soviet Foreign Minister Molotov demands £150,000,000 in war reparations from Finland. The Russians do not ask for Finnish labour to carry out reconstruction work in the USSR, as Helsinki feared, but are insisting that the 1940 border imposed by Moscow at the end of the 'Winter War' be re-established. In that conflict the Finns had invented a simple explosive device that proved effective against Russian armoured vehicles; bottles filled with petrol and capped by a flammable rag were dubbed 'Molotov Cocktails'.

> **'The British Red Cross are now sending 97,000 parcels each week to British prisoners of war. There are seven different kinds of parcel and 41 varieties of food which may be in them.'**

3 April – Naples. Against a clear blue sky the snow-capped peak of Mount Vesuvius continues to erupt in spectacular fashion.

Royal Navy Barracuda bombers from the carriers *HMS Victorious* and *HMS Furious* strike at Germany's only remaining battleship, *Tirpitz*, at Altenfjord, Norway. The vessel is damaged but not sunk.

Next day an RAF reconnaissance flight takes the first photographs of a large camp in Poland. It is identified as Auschwitz.

From Egypt come reports of a mutiny in the Greek Army Brigade. There is a crisis brewing within the free Greek forces as communists and royalists stake their claims for power in post-war Greece.

Algiers: The Head of the Committee of National Liberation, General de Gaulle, takes full control of all Free French armed forces.

In Burma around 12,000 Japanese soldiers are reported to be closing in on a mixed British – Indian force of just 1500 at Kohima.

5 April: In Britain, all military leave has been cancelled and postal and telephone services now operate under strict supervision. Even so, there are security scares. In one incident a packet sent from London to Chicago bursts open in transit to reveal secret invasion plans. An American officer had posted them to his sister by mistake. In another instance, US General George Patton is given a stern dressing-down over his loose talk of the invasion that was overheard at a party.

6 April: The UK sees the introduction of a new personal taxation system. Tax will be easier to collect and harder to dodge with the pay-as-you-earn (PAYE) system. Newspapers also report that a wartime research and development programme has led to a useful invention for the home; wallpaper which can be washed clean with soap and water thanks to a thin film of transparent plastic coating. The new product will not be available until after the war.

Up to 10% of the Allied troops in embattled Anzio are allowed leave at any one time. Four-day R&R (rest and recreation) breaks usually centre on Naples where there are ample quantities of wine, women and song. The Neapolitans much prefer their Allied customers to the Germans who occupied the city last year.

On the night of **8 April** the Volkswagen plant at Fallersleben near Hanover is bombed. Source of Hitler's famous 'Peoples Car' (better known as the Beetle), the VW factory's priority has been the manufacture of vehicles for the military.

In Moscow, Molotov announces that the USSR has no territorial designs on Rumania or the country's existing social order. They simply require the restoration of the 1940 border. A 324-gun salute in the city celebrates the First Ukrainian Front army's recent advances to the Rumanian and Czech borders. In the Crimea, only evacuation across the Black Sea can save the trapped German forces.

9 April: The Vichy authorities ban dancing in public in France. The measure is the latest in a series that keeps large groups of civilians from assembling and becoming 'politically irresponsible'.

10 April: Royal Navy midget submarines – X-Craft – are in action in Bergen harbour, Norway. X-24, commanded by Lt M H Shean, evaded German defences and placed explosives beneath the 7500 ton merchantman, *Barenfels*. X-24 escaped undetected, leaving the Germans suspecting the sinking to be the work of land-based saboteurs.

Next day sees a daring but highly successful low-level precision bombing attack by RAF Mosquito aircraft of 613 Squadron on a

WAR DIARY

April '44

building close to the Peace Palace in The Hague. The five-storey Kleizkamp Art Gallery holds detailed records relating to Dutch citizens. These records are invaluable to the Gestapo.

12 April: King Victor Emmanuel says he will give up the throne of Italy when the Allies enter Rome. This seems a distant prospect with the Allies still contained within the Anzio beach-head and unable to break through at Cassino.

On **13 April** Britain and America issue a joint demand that Sweden halt the export of ball-bearings to Germany. On the other side of the world in New Guinea, Australian troops have pushed the Japanese out of the town of Bogodjim.

Russian General Nikolai Vatutin dies today **(14 April)** in a Kiev hospital from wounds sustained in February when he was ambushed by a band of anti-Soviet Ukrainian nationalists.

A terrible accident in Bombay leaves 740 people dead when the ammunition freighter *Fort Stikine* explodes. The blast severely damages 27 other vessels and destroys 40,000 tons of food.

15 April: Flying from Foggia in the south of Italy, 448 US Flying Fortresses and Liberators escorted by 150 long-range Mustang fighters, bomb the Ploesti oilfields in Rumania. It's Germany's only substantial source of oil and is also threatened by the advancing Red Army who are only 140 miles away. RAF Wellingtons joined in to bomb key rail targets in the country.

16 April: Yalta in the Crimea recaptured. Sevastopol is now the only major port from the Germans can evacuate their trapped forces. The city's airport is already in Soviet hands and fighting ranges over the old battlefield of Balaclava where the famous Charge of the Light Brigade took place nearly a century earlier.

Next day liberated Italy finds itself without a government as Marshal Badoglio in Naples announces the resignation of his entire cabinet. He is asked to form a new government that must include communist leader Palmiro Togliatti.

The Japanese launch *Operation Ichi-Go* in China with the aim of crushing the forces of Generalissimo Chiang Kai-shek between the Yellow and Yangtze rivers and neutralising US air bases in Honan and Kwangsi provinces. The Japanese also want to open an overland supply route to their Southern Army in Thailand and Malaya. Following a personal request from President Roosevelt, Chiang Kai-shek has ordered Chinese troops to enter Burma in support of the hard-pressed Allies; now he finds his own country under renewed savage attack.

In London, the privileges of diplomats are restricted. All foreign embassies are put under surveillance in the run-up to the invasion. The only protest comes, ironically, from representatives of the Free French. Tomorrow, a new Defence Regulation - supported by the TUC - confers drastic powers for dealing with persons responsible for inciting strikes or lock-outs which interfere with essential services.

18 April: The Swiss give refuge to Giuseppe Bastianini, former Italian ambassador in pre-war London and Warsaw. The diplomat has been sentenced to death in absentia by a fascist tribunal in Verona for his role in the overthrow of Mussolini last year.

19 April: Allied raids on key transport links in France are incessant; in the last 36 hours over 7000 tons of bombs have been delivered. Unfortunately, French civilian casualties are mounting. Overnight 14 Allied aircraft were lost.

In a joint Anglo-American operation, planes from the carriers *HMS Illustrious* and *USS Saratoga* combine to bomb the important harbour of Sabang on the island of Sumatra.

On **20 April** the discovery of a set of orders on a dead Japanese NCO alerts the British to plans for enveloping the Imphal area of Assam. General Slim is able to put pressure on the Japanese who have almost encircled the hilltown of Kohima. The enemy intention to secretly divert part of their force for a march on Imphal is abandoned. Slim's 'Forgotten Fourteenth' Army includes West African troops from the Gambia and the Gold Coast.

21 April: German-controlled Paris radio claims that 641 French civilians died in an Allied air raid on Lille earlier in the month.

In England, Princess Elizabeth celebrates her 18th birthday and attends a Changing of the Guard ceremony. The popular royal is Colonel of the Grenadier Guards.

Next day a massive US Task Force under General Douglas MacArthur begins landing a 52,000 strong invasion force on Dutch New Guinea. They seize the administrative capital, Hollandia. An equally large force of Japanese are positioned elsewhere on the island at Wewak, due to faulty intelligence.

The Japanese are faring better in China where they capture Chengchow in Honan Province and rout 300,000 Nationalist troops.

23 April: Blood is shed for the first time in the Greek forces crisis. The crews of five warships at Alexandria, Egypt, have been refusing to obey orders. Unrest has spread to shore-based personnel and army units. Root cause of the trouble is dissatisfaction with the Allied-recognised Greek Government-in-Exile. Today 50 men die as Greek officers storm three of the vessels. Next day the crews of the other two ships and the First Brigade of the Greek Army end their mutiny.

24 April: Allied intelligence believes that German aircraft production for the whole of 1944 will be around the 20,000 figure. For the same period, the combined USA - British Empire output will be around 140,000 aircraft.

'Actor Ivor Novello is sentenced to eight weeks in gaol for the illegal use of a motor vehicle.'

By **25 April,** Hollandia is well on the way to becoming the biggest military base ever seen in the South West Pacific. US Construction Battalions (The Fighting Seebees) are working at a frenzied pace to build docks, airfields and housing for the 140,000 men who will augment McArthur's steady advance on the Philippines, the islands where he famously vowed, 'I will return' early in 1942.

Actor Ivor Novello is sentenced to eight weeks imprisonment for conspiring to commit an offence against the war-time restrictions on the use of motor vehicles.

Also in London, the outspoken General Patton causes controversy with congressmen back home when he tells an English audience that it is the destiny of Britain and the US to rule the world once the war is won. A later version of the speech reported in a newspaper has Patton including the USSR as a third party governing the globe.

26 April: Off the Brittany coast of France a British naval force engages a flotilla of E-Boats, sinking one. D-Day planners give attention to the potential U-Boat threat posed to the Allied invasion fleet when it finally sets sail across the English Channel. A marked reduction in recent U-Boat activity is interpreted as evidence that Admiral Donitz is preserving his strength for an all-out attack. U-Boats would have difficulty operating undetected in the shallow Channel waters but the big ships of the Allies will be tempting targets.

From midnight on **27 April** all civilian travel abroad from Britain is banned and exit visas already issued become invalid. German intelligence sources on the UK mainland are virtually non-existent but the Allies know they must be prudent and assume the worse. The Germans have imposed their own 'no go' zone for civilians along the coast of Occupied Europe from the border with Spain in the south to beyond the Arctic Circle in Norway.

28 April: US aircraft are bombing bridges on the Yellow River in China to hold up the Japanese advance.

29 April: A night-time training exercise goes wrong off South Devon, when German E-Boats out of Cherbourg intercept transports loaded with troops. In the resulting chaos hundreds of US servicemen drown or die from 'friendly fire'. Bodies will be washed up on beaches in the area for many days to come.

The last day of April sees a further increase in bombing raids over France. Trains, road and rail bridges, radar and radio installations, power stations; the entire infrastructure of France within 150 miles of the planned invasion zone is being relentlessly pummelled.

HITLER'S FORTRESS EUROPE

MAY 1944

OCCUPIED PARIS

Paris came under German control in June 1940 with the fall of France. In that month Hitler himself paid his only visit to the French capital to inspect his greatest conquest to date. The Eiffel Tower was on his tourist intinerary.

The familiar faces of Maurice Chevalier and Edith 'Little Sparrow' Piaf can be seen in two of the photographs above. Both of these celebrated singers stayed in Paris for the whole of the Occupation along with literary luminaries such as Jean Paul Sartre. Chevalier was later much criticised for entertaining audiences that included German soldiers and known collaborators.

The famous girlie shows didn't stop either and fraternisation between French women and German soldiers, sailors and airmen was not uncommon. Three photographs above show the Moulin Rouge 'Then and Now'. The famous church of Notre Dame also features in a wartime photograph here.

HITLER'S ATLANTIC WALL

'I am the greatest fortress builder of all time..'

Hitler was boasting of his vaunted Atlantic Wall. Yet the Führer's Atlantic Wall at the beginning of 1944 was largely a figment of his imagination. Certain locations - the ports such as Cherbourg, Le Havre and Dieppe and the Pas de Calais and Belgian coast - were heavily fortified. Much of the Channel Islands too - conquests highly prized by the Nazis - had been turned into concrete fastnesses bristling with guns. On Jersey they built a massive bomb-proof underground hospital. But these were the exceptions. From Denmark down to the border of France with Spain, most of the coastline was protected by a few minefields, some strands of barbed wire and poor calibre troops. Many of the latter originated from the conquered territories of Eastern Europe, men who preferred to don a German army uniform rather than endure the terrible conditions in the PoW camps. They would be unlikely to put up a fight in the event of the invasion.

Even so, by the late spring of 1944, feverish work was underway to make the Atlantic Wall a reality. The driving force was Field Marshal Erwin Rommel, the legendary 'Desert Fox' of Afrika Korps fame. He believed that the best place to stop an Allied invasion was on the beaches before armoured units could gain any substantial foothold.

Rommel shared an intuition with Hitler that the Allies would mount their main assault in Normandy, a view not shared by the Commander-in-Chief West, Field Marshal Gerd von Rundstedt, who thought the short sea crossing to the Pas-de-Calais the most likely Allied invasion route. The Todt Organisation comprising thousands of virtual slave labourers hurriedly constructed strongpoints, laid millions of mines and began covering potential landing beaches with a vast and ingenious array of obstacles - many designed by Rommel himself.

It was a race against time. A 'Second Front' to liberate Western Europe and crush the German armies between the Allies and the Russians was long overdue. But could the Germans build defences strong enough to resist the Allied invasion that must surely come in the early summer of 1944?

Top: A German sentry stands guard at Etretat near Le Havre, Normandy. The distinctive chalk arch also features in the recent colour photograph.
Centre left: Rommel pictured beside an artillery bunker.
Centre right: Another bunker designed to look like a typical Normandy house.
Bottom: A poster with a message for French civilians is seen alongside two Germans on a sand dune.

INVASION

CIMETIÈRE DES ALLIÉS

COUNTDOWN TO D-DAY

The Waiting Game..

With the advent of May 1944 and the promise of good weather, everybody in Southern England knew that the invasion of France was imminent. In ports and sheltered waters all along the coast, there was a massive assemblage of warships, transports and landing craft. Inland, fields and forests and country lanes were jammed with military vehicles of all shapes and sizes together with thousands of tanks and guns. On hundreds of airfields, fighters, bombers, gliders and transport planes were lined up waiting for the order to go into action.

Civilians were not encouraged to travel and so would miss much of the spectacle of these mighty forces, pent up in so many locations. But the thousands of vehicle convoys on the roads passed through cities, towns and villages and were there for all to see. Indeed, casualties - both civilian and military - from traffic accidents reached appalling levels due to the sheer volume on the highways and byways, coupled with the fact that so many of the drivers were unused to driving on the left and also had minimal lighting at night.

A further clue to the approach of D-Day came with the 'disappearance' of many servicemen from everyday life as most became confined to their camps and barracks. Pubs and cinemas lost lots of their best customers and public transport in London suddenly seemed empty. The final military exercises took place; after *Operation Fabius* in May was deemed a success, US commanders declared that their men were as ready as they ever would be.

Incredibly, the Germans were still guessing as to where the big assault would take place and had to maintain armies in all the likely landing areas such as the Pas de Calais; even an Allied invasion of Norway was not ruled out; a massive garrison remained stationed there until the end of the war. No reliable information filtered out from their spies and sympathisers in Southern Ireland and other neutral countries. The Luftwaffe in France was a shadow of its former self and with Allied superiority in the air total, they could mount few, if any, successful reconnaissance missions. In case they did, the Allies even had a phantom army of dummy tanks and

guns camped conspicuously in Kentish fields under the 'command' of the flamboyant General George Patton.

Of course, the Allies had to assume that their *Operation Overlord* plans were compromised, in part at least. There was the famous *Daily Telegraph* crossword coincidence when in the period between 2 May and 1 June no less than five key D-Day codenames appeared as the answers to clues on various days. And who had tipped off the German E-Boats from Cherbourg who raided Allied troop transports on exercise off South Devon earlier in the spring? This was the tragedy, veiled in secrecy for years afterwards, in which over 700 US soldiers and sailors lost their lives. It was indeed difficult for either side to discern fact from fiction when peering into the fog of war and deceit.

But as the decisive day loomed nearer, plans compromised or not and with the exception of the relentless bombing campaign against Europe's road and rail network, the gargantuan Allied war machine paused, almost as a living thing might pause to draw breath, before embarking on its mighty and long-awaited endeavour.

The Italian Campaign

May 1944. The Allied superiority in fighting men, machines, aircraft and warships must surely prevail at Cassino and Anzio.

Fifth Army General, the American Mark Clark met with the Commander-in-Chief of Allied land forces in Italy, General Sir Harold Alexander, on 1 May 1944. It was for a final briefing between the two and their senior officers and planners concerning *Operation Diadem*, a major offensive to at last crack the Gustav Line and precipitate a break-out by the Allied soldiers still penned into the Anzio beach-head.

The meeting was not a smooth one, being marked by bickering and dissent. Whilst all agreed that the trapping and destruction of the German forces south of Rome must be a primary objective of any offensive, it seemed to the British that Clark was also giving priority to ensuring that American soldiers would be the first into the Italian capital.

To overcome the Gustav Line more than 1500 artillery pieces were assembled and two million rounds stockpiled. The American Fifth and British Eighth Armies underwent a complicated switch of roles with the Fifth taking over the left flank, north of the Garigliano, and the Eighth shaping up for the major push up the Liri Valley. Infantry assaults were to breach the German defences and powerful armoured formations would exploit the breakthrough.

German intelligence of the Allied plans was meagre. Fearing another amphibious landing north of Rome, they left sorely needed reserves around Civitavecchia. The Germans also believed that their enemies had already received enough bloody noses from battering against the mountain fastnesses around Cassino that they were likely now to favour a coastal advance and accordingly reinforced

that area. To cap it all, two senior German commanders both agreed on 10 May that the Allies would not attack in the immediate future. On the very next day dawn was heralded with a thunderous artillery barrage. *Operation Diadem* had begun.

In the next six days some half a million rounds were fired off by guns supporting the British 13th Corps. One witness reported: 'In those few miles between the hills (on either side of the Liri Valley), a thousand guns let go as one and then kept on firing. We'd never seen or heard anything quite like this and could only imagine what sort of hell was falling on the German lines. It damn near deafened us.'

Yet *Diadem* failed to yield swift success and 13th Corps - comprising men from the Hampshire Regiment alongside Indians and even an Italian Motorised Group - struggled to create a decisive bridge-head. They sustained nearly 4000 casualties in driving a salient three miles deep into the German lines, a figure that would most certainly have been higher had the British artillery not smothered with smoke the German observation posts on the heights. On 17 May, Eighth Army Commander Lt-Gen Oliver Leese decided the time was right to commit the Canadian 1st Corps; they were to be the spearhead of the push up the valley.

Poles and Goums

Meanwhile there was action elsewhere on the Gustav Line. General Wladislaw Anders commanded a Polish Corps, a unit eager to do battle with the Germans and avenge the brutal invasion of their homeland in September 1939, the act that triggered World War II. The Poles were in position on the Cassino frontline. Now they were ready to assault the heights and capture the ruins of the monastery.

Their first attack went in at the beginning of *Diadem* but the paratroopers facing them seemed as implacable a foe as ever. The Germans knew the ground and had sown minefields and set up deadly cross-fires. By 13 May even the determined Anders realised the task was impossible and reluctantly pulled his men back.

Other Allies now took on a key role. General Alphonse Juin, a soldier noted for his left-handed salute (his right arm having been maimed during the Great War), commanded the French Expeditionary Corps which included three North African Divisions. Among

Right: A British armoured car in the streets of Cassino after the Germans had retreated.
Left: Two prisoners being brought in under guard amidst the ruins of the town.

them were Goums, men from the Atlas Mountains who were used to fighting in rugged terrain. They wore burnooses and carried large knives. Montgomery said of them: 'Dark men, dark night. Very hard to see coming.'

Juin's men faced the steep slopes of Monte Maio, some 15 miles south of Monte Cassino. Only light German forces defended the position for both they and the Allies had hitherto believed the area to be to be impassable by an army in strength. But Juin's Goums proved up to the task and ghosted through the mountains, ruthlessly despatching the opposition.

Too late Kesselring realised that his stubbornly-defended Gustav Line had been compromised. More bad news followed for the Germans when the US II Corps, supported by naval gunfire, made progress in the coastal region around Minturno. British units

such as the Black Watch and Royal West Kents in the Liri Valley were also fighting hard – two VCs were won in this arena. On the late afternoon of 15 May, Kesselring learnt that 100 Allied tanks, crewed in the main by Canadians, had broken through in the valley. Cassino was about to be outflanked. Orders were issued for the paratroopers to pull back from the Monastery and retreat north.

Monte Cassino captured

The Poles didn't know of the German decision. That night they attacked again and fierce fighting erupted at outlying positions such as Albaneto Farm. Mine explosions and mortar barrages, rifle and Spandau machine-gun fire ripped through the darkness. Allied tanks added the blast of their own guns. By 17 May the Poles were at last close to their objective.

Next morning Lt Casimir Gurbiel and a party of Uhlans of the Poldoski Lancers cautiously entered the ruins of the Benedictine Monastery to find only badly wounded Germans remaining in the vaults. Overnight the Germans had gone. Soon the red and white flag of Poland fluttered over the scene of devastation. The sounds of war were distant now and a kind of peace descended on the holy place. Shredded tree stumps, scattered masonry and overlapping bomb and shell craters were everywhere. Yet present also were wild flowers. Lots of them, and in a riot of colours dominated by the red of poppies. Their example would not be lost on the monks of St Benedict. Just a few years later, a new Monastery would rise from the ruins of the old.

Over 850 Poles died and 3000 were wounded in the final seven days of fighting at Cassino. The inscription at the Polish cemetery which faces the rebuilt Monastery across a valley reads: 'We Polish soldiers, for our freedom and yours, have given our souls to God, our bodies to the soil of Italy and our hearts to Poland.'

The war moved on up the 'leg' of Italy. But not very far. The Germans had another

Above left: US General Mark Clark at Borga Grappa on the morning of 25 May 1944 when troops from the south linked with troops from Anzio for the first time. Left: The memorial at Borga Grappa. This picture was taken by Sixty Years On Editor David Arnold in 1994 on the occasion of the 50th anniversary of the break-out. Anzio veteran and distinguished author Raleigh Trevelyan is seen beside the monument.

defensive position, the Adolf Hitler Line, already marked out. For a while it stalled the Eighth Army. Then the French Goums, continuing their advance on the heights to the west of the Liri Valley, forced a breach. Excellent fighters, unfortunately the North Africans were earning a reputation for rape and robbery off the battlefield. One Italian report lamented, 'The Germans took away our goats, sheep and food, but they at least respected our women.'

The Canadian 1st Corps went into the attack again on 21 – 22 May and three days later the Hitler Line caved in. On the same day the Luftwaffe put in a major effort for the first time in many weeks but to no avail; they lost 32 precious fighters. Then Formia and Gaeta on the coast were captured by the Americans while the advancing Poles took Piedimonte.

Alexander was pleased to inform Churchill that 500 square miles of Italy had been liberated in just two weeks and over 10,000 Germans taken prisoner. The Allies had developed a powerful forward momentum. Now was the time for the forces cooped up in the Anzio beach-head to burst out and cut off the enemy's line of retreat to Rome and beyond.

Breakout at Anzio

The night of 22 – 23 May was a clear, starlit night over Rome, the Alban Hills and the Latium Coast. In the blacked-out Anzio – Nettuno beach-head, 150,000 men gazed upwards at the panoply of constellations. *Operation Buffalo* – the long-awaited breakout – was imminent. Would dawn see an end to the terrors and tedium of the months of virtual trench warfare?

Not immediately. Following a massive artillery barrage that started at 05.45 hours, the massed Shermans of Maj-Gen Ernie Harmon's First Armoured Division rolled forward on a mere 2000 yard front, heading for Cisterna. By nightfall, 86 US tanks and armoured vehicles had been destroyed. The stubborn German defenders in Cisterna held out for three days; seven Congressional Medals of Honour were won by US soldiers fighting for the ruined town.

The British at Anzio had a diversionary attack role at the beginning of the breakout. The night before *Buffalo*, Raleigh Trevelyan, a young officer in the Green Howards, led a recce patrol out to scout around the mouth of the shallow Moletta River, across which the British attack would go. He and his troops walked into a minefield, where two of his men were blown up. Trevelyan reckoned he must have stepped over the very mine that killed them.

In the diversionary attack itself he wasn't so lucky. Wounds from grenades hospitalised him from where he wrote to his brother, 'Of course our barrage was quite fantastic..when I led a section round some bushes, a Spandau opened up only 10 yards away, killing the section leader behind me and badly wounding four others. I chucked a grenade and tore off, only to discover another Jerry trench just below me. The Jerry threw an egg grenade, which hit me on the nose and then bounced back on to him and exploded. The next few hours were a haze of grenade throwing and tommy-gunning, sand and bits of scrub flying everywhere. My platoon took 15 prisoners and we must have killed half a dozen others.'

Some diversion! Trevelyan went on to record his experiences in Italy in two books, *The Fortress* and *Rome '44 – The Battle for the Eternal City*.

After the fall of Cisterna, German prisoners were gathered in ever-larger numbers. Allied air power crippled their ability to move and in one aerial onslaught 15 Tiger tanks were destroyed on a short stretch of road near the town of Cori. Attention turned to Valmontone on Route Six between Rome and Naples. This town was in the heart of a now rapidly diminishing gap between the Allied soldiers advancing from Anzio and the Allies coming up from the south. Closing the gap would seal the fate of a large part of the German army in Italy, leaving but a few effective enemy forces between this place and the Alps.

It was not to be. On the seeming verge of a stunning victory, General Mark Clark changed the momentum of the attack. Instead of reinforcing the advance on Valmontone he instructed Maj-Gen Lucian Truscott – commander of the pent-up Anzio forces, most of whom had not yet been committed to battle – to march his men north. In the direction of Rome.

Controversy about Clark's decision continues to this day. It is said he suspected there was an Eighth Army plot to steal ahead and enter the Eternal City as liberators ahead of his Fifth Army. Was it vanity that made him go for Rome, to be hailed as the first warrior to enter the city from the south in 2000 years? When Churchill learnt of Clark's order he signalled Alexander, 'The glory of this

Above: Monte Cassino in May 1944. Polish dead are being removed from the battlefield. The Poles suffered many casualties in the final assault on the heights.
Right: British troops of the Fifth Army pictured in the same month. They are taking cover in a German trench whilst waiting for reinforcements before advancing.

battle, already great, will be measured not by the capture of Rome or juncture with the (forces from Anzio) but by the number of German divisions cut off.'

The French General Juin made his own comment: 'Questions of prestige are shaping events, with each one wanting to make entry into Rome. History will not fail to pass severe sentence.'

NEWS FROM ITALY

British newspapers carried no news of the D-Day build-up in May 1944. However, events in Italy were reported in detail. The map reproduced here is from the Daily Herald of 25 May 1944. It shows the Allied advance north from Cassino and the break-out from Anzio. In fact by this date, the two forces had actually linked up.

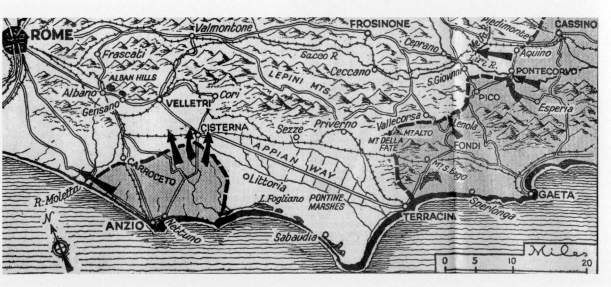

As individual instalments of Sixty Years On *were published we received numerous letters and contributions from readers. To help with the chronological flow of this omnibus book, we have, so far as possible, put the letters as close to the time they allude to.*

Anzio veteran

Writing as a veteran of the Anzio landings in 1944, you may be interested in my return to Anzio on 22 January 2004, the 60th anniversary of *Operation Shingle*. I served in the 248 Fld Coy Royal Engineers and we were one of four companies of REs in the 1st British Infantry Division. I only managed to get to the 2004 commemoration event through the kindness of Mr Geoff Smith, who was one of the survivors of *HMS Spartan*, a cruiser sunk by a glider bomb off Anzio.

I met up with him and other survivors at Stansted and travelled with them to Anzio. I then met up with Major Reg Norfolk, who was second in command of the 248 in the beach-head. The citizens of Anzio had laid on a number of remembrance ceremonies for us to attend and really did us proud. The main object for Reg and I was the laying of a wreath on the memorial at the Beach-head Cemetery, where our comrades of the 248 were buried. Of the 1st Infantry Division, which at the start of the battle consisted of 18,000 troops, we lost 8868 officers and men, killed, wounded and missing at Anzio alone.

After the break-out we entered Rome on 5 June 1944 (it was my 22nd birthday). Of course, next day, 6 June was D-Day and the Italian Campaign took a back seat and hardly got a mention in the press from then and still doesn't get much attention even today. However, the people of Anzio are most grateful and we were treated so kindly during our stay. The Mayor of Anzio presented us

with a medallion to commemorate the 60th anniversary and we were also given a Certificate of Honour which says: *'To those who fought so valiantly, without fearing for their own lives during the battle of Anzio. Lest we forget.'*

There is a wonderful museum in Anzio. If you check on my website, you will see some of the photographs, including action pictures of the battle. One is of the Flyover, a real hot spot. Being engineers we had the job of tunnelling through the left-hand embankment for observation of the enemy on the other side. This work was carried out by the sappers, most of the time under shellfire. Two of our sappers were buried whilst digging the tunnel but they were dug out; apart from being badly shook up, they were OK. The tunnel when finished was very impressive and used by spotters for the artillery. My part in this action was being a driver. I had the doubtful honour of getting the sappers up to the Flyover to carry out their work and this could only be done during darkness as we were under observation all the time. The German gunners had an 88mm gun lined up to fire through the bridge which, to say the least, was a bit scary. I had to do this trip night and morning, as it was too dangerous to leave a vehicle up there all night. The road leading to the Flyover was dead straight for a mile and with the 88 firing through the bridge we had a very rough ride at times. On getting to the bridge I had to turn left across the railway, where it was fairly safe. I then had to unload before taking the sappers who had been relieved back to our holes in the ground in the rear area - which was not much safer than being up at the front!

I have my own website which tells the story with photographs and also the story of Angelita, a little girl found on the beach-head, of which there is a book, obtainable from Anzio, *The Legend of Angelita*. I have a copy which was also given to us by the Mayor. My website is **odell.silversurfersatbedford.org.uk/anzio** Incidentally, Reg Norfolk and myself were the only two from the 248 able to attend the 2004 ceremony. Age has taken its toll.

Bob Odell (ex-248 Field Coy RE)

Left: The Flyover at Anzio pictured after the break-out in the Summer of 1944.

Memories of Minturno

I was particularly interested in the letter from Jim Pybus (page 21) who said that he intends visiting Minturno Military Cemetery in Italy. I supervised the construction of Minturno Cemetery and although it is not so beautiful as some of the others I was also involved with, it is nevertheless a quiet and tranquil place, despite being adjacent to the Rome - Naples road.

If Jim does visit (and I urge him to so do as it is very easy to get there) then I suggest he rents a car in Rome and about two hours drive will bring him to the cemetery gates. Then I ask him to pause a moment at the graves of the many very young men buried there. I seem to recall one as young as just 16 years - or perhaps he is buried at Monte Cassino; there are so many.

I myself landed at around 9am on 6 June 1944 on Juno beach in Normandy. To my horror I saw the bodies of several hundred Canadian troops lying on the shore. They were so close to each other that to my everlasting shame I was forced to tread on some of their bodies in the mad rush to get to the sea wall and away from the German machine guns.

A E Long, Peterborough

An Italian pilgrimage

War documentaries and analyses we get on TV are interesting and well done but cannot portray the reality. War on TV is safe whereas the real thing is very dangerous and frightening: indeed it is largely to do with killing people. Even at the 'effects' level, the sheer noise of battle can never be recreated (it would burst the equipment). Above all, the difference between now and then is that we now know the outcome. At the time there were those who would not live to know it.

This was the sort of reason why I (no doubt like others) was slightly uneasy about the prospect of going back in time (in my case to Salerno, Anzio and Cassino), though I very much wanted and needed to. However, in revisiting the first half of the long Italian campaign, it was for me hugely important to share the experience with my wife Janet, not to mention our elder son Giles. He was splendidly interested as well as being an attentive help to us old folk. He now understands more of what I have been unable to describe properly, and so will his three sons by degrees.

Italy is unbelievably beautiful as well as providing virtually impossible terrain for an army on the attack. To have seen again the southern battlefields (and now also the cemeteries) is to confirm one's sheer luck in coming out of it all unhurt at least in body. I knew that many friends would now be cemetery crosses, with their dates of death clustered around the dates of our battles. But there were new things still to find out or to retrieve memories long overlaid by the rapid movement of war.

For example I took on board for the first time the full story of the London Scottish private who won a VC in my 56th Division – that he was shot by a German soldier who had already surrendered to him. I heard much more from our guide than I had ever known about the shape of the battles and the part played by formations other than my own. And fighting aside, I saw more than at the time the extraordinary difficulty of organising a war and the sheer flukiness of events.

To see the mountains near Cassino brought back the foreboding we gunners felt as our infantry were sent in to capture heavily defended targets in full view of the enemy. There had been pride but also dread as we watched the Scots Guards setting out in single file up the slopes of Monte Camino to the sound of bagpipes.

Nothing on this visit could recreate the sound of the dive bombers as we came in to disembark at Salerno and later at Anzio. Not only did they come with shocking surprise, invisible out of the setting sun, but they were equipped with sirens that shrieked ever louder as they dived. And of course the bombs were visible, seeming to fall no faster than large tennis balls: where would the next one land? Bombing and shelling aside, however, once we were ashore I felt lucky to have been an artillery subaltern compared with my infantry equivalents; although we had many losses they were usually 'at arms length' and did not involve us in unnerving patrols.

I served mainly as Assistant Adjutant of my regiment (the 64th Field) with periods back at the guns to keep in practice – and my job included manning the CO's forward command post. I suspect it was unusual (at any rate in my war) for someone in this situation to have lost, as I did, two colonels out of three, killed by shellfire just after they left me to confer with the infantry brigadier. I myself had only a lot of disturbing near misses.

My first colonel, as we approached the Garigliano river, was Angus McCracken, a 48 year old territorial, typical of the citizen soldiery in our territorial regiment – a city accountant, who had told me modestly only a week or two before he died that a field telephone call just received had been to tell him about the award of his DSO. (His wife was Esther McCracken, whose popular stage plays were filling West End theatres at the time he was with the regiment). He was an old fashioned gentleman, who used a cut-throat razor that I kept and threw away only recently. The manner of his death would have seemed inconceivable in his City office a few years before. Such City links permeated this TA set-up, and one imagines pre-war evening

drills for stock jobbers, jaded after days at desks, now suddenly transformed into blood and guts for real. They were splendid people.

The second colonel I lost in a similar way in the Gothic Line, a few months later, was Col Zambra, who from his name must have died in the country of his ancestors. Only 34, he was a Regular, and this was his first command.

Our guide on the (Holts) tour last October was exceptionally good; an ex-Marine colonel (David Storrie OBE) with 34 years service, who had fought in Borneo and many other places. He had briefed himself with military thoroughness and gave potted lectures at roadsides as we frequently disembarked from the coach at this or that battle site. He was also a strict disciplinarian, getting us up by 6.30 most mornings!

I lent him my boyish diaries to lend very slight colour to the serious business of strategy and tactics. And as the only one who had been at both Salerno and Anzio (as well as the approaches to Cassino, from which my Division was sent urgently to help out at Anzio), I was occasionally invited to comment.

The others on the tour were a mixed bunch of predominantly younger people with an interest in military history. It was difficult to convey the reality of war to them. For example, one chap asked me whether we had sought the Italian farmer's permission to put our 25-pounders in his field and sleep in his buildings!

In all it was a nostalgic experience rather than a holiday. We all found it worthwhile, though for me it was discouraging to walk uncertainly across beaches where 21 year old limbs had once been so agile. Pledges to visit graves, made privately over 60 years ago, were certainly worth keeping (though they were not for me what Americans might call 'closure').
Geoffrey Cockerill, Surrey

PS. I saw Alan Whicker's very lively and riveting programme on the Italian campaign, including his account of filming at Salerno and Anzio. Out of curiosity I checked Who's Who for detail and found that he was born only in August 1925. Hence he must have been an officer aged just one month over 18 in Salerno and 19 in Milan. To be a director of the film unit in Eighth and Fifth Armies at this age is another astonishing thing one would not have guessed.

Green Howard hero

Since he died in June last year I have lodged my father's medals with the Green Howards Museum at Richmond, North Yorkshire. He came from a third family generation of soldiers who fought for their country and his medals plus those of his father and grandfather are being displayed on their own board as a tribute to their endeavours.

My point in writing is that your *Sixty Years On* series is currently reporting on the battles for Monte Cassino. My father was awarded an immediate MM in the field for commanding the bridging of the River Gari and for his work on the Bailey Bridge operation to cross the Cassino river in early May 1944. He was with the 4th (Br) Division, 13 Corps, Unit 7th Field Company RE and was just 24 years old. British Army records state:

'During the night 11-12 May Sgt Riordan was an NCO in charge of Bridge construction on Operation Congo across the River Gari, three miles south of Cassino. Under heavy machine gun, mortar and shellfire he displayed resource and courage and, under most difficult conditions never for one moment allowed the situation to get the better of him. By his inspiring leadership he kept the men under his command at work until they were ordered to withdraw.'

The records then relate how the very next night Sgt Riordan volunteered to work on a Bailey Bridge *(Operation Amazon)* in the same area and again '...displayed the highest qualities of leadership ... whilst under continual small arms and shellfire.'

My father was also at Dunkerque, helping to slow down the German advance until he was injured, eventually getting off safely at De Panne. In later years he wrote his war memoirs, *A History of the 7th Field Company 1939 – 1946.*
John Riordan, Pontefract, Yorks

John Riordan and his family pictured in the Green Howards Museum, Richmond, North Yorks, presenting medals won by three generations of Riordan servicemen, including those of his father which were awarded for exceptional bravery at Cassino in 1944.

WAR DIARY
May 1944

Prime Ministers from British Commonwealth nations gather in London at the beginning of May. Discussions centre on the progress of the war and future strategies.

On **1 May** Truk in the South Pacific is again the target of a US carrier task force; over 120 Japanese aircraft are destroyed, over half of them on the ground, in two days of raids.

On **2 May** a crossword puzzle in the *Daily Telegraph* contains a clue at 17 across: 'One of the US'. The answer is revealed as UTAH, an American state but also the code for one of the US D-Day landing beaches in Normandy.

BBC's Voice of Britain is widely listened to throughout Occupied Europe, despite harsh penalties for people caught tuning in. It carries a story concerning two U-boats attempting to fight back against an air attack that sunk the pair whilst a third U-Boat took the opportunity to submerge and escape. When German monitors pick up the story it leads to the court-martial of the U-boat's Captain. On his return to port he had claimed that his two companion vessels had declined to open fire but had been destroyed in the act of submerging, leaving his vessel on the surface to fight off the aircraft alone!

3 May: Spanish dictator Franco's refusal to join the Axis Alliance even when a fascist victory in the war seemed assured in 1940 is reaping dividends. He is courted by the Allies who turn a blind eye to Dictator's harsh repression of Spanish communists and suspected republicans. Spain now agrees to cut tungsten ore exports to Germany by one sixth in exchange for US oil. Hitler is incensed. Franco's steady concessions to the Allies have included the release of Italian ships interned in Spanish ports and the recall of Spanish volunteer forces aiding Germany against Russia.

4 May: British civilians used to seeing well-fed Americans 'over here' may not have believed that meat rationing had been

A massive bunker on the Atlantic Wall built by the slave labourers of the Todt Organisation

enforced in the USA since Pearl Harbour. But from today meat goes back on the menu right across the States, thanks to the success of beef farmers in increasing production.

On **5 May** Hitler is able to read the transcript of a conversation between Roosevelt and Churchill thanks to a rare coup by the German intelligence service. No secrets are exchanged.

6 May: That ancient city of the Tartars, Sebastopol, comes under furious attack; the Russians face desperate German defenders.

Mahatma Ghandi is released from prison in India because of ill-health. He has been held since 1942 on fears that he might, even unwittingly, encourage Indians to take a pro-Japanese stance. Despite the current Japanese threat to Assam, there has been no sign of popular support for the invaders.

British 'skytroops' on a training exercise with their gliders. An airbourne vanguard will be a key element of the Allied invasion of Europe.

WAR DIARY

The last resting place for many of the German defenders at Cassino.

In France 1800 men are deported to Dora Concentration Camp in Germany to work on the production of Nazi secret weapons. Few will survive.

A five day exercise - *Operation Fabius* - has been taking place at coastal locations in Southern England, from Littlehampton in West Sussex all the way to Slapton Sands in Devon. Allied commanders are putting their men through the final phases of training for D-Day. A second exercise, *Operation Splint*, provides experience in handling the evacuation of casualties via landing craft.

7 May: At Imphal the fighting settles into a stalemate, although it is clear the initiative lies with General Slim. Exploiting the Allied air superiority is the key to future success. In China the Japanese are still making gains; today they captured Suiping and cut the Peking – Hankow railway.

8 May: General Eisenhower sets the date for the invasion of Northern Europe: D-Day will be 5 June 1944. In Berlin tomorrow, Admiral Donitz will tell the German High Command that he doesn't believe the Allies plan a landing in the near future.

In Budapest, a cruel barter is proposed by Adolf Eichmann, Head of the Jewish Office of the Gestapo. Deportations of Jews from Hungary will be slowed, or even halted, if the Allies provide Germany with 10,000 vehicles to be used in the war against the communist Red Army. Joel Brand of the Hungarian Jewish Assistance and Rescue Committee is on his way to Turkey seeking Allied agreement to the plan.

Next day **(9 May)** the Germans declare a 10-mile exclusion zone out to sea along the entire coastline of Denmark. A similar restriction already applies to the Dutch coast. Fish to supplement the rations of the Dutch and Danes will all but disappear from sale.

It's the end for Hitler's 'Aircraft Carrier in the Black Sea' as Sebastopol surrenders to the Red Army. Around 20,000 German and Rumanian soldiers have died in the siege and nearly 25,000 are taken prisoner. Almost all of the Crimea has been freed.

10 May: It's revealed that the Americans have stockpiled vast quantities of food in England to feed the half-starved peoples of Europe in the wake of the invasion. Cereals, dried milk, powdered eggs, canned meats and dehydrated vegetables form the bulk of the growing food mountain.

11 May: *The Marx Brothers Go West* is the film most requested for screening by soldiers of the Eighth Army in Italy.

In Burma, 40,000 Chinese cross the River Salween in an offensive aimed at ejecting the Japanese from the north of the country. If successful then the Japanese on the Burma – India border will be isolated.

Next day London broadcasts messages to the leaders of Hungary, Rumania and Bulgaria urging them to quit the Axis alliance and give up fighting the Allies. Overnight six German plants manufacturing synthetic oil have been hit by a total of 900 Flying Fortresses and Liberators of the Eighth USAAF. Allied losses number 58 while 50 German aircraft are shot down.

13 May: The fourth major Allied assault of the year is underway against Cassino and the Gothic Line. *Operation Diadem* is accompanied by a gigantic artillery bombardment. Over the next six days half a million shells will be hurled at the Germans.

The only Germans now remaining in the Crimea are either killed or captured as the Russians take Cape Kherson. Even for those soldiers who escaped by sea, the ordeal was not ended; Russian submarines, torpedo boats and aircraft have sunk 190 fleeing vessels drowning around 8000 German troops. Hitler had hoped the Crimea would be a fortress where his garrison would hold out until the tide of war turned again. Instead it became a huge trap costing him 110,000 irreplaceable men and vast quantities of arms.

In the English Channel, E-boat S147 is sunk in an action with the frigate *HMS Stayning* and Free French destroyer *La Combattante*. S147's captain is Klaus Donitz, son of the German Admiral Karl Donitz, mastermind of the Nazi U-boat campaign. Klaus is the Admiral's second son to die on active service.

14 May: Britain's code-crackers have uncovered a German ploy to trick the Allies into bombing inactive Luftwaffe airfields. Details of the plan were contained in an intercepted message from Luftwaffe boss Herman Goêring. The Allies have their own elaborate deceptions underway. General George S Patton's First Army Group is massing in Kent preparing to invade France in the Pas de Calais area. At least that's what the Germans believe. In fact, Patton's army doesn't exist; fake tanks, sprawling encampments empty of men and busy radio traffic are all keeping the enemy guessing as to what Allied armies are coming and where.

15 May: Civilian travel on the rail network in France has been banned. In Algiers, the French Committee of National Liberation decides on changing its name to the Provisional Government of the French Republic with effect from 2 June. In Italy, Free French forces under General Alphonse Juin consolidate their capture of San Giorgio and Ausonia; the Gustav Line is finally beginning to crack. Juin's men include tough African Goumiers from the Atlas Mountains who are feared as much by the Italian civilian population as by the Germans.

London: The King, Prime Minister Churchill, South African Premier Jan Smuts and other Allied leaders are at St Paul's School in Kensington for a briefing on the impending invasion. In the school hall, General Eisenhower and Field Marshal Montgomery unveil a huge coloured map depicting the Normandy beaches on which the Allies will land in the next few weeks. Monty had attended St Paul's as pupil.

16 May: In Berlin orders are issued for the deployment of the secret V1 rocket-propelled 'Flying Bombs' to their launch sites that stretch from Normandy to the Dutch coast.

Next day the British Far Eastern Fleet sails close to Java and launches an air attack on oil facilities at Surabaya.

In London a conference of Prime Ministers of Britain, Canada, Australia, New Zealand and South Africa ends with the unanimous endorsement of plans for winning the war and a blueprint for post-war relations which includes the foundation of a world organisation empowered to preserve peace.

18 May: At last the Gustav Line is broken. After a six day struggle up the mountain by soldiers of the Polish II Corps, the Eagle flag of Poland flutters over the ruined monastery at Monte Cassino.

In the Turkish capital, Ankara, martial law has been declared following pro-German riots. The unrest demonstrates why the government has been cautious of openly supporting the Allies.

U-241 has been sunk off the coast of Norway by a Catalina flying boat. Two days earlier, sister submarine U-240 suffered the same fate.

In Palestine three truckloads of members of the Jewish nationalist group, *Irgun*, storm a radio station. Their plans to broadcast messages to the Jewish population of Palestine are

WAR DIARY
May 1944

thwarted by the arrival of police reinforcements in armoured cars. After a brief gun battle the Irgun men escape.

19 May: The Allied breakthrough in Italy gains momentum as the US II Corp push up the coastal Highway 7 to occupy Gaeta and Monte Grande. The Germans are putting together a new defensive position at the top end of the Liri Valley but this so-called 'Adolf Hitler Line' is unlikely to hold up the Allies for long.

In London the Government confirms that British POWs can have monetary credit balances built up in Germany made available for their families in this country. German prisoners have reciprocal rights. The rate of exchange is 15 Reichsmarks to the £.

On **20 May** the Americans initiate a two-day air blitz on Marcus Island in the South Pacific. Japanese resistance on Wakde Island near New Guinea has ended.

21 May: *Operation Chattanooga* is underway as the Allied air forces systematically bomb rail targets in France and Belgium. On one recent evening residents of an English South Coast town observed a vast formation of RAF bombers heading for the Continent; it took 35 minutes for the full stream to pass overhead.

Unknown to the general public, an embarrassing problem has occurred with some component parts to the top secret artificial harbours codenamed *Mulberry*. Massive floating concrete caissons are to be towed across the Channel and sunk off the Normandy coast to form breakwaters. Unfortunately, a number of the big caissons have stuck firmly in the mud of the Thames estuary and are proving impossible to budge.

22 May: General Mark Clark arrives at Anzio on the eve of *Operation Buffalo*, the long-awaited breakout from the beach-head. As evening comes the guns are strangely quiet as 150,000 Allied soldiers ponder what dawn will bring.

23 May: Anzio. 05.45 hours. Over 1000 guns, tanks and mortars open fire on German positions, mainly in the Cisterna area where the principal Allied thrust will begin.

In London the Ministry of Pensions is considering improving the allowances made for separated or divorced wives of men serving in the Forces. This follows representations from the Soldiers, Sailors and Airmens Association and the Officers Families Association.

The Anzio breakout **(24 May)** is being stubbornly contested at Cisterna by the LXXVI Panzer Corps. So far 86 Allied tanks and armoured vehicles have been lost to mines and artillery fire.

On this same day in Rio, President Vargas reviews men of the Brazilian Expeditionary Force who are embarking for Europe as part of a promised army that will eventually number 60,000. Brazil declared war on the Axis powers in August 1942 following the sinking of several of her ships by U-Boats in the Atlantic.

A small ship carrying 54 Germans and seven Rumanians who escaped from the Crimea has docked in Zonguldak, Northern Turkey, where the men are interned.

25 May: Over 138,000 Hungarian Jews have so far been deported to concentration camps. The Allies refused Adolf Eichmann's 'Jewish lives for Allied trucks' offer made in the spring. Retribution will befall Eichmann some 18 years later when he is kidnapped from his Argentinian hiding place and taken to Israel for trial and execution.

The siege of Anzio officially ended this morning when US troops from the beach-head linked up with the Fifth Army advancing north from Terracina. Later in the day Cisterna is captured after three days of fierce fighting.

Right: Waiting for the invasion: a German gun position on the coast of France in spring 1944.

26 May: Marshal Petain reiterates his call for prefects and civil servants in Occupied France to give 'complete and loyal help' to the German Army, citing the Armistice Convention and The Hague Convention as the corroborative authority. Allied aircraft today hit military and transport targets in Nice, Marseille, Lyons and St Etienne but there are inevitably civilian casualties.

27 May: A coded signal for the Italian partisans in the hills and towns around Rome is transmitted on London Radio. *Anna Maria e Promossa* – 'Anna Maria is Promoted' - is the signal telling the partisans that the time is right to rise up against the Germans. In Rome itself, the inhabitants are asked to be patient rather than risk the destruction of the city.

28 May: Oil facilities in Germany are the target of big American air raids. However, the enemy are showing great skill in minimising the effects of the bombing. The able and efficient Albert Speer has been in charge of armaments production since February. Production of German fighters is actually rising at present. One of Speer's innovations are the *Jagestabs* – special flying squads of skilled operatives charged with supervising the repair of factories.

In Britain the D-Day security clampdown is absolute. Everyone concerned with the invasion has been sealed within the confines of their camp. No mail is allowed in or out.

29 May: The 11,000 Japanese defenders of Biak have pinned down three US infantry regiments who had landed unopposed 18 hours earlier on this small island off the coast of New Guinea.

30 May: Berlin: A shadowy Nazi boss - Martin Bormann - believed to have considerable influence over Hitler issues a chilling directive telling local Nazi leaders that shot-down Allied aircrew can no longer consider themselves protected under the Geneva Convention due to the 'criminal combat methods' employed in bombing German cities.

Fierce fighting continues in front of the German Caesar Line at Campoleone near Anzio where the Americans have sustained 5116 casualties since 23 May.

The last day of May 1944 sees air attacks on bridges over the River Seine in Normandy but also increased bombing around Calais and Boulogne. The Luftwaffe is largely absent in France although five Focke-Wulf 190s are shot down by Allied fighter-bombers over western Germany.

Monte Artemisio in the Alban Hills to the south of Rome has been seized by the Americans and threatens the flank of the Germans holding out in their Caesar Line. The Eighth Army is coming up Route 6 and approaching Valmontone. The Germans must surely retreat. The question is, will Hitler order the destruction of Rome? The American General Mark Clark has his own vision; he seeks to lead the first army to conquer Rome from the south in nearly 2000 years.

THE LONGEST DAY DAWNS

JUNE 1944

D-DAY

D-Day and the Invasion of France unfolded on a vast scale. The landing beaches in Normandy were spread along some 60 miles of coast, almost from the mouth of the Sein in the east to the Cotentin Peninsula in the west.

Preceding the sea landings came two vast air armadas with thousands of paratroopers in transport aircraft and gliders. Bombers and fighter planes crowded the skies. The Americans came down in the area behind their two designated beaches of Omaha and Utah. The men of the 101st 'Screaming Eagles' and 82nd 'All American' Airborne Divisions suffered terribly from poor navigation and approach work by their Dakota crews. The Germans had also flooded large areas in recent days to introduce an unforeseen hazard.

The main objective of the US airborne assault was to secure the roads, bridges and causeways leading inland from the invasion beaches, particularly those of Utah, the most westerly. Despite initial confusion and heavy losses, the Americans did well with small groups who joined together to form ad hoc fighting units. A key achievement was the capture of the town of St Mere-Eglise at around 5am; this blocked the route of any German counter-attack in the first vulnerable hours of the sea landings.

How the British air landings fared are covered in more detail on the following pages.

Few of the men who took part in the events of D-Day could have seen the 'big picture'. Only those in the air could get close to gauging the enormity of it all. As dawn broke and an initially uncertain light visited the Normandy beaches, Flight Lt R H G Weighill of RAF No 2 Squadron, 35 Wing, flying a Mustang to spot the fall of shot for *HMS Glasgow*, was privileged to witness a scene without precedent in the history of war.

'The sea was littered with ships of all descriptions, ploughing doggedly towards the enemy's coast, looking very grim and determined. The bombardment was terrific and one could actually see the shells in the form of red and white lights as they left the ships and flew towards the shore. I stayed at 1000 feet and watched five of the naval vessels, about a mile offshore and turned broadside on, proceeding to belch flame and destruction.

'It was a most terrifying sight, for as they fired what I now know to be rockets, a sheet of flame 50 yards long enveloped the ship. By this time the first boat was almost ashore, and as I watched it, the front came down and the men inside jumped into the water and ran towards the beach. It was a wonderful moment when I reported that the first men had actually landed.'

Ashore in force

The RAF's Official History credits Weighill as being most probably the first aerial eye-witness of the landings. By 10.15am the Allies were ashore in force in most places. At this time, Air Commodore Geddes, also in a Mustang, traversed the beaches from one end to the other at a height of some 1000 feet. His flight caught perfectly how the fight was progressing.

In the British and Canadian sector all the beaches (Sword, Juno and Gold) seemed secured. In the centre the village of Le Hamel was shrouded in smoke and dust from which emerged vehicles and the purposeful figures of the invaders. At some places they were already three miles inland; at others half that distance.

INVASION

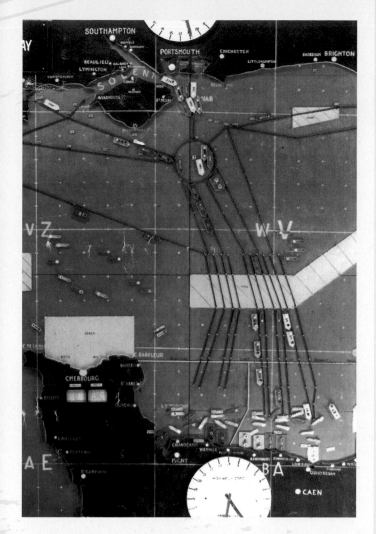

Above: *The famous wall map in Southwick House near Portsmouth is preserved in its original position with the clock set for H-Hour on D-Day.*

Left: *Two Thunderbolt aircraft pictured flying over US troops on 'Bloody' Omaha Beach on D-Day. The Americans faced the most determined German opposition on this stretch of coast and came close to ordering a withdrawal before finally breaking through. Inset is the front page of the Liberation Edition of* Yank *magazine dated 11 June 1944.*

As Geddes approached the Cherbourg (Cotentin) Peninsula, he perceived a place where the 'shore seemed to be congested with vehicles, craft and men with no sign of penetration beyond the sea wall'. This was 'Bloody Omaha' where the Americans were meeting ferocious fire from the Germans atop the steep bluffs rising up from the beach.

Geddes made another pass, this time in the opposite direction. He noticed a direct hit on a house near the harbour mouth of Port en Bessin; spouts of water where enemy return fire was ranging on the invasion fleet; several fires a short distance inland and a damaged landing craft, half awash. He witnessed the 'majestic sight' of HMS Warspite firing salvoes landward while attendant small boats bustled around her, laying a screen of smoke.

By nightfall on D-Day 6 June, the British and Canadians in the east had established a beach-head nearly 20 miles long and some five miles deep. They had secured their flank on the River Orne and were close to the outskirts of the city of Caen.

On the west, around Utah Beach, the Americans held an area nearly 10 miles wide and had spearheads more than four miles inland and in contact with the scattered paratroop units. Only in the centre at Omaha, had there been really serious trouble. But as the light faded in the late evening, even here the US troops were at last making progress and reinforcements were rapidly making good the losses of the day.

The month of June would see gains and setbacks; the German garrison in Cherbourg surrendered on 27 June, though the port was pretty much destroyed. In the east though, the British and Canadians found the going hard against strong German resistance in a countryside and terrain that very much favoured the defenders.

J D Todd of Somerset writes:

The comments and photographs of the large gun 'Anzio Annie' (page 55) brought back memories of the Normandy beaches of June '44 and provided me with the likely explanation of an incident which has been with me since those days. I was serving on a British Merchant Navy ship carrying ammunition between East Ham and the beaches.

We arrived at Sword Beach a few days after the initial assault, by which time we had control of the beaches, although there was considerable activity and much metal flying about. Some days later the ships became the target of long-range shells which we were informed came from a large gun, on rails, sited on the hills above Le Havre. Not knowing much about artillery, I felt that the range would be impossible, but the 'Anzio Annie' story confirms this could be possible with such a powerful gun.

Under darkness of night, apparently mines were being laid, probably by miniature submarines. I do not know how many ships were lost this way, but recall one morning just as we were approaching the shore the ship ahead was blown up, her back broken, and she went down rapidly. Word later went round that she had been carrying troops for landing and there was much loss of life. Sadly, we could do nothing to help.

Prior to this, there had been a Polish destroyer attempting to shell the long-range gun, but to no avail. We understood that the gun, after a brief spell of shelling, would retract into a cave or bunker. Then, much to our joy, the battleship HMS Warspite appeared and stopped not far from our ship, positioned herself, and then proceeded to pound the long-range site. She soon hoisted the 'Target Destroyed' flag and, almost as quickly as she arrived, she vanished. With our ship's telescope we could just make out a large black area where the big gun had been and there was no more shelling from that quarter.

There were many brave men on those beaches, but one group are not often mentioned - the pilots who flew Dakotas loaded with urgently needed cased fuel. Landing these planes on suitable sites was not always possible; apparently any pilot who lost his plane due to these hard landings was required to make his way back to the UK by any possible means. On several of our trips back to East Ham we were able to help. Ironically, by this time the beaches were safer than the Thames due to the daily arrival of the Doodlebugs.

G Hooper of Bedford writes:

I can explain exactly why HMS Ramillies was the first ship to open fire on D-Day. She was sailing towards Normandy, some three or four miles distant, when at about 04.30am on 6 June 1944 a shell splashed down scarcely a cable's length dead ahead.

Jerry wasn't playing by the rules. As is now well known, the show wasn't due to start until 05.00. Now, while our Captain Middleton was a gent of the old school, he did have a short fuse, especially when it came to correct procedures not being followed. At this stage I should inform readers, that in action the captain of HMS Ramillies wore a grass skirt, a gift from a Maori chief which was guaranteed to keep the ship from harm. (It seemed to work, too, because two years earlier he had taken it off and we were badly hit.) Captain Middleton also wore a monocle. Jerry continued to lob more shells while we could do nothing about it but sail straight on towards our tormentor. Captain Middleton's grass skirt was now rustling noisily, and his face was getting more and more like a monocled turkey cock. At last his short fuse patience snapped and, turning to the gunnery officer, he barked 'Give him one back Guns'. I felt sorry for Guns who was a decent sort (forgotten his name). He hadn't really got a target, but he loosed one off just the same.

And that was why HMS Ramillies became the first of the D-Day naval force to open fire.

OUT OF THE NIGHT

A crucial chain of events in the opening hours of D-Day and the subsequent link-up of British airborne forces with soldiers advancing from Sword Beach is recounted by military historian Neil Barber.

Just after midnight on 6 June 1944, a stream of British bombers began crossing the Normandy coast. Among them for disguise purposes flew the vanguard of the invasion, six Horsa gliders containing 138 men of the 2nd Battalion, Oxfordshire and Buckinghamshire Light Infantry, led by Major John Howard. Their task, to capture intact, two bridges of vital importance to the D-Day operation.

Allied planners knew that the most critical period for any seaborne landing was the early stages, when time was needed to establish a strong enough defence to allow the build up of men and matériel necessary for a break-out. The most vulnerable areas were the flanks and so prior to the landings, Airborne Forces were to be sent in to create defensive 'buffer zones'. The American 82nd and 101st Airborne Divisions were detailed for this task in the west, around Utah Beach, and the British 6th Airborne Division in the east, beyond Sword Beach.

On Sword's eastern limit lay the small port of Ouistreham, where the Caen Canal and the River Orne merged with the sea. These ran south and virtually parallel for 10 miles, until reaching the city of Caen. However, from coast to suburb, only one road crossed the waterways, five miles inland at the village of Benouville. The 6th Airborne Division, commanded by Major-General Richard 'Windy' Gale, was to establish itself to the east of the Orne, thereby making the bridges essential for the long-term re-supply of the Division via the beaches, for reinforcement and for evacuation of casualties. Also, critically, any German counter-attack from the east would have to cross them. These therefore, were the destinations for the six Horsas.

Each glider also carried a complement of six Royal Engineers to remove charges that, via information from the French Resistance, were known to be ready to destroy the structures. It was for this reason that glider troops were being employed, as they could be landed in close proximity in a very short space of time, unlike parachutists who would have to assemble before performing an assault. Split seconds could prove vital in preventing destruction.

A casemate of the Merville Battery.

Hazardous operation

At 0012 hours the gliders began casting off from the Halifax tugs at around 5000 feet and commenced their blind, curving descents using altimeters and stopwatches. Such a pinpoint landing in the dark was an extremely hazardous operation. However, their skill was such that at the Caen Canal, the first glider came to a halt around 50 yards from the eastern end of the bridge, the second and third following only yards to the right. 25 Platoon, 'D' Company, immediately silenced two dugouts, one of which contained the detonating switch, and stormed across the bridge. 24 Platoon, 'D' Company, crossed the road and cleared trenches to the north-east, while 17 Platoon, 'B' Company, reinforced 25 Platoon. Within minutes, the bridge had been secured and a small defensive perimeter established at its western end, just beyond a building known as the Café Gondrée. Surprise had been total.

Some 500 yards along the road only two gliders managed to land near the Orne Bridge, but it was not heavily guarded, and 14 Platoon, 'B' Company, arriving first, charged across, the few Germans there having fled. Both bridges had been taken within 15 minutes, for the loss of two men killed and 14 wounded. The first part of the operation had been completed. The bridges now had to be held until the 7th Parachute Battalion could get there to enlarge the defensive perimeter and ultimately, relief arrived from Sword Beach.

At 0050 hours the Division's six parachute battalions began their jumps. Unfortunately, Lieutenant Colonel Geoffrey Pine-Coffin's 7th Parachute Battalion, supposedly landing a mile further on in the fields north of Ranville, suffered a scattered drop. Those that were able, managed to take up their positions in Benouville and Le Port, west of the Canal Bridge. They were guided by the perpetual explosions emanating from a tank that had approached the Ox and Bucks from Benouville. A PIAT (Projectile Infantry Anti-Tank), fired at point blank range, had caused the memorable 'firework display'.

Merville Battery

At 0330 hours gliders containing the Divisional HQ also began landing in the Ranville fields. Amongst their loads were 17-Pounder anti-tank guns vital to the lightly armed Paras for the inevitable arrival of enemy tanks. With the various parachute battalions gradually taking up their positions, the Division's 'buffer zone' began to take shape.

To achieve success on the beaches, the Allies had to deal with Hitler's much-vaunted Atlantic Wall, and although in many places it did not warrant its reputation, for Sword Beach, part of it did indeed pose a serious threat. This was a gun battery situated inland, on high ground six miles to the east, near the small village of Merville. Its four concrete casemates each housed a gun, which from the size of the constructions, was estimated to be of 150mm calibre. Around 150 men garrisoned the Battery, which contained machine-gun positions, an anti-aircraft gun and various underground command and magazine buildings. Minefields and huge belts of barbed wire surrounded the site, and to the north-east ran a formidable anti-tank ditch. With the casemate walls being in some places up to six feet thick and covered in earth, they had proved to be almost impervious to bombing. This dictated the necessity for a land-based assault.

The landings on Sword would begin at 0720 hours and so silencing the guns prior to their commencement was of paramount importance. This was another of the 6th Airborne Division's primary tasks and was assigned to Lieutenant Colonel Terence Otway's 9th Parachute Battalion.

The 9th also began jumping at 0050 hours and like the 7th Battalion, suffered a horribly scattered drop. Out of nearly 700 men a mere 150 actually made it to the objective. The thoroughly rehearsed assault plan had to be abandoned for a hastily improvised one. The Paras put in a ferocious attack involving heavy hand-to-hand fighting, and their mixture of training, determination and extraordinary bravery prevailed. In 20 minutes the Battery was theirs. Upon inspection of the casemates they found that the main armament had not yet been fitted, and instead were faced with the destruction of Czech-built 100mm Field Guns, but whatever the calibre, Sword Beach would be spared their 'contribution'. When the survivors gathered along the road at a Calvary Cross rendezvous, only 75 men were left standing.

Pegasus Bridge as it is today.

Lord Lovat's Commandos

Those formations with the responsibility for relieving the men at the bridges came ashore on the most eastern section of Sword known as 'Red Beach', at La Breche. The initial waves, comprising the specialist beach clearing vehicles of the 22nd Dragoons, 'swimming' tanks of the 13th/18th Hussars and infantry of the 2nd East Yorks, duly began landing at around 0725 hours and immediately ran into difficulties. So much so that over an hour later, No 6 Commando and its HQ of Lord Lovat's 1st Special Service Brigade found that fighting was continuing on the sand and beachfront. The Commandos disembarked, punched their way through the defences and got off the beach.

During all of this time the depleted 7th Battalion in Benouville and Le Port had held off attacks from all directions, but with the enemy strength increasing, began to suffer heavy losses. As the morning wore on, a couple of small groups of the Ox and Bucks were moved from the bridge to reinforce the Paras in Le Port.

Small sections of Commandos that had been given specific orders to get to the bridges at all costs began arriving at the Canal Bridge during the late morning. However, it was not until around 1300 hours, that the Airborne men heard the most unexpected sound of bagpipes. They were no longer alone. The wail of the pipes caused the Germans in Le Port to simply disappear. No 6 Commando had fought its way along the roads through Colleville and St Aubin d'Arquenay, and led by Lord Lovat, began to approach the Canal Bridge. Sniper fire necessitated rapid movement, but Lovat crossed the span and exchanged greetings with Major Howard before moving on to the less hazardous Orne Bridge, where he ordered his piper, Bill Millin, to play them across.

Although German activity subsided around the bridges, the arrival of the Commandos did not entail actual relief for the men there and they continued to be pestered by small attacks and sniper fire. Not until around midnight and the arrival of the 2nd Warwickshire Battalion, did they hand over responsibility for the bridges.

Visiting Pegasus Bridge and the Merville Battery

Whether travelling to or returning from the south of France via Ouistreham, the car ferry route is along the D514. A couple of miles outside the town, exit signs appear for the historic Pegasus Bridge, and this is literally a minute's drive from the turn-off. Just before the bridge, on the right-hand side is the wonderfully atmospheric Café Gondrée, which has, since the war, evolved into the focal point for the meeting of Airborne and Commando veterans. It contains many mementos of Parachute, Glider, Commando and various formations involved in the area. To sit there with a coffee, savouring the special atmosphere, is a memorable experience.

The bridge itself was replaced with a larger a decade or so ago, however, it is very similar in appearance. Across the bridge, on the right-hand side are three marker stones on the precise spots where the three gliders landed, plus a bust of Major John Howard.

Fifty yards down on the left is the recently added attraction of the Memorial Pegasus Museum. Through film, photographs, explanation boards and exhibits, a detailed picture can be gained of what exactly went on in the Orne area. The friendly and helpful staff, who all speak English, will answer any questions. The original Pegasus Bridge is held outside, and a full-scale replica of a Horsa glider now sits beside it.

Horsa Bridge

The Merville Battery is 15 minutes further on. Turning left out of the museum, cross the Orne Bridge, now known as Horsa Bridge, and continue to the roundabout. Take the final (left) exit, remaining on the D514, heading for Merville-Franceville Plage. Pass through Sallenelles and continue until the first crossroads (traffic lights) in Merville-Franceville. Turn right into the Avenue Alexandre de Lavergne and as the road veers left, a sign for the Battery will point to a right turn. The site is at the end of this short road.

Today, the four casemates remain, with No 1 now housing an excellent museum. The walls are lined with photographs of the faces of the men of the Battalion, and a more fitting and poignant tribute is difficult to envisage. Explanations on the construction of the Battery, routine life for the German defenders, the attack itself and exhibitions of original equipment used by the Paras adorn the various rooms. A field gun of the same type that was found in the casemates points towards Sword Beach.

Ouistreham Casino

Heading back to Ouistreham on the D514, cross the flyover and go towards Colleville. Here remains the fortified underground bunkers of a position known as 'Hillman'. The 1st Suffolks, who came ashore on Queen Red before the Commandos, captured the site during the afternoon of D-Day.

Returning to Ouistreham, there are various places of D-Day interest to visit along the seafront. No 4 Commando of Lovat's Brigade captured the town, and opposite the casino, which was a German strongpoint cleared by the Free French contingent of the Commando (an action portrayed in a memorable scene in the film *The Longest Day*), is a small but very informative museum dedicated to the unit. Just past the Casino on the left-hand side of the road, amongst the sand dunes, a Memorial to No 4 Commando sits upon one of the actual steel machine gun posts that formed part of the German defences.

Further on, signs direct you to a Flak Tower Museum. This high concrete structure is an extraordinary museum. Upon every level the various rooms are filled with figures and equipment showing what daily life was like for its German occupants. On the top floor, looking out to sea, remains the large working telescope.

Neil Barber is the author of The Day the Devils Dropped In, *which details the exploits of the 9th Parachute Battalion at the Merville Battery on D-Day and during the following week in the words of the men who were actually there.*

The book was published by Pen and Sword Books Ltd.

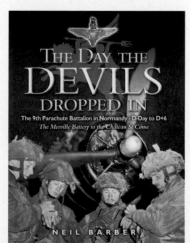

Rendezvous
ON JUNO BEACH

I was too young to serve in the Forces in 1944 but have been privileged to know many people who did, writes Ron McGill. Indeed, there are a number of veterans who are members of my golf club in Surrey. Sometimes it can be difficult to visualise that these quiet, mild-mannered and elderly men are the survivors of the brave youngsters who over 60 years ago fought so valiantly for the precious freedom we enjoy to this day.

One such man is Peter Glanville, now in his 80th year and disabled/wheelchair bound who lives at Hindhead in Surrey with Chris, his wartime WAAF sweetheart who became his wife and is now his constant care and attention officer!

Many Guildford folks will know Chris and Peter from their period in the 1970s/80s when they ran the sub-post office in the Pilgrim's Bookshop in Upper High Street, Guildford, until Peter's retirement in 1985. Even in those days, I would ponder whether this quiet and cheery sub-postmaster really was one of those men who landed on Juno Beach on the morning of 6 June 1944...playing such a vital role with his duties, calling up support fire from off-shore warships onto enemy positions holding up the advance in his sector.

Peter joined the Royal Navy in 1940. He later volunteered for Combined Operations in 1943 and was trained as a Yeoman Signaller at Plymouth prior to posting to a new craft LCT.2428 - a Landing Craft Tank that was part of the LCT 105 Flotilla. After a hazardous journey down from Scotland they eventually tied up safely at the Hamble River near Southampton to begin intensive training into the Channel - somehow surviving an attack from German E-Boats that blasted bullets through the sides of his LCT.

Pleasant surprise

Shortly before D-Day, Peter's commander called him in and proudly informed him he was regarded as the most expert wireless/signaller in the group. This was a pleasant surprise for Peter until he was told he would be staying with the Commander in his role as Flotilla Leader on the first craft of the first wave of assault craft to land at Juno Beach on 6 June. At this stage I think it more interesting to hand over to the actual wording of Peter's personal 'Overlord Diary' that he has kept to this day:

'We weighed anchor at 0600 on 5 June 1944 and proceeded down river to the Solent, all the time gradually forming into 'cruising order'. The sight was wonderful to behold...thousands of ships, all shapes and sizes, packed with tanks, guns, men and material setting off on a journey across the English Channel to invade Hitler's European Fortress - commonly known as France.

We had been finally briefed some 24 hours beforehand so all knew what we were sailing into and of course, all wondering if we would ever see the shores of our homeland again - or the ones we loved.

The weather was not ideal for the job, in fact for the small craft it was rough going. How some of them managed to stay afloat under the circumstances was a miracle - due to superb seamanship and our ship-building people. We in LCT 2428 were not having too bad a time as the ship was one of the bigger types of 'Tank Landing Craft' weighing 120 tons with an additional 100 tons of Army Tanks and Bulldozers aboard.

Hit by a mine

At 0500 hours on 6 June we were a few miles off our objective and we then formed into battle stations and went in at the coast - full speed ahead! The beach itself was a mass of obstacles and mines. One type was a huge steel gate arrangement on rollers which allowed a craft to get so far over it then the craft would stick - and they also had mines on them! Although a lot of the craft hit these things and received holes in their ballast tanks they were so constructed that it did not effect them so much.

Our ship's objective was very slightly to the right of the village of Courselles and it was known to be heavily defended. The Army lads were informed we were near and told to stand by to land. On the way over most of them had been very seasick but now they forgot all that!

We went in at the beach in a long formidable line with reinforcement craft in our wake. It must have been a sickening sight for the German defenders behind their guns on the beach. The craft I was in was hit by a mine as we went up onto the beach, a large hole was blown in our starboard side but luckily, nobody was hurt that much and we got our Army gear and infantry off safely.

The Bulldozers cleared away many of the tank traps while our guns blasted away at the enemy pillboxes. At the same time we were receiving covering fire from Landing Craft fitted with 4-inch guns - these were known as LCGs whose job it was to stay off shore and lob shells over our heads into the enemy lines. They and the rocket firing ships gave us good cover but unfortunately some fell short causing us a few casualties.

Good fighting men

It was truly hell let loose - our guns firing over our heads and the Germans firing at us. Somehow we managed it and the landing was eventually 'made'. Our men got to the barbed wire in front of the pill-boxes and then received very heavy machine-gun fire ...a lot fell dead or wounded but the rest ran on through the wire and into some trenches, having no mercy and killing as they went... it was a case of get your man or be killed yourself.

We had landed 'Marines - Kent Regiment' and 'Royal Canadian Winnipeg Rifles' - all good fighting men and the Canadians especially so. They ran at the wire, some laid flat on it while others walked over them - a sure way of getting through but not one of my choosing! Once through they slipped off their heavy packs and carried on to charge with fixed bayonets and long thin bladed knives.

'Get out and push it!'

We managed to get back to our craft and cleared the beach although she had been mined - the main thing was to get all craft clear in order that the supplies in our wake could keep coming in to land. Our poor old ship, LCT 2428, made a gallant effort to keep afloat but by midnight we realised she was doomed. It was just a matter of how long she would stay up; unfortunately, not very long! I was busy 'flashing' as many ships as I could asking them to pick us up - but they were all heading for the beaches and could not stop. Their replies included, 'Sorry Chum, cannot stop' and 'Never mind Mate, better luck next time' and even, 'Get out and push it!' One ship was a bit more polite - he flashed back 'Regret unable to help, have a date with Hitler'.

She began turning over on us and it was a scramble to the ship's side. I was still on the Bridge then but it was only a matter of seconds before I had slipped off my oilskins and joined the rest of the crew in the water. I was just thinking that 15 miles to the shore was a long way to swim when a large Tug came by and picked us up. The most welcome sight I had seen for many a day and we could relax a bit as the Tug brought us back to England and landed us at Portsmouth on the morning of 7 June. We were given hot drinks, food and clothing, then asked all sorts of questions as we were the first survivors to come back.

'What was it like?' 'What had we seen?' 'Were our lads ashore and holding?' and a 1001 other questions. We were then issued with a mattress and blanket (on loan) and slept a peaceful night's sleep... the end of a hectic 24 hours indeed!

Evening Standard

37,357   BLACK-OUT 10 57 pm to 5.0 am   MOON Rises 9.50 pm; Sets 6.29 am.   ONE PENNY

Churchill Announces Successful Massed Air Landings Behind Enemy in France

4000 SHIPS, THOUSANDS OF SMALLER VESSELS

"So Far All Goes to Plan"— 11,000 First Line Airplanes

An immense armada of more than 4000 ships, with several thousand smaller craft, has crossed the Channel, said Mr. Churchill to-day, announcing the invasion.

"MASSED AIRBORNE LANDINGS HAVE BEEN SUCCESSFULLY EFFECTED BEHIND THE ENEMY'S LINES," HE SAID.

MR. CHURCHILL DESCRIBED THE LANDINGS AS THE "FIRST OF A SERIES IN FORCE ON THE EUROPEAN CONTINENT."

"The landings on the beaches are proceeding at various points at the present time. The fire of the shore batteries has been largely quelled, said Mr. Churchill.

"The obstacles which were constructed in the sea have not proved so difficult as was apprehended.

"The Anglo-American Allies are sustained by about 11,000 first line aircraft, which can be drawn upon as may be needed for the purposes of the battle.

No. 1

At 9.30 a.m. to-day the following communiqué was issued from General Eisenhower's Supreme Headquarters:

"**U**nder the command of General Eisenhower, Allied naval forces, supported by strong air forces, began landing Allied armies this morning on the Northern coast of France."

The statement was marked "Communiqué No. 1." At the same time it was revealed that General Montgomery is in command of the Army Group carrying out the assault. This Army Group includes British, Canadian and U.S. forces.

The King on the Radio To-night

It was officially announced from Buckingham Palace to-day that the King will broadcast at 9 o'clock to-night.

HITLER IN COMMAND

Hitler is taking personal command of all the anti-invasion operations, according to news reaching London from underground sources.

His four marshals are Rundstedt, titular commander-in-chief; Rommel, Inspector-General; Sperrle, in charge of air forces; and Blaskowitz, acting deputy to Rommel.

'LANDINGS ON JERSEY, GUERNSEY'

German Overseas News Agency said this afternoon that landings have been made on the Channel Islands —Jersey and Guernsey—by Allied parachute troops.

Quoting the German High Command spokesman, the agency said: "Early to-day Allied airborne formations landed on Guernsey and Jersey.

"They were at once engaged in extremely costly battles."

SURPRISE

"There are already hopes that actual tactical surprise has been attained," said the Premier, "and we hope to furnish the enemy with a succession of surprises during the course of the fighting.

"This vast operation is undoubtedly the most complicated and difficult that has ever occurred.

"The battle which is now beginning will grow constantly in scale and in intensity for many weeks to come, and I shall not attempt to speculate upon its course.

"Complete - unity prevails throughout the Allied Armies." (Cheers.)

"There is a brotherhood in arms between us and our friends in the United States.

"There is complete confidence in the Supreme Commander, General Eisenhower, and in his lieutenants, and also in the Commander of the Expeditionary Force, General Montgomery.

"The ardour and spirit of the troops as I saw them myself embarking in these last few days was splendid.

"Nothing that equipment, science and forethought can do has been neglected, and the whole process of opening this great new front will be pursued with the utmost resolution both by the commanders and by the U.S. and British Governments whom they serve.

WHAT A PLAN!

Replying to Mr. Greenwood, Mr. Churchill said that certainly in the early part of the battle he
(Continued on Back Page, Col. Four)

Thousands Of Fighters Strafe The Nazi Guns

Since the invasion began, Allied fighter-bombers have been dive-bombing, glide-bombing and strafing German defences and communications.

They fly literally into the mouths of guns and dive within feet of the spans which hold bridges together.

A gun is silenced, a truck carrying ammunition for a company of German soldiers is blown up, a bridge is shattered, making German supply convoys detour 20 or 30 miles, a gun crew is wiped out—multiplied by thousands, the fighter-bomber attacks will help the surface forces in 1000 ways, and will have an enormous effect on the battles below.

Bomber Command last night made their heaviest attack to date on the German batteries along the French coast. In all, Bomber Command despatched more than 1300 aircraft.

SHELLED BY 640 GUNS

The Supreme Headquarters of the Allied Expeditionary Force state that over 640 naval guns, from 16in. to 4in., are bombarding the beaches and enemy strong points in support of the armies.

About 200 Allied minesweepers, with 10,000 officers and men, are engaged in the operations.

The weight of minesweeping material used amounts to 2800 tons, and the amount of sweep wire in use would reach almost exactly from London to the Isle of Wight.

The Press Association learns that enemy destroyers and E-boats are reported coming into the operational area,

'Tanks Ashore on Normandy Coast'
—SAYS BERLIN

The Allies have established beach-heads in Northern France and are driving inland, according to pilots who have flown over the battle.

This afternoon the Germans announced that landings were continuing in the Seine Bay—the stretch of the Normandy coast between the two ports of Cherbourg and Le Havre.

They reported parachute landings on Guernsey and Jersey, the two principal Channel Islands, and said that Allied troops were ashore at these points on the coast of Normandy:

ST. VAAST LE HOUGE (on the Cherbourg Peninsula): "Mass landing" supported by considerable naval forces, while strong American airborne forces jumped near Barfleur, a few miles to the north.

OUISTREHAM (at the mouth of the River Orne): "Landing barges under strong air umbrella are making landings," said the Germans.

Earlier the Germans had mentioned that Caen, a few miles inland up the Orne, was "the first local point," where sharp fighting was taking place. The Germans also reported fighting 10 miles inland.

ARROMANCHES (in the middle of the Seine Bay): Tanks have been landed there, says Berlin.

ST. MARCOUF ISLANDS (just off the coast south of Cherbourg): "New landings made before noon particularly in this area."

VIRE ESTUARY

Another focal point mentioned by the Germans was the estuary of the Vire, another river running north into the Seine Bay. Parachute landings were reported in several areas besides Barfleur—
(Continued on Back Page, Col. Two)

Stories of The Men Who Watched

Here are the stories told by men who watched the landings.

Fighter pilots returning from over the landing areas report that Allied infantry scrambled ashore at 7 a.m. in two areas of the French coast, apparently without heavy opposition. says Robert Richards, British United Press war correspondent at a U.S. Fighter Base.

One of the pilots, an American Colonel, William Curry, told me:

"I saw the first troops wading ashore about 7 a.m., from light landing craft. From the height at which I was flying they did not appear to be meeting heavy opposition and were covered by extensive and heavy naval bombardment from our warships.

"Flying Fortresses were also bombing the beach which appeared to be marshy instead of sandy.

Major John Locke, of Texas, who led a squadron of Thunderbolts, said:

"I have never seen so many ships in all my life. Flying over the harbour at one port I counted great numbers of cruisers and other craft. The constant flashes from their guns indicated that the beach was getting a heavy pounding.

"Behind this advance brigade, stretching in a never-ending stream across the Channel, came line after line of L.C.T.s (landing craft, tanks) escorted by corvettes and P.T. boats.

"We were never attacked by enemy airplanes although the flak was terrific."

Second Lieut. Benson, from Iowa, said: "The Channel waters were fairly calm and the boats bounced along smoothly. They were constantly patrolled by warships and many were towing barrage balloons."

Colonel William Schwartz added: "When I arrived over the beach our battleships brought all their fire to bear on the shore."

MULBERRY:
THE ULTIMATE BLOCKSHIPS

Kenneth Bungard went to France aboard various parts of the Royal Navy's famous Mulberry Harbours.

My D-Day experience actually began on 24 April 1944, after returning to Chatham Barracks from service with the Fleet Air Arm in Trinidad. Whilst awaiting a ship I went home to see my girl. Being a few hours adrift from my overnight pass, I was consequently put on Captain's Report. Being in the rattle and a 'black list' man, when the tannoy called for volunteers for some mysterious operations called *Party Fun* and *Party Game*, I was first in the queue, with no idea what I was letting myself in for.

'Rig of the day' was overalls, sea boots and lifebelts and it was disconcerting to be issued with red lights and batteries for our lifebelts. When asked for my Station Card, I owned up that it was in the possession of the Master at Arms. They were anxious to get us off, so I was grudgingly told to be certain to report back to the Master at Arms office as soon as the job was over. Naturally, I never did go back and ask for punishment.

Blocks of flats
We were taken to Sheerness where we were confronted by what looked like windowless blocks of flats alongside a quay. We climbed the ladder and found ourselves on top of a huge concrete egg-box type thing with no top but a bit of concrete at one end on which to stand. We were towed at night past Dover to Dungeness Bay, where we opened the sluices and part submerged the strange object. The Germans used to shell 'Hell Fire Corner', of course, and we felt very vulnerable crawling along behind a tug. Our base at this time was the dear old paddle-steamer *Queen of Thanet*, where our kit was stowed and in theory we slept.

We settled into a routine of bringing these great caissons called Phoenixes round to Dungeness and Selsey Bill. They were about 60ft high, 60ft wide, 200ft long and weighed in at around 7000 tons. When we tried to pump them out to refloat them, our pumps were useless, so civilian contractors were brought in with bigger ones, and, to our great disgust, they were paid danger money just for setting foot on the things. Some stuck firmly to the bottom, despite all our efforts, some broke in half, but most were refloated to be towed across to Normandy.

Lord Haw Haw
Naturally we were not told the purpose of these monsters, which were sunk randomly in Dungeness Bay, where they must have been visible to any German reconnaissance aircraft. Lord Haw Haw remarked that the Germans would sink them for us. Secrecy was vital, of course, and though we could receive mail, we could not send any out, and there was absolutely no leave. Some of the caissons were left sunk around Dover as part of the deception plan. I have a film which shows caissons assembled in Dungeness Bay and I can see the *Queen of Thanet* tied up to one of the pier head parts. I see that I also have the *Queen of Kent* on my naval record for that time. I believe that she was later sunk in a Belgian port by a V2.

Owing to the hard conditions under which we were living, things began to get a bit fraught, with much discontent amongst some of the men who missed their beer and women; the Captain, in his wisdom, decided to give a few hours shore leave. Visions of some of the men disappearing 'up the Smoke' etc, were soon dispelled when we were landed at Ryde on the Isle of Wight, for a single evening's fun. Unfortunately, a long pent-up thirst, plus many Americans also on a run ashore, culminated in a complete mix-up of men who found themselves on all the wrong ships for the night, something which had to be sorted out next morning. A good time was reckoned to have been had by all, even though no one could remember a thing about it.

100 miles to Arromanches
For D-Day we started off across the Channel at about four knots, towed by a tug. The 100 mile trip to Arromanches was very long, very cold and, I suppose, very dangerous. We were issued with duffel coats, but it was still freezing cold up there. The self-heating tins of soup, and I think cocoa, were very welcome. There was nowhere to sit down and in any case we had to walk round all the

time to check on whether the thing had sprung a leak. There was an Able Seaman (my rank) in charge of each Phoenix, one Naval Signaller and two Ordinary Seamen. In the middle there was an AA gun, with two soldiers to man it. It could not be fired at sea. The soldiers were lucky as they could get into a bit of shelter under the gun, but we were exposed to the freezing cold all the way.

Our caisson sprang a leak and I signalled to the tug that I had to let one of the side weights go as we were listing badly. Of course, it then rolled over the other way with the weight of the water sloshing about inside it. So I asked the tug to go as fast as possible as we were sinking and our pump was useless. We got to Arromanches in the nick of time and sank it into position. It was quite a hairy situation. I had to get down onto the narrow ledge which ran round the caisson's base. In calm weather this would have been above four or five feet above the water, but owing to the list it was well awash and the massive side of the caisson looked to me like the Leaning Tower of Pisa overhead. Two of the Phoenixes were torpedoed by E-Boats from Cherbourg or Le Havre, some broke up, some were cut adrift, some went down in the gale that hit us a few days after D-Day. As the flat front of the caisson hit the waves, it echoed like a huge drum, with a constant deep booming sound.

On arrival at Arromanches I had to give a paper to a RN Officer, as evidence of safe delivery. He could not have cared less and I wish now that I had just put it in my pocket, as it would be an interesting souvenir today. As far as I recall, it had the codename Phoenix and the number of the caisson at the top. He didn't give me a receipt. We were put on to the first available vessel back to Selsey, to bring another caisson across.

Sodden clothes

It was a really grim time. We could not wash, shave or change our sodden clothes and had just two gallons of fresh water between us per trip. All our kit was on the *Queen of Thanet* so there was no hope of dry clothes. We had

a box of rations containing self-heating cans of soup and cocoa, boiled sweets, a few cigarettes, toilet paper, bacon wrapped in foil (though we had no means of cooking!). We were also issued with 'Wakey-Wakey' tablets.

We received no news whatsoever and had no idea even what day of the week it was. After one of these delivery trips we landed back at Portsmouth Barracks, thinking we would get a shower and a meal, but instead we were put on a train with a warrant for Dungeness via London. That did it. I realised that the train would go through Woking and was determined to alight if it stopped. We all agreed that we deserved a bath and a change of underwear and agreed to meet at Victoria very early next morning.

So, I got off at Woking, filthy, smelly, unshaven; the Redcaps made a beeline for me. A little porter boy saw me and I asked him if he could get me off the station quickly as I had no ticket. He asked if I was a survivor, and when I said yes, he quickly let me out of a side gate, where I fortunately got straight on a bus for Chertsey. An army officer also got on and regarded me with increasing suspicion. I was wearing overalls and had tucked my cap inside, but suddenly realised that my lifebelt was sticking out of my pocket. I hastily alighted at St Peter's Hospital (then Botleys Park War Hospital) and hurried up to Ferndale Avenue to my fiancée's home. Her mother ran me a bath while she cycled off to my home to collect some clean underwear from my mother. I was so exhausted I kept falling asleep in the bath. When they asked what on earth I had been doing, she said I muttered something about sailing a bloody great block of flats - before falling asleep with my face in a plate of dinner. I got the first train next morning, met the others safely at Victoria in spite of the numerous Redcaps, and, clean and fragrant again, we got safely back to Dungeness, where we resumed our shuttle service. We usually came back on a tug, trying to snatch some sleep on open decks in lousy weather. One bright spot was returning on an American ocean-going tug, where we were able to go

below and could help ourselves to some marvellous food, coffee and even ice-cream.

Gliders overhead

I remember seeing gliders going overhead and one coming down in the sea. Star shells were being fired at odd intervals, in the hope of illuminating any prowling E-Boats. Two caissons were sunk by German torpedoes; the crews did not stand a chance of being rescued, as the blocks would have gone down like stones. There were buoyed swept channels going across to the landing beaches, and the E-Boats would tie up to these buoys and lie in wait. These great lumbering slow monsters were sitting ducks.

Once there was no navy vessel to bring us back, so we were sent to a merchant ship rigged out with hammocks to sleep on, as if that was possible with all the shelling going on and general racket. Early next morning we sailed back on a Norwegian merchant ship which, to our great surprise, had some females in the crew.

The saddest memory is of seeing all the bodies floating about in the water off the Normandy coast. Men with boat hooks were fishing the dead out of the water and piling the bodies up on the deck of a big launch. I realised then how lucky those of us were who came through it all unharmed.

On looking back, it was quite something to have had a part in the greatest amphibious operation of all time, though I must admit that I did not appreciate the historical importance of it in 1944. My next posting was to a new destroyer, *HMS Zenith*, on escort duty with convoys to Russia.

Left: A section of Mulberry under tow. Note the anti-aircraft gun on the top of the caisson.
Below: The Arromanches Mulberry pictured from high altitude. There was a second artificial harbour at St Laurent that was crippled in a three day storm that struck Normandy on 19 June 1944. Parts of it were salvaged and moved to the more sheltered waters at Arromanches. The harbour then stayed operational until 19 November 1944 by which time over 250,000 men and 40,000 vehicles had been landed there as well as up to 11,000 tons of stores a day.

Around the Orne!

Captain Robert Worth of the Royal Engineers landed on Sword Beach on D+3. During the battle for Caen he believes he witnessed an incident of 'friendly fire' that had a profound effect on the course of the war.

We were transported across from the port of Newhaven by an American LSI. The senior crew kindly invited the Officers into the ward room for dinner and served us with the fattest pork chops I ever saw; being subject to sea-sickness this was a good start! I took pills to stop me being sick, but oh how I wanted to be. The one good result was that the next morning as we sailed into Sword Beach, I didn't care a hoot about the shelling on the shore, all I wanted was to get my feet on dry land.

We sailed in past the bows of battle-cruiser Renown. Her big guns were firing, an ear-splitting experience. The American LSI crew wanted rid of us as soon as possible so they could pull off away from the shelling and in consequence we were landed in quite deep water. I took my platoon in advance to take up our positions around the sea-locks at the entrance to the Ouistreham-Caen Canal. We had been told that the front line would be

some two miles up the coast at Cabourg, so I was somewhat surprised to be told by the Ox and Bucks Light Infantry that our position was the frontline and the Germans were some 400 yards away on the east bank of the mouth of the River Orne. The Ox and Bucks added nonchalantly that they were pulling out under orders and it was all ours! The Sixth Airborne were also on the east bank of the Orne, but at least half a mile inland.

My platoon - men of the 937 Port Construction and Repair Company, Royal Engineers, took up the advanced position on the east side of the lock with a minefield in front of us, but with a dirt track running through towards the Germans. I felt fairly safe as the Orne was between us; that was until a local Frenchman told me that you could drive a car across at low tide, so tanks could

certainly traverse it. I often wondered if Monty knew that only a mere Port Construction Company was holding the extreme left of the line. An armoured attack could have overwhelmed us and have enjoyed an open coast road to roll up the beaches all the way to Arromanches and the Mulberry Harbour.

Dazzling gold braid

This doubt was reinforced after a few days when a number of staff cars drove to the west of the locks and out got A V Alexander, the War Minister, and a dazzling array of gold braid, red tape and all and proceeded to walk across the damaged bridges over the locks and climb onto the top of the heavy coastal gun emplacements in full view of the Germans. I remonstrated with an ADC who said they knew what they were doing. So I got all my men off work and into their slit trenches, expecting a violent German reaction, but nothing happened; perhaps they were so amazed they thought it was a trap.

When the locks and their machinery had been got into working order, the next priority was to ensure that all the lift bridges over the canal were also in working order after being inoperative for some time. We managed all successfully except the famous Pegasus Bridge which was the main access and supply

Above: A German armoured vehicle passes a wrecked British glider in the Ranville area near the River Orne on 7 June 1944.

Left: A dramatic photograph of the results of Allied bombing of Caen. The city was largely destroyed after D-Day as the Allies attempted to overcome the stubborn German resistance that centred around this part of Normandy. The Caen Canal and River Orne are the two waterways running down to the coast. Pegasus Bridge at Benouville is in the centre top area of the photograph but the bridge is too distant to be made out. This is the area where Robert Worth and his Royal Engineers platoon operated from 9 June 1944. Although obscured by smoke, Ouistreham and Sword Beach are to the left of the photograph and Cabourg is off to the top right.

> 'I felt fairly safe as the Orne was between us and the Germans; that was until a local Frenchman told me that you could drive a car across at low tide, so tanks could certainly cross..'

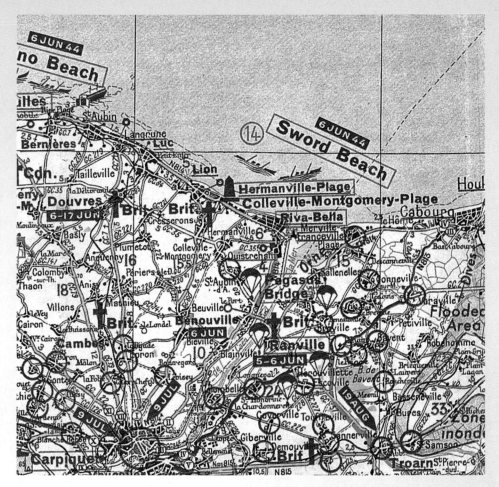

route to the Sixth Airborne Division and by then also to the 51st Highland Division. It also carried festoons of signal cables which precluded lifting the bridge without breaking them. Not being able to agree a possession of the bridge at local level we sent a request all the way up to Army Group level and down came permission for a one hour occupation.

A bridge too stuck

These bridges are hand-operated rolling bascule constructions and at the appointed time I was in the winding chamber in one of the abutments having posted sentries to stop any traffic. We wound the bridge up successfully, but when winding it down it stuck with the bridge at two feet above its closed position. Whilst I was in the winding chamber I heard the roar of an engine and the squeal of brakes and looking out saw a jeep had drawn up on the bridge carrying a very irate Airborne Officer who jumped out and – from his elevated height above the road – started to tongue-lash the little Welsh sentry below. When he finally paused for breath this little chap standing as stiff as a ram-rod, looked up at the Officer's red beret and said 'Well sir, you are Airborne aren't you?'.

When the break-out approached, we had moved up to the outskirts of Caen to build additional jetties in Caen docks. We were stationed just to the north west of Caen and all available heavy and medium guns had been drawn up in an arc to be ready for the advance over the open and higher country to the south east of the city. The guns had ample dumps of ammunition behind them. At mid-day, with a clear blue sky, we heard bombs start to come down and saw three Flying Fortresses start to plaster our own

ammo dumps – we heard later from the RAF that a Mosquito was up there too and tried to signal the Fortresses that they were bombing way off target, but with no effect. He shot one down, but by then the damage had been done. The dumps continued to explode for at least 24 hours. Therefore the break-out was delayed to allow for the dumps to be built up again.

The result was that the closure of the trap at Falaise was not total and a number of German divisions escaped though badly mauled. All this I can vouch for, but later I learned that one of the divisions which happened to be re-equipping in Arnhem at the time of the Market Garden attack in September was one of those which had escaped. It thus seems to me that

but for the Flying Fortresses and their 'friendly fire', Arnhem might have been a success and we would have been through to Berlin before Christmas, long before the Russians, with a resulting profound effect on post-war state of affairs in Europe. Perhaps for the want of a horse-shoe the battle was lost.

Above: A section of a 1947 Michelin Map showing the Normandy battlefield.

Below left and right: Two photographs taken just days before the invasion by a reconnaissance Spitfire of No 430 Squadron RAF. Both show the Dives estuary with Cabourg and Houlgate on either side. Robert Worth believed Cabourg would be the frontline on D+3 but it wasn't! Note the extensive beach obstacles – 'Rommel's asparagus' – in the photograph below. Pictures courtesy of the Macclesfield Historical Aviation Society.

Above: Barbed wire remains on the cliff top at Pointe du Hoc which US Rangers stormed on D-Day. Bunkers thought to contain heavy guns were found to be empty.

Above: Gold and Juno Beaches as they appear today can be seen in this Calvados view. British and Canadian troops came ashore on this coast on D-Day.

Above: Arromanches where the remains of the gigantic Mulberry Harbour can still be seen embedded in the sand. All pictures by John Lloyd

HISTORY LESSON

As a boy, Peter Champion had a unique view of the events leading up to the D-Day landings from his Brighton living room window. Then on 6 June 1944 his teacher allowed his class to witness history in the making from the school playing field.

To a schoolboy World War Two seemed like an everlasting comic strip series that unfolded daily into exciting episodes such as air raid sirens wailing with their undulating note and vapour trails high in the sky.

At my school, Varndean in Brighton, the sirens were welcomed by the children as it meant the immediate movement of everyone into well-built shelters dug into the ground in long tunnels behind the school; the advantage of such confinement meaning that lessons became such a haphazard affair as to be virtually non-existent. The all-clear siren was one long note, and then the whole school would troop back to the classrooms; this happened on a number of occasions on an erratic basis.

There were countless other incidents which, while terrifying to the adult population, were all part of the big 'adventure' for us schoolchildren. Nothing lasts forever… and childhood is one of those things.

My big 'adventure', together with my childhood, ended in the middle of April 1944 on a dark night over Karlsruhe, Germany, when my favourite uncle who had joined the RAF as a mid-upper gunner on Halifax bombers at the age of 40, was killed. He had volunteered at twice the normal age for aircrew because, he'd said, 'it seemed the right thing to do'.

From then on to me the war was no longer fun, but a terrible conflict that hurt people. As a reminder I still have a photograph of his gravestone in Karlsruhe Military Cemetery. Time and the war moved on and there was little time to dwell over lost loved ones; every family in Great Britain and the Commonwealth had, or was about to, lose someone.

Sherman tanks

As May 1944 moved heatedly into June, rumours of an imminent Second Front became rife, fuelled by the busy testing of Sherman tanks in huge water troughs in the parks. The tanks would rumble up a ramp and proceed through the water troughs with just the turrets showing above the water line. Large black funnels at the rear of the tanks puffed out the black exhaust fumes. This exercise tested their water-proofing; soon they would be rumbling through the shallows of the English Channel making for the landing beaches on the enemy-held shores of France. Once tested, the tanks would be loaded onto transporters and driven off.

The houses in nearly every street in Brighton seemed full of billeted troops of all nationalities, but from the 1 June they emptied, mysteriously, overnight. The atmosphere of excitement and apprehension was electric. Troops and tanks seemed to have disappeared and the whole Allied army appeared to have vanished.

A day or so later we were sitting in our classrooms talking about the approaching Second Front when we were interrupted by a huge explosion above and to the south of the school. We crowded around the windows in spite of the teacher's cry that we should lie flat on the floor. There was low scudding cloud in patches against a bright blue sky, and from one low patch of cloud fell a black object. It was an aircraft fuselage with two large radial engines plummeting earthwards, while the after fuselage and tailplane fell simultaneously from another smaller cloud. The two crew members, small black dots, fell behind some distant houses. A few seconds later a single slowly rotating Spitfire wing fluttered gently into a nearby park.

White parachute

'Look, look, up there,' shouted one of my classmates and about half a mile to the right of the debris that had just fallen to earth, at about 2000ft was a solitary white parachute.

It transpired that a twin-engined Beaufighter had collided with a Spitfire in the low cloud resulting in the death of the two Beaufighter crew; the Spitfire pilot had parachuted to safety.

The build-up to D-Day became feverish. My family lived in a top floor flat and the view from the lounge window commandeered a panoramic view of the English Channel. Nobody knew what part of the French coast was to be invaded by the liberating Allied armies; however, Allied bomber and fighter activity over Sussex had increased over the last few weeks and, by 5 June it felt as though you were waiting for a huge orchestra to begin the 1812 Overture .

It was mid-afternoon when my father called me to our window and pointed out to sea. On the horizon were four or five large white oblongs towed by tugs, themselves almost invisible owing to the distance. The oblongs were spaced at about a mile distance from one another and I would guess some 400 yards long and 40 feet high. I suggested to my father that they may be targets. 'No,' he said, 'too big and solid looking.' They moved slowly on eastwards up the Channel and eventuality went out of sight.

Coded messages

Weeks later we learned that they were sections of the prefabricated Mulberry Harbours which were towed to the D-Day beaches, joined and sunk into the sands for the landing of tanks and heavy equipment.

No popular television in those days; we followed the war on the radio and occasionally we could pick up the coded messages from the BBC to the Resistance forces in France. They sounded like nonsense to us, but contained vital information for the French Resistance. With D-Day at any moment now this radio traffic was mounting and in the late evening of 5 June, we heard quite a few.

It was 11pm; I yawned and went to bed. The weather did not look good for Tuesday 6 June. I was woken at 5am by the whoosh, whoosh, whoosh noise of aircraft engines and dashed out of bed and up to the lounge window. Gaggles of fighters were flying low over Brighton before dropping even lower over the sea as they headed southwards. This traffic continued for some minutes, followed by a lull of about five minutes and then the pattern would repeat itself.

At about 5.30am I heard the beginning of a continuous rumble of gunfire from way past the horizon. I don't remember breakfast that day but do recall the family sitting by the radio. We learnt that the invasion of Europe was under way.

My classroom window looked out on to the playing fields, behind which and to the south was Brighton and beyond that the Channel. Aircraft noise that day was constant as was the distant rumble of heavy naval guns.

At around 10am we filed into a classroom for a history lesson covering William the Conqueror and 1066. The lesson fell on deaf ears as all of us were craning our necks for views from the windows. Our exasperated History Master slammed his history book shut, cutting William the Conqueror off in mid-battle. 'I want you all to file out quietly onto the playing fields and sit in neat rows and observe what is going on; there is no point sitting in here having a history lesson when history is being made out there,' he said, pointing out of the window. We eagerly obeyed.

Watch and remember

The Master stood in front of us in his mortar board and gown and addressed us, some 30 pupils. He paused before speaking, looking up, as another wave of low flying Typhoons swept over us at no more than 100 feet altitude. After the aircraft had passed, he said: 'We can sit here for an hour. During that time I want you to watch and remember, because what you see today you will never, never see again, for as long as you live.' His voice was drowned out by more low flying aircraft.

We settled down and looked as the whole panorama spread before us. The weather was mixed; some low blobs of coastal cloud, some layered at about 10,000 feet and a few wisps of high cirrus. We thrilled to the fighters set out more or less in lines of possibly a dozen dipping low over the school. Higher up were the medium bombers in tight formations of probably nine aircraft. There were dozens of groups of these aircraft for as far as the eye could see. Between the bombers, Mitchells, Marauders and Bostons, were hundred of gliders, mostly Horsas, being towed by Dakotas and Halifaxes.

Then high up, possibly 20,000 feet plus were the heavies, the B-17 Fortresses, B-24 Liberators, Lancasters and Halifaxes exuding their white contrails. I had often seen these forming up for bombing raids and circling Brighton waiting for their fighter escort before proceeding to Germany. But there was no circling today - they were in straight lines all with their targets marked on their maps, having been finally briefed in the middle of the night before take-off.

As we watched, a 12-year-old rushed out of school and yelled: 'I just heard it on the radio - Smith of General and Practical 5 has a portable!' 'What have you heard,' we all shouted. 'We've landed in Normandy!'

'Where the hell is Normandy?' I asked the boy next to me. 'Stupid!' he replied, 'France - don't you have a war map?' I did, of course, but we had all been expecting the landings to be in the Pas de Calais area. Luckily so had the Germans.

Window on the War

I witnessed many exciting incidents from the vantage point of our high-up flat. Once I saw a Hawker Tempest chasing a V1 flying bomb and tipping its wing with its own wing. The Doodlebug went into a flat turn over Brighton and continued to throb a wide two mile circuit around the town, its pulse-jet engine giving an unmistakable signature. I ran from one room to another to watch its progress. Suddenly the pulse jet stopped and the sinister black blob fell noiselessly behind some houses in the distance... a pause... a loud explosion... but fortunately it had fallen in open country and I believe there were no casualties.

One Sunday lunchtime, I heard the staccato of machine-gun fire and looked up to see five shiny dots in a 'V' formation with another larger silver dot coming up behind. The noise was that of the slower firing German cannon guns. One silver dot from the 'V' formation hurtled vertically to earth and, as it dropped lower, the shape of a Spitfire wing was apparent. The other dots - possibly at 20,000 feet or more broke left and right and turned into the tail of the brave German Dornier 17 bomber pilot who had attacked the Spitfires. They lined up behind him and as the action got down to around 2000 feet set his port engine on fire. He tried to pancake into the Channel, but broke up as he hit the water. There were no survivors. We finished our lunch.

On another occasion my mother called out that there were two Hurricanes coming in very low over Brighton heading straight towards us. They swept over at no more than 500 feet. In fact they were two German Messerschmitt Me 109s, pilots' heads and black crosses clearly visible; they turned and disappeared out over the Channel. My kingdom for a Spitfire!

Peter Champion painted this scene of Battle of Britain Spitfires over Brighton. The famous two piers can be seen below and the detail includes the fact that in wartime gaps were created to prevent German troops using them as landing jetties. Peter was war artist for the Daily Mail during the 1982 Falklands conflict.

D-DAY TO
Tin Pan Alley

After Royal Navy service, opportunity came knocking for singing sensation David Whitfield.

The lumpy, windswept English Channel at dawn on 6 June 1944 hampered the vulnerable landing craft, but offshore lay the massive force waiting to provide naval artillery cover. Part of this group was the veteran 29,000 ton battleship *HMS Ramillies*.

Although 28 years old, her 8 x 15 inch guns were still capable of hurling massive shells far inland. She was the first ship to open fire off Sword Beach, and her particular targets included the fortified gun emplacements at Mont Canasy and the German garrison at Vierville - the shell craters are still visible today in the hills behind the beaches. At his duty station serving one of *Ramillies'* gun turrets, was a young seaman who had served a mere seven months in the Royal Navy - JX63035 Whitfield D.

After his demob in 1950, David Whitfield went on to achieve fame and fortune as one of the biggest singing stars this country has ever

David Whitfield aboard HMS Belfast *in the Far East. The ship - herself a veteran of D-Day - is now berthed in the Pool of London and is a popular tourist attraction.*

produced. He was the first British male singer ever to be awarded a Gold Disc. This was for *Cara Mia*, which stayed at the top of the charts for 10 consecutive weeks – a remarkable achievement in its day.

Singapore posting
David Whitfield was born in Hull in the Drypool area on 2 February 1926 and began his love affair with singing as a choirboy at St Peter's Church. During his early years in the Royal Navy, wartime commitments allowed little leisure time to pursue his hobby and it was not until he received a coveted posting to Singapore in 1947 that more opportunities arose. Travelling out to join *HMS Belfast*, David was a passenger on the troopship *Empress of Scotland*. The long voyage provided many chances to entertain the other passengers at concert parties and the talent of the young seaman was noticed.

His time on *Belfast* was short, as the cruiser was returning home. David was posted to the frigate *HMS Black Swan*, one of the first ships to venture up the Yangtze River, scene of the dramatic escape of *HMS Amethyst* in 1949. Visits to Shanghai, Amoy and Hong Kong provided increasing opportunities for David to spend his shore leave singing in hotels, clubs and bars, and to supplement his basic naval pay. A regular 15 minute slot on Radio Hong Kong (ZBW) paid £8 – almost two weeks pay for an able seaman at that time.

Ed Sullivan Show
David returned to the UK and was de-mobbed in 1950. He was establishing a reputation as a promising tenor, but initially found it difficult to repeat the success he'd enjoyed in the Far East. His big showbiz break came when he was admitted as a last-minute replacement to one of Hughie Green's *Opportunity Knocks* heats. Performing *Goodbye from White Horse Inn*, he won the grand final and the 'singing sailor' was finally on his way. Hughie invited him to tour with the Radio

Luxembourg *Opportunity Knocks* show for eight months.

David went on to become one of the biggest and brightest international stars this country has produced. He was the first British recording star to break into the American Top 10 and the first to achieve a US million seller. He appeared no less than eight times on the Ed Sullivan Show, and hosted his own TV shows in this country. He appeared in three Royal Command Performances, featured in the stage version of *The Desert Song*, and his recording of *I'll Find You* was the backing track for the Richard Burton and Joan Collins film *Sea Wife*. Other massive hits included *Marta, I Believe, Answer Me* and *Bridge of Sighs*.

David continued to sing for his myriad fans worldwide for many years after the halcyon days of his singing career. Indeed, he was on a tour of Australia when he died suddenly in January 1980 of a cerebral haemorrhage. His ashes were brought home to England, and were carried out into the North Sea on the frigate *HMS Sirius* – thus maintaining his link with the Royal Navy to the final chapter.

Martin Barton Smith

*The memory of David's remarkable career in entertainment lives on via The David Whitfield International Appreciation Society whose Patron is Dame Vera Lynn DBE. More information and details of how to obtain recordings of David's hits may be obtained from the secretary, Bill Wilkins on 01482 831570. Bill is curator of The David Whitfield Museum & Archives in Kingston upon Hull. Admission is free but by appointment only. Information is also available at:
www.davidwhitfield.com

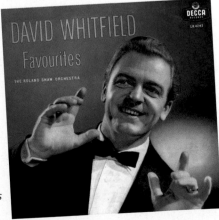

An album of David Whitfield's favourites performed with backing from the Roland Shaw Orchestra.

War Correspondence

As individual instalments of Sixty Years On *were published we received numerous letters and contributions from readers. To help with the chronological flow of this omnibus book, we have, so far as possible, put the letters as close to the time they allude to.*

Newbury memories

Born in 1933 I was too young to realise the perilous position of the nation at the time of the Dunkirk evacuation in 1940. By 1942 we were living in Newbury and one day my father called me excitedly to the window shouting 'Yanks' as a small squad of American soldiers marched by. He was obviously so relieved to see them as without their involvement he knew we had no chance of winning the war.

From that time the American presence in Newbury gradually built up. Heavy earth moving equipment set to work on Greenham Common to build the airfield which became the base of the American 101st and 17th Airborne divisions (I did not know the units at the time). The single line railway, through Newbury, from Oxford to Southampton was doubled (it is now part of the Newbury by-pass).

My mother worked at the American Red Cross Club in the centre of Newbury and during the school holidays I would work clearing the dining tables. I was struck by two things about the GIs, firstly the wasted food left on the plates and secondly the great generosity of the tips left under the plates!

The soldiers used to arrive at the club in their jeeps, which they parked in boxes improvised from the wooden crates in which the gliders arrived. This was to protect them from the inclement English weather. In 1944 I was a keen train spotter and whilst on Newbury station troop trains would come through and stop. I remember the soldiers leaning out of the carriage windows asking where they were. I would show them on my pocket map. The build-up continued and on D-Day the sky was literally filled with Dakota aircraft towing their Hengist and Horsa gliders; where they were going we did not know. The American presence in Newbury evaporated almost overnight.

Newbury racecourse was used as a large military dump with railway lines and shunting engines. A prisoner of war camp was also constructed there. I remember two older boys cycling up to the barbed wire, making the 'Heil Hitler' salute and shouting mockingly at the prisoners, 'Hitler's army!' I thought they were being very patriotic. The Germans ignored us. To my surprise at the time, but obviously not now, we were told to clear off by an American guard in his watch tower.

Following D-Day my father put up a wall map of western Europe on which we plotted daily, with little flags mounted on pins, the Allied advance. In the late summer of 1944 an old colleague, W T (Tully) Ogilvy, visited my father. The pair had been schoolmasters at Dover College before the war but at the time Tully was a padre in the Parachute Regiment. He told my father that he thought the war would soon be over but sadly, a short time later we heard that he had been killed at Arnhem.

Dr David Starr, London SE2

Eisenhower's ship

On 6 June 1944 I was 18 years of age, serving aboard the destroyer *HMS Undaunted,* lying off the coast of France. The ship had been acting as a forward artillery position. Coming off watch at 8am that morning, I was amazed at the sight of ships of every size and description, all seemingly 'throwing everything' at the coastline.

On a later occasion we were ordered to take on board Admiral Ramsey, who commanded the naval force, and General Eisenhower, and get them back to England with all speed. It was whilst on board that General Eisenhower presented the ship with a personal flag. Overall blue with five silver stars, one of which he signed with an indelible pencil.

This standard travelled with the ship wherever it sailed. This included sailing into the Pacific with the British Pacific Fleet, which had formed up in Trincomalee, Ceylon (as it was known then). At every port of call *HMS Undaunted* was referred to as 'General Eisenhower's ship'.

John Hunter, Dorset

Newport and D-Day

In early 1944 I was 17 years old and awaiting call-up to the Royal Navy under a special scheme for volunteers who were below the official conscription age. At the time I was a petty officer in the Newport Sea Cadet Corps and as such I enjoyed the privilege of being permitted to enter the closely guarded and highly secure perimeter barriers of The Alexandra Dock at Newport, South Wales. This was in order to gain access to our Brixham trawler which we sailed out at weekends into the Bristol Channel for naval training and, as a sideline, to deliver Sunday newspapers to the English and Welsh Grounds lightship.

By April we were still allowed into the docks but not to sail, only to carry out maintenance and shore training. We had our suspicions as to why this was and very soon we had confirmation. Through those early months of 1944 there had been a marked increase in the already feverish dockyard activity. Huge motorised convoys arrived and locomotives pulling long lines of trucks, all carrying mysterious tarpaulin-covered loads that were rapidly spirited away to large warehouses or to large open areas covered in camouflage netting. It was not difficult to recognise the muffled-up shapes of much of the trappings of war! Indeed, we learned after the war that, at the time of which I speak, there were 36,000 tons of ammunition and explosives secreted all around us!

Sunday, 4 June saw the docks filled to bursting. Jocularly it was said that one could cross the water by using the decks of the closely-moored ships and I can verify the near truth of this. There were freighters of all sizes, oil tankers, 'Liberty Ship' troop carriers, Royal Navy assault craft and escort vessels including a couple of 'Woolworth' aircraft carriers (conversions from merchant ships).

From then on, as each enormous channel tide gave the required depth of water, the colossal tonnage streamed through the lock gates to rendezvous in mid channel with similar fleets from the rest of the Bristol Channel ports. When they were all on station the signal to sail was given and, 30 hours later, they were off the Normandy coast, part of the largest invasion fleet the world had ever seen. My next visit to Newport Docks was on

the following Sunday, 11 June, and my incredulous eyes were greeted by a great expanse of empty water!

I was too young to have been involved in the bloodier side of World War II but I like to pride myself on the fact that I was present to see the truly miraculous preparations for D-Day only two days before the actual landings. I did, however, get to stand on the site where the war was finally ended – 14 months after D-Day, in the levelled ruins of Nagasaki.

Haydn Davis, Monmouthshire

Unexpected happenings

In 1944 I found myself staying in a young boys' recuperation home on the hills of High Salvington behind and above Worthing in West Sussex following three months of unexpected happenings.

It had started in February with my army medical - A1. Then at the end of March I had a week of professional exams held in Queen's Square, London WC1, which had been interrupted by incendiary bombs burning out the roof on the Wednesday. Friday's last exam was accompanied by acute stomach-ache. A day later I was back in the square again only this time in hospital for an emergency operation for a perforated appendix. The air raids continued but fortunately not near the hospital.

One week later I celebrated my 18th birthday and the week after that I received my call up papers. These were met with the relief that I had not been selected by lottery to be a Bevin Boy and would disappear down the mines, but with distress about the impossibility of getting to Chester in a few days time whilst I was hospitalised with the operation not healed. A doctor's certificate delayed the call up but the failure of the wound to heal left me somewhat feeble. Thus arrangements were made for me to go to the home at High Salvington for a month.

One night we were roused by the house rattling and a series of tremors that continued for some time. Later I learnt that the vibrations were caused by RAF bombers dropping some of the very heaviest of their bombs on the tunnels and caves in Northern France where Hitler's secret V-weapons were being made ready to bombard England. The shock waves from the explosions had travelled in the chalk under the Channel to reach us.

The next night we heard much rumbling but no tremors and were mystified until at 9am the radio announced that the invasion of Europe had begun. The rumbling noise had been the sound of the first 'softening up' salvoes fired by the Navy off the Normandy beaches.

Soon after breakfast a steady drone smote our ears. From the balcony I viewed the largest air armada ever. Aircraft stretched from horizon to horizon in every direction, carefully spaced, side by side and fore and aft with most of them towing a glider. It seemed ages before the last appeared over the horizon by which time I am sure the first of the gliders would already have landed.

So my two vivid memories of 6 June are of the rumble of gunfire heard from across the Channel one way and the planes in the sky with their precise spacing and constant coming, going the other way.

A week later I was allowed home. I remember how when I had left London, barrage balloons were scattered in a haphazard fashion all over the capital to thwart conventional bomber attacks. The threat of the V1 devices brought a change in tactics. Incoming doodlebugs now met a protective curtain of balloons that stretched across the North East Kent approaches to the city. Having seen a sky so full of planes just days before it was odd to see the London sky now empty of balloons.

A R Miller, Dorset

View from the Tor

On the evening of 5 June 1944 my future wife and I were on the summit of Glastonbury Tor - all alone. We heard the approach of aircraft engines, which increased to a deafening roar. We searched the skies above without success and then looked down and saw a vast number of towing craft and gliders. We could actually see the pilots in the cockpits. They were flying west

towards the Atlantic and we could only gaze in awe and wonder where they were bound. The next day we learnt they had turned south and then east and made their airborne assaults - D-Day had arrived.

J T Gibbs, Essex

The *Medusa* story

Two Harbour Defence Motor Launches left Portland Harbour about 24 hours before Eisenhower said 'Go' for *Operation Overlord* and took station on approach channel 4 to Omaha and Utah beaches. The MLs were numbered 1387 and 1383 with the former being the navigational leader. Both remained on station for the first 30 hours of the Normandy invasion, guiding the armada bound for the two American beaches and coming under US command.

In the weeks that led up to D-Day both MLs were involved in the practice assaults on Slapton Sands in Devon - codename: Fabius 1. Lt Maurice Liddiard RNVR was the skipper of ML1383 and early in 1945 she went across the to The Hague and went on to receive the surrender of the German forces at Ijmuiden. From there she navigated the North Sea Canal to Amsterdam, the first Allied ship to do so.

ML1383 was broken up long ago but ML1387 is still around and named *Medusa*. She can still steam out into the Solent at 11 knots and has the distinction of being admitted to the National Register of Historic Vessel's Core Collection. At present *Medusa* is berthed in Southampton Docks.

B G Small, Hants

Yes, I remember D-Day from 6000 miles away

In June 1944 as a member of the Royal Air Force, I was housed in a hospital in Batavia, Java. All my companions and I had been taken prisoner by the Japanese in 1942 and had been transported to the island of Haruku to build an airfield. A large proportion died under most distressing circumstances, 700 on the *Suez Maru*, torpedoed by the Allies. My group missed this boat and arrived safely in Java.

I was fortunate to find myself in St Vincentious Hospital, the only civilised place I encountered as a POW. It was run by Lt Col Maisey and the Japanese only entered for roll call check. In June 1944, I was, with others, occupying upstairs accommodation, in a large room. On one side was a ventilation grille about a foot from the floor. I was curious to learn why a couple of Hollanders would come each evening and lay full length very near this grille. We soon realised that they were listening to a Javanese news broadcast

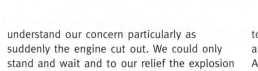

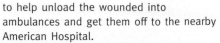

coming from a radio at ground level in the Japanese quarters.

On 6 or 7 June they passed the word around that a cross Channel invasion had been mounted on the European mainland. Though we had previously been victims of many unfounded rumours, we thought this info was reliable, considering its source. Not knowing the full details, we were not impressed.

Very shortly afterwards, some of us were moved back to a working camp and I do not recall hearing more regarding what was happening in Europe while we remained in Java. Later, a guard in Sumatra told us of the collapse of Germany in May 1945.

Though they did not know it at the time, for the participants of D-Day, the end was in sight, but involving most horrendous casualties. For us it was nowhere near the end, hundreds of us being shipped to Sumatra in July 1944, this time to build a railway. Many of the chaps I knew from St Vincentious did not arrive, being torpedoed en route to Sumatra, again by the Allies.

In Sumatra we had to manually slave away for well over another year, with many succumbing to malaria and malnutrition. Recently a book has been published recording all the RAF people who were taken prisoner in the Far East. *Unsung Heroes Of The Royal Air Force* (by Les - former POW - and Pam Stubbs, published by Barny Books) makes really sad reading. I found out that people I knew so well, had died a few months before the end of the Japanese war in August 1945, having survived captivity not for months but for three and half years.
J G Fitzgerald, Herts

The clouded sky!
On D-Day I was just 13 and living with my parents in Southend. The whole town had become a holding area for the troops awaiting the onset of the invasion. Our street was filled with military vehicles and their crews, so each evening they were invited in for tea and any biscuits and cake we could find. My father had served in the previous 'War to end Wars' and was not too well having suffered the effects of mustard gas whilst with the Royal Horse Artillery.

The visiting young men were obviously apprehensive but it was not until my father showed them his discharge papers, at their request, that I realised the strength of their concerns. They held these papers with a longing that was very touching indeed.

Later we suffered a fair number of V1 attacks and one day we were in the local cemetery collecting whatever vegetation we could to feed to my friend's pet rabbit.

The distinctive drone of an approaching V1 was heard and because of the fragmented cloud we only saw very brief glimpses of this ugly machine. However on this occasion it passed over and the sound gradually faded. We kept collecting and to our horror yet another V1 could be heard; with the cloud having thickened and lowered, it was impossible to see this machine. Anyone who has heard the distinctive engine noise will

understand our concern particularly as suddenly the engine cut out. We could only stand and wait and to our relief the explosion was at least two miles away.

My studying the clouds throughout this event had made me realise what wonderful shapes, movement and even colours one could see and admire simply by looking at the sky. I had a scientific bent and decided that I would find out more about clouds and this eventually led me to join the Met Office. I have always regarded my time in the Met Office as a very satisfying one and eventually retired in 1990.

The end to this tale is that in 1950 whilst volunteering with St Johns Ambulance I often attended Southend General Hospital Casualty Department taking in patients from accidents. I met my wife Jean there and she too had had a brush with Hitler's V2 weapons but a much more traumatic one than mine.

On her way home from school, she was waiting for a bus at Walthamstow Waterworks when a V1 exploded across the street. She was severely injured and still carries a scattering of shrapnel. In later years this would give the airport metal detectors a bit of a blip. The date of this event was 1 March 1945 so this rocket must have been one of the very last launched.
Fred Landon, Cumbria

RAF recollections
I was on a RAF Wireless Mechanics course at Holloway Road Polytechnic in London in 1944 and, walking to the college on 6 June I witnessed the traffic almost stopped due to the thunderous noise of aircraft flying towards France. Mostly bombers supported by fighters; this was the first indication that the invasion was on.

Another day while on the phone to my Dad in a kiosk outside the Albert Hall, there was the usual sound of a V1 approaching; the engine died overhead and everyone dropped to the ground. It made a direct hit on the nearby Wellington Barracks, killing hundreds of soldiers. While on the Radar Mechanics course and billeted in Exhibition Road, with lectures at the Royal College of Arts, the bombing caused so much havoc that we were all moved out to RAF Cosford near Wolverhampton.

I was later posted to a Dakota squadron in Oxfordshire, where part of their deployment was to attach glider aircraft that would transport soldiers straight to the front. I remember them blackening their faces just before entering the aircraft. Days later the tannoy requested all airmen to the tarmac

to help unload the wounded into ambulances and get them off to the nearby American Hospital.

The squadron became a mobile one and moved on to Egypt, Palestine and Italy just as VJ Day was declared – but that's another story.
Don Smart, North Somerset

Mauritius posting
Thanks to *Sixty Years On*, I am still finding out more about what happened in those never-to-be forgotten times. On D-Day 6 June 1944, it was my lot to report for service at RAF Station Khartoum after a four-day journey up the Nile (two of them on a river boat). By October, I was posted onward to East Africa and from November until VJ Day I was serving in – of all places – the lovely island of Mauritius. With all this travelling and given the distant places that I served in, it's perhaps not surprising that we knew hardly anything about what was really happening in the active war theatres.

Ironically, I was writing home to my parents as 'on active service' at a time when they were back in the air raid shelters in London ducking V1s and V2s! Censorship prevented us from knowing what was going on.
Ron Purser, Middlesex

Slim in Burma
May I add some background to the mention of General William Slim in 'Forgotten Front' (page 71 of the book). He was born in Australia in 1891. After serving in the First World War, he continued afterwards with a commission with the Gurkhas in the Indian Army. In World War II he served as a Brigadier in the East African campaign. Subsequent to this he was appointed GOC of the Fourteenth Army in Burma. After the war, uniquely for an Indian Army Officer, he became Chief of the Imperial General Staff. He ended his career as Governor General of Australia. Slim died in 1970.

I was also interested to see that the singer David Whitfield (page 103) sailed to Singapore in 1947 on board the *Empress of Scotland* (formerly the *Empress of Japan*). I sailed in this same ship in June 1941 en route to India. She carried some 3000 troops including the first batch of cadets destined for training in the Indian Army Service Corps. We went from Glasgow in a very large convoy and took two months to reach Bombay via Cape Town where we spent three days. It was a most uncomfortable journey as we slept in hammocks, packed in like sardines. However, I was pleased to learn that the vessel survived the war.
H A Carn, Bristol

ROME - OPEN CITY

In the very first days of June 1944 nobody on the Allied side knew for certain the German intentions regarding the Italian capital, Rome. Would they defend the city or destroy it in a fit of rage at being forced to retreat? The people of Rome had most to worry about. Already on the verge of starvation, what further horrors now awaited them?

In the notorious city gaol, Regina Coeli, captured British agents could hear the guns of the approaching Allies, But the Germans were still in control. As late as the afternoon of 3 June, 14 men were taken outside the city by lorry and shot. Their number included Captain John Armstrong.

For several days previously, the Allies had been fighting their way towards Rome from the Anzio beach-head in the face of desperate German resistance. With Route Six still open, the Germans facing the Eighth and Fifth Armies and the Anzio forces had taken heart and renewed the fight with grim determination. Field Marshal Kesselring regained his masterly poise in adversity. Though his men had been badly hurt they conducted an orderly retreat in early June - it was certainly no rout.

Unbeknown to the Allies, Hitler then confirmed his decision to spare Rome from destruction, declaring it a 'place of culture' and not fitting for combat operations. The Italian dictator Mussolini was not so charitable. He demanded the defence of the city street by street, railing, 'Why should the citizens of Rome have a better life than those of Cassino?'

The **Italian** **Campaign**

The Eighth Army's advance was more or less along the central mountainous spine of Italy leaving the approach to Rome to the American Fifth Army. There was mounting excitement in the latter as units neared the Eternal City. Traffic jams became almost as irritating as the enemy rearguards. On the Appian Way, a German paratrooper corporal and a handful of men with a heavy machine-gun, cut down an advance party of Americans who were unwise enough to stroll down the centre of the road.

Later captured and transported to Anzio, the same corporal realised that Germany had lost the war: 'I saw vehicles, tanks, jeeps, guns and lorries in long columns for as long as the road stretched and as far as the eye could see. Never had I seen such an array. There were even water-trucks sprinkling the ground to damp down the dust. And this was just a supply route. I was used to our lorries sprinting along under shellfire, in ones or twos or threes.'

On the night of 4 June the Americans entered Rome in force. The tanks of Maj-Gen Ernie Harmon's First Armoured Division were in the vanguard. A senior officer recalls, 'There were no Italian policemen, no directional signs, no street lights and no lights in any of the buildings ... as we moved along the dark streets we could hear people clapping their hands behind the windows of their homes but we could not see them. Later, when it became evident that the Germans had abandoned the city, men, women and children, in night dress and slippers came down into the still-dark streets to welcome the Americans.

'Some ran up and down the columns offering wine to the soldiers. After daylight the population appeared on the streets dressed for a holiday. Women and children threw flowers at passing troops.'

Vera Cacciatore was the Director of Rome's Keats-Shelley museum. She later remarked, 'How extraordinary it was to see two Armies crossing a city. Very young, worn-out and hungry German soldiers ran through Rome on foot and the people drew aside so not to trouble them in their progress.'

'This is a great day for the Fifth Army.'

Just hours later she was caught by surprise when American troops came to keep watch over the museum and guard against looters: 'One of them asked to visit the rooms where Keats lived and died in 1821 and where 10,000 volumes by poets such as Shelley, Hunt and Lord Byron are kept.'

By the time the people of Roman flocked onto the streets in large numbers in daylight to wildly celebrate their deliverance on the morning of 5 June, most of the front line soldiers had already passed through on the heels of the retreating Germans. Rear echelon troops got the glory. Just a small number of British units came through the city in the first day of liberation.

US General Mark Clark arrived on that first morning, soon making his way to the Piazzo del Campidoglio. To the press of the free world he announced, 'This is a great day for the Fifth Army.'

It was a statement which upset many, including the war correspondent Eric Sevareid. In his memoirs he wrote: 'That was the immortal remark of Rome's modern-day conqueror. It was not, apparently, a great day for the world, for the Allies, for all the suffering people who had desperately looked towards the time of peace. It was instead a great day for the Fifth Army.'

Sevareid continued, 'The men of the Eighth Army, whose sector did not happen to include Rome but without whose efforts this day could not have occurred, did not soon forget the remark.'

Commander of the mainly American Fifth Army, General Mark Clark, pictured (back centre) in a jeep in Rome on 5 June 1944. His overriding ambition to be the first into the Eternal City caused resentment amongst the other Allies.

D-DAY

Ernest 'Geoff' Huxley was a typical 'D-Day Dodger' who served with the Eighth Army first in North Africa and then Italy and who was away from home for years.

Simply getting to North Africa was an ordeal - his troopship *Strathallan* was torpedoed and sunk on the way and he, along with most of the men on board, was fortunate to survive. In Italy, Geoff went from Sicily to the Po Valley and in the course of the campaign the exploits of the 'D-Day Dodgers' were immortalised in the lyrics of a song. This was sung to the tune of *Lili Marlene*, a favourite with the German Afrika Korps that was 'borrowed' by the British. The song expresses the disappointment of the men of the Eighth and Fifth Armies at what they saw as a lack of public recognition of their contribution to the war effort compared to the huge publicity given to D-Day and the subsequent battles in Northern Europe.

WE ARE THE D-DAY DODGERS OUT IN ITALY
ALWAYS DRINKING VINO, ALWAYS ON THE SPREE
EIGHTH ARMY SHIRKERS AND THE REST
WE LIVE IN ROME AND EAT THE BEST

WE LANDED AT SALERNO, A HOLIDAY WITH PAY
JERRY SENT THE BAND OUT TO CHEER US ON OUR WAY
HE SHOWED US THE SIGHTS AND GAVE US TEA
WE ALL SANG SONGS AND THE BEER WAS FREE
FOR THE D-DAY DODGERS, OUT IN ITALY

NAPLES AND CASSINO WERE TAKEN IN OUR STRIDE
WE DIDN'T GO TO FIGHT THERE WE JUST WENT FOR A RIDE
ANZIO AND SANGRO WERE JUST A PLEASANT GAME
AND SENIO WAS REALLY JUST AS TAME
FOR WE ARE THE D-DAY DODGERS, OUT IN ITALY

DEAR LADY ASTOR, PLEASE TAKE A NOTE
DON'T STAND ON THE PLATFORM BLEATING LIKE A GOAT
YOU'RE SUCH A SWEETHEART - THE NATION'S PRIDE
BUT YOUR MOUTH IS OPEN FAR TOO WIDE
THAT'S FROM THE D-DAY DODGERS, OUT IN ITALY

IF YOU ARE IN THE MOUNTAINS IN THE MUD AND RAIN
YOU'LL SEE LOTS OF CROSSES
SOME THAT BEAR NO NAME
HEARTBREAK, TOIL AND SUFFERING
THE BOYS BENEATH SHALL NEVER SING
THAT THEY ARE THE D-DAY DODGERS, OUT IN ITALY

DODGERS!

Geoff took the opportunity to write down the words of the 'D-Day Dodgers' and eventually sent them home to his wife Betty back to Britain. The references to Bologna and the Po indicate that the songsheet was copied some time after D-Day. It's also the 'unabridged' version complete with advice for 'Dear Lady Astor' who was accused of coining the description 'D-Day Dodgers' in a less than kindly reference to the Allied forces out in Italy.

Geoff never spoke very much about the war although he did freely volunteer the information that his driving duties with the RASC (325 General Transport Company) had at one time involved him in ferrying the band leader Mantovani on a troop concert tour.

Even after the end of the war, lots of 'Dodgers' were kept overseas for many more months. It was January 1946 before Geoff got home to Betty and his four-year old son 'Geoffy'. Geoff resumed his pre-war profession of builder - and not just of houses for he and Betty made up for lost time and produced a brood of no less than nine children in their High Hurstwood, East Sussex, home. One of them - Barbara - became my wonderful wife.

Geoff died in 1985 and Betty too passed away four years later. The Huxley family are happy for me to publish Geoff's D-Day Dodger letter here together with the postcard reproduced below.

David Arnold,
Editor, *Sixty Years On*

Postcard to Italy

Betty Huxley sent this postcard to her husband, Driver Huxley, E G, on 14 May 1944. Her message aside, it's interesting to note the quote from Churchill printed on the card: 'We shall never stop, never weary and never give in.' It's unlikely Betty knew for certain that Geoff was in Italy. In a letter to her dated 9 June, he talks of getting a set of postcards to show her what '... some of the places out here look like.' But he doesn't say where these places are. When she posted the card Betty was in Ayr, Scotland, with her family and in mourning at the news of the death at Anzio of her brother George Kane of the Royal Scots Fusiliers on 18 April 1944. He is buried in the Beach-head Cemetery alongside so many of his comrades who also lost their lives.

George 'Geordie' Kane.

Christopher Portway is an accomplished travel writer and an astonishingly fit one too, for at the age of '80 something' he's still busily exploring the world on foot or by bicycle!

Christopher is also a D-Day veteran who came ashore on the beaches of Normandy on 6 June 1944 as a 21-year-old soldier in the British Army. Here are his reasons why he believes that remembering and commemorating the events of six decades and more ago is as important today as it ever was.

It was nearly 930 years ago that the conquest of England was launched by Duke William of Normandy from the small seaport of Dives. It was some 880 years later on 6 June 1944 that the greatest armada of ships ever assembled converged upon the yellow-sanded Norman beaches within a very few miles of that same little port. The two events, unconnected but strangely similar in method if not intention, offer those of our citizens who visit Normandy a uniquely close relationship to France.

The year 2004, the 60th Anniversary of D-Day and the Battle of Normandy, was a special occasion, when a diminishing band of men of many nationalities congregated upon Norman shores to relive each his private memories and remember those comrades left behind. There was pomp and ceremony. But for those who came ashore or landed by parachute or glider

Past Reunion. Christopher Portway is in the picture between the French and British flags at this reunion at Tilly sur Seulles, Normandy, in 1984.

GOINGBACK

The remains of part of an artificial Mulberry harbour on a Normandy beach.

60 years before, the most poignant moments will have been the personal pilgrimage to a fragment of a field, a corner of a village, farmhouse, hedgerow or orchard that once exuded a terror never completely erased by the years.

There is a tiny cemetery some 10 kilometres east of Bayeux that is, perhaps, the most meaningful place in the world for some. It holds a sadness that screws you up inside. Just a few dozen graves marked by Portland stone comprises the military cemetery of Little Jerusalem where a Pole and a Dorset lie side by side among a sprinkling of names from British tank and infantry units. At intervals down the years I have returned here with the surviving colleagues of my regimental association and are invariably asked to attend the simple act of remembrance by the villagers of nearby Chousain who, through the decades, have looked upon the tiny graveyard as their own.

The village band exhausts itself with spirited trumpetings. Our president, bare-headed, reads aloud his oration in stumbling French, and a line of school children with reproachful faces lay their bunches of wild flowers as if in admonishment to an earlier generation for its glory and its shame. We, who have been spared to grow old, see the flowers, the silent stones, the names, the regiments, the youthful ages preserved in a kind of waterglass. Externally we are balding, aged veterans of a war six decades past, but in our ears rise the sound of churning tank tracks in the night and Spandau bullets swishing through the corn.

What infantry soldier can forget that sickening pre-dawn hour of 'stand to', when, aroused from fitful slumber on the damp earth of a slit trench, he stands, bleary-eyed, staring into the dying night, tensed for the counter-attack the dregs of darkness so often brought. Or those silent incursions into enemy lines, devoid of anything that might rattle, with the intention of capturing a prisoner for interrogation. And, perhaps worse, those bouts of street fighting amongst the rubble of broken houses and the personal belongings of absent householders, their best china and family photographs trampled underfoot in an orgy of savagery.

Taken prisoner myself and transported to Poland, I was to witness unspeakable horrors and a cruelty so hideous that, in comparison, it made military combat positively saintly. But the threat of death or mutilation spares neither the soldier in the front line, the citizen under aerial bombardment or the captive in the charnel houses and camps of the remote hinterland.

> ❝ **We are balding, aged veterans of a war fought six decades past, but in our ears rise the sound of churning tank tracks in the night and Spandau bullets swishing through the corn.** ❞

Yet not all my memories of that time are tinged with fear. There was pathos too. Watching crew members eject from stricken Allied bombers, counting them one by one as the parachutes blossomed, our eyes streaming with tears for men we'd never met; for the inevitable few that failed to bale out.

And there was humour too. How can I forget the night while on picket duty behind the front line when two smartly-uniformed German officers emerged and asked to surrender. Nonplussed, I adopted an aggressive stance, covering them with my sten gun, whereupon one of the officers looked at me reproachfully and, in perfect English said, 'Excuse me Corporal, but you've no magazine on that gun.'

Today the memories are fading. Young families holidaying on the sandy coast of Calvados and La Manche are not concerned with the horror that swept across these pleasantly rural departments of North West France and why should they be? The museum of the landings at Arromanches, the concrete bunkers and the occasional rusting tank on its plinth are things to play over and explore in happy laughing groups. The gigantic operation that was the key to the liberation of France and Europe is but a slice of history that happened long ago. Like earlier events it was something that happened in times past; it's something to be learnt in lessons at school together with 1066 and all that.

Yet there are still a large number of us who remain and have our recollections of something real and awesome in scale. We might be the veterans of either side, or could be French civilians, perhaps in childhood at the time of the invasion. Yes, the anniversary will still be very much an authentic event for a lot of people for some considerable time to come.

Christopher Portway's amazing wartime experiences are told in his own words starting on page 197 of this book.

The Art of War

On the first day of June 1944, Resistance men and women all over France hear the BBC transmit two quotations from the poetry of Verlaine. The words signify that the invasion is imminent.

Eamon de Valera's Fianna Fail party in Eire is given a vote of confidence by the Irish people today when they return it to power with an increased representation. De Valera's strict neutrality policy, maintained in the face of British and US efforts to have him expel Axis diplomats in Eire, is believed a main reason for his party's popularity. The cost of his obstinate even-handedness has been economic isolation.

On **2 June** the Royal Navy confirm that it can have the first Mulberry harbour units moving according to schedule. The huge concrete caissons had become stuck in the Thames mud but have finally been floated free. Today also sees warships sailing from Scapa Flow, Belfast, The Clyde and other northern ports and anchorages, heading south towards the English Channel to join the invasion fleet.

Next night 99 RAF bombers drop 509 tons of bombs on the wireless intercept station at Urville Hague near Cherbourg, headquarters of the German Signals Intelligence Service in North Western France. Its loss could have a powerful influence on the course of the imminent invasion.

By **4 June** major sections of the invasion fleet are already at sea believing that D-Day is dawn on 5 June. At 04:30 hours on this Sunday morning the *Overlord* supremos of SHAEF meet to learn of a weather forecast that promises rain, high winds and fog. Eisenhower postpones the invasion for 24 hours. The ships at sea are recalled.

5 June: The Italian capital has been declared an 'Open City' and evacuated by the Germans. Today the soldiers of Mark Clark's Fifth Army enter Rome to a jubilant reception from cheering civilians thronging the streets.

At the end of this victorious day, just one hour and four minutes before midnight, the first aircraft take off and set course for Normandy. They are towing three Horsa gliders carrying Major John Howard and the men of the Ox and Bucks Light Infantry on a daring mission that will open the assault on Hitler's Occupied Europe.

Normandy, **6 June:** 00.16 hours. In what Air Vice Marshall Leigh-Mallory will describe as 'the greatest feat of flying in World War II', Major Howard's three gliders come down precisely as planned alongside the Benouville Bridge over the Canal de Caen. Within less than a minute, the men are emerging from the gliders to execute a classic *coup de main* and seize the bridge. A sentry fires a flare and is promptly cut down, the first German to die on D-Day.

A short time later large forces of British and American paratroopers drop at both ends of the invasion area during the hours of darkness. Many are scattered far away from their dropzones. Some are dropped over the sea.

At 05.30 hours the naval bombardment of the beaches begins. Just over one hour later, US infantry begin landing on Omaha and Utah beaches. A further hour after the first Americans are ashore, British and Canadian tanks and infantry begin landing on Sword, Gold and Juno beaches. Good progress is soon reported everywhere except for Omaha, where German resistance from the bluffs above the beach is fierce for many hours.

Hitler's V1 'Doodlebug' flying bomb offensive began in June 1944.

In the course of the morning of 6 June, 75,215 British and Canadian and 57,000 American troops will have landed by sea and linked up with the survivors of the 23,400 men who arrived by parachute or glider in the night. Total Allied killed, wounded or missing on D-Day number some 10,500; 114 aircraft have been lost. On the German side, casualties total 6500.

By 21.00 hours the fighting dies down along the entire Normandy front of some 60 miles. The Allies have firm footholds in many places and are hanging on determinedly in areas where German resistance has been strongest. Now the Allies must race to build up their strength before the enemy counterattacks.

Normandy **7 June:** More men and supplies pour ashore. British commandos attack Port-en-Bessin, seeking a link-up between the American and British beaches.

Next day **8 June** a set of invasion plans falls into German hands revealing that Normandy is the main thrust and not a feint. Even so, some high-ranking officers remain convinced that a further landing will be made in the Pas de Calais area.

In Italy on **9 June** the German retreat continues. Marshall Badoglio resigns and is succeeded as premier by a civilian, Ivanoe Bonomi.

10 June: The first deployment of Allied fighter aircraft to temporary airstrips in Normandy takes places as Spitfires of No 144 (RCAF) Wing fly in at Ste Crois-sur-Mer.

On **11 June** in the South Pacific Marianas islands, US naval and air forces attack Guam, Saipan and Tinian. Around 200 Japanese aircraft are destroyed.

12 June: Six days after D-Day, Montgomery informs reporters that the Allies 'have won the battle of the beaches'. Winston Churchill and South African Premier Smuts have visited the British beach-head.

On **13 June** six people are killed and nine seriously injured by an explosion caused by a strange new German 'flying bomb' which demolished a railway bridge at Grove Road, Bethnal Green.

In Sweden the authorities have impounded the wreckage of a German experimental rocket that went off course. The A4 - which will become known as the V2 - is more advanced than the V1.

14 June: General de Gaulle makes his first visit to liberated France. He tells his fellow countrymen in Bayeux: 'What the country expects of you is to keep up the fight.' A Vichy France broadcast from Paris

WAR DIARY
June 144

urges civilians to shun the Allies. Radio announcer Herold Paquis declares: 'If France is to live, England, like Carthage, must be destroyed.'

On **15 June** Tokyo radio claims six US planes shot down in the course of a raid. US sources confirm that 47 Superfortresses of their 20th Air Force based in China hit iron and steel works in Japan.

16 June: Canadian prisoners massacred by the SS on 7 June in Normandy are partly avenged today when a 16 inch shell from *HMS Rodney* lands 20 miles inland and kills the commander of the 12th SS Hitler Jugend Panzer Division.

By **17 June** Hitler's flying bombs are arriving over England in increasing numbers by night and day bringing with them the spectre of a new Blitz. People refer to these new weapons as 'doodlebugs' or 'buzz bombs' because of the drone of their engines. The authorities discourage the term 'V1' because it suggests that even more deadly weapons will follow.

Napoleon's island of exile, Elba, near Corsica, is liberated today.

18 June: In the South Pacific US marines capture Aslito on Saipan. Three days ago the Americans stormed ashore on this Marianas island in a four-mile wave of 600 amphibious craft.

German forces carry out intensive anti-partisan operations in the Lublin region of Poland.

On **19 June** a powerful storm strikes the English Channel. One casualty is the Mulberry artificial harbour off Omaha beach. Heavy seas, the worst in 40 years, decimate it.

20 June: The Battle of the Philippine Sea has been fought over the last two days and resulted in a stunning victory for the Americans. In the greatest carrier battle of the war, the Japanese have lost so many aircraft - 480 in total - that US pilots are calling the action 'The Great Marianas Turkey Shoot'. Japanese plans to destroy the American invasion fleet are in tatters and they've lost three more irreplaceable aircraft carriers plus many other ships.

The air offensive against Germany continues on **21 June** when a massive force of 1234 heavy bombers attack Berlin, Potsdam, Stendal and other targets.

22 June: Belorussia. A Russian army numbering 1.2 million men, 5200 tanks and assault guns supported by 6000 aircraft is today attacking a German force numbering just 400,000 men, 900 tanks and heavy guns and 1300 aircraft. Great gaps are torn in the German lines as the Red Army armour races towards Minsk.

23 June: There's more savage fighting on Saipan today when US and Japanese forces clash at a place dubbed 'Death Valley' near Mount Tapotchau.

On the India-Burma border, supply convoys are moving again on the Imphal to Kohima road following the lifting of the three month siege of the area. Around 30,000 Japanese have died since the start of their planned invasion of India against Allied losses of 2700 killed and 10,000 wounded. A key turning point came on 17 June when the exhausted Japanese abandoned the Mao Songsan ridges, the first time they have given up a position without a fight in the entire campaign.

Germany still has forces beyond the Arctic Circle in Norway. Desperate to keep Finland in the war, Germany's Foreign Minister, von Ribbentrop, is in Helsinki with promises of arms and troops.

24 June: North Atlantic. Flt Lt D E Hornell will be awarded the posthumous Victoria Cross for bravery in tackling a U-Boat sighted in far northern waters today. Canadian Hornell's Catalina flying boat spotted U-1225 on the surface and dived to attack. The U-Boat fought back and severely damaged the aircraft before sinking. The burning Catalina lost its starboard engine and had to land on the water. With just one serviceable dinghy, the crew took turns to sit in it or cling to the sides; two died of exhaustion in the freezing sea during the 21 hours they waited for rescue. Hornell died of exposure soon afterwards.

On **25 June**, the British Government begins free distribution to next-of-kin, of a 16-page handbook giving information about prisoners-of-war in the Far East.

26 June: Germany. Hitler emerges from seclusion to address a group of leading industrialists in Obersalzberg. Later he is described as sounding forgetful and looking ill.

Good news from Burma on **27 June** as the Chindit 77th Special Force Brigade together with two battalions of the Chinese 114th Regiment, take Mogaung. Battle and ill-health have taken their toll on the Chindits who have fewer than 600 men on their feet and able to fight. In China, however, the nationalist 10th Army retreats in disarray as the Japanese attack. An airfield used by US bombers to hit Japan has been captured.

On **28 June** there's a general strike in the Danish capital Copenhagen in protest at the German Occupation.

Today the USA cuts diplomatic ties with Finland. Most Finns want an end to the war with Russia but President Rysto Ryti, backed by a pro-German lobby, seeks to fight on.

Next day **29 June** the US Eighth Air Force Flying Fortresses are out in force raiding a score of industrial targets including the Volkswagen factory at Fallersleben, near Brunswick, where V1 flying bombs are constructed.

London: **30 June.** A V1 comes down on Bush House in the Aldwych, killing 198 people. Civilian casualties from the flying bomb offensive total 1935 dead and 5906 injured. Since D-Day, 4868 Americans, 2443 British and 393 Canadians have been killed, a total of 7704 dead. Battle fatigue takes an increasing toll - one fifth of all American casualties are attributed to exhaustion and shellshock.

Jews deported from the Greek island of Corfu arrive at Auschwitz-Birkenau after a 27-day journey in sealed boxcars. Many of the 1795 who set off have died in transit. The survivors are herded straight into the gas chambers.

Left: British airborne troops looking happy with their D-Day mission accomplished.

Battle of Normandy

JULY 1944

BATTLE

By July 1944 the Allies were firmly established in Normandy. But battling past the tenacious German defenders of the Norman landscape of dense hedgerows, sunken lanes and meandering streams would prove a costly and protracted struggle.

By daybreak on 1 July all German resistance in the northern part of the Contentin Peninsula had come to an end. Over 10,000 prisoners had been captured in Cherbourg and another 6000 surrendered in and around La Hague in the last days of June.

By this time the Germans had lost all hope of driving the Allies back into the sea. On the other hand, the fighting power of the *Wehrmacht* remained potent and it was now up to the British, American and Canadian forces to challenge that power and break it. Only once this was achieved could the Allies venture forth in confidence to liberate the rest of France and Occupied Europe.

Attention shifted to the eastern end of the bridgehead. The town of Caen, straddling the River Orne, was the key to victory. Attacks preceded by heavy bombing raids in June had come to nought. On 4 July the British General Miles Dempsey put in another assault which gained him only the part of the town on the north bank of the Orne. Then as the Allies drew breath it was noticed that the Germans were switching their reserve divisions to the west where General Omar Bradley's Americans were preparing to break out.

Operation Goodwood

To stop this German movement, the British launched another fierce armoured attack east of Caen on 18 July. This was *Operation Goodwood*. 'My whole eastern flank will burst into flames..' Montgomery told Eisenhower. The latter, haunted by the prospect of the invasion turning into a stalemate like that at Anzio near Rome earlier in the year, felt encouraged. *Goodwood* would be preceded by saturation bombing that would herald an attack by 750 tanks.

Unfortunately, the plan had some serious drawbacks. There was a reluctance to send infantry in with the tank spearheads. The British Army faced a serious manpower shortage. *Operation Epsom* at the end of June had cost some 4000 casualties in five days and the War Office warned that it could not guarantee to make good the losses for much longer. The situation caused General Miles Dempsey to later observe: 'I was prepared to lose a couple of hundred tanks. So long as I didn't lose men.'

The Germans had also prepared for defence in depth with minefields and strongpoints stretching back for 15 kilometres. The Allied bombers pummelled a depth of around eight kilometres. Even so, good initial progress was made. Until the tanks approached Cagny. Here a Luftwaffe flak battery with 88mm guns devastated the onrushing British armour. A German officer described the scene: 'One could see the shots flying through the corn like torpedoes. In the extensive fields to the north (of Cagny) stood at least 40 enemy tanks, on fire or shot up.'

Montgomery called off the attack on 20 July. Dempsey had lost over 400 tanks and sustained 5000 casualties.

For the British and American troops in and around the front line, these summer days of 1944 were a time of terror, maiming and sudden death. The Germans proved skilful and resolute in defence and made good use of the Norman Bocage country. Their weapons were very efficient and more than a match for the Allied equivalents. The range of mortars coupled with the ultra-fast firing Spandau machine-gun afforded valuable back-up for the speedy local counter-attacks in which the Germans excelled. One fearsome weapon was the *Nebelwerfer* - nicknamed 'Moaning Minnie' by the Allies - which had up to eight barrels that could be fired simultaneously accompanied by a screeching roar.

Tiger and Panthers

Their panzers too were in the main superior to those of the Allies. The latter's main battle tanks were Shermans, nicknamed 'Ronsons' by their hapless crews and 'Tommy-cookers' by the enemy. Outgunned by the mighty Tigers and Panthers of the Germans, the Allies most often relied on sheer weight of numbers to force the issue.

In the 88mm gun, an anti-aircraft weapon which the Afrika Korps had found even more deadly when utilised in an anti-tank role, the Germans had a powerful, high velocity killing machine. With the benefit of hindsight, one wonders why the Allies didn't simply produce copies of 88mm and thus even up the odds on the battlefield. The Bren Gun, after all, wasn't a British design; it was named after the Czech town of Brno where it was conceived and the British town of Enfield where it was later manufactured. Besides, in wartime, enemy patents don't count for much!

In the air, it was a totally different story. The Allies had total supremacy of the skies over Normandy, an advantage only annulled when rain and low clouds grounded aircraft. Rocket-firing Typhoons and all kinds of fighters roamed behind enemy lines or waited in 'cab ranks' to be called down on targets picked out by spotter aircraft or observers on the ground.

Eisenhower said of the Allied air efforts, 'The spectacle of our mighty air fleets roaring in over their heads had a most heartening effect upon our men.' Rommel himself fell victim of RAF Squadron-Leader J J Le Roux on 17 July when his staff car was shot up near Bernay. The wounded Field Marshal was succeeded by von Kluge,

IN THE BOCAGE

"FOR THE FIRST TIME IN THE HISTORY OF WAR, AN ARMY IS ATTACKING IN ALL FOUR DIRECTIONS AT ONCE!"

who quickly reported to Hitler that, 'There is no way by which, in the face of the enemy air forces' complete command of the air, we can discover a form of strategy to counter-balance its annihilating effect.'

Ring of Destruction

Before July was out, heavy and medium bombers had traced a ring of destruction around the battle area. It ran along the Seine and the Loire; bridges were blown up and rail links interdicted on a massive scale. The Germans were forced to detrain reinforcements, taken from the Russian Front, as far east as Nancy and Mulhouse. From here the troops marched or wobbled on bicycles towards the battle, hoping their heavy equipment would somehow find a passage behind them. Ironically, Hitler had a formidable reserve force much closer to Normandy. Fortunately for the Allies, he kept the well-armed 15th Army intact and in place around the Pas de Calais, awaiting a further seaborne assault which would never come.

American attention became focused on Saint-Lô on the River Vire, almost in the centre of the bridgehead perimeter. Perceived to be the gateway to the interior of France and already badly smashed up in the opening days of the invasion, the town and locale - stoutly defended by German paratroops - came in for further intense pounding from bombers and artillery. Such was the ferocity of the fighting that Saint-Lô was dubbed 'the Cassino of the north'. Indeed, the lessons of Cassino were having to be learnt the hard way all over again at many places in Normandy. Devastating bombing raids on towns all too often simply made the streets impassable to armoured vehicles and prevented the Allies pressing home their advantage of weight of numbers.

Colourful reputation

By 18 July they had achieved their goal and captured Saint-Lô. The scene was set for *Operation Cobra*, a large-scale south and eastward dash spilling armoured forces out of the Contentin Peninsula and onto a broader landscape more suited to a mobile war. Another huge air assault preceded the advance. Unfortunately it was marred by several instances of bomb 'carpets' falling short amidst the forward American units. Nevertheless, the crust of German resistance was broken and by 30 July Avranches had fallen.

Within days US columns were racing at high speed into Brittany. Rennes was liberated on 4 August, Lorient and Brest on the Bay of Biscay were reached on 7 August. The nightmare of the close quarter fighting in the Bocage seemed over as distant objectives, such as Orleans and St Nazaire, became suddenly attainable. Now a new name sporting a colourful reputation, hard-earned in North Africa and Sicily, appeared on the scene: General George S Patton soon found a phrase to describe the lightning manoeuvres of the armoured Third Army as it undertook a colossal turning movement in the direction of Le Mans: '...For the first time in the history of war, an army is attacking in all four directions at once!'

Left: A young German soldier looking out for Allied aircraft in Normandy.
Above: Two children survey the wreckage of St-Lô while US transport trundles through.
Below: A German despatch rider checks his map. Note the bomb damage in the background.

GUARD AFRICAN SKIES

GOLD COAST TO NORMANDY

Renee Pay's life in the Army took her to the Gold Coast of West Africa and later to the killing fields of Normandy in the summer of 1944.

Renee Pay (nee Morris and known as Katherine to some) was born in 1912, the first and eldest child of what would become a large Herefordshire farming family of eight girls and two boys. She was educated at Hereford High School for Girls, and then trained as a nurse, subsequently joining the Army as a Queen Alexandra nurse in 1940. During the next tumultuous years of a world at war, Renee's life was colourful, adventurous and often dangerous, serving as she did in West Africa from 1941-1943 before returning to England to prepare for and take part, as a nurse in the June 1944 Normandy landings.

Through these extracts from her memoirs we can glimpse a woman of courage, determination and lively personality. She seems to embody all that we owe to that special wartime generation. We begin with the story of a perilous 1941 sea voyage from Glasgow to West Africa, sailing in a convoy into the North Atlantic and subsequently zig-zagging southwards to escape the attentions of prowling U-Boats:

'Luxury was now the order of the day. I shared a two-berth cabin, own bathroom, and the food was absolutely super - at least it seemed so to us. We found we were part of a very large convoy with three large liners crammed with troops and of course many merchant ships. *HMS Ark Royal, Hood* and *Warspite*, I remember as being part of our escort, together with destroyers and corvettes. The war at sea was going very badly at this time. Our losses were enormous. There was no question of going

Left: The artist who created this illustration of a Hurricane fighter flying over a typical West African town is unknown. The colours are bright to reflect the style of the region and would have been displayed to show the local population that the RAF was there to protect them. West Africans supported the British war effort in large numbers, serving with distinction in the Burma theatre. Prior to the Germans and Italians being expelled from North Africa, Lagos in Nigeria, for example, was a vital staging post for aircraft flying over Africa to reinforce the RAF in the eastern Mediterranean, Egypt and the Far East.

straight down south - we found ourselves getting colder and colder and it was obvious ships were missing from the convoy. To my cost, I found I was the most terrible sailor. One morning, very early, there was a terrific bang followed by a shudder. Alarm bells went off, the engines stopped and the ship seemed to tilt. I was so incapacitated by sea-sickness I couldn't stand. I remember the steward rushed in, pushed me into my greatcoat and life jacket and propelled me towards the deck. Here we confronted nothing but mountainous seas with no convoy on the horizon - nothing but one little corvette. We had been bombed by a solitary plane. We huddled on deck for about 24 hours, feeling like a target for any submarine or for the returning hostile aircraft. Word came through that the German battleship *Bismarck* had been sunk by some of our escort. Later we learnt that *HMS Hood* had been lost earlier in the action.'

Renee provides an amusing description of the final lap of her voyage and her arrival in Ghana, then called the Gold Coast and described, encouragingly, as 'The White Man's Grave'!

'We were escorted down the coast of Africa by a destroyer and a little corvette. Upon arrival offshore, we were put into bark-like canoes rowed by nearly-nude Africans. This really was like something from a film with the Natives singing in time to their rowing against the surf. As our canoes rushed towards the beach, I thought we were in for a soaking. But no. Suddenly I was lifted in the arms of an African, rushed to the beach and plonked down safe and dry!'

Strict security

Renee's memoirs later provide a vivid glimpse of her experiences preparing for and participating in the Normandy landings:

'As a British General Hospital, we mobilised at an unused orphanage in Watford in December 1943. Doctors, RAMC Orderlies and Sisters; some of us knew the ropes, military hospital-wise, and the Orderlies were partly trained. These were the days before plastics so every dish, bowl, syringe, instrument and each piece of equipment had to be greased and wrapped in oiled paper, then packed in chests. Mattresses and bedding etc, were

rolled in oiled paper and stitched into hessian. I remember this as being very hard work.

'About the end of February 1944 we went up to Peebles for physical training. It was realised that we would have to be at a peak of physical fitness. We soon got the message that assembling for anything as an unruly gaggle of girls, was definitely out. We were also, by now, wearing scratchy AV (anti-vermin) battledress, boots and gaiters. Daily drill and route marches together with lectures on possible dangers, were our routine. Here we saw the last of tin trunks and grey and scarlet uniforms for a long time. I don't think they caught up with us again until we were in Eindhoven, Holland, in September.

'I've been back to Peebles to find the hill our drill sergeant used to make us walk up, wearing gas masks, and the streams he made us long jump over. Towards the end of April, we went as a unit to the village of Peasonhall in a quiet part of Suffolk. Security was strict. We took over three empty houses. Here camp beds and everything except the barest necessities were sent away. Now we were really getting down to basics, using the same mess tins, plus tin mugs, as the men and what we learned to call eating irons. Heaven help anyone who lost these essentials. Two blankets only. No camp bed!

'Fortunately it was a lovely spring in 1944, I remember, but the whole area was one armed camp. The villagers of Peasonhall were especially good to us. The WI gave us a party in the tiny village hall. During May, the unit had a Drum Head service in the middle of a forest. Monty came and gave a 'pep talk' at the end. On 12 June we entrained for our embarkation area. Here again, the organisation was meticulous. Now we spent a night in an American assembly area. Then to Southampton - by now everything neatly packed on back or front, leaving both hands free.

A cheer for the Sisters

'When we got out of the buses at the assembly sheds, had fallen in, and started to march towards the ship's gangway, we saw that hundreds of troops were drawn up, waiting to embark. As we marched towards the gangway, we could hear the murmur "They are Sisters". Cheering started and only finished

Left: 'Bitsy' by Clixy Watson. It's a cartoon depicting a glamorously uniformed nurse who has just given a bedridden sailor a signed photograph of herself. 'With all my Love - Nearly' reveals that she gives the same photograph to all her patients. The cartoon appeared in Ditty Box, *the Royal Navy's own magazine aimed at boosting morale. It was published monthly from July 1944 to January 1949. National Archives.*

when we were on board. It was then that we truly realised we were privileged to be part of the much-heralded invasion. Across the Channel and the landing craft were quickly alongside. Scramble nets went over the side and then laden with all the gear, we went down to the very unsteady boat.

'It was just a short distance to the beach. Nearly dark by now, we had to leap up on to the tail-board of a Utility truck that whisked us quickly away to an orchard. "What a day" said our escort, "Winston this morning and Sisters this evening!".

'Early next morning, we boarded a truck for the journey to our hospital site. There were mounds of earth alongside the road, topped with tin hats on top of wooden crosses with identity discs hanging there. Burnt-out tanks and equipment along a recently-made track running parallel with the road. Cows with legs chained. Dereliction and damage. Then we went down a lane leading to a largish house. This was it. Here our advance party were putting up marquees. From now on, it was a matter of getting ready to admit casualties in the next 36 or at most 48 hours.

'The organisation and back-up were excellent. Equipment we had packed back in January was there and even our own camp beds and the kit bags. It all seemed unreal what with troops glimpsed through the hedges around us and the continuous noise of vehicles. We began admitting casualties at the end of the second day, but nothing had prepared us for the scale of events. We got used to the grind of ambulances coming up the track, the walking wounded being helped along. On bad days, we would admit 600 and evacuate probably 500. On one especially

awful day, the number of admissions reached 1000. I remember Dillon, our Batman, coming round that night with the rum ration in cocoa. It had been raining most of the day and we certainly needed it.

'The routine was to get everybody to the beach-head as soon as possible. We kept only casualties with severe abdominal wounds. In theatre we simply didn't know who was going to be on the table next. There was no water coming out of the taps, no automatic turning on of a switch for electricity. I well remember the day our water tanker was hit. Imagine a theatre with three tables working and only four Jerricans of water. I thought, thank heavens for Penicillin powder, as I washed instruments again and again in the same water. Our sterilisation was done by boiling on Primus stoves.

'About this time, which was probably late June, Monty came to the theatre. He told us which road we were on and also said that they'd thought they would have to evacuate us the previous night because just four kilometres down the road was the German Seventh Panzer Division. Only later do these things register - we were much too busy at the time. Meanwhile, wards and the reception area had their own problems. The three Padres attached to us worked in the reception area and also as stretcher bearers when the need arose. The spirit and camaraderie were superb. We became used to the sound of gunfire, but nights were hideous. The Navy were shelling targets beyond us and the return fire was continuous. Shrapnel fell everywhere at night. It was decided we should sleep in the deepened ditch running around the field - I don't know which was worse, and can only say that any degree of personal comfort was not a feature of our lives.

'Towards the end of June, three other hospitals began taking casualties. Things didn't get much better, though, until Caen had been taken in late July. I was grateful for having been part of it all and for coming through unscathed.'

Renee (nee Morris and also known to some as Katherine) died in April 2004. The story here was provided by her niece Mrs Christina Backholer of Haywards Heath, West Sussex. It is based on notes Renee had written for various talks about her experiences.

Left: A convoy of ambulances approaches a hospital ship anchored at the Mulberry Harbour at Arromanches. Allied soldiers knew that if they survived the initial impact of a bullet or shrapnel wound then the casualty evacuation system gave them a good chance of survival.

FROM ROME to Florence

For the first three weeks of June 1944 the German forces in Italy were in retreat. But by the time Rome was some 130 miles in the rear, the Allied armies faced stiffening resistance.

By 20 June crack Panzergreadier and Parachute units were drawn up close by Lake Trasimeno in the centre of a line which ran from the River Chienti in the east and across the Apennines before taking advantage of other river barriers in the west.

The battle of Lake Trasimeno lasted some 10 days. The Eighth Army found itself fighting on ground which had witnessed the rout of Flaminus and his Roman legions by Hannibal over 2000 years earlier. As July dawned,

Above: A German propaganda leaflet from the summer of 1944. It invites the Allies to partake of the pleasures of the Po Valley. On the reverse side, however, the scene is one of death and destruction and depicts the real welcome the Germans were preparing for the men of the Eighth and Fifth Armies.

General Oliver Leese reported that the Germans had been driven north. They didn't retreat very far. Kesselring had marked a series of phase lines in front of the Arno river and Florence where rearguard actions could be mounted. Each line was known by a girl's name such as Karin, Olga and Paula and the Germans did just enough at each one to hold up the advance of the Allies by a day or two. On 16 July Arezzo fell and on the next day the Arno, south of Pisa, was reached. On 18 July the Poles liberated Ancona and next day US troops entered Leghorn.

The Allies were still around 20 miles south of Kesselring's main defensive position. Called the Gothic Line, it ran along the last barrier of mountains before the terrain opened out into the wide plains of the Po Valley. The wily German commander – master of the spoiling flight – had been

using the time bought by the stubborn resistance of his troops in the face of the Allied advance to strengthen and reinforce the position. At the same time the Allies were diverting considerable land, sea and air forces away from the fighting in Italy in preparation for an invasion of the South of France.

The Po bridges had up to now been immune to Allied bombing in anticipation of needing them intact for the advance of the Eighth and Fifth Armies. But in late July they began to destroy the bridges, hoping to trap German forces to the south of the river. Implicit in this change of strategy was an admission that further rapid victories in Italy were unlikely before the autumn.

On 4 August elements of the Fifth Army entered Florence. The Germans had abandoned the city but before departing had blown up all the bridges apart from the most famous one, Ponte Vecchio. But at least the Allies were now in striking distance of the Gothic Line.

The Italian Campaign

Guns, Mountains and Mules

For almost the whole of 1944 and 1945 until the hostilities ceased, Jack Perris* was in Italy as a member of a Mountain Artillery Regiment. This is his story.

I think our unit was unique in this theatre of war. Our guns broke down into a number of component parts and were carried on the backs of mules along with the ammunition. The mules were driven by Basuto tribesmen who had been recruited in Africa.

The weapons were known as 'screw guns' by the gunners and our job was to work in the mountains of Italy in areas not normally accessible to guns towed by vehicles. The gunners walked with the mules. Sometimes we would traverse metalled roads but more usually would traverse the valleys and hills and cross streams and rivers, wading along with the mules, often hanging on to the mule's tail for safety. We covered quite long distances, often 20 or 30 miles, marching by night to avoid German aircraft. Since we had to carry all our equipment, blankets were not included and many nights were spent sleeping in snow and ice with twigs and bracken instead of blankets for comfort.

I was known as a Specialist, a technical assistant to aid the officers in siting the guns and to control their firing from observation points, using trigonometry to transfer information from maps and relay that information to the men manning the guns.

We did not engage in any 'big' battles such as those at Cassino and Anzio but instead acted more like guerrillas, harassing the enemy from unexpected quarters. There were many hair-raising and dangerous incidents, of course, as the Regimental Roll of Honour and list of Citations in the diary proves. For example, Gunner Sydney Roden was awarded the MM on 26 December 1944. The Citation reads: 'During the Monte Cavallo operations, line signaller Gnr Roden was sent back to guide the ration party up to the OP. While crossing a spur, he came under artillery fire and ran towards a house to take cover. When he was close to it he suddenly noticed two Spandau (machine guns) at the ground-floor windows and, a moment later, saw a German cross the open doorway.

He at once drew his revolver and charged the house, calling loudly to non-existent men behind him to come on. The German promptly came out and surrendered. Gnr Roden drove him into the house at the point of his revolver and there found another 12 armed Germans with an NCO, eating around a table. He called on them to surrender which they did and then he forced the NCO to disarm them all. Subsequently he made them march off, carrying their Spandaus, and handed the whole party over to the nearest Battalion HQ.'

When the fighting ended I was posted to GHQ in Naples and lived in well ordered barracks. Obviously the soft living after the snow and ice of the mountains did not agree with me and I spent three weeks in hospital with pneumonia.

*Jack Perris lives in Cheshire.

EYE WITNESS

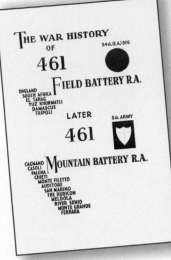

THE WAR HISTORY
OF
461
FIELD BATTERY R.A.

54th (E.A.) DIV.

ENGLAND
SOUTH AFRICA
EL TAHAG
TUZ KHURMATLI
DAMASCUS
TRIPOLI

LATER

8th ARMY

461

CAGNANO
CASOLI
PALENA
CHIETI
MONTE FILETTO
AUDITORE
SAN MARINO
THE RUBICON
MELDOLA
RIVER SENIO
MONTE GRANDE
FERRARA

MOUNTAIN BATTERY R.A.

This is the frontispiece for a diary containing an account of 461 Battery's war service from its official formation on 15 January 1941 through to disbandment in 1945. Below we highlight a number of entries.

The unit sailed from Belfast in October 1942, first stopping at Freetown, Sierra Leone - 'Green, damp and strange. Natives diving for coins' - before passing Capetown and Table Mountain on the way to Durban and some time ashore. The book then records, 'Leave Durban. Rough for four days. Rumours of submarines.'

The unit landed in Egypt and in a series of hops made its way across the Middle East to a camp near Baghdad: 'Visit Babylon. Good food - more smells. Cold nights and sandstorms. Flies - and more flies. Dates, locusts, melons, scorpions, spiders.'

By August 1943 the men were in camp near Tripoli in Syria and a few months later the mules and their Basuto drivers arrived. In February 1944 the Advance Party sailed from Beirut to Bari in Italy and by 7 March they were at Naples. The Mule Party meanwhile sailed from Tripoli to Bari via Port Said in Egypt. The Main Party also went first to Egypt and Tahag Camp where the book records: 'Arrive on same plot of sand we left over a year before in January 1943!'

10 March: 'Embark on *Franconia* and travel with ENSA company and Poles, male and female, and also 600 Basutos - nearly all sick but cheerfully so.' Six days later they arrived at Taranto: 'Cold and rain, chaos unloading stores.'

On 11 May 1944, the entry reads: 'Hear Cassino offensive starts at 23.00 hours tonight! Guns moved forward, Just get in by daylight. First casualties by enemy action.'

11 June: 'Battery move up Fara Gorge. Climb 5000 feet in two and a half hours. OP moves up another 1000 feet after an hour's rest.'

29 June: 'Visit Cassino. Description of battle given by Second-in-Command.'

In the summer of 1944 the unit played a role in breaking through the German defenses known as the Gothic Line. 24 August: 'Cagli bridge (blown) had proclamation on it dated June saying hostages would be shot if Partisans continued to interfere with mining of bridge.'

26 August: '338 Battery OP shelled and three signallers killed. Pink airburst fired by enemy over road demolitions.'

The Basuto mule drivers were an invaluable component to the artillery unit. Several of them feature in the Citations in the War History of 461 Battery RA. Gunner (L/Bdr) Mobuoa Mahase was awarded an MM (Military Medal) on 29 December 1944 for managing to get across the seemingly impassable swollen rivers Ronco and Voltre, with his mule, to re-establish communications with two forward Companies of infantry. The entry concludes: 'L/Bdr Mahase's successful crossing of both rivers, alone and after being separated from the British signallers with whom he normally works, showed an exceptional degree of initiative and determination which are worthy of the highest praise. His conduct on this occasion went far beyond his ordinary duty and forms an outstanding example of the soldierly qualities which have distinguished the Basutos since they became mule drivers in the Mountain Artillery.'

3 - 4 September: 'Warning from Adjutant not to eat grapes because of arsenic insecticide. Allied medium bomber comes down in flames, most spectacularly.'

22 September: 'Officers went up to San Marino, saw girl wearing silk stockings. San Marino a quite astonishing place and like all good Italian towns had no sewage system.'

30 September: 'Move to Secchiano - more river crossings. Popski's Private Army there. Captain N Barras came out to see us. And then we went into action again.'

1 October: 'Fairish bit of shooting at San Donato and other features. 1 / 2 Punjabs of 10 Indian Division came up and we had to wear tin hats, as they mistook us for Huns in our mountain caps. Went on to attack San Donato.' 29 October: 'OP moved up to house, later found to be within 350 yards of enemy. Considerable firing.'

28 March 1945: 'OP shelled with heavy stuff. After first round, Lt Lowry orders evacuation of OP room. Two minutes later, direct hit completely demolishes room.'

16 April: 'Two platoon attack on Monte Castellaro supported. Counter-attacked on objective, withdrew with 21 casualties.'

8 May: 'VE Day. Bonfires and barrels. Plenty of fireworks.'

The final entry for 1945 reads: 'The Regiment summered in pleasant parts, mainly at Pesaro on the Adriatic Coast south of Rimini. Disbandment started. The aged returned home for release to civilian life, the younger ones were posted to other units and the Basutos started on their way back to Basutoland. A time of parties and partings of old friends and the end of a great comradeship.'

" **Baghdad. Flies and more flies. Dates, locusts, melons, scorpions and spiders.** "

DOODLEBUG

SUMMER

A deadly hail of Hitler's secret 'V for Vengeance' weapons falls on England in the weeks following D-Day. Martin Barton-Smith, a London schoolboy at the time, recalls his own experiences and records the memories of others who found themselves in harm's way on the Home Front.

The summer of 1944 was an exciting time for an eight-year-old schoolboy. Nearly five years of war had accustomed our family to the ever-present threat of German bombers, but to me the 'threat' always seemed slightly unreal - after all, bombs usually fell on other people.

The Surrey Hounds pub at Clapham Junction 'caught it' on 17 June 1944. This photograph was taken just three minutes after the V1 struck and shows the firemen setting up their hoses.

My school friends and I had become expert in the identification of aircraft and other military equipment. There was always something going on, raids at night, huddling in the Morrison shelter, and then the excitement of going out next morning to pick up shiny pieces of shrapnel, still hot to the touch. Best of all, school was often disrupted. On reflection, it seems curious that eight-year-old boys were allowed to go out unaccompanied to examine craters containing unexploded bombs and gawp at houses ripped in two, but we did. The bomb damage in north London was less than further south in the capital, but there were still plenty of incidents to examine at close quarters until we were chased away by zealous ARP wardens (Mr Hodges really did exist!).

In the spring vast quantities of American lorries began to appear in our road, huge tractor units pulling low loader trailers with brand new tanks. Best of all, these units were manned by the fascinating mix of humanity which made up the US army - accents from all parts of North America, soldiers of all types and sizes. We were in seventh heaven, and the legendary generosity of American servicemen towards small children is not exaggerated. At night mobile ack-ack guns would open up and rattle the windows and doors. In the morning more booty, until I was forbidden to bring any more metal into the house!

With the advent of D-Day, our friends moved on to be replaced by a whole mixture of other units. Most of these only stayed overnight en route to the channel ports, and there was a noticeable stiffening of military discipline, particularly when it came to denying access to small boys climbing on lorries. A week after the excitement of the invasion, another event came along which occupied our attention and which, ultimately, changed the direction of many lives. The 'Doodlebugs' started to appear. Quite how they came to be called as such is unclear; maybe the larva of a tropical insect, the antlion (doodlebug), resembled the German flying bomb? The Germans had a rather more prosaic name, calling it V1 (V for *Vergeltungswaffe* or 'Reprisal Weapon').

To we amateur 'spotters' of North London, these were a revelation. The noise of their approach was unmistakable, a sort of stuttering staccato popping noise that led to another nickname - 'Buzz Bomb'. It wasn't long before we realised that when the engine noise stopped it was time to take cover! Because of their primitive guidance system, the bombs were inaccurate and were aimed at London indiscriminately in an effort to undermine civilian morale. They crossed the coast of Sussex and Kent and winged their way to the capital up 'Doodlebug Alley' where most of the damage was done and where most of the defences against them were mounted.

My memories are but a tiny glimpse of that fateful summer. They are a schoolboy's memories, and not tainted by the close reality of death and injury which afflicted so many. Others were not so lucky. Marlene Heselden of Walmer writes in her autobiography how she was visiting her married sister in Lewisham one Saturday in June: 'There had been an unusually large number of air raid warnings that morning. We heard a flying bomb approaching sounding quite close. The engine cut out and at that moment the door bell rang - 'Go and answer the door, Albert must have forgotten his key'. Those were the last words my sister Doris spoke to me. There was a rush of warm air, then black, hot, suffocation, the smell of burnt dust and the taste of it choking me. I was aware of an ambulance bell ringing, and then, thankfully, passed out.'

New wonder drug

Marlene was the only survivor from the six people in the flat. She spent over a year in hospitals and convalescent homes being treated for severe wounds. She attributes her survival to the new 'wonder' drug, penicillin.

Frank Busby of Knaresborough was also an eight-year-old in 1944, living near Croydon Airport. He recalls: 'These rockets seemed to come over continuously, houses all round were blown apart. Our house was not hit, although windows were out, ceilings were down and there was a lot of other damage. One day I was in the garden when a Doodlebug came over. The engine cut out and I started to run indoors but tripped and fell. I lay on the ground watching the bomb, and I swear to this day if the wind had not blown it off course it would have landed right on top of me. In fact, it landed in the local cemetery!'

Two near misses were reported by Roy Lawrance of Whitstable, this time in the

Harringay area of London: 'I was cycling home from school at about 4.30pm when something caught my eye and I looked up. To my astonishment there was a V1 floating through the air immediately above me, moving like a falling leaf and slowly dipping from side to side. It was heading directly for the shopping centre in Green Lanes, but at the last minute side-slipped into the American Gardens in Finsbury Park where it demolished some houses. I wonder how many of the shoppers that day realised how close they had been to disaster?' On another occasion, Roy was again on his bicycle, this time in thick mist which made the unseen approach of a bomb doubly unnerving: 'I did not know what to do for the best. I remember riding round in circles not knowing which way to go to avoid it. I had just decided to lie down next to a hospital wall when the thing went off with a bang in the distance. I got back on my bike and continued to school'.

The reporting of the first wave of bombs in June was heavily censored. The authorities did not wish to give the Germans the slightest opportunity to plot the detonations and thus assess their accuracy. The guidance system was primitive, being based on a gyro compass and the amount of fuel fed to the engine. However, since these were essentially 'terror weapons', the uncertainty which surrounded their arrival contributed to the nervousness of the civilian population. The first recorded bomb struck a railway bridge in Bow in London and the second fell near Cuckfield in Sussex, some 50 miles away.

No trace of damage

Others recall the widespread sightings of these devices. Gil Graves of Wellington, Somerset writes: 'We arrived for work one morning and one of our colleagues who lived in Newbury said something had exploded near the A4 London Road. It appears it was a V1, but there was no mention in the papers or on the radio about it. Hitler's mob were obviously still testing them for range and direction. A few days later another device landed at Harwell airfield and destroyed a Stirling bomber and left a large crater. By dawn all traces of the damage had been removed and Harwell denied all knowledge of it.' Obviously government 'spin doctoring' is not a new science.

Charmaine Burgess' parents had a smallholding on the Essex marshes: 'There was a very dear neighbour who was very nervous about everything at this time, and came running to be with my mother whenever there was a raid. One day, Mum had cooked a huge boiler full of potatoes for the pigs and put them outside the door to cool. A Flying Bomb passed overhead and the neighbour came screaming up the road, and then screamed even louder, "I've been shot, oh help, I've been shot". Mother ran to get the first aid kit, but neighbour Nell had stepped in the boiling potatoes and only needed cooling down!'

IN PARIS

While London and the Home Counties suffered under the V1 rocket onslaught, Occupied Paris was relatively quiet in July 1944 with the Allies reluctant to bomb the city even though it was a very important transit point for German reinforcements headed for Normandy.

Some of those Frenchmen and women who had thrown in their lot with the Nazis still remained stubbornly convinced of an ultimate victory for Hitler. The Collaborationist press highlighted with great gusto the advent of the secret weapons of which the V1 was just the first. Berlin was already announcing the coming of the V2, faster and even more destructive. One broadsheet printed: 'They used to write Vs on the walls. Now write V1, V2 and V3...'

The July weather was superb. Resistance and Collaborators seemed to agree on one thing: the wonderful legs of Parisian girls. Gilles Perrault was 13 years old at the time and remembers the pretty women with skirts billowing in the updraft of passing German trucks: 'I felt life held great promise', he wrote later.

On 20 July, roadblocks went up all over the city and German tanks took up positions outside key buildings. It was the day of the failed bomb plot against Hitler and some senior Wehrmacht officers had showed their hands too early. When it was clear that Hitler had survived, the soldiers hastily assured the Fuhrer of their continued loyalty. Not all of them were convincing enough in their reasons for confining the SS to barracks and were summarily executed. Even the legendary Field Marshal Erwin Rommel, he who had predicted that the success or failure of the Allied invasion would be decided on the landing beaches in the first 24 hours - The Longest Day, was implicated. He later took poison on the understanding that his family would be spared retribution.

In the days following 25 July news reached Paris that the American General Patton had broken through at Avranches and was surging into Brittany. A Collaborator reporter in the city wrote the comforting words: 'This is because it is the only way open to them.'

Very few inhabitants of Paris believed him. But they did wonder just how long it would be before their liberators would arrive.

20 JULY

A group of dedicated German anti-Nazis attempted to dispose of Adolf Hitler on 20 July 1944. The desolating story of the failed attempt has been told many times, but what is not universally known is the fact that the attempt was the third that same month, all involving the staunch and courageous Count Claus von Stauffenberg. The first was planned for 11 July at Berchtesgaden when both Himmler and Goring were to join Hitler at a conference. About this time, 'Stauffenberg' had been promoted to be Chief of Staff and deputy to fellow-conspirator Colonel General Fredrich Fromm. This gave him access to certain conferences attended by Fuhrer. In the event, neither Himmler nor Goering attended, so Stauffenbery took it upon himself to delay setting off the bomb he carried in his briefcase; a perfectionist impulse that, in retrospect, proved a fatal error.

WOLF'S LAIR

The second attempt was arranged for a conference to be held at the *Wolfsschanze* - Wolf's Lair - in East Prussia four days later, but again Stauffenberg failed to ignite the bomb in his briefcase. This was because at the last moment he was called upon to address the gathering which threw out his plans for seeing off the explosive; a fiddly task that had always presented difficulties to him resulting from the loss of one hand and injury to the other sustained whilst serving on the Eastern Front.

At the 20 July meeting, all went well initially and the loaded and primed briefcase was placed on the floor on the inner side of the leg of the big oak table close to Hitler. Stauffenberg then left the room on the pretext of making a telephone call. A few moments later Colonel Brandt, General Heusinger's Chief-of-Staff, found the briefcase in his way and moved it a few inches to the far side of the table leg from Hitler. At 12.45 the bomb exploded killing, amongst others, the unfortunate Colonel Brandt, another of the anti-Nazi plotters who, a year before, had attempted to carry aboard Hitler's aeroplane

a couple of brandy bottles primed with explosive. Thus Hitler escaped death on that fateful July day through the inadvertent action of one of the very men wanting him dead.

Conflicting reports emerged from the Wolf's Lair concerning the fate of Hitler resulted in some of the plotters revealing themselves prematurely. One who was more cautious was General Fromm and, upon learning of the failure of the plot, reneged on his fellow-plotters, seeing to it that as many as possible were instantly shot. Then the Gestapo intervened, wanting interrogations before execution. Thus Fromm's efforts to remove all those who were aware of his earlier flirtations with the enemies of the Fuhrer, whose favour he now sought at the last minute, were unsuccessful. The wretched man was finally arrested and executed eight months later, having experienced in the meantime the worst cruelties of which the system which he had helped to create, was capable.

INNOCENT VICTIMS

The effect of the attempt on Hitler was like that of a wound inflicted upon some savage creature at bay. He gave orders for a policy of *sippenhaft* or 'kindred seizure' which entailed all near-relatives of the conspirators being arrested and executed as a sacrifice to the wrath of the insulted divinity of the *Wolfsschanze*. Their number is not known though many wholly innocent victims died in the ensuing massacre.

We should remember Stauffenberg in a good light. He was a professional soldier of fine physique, striking good looks and an infectious laugh. He and his fellow conspirators belonged to an exclusive clique of brave men whose love of their country transcended the evil of Nazism. Their hanging, on Hitler's orders, was performed in the most brutal and agonising fashion, intended to obliterate the memory of those who dared to oppose him. Instead it lit a beacon in the satanic darkness of unspeakable barbarity.

Christopher Portway

DEATH OF A PANZER ACE

On 25 July, three days after the attempt on his life, Hitler met with SS Obersturmfuhrer Michael Wittmann, to personally confer on him the Swords to accompany the Knights Cross with Oak Leaves he already possessed.

This new honour recognised Wittman's outstanding conduct in the course of the Battle of Normandy where, with just five Tiger tanks, in the course of a single day he oversaw the destruction of 30 British tanks and scores of vehicles.

With the Fatherland being battered by Allied bombs, to boost morale, the Nazis needed heroes and they didn't come much larger than life than Wittmann. Yet within a fortnight of the meeting with Hitler, the panzer ace would be dead, a victim of Allied air power. Indeed, Wittman's life and death in Normandy, mirrors the fate that befell much of the German Army west of the Seine in the summer of 1944.

VASTLY OUTNUMBERED

Wittmann's tally of 'kills' since 1939 amounted to 138 enemy tanks and assault guns together with 132 anti-tank guns before his transfer to the newly formed Waffen-SS 101st Heavy Tank Battalion, stationed in France in anticipation of an Allied invasion.

After D-Day Wittmann's unit was soon in the thick of the fighting. On 13 June his small command found themselves vastly outnumbered at the key junction town of Villers-Bocage. Fortunately for Wittmann, his presence went unobserved and when the British column halted and the crews vacated their vehicles, he at once raced his 60-ton Tiger down the column, wrecking tanks and trucks with shell after shell fired at point-blank range.

Wittmann's force was eventually overwhelmed and he and his crew had to abandon their tank and escape on foot. But they'd succeeded in blunting the British attack; Villers-Bocage would not be liberated until 4 August.

TYPHOON NEMESIS

By this time the Allied breakout was in full swing. Four days later on 8 August Wittmann was in one of a trio of Tigers keeping open an escape route for the *Wehrmacht* forces facing encirclement around Falaise. His tank was hit and set on fire; Wittmann died in the explosion.

For years it was claimed that Sherman Firefly tanks had destroyed Wittman's Tiger. Then some two decades ago, a French farmer, Serge Varin, said he had actually examined Wittmann's Tiger (No 007) after the action. He'd seen no shell damage but noted a big hole in the rear of the tank caused by a rocket fired from the air.

Rocket-firing Typhoons were the nemesis of thousands of German soldiers and vehicles in Normandy in 1944. It seems as though Germany's greatest panzer ace shared that same fate.

War Correspondence

High drama over Essex

19 June 1944 was a fine summer's day over Southern England but the war was about to come home to the people of Canvey Island, Essex. Above the Thames estuary the 379th Bomb Group of the 8th USAAF was returning to Kimbolton after a raid on V1 launch sites near Calais. At the age of only 19, Lt Lloyd Burns, piloting a B17 Flying Fortress, was flying his 24th mission; one more and he could go home. Over the Channel, Lloyd had swapped seats with his co-pilot, Lt Fred Kauffman, so that Fred could gain some 'First Pilot' experience.

Above and behind them another B17 pilot, Lt Ramacitti, fought for control of his aircraft. Having taken enemy fire over the target, one of his engines was giving trouble and the plane was seen weaving about. Suddenly Ramacitti's B17 slammed into the top of Burns' aircraft, killing Fred Kauffman instantly. Lloyd tried the controls, which were useless and ordered the crew to bale out. He tried to rouse Fred, but he was obviously dead.

The radio room, behind the cockpit, was also squashed down but with enough room for the radio operator, Leroy Monk, to squeeze out and put his parachute on before he jumped. In the nose, bombardier Jack Gray was shocked to see the Plexiglas nosecone popped clean off the plane by the impact and found himself staring into space and without a parachute. He managed to scramble back for his 'chute, put it on and jumped.

Underneath the B17 was a gun turret shaped like a ball. The gunner, Bill Farmer, saw that his plane was falling to pieces and baled out. Richard Andrews, normally the waist gunner, was one of the tail guns that day and baled out of the escape hatch. The usual tail gunner, Louis Schulte, also jumped but sadly he drowned in the water.

Moments before the collision, Len Gibbs, the flight engineer/top turret gunner, had climbed down from his turret suffering from an earache and when he picked himself up from the floor he too jumped, to be followed by the last man out, pilot Burns.

Onlookers saw the doomed B17 turn away from the island before crashing into the marshy area known locally as 'The Point'. Many believed that a body recovered from the wreck was that of the pilot who had stayed at the controls to avoid the houses. In fact it was the forces of aerodynamics that steered the aircraft away from Canvey and the body was that of the navigator, Ed Sadler, who never made it out.

Sadly there was only one survivor from the other B17, bombardier Theo Chronopolos. Theo was thrown out when the plane broke in half as it spun down to crash on the Kent side of the river. He landed safely by parachute.

Lloyd Burns flew his 25th mission three days later, but stayed in the air force and went to the Pacific to fly the mighty B29 Superfortress in the war against Japan.

As a boy in the 1970s I dug up some parts of this B17 bomber from the mud of the Thames and was nearly drowned in the process. I knew nothing about the crash until last year when I came across research carried out by an eye-witness called Stan Pierce who was himself just a small boy when he saw the incident take place.
Mark Etheridge, Lancashire

Left: A Fieseler Storch of the kind encountered by Philip Mead in the sky over Normandy in the summer of 1944.

Pistols at 2000 feet!

It was March 1944 when I finished my training as a Navigator in the Royal Air Force. After 200 hours of night flying from RAF Mona Anglesey we expected to be posted to Bomber Command but it was not to be. The whole course of Navigators was sent to an airfield near Cardiff and put in a hanger with a similar number of pilots and ordered to 'pair off'. Then each pair as a crew was allotted an Avro Anson. The Anson was a low wing twin engine aeroplane with a wing span of almost 60 feet used by Coastal Command with a crew of perhaps six but we were to fly as transport aircraft with just pilot and navigator.

As D-Day approached we were told our planes were part of 1311 T Flight Transport Command but this was later changed to 84 Group Support Unit 2nd Tactical Air Force and our job was to keep the British and Canadian forces supplied after they landed in Normandy. Unarmed and heavily loaded we took off from bases near the South Coast and flew across the Channel at 2000 feet looking for temporary airfields just our side of the front line (which was of course advancing all the time).

One day in the summer of 1944 when the Allied troops had advanced east of Caen we had taken off and flown towards the French coast. I had given a course to fly to an airfield captured by the Canadians and at 2000 feet was map reading. Suddenly I observed a small black spot moving below us. Gradually it got bigger until I could identify a Fieseler Storch German reconnaissance aircraft coming up from below. It was a sinister looking high wing monoplane painted all in black with white swastikas and formatted a few feet from our right wing tip. The pilot was wearing a black flying helmet and goggles. He looked across at us and stared and then took out and waved his service revolver at us!

We had also been issued with revolvers for protection if we crashed in enemy territory so we both drew out revolvers and shook them back at him! The German then waggled his wings and slowly descended until he was finally lost above the trees below us.

Our Anson slowly plodded its way on at 140 knots until we spotted the allied airfield where we landed safely.
Philip Mead, Surrey

Mr Mead was WO Navigator 1805100 in the RAF 1942-1946.

WAR DIARY
July 1944

The beginning of July sees a surge of recruits to the Italian partisan movements. Since the liberation of Rome early last month thousands of men have taken to the mountains and hills to join bands of guerrillas - mainly communist-led - who are carrying out sabotage operations and hit-and-run raids on the German lines of communication.

On **2 July** 5000 men of the Brazilian Expeditionary Force are at sea. This first contingent is bound for Naples where it will join Allied forces fighting north of Rome. Brazil declared war on the Axis in August 1942 but the country's role in the conflict to date has been confined to assisting the battle against the U-Boat menace in the Southern Atlantic.

The following day in Normandy, two squadrons of Northrop P-61 Black Widow nightfighters begin operations over the Allied bridgehead. The Allied air forces have complete command of the air by day and the arrival of significant numbers of nightfighters will reduce the Luftwaffe's ability to mount raids after darkness.

4 July: US aircraft from Task Force 58 raid Japanese bases on the islands of Guam, Iwo Jima and Chichi Jima.

In London the flying bomb offensive has led to a new evacuation of the capital. Mothers of children under five and expectant mothers as well as schoolchildren are to be moved to the country.

5 July: British soldiers in the invasion forces have been allowed to take no more than 10 bob with them to France. This low sum has been fixed to prevent a 'run' on commodities in the newly liberated territory.

By **6 July** the island of Saipan in the Marianas is close to being secured by the Americans. The Japanese commanders Admiral Nagumo and General Saito, both commit ritual suicide rather than surrender. Some 8000 Japanese - soldiers and civilians - follow their example.

7 July: The Red Army enters Vilnius in Lithuania after overcoming fanatical resistance by SS men and paratroops on a 'stand or die' mission. Whilst the Lithuanians and citizens of the other Baltic states of Estonia and Latvia have been treated badly by their Nazi occupiers, many of them do not wish to be 'liberated' by the Russians and are deeply wary of Stalin's intentions.

The following day in Burma, Ukhrul falls to the Allies; the Japanese are still in retreat following the repulse of their invasion of India.

On **9 July** bandleader Glenn Miller - already a showbiz legend - gives the first concert of his British tour.

10 July: The British newspapers look to have won a campaign to have a ban on weather reports lifted. Imposed at a time when the UK was under constant threat of daylight bombing, the weather gag infuriated farmers.

By **11 July** some 41,000 mothers and children have been evacuated from London in the face of the V1 offensive.

By **12 July,** some two months after the breaking of the Gustav Line and the capture of Monte Cassino, the men of the Fifth and Eighth armies are 250 miles north of the start line and are approaching Florence. German resistance begins to harden along their Gothic Line.

A German nightfighter based at Deelen in Holland landed at RAF Woodbridge in Suffolk on **13 July** after an apparent navigational error. The Ju88G carried three different radar sets, all designed to negate the RAF's sophisticated electronic counter-measures equipment. British scientists are surprised to see how up-to-date the German devices are.

14 July: Bastille Day in those parts of France that are liberated is marked by the settling of old scores against many Frenchmen and women who collaborated with the Germans.

By **15 July** it becomes clear that U-Boats pose no threat to the Allied supply ship lifeline across the Channel. The vessels of Admiral Dönitz are being sunk on an almost daily basis in the Atlantic, North Sea and Bay of Biscay.

On **16 July** US troops continue to inch their way towards St Lô and are within sight of the town's outskirts.

17 July: Field Marshal Erwin Rommel fell victim to the RAF today when a fighter flown by Squadron Leader J J Le Roux of 602 Squadron strafed the staff car carrying the legendary German commander near Bernay. The incident has left Rommel seriously injured and unconscious in hospital. Ironically, Rommel is fortunate to have been attacked by conventional weapons. Elsewhere in Normandy US aircraft drop napalm for the first time.

On **18 July** VHF radio equipment is introduced into Sherman tanks to provide a direct ground-air link between British armour and rocket-firing Typhoons of the Second Tactical Air Force.

19 July: In London it's estimated that so far 200,000 homes have been damaged by the doodlebugs. Daring fighter pilots have been developing a technique for 'tipping' the doodlebugs off course. This involves the hazardous operation of diving down and alongside one of the pilotless rocket devices and then close enough to cause it to veer off through slipstream turbulence.

Hitler survives an assassination attempt today **(20 July)** when a briefcase bomb explodes in his Rastenburg HQ during a briefing. A table shielded Hitler from the full force of the blast.

21 July: In Italy some 100,000 troops are being pulled out of the front line and sent back to Naples in preparation for the invasion of Southern France.

Today in the South Pacific **(22 July)** US marines reinforce their beachheads on Guam following yesterday's initial landings.

23 July: General Henry Crerar's First Canadian Army becomes operational.

On **24 July** the Red Army is advancing into Poland. Yesterday the cities of Lublin and Pskov were captured. Today the Russians come across the first of Hitler's rumoured concentration camps and liberate the inmates.

25 July: In the Indian Ocean the British Eastern Fleet has been attacking Japanese installations at Sabang.

26 July: In Germany a massive hunt for the Hitler bomb plot conspirators and sympathisers is underway and some 7000 suspects have been rounded up by the Gestapo.

27 July: A succession of key positions held by the Germans are falling to the Soviets. Today Lwow and Bialystok are liberated.

28 July: Japanese defences at Ibdi on Biak, New Guinea, have been crushed by US forces.

By **29 July** the Russian advance into Poland has covered some 450 miles in just five weeks of combat. The Polish capital Warsaw lies just a few score miles from the Red Army tank spearheads.

30 July: US forces have landed on Middleburg and Amsterdam islands in the Far East.

31 July: US Naval commanders back General Douglas MacArthur's plan for the liberation of the Philippines as a priority rather than bypassing the islands and invading Formosa or Okinawa.

Smiles ahead!

...as the Allies advance in France

AUGUST 1944

BREAKOUT

At last a war of movement is open to the Allies in France. A stubborn Hitler fails to see the danger.

On 7 August 1944 the 117th Regiment of the 30th American Division near Mortain in the extreme west of Normandy, saw, clanking through the morning mist, the vague outlines of German tanks. They at once engaged the enemy with bazookas and 57mm guns but with limited effect. The panzers ground their way forward, the vanguard of some 400 others. On Hitler's personal orders the *Wehrmacht* was mounting a desperate counter-attack aimed at cutting off Patton's rampant Third Army, now charging into Britanny and beyond.

Mont St Michel, Normandy, in 1944 and as it is today.

With the situation critical by noon, the sun came to the aid of the Allies. As the last of the mist burnt off, British Typhoons of the Second Tactical Air Force appeared overhead. Between 12.30 hours and dusk they flew 294 sorties and knocked the stuffing out of the German armour. 'Suddenly the fighter bombers swooped out of the sky' reported panzer commander General von Luttwitz later, 'they came down in hundreds, firing their rockets at concentrated tanks and vehicles. We could do nothing against

them and could make no further progress. By 9 August, the Division was back where it started, having lost 30 tanks and 800 men.'

It was a similar story for all the German units involved in the counterattack. Five years later the *Wehrmacht's* General Speidel stated: 'The armoured operation was completely wrecked exclusively by the Allied air forces, supported by a highly trained ground wireless organisation.' There's a measure of truth in Speidel's words but they do seem today to be largely grounded in a desire to blame the *Wehrmacht's* reverse on circumstances beyond their control. In other words, Allied soldiers had nothing to do with the defeat of the German Army - it was all down to the dreaded *jabos*, the fighter-bombers.

On the same day that the Mortain attack was blunted, American tanks were in Le Mans. Back in Normandy, General Pat Crerar's Canadians were moving slowly on Falaise which they reached and cleared by 17 August despite a bloody check north of the River Laison. Meanwhile, General Omar Bradley's US forces had turned north. In consequence a pocket had been formed of which the northern side, ending in Falaise, was held by the British and Canadians, and the southern, ending at Argentan, by the Americans.

In the pocket were the remnants of 16 German divisions, including nine panzer divisions. Not until 13 August had Hitler given permission for them to retreat across the River Seine. By then for most it was already far too late to escape. Soon the mouth of the pocket was just 25 miles wide and shrinking almost by the hour.

Fierce action near Chamois

Those outside the pocket were intent on headlong retreat while the Germans caught inside seemed made of sterner stuff. They could have surrendered but instead fought on. On 18 August a fierce action developed near Chamois - a place swiftly dubbed 'Shambles' by the Tommies - when the Germans brought up their few fresh troops in a bid to allow the remaining panzers to escape. Around 48 hours later the Polish Armoured Brigade found itself under pressure from an encircled enemy tank force greater in numbers than themselves. Timely air support decided the issue.

Air Marshal Sir Arthur Coningham's team had brought the air force to the highest pitch. From dusty air strips just a few miles from the Normandy shores the Typhoons and Spitfires with their eager pilots went about their deadly business. No doubt Hitler failed to appreciate the irony that what he had begun in crowing triumph in Warsaw and Rotterdam back in 1939-40 was now being visited on his *Wehrmacht* many times over in this little corner of Normandy.

The retreating Germans found themselves trapped in a scene from Dante's *Inferno*. In vain they took to the woods. These became death traps into which bombs, rockets and shells were poured. 'When an air attack developed' recounted a French farmer, caught in the maelstrom, 'and it seemed to me that there was one every half hour at least, the Germans would run from their vehicles looking for any kind of cover to escape the eyes of the pilots. The rockets coming from the British fighters looked from the ground as though shooting stars were rushing upon the earth. Any vehicle hit burst into instant flame.'

Doors of vehicles removed

'In order to leave their vehicles as quickly as possible, the German soldiers had removed the doors and one of their number always lay on one of the front mudguards looking upwards and scanning the sky.'

Away from the main road there were many deep-cut lanes. They remain today where great stretches of beeches and other trees form funnels of green overhead. In the summer of 1944 the Germans attempted to hide beneath these same canopies of foliage, to little avail. The slightest glint of metal glimpsed through a vehicle's additional camouflage of fresh-cut branches would bring down death and destruction from above.

Right: The statue of William the Conqueror in Falaise pictured today and (below) with two British soldiers in front of it in 1944.

Frank Wootton's famous painting of the carnage wrought by Typhoons in the Falaise Gap is reproduced on page 202 of this book.

When it was all over, a witness who toured the Pocket wrote: 'I soon abandoned my jeep for it was impossible to make progress on the secondary roads. Where the retreating Germans had been caught in the open, they lay in irregular swathes mostly in shallow ditches. Their transport was mixed. Cars of every description, many of them Citroens, Renaults and other French makes, strewed the fields, mingled with horses dead in the shafts of stolen carts.

'I noticed one modern limousine painted with the stippled green and brown camouflage effected by the Germans. It contained on the back seat a colonel and his smartly dressed mistress. Each had been shot through the chest with cannon shells. At the entrance to the next leafy lane a tank, its gun pointing skywards, straddled the road. From the turret hung a dead German.

'In the sunken lane under the semi-darkness of the arching trees in full August leaf the picture of destruction was complete and terrible to the last detail. It was obvious what had happened. Typhoons had spotted the column and destroyed the leading and end vehicles, in this case two armoured cars. They had then passed up and down the lane using rockets and cannons. The vehicles were jammed bumper to bumper and each bore the signature of the Second Tactical Air Force - a gaping hole in side or turret. Grey-clad, dust-powdered bodies were sprawled everywhere. I gave up trying to walk over this mile of utter destruction and made a wide detour only to find another lane equally impassable.'

On the original *Operation Overlord* timetable, Paris was to be liberated well over four months after D-Day. Now, suddenly, Allied advances of breathtaking magnitude looked imminent. Paris? Brussels? The borders of the Reich itself? Nothing seemed impossible. 'The Great Swan' was taking flight.

Normandy

Man and beast get a respite from the fighting in Normandy in August 1944. The photograph above shows cows ambling leisurely past a British field gun on their way to the milking shed. Thousands of farm animals died in the fighting but the plentiful fresh milk was appreciated by the Allied and German forces.
In the photograph below, after taking a shower, British soldiers line up for an issue of fresh underwear from a mobile laundry. The sign in the foreground reads: 'Brighton. Grand August by the sea. Bank Holiday afternoon. Baths will be free. Bring your tanks and bulldozers.'

...in the Summer of '44

THE SECOND D-DAY
INVASION OF THE SOUTH OF FRANCE

The Mediterranean coast of France was a popular posting for the men of the Wehrmacht. Even in early August 1944 it was a world away from the grim realities of war in Italy, on the Eastern Front and in Northern France, although the 250,000 men of the German 19th Army surely knew their enemy must one day come their way.

Yet if Winston Churchill could have had his way that day would have been put off for quite some time. The British premier wanted the husbanded forces in the Mediterranean to strike instead in the Balkans in a campaign that might have seen the Western Allies first into the capitals of countries like Austria and Hungary before the Red Army arrived to impose Stalin's will.

At this time the Americans were far less suspicious of Russian intentions than were the British. Dismissive of Churchill's 'adventurism', they, along with General de Gaulle and his resurgent French forces, backed *Operation Anvil*, the southern arm of a giant pincer movement to crush the Nazi forces in France.

Out of the darkness

The US view prevailed. So it was that two months and nine days after the Normandy landings came the invasion of the South of France (with a change of codename to *Operation Dragoon*) on Tuesday 15 August 1944. Out of the darkness of a warm Mediterranean night steamed 250 fighting ships (including many Royal Navy vessels such as *HMS Black Prince* and *HMS Ajax*) escorting 1000 transport vessels carrying close to 300,000 Allied soldiers, mainly Americans but also French, Canadian and British. Thousands more men floated down by parachute or were glider-borne to land amidst the fields and vineyards of Provence and the Côte d'Azur.

The main landings were concentrated on the coast between Cannes and Hyeres with the normally quiet fishing port of St Tropez being right in the centre of the action. The light German defences along the resort's now famous Pampelonne and Tahiti beaches and those further west at Cavalaire were softened up by naval gunfire before a phalanx of landing craft and amphibious DUKWs brought the fighting men ashore. Progress was swift in most places; only at Frejus and St Raphael did the Germans put up a stubborn but ultimately futile fight.

A section of a 1947 Michelin Map depicting the landings in the South of France is reproduced below. In the picture above note the St Raphael town sign. The resort of Croix Valmer featured in the plaque (below left) is just north of Cavalaire at the bottom of the map.

Shower of grenades

The defenders were in the main a ragbag army. As in Normandy, many were volunteers from places like Armenia, Georgia and the Ukraine, all at one time glad to be freed from Stalin's tyranny but now finding themselves subject to the whim of another dictator - and worse, expected to fight for a country that was clearly losing the war. The understrength 11th Panzer Division was the only tank force still in the south. But it was in the wrong place around Albi and Languedoc and also came under Hitler's private control.

SUR CETTE PLAGE
LE 15 AOUT 1944 A 6 H^{RES}
DEBARQUERENT LES ARMEES
ALLIEES LIBERATRICES QUI
DELIVRERENT CROIX VALMER

"Aboard *HMS Kimberley* as she closed in on the South of France coast that morning was Winston Churchill, seeing for himself how the invasion fared..."

There were some tragedies. A group of French African Commandos found themselves at the foot of the 350 feet high cliffs of Cap Negre which was topped by a German strongpoint. Sentries spotted their assailants and broke up the attack with a shower of grenades and bullets before it could even get started. Another 700 French Commandos landed to block the highway between Cavalaire and Le Lavandou. Others attacked pillboxes at Rayol and La Canadel.

Douglas Fairbanks Jr's war

Hollywood screen star Lt Commander Douglas Fairbanks Jr led a diversionary attack near Cannes to the east of the real invasion zone where the British gunboats *Aphis* and *Scarab* went close inshore to lob shells at the coastal highway.

Large numbers of the 5000 paratroopers involved landed around Le Muy and Draguignan amidst an eerie low-lying fog covering the valleys and plains; hills and even some houses protruded through the murk. Others were scattered all over the hills of the Maures and Esterel ranges but sowed chaos and confusion in the enemy. At 5.10am a substantial detachment of the British Second Independent Parachute Brigade touched down in the hills of Le Rouet. Eighty of them missed the target but nevertheless managed to destroy a German motorised column with the aid of bazookas and light weapons.

Aboard *HMS Kimberley* as she closed in on the French coast that morning was Winston Churchill, seeing for himself how the invasion fared.

Jaque Robichon's excellent book, *The Second D-Day*, (first published in the UK by Arthur Barker in 1969) tells a story which echoes the old joke about one Scotsman being worth 10 of any other nation's soldiers. He recounts how a jeepload of seven Scots turned up in the nick of time to ambush a German column of reinforcements on the road between Callas and Le Muy. Stripped to the waist in the searing heat of a Provencal August, the Scots blasted away with sten guns and killed 60 of the enemy before piling back into their vehicle and driving off. The whole scene was witnessed by a French farmer. He had his home burnt down in retaliation and livestock slaughtered but he did, at least, live to tell the tale.

St Tropez liberated

Apart from the odd sniper, St Tropez was liberated by late afternoon with the aid of the local French Resistance. The nearby hilltop towns of Gassin and Ramatuelle were also captured. It was an unequal battle. Aix-en-Provence fell on 21 August and three days later the Allies were as far north as Grenoble in the French Alps. Marseille and Toulon surrendered on 28 August. With the whole of the South of France clear of the enemy, the Allies set off in pursuit of the fleeing Germans as they retreated up the Rhone Valley, past Lyon.

Background illustration: Allied warships in St Tropez harbour fire at Luftwaffe raiders shortly after the town was liberated.
Inset: A US soldier standing on the deck of a French warship that had been scuttled in Toulon harbour in November 1942 following the German takeover of the previously Vichy controlled South of France.

NAPOLEON'S BIRTHDAY!

15 August

Was it coincidence that 15 August was also Napoleon's birthday? The French Maquis obviously knew it - their local codename for the landings was that of France's most famous leader. The South of France was where Napoleon came ashore from exile in 1815. Winding northwards through the mountains lies the famous Route Napoleon, passing through Grasse, Sisteron and Gap on the road taken by his fast-growing army which would eventually enter Paris in triumph. In 1944 Allied troops followed north in Napoleon's footsteps. We wonder if patriotic Frenchmen six decades ago would have appreciated the irony in Mr Bonaparte's fate - a crushing defeat at Waterloo by a combined army of British, Belgians and ... Prussians!

St Tropez AT WAR

Commander Stanley A Nettle was a Royal Navy Beachmaster for Delta Force during the invasion of Southern France. He landed on 15 August 1944 on Pampelonne beach to the west of St Tropez. This is his story.

My original role in *Operation Dragoon* was a planning one as I was Assistant Staff Officer, Operations, at GHQ in Italy. The ships were already in their loading ports when I was told I was to go with them as a Beachmaster. The British transport vessels involved in the landings comprised 17 troop carriers and 42 store ships. I was on board the *Dunera*, a passenger ship with landing craft slung from stem to stern on both sides. We were to land soon after H-Hour on D-Day itself and quickly learnt that there were 12 hospital ships also detailed to rendezvous in the target area, ready to be called forward as necessary. Perhaps it was the knowledge of those hospital ships that made me suddenly very much aware of my white naval cap cover. I thought it would make a tempting target for snipers and so, just before arrival off the coast, I dyed it with the aid of a cup of coffee!

Orange flashes

We were lying quite close to the beach and just before dawn the bombardment of the coast from the warships began. It was a most impressive spectacle to see the orange flashes of the naval guns, feel the swoosh of the shells as they passed overhead and then to see and hear the crash as they exploded on the beaches and beyond. We prayed that none would fall short.

The LCAs (Landing Craft Assault) had been lowered and then the first wave went ashore to clear any minefields and place white tapes to show the safe passages. Once ashore, I hitched a lift to St Tropez in a jeep with an American Lieutenant. On a country road en route there were half a dozen soldiers lying in a ditch. The Lieutenant stopped and asked what was going on. 'There's snipers in them there trees, Sir' said one of them in a real Southern accent. On hearing this the Lieutenant shouted, 'Then what are we waiting for? Get goin'!' and we rushed off. I was glad about my inconspicuous coffee-dyed hat.

I joined up with fellow staff at our HQ and we were allotted an empty farmhouse as a Mess. Next day we started organising the ships for discharge over the beaches according to requirements for the different sorts of cargo. My sector was between St Tropez and St Raphael and I had to thumb my way out to the ships in DUKWs or landing craft. Then the French requisitioned some fishing boats for us to use as boarding vessels which made things a lot easier.

Cross of Lorraine

In 1940 after Dunkirk I had signed up as a supporter of General de Gaulle's Free French Forces and I wore the Free French brooch with the Cross of Lorraine on the lapel of my uniform. This made quite a difference when I met the Mayor of St Tropez, Monsieur Rene Girard. A leader of the local Resistance force, he had been advised in advance of the landings by messengers landed from a submarine. He and his men of the FFI (*Forces Francaises de l'Interieur*) with their armbands and assorted weaponry were out from 4am on D-Day to warn the Allies of German concentrations and any mined roads.

His daughter, Mimi, a charming girl, had been one of the couriers passing messages to the different Resistance cells. Messages were put inside the tyre of her bicycle which she then rode to a prearranged spot in a village where she would leave it whilst she visited someone or called into the shops. In the meantime a Resistance man would take her bicycle, remove the message and insert a response before returning it. Later, Mimi would simply ride it home.

The German troops in this area had been a mixture of admin units and soldiers on leave from the Normandy Front for rest and recuperation. This, together with the information from the Resistance forces, made the Allied advance quicker in my sector than in other parts of the coast. Intelligence passed on by the FFI not only included the locations of fighting troops, but also pinpointed innocent looking houses near main roads which had been turned into well-defended strongholds.

Snipers in St Tropez

Even though St Tropez was captured quite quickly, there were snipers still around and it was dangerous to be alone in the town, particularly at night. The speed of our advance also required us to change the priority of discharge from the ships to the beaches. Now, instead of ammunition, they needed fuel for the vehicles to maintain the chase.

Above: An American paratrooper pictured with St Tropez Resistance leader Marc Rainaut. The girl in the centre, Mademoiselle Nicola Celebonovitch, warned the Americans of the location of a group of Germans waiting to ambush them.

I went out to one ship loaded with ammunition to tell him to move further out to sea as we didn't need his cargo straight away. The Captain was more than a little upset and said he wanted his cargo discharged at once as it was unsafe. They had loaded it in Naples without sealing the bulkhead between No 3 hold and the engine room. He'd protested, but had got the standard reply of 'don't you know there's a war on!'. I finally persuaded him to anchor further offshore and I brought in the ships with the fuel. There were German air raids mainly at night and although some ships were hit, none were sunk.

Alpha Beach closed at D+25, but my beach at St Tropez and the others to the east stayed 'in business' until Marseilles was captured. Soon after this I learned that I had been promoted to Lieutenant Commander. As the pressure eased in Marseilles, the Resistance took their revenge on those deemed to have collaborated with the Nazis. Men simply disappeared from circulation. Women were sat in a chair in a public place surrounded by armed Resistance fighters while they had their heads shaved and not too gently either.

Our landing at Pampelonne had been relatively quiet and it was not until later that we heard of the intense fighting and loss of life at the landing places to the east of us where navigational errors in the dark put some of our Allies on to heavily defended points. Altogether though, *Dragoon* was a satisfactory effort leading to the army from the Mediterranean being able to join up with the forces from Northern France in a very short space of time.

THE LIFE-LINE IS FIRM

After this superb work of art by Charles Wood was refined from the original reproduced here, it became a window poster from 1942 onwards. The message supported the vital role of Britain's Merchant Navy. A coxswain mans the ship's wheel while an officer with binoculars keeps watch.

RED DUSTER

'Records indicate that by the end of the Second World War some 30,248 British merchant seamen had lost their lives, 4707 were injured, 5720 had been taken as Prisoners of War and 530 had been declared missing. These men, or their bereaved dependents, would not be entitled to any compensation, nor would they receive a pension. Merchant seamen were "civilians" according to the War Ministry.'

Thus reads the preface to a 2004 book of wartime memoirs by Ron Tubb - *Red Duster Recollections - A Merchant Seaman's Experiences in World War II* (Woodfield Publishing).

Dedicated to Ron's many training school colleagues and shipmates who lost their lives in the service of their country, here is a fascinating story of an aspect of the war little has been written about.

Born in Bridgend in 1916, the sea was very much Ron's destiny as soon as he enrolled at a Nautical Training School at the age of 12. Ron's experience of war included witnessing the Liverpool Blitz, the U-Boat menace and attacks at sea by enemy aircraft. By 1942 he had gained his Master Mariner's Certificate and subsequently served on troop ships and tankers. He sailed to Australia and the Far East, North America and the Caribbean, gradually rising in rank along the way.

On one crossing of the Atlantic he recalls his convoy being three days in dense fog: 'Even though ships were within a couple of cables of each other, none could be seen. At one point a passenger liner was on our port side and we could hear children laughing and shouting, but the liner was invisible. Eventually we came out of the fog at an angle and saw ship after ship eerily emerging. The fog bank resembled a vertical wall.'

In the spirit of *Sixty Years On* we reprint here an extract from the book that covers a period in 1944, the year in which Ron's war service ended on health grounds.

Curacao diesel

'Promoted to First Officer, in March 1944 I signed on the *MV Dipladon*, sailing for the West Indies, to load diesel in Curacao. We

Above: French warships scuttled in Toulon harbour. Ron Tubb's merchantman tied up alongside one of these vessels in the summer of 1944.

were then ordered to proceed to the Mediterranean to await further orders. As Gibraltar was full of naval ships, we anchored off Oran in North Africa where we waited for a few days before proceeding to Marseille to discharge part of our cargo of diesel and wait again for orders. From information received on the wireless, it was evident that the Allies were liberating the South of France, but encountering stiff resistance.

'At Toulon, we tied up alongside a French warship, one of many scuttled earlier in the war so that the Germans could not use them. I was told that some German forces had been cut off and trapped on Toulon Island and a fierce battle had ensued with Senegalese troops, under French command. No Germans had survived to leave the island.

'We managed to connect a pipeline over the warships which in turn connected to another line leading into a tunnel. I went ashore, to find that the area was honeycombed with tunnels and all oil tanks were housed underground. In one tunnel there were four large, high-speed diesel engines, the type used in German E-Boats: all booby trapped. One had to tread very gingerly, as there were piles of ammunition and guns everywhere and signs warning against mines.

Bomb blast

'We next proceeded along the South Coast of France, oiling various British and American men-of-war, until we received a warning of enemy aircraft. I remember we sighted some planes, but recall nothing that happened afterwards. I must have lost consciousness for a while and was subsequently told that there had been a massive bomb blast.

'Having discharged all our cargo we headed back across the Atlantic without escort. I became unwell during this passage with the recurrence of a previous medical problem. When we arrived at Galveston, Texas, I was told that I needed surgery. My wife was asked whether she would agree to my entering hospital in America, or whether I should be brought home. Without any hesitation, Gwynneth said, "Bring him home".

'My journey homeward was by Pullman to New York where I joined the *MV Amastra*, as acting Master. Our voyage was without incident and we arrived safely in Liverpool. I soon underwent an operation in Bridgend Hospital and, after three months convalescence, was told to attend the Ministry of Transport doctor. After he'd looked at me, then at my history, he stated that he would not recommend me for further sea duties. This was devastating news.'

*Post-war Ron Tubb had a long career with the Inland Revenue. His beloved wife Gwynneth passed away in 1993. Ron remains active today, being computer-literate and studying French 'in order to be able to speak it more fluently on my trips there.' The final sentence of Ron's book reads, 'All in all I am glad to say that I have had, and am still having, a very good life.'

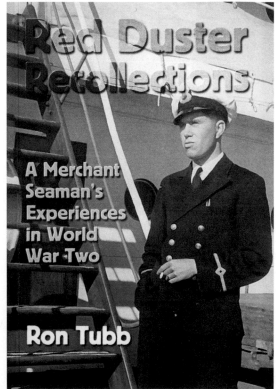

LIBERATION
of Paris

As the sultry days of August came to the French capital, all Parisians were aware that the Germans were losing the fight in Normandy. Convoys of ambulances full of Wehrmacht wounded flowed over the Seine bridges and through the city along with trucks towing artillery pieces and hundreds of horse-drawn vehicles and carts. It was in stark contrast to the weeks following D-Day when an endless stream of reinforcements passed through in the opposite direction heading for the '*Zur Normandie Front*'.

The Allies spared the city centre from bombing. Hitler had other plans. His orders to the Commandant of Gros-Paris, General Dietrich von Choltitz, were unequivocal: 'Paris must not fall to the enemy - or the enemy must find it reduced to rubble.'

On 10 August, railway workers came out on a patriotic strike. Three days later the nervous Germans began disarming the city's 20,000 policemen. Posters urging insurrection began to appear on walls. The Germans countered with stickers of their own: 'Achtung! Be warned. The fate of Paris is in your hands.'

Patriotic uprising

Despite the strong words, the German response was muted by their ruthless standards. For one thing, they were anxious to keep the Paris bridges open and intact for their retreating forces and for another, von Choltitz seemed to be wavering in the face of orders to destroy such a beautiful city. The Swedish Consul, Raoul Nordling, was also making strenuous efforts to broker a truce.

On 19 August a call went out for all male Parisians between 18 and 55 to take up arms. Incredibly, many Germans were taken by surprise as Wehrmacht transport was stopped and weapons seized. Public buildings were occupied by the Resistance and more and more policemen cast their lot with the Free French. The Tricolore was hoisted over the Prefecture near Notre Dame and people sang *The Marseillaise*. For the first time in the history of Paris - a city famous for popular uprisings - police and insurgents found themselves fighting on the same side.

Resistance newspapers were published openly on 21 August with big bold headlines urging 'Mort aux Boches et aux Traitres'. Even so, the Germans in the main stayed in their strongpoints and it was clear to rebel leaders that the Liberation of Paris needed help from outside.

Messages were sent to the Allies pleading for intervention. Eisenhower and his commanders had intended bypassing the city but now minds were changed and Maj-Gen Philippe Leclerc's Free French 2nd Armoured Division with 200 tanks and 15,000 men began the race to Paris. In just 40 hours the huge motorised column covered 150 miles. On the evening of 24 August the first armoured vehicles nosed through the Porte d'Orleans and made their way to the Place de l'Hotel de Ville.

Death and gunpowder

SS men in the Luxembourg Garden put up the fiercest resistance but by the afternoon of 25 August the Germans were surrendering in large numbers to the regular French troops rather than the Resistance who had many a score to settle. Von Choltitz kept his dignity and gave up after a two-hour siege of his Hotel Meurice HQ. He would tell his captors that he'd lost faith in the Nazi system since the attempt, albeit failed, on Hitler's life on 20 June.

The fight for Paris cost Leclerc 901 dead while the German losses were estimated at around 2000. In addition some 1000 insurgents and 600 non-combatant Parisians died.

Gilles Perrault was a youngster in Paris during those heady August days of 1944. He remembers: 'We had lumps in our throats as we contemplated the tank drivers who smiled at our show of feeling. Then their radios crackled and we were calmly advised to move away a little by a tank commander. Ten seconds later he opened fire on a German armoured car that loomed up in front of us. It managed to get away, leaving a trail of blood. That night Paris smelled of death and gunpowder. Four years and 46 days had gone by since the Germans had marched into the city.'

On 26 August Perrault, part of an enormous crowd, watched de Gaulle's triumphant parade: 'We were drunk with emotion, drowning in happiness...Night fell and I took a walk along the banks of the Seine under the Tuileries where Leclerc's troops were bivouacked, and heard a strange refrain. The melody was interwoven with a profusion of long sighs, brief moanings and stifled cries. It took me a little while to understand that hundreds of men and women were up there in bed together. Transfixed with near-religious feeling, I spent a long moment there listening to Paris make love.'

Top Left: A tank from the Free French forces under General Leclerc's command pictured outside Notre Dame.

Above: The present-day view of Paris from the top of the famous church.

1 August: Kovno in Lithuania has been taken by the Russians, effectively isolating the Baltic States from East Prussia. Evacuation by sea and air is the only escape route open to Germans trapped in the north.

2 August: Half of the island of Guam has now been captured by US forces. Tinian in the Marianas has also been taken at a cost of 394 American dead and 1961 wounded.

In the English Channel mini-submarines piloted by German volunteers are being used against the invasion fleet off the Normandy coast. Called *Marders,* the craft weigh some three tons, have a top speed of less than three knots and carry a single torpedo slung below the hull. Attempts to use them at Anzio earlier in the year ended in failure but today (**3 August**) a success is recorded when the destroyer *HMS Quorn* is hit and sunk.

On **4 August** in Amsterdam, following a tip-off Gestapo agents raid a house and arrest the Frank family who have been hiding in an attic since 1942. The Jewish family includes 14-year-old Anne who has been keeping a diary of her thoughts and experiences.

5 August: In Australia over 1000 Japanese POWs have staged a mass breakout at Cowra camp just before dawn. Wielding improvised weapons, they rushed the compound wire. Three guards were killed but the Japanese lost 234 killed and 108 wounded. Over 300 prisoners succeeded in escaping and a big effort is being mounted to capture them.

South African troops entered Florence today after the retreating Germans declared it an 'open city'.

6 August: Montgomery issues orders for the destruction of the German Army west of the Seine and north of the Loire. Field Marshal von Kluge opens a German counter-attack in the direction of Avranches, Normandy.

7 August: Eisenhower transfers his headquarters from London to Granville, France.

8 August sees the climax of an eight-week struggle by the Japanese to capture the important rail junction at Hengyang, China.

9 August: St Malo and Angers are liberated as the Allies spread out regardless of the threat posed by von Kluge's counter-attack in their rear. Meanwhile the Free French under de Gaulle have declared the Vichy Government null and void in a

The Germans tried to recruit Dutchmen in Occupied Holland into their SS forces. The poster on the right says that the fight is against Bolshevism. Though some Dutch did join up many, many more fought with the Allies. The poster below was distributed in Britain and praised the contribution of the Dutch naval forces.

> " In Australia 234 Japanese POWs are killed when over 1000 of them stage a mass break-out from their prison camp at Cowra. "

proclamation issued from Algiers.

10 August: In Paris rail workers have gone on strike at the urging of communist Resistance leaders. The effect is one of almost total paralysis of the rail network. Hitler is determined that the city should not be spared destruction in the way Rome was.

11 August: The Germans are sending heavily armed units into the Polish capital, Warsaw, to crush an insurrection by the lightly armed men and women of the Home Army.

By **12 August** Patton's Third Army has captured Le Mans and Alencon and bottled up German garrisons in the Brittany ports of Brest, Lorient and St Nazaire.

On **13 August** the American XV Corps halts at Argentan and waits for the Canadian push southwards to start. The area around Falaise is the centre of a pocket through which runs the only escape route for a large number of German units who were previously containing the Allied bridgehead.

The following day (**14 August**) sees the French police join the strikes now crippling Paris. With the Allies clearly winning the police have decided to throw their lot in with the Resistance.

15 August: The French Riviera is the scene of 'The Second D-Day' today when *Operation Dragoon* commences. Troops of

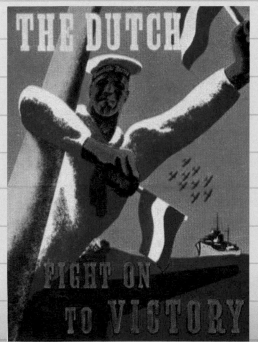

THE DUTCH
FIGHT ON TO VICTORY

NEDERLANDERS
VOOR UW EER EN GEWETEN OP ! - TEGEN HET BOLSJEWISME
DE WAFFEN ⚡⚡ ROEPT U !

WAR DIARY
August 1944

the US Seventh Army and French Army B storm ashore on beaches between Cannes and Cavalaire. A large naval force backed up the landings with a terrific barrage aimed at German gun emplacements. Paratroopers have been dropped behind the coast as far inland as Draguignan.

16 August: Resistance groups in the Savoy region have launched a general uprising in support of the landings in the South of France. American and Free French forces are making rapid progress in all directions under clear blue August skies.

On **17 August** the Canadian's new push results in the capture of Falaise. The Germans are in a trap - the 'Falaise Pocket' - and there is just one route of escape. Roads congested with vehicles, horse-drawn carts, tanks and men present easy targets for the 'cab ranks' of Typhoons in the Normandy skies.

18 August: The Red Army reaches the border of the Fatherland in East Prussia.

19 August: In Paris the prospect of liberation is causing growing excitement. At 7am this morning a large force of gendarmes took control of the Prefecture of Police and fought off a German counter-attack. Paris commander General von Choltitz has been ordered to turn the city into a 'field of ruins' by Hitler.

20 August: Japanese resistance ends on the island of Biak, New Guinea. The US has suffered 2550 casualties whilst the enemy dead are estimated at 4700.

21 August: The Battle of Normandy is almost at an end with the sealing of the Falaise Pocket today. Although 30,000 of the enemy are thought to have escaped across the Seine at least 50,000 Germans have been captured. The air power of the Allies was a key factor in victory. It's now all-out for Paris where the Resistance and police are leading a popular uprising.

22 August: Allied forces from Southern France have advanced northwards through the Maritime Alps against minimal German resistance and have now entered Grenoble unopposed.

23 August: The Battle of the Flying Bombs is being won but at a terrible price. A single V1 impact in East Barnet today kills 211 civilians.

24 August: France rejoices as Sherman tanks and mobile units of General Leclerc's 2nd Armoured Division roll into Paris this evening, to be greeted by delirious crowds. De Gaulle's decision to send Leclerc's forces in against the advice of Eisenhower is about to pay off.

The following day **(25 August)** Paris is officially liberated when General Choltitz surrenders. Today also sees Roumania quit the Axis and the King's new Government declare war on Germany.

26 August: In Southern France, Marseille and Toulon continue to hold out but the Germans have been chased out of Avignon and now the Allies are set for a swift advance up the Rhône valley.

27 August: RAF Bomber Command undertake their first major daylight raid over Germany since August 1941. The synthetic oil refinery at Meerbeck near Homberg is the target of 243 assorted Halifaxes, Lancasters and Mosquitos. The Nazi war machine is running out of fuel - the Luftwaffe alone requires 160,000 tons of aviation fuel each month but is lucky to receive 10,000 tons these days.

28 August: Marseille surrenders to Free French forces following the fall of Toulon yesterday. In the north Rheims and Soissons have been liberated by US forces.

29 August: Partisans in Slovakia have issued a general call to arms and today declared the formation of a free Czechoslovak republic. Great swathes of Occupied Europe are rising up against the Germans.

On **30 August** in Northern Italy the British V and Canadian I Corp crossed the Foglia river this morning to begin their attack on the Gothic Line. The Russians have captured the Rumanian oilfields at Ploesti to deny the Germans their major source of oil.

31 August: Allied spearheads and Resistance fighters capture all the bridges over the Somme. The Rumanian capital falls to the Russians.

The Allied supply chain via Normandy is too long to permit offensive operations for all units and Eisenhower wants to keep the momentum of Patton's Third Army thrust going at all costs. Montgomery favours a single concentrated push on the left through Belgium and Holland, across the Rhine and into the Ruhr, Germany's industrial heart. Monty believes his plan could end the war before Christmas.

Above: Allied artillery on the move as the breakout gathers pace. As can be seen from the graveyard, many Germans will never leave Normandy.

EPIC
OF THE
SKY
TROOPS

SEPTEMBER 1944

ROCKET SCIENCE

Above: A V2 prepared for launch. There was no defence against these rockets which fell at supersonic speed from the edge of space. The silhouettes on the left are taken from an amazing photograph of a Spitfire flying alongside a Doodlebug in an attempt to deflect the flying bomb off course.

More of your memories of the 'Doodlebug Summer' of 1944, compiled by Martin Barton-Smith, himself a London schoolboy at the time. This second instalment includes eye-witness accounts of the coming of the V2 rockets.

John Cross from Newmarket recalls: 'One night we heard this unusual sounding engine which suddenly stopped. I looked out of the window, and this 'thing' went down the middle of the road somehow missing the houses. I believe it hit our school because I only had lessons for one afternoon a week after that in somebody's front room. Another time I was talking to a neighbour when we heard two cut out together; one landed in playing fields 200 yards away, but we lost sight of the other.

A neighbour, Mr Towner, jumped into his fish pond and I hid behind our dustbins! Sirens often didn't sound for Doodlebugs and I used to stand on top of the Anderson Shelter and shout a warning to the neighbours if I heard one cut out.'

Obviously, many of our recollections come from those who were only schoolchildren or teenagers in 1944. David Hollamby from St Leonards-on-Sea remembers staying with his grandparents in Hastings, right in 'Doodlebug Alley': 'My grandfather would take me upstairs into his bedroom from where we could see these evil machines, with their tails ablaze, soaring directly over the house. I had no concept of the fact that immediately their engines stopped they fell to earth with loud explosions, doing untold damage. To minimise the damage to my young mind, my grandfather told me they were fireworks going off.'

Tears at a wedding

John Newcomb from Orpington also recalls the first night of the flying bombs: 'A totally different sound emanated from their crude jet engines. In the morning we could see the things clearly and the word soon got around - 'only duck if the engine cuts out' became the watchwords. And then came the V2s, one fell a few miles away and we found a long length of thin, oily, wire on the driveway. It came in very useful for the raspberry plants.'

A R Coulter from Bury St Edmunds was awaiting the opportunity to get married in 1944. As an army signals analyst, he was still based in England passing intelligence to Bletchley Park: 'Fortunately I was still around on 17 June, so I set off in the OC's car to catch a train to Liverpool Street. Unfortunately the first Doodlebug to reach London had struck the rail bridge at Bow so I only just managed to make the church by the deadline of 2pm. My kid sister got blast concussion from the same bomb, so we had a smiling bridesmaid apologising for her uncontrolled constant tears.'

Although the bombs themselves destroyed hundreds of houses and other buildings, there were other hazards. Bill Beazley from Bexley Heath was a 16-year-old trainee Post Office engineer: 'Barrage balloons sometimes needed to be lowered very quickly. If a storm developed, lightning could strike one balloon and travel to adjacent ones, bringing the whole lot down. Falling cables could drape across high voltage power lines, which in turn could fuse telephone lines into people's homes. I was working on a control box at Longfield Hill and a wheatfield lay several feet lower by the pavement. A Doodlebug came over and I knew there were several balloon sites in the vicinity. I dived into the field in case the bomb hit a cable. It sailed through them and I am sorry to say I waved it on its way!'

Costly tactic

The main onslaught of the V1s lasted approximately 80 days during which time fighter aircraft claimed 1850 (the New Zealand squadrons alone accounted for 249), AA fire and rockets 1878, and 232 fell to the barrage balloon defences. After the launch sites in the North of France and along the Belgium coast were overrun by the advancing Allies, the resourceful Germans continued the offensive with bombs launched from Heinkel 111 aircraft. This tactic proved to be too costly in aircraft and pilots and was soon abandoned.

A short campaign using long range V1s was mounted from 3 to 29 March 1945, but by this time the British defences had got their measure, and only 13 bombs succeeded in reaching London. It is not always realised that some 6500 bombs were launched against Allied controlled areas in Europe from October 1944 onwards. If these are added to the estimated 8000 launched against Britain, some idea can be gained of the huge effort put into the production and deployment of these weapons.

We have mentioned earlier the awesome power of the V2 weapon, and its virtually unannounced arrival. There was no defence against a rocket which travelled at Mach 3. However, our last eye-witness account is particularly intriguing. R F Payne of Shepperton writes: 'As a young lad in 1944 I can recall people talking in the summer about a rocket the Germans were supposedly developing. They said it was as tall as a telegraph pole and weighed 10 tons. At the time just another rumour going around. One bright evening in September, I was on Putney Common watching some lads playing football, when I noticed a puff of smoke high in the sky and from the smoke a vapour trail appeared at the end of which something like a needle was glinting in the sunlight. Just moments later a huge explosion shook the quiet of the evening. I had witnessed the first V2 to fall on this country. It landed on Chiswick. Thinking back, I might have been the only person to have witnessed it.'

The V1s and V2s proved to be a final gamble by Hitler to preserve his crumbling regime. There is no doubt that the V2s were technically very sophisticated and dangerous weapons. Ironically, when the war ended, many of the scientists involved were later to form the core of the American NASA space programme including the scientist Dr Werner von Braun.

THE GREAT SWAN

The very end of August and first week of September 1944 saw an Allied advance of astonishing rapidity across France and into Belgium. For a few euphoric days it seemed to the British and Canadians in Montgomery's 21st Army Group that the end of the war was in sight.

'The August battles (in Normandy) have done it,' stated one senior intelligence officer reporting at the time to General Eisenhower, 'and the enemy in the West has had it... The end of the war is within sight, almost within reach.'

The grim realisation imposed in the post-D-Day weeks of June and July, when the war in the Normandy hedgerows had settled into a deadly slogging match, was quickly changed into a mood of expectation for the Allies following the crushing defeat of the Germans at Falaise. Paris was liberated on 25 August; the city was at the centre of a broad front of advance by the US 12th Army Group under General Omar Bradley. His forces included Patton's Third Army. 'The man with the ball' - as Montgomery described him - was racing eastwards towards Metz and the Saar Valley.

On an 80-mile front spread in the direction of Paris from south of the Seine Estuary in the area of Honfleur and the present-day Pont de Normandie and Tancarville bridges, the British 21st Army Group was poised to set off in pursuit of the Germans. The latter had salvaged what they could from the battle at Falaise; it was estimated that some 20,000 troops, two dozen tanks and just 60 guns escaped across the Seine.

Over the Seine
Military historians still argue over the Allied strategy at this point in the war. Montgomery wanted an advance on a narrow front through Northern France and Belgium to be sustained all the way into Germany where a 'knock-out' blow would be delivered in the vital Ruhr industrial region. Eisenhower - conscious of the political requirement that the US forces too should play an offensive role - allowed a broad front policy to prevail. The repercussions of this on the rapidly extending supply lines would be felt all too soon. Losing the argument perhaps also influenced Monty to later push so hard for the Arnhem air landings, a high-risk operation of a kind anathema to his character. Some would claim that Britain's top general was determined to have his own way regardless of the changed circumstances.

Perhaps. But on 26 August 1944, when Sir Brian Horrocks took command, if anyone had

Above: After winning the grinding battle of attrition in the Normandy countryside in the summer of 1944, Montgomery was keen to pursue an attack on a narrow front parallel to the French and Belgium Channel coast with the aim of punching into the German heartland as quickly as possible.

told the men of the 21st Army Group's XXX Corps that within three weeks they would be on the Dutch border and little more than 30 miles from Germany, they would have laughed out loud. Then came the Great Swan.

For the men of the famous 11th Armoured 'Black Bull' Division, the chase began early on 28 August at Vernon where, a few days earlier, 43rd Division had forced a crossing to create a bridgehead on the north bank of the Seine. The tankmen and their supporting infantry had experienced a hard time in the grinding attrition of the Normandy battles but were now rejuvenated and ready to roll.

'We motored in blinding dust and crossed the Seine at Vernon over a Class 9 pontoon bridge in total darkness - a strange experience - and then wondered where the hell to go next,' wrote W Steele Brownlie, a Troop Leader with the 2nd Fife and Forfarshire Yeomanry, 'We passed two burning scout cars and then a burning Tiger before eventually we found the regimental harbour. Our orders were to move north at first light with all speed.'

By the second day the advance was gathering momentum with 3 RTR (Royal Tank Regiment) 'swanning' an amazing 60 miles northwards from Tilley. Pockets of German resistance at this stage proved troublesome in places but elsewhere the Allied tanks revelled in the open country, fairly belting along.

'Amiens tonight'
As dusk fell on the third day, 11th Armoured forward units were within 20 miles of Amiens, having been greeted by joyous local populations in towns and villages throughout the day. The only unhappy faces belonged to the collaborators who had failed to leave when the Germans quit - instances of summary justice were commonplace, often carried out in full view of the liberators.

'Drinks of all sorts were pressed on us' tankman Roland Jefferson recalled, 'The French called us Tommy and we realised that we were now into the battlezone of the First World War which our fathers had known so well. A common joke was: "Come away from her, she's probably your sister".'

11th Armoured commander, General 'Pip' Roberts, was told to seize the Somme bridges in Amiens in the course of a night dash. 'It was quite simple,' he recalled, 'Ike said to Monty "Amiens tonight"; Monty said to Bimbo (Dempsey) "Amiens tonight"; Bimbo said to Jorrocks (Horrocks)

"Amiens tonight" and Jorrocks said to 'Pip' Roberts "Amiens tonight"; and then the planning started.'

The subsequent daring attack started at 2300hrs in pouring rain. Occasional German vehicles joined the convoy in error and were despatched with thoroughness, although some tagged on oblivious and unobserved for quite a few miles. The Division's Shermans navigated in the main by simply following the dull red exhaust of the tank in front.

Amiens was approached just before dawn and much German vehicle movement throughout the town was observed. Civilians warned the British that around 5000 of the enemy were still around and lots of small individual actions ensued. A King Tiger and 15 ack-ack guns were destroyed in one battle and prisoners came in by the hundred. More importantly, the main bridge and a couple of smaller ones over the Somme were captured intact and the way ahead remained open.

Hail of flowers

Arras, Vimy and Lens were liberated and once more the tankmen were subjected to a hail of flowers, fruit, biscuits and assorted 'friendly' missiles - as the latter might include bottles of wine and beer, the wearing of steel helmets was a sound precaution! Greeting the Local Resistance could also be hazardous to health. The historian of the 23rd Hussars recorded how, 'They would advance in the most friendly manner to shake hands, while in the left hand a fully loaded rifle pointed at one's stomach. In their enthusiasm they were the most dangerous individuals we met.'

Many Germans were anxious to surrender. Patrick Delaforce tells the story of 'Ginger' Wilson, a young Lieutenant in the RAMC who was summoned by an excitable French farmer who asked him to sort out some Germans hiding in his haystacks. Despite being

technically non-combatants, Wilson and some of his men armed themselves and set off in pouring rain across the fields to a spot where eight sorry-looking members of the Wehrmacht were discovered, all of whom seemed relieved to be made prisoners.

'A cynical name for the RAMC,' writes Delaforce in his book *The Black Bull* (Alan Sutton Publishing, 1993), 'was Rob All My Comrades. On this occasion the enemy were relieved of a pair of jack-boots, a camera, a compass and a pair of scissors.'

For XXX Corps, the days of the Swan were unforgettable. It was a time when a tank or jeep taking a wrong turning might end the day being hailed as liberators by the occupants of a village or even a whole town. Girls would fling themselves at the soldiers, many obviously willing to consummate freedom with the ultimate act of joy. Following a sharp encounter with German 88s at Seclin, Black Bull tankmen relieved the enemy of a large stock of looted wine and spirits; the advance continued with crates of brandy or champagne stowed behind the turrets of the Shermans.

Target Antwerp

Roland Jefferson remembers passing four huge cemeteries from the 1914-1918 war - 'They all looked so neat and tidy even though they had been under German occupation for over four years. There was an air of stillness and reverence as we passed them'

By the fifth day of The Great Swan it became clear that the site of a British airborne drop on Tournai planned for 3 September was now actually behind the new Allied lines; accordingly the operation was cancelled. US troops moved into the area very early on this same day on the assumption that the British hadn't advanced as quickly as the Americans. In fact the Guards Armoured Division would be in

Brussels, 40 miles further on, at almost the exact same time!

The largest surrender of German troops also occurred on 3 September when 25,000 went 'in the bag' around the same Belgian town where, 30 years earlier, British Tommies were reported in their exhaustion to have seen the 'Guardian Angel of Mons.'

The 11th Armoured's progress in leaps and bounds led them to believe Brussels was their objective. Now they learnt that the fleshpots of the Belgian capital were the preserve of the rival Guards Armoured. They soberly contemplated their own target Antwerp, far more important in strategic terms than the Belgian capital, but ringed by forts all likely to be heavily defended.

Torture and interrogation

The columns raced over the border, the welcome as rapturous as ever. The flags changed from red, white and blue to the red, yellow and black of Belgium. Patrick Delaforce tells how at 3am on 4 September after an 87-mile surge forward, 2nd Fife and Forfarshire 'avoiding flying plums, jet-propelled apples and rocket-projected pears, reached Aalst, 20 miles north-west of Brussels. All the cafes were open and Corporal Vallance's Sherman had run out of petrol in the town square where he was observed to be getting on very well with the natives.'

The Germans were falling back but still found time for reprisals. Delaforce went through Breendonk, seven miles east of Malines. Here armed civilians begged him to have a look in a large sinister grey fortress. He discovered that 50 members of the Belgian White Army had been handed over to the Gestapo here for torture and interrogation. The bodies, the blood and the smell of horrible death were still all too real on the morning of 4 September.

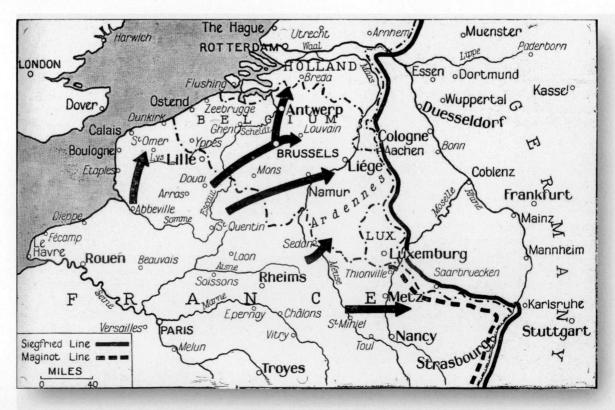

This contemporary map illustrates the directions of the Allied thrusts in September 1944. The Canadians came up the Channel coast whilst British spearheads can be seen liberating Brussels and Antwerp in the course of the 'The Great Swan'. The Americans and Free French forces fanned out across the rest of France and closed on the Siegfried Line beyond Liege, the Ardennes, Metz and Nancy. The Dutch city of Arnhem can be seen at the top of the map and it can be seen as a logical point of advance for the Allies seeking to enter the industrial centre of the Reich.

At about this same time the spearhead of the 11th Armoured Division was moving into Antwerp having made a fighting advance of 230 miles in the six days since crossing the Seine at Vernon. The city and environs were defended by 15,000 Germans widely scattered, poorly equipped and all shocked to find the Allies closing in so quickly. Even so, many were determined to mount a defence.

Major Noel Bell MC in his *Beaches to the Baltic* book recalls arriving in the city to the sound of rifle fire. 'Germans began throwing grenades at us from a window of a high building nearby. Then 20mm guns opened up and we knew we should have to fight for it. The main streets were densely packed with crowds waiting for us. Our vehicles were unable to move and were smothered with people; we were overwhelmed by flowers, bottles and kisses. Everyone had gone mad. We had to get to the docks at all costs to save them from being destroyed by the Germans who might now be getting organised.'

Glasses of wine

The mixture of euphoric crowds and German sniper and panzerfaust (bazooka) fire was bewildering. Fellow tankman John Dunlop is quoted by Patrick Delaforce: 'We never closed the lids of our turrets, because we then became so blind and so deaf that we felt too vulnerable. We felt a lot safer with them open. But that afternoon I seriously considered closing down. Sporadic firing from upper windows, bursts of small arms fire and an occasional grenade would scatter the civilians climbing over our tanks.'

Colonel Ivor Rees entered Antwerp on the same day to find, '...this mass of populace crowding around, still kissing you, asking you to post a letter to America, to give them some petrol, some more arms for the White Brigade, holding a baby under your nose to be kissed, trying to give you a drink, inviting you to your house, trying to carry you away, offering information about the enemy, just had to be seen to be understood.'

Even in combat the civilians were often present. Two tanks busily blasting the SS HQ earned the attention of celebrating Belgian civilians. 'Each time an empty shell case was pushed out of the tank's open port, a hand would come in bearing a large glass of wine!' records Delaforce.

Out in the River Scheldt a small steamer of fleeing Germans ran aground in a cloud of steam after being hit by armour-piercing shells from a troop of Shermans.

A German column of horse-drawn vehicles was attacked; later the dead horse were hung, skinned and quartered by a local butcher. 'It was unrestrained joy - mad and crazy', said Captain CKO Spence of the Ayrshire Yeomanry, 'and all the time sporadic firing against the stubborn remnants of resisting Germans.' His own effort to 'liberate' a beautiful Mercedes staff car was thwarted when the Belgians got there first.

Collaborators in cages

That night a Bren carrier painted white roared around a district in the city. Manned by

British units crossing the River Seine on pontoon bridges at Vernon.

Resistance, the vehicle had been hidden but kept in working order since the day it had been abandoned by the BEF in 1940! Café parties and dancing in the streets went on until dawn, punctuated by sniper fire and explosions.

The city zoo was turned into a prison. Patrick Delaforce was able to visit the lion house where he watched two pretty Belgian girls checking in the new arrivals. Each cage had a different category of prisoners ranging from German officers through to important Belgian traitors. A large crowd outside the zoo jeered the new inmates. A German officer explained that the Germans (who numbered some 6000 by the 5th) would be handed over to the British in due course; as for the collaborators, they were to be shot that night, 'after a fair trial'. Military historian Alan Moorehead also saw the zoo and recorded that the scenes there must compare with the Colosseum in Rome at the time of Emperor Caligula.

In the chaos and confusion a serious planning error had come to light. The Albert Canal was thought to run through the city centre but in fact it was located to the north. It was important to get across this 60 yards wide waterway before the Germans could put a defensive line along it. There was no way on land around to the north bank of the Scheldt without crossing the canal and until the Allies controlled both the north and south banks of the river there would be no access for shipping to the huge Antwerp docks. 'Pip' Roberts got news that the main bridge over the canal had been blown up at 9am on 5 September. This same day three companies of the King's Shropshire Light Infantry got across by boat to form a bridgehead in the northern suburb of Merxem. But they were

too lightly armed to mount an effective defence against the panzers and heavy weapons mustered by the Germans and on 7 September the decision was made to bring the survivors back, a mission accomplished within 15 minutes without a single casualty. In the previous 48 hours the KSLI had taken 150 casualties including 31 killed and their Colonel Ivor Reeves seriously wounded. The fight for the Merxem bridgehead is a significant KSLI battle honour.

Cointreau and heartburn

For 11th Armoured Division the Great Swan was now definitely ended. German resistance was hardening as their own supply lines shortened whilst those of the Allies stretched longer and longer. More than this, with the borders of the Reich itself just a few score miles away from the British and Americans, the Germans seemed to have rekindled the will to fight. Though the tankmen and their infantry support had won the battle for Antwerp, the battle for the city's port would continue until November before the Scheldt estuary and the islands of Walcheren and South Beveland were captured at great cost by the Canadians.

A final bright spot for the Division before leaving the city was their occupation of Antwerp Customs House and the liberation of the spoils of war within. Each regiment received 800 bottles of wine and 8000 cigars - enough for a bottle and 10 cigars per man. Patrick Delaforce remembers how his half track crew all stood five inches taller when they left Antwerp than when they went in as they were all standing on cases of Cointreau - '...a delicious liqueur, but taken in abundance it produces heartburn.'

Top: A German gun fires across the Straits of Dover at England. Over 3500 shells fell on Dover and the Kent countryside in the time from 12 August 1940 to mid-September 1944 when the enemy guns fell silent.

September days of 1944 the Scots were returning in triumph.

For the Canadians there was a turning of the tables too. At Dieppe on 19 August 1942 they had lost thousands of men killed or captured in the 'reconnaissance in force' raid on this Upper Normandy port. On 1 September 1944 they took the surrender of the port and town. Following the 1942 attack Hitler had ordered an immense ring of concrete bunkers and gun emplacements to be built around Dieppe but in the event the German garrison lacked the will to fight.

Calais and Boulogne proved tougher nuts to crack. September 1944 saw the firing of the last rounds across the Channel by the big German guns on the cliffs in the Pas de Calais area. Dover and the surrounding Kentish towns and the countryside had borne the brunt to the barrage that had begun on 12 August 1940 and continued right through the war years. The casualty toll from the 3514 shells fired in total included 400 civilians injured and 100 killed.

On 1 September a German flotilla of small vessels sailed out of Boulogne carrying personnel not required for the port's defence. Giving covering fire, the German batteries opened up on the sites of Britain's own big guns on the Dover cliffs. A cross-Channel duel resulted which lasted - on and off - until the middle of the month when the Canadians closed in after a series of heavy bomber attacks on the ring of concrete bunkers around the town.

The last shots were fired by the British batteries on 19 September after which barrel wear made further accurate shooting impossible. A German battery that emerged unscathed from the attention of the Allied bombers continued firing for a few days more. On 29 September an attack by Canadian infantry and tanks, including the 'Crocodile' flamethrower variety, finally forced the surrender of the Boulogne garrison.

The Germans in Calais surrendered the next day, 30 September. In the end, holding on to the Channel ports cost Hitler 120,000 men. Thousands more found themselves surrounded in a number of ports in Brittany and on the Atlantic Coast of France. The Allies were in no hurry to storm these fortresses; with time and the tide of war on their side they were content to play the waiting game.

ROLLING UP 'La Manche'

The Canadian First Army was tasked with rolling up the German defences in the various ports and towns along the Channel coast from the mouth of the Seine to the border with Belgium.

They were assisted by the English 49th Division and the 51st Highland Division, the latter two units being given the thankless task of reducing the fortress of Le Havre in which 11,000 Germans had sought refuge. Seven heavy bomber raids were made on the town; on 5 September alone 348 Lancasters,

Stirlings and Mosquitos dropped 1812 tons of bombs. As many as 3000 civilians died before the Germans surrendered on 12 September. The welcome given by the inhabitants to their British liberators was understandably muted.

Where the fighting wasn't light and war damage limited, it was a different story. At Etretat where the famous chalk arch is still a major landmark on this part of the Norman coast, the Scots had been greeted with joyful scenes on 2 September. At St Valery en Caux the arrival of the 51st Highland Division was especially poignant. In 1940 the Division had made a historic stand around the tiny port before being forced to surrender to the victorious panzer forces of the then unknown General Erwin Rommel. Now in these early

Right: The painting depicts 'British Coastal Artillery'. It is the work of the artist and illustrator Terence Cuneo who went on to find post-war fame as a brilliant painter of trains, racing cars, jet aircraft and action scenes of all kinds. His trademark was the inclusion of a tiny mouse in many of his paintings. The work reproduced here pre-dates 1944 and shows the crew of a coastal artillery piece loading their gun. In the background another gun engages the unseen enemy - most likely a ship or E-Boat as the weapon does not look big enough to fire all the way across the Channel to Occupied France. The white cliffs are presumably those of Dover. The piece was used in a campaign titled 'Help Britain Finish the Job' that was aimed at the USA and the Dominions (National Archives - Art of War). Terence Cuneo died in 1996.

COASTAL ARTILLERY
A PAINTING BY TERENCE CUNEO

BRUSSELS IS FREE!

The quote on the opposite page are the words of a participant in the astonishing Allied dash from the Seine to the Belgian capital Brussels and beyond accomplished in a matter of days late in the summer of 1944. The British Second Army of General Miles Dempsey was on the move and picking up momentum. Suddenly territorial advances in leaps and bounds unimaginable just a month before became commonplace. Starring role in the liberation of Brussels went to the Guards Armoured Division, part of General Horrock's XXX Corps. On 31 August he'd told the Guards he wanted them in the Belgian capital within four days. On the evening of 2 September in Douai he reiterated his order - they were to make Brussels the very next day, traversing the intervening 70 miles or so.

Horrocks clearly gave the advance all the trappings of a madcap race by setting his two brigades (5th and 32nd) with Grenadier and Welsh Guards respectively, different routes but a common 'winning post' at their appointed junction spot before the capital. Other famous units participating in the historic move forward were the Coldstreams, the Irish Guards - under the dashing Colonel 'Joe' Vandeleur - and a squadron of armoured vehicles of the Household Cavalry.

Madcap race

But the race had deadly handicaps. Pockets of the enemy would stand and fight, usually just long enough to inflict casualties amongst the men in the 'point' vehicles. Then the Germans either surrendered or ran. The Grenadiers initially took the lead and looked all over the likely winners. But at Lessines they had to first crack a German strongpoint and then were held up on the outskirts of Brussels by fighting and the need for fuel for their Shermans. Meanwhile the Welsh Guards, their faster Cromwell tanks bowling along at up to 50mph, ate up the miles to make it to the 'winning post' just ahead of their rivals.

An armoured car of the Household Cavalry commanded by Lance-Corporal I W Dewar, was the first Allied vehicle to nose into the heart of the city. Initially hesitant in case it turned out to contain more retreating Germans, the population soon broke into open rejoicing and quickly swarmed all over the car, grabbing any part of it which could be prised off or removed. The aerial antenna quickly disappeared, leaving Dewar unable to radio his position to base. Fearing that the armoured car's wheels were next on the agenda of the souvenir hunters, the crew heaved sighs of relief when a couple of policemen arrived to restore order.

The scene was visited on other liberators a thousand times over. Flowers and even pots of geraniums decorated the mobile weapons of war and Brussels drank deep of the heady draught of freedom. Unbridled joy filled the air; men, women and children cried with happiness. But the Germans were still around and occasional outbreaks of firing scattered the crowds. When the first Welsh Guards tanks entered the city, the Cromwell of Lt John A Dent came across a Panzer Mk IV in the Rue de la Loi and a German bus which was promptly set on fire. Other British tanks in the Rue des Colonies and Rue Royale made for the Cinqauntenaire, where, guns blazing, they took on the enemy.

Battles in the darkness

With nightfall came rumours of a German counter-attack - in fact one was planned but stalled through lack of transport. But small-scale battles erupted all through the hours of darkness as Resistants hunted for Germans to fight. The crowds grew bolder and even attempted to pillage a warehouse still occupied by the enemy. Firing by the latter and the explosion of train wagons filled with munitions killed some 30 civilians - other Resistants died in clashes with retreating Germans. The British - impeded by the crowds - had still not arrived in strength and had hardly more than 30 tanks in the city by 1am.

Next day the celebrations picked up where they left off with seemingly even more people out on the streets. Horrocks himself hurried to Brussels and Piron's men also moved in. The Belgian Roger Dewandre and his tanks arrived at Laeken via the Bourse, escorting General Horrocks. Here they were received by Queen Elizabeth, the only member of the Belgian Royal Family remaining in the capital.

Champagne campaign

Brussels airfield was still under shellfire but the city was fairly bursting with joy. On the outskirts, a huge cache of champagne and liquor was 'liberated' by a special detail aptly led by Major Hennessy of the famous cognac family. Also in the 'drinks' party was the future Lord Carrington.

Meanwhile in the city the inevitable retribution began as collaborators and suspected traitors were apprehended.

Another night went by and the exuberance barely abated and indeed was whipped up to new heights following an announcement at 11am on 5 September that Germany was seeking an armistice following the suicide of Adolf Hitler. Loudspeaker vans touring the streets denied the story.

Another spontaneous wave of enthusiasm broke on 7 September when Montgomery in person was welcomed to Brussels; he made a public appearance in the Grand Place. After this it seemed that at last even this city of unrestrained happiness must pause and draw breath again. When the Belgian Government-in-Exile returned 24 hours later the welcome, although warm, was muted by comparison with that afforded the men of XXX Corps.

The liberation of Brussels and the resulting celebrations swiftly took on a legendary status within the British Army. Given a choice of Continental leave destinations in the following months, the Guards (and men of many other units) would inevitably select this city where they were always sure of finding a host family. From humble private to high-ranking officer, the freeing of the Belgian capital was an indelible event in their lives. As General Sir Brian Horrocks went on record in his memoirs: 'There were flowers, fruit, champagne and girls all over our vehicles and kissing such as never before seen. We had become connoisseurs of Liberation, with all the towns and villages we had come through since we crossed the Seine.

'But everyone agreed that the welcome offered by the citizens of Brussels was unparalleled...'

'Villages began to slip by. Most of the inhabitants realised that the British were across the Seine and on their way forward, but none imagined they could be arriving so soon and in the middle of the night. They believed that the Germans were still passing through and not many stirred from their beds. But occasionally a keen-eared patriot would detect a different sound of fleeing enemy transport and the more sustained roar of the pursuing British armoured cars and then he knew that it must be 'Les Anglais'. We saw them stir, silhouetted figures pulled back the curtains, flung open their bedroom windows and shouted their heartfelt feelings.'

Above: A British tank advances into the Belgian capital. Left: Grand Place, Brussels. Montgomery made a triumphant appearance here on 7 September 1944.

149

Me and Vera Lynn

The background to my meeting the lovely Vera Lynn began with a walk into Burma in 1944 with 16 Brigade, Chindits. I was fortunate eventually to be flown out to land at Comilla where there was a large hospital sorted into 'sick' and 'wounded'. Tagged 'sick', I was given hospital pyjamas, washed with very strong soap and told I'd be on 'Double Convalescent Rations' comprising a bonus tin of evaporated milk and a small bottle of rum each day. I was expected to have my hair cut and beard shaved off as soon as possible. A few of us wandered around and tracked down the rest of the blokes from our plane and were amazed to find that the 'wounded' were not on rum.

A collection was made to rectify this omission. My contribution was to deliver six small bottles to friends in the 'wounded' ward - all on a 50-yard veranda, facing the sun. Having settled down on one of the beds I realised that we had visitors - and a great deal of Red Tape. The best advice was for me to lie down and spread the bottles round so that they did not rattle!

An orderly came ahead of this group to tell us that 'Force's Sweetheart' Vera Lynn was here and would we please contribute to the conversation. I tried to be anonymous but of course she had to stop at my bed where there was no board detailing the nature of my wounds/sickness at the end of it. Luckily I had seen her on stage a couple of times and we discussed the finer points of the Shepherd's Bush Empire.

She moved on to talk to other men. I was in the middle of the ward and as the main party eventually left I saw one orderly turn and head back purposely in my direction! Fortunately, friends in the ward had already briefed me on the best way to escape. The orderly had passed about three beds, when one of the occupants let out a loud yell of pain. Being a true professional, the orderly turned to attend to the wounded soldier giving me just enough time to nip into the next ward and safety.

As one of the lads from our evacuation flight put it: 'They couldn't have sent you back, we were on the last plane out!'
Jack Reddy, Northants

Boy Scouts almost caused a strike!

In 1941 the authorities started supplying Morrison table shelters which were erected inside the house and made a pleasant change from the cold and damp Anderson shelters buried in the garden. The Morrison shelter was six feet long, four feet wide and about two feet six inches high. Four steel legs, secured to four steel beams along the sides, supported the steel table top. Steel springs across the bottom provided a base for a bed and strong wire sides protected the occupants from the falling debris of a bombed house. These saved many lives. But it took four council workmen four hours to erect one and they got paid to build two a

day. We Boy Scouts were asked to erect the shelters for the elderly and disabled on an unpaid and voluntary basis. We gave up our Saturday mornings and soon found that three Scouts (aged from 12 to 16) could erect a shelter in less than an hour. Teams of us could erect two or three in a single morning. This did not please the workmen and they threatened to go on strike, if the Scouts continued their work. The council gave in, the Scouts were withdrawn and many elderly people were denied their Morrison shelters. So much for the war effort.

Many 14 and 15-year-olds lied about their ages and claimed to be 16 in order to join the Civil Defence as messengers. No one asked too many questions. Some joined the fire service, some the wardens and some the hospital service. We were supplied with tin hats and special gas masks and when the sirens sounded would jump on our bikes and rush to our posts. We had an exciting time and some narrow escapes. After a night raid, school started later at 10am. Daylight raids provided a good dodge to avoid lessons until the Headmaster found out that it took us about five minutes to reach our posts, but over 45 minutes to return, particularly if the lesson was unpopular. The Headmaster put a stop to this particular wheeze. Our school exam results may not have been very good

but I think we learnt much more of use in later life in respect of dealing with emergencies and problems.

In the summer of 1940, we were camping in camouflaged tents on the outskirts of our town. When anti-aircraft gunfire started we dived for shelters. On the 'all clear' we would find shrapnel fallen through our tents; these fragments made prize possessions. In August of that year our summer camp was at Brynbach on the Denbigh Moors. On arrival there, we found about 400 French youngsters (aged 16 and older) already in residence. They had escaped from Occupied France and were waiting to join the Free French forces. One day they were expecting a visit from some VIP. No troops were available to guard the access to the camp, so we Boy Scouts were called upon to man the perimeter against possible German invasion (perhaps paratroops disguised as nuns!). I was on the main gate, when a large open top car arrived, the Cross of Lorraine pennant flying from the bonnet. The occupant, a then unknown French officer called Charles de Gaulle, spent some minutes chatting with us before going on to meet his countrymen. That evening we heard the French in full voice singing *The Marseillaise*. Those lads did not know when or whether they would ever see their homeland again. A poignant memory. We used to play the French at rugby and had many catapult wars, the occasional wounded being treated by a French doctor.

Nobody worried about Health and Safety Regulations in those days, we just got on with whatever was necessary and did not suffer from it. At the time, potential 'yobs' were fighting the Japanese in Burma, parachuting from burning aircraft or drowning in the freezing North Atlantic. It should be remembered that many others suffered a lot worse. We would not wish our grandchildren to go through what we experienced, but perhaps our present-day law-makers would do well to study such events prior to framing their next piece of 'nanny state' legislation.
Brian Jones, East Yorkshire
* Mr Jones later took part in the Liberation of Jersey in May 1945. See pages 272 - 273.

MARKET GARDEN

Monty's plan to end the war by Christmas

Vital though it was for the Allied advance upon Germany to clear the Scheldt estuary and get the port of Antwerp working, both Eisenhower and Montgomery agreed to give priority to securing a bridgehead across the great natural barrier of the Rhine. But the move had to be made quickly, before the Germans had the chance to recover from their summer of dramatic reversals on the battlefield.

Montgomery was ready with a plan, an unusually bold and audacious one and, uncharacteristically for this commander who had hitherto frowned on military gambles, one that was clearly dependent on a large helping of good fortune. It involved the British 21st Army Group together with the Allied First Airborne Army which consisted of two American airborne divisions, the British 1st Airborne Division and a Polish airborne brigade.

Airborne carpet

The British 'sky men' had been thirsting for action since long before D-Day when the Division discovered that they didn't figure in the *Overlord* plans - the British airborne role in Normandy going to the 'rival' 6th Airborne. During July, August and early September the Division had been readied for a whole series of mooted drops on objectives just ahead of the advancing Allied armies. Each operation was cancelled in the face of the astonishing progress by the ground forces.

But now the 1st Airborne were being given the key role in Montgomery's plan, *Operation Market Garden*. They would be the spearhead of a 'carpet' of airborne troops landing across Holland. The British paratroopers, later to be reinforced by the Poles, were to descend on the Arnhem area, more than 60 miles from the British front-line troops east of Antwerp. While the British and Polish airborne forces held the bridge over the Lower Rhine (the river was also erroneously referred to as the Lek in some accounts written at the time), the British XXX Corps would drive northwards up a narrow 'corridor' through Belgium and Holland to link up with them and cut off all German troops of the Fifteenth Army to the west.

From their salient north of the Rhine the Allies would then push on into Germany before swinging south into the vital industrial region of the Ruhr, heart of Hitler's faltering war machine. Capturing the Ruhr must hasten the end of the war, perhaps even securing

Gliders on their way to Arnhem, September 1944.

victory before Christmas. In also liberating the rest of the Netherlands the Allies would capture the German V1 and V2 launch sites on the Dutch North Sea coast and put an end to the barrage of rockets falling on England.

To help British ground troops in their advance through the difficult network of canals and rivers between the British front and Arnhem, the American 82nd Airborne Division would land and seize the bridges over the Rivers Waal and Maas near Nijmegen, while the 101st Airborne were detailed to capture and hold bridges over the canals near Eindhoven.

British spearhead

The operation began on 17 September. The British 1st Airborne landed some six - eight miles from the bridge at Arnhem, while the two American divisions dropped much nearer their objectives. The Guards Armoured Division were the spearhead of the northward drive by the British XXX Corps. In the first few hours things seemed to be going well.

The good news didn't last. The weather turned bad; for many days supplies and follow-up forces could not be flown to Arnhem. Meanwhile the troops there discovered that the Germans were in the area in force and were able to quickly bring tanks and self-propelled guns into action against the lightly armed airborne. Soon the British sky men were cut into two separated groups; a single besieged battalion holding on to the north end of the Arnhem bridge with the rest of the Division trapped in a

horseshoe-shaped enclave around the small town of Oosterbeek, a half a dozen miles away on the north bank of the Rhine.

Both the Germans and the Allies fought hard and desperately. The two American divisions that held the bridges at Nijmegen and Eindhoven suffered heavy losses in the face of German counter-attacks, while the British paratroopers of the 1st Airborne Division held out for nearly five days at the bridge before the survivors were forced to surrender. Four days later the remaining men within the Oosterbeek perimeter - the latter called *Der Kessel* (The Cauldron) by the Germans - withdrew as best they could across the fast flowing Rhine to the relative safety of the southern bank.

Of the 10,000 men who had gone in, just over 2000 came back in the course of the overnight evacuation. Many hundreds more would make their way back into Allied hands during the following weeks and months, thanks in large part to the bravery of the Dutch people who aided them. But at least 1500 dead would never return and for over 6000 others, many of them wounded, the rest of the war would be sat out in POW camps.

Grievous losses

To the grievous losses of British and Polish sky men and RAF crews must be added the toll of American paratroopers and the tankmen and infantry of XXX Corps. The Americans, indeed, were left in the line until November and suffered a further 3400 casualties in this period in addition to the 3542 dead and wounded during the time of *Market Garden*. It's estimated that something like 10,000 Dutch civilians died during the fighting in mid-September or in the bitter winter of starvation that followed.

Montgomery's plan had not been a complete failure but neither could it be called a success. A deep wedge had been driven into the German line, but that line had not been broken. Allied attention shifted westward to concentrate on a step-by-step advance along the River Scheldt aimed at prising open the approaches to Antwerp.

On 28 September 1944 the Field Marshal ordered a letter to be read out to the survivors of the 1st Airborne as they reassembled in England. The letter included the lines: 'In the years to come it will be a great thing for a man to be able to say, "I fought at Arnhem".'

BATTLE FOR THE
BRIDGES

Christopher Portway recently
paid a visit to this pleasant and
peaceful Dutch city of Arnhem
to remember a time in
September 1944 when death
and destruction was all around.

The capital of the Dutch province of
Gelderland is Arnhem, one of the best-known
names in Holland, at least to the more
mature of us. This because of the ill-fated
Allied airborne attack in September 1944 that
was intended to greatly hasten the end of
World War II in Europe.

Operation Market Garden hinged on the
capture of the river crossings at Arnhem (the
farthest bridge), Nijmegen, Eindhoven and
Grave, so turning the defence-line of the
Rhine and cutting off 100,000 German troops
in Holland. The epic battle has passed into
legend but of that legend, the work of a
workaday country regiment's infantry
battalion - the 4th Dorsets - on the night of
24 September 1944 and onwards formed an
indelible part.

Ordered to cross the Neder Rijn, or Lower
Rhine, to the south west of Arnhem and
cover the evacuation of the survivors of the
1st British Airborne Division, they made their
way under annihilating fire athwart a strong
current in foundering boats. About 300 of
the battalion made it and held on for 36
hours while, with unimaginable difficulty,
some 2400 paratroopers were ferried back.
Very few of the 4th Dorsets, however, made
that nightmare return journey and their
desperate courage was specifically
acknowledged by Viscount Montgomery in
his book *Normandy to the Baltic*.

One reason I mention this is that the
4th Dorsets was my battalion which had been
fighting its way from Normandy to Holland as
part of the 43rd Wessex Division attempting
to relieve the hard-pressed airborne troops.
Had I not been taken prisoner outside the
Normandy city of Caen I too would have been
involved in this bloody action. Instead, by the
grace of God and the 12th
SS Panzer Division, who
were my captors, I avoided,
in all likelihood, becoming
one more name on a
war memorial.

Explicit order
The story of the landing
from the sky of the 1st
Airborne Division led by
Major General Urquhart,
together with the 1st
Polish Independent
Brigade under Major
General Sosabowski, is
well-known, the epicure of
the battle being featured
in the celebrated film *A
Bridge Too Far*. Given a
short explicit order
'Capture Arnhem Bridge
and hold it', there was,
once airborne, no going
back even when it was
discovered that two
German tank divisions
were quartered in
the area.

The bridge, as a major crossing of the
Rhine, was of vital importance and the hilly
wooded country north of the river, together
with the flat terrain of open roads along
dykes to the south, explains the failure of
the main Allied forces to relieve their
airborne colleagues attempting to hold the
bridge intact. During and after the
unsuccessful operation until liberation after
bitter fighting in April 1945, Arnhem was
subjected to heavy shelling from across the
Rhine, and the present town has been
almost completely rebuilt since then. The
famous bridge, renamed after John Frost, the
British Parachute Brigadier, whose unit held
it in 1944, is, today, a modern structure but
of similar design to the earlier one broken
by savage fighting and bombardment.

The older buildings of the town have all
been restored or rebuilt following the
damage inflicted and these include the Grote,
or Eusebius Church, originally constructed
between 1452 and 1650, its 98-metre high
tower being a replacement fort that was
destroyed during the fighting in 1944. Nearby
is the former Stadthuis (Town Hall) of 1545
vintage, while the Sabelspoor is the only
remnant of the fortifications of 1440. A
similar martial remnant of a more recent date
marks the centre of the Airborneplein, a
sunken garden at the heart of a busy
roundabout in which a broken column from
the ruins of Arnhem bears the date 17
September 1944.

In the immediate vicinity of Arnhem is an
assortment of museums. One that deals
exclusively with the events of 1944 is the
Airborne Museum at Oosterbeek housed in
the old Hotel Hartenstein, the one-time
headquarters of the 1st Airborne Division.
For today's visitors the events of the battle
are made abundantly clear through a cleverly
arranged series of models, photographs and
dioramas which, together with the spoken
commentaries, explain the details of the
operation and its tragic consequences.
A substantial stone Airborne memorial stands
just outside the pleasant park in which the
museum is situated.

Tranquil woodland
War cemeteries of both First and Second World
Wars are places of great beauty and evocation
anywhere and that of Oosterbeek's Airborne
Cemetery is no exception. Here lies the last
resting-place for 2000 British and Allied
soldiers in a tranquil landscaped woodland.

Those visitors to Arnhem who wish to
continue their Second World War theme of
exploration might care to partake of a meal
at the Cafe-Restaurant Schooroord in
Oosterbeek, the original building of which
was used by the 1st Airborne Division as a
main dressing station where more than 500
wounded men were tended. Heavily damaged
and since rebuilt after 1945 it has become a
meeting place for many an Arnhem veteran.

Another wartime museum of considerable
interest is that simply titled '40 - 45'
situated just outside the township in an old
village school. Here a huge variety of
exhibits telling the whole wartime story of

Holland. For me the most intriguing item is a 'secret room' lodged behind a bookcase and used to conceal those who were likely to be deported to work in Germany or, worse, to concentration camps. Long after the war ended the new owner of the building never discovered this extra room in his own house! Surrounded by rusting artillery pieces and scarred T54 tanks the museum is a labour of love of Rob Pogge, its curator and founder.

Oosterbeek Church

And so to neighbouring Nijmegen, one of the oldest towns in the Netherlands with a history going back to Roman times. Because of its strategic position on a bend of the river Waal, just to the west of its junction with the Rhine and spanned by another similarly-designed bridge to that of Arnhem but with a slightly happier fate, the town has often been the scene of sieges and battles, culminating in the action to secure the vital river crossings in 1944 during which it was, likewise, virtually destroyed. Rebuilt in modern style with, again, many well-kept parks and gardens, there are still sizeable fragments of the old fortifications to be seen and these are marked by a circular tower overlooking the river and bridge. Close to the luxurious but good-value Scandic Sanadome Hotel with its superbly equipped spa, lies Jonkerbus Military Cemetery, another wooded resting place for some 2000 souls. Yet a further such cemetery - this one for Canadian dead - crowns a hill near the sizeable village of Groesbeek, site of *Operation Veritable* which, in February 1945, ultimately led to the conquering of the left bank of the Rhine.

Also close to Groesbeek stands the uniquely-designed National Liberation Museum again bringing history back to life but, this time, giving the younger generation a taste of what it was like to have one's country occupied by a hated and ruthless foreign power.

Following the landing of the American 82nd Airborne Division during *Operation Market Garden*, the front line ran around Groesbeek and, today, this wide open countryside is known as Little America where the 82nd rained down from the sky to fight their way to the Waal bridge at Nijmegen.

Perhaps the most evocative wartime site of all is to be found in Oosterbeek where a simple 1000 year old church and its nearby vicarage formed part of the 1944 front line. Here wounded soldiers found refuge, there to be looked after by Mr and Mrs Ter Horst even during the heat of battle. 'These men are like our own boys,' they declared, and many a surviving veteran will never

forget them. Outside the church is an old lime tree, also a casualty of war and so badly damaged by bullet and shell splinters it was due to be cut down. But signs of life persisted and now, flaunting its scars, that tree is once more in full growth.

Arnhem, Nijmegen and the surrounding villages likewise nearly died only to rise again from their ashes to become thriving urban centres looking backwards to a recent past as well as forwards into a bright future.

Top and right: British troops pictured at Nijmegen bridge in September 1944.

PRIORITY TELEGRAM

Ron McGill was a spectator of the Arnhem air armada and later witnessed first hand the awful consequences of war.

On Sunday morning 17 September 1944 I was a young teenage helper for our local milkman, delivering and collecting milk bottles in the Doverhouse Road area of Roehampton in SW London.

As we clattered and scurried around doorways at the top of the hill we suddenly became aware of thunder in the bright sky and the ground seemed to begin to shake. We were quite transfixed to suddenly see formation after formation of C47/Dakotas passing fairly low and flying in an easterly direction. Young lads at this time of the war were fascinated by the constant air activity in the English skies and we were all experts in aircraft recognition. The D-Day formations earlier in June were still fresh in our minds - but this vast panorama of comparatively slow and drab coloured aircraft was clearly something different - taking many minutes to pass over us with the sound of their engines throbbing on for a long time.

Grim battle

The noise brought people from their homes and they quietly gathered in the streets; few had any doubts it was yet another stage in the battle against Nazi Germany and that young men would be lost during the day. If I recall correctly, it was not until the evening that we heard on the radio an Allied Airborne Force had parachuted into Holland, at a place we had never heard of - Arnhem - in an attempt to bring the dreadful war to a close. At school the next morning our teacher, a Great War veteran with a bad limp, called us all to attention and quietly asked us to stand and think for a few minutes about the young men fighting a grim battle that very day, deep in Occupied Holland.

I remember it was difficult to concentrate for the rest of that day and I think in the end we were all sent home early - alive to the excitement of it all.

Now move forward to the last day, but one, of December 1944. It is tucked away in my memory for an incident of pure misery that brought home to me the tragic impact of war.

On reaching my 14th birthday in October, I joined the Post Office as a Boy Messenger (or Telegram Boy as they were known) and I was appointed to the busy office at Hammersmith Broadway. Out in all weathers, pushing heavy red bikes around for long hours, always alert

for the staggering explosions of the German V2 rockets and literally swamped with the volume of wartime telegrams, it was not that easy a job for less than £1 per week.

The incident in question came in the afternoon of that December day when I happened to be the first boy back in from delivery when yet another of the Priority 'war casualty' telegrams was brought down from the Instrument Room by the lady telegraphist. It was the sensible practice to hand these to the older boys to try and seek neighbourly help prior to the actual delivery, but as I was the only one there, I had the briefing and left for the first of my Priority calls without delay.

An Arnhem casualty

The address was in a small row of 19th century houses on the left-hand side of the Hammersmith Bridge Road, very near to the bridge itself. The house had the usual flight of concrete steps up and over the basement flat to a front door and two further flats above. I propped my heavy bike against the gateway of the house I wanted and before I

could do any more, the door opened to show a pretty young woman with a small child hanging on to her dress. She took one look at me, slumped back hard against the wall and slowly crumpled down to the floor in a dead faint.

I rushed up the steps and somehow righted her against the wall, moved the baby back further into the hallway and ran for help. I was able to bring an older woman from another house and together we managed to get the stricken lady to a chair where she finally came round and opened the most anguished of blue eyes that I had ever seen in my young life. The neighbour opened the telegram and confirmed to me the death in action of her Airborne husband who had, apparently, been missing since the Arnhem drop back in September. She also told me that the young woman was going to have a second baby and she asked me to stay while she made urgent arrangements for her care.

Feeling of guilt

I stayed with the young woman for about 20 minutes and she never took her eyes off me and quite pitifully, was unable to speak or cry. Then other ladies came in and I was able to leave and cycle back to the office, quite shattered by this contact with the grief that I had brought to this household.

I had a dreadful feeling of guilt and that evening, after telling my father about the episode, I suggested this first-hand misery was not for me and perhaps I should seek factory work? He simply said, 'Somebody has to do it son,' and persuaded me to stay. This I did and greatly enjoyed the humour and companionship of the other 20 boys, some of whom have remained friends to this day.

In later years, I could never pass that small terrraced house without a twinge, particularly if the young children were playing on the steps. Then came a moment in the late 1960s when I was driving back through Hammersmith and gave my usual glance at the house...only to see that the whole row had gone, cleared in the redevelopment of Hammersmith Bridge and its approaches.

It is over 60 years ago now, but I can still recall the pure misery of those unforgettable blue eyes and the delivery of my first Priority Telegram.

Remembrance

My most recent trip to Holland to see relatives who live at Breda allowed for a brief visit to Arnhem to see the Bridge and tour the Hartenstein Hotel in Oosterbeek. Once the HQ of the British Skytroops, it is now a superb museum dedicated to the historic battle fought around it.

We ended with a stroll through the now delightful streets and went to the nearby Airborne Cemetery.

Walking around the rows of headstones we were struck that so many were for

19 or 20 year olds and that other than those from all parts of Britain, there were a few Australian and New Zealand soldiers, together with so many Polish men. In the tranquillity and peace of the grassy walkways and white headstones of Oosterbeek I could but reflect that I had seen them pass overhead in that vast air armada, only to lose their lives in the next few days.

Now, after all those years had passed, I was able to stand at their graves and personally remember them.

RETURN TO ARNHEM

On the 60th anniversary of Operation Market Garden, the Dutch warmly welcomed many hundreds of veterans to the Netherlands for a series of moving commemorative events centred on Arnhem and Oosterbeek. One of the returning soldiers was Gerald Levy who may well have been the youngest of the 'Sky Troops' to parachute into the battle. This is his story.

Gerald Levy volunteered for the Army just three months after his 17th birthday in 1944. He was admitted to the ranks under a special scheme for War Office-recognised members of the Army Cadet Force. With experience as a sergeant in the 2nd Cadet Battalion (JLB) Royal Fusiliers, Gerald was asked to swear an oath of allegiance to Crown and duly received the King's Shilling.

Posted to a recruit depot in Hamilton, Scotland, he and his fellows were kitted out and next day marched to the railway station with a pipe band at their head. In full marching order they looked like a parade of heroes even though they had been in uniform for just 24 hours. They certainly impressed the locals who turned out to shower them with sweets, chocolates and biscuits.

Posted to barracks set up in a disused dye works at Alexandria near Dumbarton, Gerald was one of 90 volunteers known initially as the 'Milk Boys' because, being under 18 years, at mid-morning NAAFI break they were

The 60th anniversary of Operation Market Garden was marked by a series of poignant commemorative events in and around Arnhem in September 2004. But of course, the many veterans who made the trip to Holland found time for some fun. Enjoying a refreshing beer in the Kleyn Hartenstein Restaurant in Oosterbeek are (left to right): Arthur Sobey, Norman Jones, Ronald Hare, Gerald Levy and Len Wilson who were in a party invited to Holland by P&O Ferries and the Arnhem and Nijmegen Tourist Board.

Below left: Gerald and his grand-daughter Nina Dawson pictured at the John Frost Bridge in Arnhem.

Below right: The veterans on the bridge to view a parade were treated to sweets by men of a military re-enactment unit dressed in authentic 1944 paratroop uniforms.

marched to the cookhouse for milk and buns. Such wholesome sustenance worked wonders. They started to win every competition going (except the one for barrack room cleanliness!) and earned the description 'The Mad Ninety' in the process.

Parachute Regiment

After completing the recruit training (volunteers did six weeks and conscripts eight), Gerald volunteered for the Parachute Regiment and was posted first to Aldershot and then Newark for jump training. They had

RETURN TO ARNHEM

not seen anyone as short as 5ft 4ins but he was allowed in provided he passed all the physical and mental tests. Eventually he was posted to the Third Battalion The Parachute Regiment in time to take part in the airborne assault to capture the bridges (rail and road) at Arnhem.

On Sunday 17 September 1944 Gerald dropped with his fellow paratroopers onto Wolfhezen (DZ X), quite a few miles west of Arnhem. They formed the *Market* part of *Operation Market Garden* with *Garden* being ground forces charged with breaking through the German defences to link up with First Airborne Division. Arnhem was around 60 miles from the Garden startline on the Belgium border.

Gerald remembers it as a fairly good drop and the First, Second and Third Battalions duly formed up and made for the Arnhem bridges (road and rail), each by a different route. The rail bridge was blown up by the Germans early in the battle. The Second Battalion under Colonel John Frost made it to the north side of the roadbridge and held on tenaciously for four days under heavy tank and artillery bombardment until finally being over-run and killed or captured.

Below: Skytroops pictured in a trench with rifles at the ready. They are defending the horseshoe-shaped perimeter at Oosterbeek against heavily armed Germans backed by panzers and self-propelled guns.
Above right: 'In the bag' but still defiant! A British paratrooper is led off into captivity.

The Third Battalion advanced to the outskirts of Arnhem where they were driven back by the 9th SS Panzer Division, sustaining many casualties. The Battalion was decimated to the point where it was merged with other troops to form 'Lonsdale Force' under Major Dickie Lonsdale.

Lightly armed

Their task then was to hold the south-east corner of the horseshoe-shaped perimeter around Oosterbeek in which the remaining lightly armed troops of the First Airborne and their glider pilots found themselves trapped by troops of the Ninth and Tenth SS Panzer Divisions who were armed with tanks, self-propelled guns and flame-throwers.

The Division had been told to expect relief within a couple of days at most. It held out for nine. Life inside the perimeter was nightmarish. Incessant shelling, mortaring and raking small-arms fire poured in at all hours. The Germans called it *Der Kessel* (The Cauldron). Not even the arrival of small numbers of Polish paras from across the Rhine (and a brave attempt at reinforcing the bridgehead by men of the Dorset Regiment) could alter the outcome.

Polish rearguard

Eventually, on the dark rainy night of 25/26 September, an evacuation was put in train. From all around the enclave into which the remnants of the Division had been squeezed men were assigned to marked routes leading to the banks of the Rhine to the south. Those to the north, farthest from the river, were evacuated first, so Gerald's unit was one of the last to leave its position, the Poles forming part of the rearguard.

At the river they slid down the bank into the mud to await their turn to board the small boats, which diminished alarmingly in numbers as the dawn approached and German fire and the swift current took their toll. Gerald had sustained a head injury during the battle and was brought out by comrades who had looked after him for three days; he was lucky for many of the more seriously wounded had to be left behind.

Gerald spent some weeks recovering in hospital. No longer fit enough for airborne duty, he was transferred to the transport side of the Royal Army Service Corps where eventually he was appointed Divisional Chief Clerk 1. But that, as Gerald says, is another story.

A wonderful welcome

As Editor of the *Sixty Years On* series, I was invited to accompany a veteran back to the Netherlands by P&O Ferries and Gelderland Tourism for the 60th anniversary of the air landings in September 2004.

Ten years ago I had made a similar pilgrimage with Third Para veteran Gerald Levy who returned to Arnhem for the first time in half a century though we went a few months ahead of the actual airborne landing anniversary date. It seemed appropriate that Gerald – still amazingly active and spritely at the age of 78 – should this time be present at the actual commemorations. Gerald was understandably very keen to make the trip and his grand-daughter Nina Dawson was equally delighted to come along as a carer/companion.

Gerald lives in Polegate, East Sussex, so it felt a little odd to make the long journey north to Hull to join the P&O Ferries overnight sailing to Rotterdam. However, it meant we were able to join the rest of the party that included four other *Market Garden* veterans and their escorts. The party leader was P&O man Jim Pybus. By coincidence, Jim had himself already made a contribution to *Sixty Years On* in respect of an uncle who was killed in Italy early in 1944 near the Minturno river (see page 21 of this book).

It's less than a couple of hours drive from Rotterdam to Arnhem and upon driving into the area on the Thursday it was obvious from the atmosphere that something very special

Top right: A rifle marks a temporary grave.
Below right: A medic kneels beside another grave.
Below: Scenes in the Commonwealth War Cemetery, Oosterbeek, on Sunday 19 September 2004. Market Garden veterans can be seen carrying in their standards in the top picture while the bottom picture shows some of the many hundreds of Dutch schoolchildren who laid wreaths on each and every grave.

was going on. Veterans proudly sporting their red berets were everywhere and there were jeeps and World War II vehicles galore on the roads. As soon as we took to the streets, we could literally feel the friendship and goodwill radiating from the Dutch people of all ages towards these men who had passed this way so many years before.

A slightly puzzled Gerald asked one Dutchman why the paras were so warmly welcome when, after all, *Market Garden* had been a failure in terms of liberating Arnhem and had led to the death of many civilians and utter destruction of the town and surroundings. 'After years of despair you gave us hope,' was the simple and heartfelt response, a view espoused by many others during the course of the weekend.

The commemorative events were varied in size and scope and ranged from a massive parade over the Arnhem 'Bridge Too Far', to a simple early morning ceremony at the Airborne memorial a couple of hundred yards from the Hartenstein Hotel, HQ for the paras during the bitter fight for survival in Oosterbeek. On the Saturday morning, we witnessed 1600 paratroops re-enact the landing on Ginkel Heath. Their number included half a dozen veterans.

On the Sunday morning several thousand people together with all the veterans assembled in the Airborne Cemetery at Oosterbeek for a service of remembrance in the presence of HRH The Prince of Wales, Colonel-in-Chief of the Parachute Regiment. It was a moving and emotive occasion in which the Dutch people again expressed their thanks as over 2000 schoolchildren placed

bouquets of flowers on every single grave in the cemetery.

A big thank you...

I'm sure I speak for all the veterans in our party in giving a big 'thank you' to the Arnhem – Nijmegen Regional Tourist Board for putting this trip together in conjunction with Jim Pybus and P&O Ferries. The manager and staff of the four-star Scandic Sanadome Spa Hotel in Nijmegen were also wonderful hosts, even going to the trouble of mounting a photo exhibition in the hotel lobby commemorating the events of 1944 and saluting the returning veterans.

David Arnold

For information on all of Holland and the Arnhem / Nijmegen area in particular visit: **www.holland.com/uk**

Three Pals and Vera

Leslie Sumption, Stanley Johnson and John Ashby were three ordinary men leading ordinary lives when the war came along. Fate brought them together in the Far East and the trio became firm friends. Some sixty years on they were reunited with a very special person they'd last seen in a jungle clearing in Burma.

Les worked as an engineering apprentice in Lambeth, South London, and had joined the RAFVR (Royal Air Force Volunteer Reserve) in 1938. Stan worked at a steel works in Grangetown near Middlesborough by day and, as a member of the local Home Guard, kept watch over the works by night, thus spending almost 24 hours a day on site. John was working as an apprentice carpenter with a small firm in Sutton, Surrey. All three were 19 when they joined the RAF.

Les joined in 1939. Two years later he was an Engine Fitter with No 31 Squadron at Lahore, in the Punjab. On the way out from Glasgow his troopship was involved in a collision with another ship in the convoy. The badly damaged vessel limped to Cape Town alone, Les and everyone on board acutely aware of the U-Boat menace.

Around the time Les was joining '31' Stan was called up. He went to Technical Training School No 12 at Melksham. After qualifying as an Instrument Repairer he served on Nos 255 and 257 Night Fighter Squadrons, operating Beaufighters and Typhoons. In April 1943 Stan left Liverpool for Bombay on the *Auorangi*.

John joined the RAF in 1942 and in March 1943 sailed for Bombay via Freetown in Sierra Leone and Durban, South Africa. From Bombay he made the four-day train journey across India to Kharagpur, where he joined No 31 as an Engine Fitter on 25 June - his 20th birthday. Stan joined the Squadron a month or so later and it was at Kharagpur where the three men first met.

Les had already been with '31' for two years, working first on a DC-2, 'V' for Victory, then DC-3's, followed by the more reliable military version, the Dakota. At this time fitters and riggers took an active part as dispatchers, pushing and kicking the supplies out of the rear door of the aircraft. Les recalls never being given a parachute as 'there were none on the Squadron'. Although he was told he would get an extra 1/6d a day for flying duties, despite clocking up well over 300 hours in the air, he never received a penny!

Having initially been on a six month detachment in the Middle East the Squadron moved to Chittagong, North East India, where they were in constant action dropping supplies to refugees and Allied troops retreating from Burma in the face of the advancing Japanese. Once the Japanese progress had been halted near Imphal in Bengal, Brigadier Orde Wingate's famous Chindits undertook operations deep behind enemy lines in Burma. '31' had the task of keeping the supply lines open from the air. Each Chindit column had an RAF Wireless Operator assigned to it. When the column Commander selected a jungle clearing suitable for a drop, the WO would radio base with their requirements, anything from food and medical supplies to arms and ammunition. Loads were normally mixed with free-fall items such as sacks of rice pushed out at low level, whilst medical supplies and arms required a parachute drop, normally from 600 feet. Time over the Drop Zone could be as much as 30 minutes with on average six or seven passes. One supply drop Les remembers well entailed getting a replacement monocle to a Brigadier Ferguson of the Black Watch. To avoid damage the monocle was concealed in a sack of rice; they later learnt that finding it proved extremely difficult for the recipient!

Japanese zero fighters

There were encounters with Japanese fighters. Les remembers completing a drop over Myitkyina in Burma. As DC-3 'J' was cruising peacefully back to Dinjan he noticed, off the port wing, two low-winged, radial-engine monoplanes closing fast. At first he thought they must be a pair of Mohawk fighters of No 5 Squadron. Then he remembered they had no fighter escort that day; these must be Japanese Zeros! Les hurriedly notified Pilot Officer Williams who, after swearing and casting aspersions as to Les's legitimacy, plunged the 'Dak' into a dive and headed for a bank of cloud. The cloud proved too thin and the Zeros homed in again, this time from astern. Les recalls manning the Dak's single Thompson machine-gun, but having no idea how to operate it. Fortunately, they were able to dive into another cloud bank and dropped down almost to tree-top level as they made their escape.

Later, on the island of Akyab in the Bay of Bengal, Les and his crew flew a night operation to rescue 11 British soldiers from an expected Japanese incursion. Of two runways on the airstrip one had been bomb damaged. Unfortunately, in the dark, the pilot 'got a bit mixed up', chose the wrong one and wrote off the aircraft in a bomb crater. The rescuers needed rescuing! Over the next two days Les survived a strafing by a Zero as he crossed the airfield in an attempt to retrieve the one machine-gun from the aircraft and the attentions of several Japanese bombers. Rescue for all finally came in the form of another 31 Squadron Dakota flying in at night and making a rapid turn-around.

By the time John and Stan arrived on the Squadron the rules regarding ground crew acting as dispatchers had changed; now only air crew carried out these duties. That's not to say there was no flying for the two men. The Squadron moved around on various detachments and even took rest breaks away from the Burma front line. John's main flying duties consisted of the regular mail runs between Calcutta and Imphal, normally on 'U' for Uncle, 'his' aircraft. His one and only supply drop involved a daytime landing at Taro, an airstrip behind enemy lines, between Imphal and Myitkyina. The purpose of the landing was two-fold; five Army officers, 'all dressed in identical green and sporting identical beards' were to be dropped off and a political prisoner was to be brought out.

Behind enemy lines

On another occasion when the Squadron was on detachment at Sylhet and engaged in night supply drops, John was given a day off by Sqn Ldr Honeyman. Along with a pal, 'Blackie' Goodwin, John went shooting for the day and met up with two Americans doing the same. An invite back to the US base for a meal led to a somewhat later than planned return to their own airfield where they were met by an angry Scottish Flight Sergeant 'doing his nut'. It turned out that the whole detachment had left Sylhet and returned to Agatarla, leaving one aircraft, the flight Sergeant and the CO behind because they had no crew! Fortunately, Sqn Ldr Honeyman stepped in and vouched for the men.

Stan remembers a couple of special assignments vividly. One involved a flight to a jungle airstrip, guarded by one Army Sergeant and a number of Ghurkas, where an abandoned aircraft had been spotted by an over-flying, returning '31' aircrew. Stan and colleagues were to cannibalise the abandoned aircraft. He recalls they 'landed like vultures' and stripped out spares galore.

On another occasion Stan never actually left the ground. It seems it wasn't always the practice to check an aircraft's 'payload'. This particular day saw him standing at the front of the Dakota, between the two pilot's seats, with boxes stacked high on either side of the fuselage. The pilot throttled up the engines

It was the publication of the photograph here in the Sixty Years On *series that led to the reuniting of three of the RAF men who witnessed a Vera Lynn concert in Burma in 1944. Stanley Johnson is standing on the left with his hands clasped. John Ashby is in the back row with the wavy fair hair to the right centre. Leslie Sumption was present but wasn't wearing a shirt and so was banished from the photo! The story of the trio's Burma experiences has been compiled by Malcolm Ashby, John's son. All three veterans came along to a special* Sixty Years On - We'll Meet Again *air show / concert held in May 2005 where they met with Dame Vera Lynn on stage and sang together the song she made her very own. More about this event and other* Sixty Years On *happenings can be be found in the 'Scrapbook' section starting on page 320.*

and they set off down the runway. Normal 'rotation' speed was reached and the pilot pulled back the stick but nothing happened; no response. Another attempt and still nothing. Running out of runway, the pilot cut the power and applied the brakes whereupon the aircraft failed to stop, left the runway, careered across the grass and crashed into a ditch. Inside the aircraft the abrupt halt had stopped everything except the heavy load and Stan remembers the supplies flying forward, forcing the bulkheads to collapse and pinning the two pilots in their seats! Fortunately every man on board walked away from the aircraft.

Calcutta Cathedral

Stan regularly visited a COE church in Kharagpur, where he attended confirmation classes. However, the nearest Bishop authorised to perform confirmations was in Calcutta. One day Stan 'hitch-hiked' on an aircraft bound for Dum Dum, Calcutta's airport, where he stayed with the Bishop before being confirmed in Calcutta Cathedral.

Kharagpur, Agatarla, Sylhet, Chittagong, Aykab and Dum Dum are all names that come flooding back and all three men have many tales and memories of their bases. Of the Kite-Hawks raiding any uncovered food. Of the Bamboo Basha huts, the heat, the

damp and mould during the monsoon season and of the white ants eating anything and everything, including 'the soles of your boots'! With new recruits, one game often played was to send them to the canteen for sandwiches, only to watch them being stolen by the Kite-Hawks, much to the amusement of the veterans.

The one outstanding bright moment of the campaign was the visit of Vera Lynn to the Squadron, with an ENSA party, on 10 May 1944. It was 'as if a breath of England had descended upon their jungle outpost' and 'one of their own family members had visited them', the three Vets recall. The visit included a tour of the sick quarters to greet airmen of all ranks, lunch with the 'boys', declining the invitation of the Officers, and a show in the bamboo theatre in the evening. Word had got out; Stan notes an entry in his diary on the 9th: 'Vera Lynn definitely coming tomorrow.' John, it seems, was not so well informed, though he remembers thinking 'something was happening' as there were flowers placed on all the mess tables. They all recall the photo-shoot, completed without Les as he scurried from his place of work without his shirt (not the done thing in front of a lady and especially when Squadron photos were being taken). John remembers the gathering of jungle flowers for the bouquet presented

to Vera, and they all remember the queues for her autograph, many written on one rupee notes. Sadly John spent his, though he was to take full advantage in reclaiming Dame Vera's signature once more, over 60 years later!

And so to the *Sixty Years On* lovely reunion, on a bright and breezy day in May 2005 at Glynde Place in East Sussex. Les, Stan and John were overwhelmed at being able to meet with Dame Vera once more. They remember her with such affection; she really was their 'Forces Sweetheart'. To sing *We'll Meet Again* with Vera on stage in front of thousands was a memorable experience. All three thoroughly enjoyed every minute of the day, and were made to feel like 'stars' themselves!

What of the other 'bird' in their lives all those years ago in the Far East, the venerable Dakota? 'We loved it, so easy to maintain, so reliable and capable of safely carrying a load even on one engine. All you needed were a couple of elastic bands in your tool kit and you could keep her flying forever' they all agreed. To this day the sound of the Pratt & Whitney radials are as easily discernable to these veterans as they were six-something decades ago.

Les, Stan, John, Dame Vera and all on No 31: 'Thank you', one and all.
Malcolm Ashby

HEROES RETURN

John Tebbut paid a visit to a quiet little place in Belgium where the fallen do not grow old.

Let me make it clear; I do not claim to be a hero. The title is taken from the Big Lottery Fund scheme, Heroes Return, that enabled ex-servicemen and women who saw active service overseas during the 1939-45 conflicts, to visit one or more of the war cemeteries. Grants were available to visit such cemeteries in Europe, Egypt and the Far East with additional grants for accompanying wives and also carers. It was an excellent initiative but unfortunately is now no longer available.

My own visit in October 2004 was prompted by a long-held desire to find out more about my late wife's cousin and if possible, to visit his grave, but I had very little information about him other than that he was in a Scottish regiment, although he himself hailed from Sheerness in Kent.

I first went to the War Graves Commission website. Reference to this gave me, in five minutes, all I wanted to know; regiment, army number, date of birth (his age 26) and very importantly, his burial site.

I was mystified that he was buried in Belgium, east of Antwerp, in the small village (now a small town) of Kasterlee. The information went against previous family beliefs that he was killed shortly after D-Day, but his date of death was 25 September 1944, three months later, far into the battle zones.

Above: John Tebbut today and, top right, pictured in 1940.

Gleaming headstone

I found the Kasterlee Cemetery, which is a very small one, with just 100 graves. As with every other Commonwealth Graves Commission War Cemetery I have visited, whether in Italy, France, Belgium or Holland, it was absolutely immaculate, so wonderfully maintained. It may be the wrong adjective, but I can only describe it as beautiful and peaceful in a small corner of cleared woodland overlooked, as if on guard, by a very large (non-working) windmill.

From the cemetery register – one is always kept in a waterproof compartment – I quickly found the grave's position and went to it. There it was, a gleaming white headstone. Alongside were those of his comrades and others probably unknown to him, Officers and other ranks, mostly from various Scottish Regiments although many were not Scottish. One even bore an inscription and a posy of flowers: 'He was only a simple Norfolk lad.' Other headstones indicated members of a Canadian regiment.

I was approached by an old Belgian man who I found often visits the graves. Unfortunately he could only speak Flemish (I had hoped to speak in French with him), but he could manage a few words in English, and with difficulty, was able to tell me how the soldiers lying there were killed.

He even showed me the river – he called it the canal – which the soldiers had been trying to cross with tragic results. I was very emotional; he had tears as he spoke with me, pointing out, on the headstones, the ages of the fallen, ranging from just 19 to one 'old man of his regiment', just 30 years of age.

What had attracted him to visit and revisit what I call a 'haven of peace'? I could only think that being of my generation, he really did appreciate what had been done for him and his family.

Allied comrades

The headstone I had come to see of Cousin Billy Isles, reads: 'Now that the job has been done I can rest in peace.' May God bless his soul in that far-off part of what is, although in Belgium, part of our Commonwealth. There are also many graves of Polish men, who although they were killed alongside their Allied comrades, were refused admittance to Poland because of some Polish problems. No doubt behind each headstone lies a very interesting story, which we will never know.

The cemetery at El Alamein.

My own war service took me to Egypt in 1940. On Remembrance Day each year at 11am, my thoughts immediately go back to the very first war grave I saw, in what was known as Libya. It was a hastily dug temporary grave with an improvised wooden cross bearing the name or number of a trooper of the 11th Hussars. He lay beside an overturned shell-ridden hulk of an armoured car. The wooden cross was surmounted by his helmet. I still remember vividly that first grave, but my latest visit to Kasterlee and Arnhem (I went on to Holland in the course of the same trip) have given me further cause to ponder.

I have to remember my own unwritten inscription: 'But for the grace of God, I could be lying in one of those war cemeteries instead of just visiting, standing and very emotionally, paying my respects.'

WAR DIARY
September 1944

By **1 September** 'The Great Swan' has been underway for four days. It's the name given by the British - notably the men of the 11th Armoured 'Black Bull' Division - to their rapid advance through Northern France in pursuit of the retreating Germans. The Allied progress since the breakout from the Normandy bridgehead a month ago has been astonishing. Some units are covering 60 miles or more in a day and are close to the Belgian border.

The following day the Finns finally accept Stalin's peace terms. Marshall Mannerheim believes that to delay an armistice any longer can only result in even more stringent Russian demands.

3 September: German troops have quit Brussels ahead of the arrival of the Guards Armoured Division. British units crossed the border in force over the last 24 hours to be welcomed by cheering crowds waving the red, yellow and black flag of Belgium.

The British 11th Armoured Division enters the port of Antwerp today **(4 September)**. Crowds of joyful civilians are out on the streets despite the presence of a large German garrison determined to make a stand. Bullets, shells and grenades fly in some parts of the city whilst close by, Allied fighting vehicles and their crews are mobbed by people offering flowers, bottles and kisses to their liberators. The Allies are desperate to secure a large port on the North Sea in order to shorten their supply lines which now stretch all the way back to Normandy.

5 September: In London the Government has decided that all Soviet citizens captured by British forces are to be repatriated to the USSR whether they want to go or not. Some 12,000 are currently being held in camps in the UK and hundreds more are being captured daily. Many of these Russians volunteered to fight with the *Wehrmacht* but the majority simply wanted to get out of the German POW camps where they had been starved and treated terribly. Thousands manned Hitler's Atlantic Wall but when the Allied invasion came most gave themselves up as quickly as they could.

On **6 September** blackout conditions in towns and cities across Britain have been relaxed and the Home Guard are told to partially stand down. German aircraft are no longer a threat and the blackout is no deterrent to the V1s.

7 September: Sedan is captured and the Moselle river crossed by the Allies. The town was the scene of the *Wehrmacht's* breakthrough in May 1940 when Hitler unleashed Blitzkrieg on France and Belgium. Now it is the Germans who are on the

This illustration by Leslie Ashwell-Wood depicts the fighting abilities of the M4 Sherman tank optimistically suggesting it could destroy the heavily armoured German Tiger and Panther tanks (National Archives - Art of War).

receiving end of 'Lightning War'.

A new type of German rocket - the V2 - plunged out of the early evening sky above Chiswick, West London, today **(8 September)**. Despite the resulting massive explosion, which left an enormous crater, just three people were killed. The noise of the blast was terrific - witnesses described it as like 'double thunderclaps followed by the rush of an express train'. These new weapons take just minutes to reach their targets hundreds of miles away. Unlike the V1, the V2 is a true rocket which ascends to the edge of space before hurtling back to earth.

On **9 September** the Allies enter Dutch territory when US forces drive into Maastricht. Further south in Lorraine there are supply problems for Patton's Third Army. There is no fuel for the tanks, which have halted on the banks of the Moselle, a tantalisingly short distance from the German border.

10 September: The first Allied vehicle, a US jeep crosses into German territory. The following day 20,000 surrounded Germans in Orleans surrender to the 83rd US Infantry Division.

11 September: Churchill and Roosevelt begin the 'Octagon' conference in Quebec. An important item on the agenda is the development of the top-secret atomic bomb.

On this day **(12 September)**, three months and one week after the first Allied soldier had set foot on French soil, the historic junction takes place of *Operation Overlord* and *Operation Dragoon* when soldiers from the Normandy beaches meet with soldiers from the South of France landings. The meeting takes place at Nod-sur-Seine, 150 miles south of Paris.

13 September: The British Eighth Army is hampered by the weather and terrain in their attacks on the Gothic Line in Italy.

Today **(14 September)** a daring underwater raid on Bergen, by a midget submarine, succeeded in destroying a huge floating dock. X24 commanded by Lt H P Westmacott negotiated 30 miles of offshore islands and mine fields before slipping into the Norwegian harbour.

The following day the *Arundel Castle* docks at Liverpool with over 1000 repatriated POWs returning home after, in some cases, four years of captivity.

16 September: After an 11-day lull the doodlebugs are back in southern England. This time they are being launched from aircraft flying from airfields in Holland.

On **17 September** *Operation Market Garden* is launched. In a bid to deliver a decisive blow to Germany and end the war early, Allied paratroopers drop into Holland to secure a series of bridges and waterways which form a corridor to the German border. Along it, according to Montgomery, will pour Allied

WAR DIARY
September 1944

Florence was freed from German oppression by 22 August 1944. Here we see men of the Eighth Army marching through the city. In the background is Il Duomo, fourth largest church in the world, dating from 1298. Largely spared destruction, the famous city quickly became a popular destination for Allied soldiers on leave. In September the Allies continued to make progress in breaking down the Gothic Line north of Florence and by the end of the month bridgeheads had been forced across the River Uso - the famous Rubicon of Julius Caesar. Rimini on the Adriatic coast was liberated and the Fifth Army had closed to within 15 miles of Bologna.

German self-propelled gun parked outside.

19 September: In New York Churchill and Roosevelt have been discussing the military applications for atomic energy and have agreed on full collaboration between their two countries. A decision is secretly made to use the atomic bomb on Japan as quickly as possible after the detonation of a test device.

By **20 September** US airborne troops have taken Eindhoven and Nijmegen. The 'corridor' is now in place but its narrowness is causing problems for the British armour advancing along it. The one main road is extremely vulnerable to attack from the flanks and a single tank or field gun can hold up an entire army.

There is now no hope of relief for Frost's men at Arnhem Bridge. Although Urquhart has escaped from his bolthole all he can do is form a defensive horseshoe around the village of Oosterbeek. German tanks are now pressing in on the lightly armed 'Red Devils'

On **21 September** British tanks cross the Waal bridge at Nijmegen but it is too late for 2nd Battalion at Arnhem bridge, who have been forced to surrender - Frost himself is amongst the wounded.

22 September: In the Pacific, Admiral Halsey's Third Fleet claims 205 Japanese aircraft destroyed both on the ground and in the air against 15 American losses.

23 September: Supreme Allied Commanders HQ is being moved from Normandy to Versailles. Since the invasion of France the Germans have lost upwards of a million men, over half of them captured.

On **24 September,** in the Pacific the Japanese launch a determined attack on US positions on Peleiu. Meanwhile in the Caroline Islands, on the atoll of Ulithi, the Americans are constructing a port in the safe haven of an enormous lagoon.

25 September: Montgomery authorises the withdrawal of British and Polish paratroops from the north bank of the Rhine.

The following day in Italy the Eighth Army crosses the **Rubicon,** the legendary river known to Caesar's legionnaires. The British are heading in the opposite direction to Caesar but hope their action will prove as decisive in ending a war.

On **27 September** the remaining British and Polish troops, many of them wounded, trapped on the north bank of the Rhine surrendered in the last hours of the nine-day battle to hold the bridgehead around Oosterbeek and Arnhem. Only 2400 of the 10,000 who took part in the operation escaped by boat or by swimming the river.

By **28 September** British troops are based on the Dalmatian islands in the Adriatic and are supporting Tito's partisans in preparation for an invasion of mainland Yugoslavia.

29 September: Dover need fear the 'big guns' of the Germans no more as Canadian troops capture the great batteries in the Cap Gris Nez area near Calais. Since 1940 the Germans have been able to hurl shells at the harbours and towns around Kent's white cliffs.

On **30 September** the surviving 7000 Germans of the Calais garrison surrender, despite brave displays of resistance which suggested they would fight on to the last man. Almost all of France is now free.

armies into Germany's lightly defended interior. The swift capture of the Ruhr industrial area will cripple German military capabilities and topple the Nazis.

The operation begins well as American paratroopers attack and secure bridges across the Maas and Waal rivers. At the northern end of the corridor first Airborne Division land against light opposition some eight miles from their target, the bridges at Arnhem. However jeep-carrying gliders fail to arrive and those that do are caught in an ambush. As Lt Col John Frost's 2nd Battalion nears the northern end of the road bridge at twilight there are ominous signs that a German reaction will not be long in making itself felt.

18 September: Lt Col Frost and 2nd Battalion have formed defensive positions overnight. Radio contact is erratic and reinforcements have failed to reach them, the Germans are approaching from the north and also have a tight grip on the southern end of the bridge. The commanding officer Maj-Gen Urquhart is currently hiding in the attic of a Dutch house with a

WARSAW'S AGONY
...dreams of freedom crushed

OCTOBER 1944

THE WARSAW UPRISING

was already free of the hated Nazi occupiers. Surely all the freedom fighters of the Home Army needed to do was wait a few weeks more for liberation from the East? Why did they risk needless confrontation with a ruthless and unpredictable German enemy who had no apparent choice but to retreat in the face of Stalin's limitless legions?

Polish loyalties

The key to the tragedy lay in divided loyalties. General Bor and the Home Army owed allegiance to the Polish Government-in-Exile based in London since the occupation of their country by the Germans (and until Hitler turned on them too, in part by the Russians) in 1939. By 1944 however, Stalin had built up a large army of Polish Communists who had appointed their own political leadership. Bor and the London Poles had good grounds for suspecting that Stalin's intentions for post-war Poland did not allow for democracy.

Churchill and other Western leaders shared their suspicions but geography alone ruled out any hope of large-scale assistance for the Home Army. The latter perceived that their only hope of asserting independence lay in freeing themselves from Nazi rule before the Russians and Communist Poles were able to. An uprising was inevitable.

In the first week the lightly armed Poles - buoyed up by enthusiasm and the knowledge that the Russians were close by - were successful. Key points and buildings all over the city were captured and much of the German garrison fled or was captured. But once the Germans had recovered from their surprise they reacted strongly. Hitler gave priority to the crushing of the rebellion. He allowed Himmler to divert precious land and air forces to carry out the task. Amongst the units selected by the SS supremo were SS police units, a brigade of Russian ex-POWs and a brigade of ex-convicts, all of whom were already notorious for their cruelty and excesses to soldiers and civilians alike. With relish this well-armed army, backed by powerful artillery and panzer support, set about reducing Warsaw to ruins.

Just as the German guns began to pound the city, block by block, so the guns of the

'Soldiers of the capital! I have today issued the order which you desire, for open warfare against Poland's age-old enemy, the German invader. After nearly five years of ceaseless struggle, carried on in secret, you stand today openly with arms in your hand, to restore freedom to our country, and to mete out fitting punishment to the German criminals for the terror and crimes committed by them on Polish soil.'

With these ringing words General Bor-Komorowski, Commander-in-Chief of the Polish Home Army, signalled the start of the Warsaw Uprising on 1 August 1944. A little over two months later, on 2 October, this same leader, with a sad and heavy heart, ordered his remaining fighters to lay down their arms and submit to the Germans. In the intervening period the beautiful Polish capital had been transformed into a desolate heap of rubble. And around 250,000 people, including at least 40,000 civilians, had lost their lives.

Even as part of a world war full of numbing brutality and mindless destruction, the crucifixion of Warsaw must be considered the most pointless exercise in violence. After all, by the end of July 1944 the guns over the ever-advancing Red Army could be heard by the Poles even from the banks of the Vistula and a broad sweep of Polish territory

Red Army close by fell silent. The Russians would make no attempt to support Bor's uprising. Indeed, for some time they even refused to allow British and American aircraft engaged in supplying arms to Warsaw to make emergency landings - let alone stops to refuel - in Russian-held territory.

Cry for help

Beleaguered Bor and the London Poles could only plead with the Western Allies. Three of their demands were simply not feasible - Allied bombing of the Warsaw area, the despatch of Polish fighter squadrons from France to the Warsaw area and the dropping of the Polish parachute brigade into the capital, even though in the latter case the men were anxious to go to the aid of their fellow countrymen.

A fourth request, a considerable increase in the air supply of arms and ammunition, was scarcely less formidable but was undertaken. The task fell upon the Allied air forces in Italy and the 1,759 mile round trips were probably the most hazardous of any made by Allied aircraft during the war in Europe. On five nights between 12 - 17 August out of 93 aircraft despatched, 17 failed to return.

The introduction of delayed-drop parachutes later enabled containers to be released above the range of the considerable light flak in position in and around the city. Bad weather meant many cancelled flights. When, six weeks after the uprising began the Russians finally permitted aircraft to land in their territory it was a case of too little too late despite a large-scale escorted operation by US aircraft flying a 'supply shuttle' out of UK bases and the start of nightly arms drops by planes of the Red Air Force.

Hopeless struggle

On the ground the Poles fought desperately against an enemy who brought Tiger and Panther tanks and flame-throwers to bear on houses and strongpoints where the defenders often only had rifles and pistols with which to defend themselves. Warsaw's Old Town - preserved since medieval times - was obliterated. Himmler wanted the fate of the city to be a terrifying warning to the rest of Europe.

Polish messenger women and children - the sole means of communication for the Home Army - took to the sewers. These same tunnels had become the distribution route for the dwindling supplies of food

Opposite page: Polish barricade on Chlodna Street, scene of a German counter-attack on 6 August 1944.
Above: An SS man surrenders - one of 115 taken prisoner by the Polish Home Army when the SS stronghold in Warsaw capitulated.

and ammunition. But the Poles never lacked courage in the face of the daunting odds and thousands died manning their street barricades to the very end. Blizzards of artillery fire followed by Stuka dive-bombing would be concentrated on different districts day after day. Remote-controlled Goliath mini-tanks packed with explosives were deployed against Home Army strongpoints.

Massacres of captured insurgents and civilians alike were reported. Early in the Uprising a young woman named Wanda was seized while taking shelter with others in the Ministry of Commerce building in Elektoralna Street. Narrowly escaping rape, she was driven with a procession of mostly young women with children towards the district of Wola. At one point German troops ordered them all to lie down from one side of the street to the other to form a human barricade against insurgent fire.

'We were all prepared to die' she later told George Bruce, author of *The Warsaw Uprising* (Rupert Hart-Davis Ltd, 1972), 'Bullets whistled over our heads or past our ears. As if by some miracle they only hit the Germans...They were bewildered by the fact that only they were falling and we thought that they would most certainly take their revenge on us. Stupefied and astonished they looked towards the insurgent posts and then at our quiet, resigned attitude, and the children clinging to their mothers. At last they let us go.'

Others were not so fortunate. It's estimated that as part of a deliberate plan based on Himmler's orders nearly 40,000 civilians were killed in the uprising.

Rights of combatants

The end was not far away. On 1 October General Bor declared in a message to the London Government, 'I have decided to enter into negotiations for surrender with full combatant rights, which the Germans fully recognise.'

Astonishingly, the latter part was true. The heroic resistance had forced their enemy to confer Geneva Convention statutes upon the Poles, fighters and civilians alike. German General von dem Bach praised the valour and courage of the Home Army. Of course the Germans also knew that very soon the Russian offensive must resume whereupon besieged Warsaw would be relieved. The eyes of the world would then see a victory for an enslaved people over their one-time masters.

The next day the Poles began marching out of Warsaw to lay down their arms outside of the city. By 6 October the whole place had been evacuated. Now the wholesale destruction of those parts not already razed in the fighting began. It only ended once Warsaw had been destroyed as no city had ever been destroyed before.

Yet Warsaw was destined to be no Carthage. Within a year work commenced on reconstruction of this one-time city of life and light astride the Vistula. The project turned into a national saga with the entire Old Town being re-erected street by street and house by house, even to the carvings and mural designs.

Today, Poland is a democracy once more. More than six decades on, Warsaw must count as the embodiment of this proud nation's will to survive and go forward.

Two women of WARSAW

Ingrid Pitt tells the story of two Polish women who lived through the Warsaw Uprising.

Coming from a Polish background I thought I knew, *mas o menos*, what had happened to Poland in the Second World War. I accepted the 'facts' because they came from reliable Allied sources. When the Germans invaded Poland on 1 September 1939, I thought it wonderful how the British had told them to get out. When, three days later, they were still pouring troops into that sovereign country, Prime Minister Chamberlain, forgetting his mantra of 'Peace in our Time', courageously and quixotically put the country and his own future at risk by declaring war on the Nazi Reich.

Pure simple stuff. What came after didn't bother me a lot. Of course there was the Jewish Ghetto Uprising in April 1943. Everyone knew about that. And occasionally there were stories about the Polish airmen who fought so gallantly in the Battle of Britain. Infrequently I heard rumours peddled about how the English and the Americans had more or less ignored what was going on in Poland and then, after the war, sold the country out for a saccharine smile from Uncle Joe Stalin. Nasty stories that seemed like a particularly noxious bunch of sour grapes.

Then I read *Rising '44: The Battle for Poland*, published by Pan Books in May 2004. The book laid bare as facts some of the things I'd taken for nasty rumours. Most upsetting was the revelation that the Poles, who had fought so ferociously for the Allies and had been a large factor in there still being a Britain to fight for after the Battle of Britain

in 1940, were denied the honour of appearing in the Victory Parade after the war. Why? Because the Allies didn't want to offend the Soviet Union.

The fear of upsetting Stalin went way back. It was one of the prime reasons that the Allies stood aside when the Polish Home Army rallied the troops and took on the might of the ruthless Nazi battalions in the Warsaw Uprising that began on 1 August 1944. The Soviet Army had fought its way through eastern Europe and were encamped on the east side of the Vistula, the wide river which divides Warsaw. Stalin had already made a pact with the Allies to honour the treaty the Russians had made with Germany, when they were still buddies, to deliver to them territories in the east of Poland. However, Polish Home Army General Bor-Komorowski, reasoned that if they could liberate themselves from the Germans before the Russians arrived they would be able to engage the sympathy of the Allies and keep at least their capital city from Soviet occupation. He set 1 August as Liberation Day.

Clandestine hospital

Maria Fiszer knew little of the politics that had decided the leaders of the Home Army to fight at that particular time. She had heard that the Russians were just across the river and listened to many arguments for and against taking the fight to the Germans. Maria was born in Warsaw on 11 October 1911. When she was two years old her mother died. Her father served in the First World War and was killed. Her upbringing was taken over by the Nuns at a convent on the

outskirts of the Polish capital city.

For years Maria had avoided contact with the German occupiers as much as possible. She had been a nurse in a hospital where the Nazis had dismissed the staff and thrown out the patients. The Polish Home Army ordered her to set up a hospital in a safe house. These hospitals were for treating the civilian population denied medical care by their oppressors and also to treat any Home Army soldiers who might be unfortunate enough to be wounded in action against the enemy. She was a Catholic girl with a Catholic girl's education. She had taken up nursing because she felt it was a profession of which she could be proud to be a member. Nothing had prepared her for the nightmare that was to come.

The day before the Uprising she was told to report to the house they were using as a hospital. It was on the far side of the city and about as far away from the river front separating the Poles from the advancing Russians as you could get. When she got there she realised that this wasn't just routine. Extra beds were being brought in and those already there were rearranged so that more could be squeezed in. Everyone was rolling bandages, making up beds and doing all the things that have to be done on the eve of battle. Nobody was allowed to leave. Everybody had their own idea of what was going on but not even the Home Army Captain in charge of the hospital knew the details.

Flood of casualties

The following morning the city was unusually quiet. The fighting on the east bank of the Vistula had stopped and there was an uneasy feeling that the Russians might start a bombardment on the Germans still holding the city. It was not a nice feeling. The Poles wanted to be free of the hated Hun but it would mean vicious street by street fighting and artillery bombardments that would kill many of the city's civilian population. The quiet lasted through the afternoon. Many of the hospital staff found themselves a bed and got some sleep. To Maria it seemed that she had hardly closed her eyes when she was jerked awake by the sound of gunfire. She jumped up and ran to the window. There was nothing to be seen but the muted sound of distant battle was in the air. The Sisters drove the nurses back to work. The Captain, clad in his Home Army uniform, gathered everyone in the hall. He told them this was the day they had all been waiting for - Liberation Day. Soon the city would once again be in Polish hands. But before that glorious day they would have a lot of work to do. There were bound to be casualties and it was their duty to work unceasingly to see that the injured and dying received the very best treatment.

Before midnight the casualties of the fighting began to trickle in. As many civilians as Home Army soldiers. The trickle became a flood. Maria was used to seeing injuries caused by road accidents or fires but the bodies brought into the secret and

Above and right: Maria Fiszer pictured in Warsaw with nurses and ready to go into action during the Uprising.

ill-equipped hospital stretched her ability to cope. Several times she wanted to quit. To tell the doctors that she couldn't take it. But she stayed. She never lost that feeling of inadequacy all through the brutal 63 days of the Uprising. But like hundreds of thousands of others thrust into the carnage of war she was able to control her own horror and try to alleviate the suffering of others.

When the fighting had started General Bor had thought it would all be over in a couple of days. What did the Germans have to fight for? The Russians were a few miles to the east sunning themselves on the cooling banks of the Vistula and the Allied forces were bludgeoning their way from the west against stiff opposition. It seemed to the Polish high command that when they became aware of the situation the pragmatic Germans wouldn't waste time fighting for a city they were bound to lose in the long run. It was logical that they would extricate what troops they could and re-deploy them in a position where they could take the fight to the Allies with a chance of a modicum of success. The Poles hadn't taken into account that the enemy thought that it would be unforgivable for crack Nazi battalions to be defeated by a group of ragged, ill-equipped Poles.

Typhoid ruse

The Russians, for their part, were quite willing to let the Germans wipe out the city. They wanted to add Warsaw to their empire and if they didn't have to fight for it so much the better. In London and Washington Polish diplomats in exile begged the authorities to intervene. Very little was done. The British tried to cut a deal with Stalin to use bases behind the Soviet lines from which they could make parachute drops but Stalin said 'Niet'. They attempted to fly in supplies from Italian bases but the logistics were against them and they were forced to give up. The Poles would have to go it alone. Maria wanted to do more. She inveigled one of the doctors into giving her a certificate which said he suspected her of having contracted typhoid and covered it with a letter saying that she was on her way to see another doctor for a second opinion. The letter was in her underground name of Skofia so that there could be no trace of her origins if she was interrogated. Maria was able to move about the city distributing food and ammunition hidden under her coat. When stopped she waved her letter saying she had typhoid and the Germans backed off.

The sewers had become the Resistance highways as well as safe havens for the Poles and the few remaining Jews hiding from the Nazis. Maria used them extensively to distribute the arms, ammunition and food she was entrusted by the Home Army to carry. She worked most nights and had to snatch catnaps during the day so that she could keep going.

While Maria worked ceaselessly to alleviate the suffering of the victims of the fighting, Eva Buterlewicz had other problems. Her father had worked for a Polish/Russian company, based in Moscow. Eva was born there in 1916. When the Germans invaded Poland her father went home taking Eva and his wife, heavily pregnant with their second baby, with him. Eva was a newly qualified teacher when the Germans made their violent move on Poland. She had to stand back and watch as the Nazis forced their way into the universities and schools. In the first days of the occupation over a thousand Intellectuals and teachers were slaughtered. All the schools were commandeered and Polish children were banned. Eva was saved by her lowly position in the school - at this time she was little more than a class helper.

With others from her school she had joined the Polish Home Army. For a laugh. It seemed absurd to think of themselves, little more than a gaggle of giggling schoolgirls, as soldiers. When the Nazis moved in the giggling stopped. They were gathered together and told what was expected of them. Eva was made a courier - a message carrier between the various recognised sections of the Polish community and the Nazi military command. She was small and petite and looked suitably inoffensive for the role. Her secondary, and secret, occupation would be continuing the education of the children in spite of the German ban. It meant frequent changes of location and the constant fear that a German patrol might stumble upon their hideaway or that one of the children might inadvertently give away their location. As she became more experienced she was able to bring in people who could tell the children what was going on in the outside world and assure them that soon the Germans would be overthrown and they would be able to get on with their lives in peace and freedom.

Took to the sewers

Her position as a messenger gave her an inside view of what was going on. As the Russians approached she was aware that big decisions were being made amongst the leaders of the Home Army although she had no idea what they were. On 31 July she was told that the classes for the children were to be abandoned and their parents urged to

Above right: Eva Buterlewicz. During the Warsaw Uprising she was a messenger for the Polish Home Army.

Above left: A document of the Home Army dated 23 September 1944. Both Eva and Maria survived the war.

send them out of the city. Eva was ordered to be on standby to deliver some important messages. She was also given the rank of Second Lieutenant.

All day on 1 August 1944 she scuttled around the city delivering messages and orders to the local members of the Home Army. In her pocket she had a piece of paper which she hoped would keep her safe. It was a pass signed by the Nazis which gave her permission to move around the city. Several times she was stopped by patrols but once she was able to produce the pass she was waved on without being searched. At 5pm that afternoon the piece of paper became useless. When the Polish Uprising began the German Commandant, Eric Von Dem Bach, gave the order that 'civilian' Poles suspected of aiding the rebellion should be shot on sight. Some 35,000 men, women and children paid the price for their birthright. Eva now had to be careful that she did not run into the patrols. Like thousands of her fellow insurgents she took to the sewers beneath the city which had served the Jews so well only 13 months earlier when they put up their heroic but ultimately vain attempt to fight off the Germans.

By the end of September, with Warsaw a flattened and burned out moonscape, General Bor realised that the gallant Polish fighters had given all they had to give and reluctantly he began negotiations for peace with the Germans. While the Russian Army watched from across the river, thousands of Polish men, women and children died. The Russians finally made their move on 17 January 1945 - five and a half months after the Uprising.

Ingrid Pitt is an author and actress who made her name in the famous film **Where Eagles Dare with Richard Burton and Clint Eastwood. She is also well known from the legendary Hammer Horror movies of the Sixties and Seventies.*

Art Direction

Evolution of a Wartime Poster Painting

Clive Uptton painted the two pictures displayed on these pages. His first version (above) was the one reproduced in a smaller size to the other. Dating from mid-1944 it shows three British soldiers, dressed in jungle fatigues and carrying Thompson sub machine guns, wading through a jungle swamp that's almost certainly in Burma.

Mr W Embleton of the Ministry of Information has written some notes for the artist on the painting to the effect: 'Dear Uptton. This looks very promising indeed - thanks a lot. My only comments are that the leading figure should look more "urgent" - at present he looks a little unreal and is asking to be shot at. Could he not be clambering forward like the chaps following him? Also watch carefully the position of the gun which should be held under his right arm surely? As title is to be overprinted in black I think we doctor the background a little don't you? Otherwise fine - Embleton.'

Clive Uptton took on board the Man from the Ministry's suggestions (or, rather, his polite directions!) and produced the second version seen on the page opposite (National Archives - The Art of War).

CHOCOLATE STAIRCASE
AND THE
VALLEY OF DEATH

In September and October 1944 the importance of Allied air power in helping the troops on the ground defeat the Japanese in Burma was demonstrated forcefully on the Tiddim Road and Kabaw valley. The latter name means 'Valley of Death' and the area is said to be one of the most highly malarial places in the world as well as being home to the scrub typhus mite.

Throughout the two months in question, 11th East African Division made steady progress against a retreating enemy. Appalling weather brought mud and floods and the potential for epidemics amongst the troops was enormous. However, a combination of good hygiene discipline and the fact that the whole length of the road was sprayed with DDT from the air by fighter-bombers, kept Allied casualties from both malaria and typhus to a minimum. The Japanese, on the other hand, perished in their hundreds from these diseases.

Supplied by air

Parallel to this advance, Fifth Indian Division was advancing south down the Tiddim Road. After crossing the Manipur River in mid-September, continuous landslides on the road behind made re-supply by road impossible and the Division had to be supplied entirely by air – even down to spare jeep engines. Everything came down by parachute as there were no landing strips and in the monsoon conditions it was impossible to construct any.

At the beginning of October the battle for Tiddim began. The final approach to the town from the north was very difficult especially once the road leaves the valley of the Manipur River and climbs 3700 feet in 10 miles, the first six consisting of 36 steep hairpin bends known as the 'Chocolate Staircase'. Tiddim itself is 162 miles from Imphal and lies 5600 feet above sea level.

Having failed to hold the river line it quickly became clear that the Japanese thought they stood a good chance of holding Tiddim and their troops constructed strong positions at just about every milestone in the road. Hurricane fighter-bombers intervened at every opportunity – when not blasting the enemy with bombs the noise of the low-flying aircraft helped hide the rumble of advancing tanks. Heartened by such effective support, the Indian Division pressed their attack with great vigour with the result that Tiddim was occupied on 18 October.

British soldiers of the Fourteenth Army enjoy a game of cards just 300 yards from the Japanese positions.

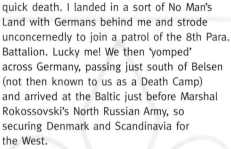

War Correspondence

Not bad for a 'Conshy'

I hold a hat trick of Doodlebugs! I witnessed a launching site, the over-flight of a V1 in the Ardennes and one exploding on descent in London. Your excellent *Sixty Years On* has brought it all back to mind.

On 5 October 1944 I had at last secured an interview at 100 Eaton Square before a board of three Airborne officers following my volunteering to serve as an unarmed medic with the Paras. I should explain that I was a 'conshy' and being awarded non-combatant status in the Army, had, on call up in October 1941, volunteered for Bomb Disposal. I served in London from 1941-1943, with the object of relieving the civilian population who were evacuated from their homes under the threat of UXBs (Unexploded Bombs).

Probably because I was extremely short-sighted, my first application for the Paras failed in June 1943. This second time when challenged about my sight – 'How can you expect to land behind enemy lines without your glasses?' - I insisted that I could stick my army steel specs to the side of my face with surgical tape and was accepted for training. As so many medics had been lost on D-Day and even more at Arnhem, I suspect that on this occasion they might have taken me with a tin leg!

While down in London I called to see 'Olly' Beech at his home in Herne Hill (he had been our Despatch Rider in Bomb Disposal) and during an air raid we took shelter in his basement. We held our breath waiting for the chug chugging of a V1 to stop and foretell the descent and explosion and breathed a sigh of relief when it missed us. Later in the Ardennes, I was detailed from 224 Para. Field Ambulance to staff a Casualty Clearing Station with the 1st Canadian Para Battalion (part of our 3rd Para. Brigade) fighting on the northern flank of the 'Bulge'. En route we had time to crawl over a bombed V1 launching platform surrounded by broken rockets and shattered cylinders of propellant. Later we saw V1s chugging overhead from Holland or Germany bound for London and were bombed by screaming Stuka dive bombers. The latter were designed to terrify us and this they did. Thus in the space of three months or so I had taken shelter at the 'business end', visited a launch site and seen V1s in transit overhead.

Later I was on *Operation Varsity Challenge* over the Rhine on 24 March 1945 and remember changing places with a man consumed with superstition, who couldn't jump as No 13. He took my number, dropped in the trees and was a sitting target for rifle and machine gun fire, so it was a quick death. I landed in a sort of No Man's Land with Germans behind me and strode unconcernedly to join a patrol of the 8th Para. Battalion. Lucky me! We then 'yomped' across Germany, passing just south of Belsen (not then known to us as a Death Camp) and arrived at the Baltic just before Marshal Rokossovski's North Russian Army, so securing Denmark and Scandinavia for the West.

Upon returning home we had 29 days leave prior to embarkation for the Far East and the ultimate assault on Japan (which I reckoned would be my come-uppence). But the atom bombs that killed so many thousands, most probably did save our lives. Instead we were sent to Palestine to try and calm the Jewish struggle for independence. I had an interesting time there with various 'specials' for 12 months before demob in the autumn of 1946.

Not bad really for a 'conshy'. I had spent four out of five years in the Army in voluntary service. But I'm not a bloody hero, nor I hope a coward, though I often think I could have done so much more. I suppose I'm what might be described as a 'freethinker'. My only faith is in the power of conscience. War is not the glorious adventure depicted on films; it's cruel, destructive and worst of all, indiscriminate in the slaughter and maiming of women and children and non combatants who play no part in the conflict. Did I do the right thing? I'll never know, but undoubtedly I had interesting experiences, especially being part of the camaraderie in those two very worthwhile jobs.

I am writing up my memoirs and have so far completed my first 40 years. Another 40 to go to cover travel, mountaineering, rock climbing, marriage to my loving and caring wife, continental camping, rambling, mountain walking in Austria and Switzerland, and then a serious illness which now prevents me from too much walking. Shall I live long enough to finish it? My mother lived to 101, so I'm hoping for a decade or so yet.
Chris Saunders, Hants

British in Belsen

The War Diary entry for 15 April 1945 (page 258) says that there was just one Englishman amongst the 60,000 inmates of the concentration camp at Bergen freed on that day. My father-in-law crossed into France on D Day +1 as a heavy goods driver with the artillery. Later he was part of the convoy that followed just behind the tanks in the course of Operation Market Garden in September 1944.

Then early in 1945, whilst recovering vehicles to the west of Celle, he and some of his troop, were captured and taken to Bergen-Belsen as this was very close by. He stayed there until the camp was liberated by his own joint British Canadian unit. The stories he has told us about conditions in the camp during this period are unimaginable. After being freed and enjoying a short period of 'R&R' he found himself once again back in the camp helping dispose of the bodies into large pits by use of a bulldozer. He also brought water tankers into the camp. I know from his accounts of this period that he was not the only British person there.
Dave Pickerell, Exeter

D-Day Dodgers

I was very interested in the article about the D-Day Dodgers song in June's *Sixty Years On* (see pages 108-109). Readers may not be aware that the writer of the words, Captain Hamish Henderson, was at that time an intelligence officer serving in Italy with the 51st Highland Division. He in fact accepted the surrender in Italy on 29 April 1945. He wrote many other songs and poems and was very much involved in the School of Scottish Studies at Edinburgh University. He died in 2002 after a very rich and full life. There are many websites giving information about him and there is an excellent tribute CD entitled *A' the Bairns O'Adam* which gives a little of his history. The first track on the CD is the authentic *Ballad of the D-Day Dodgers* (Greentrax Recordings Ltd, CDTRAX244. Tel: 01875 814155. E-mail: iangtrax@aol.com).
Duncan P MacGregor, Dundee

WAR DIARY

October 1944

The first day of **October 1944** sees the US 7th Armoured Division getting a bloody nose in the course of an attack around Overloon and Venray in Holland. The Americans are fighting in the same area as the British 11th Armoured but lack the latter's combat experience and progress is less than three miles in a week.

On **2 October** at 10pm the guns stop firing in Warsaw, 63 days after the uprising began. The Polish Home Army is out of ammunition and food and without hope of Russian relief. Some 15,000 Polish fighters have died along with an estimated 200,000 civilians and 10,000 SS and Wehrmacht troops. Surrendering Polish fighters are being treated as prisoners of war rather than rebels.

3 October: Fighting on the Channel coast continues. In Dunkirk the Germans agree to a truce to allow the civilian population to be evacuated. In Italy the US Fifth Army is nearing Bologna but casualties are high, 550 killed or wounded a day.

4 October: Britain is still under bombardment from V2 rockets. It was hoped that *Operation Market Garden* would remove or at least restrict this threat. It is believed they are being launched from Denmark.

5 October: Today the British landed on mainland Greece by sea. It seems the Germans are evacuating the country as fast as possible; the British are moving quickly to trap the 10,000-strong German garrison in Athens. It will be another two days before Hitler gives the order for his men to pull out.

6 October: In Burma the battle for Tiddim continues with tanks and air support proving to be the Allied 'ace' as the 5th Indian Division advances. The men of the Japanese 15th Army are resolutely defending every bend in the road.

7 October: The inmates of Auschwitz-Birkenau Concentration Camp stage a mass revolt against their tormentors today. With hammers and pickaxes for weapons they managed to overpower some guards and the revolt quickly spreads. SS reinforcements are quickly on the scene and set about ruthlessly crushing the revolt. Few of those involved in the uprising will live to tell the tale.

8 October: US forces are moving on Aachen in Germany in a pincer movement.

By next day advance parties of Land Forces, Adriatic, are within sight of Megara airfield, 20 miles west of Athens. In the next two days convoys from Italy and the Middle East will put to sea, heading for the Greek capital.

10 October: The Dumbarton Oaks conference in Washington has not fully resolved the deep differences of opinions between the US, USSR and Britain.

Today **(11 October)**, four Gloster Meteors of No 616 Sqdn are carrying out a week-long programme of fighter affiliation exercises with Eighth USAAF to give the bomber crews experience of jet fighter attacks. This is in response to the activation of the first operational German jet fighter unit.

12 October: In the East China Sea, Admiral Halsey's Third US Fleet is attacking Formosa with carrier-based aircraft.

On **13 October** King George VI visits VIII Corps HQ in the Netherlands and meets General 'Pip' Roberts of 11th Armoured Division and other commanding officers.

14 October: Germany's greatest military hero of the war, Field Marshall Erwin Rommel, dies. He was visited at his home by two senior officers sent personally by Hitler. They told the 'Desert Fox' that he could either take his own life at once or be arrested for implication in the 20 July bomb plot against Hitler. He was able to say farewell to his family before taking poison.

Athens and the Greek capital's port, Piraeus are occupied by British troops.

15 October: The industrial heartland of Germany, the Ruhr, has been the target for a massive bombing campaign over the last few days. Duisburg was hit by 1013 RAF Lancasters and Halifaxes and 1251 USAAF Flying Fortresses and Liberators.

With the Russians already inside his country, Hungarian Regent, 73-year-old Admiral Nikolaus Horthy von Nagybanya, announces on the radio his intention to seek an armistice with Stalin. Within hours he is in the custody of German commandos led by SS Colonel Otto 'Scarface' Skorzeny. The Nazis appoint an 'Acting Regent' who orders Hungarian forces to fight on against the Red Army.

In the Netherlands the Churchill tanks of the Guards take Overloon on **16 October.** A Victoria Cross has been won by Sgt George Eardley of the King's Shropshire Light Infantry for undertaking under heavy fire three brave actions against enemy machine-gun posts.

17 October - Norway. Grand Admiral Dönitz is determined to resurrect the U-Boat threat to Allied shipping by utilising new technology. A new and improved version of the Schnorkel allows submarines to replenish their air supply whilst remaining

Right: A 1944 advertisement for a popular brand of custard.

WAR DIARY
October 1944

submerged and out of sight of vigilant Allied aircraft.

18 October: In Germany all able-bodied men between 16 and 60 are being called-up for the *Volkssturm* (People's Front) home guard in defence of the Reich.

Today **(19 October)** the start of a major Russian push into East Prussia is reported. In Burma Indian troops of the Fourteenth Army have taken Tiddim.

20 October: In early 1942 General MacArthur vowed 'I shall return' when forced to leave the Philippines. Today he fulfilled that vow when at noon he walked through the surf onto the beach at Leyte. The 600-ship US invasion force was not due to attack for another two months but when large gaps in the Japanese defences were noticed it was decided to go in early. By the end of the day 100,000 US troops will be ashore.

21 October: Belgrade is still celebrating after the entry into the city of the First Proletarian Division of Tito's Army of National Liberation 24 hours ago. The escape route out of Yugoslavia for German Army Group E is threatened.

On **22 October** the Red Army invading Prussia stops just 45 miles short of Hitler's Rastenburg 'Wolf's Lair' Headquarters. Meanwhile Second Tactical Air Force is conducting a bombing campaign against known launch sites for V2 rockets in the Netherlands.

The following day **(23 October)** the Battle of Leyte Gulf opened with the sinking of two Japanese heavy cruisers and a light cruiser by US submarines waiting in ambush.

Moscow reports making further gains in Northern Transylvania, Hungary, Czechoslovakia and Yugoslavia.

24 October: In what may turn out to be the greatest naval battle ever fought, a total of 282 American and Japanese vessels are locked in combat today. The US Navy have superior numbers but sustain an early setback with the loss of the carrier USS *Princeton*, sunk by dive-bombers. Over 1000 Japanese sailors perish as their battleship *Musashi* goes down.

25 October: In the Netherlands the Germans are counting the cost of a low-level bombing raid carried out by RAF Typhoons on a building housing a conference of high-ranking officers. Two generals and 92 German officers and other ranks died.

Soviet forces advancing from Lapland have crossed into German-occupied Norway to seize the port of Kirkenes in the far north of the country.

On **26 October** the Battle of Leyte Gulf ends in a crushing defeat for the Imperial Japanese Navy - they have lost 28 ships including their last four carriers against a toll of four US vessels sunk. It puts an end to Japanese hopes of stemming the US advance on the home islands. The battle produced an ominous portent for the Americans when suicide pilots - *Kamikaze* (Divine Wind) - claim their first victim, the escort carrier *St Lo*.

27 October: It seems the Allies must spend another winter in Italy as the bad weather has scuppered the offensive plans of the Eighth and Fifth Armies on either side of the Apennines.

The next day Bulgaria and the Russians sign an armistice giving control of the country's armed forces to the Red Army.

29 October: The battleship *Tirpitz*, moored in Norway, is once again the target of an RAF airstrike. Even though 32 massive 12,00lb Tallboy bombs are dropped, poor visibility prevents any hits being scored.

The Hungarian Third Army has disintegrated in the face of a powerful assault by Russia's 6th Guards Tank Army leaving the road to Budapest wide open. But even as the Russians approach the capital, the SS - organised by the notorious Adolf Eichmann - continue the deportation of Hungarian Jews destined for the death camps in Germany.

On **30 October** US ground forces on Leyte capture Dagami. Out at sea the Kamikaze have been attacking US aircraft carriers. In the last two days the *Intrepid*, *Franklin* and *Belleau Wood* have all been hit.

31 October: The Japanese prepare to release 9000 balloons, each carrying an explosive charge, in the hope that the prevailing wind will carry them 6000 miles across the Pacific to detonate in the USA. The vast majority of the balloons will never make it but a few will cause minor casualties.

Below: The Gestapo HQ at Aarhus in Denmark still smoking after an attack on 31 October 1944 by 25 Mosquito fighter-bombers of RAF No 12 Group. The raid destroyed Gestapo records and enabled a young pastor, Harald Sandbaek, to escape from a torture chamber. The aircraft flew so low that one of them hit the roof of the building, losing its tail wheel and the port half of the tail plane. Even so, the sturdy machine managed to make it back to base.

MOVING
UP TO THE
SIEGFRIED LINE

NOVEMBER 1944

Battle for Walcheren

As the autumn of 1944 gave way to winter on the Dutch - German border the weather became cold and damp. In the low-lying Peel Country, troops on both sides found their slit trenches quickly filling up with water. Lots of small but nonetheless deadly dangerous operations took place as the British felt their way forward to the strong points and bunkers of the Siegfried Line.

One important battle was the British assault on Walcheren Island that began on 1 November at dawn in atrocious weather. The island was important because it commanded the Scheldt and so long as the Germans held it the Allies could not use the river to gain access to the vital port of Antwerp.

An eight day struggle ensued before the last of the German defences were overcome. Minesweeping of the Scheldt began on 4 November and the first convoy sailed into Antwerp on 28 November.

Along the whole Western Front the Germans fought hard though a steady stream of prisoners came in. Very often these men proved not to be German at all. In his book *Churchill's Desert Rats – from Normandy to Berlin with the 7th Armoured Division* (Alan Sutton Publishing, 1994) Patrick Delaforce quotes one tankman's view of a batch: 'This lot were a rabble and included a couple of Mongolians, ex-Russians who were used as stooges and general dogsbodies of *Wehrmacht* men who were themselves a more contemptible shower. One skinny 12-year-old Hitler *Jugend* from the Langemark Division, blubbered and writhed when captured yet this dangerous lad had a Schmeisser machine pistol, a Luger, three potato masher grenades and a wicked paratrooper knife. The culprit received a damned good spanking and was sent off to a POW cage.'

Hurtgen Forest

To the south in late October, Aachen had been the first German city to fall in the west. Its capture also involved the first breaching of the Siegfried Line, Hitler's last major defensive bastion before the River Rhine itself. But beyond Aachen the Americans became embroiled in bloody fighting in the Hurtgen Forest. So fierce and gruelling was the conflict that a number of units were withdrawn and sent south to the quiet Ardennes sector for rest and recuperation.

In Alsace the US Seventh Army and First French Army had closed on the Siegfried Line in a number of places in November and December. The city of Strasbourg on the River Rhine itself was captured by General Leclerc's men on 23 November. Around the town of Bitche, the Germans had taken over a section of the old French Maginot Line, which had been designed to afford all-round defence.

Shermans outgunned

A large pocket of Germans remained on French territory in the area of Colmar and southwards to the border with Switzerland. The Vosges Mountains around here – today so popular with tourists and famous for wines produced on the gentle slopes facing the Rhine – made it easy to defend the roads leading to Germany. Hitler was determined to hold on to Alsace – a region which had long been a cause of strife between the French and Germans. He sent in powerful Panther and Jagdpanther tanks which outgunned the Shermans of the French First Army. Progress was slow and costly; it took to the end of 1944 to liberate most of Alsace and even then parts of the Colmar pocket remained in German hands.

Meanwhile, in the approximate centre of the Western Front, below Luxembourg, Patton's third US Army was driving towards the Saar region of Germany. In his way lay the French city of Metz, fortified and garrisoned under the command of a tough Nazi who was determined to obey Hitler's order to fight to the last man. It was not until 18 November that the first Americans entered Metz; it took another four days before the Germans finally surrendered.

An unidentified British General in front of a formation of Sherman tanks (National Archives - Art of War).

THE BIGGEST BANG IN BRITAIN?

What may well have been the loudest explosion ever heard in Britain, occurred at about 5am on 22 November 1944, near the foot of the cliffs beneath Newhaven Fort in East Sussex. The massive blast damaged almost every building in the town and around the harbour and blew out scores of windows in Lewes, some seven miles away. It was audible up to 30 miles inland and was heard in Dieppe, 70 miles away on the other side of the English Channel.

The explosion, at first thought to be due to enemy action, was found to be caused by a British barge loaded with over 180 tons of a very high explosive. It was being towed up the Channel and broke away from a tug in a heavy storm, drifting ashore under the high cliffs slightly to the west of Newhaven, where it struck a landmine.

In Newhaven itself, hundreds of residents were blown completely out of their beds, or had furniture, glass and ceilings crashing down on them, yet among the hundreds of casualties, there were very few serious ones, just seven people being detained in hospital. There was one fatality, a naval rating killed by a falling wall. The fact that the explosion happened so early in the morning saved many lives; streets and residential roads were left littered with glass and debris. Altogether, a total of 1760 houses and shops were damaged and nearly 4000 persons affected.

Keith Baker of the Sussex Royal British Legion was a youngster living in the village of Rodmell, less than four miles from the scene of the blast. He remembers how it brought ceilings in houses down and blew out many cottage windows in the vicinity.

The 'Bloomsbury Set' novelist Virginia Woolf had earlier chosen to live in Rodmell because it was so peaceful!

By coincidence, the Newhaven blast's epicentre was within 15 yards of a crater caused by the explosion of a V1 bomb which had crashed into the cliffs on 30 July. On that occasion, there had been slight injuries caused to three people and damage to 24 houses although none to the fort itself.

War Correspondence

In the course of publishing the Sixty Years On *series we received many contributions from people who grew up as children in the war years. We print a selection of these letters on the following pages.*

Affection for flying

As a seven-year-old schoolboy in NW London during the war, one morning playtime an Allied aircraft flew overhead trailing smoke. The crew were bailing out and I believe the pilot died in the crash not far away. After the midday break, on returning to school, a mate told me that one of the crew had landed in a tree and his mother had rescued him and taken him for a 'cuppa'. I was most envious and wished it had been my back garden.

This incident left me with a long affection for flying and development of the jet age. I just managed National Service in the RAF.
John Cameron, Torpoint, Cornwall

Wimbledon at War

My mother's family led by my grandmother decided in 1938 to move from the East End of London to Wimbledon for convenience of my uncle who had a protected trade, I being a mere 18 months old. It was a large house that catered for my mother and father and older brother, my single uncle, another young newly married aunt and uncle and grandmother.

I do not remember the early years of the war but my first vivid memory is of the time when iron was required for making armaments. Lorries were sent down our road collecting any metal objects. My three wheel bike was hidden away but an old tin peddle car was forfeited along with the lovely ornate iron railings in front of the house.

There was a large gun on Wimbledon Common in front of the windmill which proved to be quite noisy when enemy aircraft were spotted. We may have been lucky to have moved out of the East End but our garden at the new house backed on to Wimbledon Station. This proved to be a hazardous location as the armaments going down to Portsmouth by rail proved to be a prime target for the Luftwaffe. One night I was awakened in the Morrison shelter by a loud bang followed by falling glass. This was a result of the side of the station being hit by a bomb. Great excitement the next morning with a WVS canteen wagon serving tea and buns.

One day my friend and I were on our bikes a long way along the road when the sirens sounded and a Doodlebug followed us dead in line with the road. On reaching home we ran into the outside loo and cuddled each other until it went off with a bang. There were many more to follow. My dad and married uncle were away in the army and the single uncle was in Dad's Army like Pike, whilst my mother was on war work building parts for Spitfires.

After the near miss it was decide to move down into the cellar which was carpeted and bedded where it was hoped we would stand more chance of survival. As things got worse and the V1s were being superseded by V2s it was time to evacuate to the Midlands where some relatives made arrangements for our accommodation. When the bombing stopped we came home and VE Day dawned with family celebrations up in Trafalgar Square. By the time the Japanese surrendered I was in hospital with suspected TB but was carried out by nurses to celebrate world peace. In latter years as a boating enthusiast I was pleased to be in attendance with the flotillas of private boats invited to take part in the 50th and 60th Dunkirk Evacuation commemorations.
Bob Wootton (via e-mail)

Rising to the challenge

I have been reading *Sixty Years On* with great interest. My own father (George Keen) was approaching his 40th birthday at the outbreak of war and was not immediately drafted into the forces. I was almost three years old in 1939 so inevitably there are some things I remember and other details have emerged subsequently.

When the air raids began on London my parents and I lived in Mitcham. We trooped off every night to the large underground shelter built on playing fields at the end of our road. It was all a bit of a joke early on and my father would keep the neighbours in hysterics by - amongst other things - dressing up as a ghost!

Then one morning returning home in the half-light of dawn, I can remember my parents taking one of my hands and hauling me over piles of bricks and twisted metal. Thankfully our house was intact but several people were killed in the corner shop; they had drowned in the cellar where they had taken refuge. Maybe this triggered something in my father because thereafter he decided against shelters. During air raids he would sit in the kitchen with a cup of tea and a newspaper quietly waiting for the 'all clear'. Meanwhile my mother rushed me into the Anderson Shelter in the back garden. I still remember occasions when her knees knocked so violently that I almost fell through them when sitting on her lap.

When my father was called up he was sent to North Africa with the Eighth Army and was assigned to petrol supply duties. He later spoke very little of his experiences there although he did relate a few events to me.

During the breakout from Anzio and the advance on Rome he was confronted in the early hours of the morning by a drunken American Colonel accompanied by two Italian women demanding petrol. When my father refused the Colonel began waving his pistol around. My father told me he was shocked but unfazed and called forward two of his men to take aim. The Colonel withdrew empty handed. I have often since wondered on the outcome of any Court Martial which may have followed.

One incident that really stuck in my father's gut was the issue of Trieste, a port that had always been a bone of contention between Italy and Yugoslavia. Marshal Tito and his partisans were giving the Germans one hell of a fight. I have never seen any reference to the collapse of the Italian Resistance that occupied Trieste in 1945. The Americans and British are said to have issued an ultimatum, giving them 24 hours to leave. This was backed up by rows of tanks from the New Zealand Armoured Division drawn up along the approaches into the city. The threat succeeded but much to the disgust of many British troops. A recent obituary in *The Daily Telegraph* suggested the intervention in Trieste was carried out by separate feuding factions of partisan forces. I can assure you this was not how British soldiers saw it on the ground.

My father must have carried out his duties in an exemplary fashion as, with the war in

LEAVE HITLER TO ME SONNY — YOU OUGHT TO BE OUT OF LONDON

ISSUED BY THE MINISTRY OF HEALTH

GOOD ADVICE FROM THE MINISTRY

This Ministry of Health poster by Dudley S Cowes dates from late 1940. It reinforces the message that children should be evacuated. The background is a blitzed street with the Union flag flying defiantly from the rubble.

Italy won, he was summoned before the Army Board to offer him a Commission in a re-organised post-war British Army. When he refused the offer out of hand the Brigadier exploded, 'Good God man! Do you realise what you're throwing away?' He did not, of course, and his return to civilian life as an unskilled worker did him no favours.

All I now possess as a reminder of that era is a local newspaper, a clutch of medals (which I applied for as my father refused to do so) and an Italian coin pressed into solidified lava from Mount Vesuvius and bought as a souvenir in 1944.

Now as I read newspaper obituaries it amazes me the incredible feats that were performed by such ordinary people. I wonder if my generation could rise to the challenge. Thankfully most of us have been spared the test. Make no mistake about it - those were not the 'good old days'.

T Keen, East Sussex

Wartime memories

I have read every page of the *Sixty Years On* series avidly and you are to be heartily complimented on putting together this unique eye witness record of those momentous days.

I was but a child at the time (born in 1937) but have some clear memories of what for us all then were the 'normal' events of the times. For example, I recall emerging from the Anderson Shelter in our garden in Yeovil to see a massed armada of German bombers filling the skies on their way to blast the hell out of poor Bristol; bombing raids on Westlands Aircraft Company with stray bombs demolishing nearby houses; collecting shrapnel which had broken our conservatory windows and taking some to swap at school; the arrival of US troops in the months before D-Day, including black men (that we had only ever seen before in Hollywood films at the Saturday morning pictures) and their kindnesses to us kids with unaccustomed gifts of chewing gum and other goodies!

It is curious to recollect that although there was a war on we enjoyed far more freedom to roam without supervision than children typically do today. Of course there were no computers or television, there could be no trips to the seaside and for the most part we had to make our own amusement. I have fond memories of cycle rides with friends out to the local airfield for some plane spotting, or down to the railway line for train spotting, or out to the countryside for scrumping, mushrooming or gathering chestnuts. These were common activities for seven and eight-year-olds then.

It is true that there were very few cars on the roads – even the minority who owned a car could not use it for pleasure trips due to the petrol rationing – but parents did not have the same fears for the safety of their children that unfortunately have become so prevalent today. And despite all the privations of total warfare, with food, clothing and much else severely rationed, I think we were generally much healthier than

children are today – there was certainly no childhood obesity!

Peter Parker CBE, Surrey

Witness to tragedy

I was a child evacuee during the war. Contrary to popular belief, most evacuees did not go to wonderful loving homes, but had a wretched time. I suffered along with the majority of evacuees. My story, though, concerns an incident in September 1942 when I was seven years old.

I had been evacuated to Haslemere, Surrey. One evening, at about 6pm we were surprised by a very dark-coloured aeroplane that descended out of the cloud layer with a terrible grinding noise coming from its engines. It flew directly over our house towards the centre of Haslemere. It was gradually losing height and, as we watched, it broke into three pieces and fell to earth.

It fell on and around the Rex Cinema in the town. One part went through the roof, but no civilians were seriously injured as the cinema was almost empty at that time in the evening. As a child I was deeply shocked because I realised that I had witnessed someone dying.

A few years ago I undertook some research on this incident. The aeroplane was a British Havoc Mark III from Flight 1455 based, I believe, in Lincolnshire. It was a night stalker and was painted black. It had a searchlight in the nose. When it found a German bomber in the dark it would train its searchlight on it so that the night fighters could home in. The crew, who all perished, were Flying Officer W Winter, Pilot Officer J Lindley and Flight Sergeant W Cleall.

The cause of the crash has been ascribed to mechanical failure, but even in those days aeroplanes did not fall out of the sky for no reason, and the noise that it made indicated that the engines were damaged. I believe it had encountered a lone German fighter above the clouds and was badly shot up.

I still get upset when I think about it.

Peter Lane, Milton Keynes

Seashore memories

At the beginning of the war I lived very near the sea in Wales and enjoyed all that a huge beach provides for children during the summer months. It was idyllic, apart from the chilly sea – but that was accepted in view of the fact that we had no other experience of any warmer waters.

You can't imagine the shock then, when going for a stroll to our beach, we found it out of bounds to the public and guarded by troops. It was soon covered by mines and spikes and barbed wire. How sad a sight.

Months later and rationing began to bite seriously (especially for my poor mother trying to make meals). One day I was walking on the promenade overlooking the sea and was horrified to see the incoming tide bringing in broken boxes and hundreds of oranges, swollen in size by the water. I remember I nearly cried because this fruit was what we really needed

but these oranges would never be eaten; they would return to the sea on the outgoing tide.

I suddenly felt a shudder when I realised that there must be seamen from sunken ships many miles out to sea, struggling in the icy cold water with little chance of rescue. On telling my father of what I had seen, he said, 'Let's all say a prayer for the poor men who will have given their lives in an effort to keep us fed.'

This is in memory of those who died.

Mrs C Walker, Kent

Memories of the Blitz

I doubt that you realised when the *Sixty Years On* series started that you were initiating such a significant archive. Your contributors and the varied correspondence from readers have created a unique body of first-hand accounts which remind, and give a new perspective, to those who lived through the times and informed those who were saved the awfulness by later birth.

It has taken me many months to realise that I might have a small part to play in recording the period, but I was almost seven years old when Hitler enforced my evacuation from London, label and gas-mask round my neck, carrying a little brown case. I spent a couple of months with a large family in Dunmow in amazement at their happy noisiness before the authorities realised that this was exactly below the flight path of German bombers jettisoning their loads when they couldn't get through to London. With a pleasant young couple in Kings Lynn I lived another life, although I was regularly slyly pinched and kicked by the son of the house who saw me as threatening his domain.

Getting back to my London home was a welcome relief, at a time of low blitzing, and I joined with relish in the occasional night-time adventures of wailing sirens and rushing down to the Anderson semi-underground shelter in our garden, or for a social change to neighbours' shelters, where grown ups played cards as I lay on a bunk listening to the whistle and crump of bombs and noisy machine gun fire.

Returning home in the dawn, with the soothing steady all-clear, it was always necessary to climb over mounds of broken glass even when there had been no nearby bombs – was it caused by the mobile anti-aircraft batteries?

As the Blitz reached new levels I was off again, this time to a family in a large Council house on the edge of Cullompton in Devon. With Mr and Mrs, Grandpa and son Jimmy I settled in to rural life for several years

lend a hand with the potato harvest

at a farming holiday camp

OCT AND NOV FREE TRAVEL AND REDUCED ACCOMODATION TERMS

This original artwork by Eileen Evans became part of the 'Lend a Hand on the Land' campaign that encouraged urban workers to take working breaks on Britain's farms in 1944 - 45. The idea had great appeal for families with children who would otherwise have no chance of a holiday. Post-war the tradition continued for many years with thousands of Londoners going hop-picking in Kent. Spot the spelling error that was corrected for the finished poster!

occasional free day.

A summer Sunday in 1944 comes to mind when we cycled from Blackfriars to Detling near Maidstone, a journey of 35 miles or so each way, to visit two of Joe's cousins who were in the Women's Land Army working on a farm down there. We had a comfortable ride down without punctures or mishaps and reached the farm in the early afternoon on a gloriously sunny day to find the girls billeted in a caravan at the edge of a field. We ate our packed lunch and enjoyed other refreshments provided by the girls and with no enemy air activity to disturb the peace of the Garden of England that day we relaxed in the warm sunshine listening to the birdsong from the hedgerows. We had no thoughts in our minds that idyllic afternoon that the Germans still occupied the land just 40 miles or so to the east. Too soon the girls were waving us off on our journey home with the prospect of the dreaded Wrotham Hill to climb - I think we walked up. Once over the summit, where the Wrotham TV mast now stands, it was mostly downhill all the way home but the last mile or two from New Cross along the Old Kent Road sorely tested our tired young legs, not to mention bottoms!

So what has this to do with fighting Hitler? Well, Joe was a year older than me and was shortly called up to a Scottish infantry regiment, which was full of cockneys. Nine months later I visited Joe in a military hospital near Epsom where he was recovering from the effects of German bullet wounds to one of his knees. He told me that when he was wounded he became separated from his comrades. A German patrol then found him and tried to lift him but his knee bent the opposite way to which nature had intended, so the Germans left him for his mates to come back and find. The knee had been rebuilt by army surgeons but was rendered permanently rigid and that was the end of his cycling days.

I will never forget that summer bike ride and the subsequent sacrifices of Joe and millions like him and how lucky I was to come through unscathed.
Tom Flawn, Kent (via e-mail)

Dinner with the enemy
I can remember two or three German POWs coming to our house for Christmas dinner. I think it was the year 1945. I have always admired my parents for welcoming the POWs into their home, especially as they were poor even by the standards of those days and it must have stretched the budget. My father fought with the Canadian Expeditionary Force in the Great War and I wonder if it was a result of his experiences then that coloured his actions that Christmas.

From what I remember, the German POWs were billeted at the back of the local steam laundry and worked on concreting a large area. I do recall them teaching me the German numbers, something that came in useful much later when I spent some time in Berlin.
Mrs J Z Chambers, North Yorks

so that when my mother made her occasional visit – travelling in wartime trains was no easy or safe life – she could barely understand my accent.

As things calmed down I joined my family in Caversham, near Reading, where I happily lived with my parents, sister and brother in a single room with a cold water tap and an outside loo. Looking back I am amazed we all coped so well and easily with such conditions. Reading was not immune from Nazi raiders and a single bomb, falling at lunch time on the town's British Restaurant, killed hundreds. My primary school in Hemdean Road was a between-the-wars single storey building with large asphalt playgrounds. It was so obviously a school

but a Nazi fighter thought it a good idea to strafe it one Wednesday afternoon which thankfully was a half day off – certainly lucky for me for when I came in next morning I found a machine gun bullet had passed through the lid of my desk.
Tony Lake, Hertford

A summers bike ride
My mate Joe and I were working teenagers, he a photographic news agency cycle messenger and me in Post Office Telegraphs. We lived in Blackfriars in the centre of London and after a six-day working week, plus a duty every other Sunday, we would get on our bikes and cycle into the countryside of Kent or Surrey on the

Flying start

" Our mission was to carry 'weeping' bombs, too dangerous to transport by land, and dump them into the sea. Imagine that today; the RAF taking schoolchildren on a low-level flight with unstable explosives on board! **"**

I was just 10 when war broke out in 1939. As a youngster in Fairfield, Buxton, 1000 feet up In the Peak District of Derbyshire and seemingly far from any action, I found to my excitement that all sorts of new things were going on.

All manner of interesting equipment appeared in print and for real; strange new shapes in the skies and lots of activity on the ground. I remember a Tiger Moth flying overhead with a somewhat spluttering engine. It appeared to be approaching Combs Edge, the top of which was higher than the plane was flying! Its engine spluttered and stopped and the craft started to glide down steeply and disappeared.

I grabbed my bike and took off helter skelter until I ran out of track, abandoned my steed and hot-footed it over gates, walls and rough grass until I could just see the top of a yellow wing beyond a stone wall - success! In my mind I was already telling my friends about how I had been the first on the scene and had rescued a dazed pilot from the wreckage of his aircraft when, to my dismay, I saw a policeman standing importantly beside the apparently undamaged fuselage embedded in the bog with no pilot to be seen. How he got there so quickly I never knew. I was told in no uncertain terms to scarper. Deflation!

Once we were sitting on the cellar steps after an air raid warning and heard a nearby crump; apparently a German bomber had been attacking Manchester and the pilot had dumped his last bomb as he tried to make a fast getaway over the Pennines. The device landed in a field near to a farm.

Parade twice weekly

I soon joined the Buxton College Air Training Corps Nº 1504 Squadron and proudly paraded twice weekly in my smart new uniform. I was learning how to be an airman, especially on how to recognise aircraft from all angles. It was exciting to watch a Westland Lysander cruising slowly over the town so that the anti-aircraft troops could practice aiming at it - no real ammunition allowed.

Once I saw something I could not identify, flying not too far away, near Loughborough. It looked like a Boston, but was much more angular. I quickly sketched it. That evening two Observer Corps men gave the ATC a lecture on aircraft recognition. After it finished I produced my sketch and asked one of the men for help identifying it. He whispered, 'I'll get shot if someone finds out, because it's still on the secret list; but I'll tell you if you promise to keep quiet.' I had seen my first Douglas Invader.

I had a collection of model aircraft, all built to a 1:72nd scale, constructed from bits of scrounged wood and cellophane - the wheels and dope [paint] were the only bits that I bought. When building them I referred constantly to my most treasured possessions; the *Aircraft of the Fighting Powers* volumes published annually throughout the war.

Wings for Victory Week

One year I was invited by local toy shop, Elliots, to produce a window display to mark the Wings for Victory Week (a week every year when people were encouraged to save funds to help the war effort). It was of a British airfield and overhead was a Heinkel 111 falling steeply with a tuft of pink cotton wool tinged with red and black at the rear of an engine, closely followed by a Westland Whirlwind which had shot it down. A crew member was descending by parachute.

I had suspended 140-odd home-made black silhouette-sized models of aircraft at various angles from my bedroom ceiling, so that I could memorise them at all angles. When my cousin Ronald came to stay we lay in bed and tried to shoot the aircraft down with dried peas.

Another year it was the turn of the Army to benefit from a savings campaign, and a local playing field was used for a demonstration by the Parachute Regiment. They had some tiny motor bikes for dropping from aircraft and we youngsters were allowed to sit on them. When my turn came my friend said, 'bet you can't start it!' What a challenge! I zoomed towards the audience, but mercifully a burly paratrooper grabbed hold of me before I hit anyone.

Later we ATC Cadets were treated to our first weekend camp at RAF Ashbourne, an airfield just south of Buxton. We were promised our first flight - in an Anson. However, as it was a few days after D-Day every available flying machine was being used to carry supplies to the south of England and beyond so you can imagine our disappointment.

In the summer of 1945 our camp was at RAF Syerston between Newark and Leicester, a Lancaster base where we did indeed achieve our first flight (mother had bravely signed the 'blood chit' allowing her plane-mad - and only child - to fly with the RAF). I will never forget being strapped in to the mid-upper turret of a real Lancaster complete with guns; I can still see the runway dropping away below us. We set off westwards at a few hundred feet altitude and saw the familiar ground of Dovedale guarded by Thorpe Cloud where the river turned west, and the famous stepping stones where we had often crossed the river.

We traversed Cardigan Bay and flew out into the Irish Sea. Our mission was to carry 'weeping' bombs, too dangerous to transport by land, and dump them into the sea where they were deemed to be out of harm's way. Imagine that today; the RAF taking schoolchildren on a low-level flight with unstable explosives on board. Thank goodness mother knew nothing of this. After dropping our dangerous cargo the co-pilot reported that one of the bombs had exploded as it entered the water, a fair measure of the instability of the contents.

Aircraft awaiting disposal

The following year the camp was again at Syerston, but by then it had become a Dakota station, stacked with unwanted aircraft awaiting disposal. One day we were flown to RAF Silloth on the Solway coast where dozens of old Dakotas were lined up prior to dismantling. On board on the return journey were the crews of several now-dumped Dakotas, who were returning to Syerston.

The following day, the end of our camp, we were all flown in a Dakota to Ringway (now Manchester Airport) so that we could be driven home, whilst some of our ATC flight who lived nearer to Syerston than Ringway were to be returned to Syerston by plane. We sat at Ringway in a bus, waiting until our chums took off before departing ourselves. However, to our horror just after the Dakota became airborne one engine cut out and the pilot made a split-second decision to abort the take-off and came to an abrupt stop off the end of the runway. Our hearts were in our mouths at seeing the near demise of our chums but, thankfully, all ended well.

Even in Northern England later in the war we too were subjected to bombardment by V1s. They were air-launched over the North Sea from Heinkel 111 bombers. We heard and saw several going overhead on Boxing Day night 1944 and, although we were 25 miles from Manchester, we heard one engine cut out followed by the crump as it crashed harmlessly on the moors just to our west - obviously filled with too little fuel or released much too early.

To a schoolboy the war was an interesting and exciting time, although it was badly tinged in the early days by the knowledge that my favourite woodwork teacher had been killed in North Africa, not by enemy action but in a road accident.

The war, even to a youngster, had its ghastly side.

Laurence Draper

WAR DIARY

The beginning of **November 1944** sees fuel shortages bringing the advance of General Patton's Third Army to a virtual standstill along the Moselle River. In the Vosges Mountains on the Franco-German border north of Switzerland, the French First Army is closing on Strasbourg.

2 November: The Eighth Army's main enemy is now the Italian winter. Since July they have sustained over 20,000 casualties and every infantry battalion has required reorganisation. Around 400 tanks have been lost in action or simply worn out.

3 November: The Allies finally secure both sides of the Scheldt Estuary. Canadian troops on the south bank take the surrender of 12,500 Germans around the town of Breskens. Within a few hours minesweepers will begin clearing the waterway to the vital port of Antwerp.

On **4 November** the Russians are halted 40 miles from Budapest by a combination of rain, extended supply lines and stiffening German resistance.

The following day Zionist extremists demanding a Jewish homeland in Palestine assassinate Lord Moyne, British Minister-Resident in the Middle East, outside his home in Cairo.

6 November: The town of Middleburg in the centre of Walcheren island is liberated.

Tokyo **7 November:** The spy Richard Sorge is executed in Sugamo prison. Over a period of eight years, Sorge supplied the Kremlin with secret Axis political and military plans. His greatest coup was assuring Stalin that the Japanese had no plans to attack the USSR. Stalin was able to move large numbers of troops from the Far East to join the fight against Hitler.

On **8 November** the famous German air ace Major Walter Nowotny dies when his Me262 jet fighter crashes. He was credited with 258 'kills' made mainly on the Eastern Front.

9 November: Patton's Third Army crosses the Moselle on a broad front and is heading for the German border just a few miles away.

10 November: In Poland a Red Cross party has been allowed access to the concentration camp of Auschwitz-Birkenau. The camp authorities carefully conceal areas where mass murder has been turned into a production line industry.

Winston Churchill is in Paris for the Armistice Day celebrations **(11 November)** and is buoyed up by the warm welcome from the populace.

On **12 November** in Norway the biggest single menace to Allied shipping in northern waters is eliminated when the *Tirpitz* is sunk by 12,000lb 'Tallboy' bombs in a raid by 30 Lancasters.

13 November: In Yugoslavia the *Wehrmacht* have pulled out of Skopje, site of their headquarters for the southern province of Macedonia.

French Alps **14 November:** Air Chief Marshall Sir Trafford Leigh-Mallory and his wife die in an air crash en route to Ceylon.

15 November: A general strike by workers is underway in Turin and attacks by Italian partisans fighters are increasing.

16 November: Antwerp has become a major target for Hitler's V-Weapons. Ten flying bombs crashed down onto the streets and houses today, killing 263 civilians.

On **17 November** the last few Germans in the Albanian capital, Tirana, surrender as the city awaits the arrival of Communist Partisan leader Enver Hoxha.

19 November: During an air raid on the bridge at Venlo on the Dutch-German border an RAF Mitchell bomber is hit by flak causing the tail-plane and turret to break off. Inside it the rear gunner, Warrant Officer Cote, a French Canadian, 'fluttered down to earth like a leaf', and miraculously suffered no worse injury than a broken leg. He is made a PoW.

The US Treasury estimates that waging world war is costing the country $250m for each day of conflict.

20 November: After five years, the blackout ends tonight with the switching on of streetlights in Piccadilly and the Strand and various other thoroughfares and squares in the capital.

21 November: In Italy General Alexander stands the Allied armies down for the winter. Air sorties, artillery duels and fighting patrols will be the pattern of the war here until the spring.

22 November: Today the men of Patton's Third Army liberate the ancient capital of Alsace-Lorraine, Metz.

23 November: In a surprise attack, Free French troops, under the command of Generals Leclerc and de Lattre, enter Strasbourg today. Around 3000 Germans are captured whilst many more hastily retreat across the Rhine.

On **24 November** American B-29 Superfortresses out of Saipan bomb Tokyo in daylight for the first time. Just 24 out of 111 participating aircraft found the target.

The following day a V2 rocket brings carnage to New Cross Road in South London when it crashes down on a busy Woolworth store killing 160 people and injuring 135 others.

26 November: General Sir Harold Alexander, top Allied commander in Italy, is promoted to Field Marshal. The appointment has been backdated to 4 June so that he is now technically senior in rank to Montgomery.

27 November: A German ship sailing from Norway is sunk by British aircraft from the Fleet Air Arm. Unknown to the airmen, the vessel was transporting 2248 Russian prisoners. Just 415 survive.

28 November: The first Allied convoy will dock in the port of Antwerp today. Supplies can now be landed within 60 miles of the British forces facing the Germans along the River Maas.

29 November: A US submarine torpedoes Japan's 'unsinkable' aircraft carrier, *Shinano*, in the Kumano Sea off Japan.

RAF bombers are in action in the early hours of **30 November** over Dortmund. UK munitions factories are finding it hard to keep up with the demand for bombs to smash the Nazi war machine.

In 1944 the Allies ran an air transport service from India to China in support of the Chinese forces fighting the Japanese. There were also a number of US airfields on Chinese territory. The supply flights had to cross the Himalayan Mountains - known as 'The Hump' to the pilots. For loading and unloading the aircraft, elephants were found to be faster and more efficient than men. Here an elephant loads 55-gallon drums of petrol from a truck to a C-46 in India.

BATTLE OF THE BULGE

DECEMBER 1944

SOUVENIR
of the
HOME GUARD
STAND DOWN
CONCERT

Given by the
DAILY MAIL,
SUNDAY DISPATCH
AND LONDON
EVENING NEWS

at THE ROYAL
ALBERT HALL
DEC. 3rd, 1944

Manager ; C. S. TAYLOR

Cyril Beavor represented C Company, 46th West Riding Battalion, in the last parade of the Home Guard before the King in London on 3 December 1944. Here are his memories of the occasion.

I was on the 'Stand Down' parade of the Home Guard on 3 December 1944 and remember it well. My role was as representative of the 46th West Riding Battalion of the King's Own Yorkshire Light Infantry and I had been given the honour of 'Private most worthy of the honour of representing the Battalion.'

At least that is what it said in the letter I received from its Adjutant. The Battalion had been given a quota of one Second Lieutenant, one Lower Corporal and one Private.

Above: Private Cyril John Beavor in 1944.

Left: Cyril has kept the 'Stand Down' Concert Souvenir Programme for over 60 years.

Below: The Doncaster Sector Detachment about to entrain for London at Doncaster Station on 2 December 1944. Private Beavor is fourth from the right.

THE HOME GUARD

We, at least, had decided that the personnel to be duly honoured to parade in the capital in front of a crowd of many thousands should be chosen from men of existing ranks. However, I later met men on the parade who had been demoted from officer rank to private, just so they could have a place in history!

Each company made its recommendations to a committee of senior officers. I was told by my Company Commander that the choice of Private had finally come down to one of two men. I was one and the other was a man well known to like his liquor. I learned later that what tipped the balance in my favour was my being teetotal; I was therefore unlikely to besmirch the honour of the regiment, whereas the other private was very likely to get drunk if let loose in London.

Three events during the parade itself stick out in my memory. The first was that we did not know who would take the salute, so it was a surprise when on the command 'eyes left' for the salute I saw that the King himself was taking it and that he was accompanied by the Queen and the two Princesses. I am not an ardent royalist but my step certainly became lighter.

The second memory was of nearly losing my footing on wet wooden flooring laid down, I believe, near Piccadilly Circus. The third was the wheeling column receiving the sharp edge of a Regular Sergeant of the Guard's tongue, as it drifted out of line.

I recall while I was in London that I slept two nights in the cavalry barracks in Knightsbridge and heard at least one V2 rocket land.

In the evening of the parade there was a concert in the Albert Hall for which I was lucky enough to get a seat. The concert cast included Tommy Trinder, Vera Lynn and Cicely Courtnedge. I was right up in the back row of the 'gods'.

On the printed programme was a poem written by a member of the Home Guard who had heard the news that a German General had just inspected a parade of the Volkssturm, the German Home Guard. It was reported that his car had driven up, he had got out, taken one look at the men on parade and promptly suffered a nervous breakdown!

Cyril Beavor lives in Birmingham. For further information on the role of the Home Guard visit: www.home-guard.org.uk

The poem and illustrations printed here were contained within the 'Stand Down' Concert Programme.

The Unkindest Cut

After inspecting the new German Home Guard the Commander has had a nervous breakdown. (Unkind but factual summary of Berlin radio announcements.)

I am far from a lover of Germans ;
I view them as pestilent hogs,
As each of them perished
The news I have relished—
Though sometimes I felt for their dogs.

But as one Home Guard now to another,
I feel Jerry's had a raw deal,
If there'd been all this fuss
After someone saw us—
Well, I think I know just how we'd feel.

We've been stood down, stood up, and stood sideways,
We've been turned inside out or laid flat ;
We've been bothered, bewitched
And bewildered and ditched,
But we've not been insulted like that !

Lester B. Wilson

(From the *Sunday Dispatch*)

"He complains that every time he goes to shoot, a Russian creeps up and breathes on his glasses."
—*by Neb.*

FAITHFUL TO THE END

183

'CONSTANT ENDEAVOUR'

Throughout World War II the aircrew of Coastal Command played a vital role in keeping the U-Boat menace at bay. On 16 March 2004 HM The Queen paid tribute to these men of the RAF – motto: 'Constant Endeavour' - when she unveiled the first national monument dedicated to their memory in the South Cloister of Westminster Abbey.

I was there. More importantly, during the weeks before and after D-Day I was one of the pilots involved in the aptly named *Operation Cork* which had the task of blocking the western end of the English Channel to prevent U-Boats attacking the Allied invasion shipping. This was achieved by setting up three 'endless chain' patrols between the French and English coasts, so spaced that a U-Boat could not cross the area from West to East without surfacing to recharge batteries. The Liberator aircraft involved flew to a strict timetable exactly 30 minutes apart. We maintained this pattern day and night for six weeks. On the only two days when sea fog closed our Cornish base, the patrols were covered from Northern Ireland.

The U-Boats made no attempt to penetrate this screen in daylight, but made several attempts to 'run the gauntlet' at night. The most outstanding success was achieved by a crew captained by Canadian Flying Officer K O Moore of 224 Squadron, which on one patrol sank two U-Boats in 22 minutes!

Later my squadron (206) moved to Scotland and for the rest of the war continued the anti-U-Boat campaign between the Shetlands and Faroes, off the coast of Norway and even penetrating into the Baltic.

The watercolour below depicting a Liberator from 206 Squadron over Trevose Head, Cornwall, was painted by R W Davies around the time of D-Day 1944. I didn't myself fly this particular aircraft - EV885, M/206 – but I can tell, sadly, of its end. On the night of 27/28 September 1944 my crew and I spent nine hours, in darkness, carrying out a north – south rectangular patrol off the coast of Norway. Seven times we completed the circuit and each time, near its southern extremity, we passed near Sola, the airfield for Stavanger, which was then a German fighter station. Twice they put up aircraft to intercept us and on both occasions I avoided them by getting down low on the water. I knew they would not fire their guns so close to the surface at night; the combination of being dazzled by the flashes from their guns and the momentary loss of control from the recoil of their cannons would pose a real danger of their hitting the sea. So both times they shadowed us from above for a period before turning away.

At the end of my time in the area I was relieved by M/206, captained by Flying Officer Carlisle. Dawn came by the time we were halfway back to base and with it my wireless operator picked up an SOS from 'M'. The fighters that didn't fire at me in the dark came out with the daylight and shot my relief into the sea. Unfortunately there were no survivors.

Jim Glazebrook F/Lt, DFC, RAFVR (retd)

Naught Escapes Us by Peter B Gunn is the story of No 206 Squadron, RAF. It was published in May 2004 by The 206 Squadron Association, Wellhead Cottage, Fountain Road, Selbourne, Hants GU34 3DA. Hardback 200 pages. Price £15 + £3 p&p.

Top: Some of the crew of Jim Glazebrook's Coastal Command Liberator who flew with him in the period August – December 1944 pictured in front of their aircraft at RAF Leuchars, Scotland. Left to right: F/S 'Johnny' Boorman, F/S 'Nick' Nicholson, 'Skipper' Jim Glazebrook, Air Gunner Sgt George Ellison and Wireless Operator/Mechanic F/S 'Jock' Bain. Jim Glazebrook today lives in Knutsford, Cheshire. Coastal Command lost more than 2000 aircraft in the war. A Book of Remembrance dedicated in Liverpool Cathedral contains 10,875 names of those who lost their lives in Coastal Command operations during World War II. The aircrew were drawn from RAF, Commonwealth and Allied squadrons. Coastal Command aircraft sank 189 U-Boats and participated with surface forces in the sinking of a further 24.

Right: The 1944 painting of a Liberator over Trevose Head, Cornwall. The aircraft in question was shot down off the coast of Norway in late September 1944.

Left: This painting by W Krogman depicts a famous incident when a Lockheed Hudson of Coastal Command secured the capture of U-570 in the North Atlantic in 1941. The aircraft damaged the submarine and it was unable to dive. The crew surrendered and can be seen waving a white flag. An armed trawler towed the vessel to Iceland. On 19 September 1941 the U-Boat was re-named HMS Graph and entered service with the British Navy (National Archives - Art of War).

Hitler's last gamble with a major offensive in the West meets with initial success but ultimate failure in the face of stubborn Allied resistance.

In the foggy and wintry dawn of 16 December 1944, in the rugged and heavily forested Belgian Ardennes region, Hitler began a massive gamble that hinged on history repeating itself. For it was from this same area in 1940 that he launched his Blitzkrieg on the West, a campaign that crushed the armies of France, Belgium and Holland in a matter of weeks and had bundled the British Expeditionary Force in total disarray off the bomb blasted beaches of Dunkirk by the beginning of June.

Now the Fuhrer was determined to make it happen again. Against all Allied expectations he'd succeeded in putting together a mighty new Panzer army with orders to break through the lightly-held Ardennes front, cross the River Meuse and drive for Antwerp, splitting the British and American forces asunder in the process. Backing the assault would be a rain of V1 flying bombs and V2 rockets directed against London and Antwerp, the latter a vital supply port for the Allies.

The German units included seasoned, crack troops, equipped with powerful tanks and the latest weaponry. In the skies, pilots of the new jet fighters were confident they would soon win back air superiority for the Luftwaffe.

Earlier triumph

But now it was a vastly different Europe, over four years on from the earlier triumph of German arms. Vast Allied armies and air forces were encamped before the German line of defence that stretched from the North Sea to the Swiss frontier. From positions in Holland, Belgium and France they were poised to roll over Germany's last bastions before the Rhine - the fortifications of the Siegfried Line. Around Aachen, the Americans had already breached this Westwall and were fighting on German soil.

Yet the Allies couldn't be strong everywhere and the inhospitable Ardennes was one part of the Allied line where their forces were spread thinly. Ironically, though the Germans did not know it, the Ardennes was also the main storage area for the Allied fuel supplies for the Western Front; fuel was a commodity the Wehrmacht was desperately short of. Indeed, the panzers would run dry within days of the offensive starting unless they could capture large quantities.

In places green and inexperienced American units reacted in bewilderment and confusion to the surprise assault by panzers and infantry erupting out of the quiet forests. But in key sectors, the Americans recovered quickly and stubbornly held their ground. The attack by Sixth Panzer Army was the first to be blunted as, in the centre, Fifth Panzer Army made the greatest progress but at the critical price of leaving the town of Bastogne in the hands of the US 101st Airborne Division and a scratch force of defenders.

Bastogne beseiged

Glaring newspaper headlines in Britain and America stirred up much public apprehension but there was much less alarm amongst the Allied fighting troops. Eisenhower, Montgomery and the other Allied commanders reacted coolly and efficiently in the face of initial confusion and rumour. The Germans soon found themselves vainly pushing at the shoulders of the 'Bulge'; thus their advance was funnelled through a relatively narrow base. The British XXX Corp moved south to guard the Meuse crossings. Hitler refused to reinforce the partially successful Fifth Panzer's advance at the expense of the stalled Sixth. Meanwhile the commander of the American stronghold at Bastogne, sustained by airdrops, turned down a German surrender ultimatum with one contemptuous word: 'Nuts!'

Patton's Third Army then struck a powerful blow against the Bulge from the south and on the day after Christmas one of his armoured divisions drove through ice and snow to break the lines around the

BATTLE OF THE BULGE

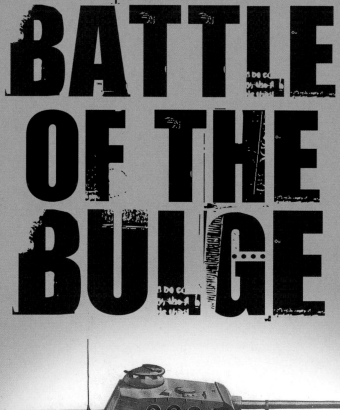

Top: At the start of the offensive, morale was high in the German ranks. They had received large numbers of new 45 ton Panther tanks (illustrated here) with superior firepower to any Allied tank.

Above: At the end of the battle, thousands of German soldiers surrendered to the Allies.

Right: This 30 ton Sherman tank is on display in the town of Bastogne, a key defence position for the US forces who blunted the German attack.

101st Division. Hitler's last great offensive in the west was doomed, a fate confirmed when, with improving weather, the Allied air forces joined in the attack with a vengeance.

Now the Fatherland's radio and newspapers prepared their audience for the worst. On 28 December the German News Agency issued a statement: 'The Allied High Command has now concentrated 24 tank divisions and heavily armed shock formations in the Ardennes.

'Among them are the 51st (Highland) British Infantry Division, renowned as a crack unit since the Africa campaign. They have gone in to the line east of Dinant.

'General Eisenhower has considerably reinforced the firepower of the First and Third Armies by supplying them with additional batteries of the biggest calibre. This strength, in conjunction with close-range air support, has caused the battle to become stationary.

'The German spearheads have been taken back according to plan...to avoid unnecessary losses and enable us to meet the American counter-attacks with compact strength. German forces found themselves forced to give up some ground in the face of ferocious battles against Americans attacking in masses all along the far-flung southern shoulder of the German salient. A policy of elastic defence is being followed between Bastogne and Echternach.'

Back to the start line

The battle continued into the New Year with undiminished intensity. But now it was the Americans, supported by British units including the 6th Airborne Division, who were attacking while the enemy grimly tried to hold on to what they had won. Slowly the Germans fell back.

By 16 January 1945, after a month of bitter fighting in the grip of a winter far colder than usual, the Germans found themselves once more lined up more or less on their own frontier, almost the original start line for the offensive. The planned Allied drive into Germany was delayed by perhaps six weeks or so but the Ardennes Offensive had cost Hitler dearly in scores of thousands of irreplaceable men; even more significantly, Germany's panzer forces in the West had been decimated.

THE BRITISH IN THE ARDENNES

At the time the British did not refer to it as 'The Bulge'. They knew it as the Battle of the Ardennes. In the early days of the German offensive it was the Americans who bore the brunt of the fighting. Indeed, in the House of Commons on 18 January 1945, Premier Winston Churchill referred to the episode as 'the greatest American battle of the war'. There were around 40 US troops involved for each British soldier and the Americans lost around 70 men for each British casualty.

Nevertheless, as the battle progressed, the British arrived in numbers to play an important role. On the following pages we publish the stories of some of the British soldiers involved in that bitter winter battle, beginning with this account by A C Jenkins of Ilford, Essex: In early December 1944, I was serving in A Company, 7th Battalion, Argyll & Sutherland Highlanders, a posting I reckon amounted to one of the toughest jobs around at the time. We were part of the 51st Highland Division (although a hell of a lot of us were actually English!) and were comfortably billeted in a seminary in the south of Holland.

THE BRITISH IN THE ARDENNES

Although not aware of it at the time, we were undergoing training for the forthcoming Reichswald offensive. Against regulations, I kept a diary and this records that on 16 December, on the very day that the German attack in the Ardennes opened, we all attended a performance by the Divisional Concert Party - 'The Balmorals'- and, of possibly more significance, that a large number of V1 flying bombs were observed flying overhead.

At 11pm on the following night, after a quiet day, we suddenly found ourselves on the move. Over the next couple of days we went into Belgium, passing over the 1815 battlefield of Waterloo, then back into Holland, finally ending up at the small town of Valkenburg where we were supposed to relieve a US outfit. They, however, had other ideas and refused to give way to a bunch of Limeys. Notwithstanding, it looked as if we were to be there for some time and so laid plans for a slap-up sit-down Christmas Dinner.

Alas for the best-laid plans; on Christmas morning we were put on an hour's notice to move out, fully kitted up. Thus we ended up eating our dinner out of mess tins, standing up in the open air. Merry Christmas! We eventually moved on to a suburb of Liege, where several of us were billeted with a family. It was touching to read the hand-written banner strung up in their living room - 'Welcome to our Liberators. Welcome to brave English soldiers'. If similar banners were hung in all the houses, I'm not sure what the true Highlanders would of made of the sentiments!

Meuse bridge guard

On 29 December we moved to the western side of the city to guard a bridge over the River Meuse. Our new billet was with another family in a farmhouse of the kind common in that area of Belgium; it had a cow and a few pigs in winter housing in one part of the building and living quarters in the rest. We duly passed our compo rations onto 'Mum' who promptly responded that this kind of fare might be alright for the pigs, but wasn't fit for humans. For the rest of our stay she fed us, Lord knows how, on her own supplies. Perhaps her husband being in the Resistance helped. We had a memorable New Year's Eve with them. On 7 January we were ordered to move. The lady of the house couldn't understand why we were leaving and my last memory is of her refusing to let our successors - some Seaforths - into the house in our place!

Prolonged snowfalls caused drifts that made it difficult to follow the roads. Our destination was the village of Grimbiemont, where we relieved an East Lancs battalion. The place had seen some hard

Above: 'Roll of Honour' memorial erected at La Roche-en-Ardennes to the memory of the 54 Scots killed during the Battle of the Ardennes.

fighting and was still subject to shelling. Taking shelter in a ruined house we discovered the bodies of three unfortunate East Lancs boys; next day, despite the ground being frozen, we managed to give them some sort of burial in the churchyard.

Expecting an attack

It was cold, so much so that the oil on our rifle bolts froze and orders came down to wipe every trace of the substance from our weapons. It was the second time in the war that I'd received such a command, the first being at Blackpool when I was in the Essex Regiment and the sand used to jam our rifles.

Within 24 hours we were told to expect an attack from German infantry and tanks. We anticipated an assault by the terrible King Tigers of awesome reputation but all that happened was that a press-ganged Pole from the 116th Panzer Division crossed the lines to surrender. We heard movement from the general direction of the enemy but that was all.

After a miserable freezing night spent trying to keep warm, we were relieved (on 10 January) by units of the Sixth Airborne Division and withdrew to Hotton for a night's rest in a barn. Sheer luxury!

The plan next day was for a Black Watch battalion in our own 154 Brigade to take La Roche-en-Ardennes and for us to then pass through them. But the Black Watch were held up and we spent the entire day on the road. Tragedy almost intervened when the three tonner carrying 9 Platoon skidded off the icy road and landed up on its side. How we 30 men in that truck escaped injury I shall never understand.

Another night, another barn and more gentle snowfall; in the morning we were driven to the outskirts of La Roche, by now taken by the Black Watch, and then marched down a winding river valley towards Hives, several miles south of La Roche. I remember the pine tree branches, blasted down by shellfire, and the pine needles and debris frozen such that it felt like walking over ball bearings.

Panther tanks

Amidst sporadic shelling, we reached a crossroads where there was yet another barn to afford shelter from the biting wind and cold. Our first section headed on down the road, descending into a shallow valley with a stone hut at the bottom. As the leading man reached this, there was a burst of machine gun fire and the crump of exploding shells which between them killed and wounded several of our men. Some of the latter somehow struggled back, despite being badly hit. Perhaps the cold served to dull the pain.

Another section went down only to meet the same fierce reception. By now a scout car from the Derbyshire Yeomanry had spotted the source of the firing; two dug-in Panther tanks on the high ground ahead. Our own turn to advance was coming up and our Company Commander, Major Samwell MC, decided to accompany us with two Shermans of the Northants Yeomanry also lending support. Somewhat reluctantly we all moved out. Just a few yards later, seconds after Major Samwell had ducked behind the lead tank to report back via the telephone link carried at the Sherman's rear for just that purpose, there was a blinding flash and a shower of sparks and metal fragments, some of which must also have hit L/Cpl McCormick just in front of me. An 'old soldier' in the best and worst meaning of the word, McCormick was the bane of the Sergeant Major's life and at 33 years of age he seemed almost a grandfather to we mere 19 year olds. With a wife and several children back in Glasgow, he should never have been serving in a rifle company.

Understandably, the rest of us legged it back to the barn as fast as we could. For their part, the Panthers and our own tanks backed off. By this time the powers that be realised that there was no way

forward down our road; B Company later advanced via a different route. We were withdrawn to the village for another miserable night with no blankets and only a can of self-heating soup for comfort. In an nearby outhouse lay the body of a poor old Belgian woman killed by shellfire. Jaundice had been stalking me for several days and on the following morning, I reported sick. Before departing for the 25th British General Hospital in Brussels, I just had time to bid a hardly fond farewell to the Ardennes.

Abiding Memory

Writing in 1994, Ardennes veteran D H Walker of Blackpool, Lancashire, recalled: My unit, the 147 Regt RAC, 34th Tank Brigade, was stationary just north of Aachen in December 1944 when we received sudden orders late one evening to proceed westward at once. At midnight, we were loading our Mark 7 Churchill tanks onto rail transporters and at dawn found ourselves off-loading them in the Ardennes. We wound our way through the hilly terrain, in deep snow, and then came to a stretch of flat countryside. At dusk we reached Dinant on the River Meuse.

Here the bridge, mined by the Americans, was crowded with civilians crossing to the 'safer' west bank. We eventually crossed to the east and found billets in the hotels along the river bank. That night the Germans bombed the town. I collected a gash on my forehead and four stitches; 'done' right away!

Later we moved out eastwards, over hills blanketed with snow, passing white-clad Airborne troops, Signals men and others. Once we made contact with the Germans we began to lose tanks. I was lucky.

An abiding memory is of Christmas Day spent in a snow-covered roadside ditch, with our wheeled transport bringing up Christmas dinner!

Brussels in turmoil

On the night of 23 December lead elements of three British divisions were moving up to their allotted positions. Troop Leader W S Brownlie of the 11th Armoured 'Black Bull' Division remembered:

We were to move to the Ardennes soonest. Forget waiting for the new Comet tanks, leave all heavy kit behind, pick up old Shermans in Brussels, get to the Meuse and help stop the Jerries. Cups of coffee in Aalst; Brussels in turmoil, population very scared. It was cold and pouring with rain, V1s were passing overhead, very depressing.

Defence of Dinant

When *Sixty Years On* was published as a series, reader Ken Baldwin read of an incident at Dinant on the Meuse in which his father, Sgt G W 'Tiny' Baldwin figured. Ken wrote to give more details of what occurred:

My father was with G Company, 8th Rifle Brigade, 11th Armoured. He was involved in the push through Belgium and Germany and was among the first troops to arrive at the Baltic.

One night an incident occurred which did nothing to reduce the tension. On the far bank of the Meuse there was a road running alongside the river. This road passed through a hole carved out of the rock through which a Sherman tank could just squeeze its way. Sergeant Baldwin's carrier section manned a post at the rock whose function it was to stop all passers-by and vehicles and examine their papers. The sentries doing the checking had a Very-light pistol which they were to fire if any vehicle would not stop, whereupon Sergeant Baldwin was to pull a string of mines across the road at the exit to the hole in the rock. It was an arrangement of which any Boy Scout might well have been proud.

At about midnight a Very-light went up. The mines were set off and there was a deafening explosion which all asleep in the neighbourhood took to be the bridge itself. When the smoke and dust had cleared away the remains of a shattered jeep were found and by it the bodies of three dead Germans. They had been travelling in a captured American jeep and were wearing American greatcoats over their German uniforms, in the pockets of which were found very detailed plans of our defences. When challenged they had refused to stop. In one respect the episode was less fortunate, for Sergeant Baldwin's mines had gone up with such a bang that an American standing some considerable distance away had had his jaw broken.

NO. 8 DECEMBER • 1944 • STALAG IV B • GERMANY

> **And so another one comes round. This time – for luck – we refuse to say 'the last behind the wire'... Some of us have said it too often.**

These are the opening words to *The Flywheel* 'Xmas Number' of December 1944, a remarkable hand-written magazine produced by British POWs in Stalag IVB in the period from May 1944 to March 1945.

It was the product of the 'Muhlberg Motor Club', who comprised several hundred motoring enthusiasts incarcerated in the camp which was situated near Muhlberg-on-Elbe, Germany, some 80 miles south of Berlin. Built to house 15,000 prisoners, at times nearer 30,000 Allied servicemen were crammed in the cold, filthy and verminous wooden huts of the camp.

Thomas Swallow, 86, who was captured near Tobruk in 1942, was the co-editor. He remembers how it was virtually impossible to escape from the camp so the inmates had to make their own entertainment.

'There was a passion for motorbikes and motorcars so we set up the club. It was our way of saying to the Germans, we can beat you. We had classes for everything imaginable – musical appreciation, business methods. We even had German lessons.'

The Flywheel was produced entirely by hand including all the wonderful illustrations of machines and landscapes. Many were drawn from memory but there were also outside sources. Tom's mum, for instance, regularly sent cuttings from home of current magazines with reports of wartime motoring events that helped the club keep track of the outside world.

All the paper and materials used in the production of the magazine was obtained through a system of 'beg, borrow, buy or barter – stealing from Jerry was taken for granted'.

The Flywheel – Memories of the Open Road from Stalag IVB was published in book format in 1987 and is credited to Tom Swallow (President) and Arthur H Pill (Chairman) and the members of the Muhlberg Motor Club 1944 – 1945.

The 1944 Motor Show as imagined by the POW producers of The Flywheel.

THE RED CROSS & ST. JOHN WAR-ORGANISATION

SWEDEN

Bornholm

STALAG LUFT
ROSTOCK

STETTIN

STALAG IID

KOENIGSBERG

G. of Danzig

DANZIG

EAST PRUSSIA

MARIENBURG
MARIENBURG
STALAG XXB

BYDGOSZCZ

STALAG 357
TORUN (THORN)
STALAG XX A

OFLAG 64

R. Vistula

R. Bug

WARSAW

BERLIN

STALAG II D
NEUKOELLN 119
BIESDORF 128

STALAG XI A
MAGDEBURG

WOLLSTEIN

POZNAN (POSEN)
STALAG XXI D

P O L A N D

LODZ

STALAG IV D/Z

STALAG VIII C
STALAGLUFT III
STALAGLUFT IV

R. Elbe
STALAG IV D
STALAG IV B
SCHMORKAU
KOENIGSWARTHA
LEIPZIG
WURZEN
STALAG IV G
ELSTERHORST
OFLAG IV C
DRESDEN
HOHENSTEIN-ERNSTAHL
STALAG IV A
OFLAG IV B
STALAG IV F

STALAG VIII A

BRESLAU

ILAG KREUZBURG
STALAGLUFT VII
B.A.B. 20

STALAG 344
B.A.B. 21
COSEL

KRAKOW

HAUSEN
BILIN
STALAG IV C

PRAGUE

PILSEN

C Z E C H O S L O V A K I A

STALAG VIII B

BERG-LANGWASSER

STALAG 383
REGENSBURG

BRNO

R. Danube

STALAG VII A

LINZ
ILAG VII H

STALAG XVII B
VIENNA
IIA VIENNA
STALAG 398
STALAG XVII A
KAYSERSTEINBRUCH
L. of Neusiedl

BRATISLAVA

R. Danube

BUDAPEST

H U N G A R Y

BRUCK
LAG 31

REFERENCE TO MAP

190

Five years 'In the Bag'

As a Youth in Training in the Post Office Engineering Department in 1939 I was conscripted into the Royal Corps of Signals as Signalman 2364104 and spent the next six months training in Hampshire and Yorkshire. Subsequently I was attached to the 30th Infantry Brigade formed as a diversionary force for the defence of Calais and the evacuation of the BEF from Dunkirk.

Captured at the fall of Calais on 26 May 1940, myself and other survivors of that battle were taken to Stalag XXA at Thorn in Poland where I was designated *Kriegsgefangenen* 11870. We spent the next 18 months working in various POW Camps around that city undertaking house demolition work, road and sewer construction and other labouring tasks.

In the autumn of 1941 I was one of about 250 British POWs transferred to Stalag XXB at Marienberg in East Prussia. After a short stay there I was 'posted' along with 22 other POWs and two German guards, to a 5000 acre State Farm in a small village called Faulen in East Prussia near the Estonian border.

The next three years were spent on a variety of farming activities, but all this came to a sudden end in January 1945 when the entire farm, POWs and civilians, was evacuated in front of the Russian winter offensive. All British POWs were marched westwards (crossing the River Vistula over the ice!) and traversed northern Germany under pretty atrocious winter conditions living off meagre German army rations and what we could scrounge from a partially evacuated countryside.

After a cross-country march of about 700 miles, crossing the Rivers Oder and Elbe in the process, we eventually reached the town of Lehrte in West Germany midway between Brunswick and Hanover, an area under attack by the advancing American forces. Our stay in Lehrte in a displaced persons camp was comparatively short; the town was captured by the Americans and we were freed.

A workparty of 27 British POWs at Faulen, East Prussia. They were employed on a State Farm from October 1942 to January 1945. Robert Marks is one of the party. He's also featured left in a recent photo.

Looked after by the Americans and enjoying their hospitality fully, after about 10 days all British POWs were loaded into Lancaster bombers returning from missions over South East Germany and we finally reached home after being away from our families' and loved ones for almost six long years.

In conclusion one must always remember the Red Cross who helped us to survive those years in captivity with gifts of food parcels and clothing, through some very difficult and never to be forgotten times.

Robert M Marks, Cheltenham, Glos

*The various camps which held Mr Marks can be seen on the map.

The POW Camps

Maps prepared by the Red Cross and St John War Organisation were provided to ensure that the whereabouts of British and Commonwealth prisoners-of-war were known throughout the conflict. Red Cross officials visited all camps to ensure that the terms of the Geneva Convention were being honoured. The Red Cross also provided food parcels which were a vital supplement to the sparse rations provided by the Germans.

Letters sent by loved ones back home were, of course, treasured by those 'In the Bag' as were messages sent in reply. The comfort of knowing the location of POWs was a boost for morale.

The map reproduced here is shown without the legend as the original is now very fragile. It's dated 30 June 1944 and was made available for *Sixty Years On* by Diana Gant. Her father, Private Edward Thompson, was captured in the North African desert on 20 June 1942. Private Thompson was in the Royal Artillery and was in the process of changing a lorry tyre when the sudden appearance of the enemy changed his life instead. He spent the rest of the war in Stalag XVIIA, east of Vienna in Austria.

Stalag Luft III (scene of 'The Great Escape' in March 1944) can be seen in the centre of the map midway between Berlin and Breslau. Colditz Castle is actually designated as Oflag IV C and features on the map between Leipzig and Dresden.

Tony Graves

British soldiers captured in 1940 around the Pas de Calais region of Northern France.

THE GLENN MILLER MYSTERY

Benny Goodman. Pollack moved to New York and introduced Glenn to a wider musical scene. During the next few years he worked as arranger, organiser and performer with such names as Ray Noble, The Dorsey Brothers and Red Nichols.

Miller dreamed of forming his own band as a showcase for his developing style of swing music. His growing popularity enabled him to recruit a group of players in 1937 but his financial acumen proved unequal to musical ability and the band folded the next year. Undeterred, Miller tried again. A prestigious summer season booking at the Glen Island Casino in New Rochelle led to another important engagement at Meadowbrook, New Jersey. The huge 'plus' of these bookings was that they offered frequent radio broadcasts and the Miller Orchestra soon developed a nationwide following. In 1939 Chesterfield cigarettes commissioned a series of broadcasts featuring such classics as *Chattanooga Choo Choo*, *String of Pearls* and *Moonlight Serenade*. Two films were also made, *Sun Valley Serenade* (1941) and *Orchestra Wives* (1942). Both were of minimal dramatic quality but provided an excellent platform for Miller to extend his blossoming fan club.

Spring in the step

In October 1942, at the height of his domestic success, Miller decided that he could best support the American war effort by donning uniform and bringing music to the troops wherever he could. By now he was 38-years-old and beyond the age for active call up; it took a personal appeal to Brigadier Charles Young before the army would consent to his plans to reorganise and modernise military music and 'put a little more spring into the step of marching men'. Not content with performing in America, Miller arranged for overseas duty and shipped his band to England where they were billeted at 25 Sloane Street in London.

Concerned at the ferocity of the V1 attacks taking place in the summer of 1944, Miller moved the band to safer quarters in Bedford on 2 July. The very next day a bomb destroyed the Sloane Street building killing 100 people.

Miller's popularity was now at its height. In one month in late 1944 The Glenn Miller Army Air Force Band played in 35 different bases and made no less than 40 radio broadcasts. His relaxed style made the music suitable for listening or dancing to and thousands of service men and women were able to forget the rigours of war, if only for a few hours. His contribution to raising morale was immense. By now promoted to Major, Glenn Miller began to plan for a Christmas 1944 broadcast to be made from Paris and on 15 December commenced his fateful journey.

He is remembered for his unique musical style, his professionalism and his showmanship. Indeed, Miller has built up a whole new generations of fans in the decades following the Forties. Above all, his patriotism in giving up his number one civilian band to enlist in the US Army Air Corps ensures his place as a true war hero.

Martin Barton-Smith tells the story of America's most famous bandleader who disappeared without trace in December 1944.

At 13.40 hours on 15 December 1944, a Noorduyn Norseman C-64 aircraft took off from RAF Twinwood Farm near Bedford bound for Paris. The Norseman was a single engine high wing monoplane powered by a 650hp Wasp engine and was used frequently on short range communication flights in many theatres of the war.

This flight never reached its destination and for the six decades since much speculation has surrounded its fate – poor visibility, icing, enemy action, even friendly fire. This is because one of the three passengers on board was Major Glenn Miller, USAAF, the founder and leader of the best known band of 'The Big Band' era. Indeed, Glenn Miller's music for many is the evocative soundtrack of World War II; his arrangements and compositions remain 'standards' to this day.

Alton Glenn Miller was born in Clarinda, Iowa, on 1 March 1904 to solid 'Mid-Western' parents who moved home with some frequency seeking to better themselves. During Glenn's younger life, living conditions were hard and the family was often isolated; music was the prime means of softening the harshness. An early interest in music built into a lasting enthusiasm. In 1918, Glenn was in high school in Fort Morgan, Colorado, where his twin hobbies were football and a new innovation called dance band music. His penchant for the latter did not endear him to his principal who remarked on presenting the graduation diploma to Glenn's mother (Miller was away playing in a band!), 'Maybe you're the one who should get it anyway, you probably worked harder on it than he did!'

Growing popularity

By now it was clear where Glenn's future lay and he joined a band called 'Senter's Sentapeeds' in Denver and eventually abandoned his university studies to seek his fortune on the West Coast as a musician. His first big break came with Ben Pollack's orchestra in 1927 where he roomed with another rising star, clarinet player

WHAT HAPPENED TO MILLER'S AIRCRAFT

All sorts of theories have been put forward about the mysterious disappearance of the aircraft in which Glenn Miller was flying to Paris - including a claim that he never actually boarded the plane. However, the most likely explanation is that the aircraft was hit in mid-air by bombs jettisoned by Allied aircraft returning from an aborted air raid on a target in Germany. It was quite common for bad weather to cause bomber crews to turn back and the usual practice was to drop their ordnance over water as it was unsafe to land with a full bomb load. Sad, but most likely true, Glenn Miller was killed by 'friendly fire'. Given Glenn's celebrity popularity it was unlikely that the Allies would admit to such a possibility in wartime.

Unforgettable

J Jenkins shares memories of wartime in far-flung places.

In March 1942 after training as a wireless mechanic in the RAF I embarked with about 3000 other men on the Belgian ship *Leopoldville*. The convoy assembled off Gourock and I recall one of the other ships as the *Arbosso*. Conditions were cramped with hammocks slung jammed together. Later in the hot latitudes the foetid atmosphere became unbearable, making it imperative to find a bed space out in the open decks, crowded though they were.

We made it undamaged to Freetown, Sierra Leone, from where we sailed unaccompanied to Capetown. This was Paradise! I was entertained by a middle-aged couple who lived in an opulent house on the lower slopes of Table Mountain. Unfortunately, the idyll had to end and all too soon it was back at sea again for a fast solo run up the east coast of Africa to Egypt on the *Niew Amsterdam*, a large Dutch liner. Once in Egypt I was posted to Aden and so it wasn't long before I was re-tracing my passage back south down the Red Sea, a comfortable trip on a ship carrying a large number of Italian POWs who foregathered each evening and sang excerpts from various operas.

East and *West* Link

Unfortunately for me, my destination was not the well established and well endowed Aden HQ, but was a tiny unit out on the lonely isthmus connecting the base to the mainland. My new home consisted of a couple of parallel bungalow buildings, one housing the technical staff of about a dozen men, the other the sergeant in charge, the cook and the cookhouse. Transport amounted to a single open three ton truck and a driver. About a quarter of a mile away across the sand was the purpose of the unit's existence. A three foot thick stone wall surrounded a half buried wholly enclosed building, which housed the transmitting hall and associated workshop. About a dozen large transmitters were ranged around the hall. Their purpose was to transmit signals sent by landline from Aden HQ on one side and RAF Khormaksar on the mainland on the other side. The function of the staff was to attend these transmitters 24 hours a day, re-tuning and repairing as necessary. The station worked Karachi in India (now Pakistan) on one side and Asmara in Eritrea and Cairo in Egypt on the other, making a link between East and West. On one occasion, sleepily re-tuning a transmitter in the middle of the night, I didn't follow the proper procedure and was knocked unconscious with 3500 volts across the chest.

Palpable silence at night

Although it was only a short distance from the base to the apex of the isthmus, it felt as though we were in the middle of the desert. The temperature was no more than about 100F but the humidity approached 100% and the atmosphere was soaked with as much moisture as it could hold; perspiration simply could not dry off from the body. The silence at night was palpable, pressing in like a heavy blanket.

I left Aden in April 1943 for another trip up the Red Sea to a unit near Haifa in what was then Palestine. We were ordered to take a Commando training course, soon learning that it was in preparation for the invasion of Sicily. For a few weeks it was all cross country runs, physical jerks, bayonet charges and other toughening up exercises. The pervading smell of orange blossom in the fresh springtime air was a compensation and I had some evenings off in Haifa and also visited Nazareth before the powers that be decided we would be better employed on the technical jobs we were trained for. So then it was back across the Sinai wilderness and into Egypt, a journey illuminated by a silvery moon.

I was next kept busy preparing 15cwt vans housing radio gear. These vehicles were allegedly waterproofed to enable them to ascend a beach covered by two or three feet of water, but I doubted whether they would stand the strain. I never did find out if they could because I was posted off the unit and never got to Sicily. Instead I kicked my heels for some months in a transit camp near Helwan, south of Cairo. The compensations here were a visit to the Pyramids and a number of trips into Cairo where there were various forms of entertainment. The camp was on the edge of the desert but it might as well have been in the middle of it given the heat, the flies and the sandstorms.

A curious phenomenon I noticed was that any individual or group walking across a wide, empty stretch of sand would start off in the right direction, but would slowly veer round, always clockwise, until they were walking at right angles to the route they should have been taking. Whenever this was pointed out to them they expressed surprise. I'm sure this natural human tendency must account for many people getting lost in the desert.

Tour of Pompeii

After an eternity of waiting, in March 1944 I was very relieved to be posted to a unit on the Adriatic coast of Italy, a new establishment conducting operations over Yugoslavia in support of Tito's partisans battling the occupying Germans. Our transmitters were housed in cabins mounted on the backs of trucks parked at a distance from the living quarters and the metal airstrip laid down like a carpet. Leave allowed me to visit Sorrento from where I went on a tour of Pompei - doubtless escorted by the same guides who had earlier showed German soldiers around - and I also wandered through the streets of Naples where the Black Market was rife. Later in Rome I had another guided tour round a

EVE OF DESTRUCTION

J Jenkins, story above opens with his sailing off to war on the Belgian troopship *Leopoldville*. Nearly three years later, on Christmas Eve 1944, the same vessel was torpedoed and sunk by a U-Boat just a few miles off the port of Cherbourg. As a result nearly 800 US soldiers drowned in the freezing cold waters of the English Channel.

German submarines had not made much impression in hindering the vast naval and merchant ship traffic between British ports and Normandy in the months following D-Day. RAF Coastal Command and the British and US navies were vigilant and increasingly successful in steadily reducing the number of enemy U-Boats in the Western Approaches.

Few dared come close to the shore. An exception occurred on that fateful Christmas Eve. The US 66th Infantry Division - 'The Black Panthers' - were on their way to back up the Allied forces engaged in the Battle of the Bulge. The only vessel available to transport them was the *Leopoldville*, not the fastest or most modern of ships. She was still crewed by Belgians.

It was early evening at 5.45pm about six miles away from Cherbourg and the safety of land when the torpedo struck. The *Leopoldville* began to sink quite slowly at first. Though the soldiers lined up on deck it appears that no orders were initially forthcoming to take to the boats. Nor had any lifeboat drill been held prior to sailing. By the time it became clear that they would have to abandon ship the men found that many of the lifeboats had fitments that were rusty and impossible to move.

The destroyer *HMS Brilliant* came alongside and soldiers began leaping from one ship to the other. Many fell into the sea. Thousands of men were rescued but almost 800 perished.

To this day there is no reference to this disaster either in the Royal Navy history or in US military records.

virtually empty Vatican - a very different experience from when I visited it years afterwards as a holidaymaker, when the madding crowd destroyed all the beauties of the place. I attended an audience given by the Pope, but did not join those who went up to receive the Papal blessing. My final spell out of camp was on a course in the beautiful baroque town of Lecce, in the south, where it was delight enough just to wander round the streets.

The winter of 1944-45 was bitterly cold. Tents collapsed under the weight of snow and the wooden boards which made our improvised beds developed a tendency to float out of the tent. Gumboots did nothing to keep feet warm in the icy slush. It was best to go on the overnight shift well flushed with wine, which we tended to try to consume in the quantities in which we had swigged beer in North Africa, usually with disastrous results. I recall one of the big five ton trucks sank up to its haunches in the mud.

Strange aircraft
Early in 1945 I was posted to Malta and switched from working on heavy ground-based transmitters to those on aircraft of great variety. Malta was an important staging post between Europe and the Middle and Far East. It was common to go on duty in the evening and be faced with up to 40 aeroplanes requiring servicing by morning. I remember one time when a very large aircraft appeared over the airfield of a type no one on the ground had seen before. It was an American Skymaster, one of the ambitiously large experimental aeroplanes that were being produced at that time, post-war soon to be overtaken by jet propelled airliners. The buzz went round that it was stopping only to refuel. Sighs of relief all round. But when it finally came to a halt, a head popped out of a window up in the lofty fuselage and an American voice called out: 'Any wireless people down there?' Thus I was faced with a repair job in a totally strange aircraft, a task I accomplished in fear and trembling lest I should do something wrong and flop the Colossus down on its belly or something equally dire.

Off duty, Malta had considerable compensations. At that time, long before the island was covered in holiday hotels, there were many beauty spots, wonderful swimming and animated life to enjoy. The war ended in the summer of 1945 but for me duty and leisure on Malta went on in the same way until October when my tour of duty abroad came to an end and I returned home. I was demobbed in June 1946, going with that sense of being cast adrift in an unknown world. I suppose it was a common experience. Looking back, I had a safe and a relatively comfortable war but it remains an unforgettable episode in my life.

J Jenkins today lives in East Grinstead, West Sussex.

Christmas Dinner

Elizabeth Riddiough remembers German POWs visiting her home.

It was a brilliant summer's day. It couldn't really be anything else, for looking back on childhood it never rained in the summer; it was scarcely even overcast. That day I was watching the man digging over a piece of ground that had recently been cleared. The sun was hot and he wore no shirt. Sweat glistened on his bronzed back as he swung the spade with a strong easy motion.

I regarded him curiously for my father never appeared without his shirt however hot it was. The last man who came did not remove his shirt, nor the one before that. This man seemed unperturbed by my uncompromising five-year-old stare. He gave me a friendly smile and continued to dig. Later my father called him and placed a tray on the wide stone steps that led down to the lawn. He attempted a little conversation with the man but it was hard work. He spoke very little English but made clear his thanks for the cup of tea and slices of bread. There was no cake because all the ingredients were rationed and certainly there was no cake to spare for casual labour.

I sat on the steps with the man and stared at him as he ate. He said nothing but smiled at me again. As soon as he had finished he rose immediately and returned to work. As the heat fell away from the afternoon the big truck with canvas sides waited at our gate. The man pulled on his shirt and jacket. Although this was the first time he had worked for us, my father gave him the usual bonus of 10 cigarettes. This produced a voluble torrent of German which even I realised was effusive thanks. He joined the row of pinched faces peering from the back of the truck, gave me a wave, and was gone.

Digging in the garden
Of course I knew about the war. I had never known anything else. I gradually came to realise that our obliging labourers, all dressed alike in tatty grey uniforms, were German prisoners of war. Anyone who wanted outdoor work done could have one for a few hours at a time by applying to the commandant of the local camp. We had a very large garden so help was often needed, particularly as the autumn advanced. There was much seasonal cleaning to be done and the winter digging to start. Most of our garden was given over to vegetables in which we were virtually self-sufficient. Naturally there was no question of payment. In fact they were not even supposed to receive cigarettes

but I didn't realise this at the time. I think, on reflection, they probably thought that anything was preferable to the boredom of the camp.

There was the usual general excitement as Christmas approached. On Christmas Eve mine was even more increased as my father explained to me that the gardeners would be coming to have Christmas dinner with us. I was quite intrigued by this idea and turned it over in my mind at length. The next morning the truck delivered our three regulars. It was obvious even to me that they had made an effort to be clean and tidy. They stood awkwardly, looking very shy for they had rarely entered the house before and certainly not on any kind of formal basis. At last dinner was ready and we all sat down. Gradually they became more at ease as everyone busied themselves with serving and eating. By this time their English had improved and we were able to converse. I listened, spellbound by the heavy accents, as they spoke of their families and how Christmas would be in Germany. To me, a small child, they were men, but my parents of course saw them for what they really were - bewildered, overgrown boys who just wanted to go home.

Pictures of children
Over the years it has greatly interested me to observe the reactions of people I tell about Christmas 1944. There's everything from understanding nods to pursed lips of disapproval. It depends on their age group of course. My father had said he hoped they would go home and tell their families that the English were kind.

For years after the war three letters arrived every Christmas without fail. I was fascinated by the strange spiky handwriting on the envelopes and wondered how Germans actually understood what they wrote to each other as the closely written sheets were unfolded. At first the accompanying photos showed our gardeners formally arm in arm with smiling girls. Later came pictures of children. I do not know how the correspondence died. I suppose it was the language barrier eventually for we always had to find a translator and no doubt they did too.

All that was over 60 years ago now. Not long ago I told someone that we were going to Hanover to stay with our mutual friend. 'It's a good job you're only going for the weekend', he said. I was puzzled. 'You'll find Birgit is a charming hostess,' he continued, 'But if you stay any longer she'll take you to visit Belsen.' He mimicked her accent. 'Everyone must visit here. Everyone must know vot heppened here. Zese terrible zings must never heppen again. Wars are shtupid.'

'Don't worry,' I laughed, 'She won't try to educate me, she doesn't need to. I've already got international cred with Birgit.'

And I told him about my Christmas dinner of 1944.

WAR DIARY
December

By **1 December** most of the Western Front is now situated on the territory of the Reich. Patton's Third Army has moved up to the main German defensive line along the Saar River.

Laurence Olivier's *Henry V* is drawing huge audiences in the West End even though the critics have not been universal in their praise of Shakespeare on celluloid.

2 December: General de Gaulle is in Moscow for talks with Stalin. The French leader is keen to re-establish his country's political role as a major power.

On **3 December** Home Guard units from all over the country hold a final parade in the centre of London, marching past King George who is giving their farewell salute.

4 December: In a rare winter attack, the Eighth Army makes a forward movement into Ravenna on Italy's Adriatic coast.

5 December: All German women over 18 are asked to volunteer as auxiliaries for the armed forces in order to free up men for front line duty. Reich women's leader Gertrud Scholtz-Klink makes the appeal.

Queen Elizabeth singles out the women of Britain for praise in a speech on **6 December,** citing their war work as a major factor in making possible the Allied victories to date.

The following day US forces extend their grip on the Philippines with successful landings at Ormoc Bay on Leyte in the face of *Kamikaze* air attacks.

8 December: US warships and aircraft are targeting a new 'stepping stone' to the Japanese homeland. Iwo Jima – halfway between the Marianas and Japan – is to be invaded.

Hungary - **9 December:** The Red Army has penetrated to the banks of the Danube north of Budapest where the city garrison is preparing for a siege.

10 December: In a superb feat of engineering, men of General Slim's Fourteenth Army in Burma have built the world's largest Bailey Bridge. At 1154ft, the structure spans the Chindwin River.

On **11 December,** senior German officers are shocked at Hitler's exhausted appearance and uncontrollable trembling as he unveils plans for a surprise offensive out of the Belgian Ardennes.

12 December: After a remarkable four month voyage half-way around the world, a German transport U-Boat has reached the Japanese-held port of Djakarta in the East Indies. The crew are stretching their legs on dry land for the first time since sailing from besieged Bordeaux in late August.

13 December: Kamikaze attacks in the Philippines damage a US destroyer and the cruiser *Nashville*. Nature too, adds to the toll when a tropical storm producing 75-foot waves sinks three destroyers with the loss of 719 men.

London - **14 December:** Post-war planning for the capital is aired with the publication of the Greater London Plan which supports the creation of a 'green belt' around the city and the setting up of 10 new towns to absorb the expected population boom.

15 December: In the thick Ardennes forests the *Wehrmacht* have secretly assembled a large army including hundreds of panzers and a vast array of artillery.

16 December: Just before dawn sees the start of the Ardennes Offensive. The Allies are caught by complete surprise as strong German forces erupt out of the forest heading west.

Antwerp is the ultimate goal of the attack. Today that city is the target of a V2 rocket that falls on a packed cinema, killing 567 people including 296 Allied servicemen and women.

In Athens fighting continues in the area of the Acropolis between British paratroopers and communist ELAS rebels.

17 December: A top secret US unit at Wendover Air Force base, Utah, continues training flights over the Great Salt Lake. The airmen know only that they will most likely eventually be dropping a bomb of exceptional power on a target in Japan.

Belgium: 125 captured GIs have been massacred by SS troops under the command of Lt-Col Joachim Peiper near the town of Malmedy.

18 December: In the Baltic, RAF bombers sink eight enemy ships and damage a ninth. The vessels were carrying German evacuees from East Prussia - thousands of civilians die.

19 December: Panic over German infiltration behind the Allied lines spreads as far to the rear as Eisenhower's Versailles HQ where the Supreme Allied Commander is confined to his office.

In the Schnee Eifel area of the Ardennes, 6000 American soldiers are surrendering to encircling German forces.

Next day **(20 December)** the Germans reach the important crossroads town of Bastogne and begin to surround the American 101st Airborne and 10th Armoured Divisions.

21 December: Snow is falling over large parts of the Ardennes as bad weather keeps the powerful Allied air forces grounded.

22 December: Britain's Home Front war effort is being aided by the efforts of carefully selected German POWs who are being paid up to six shillings a week to dig potatoes and harvest sugar-beet.

23 December: German forces together with two Italian Divisions still loyal to Mussolini launch a surprise counter-attack in the direction of Pisa and the port of Leghorn on Italy's north west coast as Allied aircraft are grounded by bad weather.

24 December: A swarm of doodlebugs are launched in mid-air from modified Heinkel bombers over the North Sea. Just 17 out of 31 of the V1 weapons reach their Manchester target, killing 32 civilians and injuring 49 others.

Clearing skies over the Ardennes allows the Allied air forces to decisively intervene in the Battle of the Bulge. For the Luftwaffe Arado 234 'Blitz' jet bombers make two successful raids on rail yards at Liege.

25 December: British units are helping contain the Germans in the 'Bulge'. Near Neuville in Belgium, 'A' Squadron 23rd Hussars, enjoy a Christmas dinner consisting of 'iced bully beef and frozen cheese sandwiches'.

26 December: German Field Marshal Gerd von Rundstedt responds to the Fuhrer's refusal to call off the Ardennes Offensive with the remark, 'This is Stalingrad Number Two'.

27 December: Winston Churchill has spent Christmas in the Greek capital trying to broker a ceasefire in the civil war. In one incident when ELAS sniper fire hit the British Embassy whilst Churchill was inside, the statesman exclaimed, 'Cheek!'.

28 December: Bastogne is the focus of renewed attacks by the encircling German forces.

29 December: The Russian-sponsored Committee of National Liberation in Lublin has declared itself to be the Provisional Government of Poland. Free Poles in London protest that the Lublin move is illegal.

30 December: Newspapers report on a domestic fuel crisis predicted to last until at least the end of February 1945. Mainly caused by the very cold weather, consumers are warned they 'must cut down or be cut out'. Ironically, it has only been six weeks since the blackout rules were relaxed.

On **New Year's Eve** 1944, the British inhabitants of the Channel Islands are about to enter a fifth year under Nazi Occupation. The Allies are reluctant to bomb or invade because of the risk to civilians. Besides which, the islands have been turned into formidable fortresses bristling with concrete gun emplacements. With food in short supply, Christmas was a cheerless time and with the news of the Ardennes Offensive, the islanders must wonder whether deliverance will ever come. The very first Red Cross supply ship, the *Vega*, from Portugal has just arrived.

A PROMISE TO THE NATION

This is the kind of poster that Christopher Portway (see following story, 'One Man's War') would have seen prior to joining the British Army. It's the work of Pat Keely and depicts a Great War infantryman behind a Second World War machine gunner. The clear message is encouragement for the population to carry on the fight regardless of setbacks. This is the artist's original concept complete with hand-fashioned lettering (National Archives - The Art of War).

ONE MAN'S WAR

1944 REMEMBERED 1945

An infantryman in the British Army, Christopher Portway came ashore on Gold Beach on D-Day and was captured in the subsequent Battle of Normandy. Put to work as a slave labourer, he

escaped from the Germans twice and on one occasion was incarcerated in the infamous Auschwitz - Birkenau Concentration Camp. In the last weeks of the war, Christopher rode on the tanks of General 'Blood and Guts' Patton's Third Army as they mopped up German resistance in Bavaria. In his own words, this is the full story of one man's remarkable war.

Though I was born into a military-minded family - my father and uncle were colonels, the former winning a Military Cross in the First World War, and my younger brother consistently outranking me in later years - I never had the ambition to make an efficient soldier. Alas, I was the black sheep of the family - the runt of the litter, if you like - in other vocations too, but particularly when it came to matters military.

I suppose a penchant for 'playing soldiers' and parading my toy army on the nursery table encouraged father in his belief that there might be a Field-Marshal's baton in his elder son's knapsack. As a schoolboy I had the choice of joining the scouts or 'The Corps' (The Officer's Training Corps), but of course my choice had to be 'The Corps' and, quite honestly, I hated it. With the outbreak of war in 1939, I became a member of the LDV - Local Defence Volunteers, the forerunner of the Home Guard, today known as 'Dad's Army' and this I enjoyed since most of its members were equally unsoldierlike.

My trouble too was that I was born at the wrong time with the second half of that war catching me just as I left school. Father was anxious I should be in his regiment - the Essex - so I was persuaded to volunteer; an act which offered the chance of joining the regiment of one's choice, and so found myself a raw recruit in an infantry training centre at Warley Barracks, Brentwood, of which Dad was second-in-command. This seemingly cosy arrangement was not a good idea at all since sundry sergeant-majors took it out on me for what they perceived as injustices perpetrated by him and I could never get used to saluting my own Father.

Pronounced a soldier after four months square-bashing, trying to hit a target with an assortment of weapons - some with vicious kicks - and throwing myself onto coils of concertina barbed-wire so that my colleagues could pass unhindered over my prostrate and bleeding body (a fiendish adjunct to the process of becoming a soldier), I was passed onto a unit called a young soldier's battalion, stationed near Epping, and from there, if I remember rightly, to the Suffolk coast.

From thence onward, there might just as well have been no war so far as I was concerned, though we seemed to do a lot of preparing for it. I have vague memories of billets in such diverse locations as prim seaside villas in Leigh-on-Sea and rusty Nissen huts in Hutton's Ambo, an extremely rural Yorkshire village. The war did intrude twice; in Leigh-on-Sea when Southend was bombed by the Luftwaffe and Dover when German long-range guns shelled it. While on the Isle of Wight I remember nights atop Boniface Down waiting for German paratroops who never came. Issued with five rounds of ammunition and a telephone it was the job of just two of us to scream down the 'blower', 'They're coming!', to warn the battalion sleeping comfortably in Shanklin of the invasion from the sky. What we were supposed to do thereafter I was never quite sure, die like heroes taking five each of the buggers with us or run like hell?

Still carrying on training between these interludes, I began to smell a rat. Father knew my various commanding officers and I envisaged the idea; I was being held back for eventual transfer to OCTU for officer training, I having been pronounced 'officer material'. Colleagues kept leaving for other units and exotic locations like North Africa and India, but I was always left behind.

Then came a decision. My colonel had me before him one day to ask if I'd prefer to be transferred to an officer's training unit or a combat battalion preparing for what everybody was referring to as the 'Big Show', the opening of the long-awaited 'Second Front'. It was entirely my choice this time and I wasn't all that keen to become an officer anyway.

Thus I found myself occupying another villa, this one on Bexhill seafront, as a corporal in the Dorset Regiment. With my new unit the training continued unabated, long route marches with full equipment becoming the norm. Fortunately, I like walking.

I well remember the two big springtime 1944 exercises involving much of the British, US and Canadian armies that gave me an even more uncomfortable time physically than experienced against the real enemy later in Normandy.

These exercises were code-named *Spartan* and *Tiger* and, in those days, the military accepted a 5% (real) casualty rate, a figure that would in no way be tolerated today. I was present at one incident contributing to such casualties during what became known as the 'Battle of Sonning Bridge' when over-enthusiastic Canadians opened up with live instead of blank ammunition; we British retaliated by tipping some of their bren-gun carriers into the Thames.

For part of *Tiger* I became a very junior umpire. Just you try to stop a determined Canadian tank from crossing a 'blown' bridge if it wants to. Lying down in front of it was no use, it'd just roll over you.

Though I had experienced being on the receiving end of that air raid at Leigh-on-Sea in Essex and cross-Channel shelling at Dover, I was not to see the whites of the enemy's eyes until June 1944. For a week or more prior to this we soldiers were herded into overcrowded tented camps along the South Coast of England guarded by military police who had orders to shoot to kill anyone attempting to leave without authority. I was so accommodated somewhere near the coast in Hampshire.

I seem to remember it was raining steadily for much of the time and it was a somewhat miserable and waterlogged bunch of crusaders that finally emerged from sodden tents to embark on the Liberation of Europe.

Then things began to happen. An inspection of the battalion by Prime Minister Winston Churchill, together with all the Empire Prime Ministers - Smuts of South Africa, Menzies of Australia, et al - plus the Chief of the General Staff, had us all lined up in our best uniforms. The Prime Ministerial party processed ponderously down the front rank of rigid soldiers - and stopped opposite me.

'Corporal,' said Churchill, pointing to my beret, 'What does the inscription on your regimental badge stand for?' It's not often that

words fail me, but they did this time. Though I was never a Latin scholar, I did know that *'Primus in Indis'* was 'First in India', but I was struck dumb.

Churchill turned to my colonel who was vainly trying to prompt me with his lips. 'See that this soldier knows the words of the regimental badge,' he barked. Then he turned and gave me a conspiratorial wink.

A few days later I was abruptly moved to brigade HQ of another division who found themselves short of signallers - not that I was a signaller in the first place, but the army never worry about details like that. With a group of men I'd never met before I went to war.

A day or two caged behind barbed wire in a gigantic camp 'somewhere off the Solent' - I think it was Gosport - and we embarked at night onto one of a vast armada of ships.

Details elude me, but I think ours was one of the larger cross-channel ferries. Aboard, each man sought to create his tiny island of privacy amidst the great mass of humanity crowded below decks. We knew now the landfall was to be Normandy and, whatever awaited us, there surely couldn't be worse conditions than on that stormy voyage; being constantly sick, watching everyone else being sick, and slithering about on a deck awash with vomit.

Before dawn, the French coast was lit by flares and flashes as the naval guns pounded the defences; explosions rippling up and down the shoreline while the tearing rasp of rocket batteries propelled what sounded like express trains screeching overhead. I think it was the noise that I remember more than anything else. It stunned the senses.

Whilst all this was going on we lined up to descend the 'scrambling nets' unrolled over the side of the ship. This is difficult enough even without the heavy loads we were carrying and the pitching and rolling of both mothership and the bobbing LCAs (Landing Craft Assault) into which we had to leap at the correct moment. Some men fell between the ship and the landing craft never to be seen again.

Each craft when loaded made for the shore. The floundering vessels - plus sheer terror - meant most of us were retching over each other's backs as we crouched in tight rows facing the bow, longing for the ramp to drop so that we could feel terra firma beneath our feet.

> " **'Corporal' said Churchill, pointing at my beret, 'what does the inscription on your regimental badge stand for?' It's not often that words fail me, but they did this time.** "

Then we grounded on the sand and gratefully waded ashore. The noise had abated slightly and we could make out machine-gun fire and the 'crump' of German 88s coming from ahead of us, but for me, it didn't really register; it all seemed unreal. On each side of me men sank to the ground as we advanced in quite leisurely fashion up and off the beach into some rough ground containing a few ruined houses. Smoke billowed across the front and a Frenchman suddenly appeared waving a small tricolour, tears running down his face. From a soldier I had made the transformation to a crusader, a liberator of Europe.

Memory is a fickle ability particularly when one has reached the age of 80, as I have. Recollections of the past become hazier with each passing year, yet instances - even those of the smallest consequence - stand out with startling clarity. Such is the case of the summer of 1944, as the Allied armies struggled to hold, expand and break out of the precarious Normandy bridgehead.

A portrait of Winston Churchill by an unknown artist. Pictures of the British Premier were widely displayed in workplaces. 'The Front Line runs through the factories' said Churchill, where the workers were 'soldiers with different weapons but with the same courage'.

Men of the 4th Dorset Regiment pause during their advance in Normandy, July 1944.

Being always good at remembering geographical locations, place-names invariably come floating into my subconscious; villages with names such as Asnelles, Hottot, Tilly-sur-Seulles, Cheux, Verson and Maltot, and towns like Villers-Bocage and, of course, historic Bayeux, which, by a miracle, escaped relatively unscathed where everywhere else was pulverised into dust.

The country over which we advanced resembled parts of Devon. Fields of standing corn alternated with pastures surrounded by high hedges and old dry ditches. Many of the minor roads and tracks were sunken, offering perfect cover to a resolute defender - and the German defenders were resolute, make no mistake. The numerous villages were strongly built with narrow passages between the farms and houses set amidst orchards. The terrain is known as *bocage* and had to be fought over hedgerow by hedgerow.

In the east, open cornfields stretched towards the heights overlooking Caen, the city that held the key to Normandy. Storm and capture those heights and Caen would fall into Allied hands like an overripe plum, we were told. The Wehrmacht, of course were aware of this too and held the high ground with great tenacity. But first we had to reach them.

Instances of those weeks 'reaching them' are fragmentary in my memory. Managing to transfer back to my own Dorset battalion soon after their arrival in Normandy confuses my recollections still further, but small episodes during street fighting amongst heavily-damaged buildings remain vivid in the mind. Advancing from house to house, crouched low to make oneself a smaller target for the enemy snipers and taking cover in every doorway from the incessant tank and small arms fire that exploded, whistled and ricocheted in those lethal streets. And in the occasional house itself small, vicious and intensely-personal battles between German and Brit ensued among the debris of French furniture with grenades exploding to shatter still further the best china and family photographs arrayed on the shelves.

Neither do I forget those pre-dawn patrols on which we were sent to capture a prisoner for interrogation. Devoid of all items of equipment except weapons, a dozen or so of us would sneak through German lines in semi-darkness, ears alert for the slightest sound; eyes straining to see what lay ahead, imagination transforming commonplace objects into sources of the direst peril. On one such patrol proceeding in the opposite direction on the other side of a thick hedgerow was an enemy patrol. Only as the last man of each patrol went by was the situation revealed and a ferocious back-to-front battle resulted.

I can still bring to mind instances of life behind the front line. The compulsory 'rest parades' when everyone lay in ranks in open fields under a warm sun to obtain as much relaxation as possible and 'MT guard' wherein, with four hours 'on' and two hours 'off', we would individually patrol our battalion motor transport park throughout the night. Then there was the comparative luxury of a cooked meal - the stew and 'spotted dick' pudding slopped into one's mess tins together with tea strong enough in which to stand a spoon. This fodder compared favourably to the 'dog biscuits' and jam which initially was a basic ingredient of nourishment in the front line. I also seem to remember a fiendish connection contained in a self-heating tin that was reputed to be a mixture of tea, milk and sugar. And, back in action again, I shall never forget the one and only time I fired in anger that most despised of weapons, the PIAT (Projector Infantry Anti-Tank) at an oncoming armoured car. But I got the range wrong and the shell exploded harmlessly in front of the vehicle while the recoil all but dislocated my shoulder. Recovering, I could think of nothing more effective to do than run like hell, encouraged to do so by long bursts of Spandau fire.

The first - and for me, last - major battle in which I participated, was I think, code-named *Jupiter*. My brigade had fought its way forward to the base of the hills overlooking Caen of which the highest became known as Hill 112. The brigade's objective was a trio of villages that lay on the ridge, namely Chateau de Fontaine, Eterville and Maltot. We advanced through fields of waving corn, which while providing some cover from view, failed to deflect the scythe of machine-gun fire that felled men left, right and centre.

From this treacherous ground my battalion moved into trees on the flank of Eterville to finally capture the remains of the village. Around the church I became involved in a private dispute with a squad of enemy soldiers as we fired at one another at point blank range from the cover of gravestones, they finally being put to flight with a couple of grenades. Consolidating our position and 'digging in' as we called the task of excavating two man slit trenches, I lost a couple of my section from sniper-fire including my partner who was taking cover at one end of our half-completed hole while I was standing up digging furiously at the other. The poor chap died with a bullet in the throat, gurgling his life away.

Though we had taken our objective, the Royal Hampshires had not been so lucky with Maltot. The battalion had run into a heavily fortified position comprising of dug-in Tiger tanks and had been virtually wiped out. We were thus called upon to go to their aid, so resumed the advance only to run into a storm of 88mm and heavy machine-gun fire from the enemy tanks against which we had no support. My company, caught in an orchard that suddenly dissolved into flame and smoke, reached the middle of the village, even occupying a recently abandoned Tiger pit, which was promptly counter-attacked by the Germans

The order to withdraw never reached the leading companies; all we knew about it was when Allied artillery put down a massive barrage on our position. Leaping into an enemy trench followed by half a dozen colleagues assuredly saved my life as the inferno of shellfire burst around us and flattened what was left of Maltot. In the uncanny silence that marked the lifting of the barrage I pushed my way out of the trench through the knot of my now mostly dead companions only to find myself starring down the barrel of a Schmeisser submachine pistol held unwaveringly by a sergeant of our long time adversary, the 12th Panzer Division.

With my hands clasped above my steel helmet I was marched through the burning village, dead and dying Dorsets strewn about its shattered streets. That I had become a prisoner of war failed, at first, to register even though the SS sergeant had actually said to me in English, 'For you, Tommy, the war is over'.

Actually it had only just begun.

My first hours of capture remain a blur of memory. The German frontline troops, though belonging to a crack SS division - 12th Panzer - treated us well enough, even offering cigarettes. Our small group of prisoners were then escorted through the blazing village of Maltot and I remember taking my turn to help carry the stretcher of a badly wounded German soldier.

A mile or so east of the village we were handed over to the Feldgendarmerie - a force equivalent to our military police. Our new escorts marched us well into the night with our hands raised painfully atop our steel-flanged helmets; any attempt at lowering them being met with a jab from a rifle butt. I began wistfully thinking of the despised biscuits and jam that reposed in my discarded haversack, some of which had been my sole culinary intake of that day.

Midnight found us outside a sizeable chateau utilised as a military HQ where, one by one, the officers and NCOs of our group were taken before a well-decorated SS captain who sardonically interrogated us. Our refusal to divulge more than name, rank and number was met by heavy doses of sarcasm and every conceivable fact about our units 30 years later, during an anniversary visit to Normandy, I was to meet this self-same officer. Needless to say, my feelings were mixed.

For what remained of the night we were herded into an out-house on the straw-covered floor on which lay about a hundred other British captives. It was pitch dark and our arrival provoked curses, many from the men suffering from unattended wounds. Feeling my way carefully I found a small space in which to curl up. The stench of blood together with the moans of the wounded made sleep impossible while morning did no more than reveal a scene mercifully hidden by the night.

Beside me lay a tank sergeant, a gaping hole festering in his side, whilst two members of his crew with horribly burnt arms and faces writhed nearby. Feeling sick I turned away to contemplate the less gruesome sight of a Canadian corporal darning his socks. Some of the men had been here for more than two days with no food, water or medical attention.

Following another search in which our last remaining possessions were removed, the Germans began loading us onto a fleet of civilian lorries, which they had gradually accumulated. But there were not enough so priority was given to those of the wounded who couldn't stand. The rest of us were marched eastwards away from the battlefront under a burning sun and with still no food to placate our rumbling stomachs. Only in the late afternoon was an issue made of stale bread, green with mould, and we were permitted water from a village pump. Then our transport returned to carry us to the first prison cage of a series that would eventually lead me to faraway Poland.

My first POW transit cage comprised of a well-equipped (for horses) French thoroughbred stables east of the town of Falaise, each loose box containing upwards of 40 men. These became our dormitories, straw our bedding and a yard about the size of a football pitch our exercise area.

Food - a vital factor in the life of a POW - was quite good when related to that of later camps, being basically potato soup, bread with margarine and ersatz 'jam' together with acorn 'coffee'. French civilians occasionally brought us cherries. Escape would not have been all that difficult, but as yet, I was not in a state of mind to attempt such measures, though, in later months I was to regret the lost opportunities.

Our stay here lasted a little more than a week, but with the Allied build-up to the closing of the so-called 'Falaise Gap' imminent, we were moved eastwards again. Transportation was by another fleet of lorries but this time progress was interrupted by incessant air attack; roving RAF Typhoons creating havoc on the roads. Time and time again both captors and captives were forced to leap for their lives from the lorries as these aircraft hurled themselves at anything that moved, squirting a hail of rockets which exploded all around us. Occasionally sympathetic but unwary French folk would give us a 'V' sign as we trundled by, only to be fired upon by our nervous guards, while in one case a village priest was picked up and deposited 30 kilometres away for his indiscretion.

Alencon was the closest town to our next cage, a heavily wired enclosure consisting of decayed barrack rooms containing double-tier bunks - mostly broken; the whole encircled by guard towers originally designed to keep people out but now adapted to keep them in. The culinary speciality here was tripe; not the celebrated Caen tripe but the stuff used to feed the dogs. The latrines were a disgrace; so bad in fact that mostly we used our steel helmets with the lining removed, or better still someone else's! Water too was scarce; the one receptacle we had for the collecting it from the single tap being the self-same helmet.

Not surprisingly perhaps, I went down with a vicious dose of dysentery and, for nearly a week, was unable to hold down a morsel of food while lying miserably on my hard bunk under my threadbare blanket listening to the rats scurrying about beneath

> **Crossing the Elbe River at Dresden we were attacked by American fighters, but sustained no casualties though the Germans, in compensation, painted large red crosses on the wagon roof and added half a dozen ammunition trucks to the rear of the train.**

Soon after Christopher Portway was moved from the Falaise area it became the scene of the decisive defeat of the German army in Normandy. 'Falaise Gap, August 1944' is by Frank Wootton and depicts rocket-firing Typhoons wreaking havoc on a German column of tanks and trucks. Reproduced by kind permission of Mrs Virginia Wootton.

the floor. The one consolation was vested in the RAF and USAAF who laid on some spectacular strafing raids which cheered us up no end - though sometimes they were a little too close for comfort.

Weak but recovered 10 days later and it was the city of Chartres' turn to play host. We were 250 to a concrete warehouse, straw again our bedding with the same inadequate water supply and a lousy cuisine supplemented by a surprising issue of Red Cross parcels - one between seven men.

There followed a journey by train that can only be described as horrific. At Chartres railway station we were herded onto cattle wagons, 55 or 60 per wagon, and the doors closed and bolted. Barbed wire stretched across the small window slits. The first part of the hellish ride took five days, the warm sun baking us by day; the cold freezing us by night. Too cramped to lie or even sit down, deficient of sanitary facilities, a bucket of water to last us a full day with salt beef our only provisions causing only increased thirst, the train rumbled east - the air in the wagons fetid. On top of this the train was repeatedly attacked by the Allied air forces, several prisoners being killed and wounded as bombs, rockets and bullets thudded around while we cringed like rats caught in a trap. At Metz a Red Cross delegate objected in vain on our behalf but at least the dead and wounded were removed at the station. Several French Canadians went mad, their personal water supply being fought over by thirst-crazed fellow prisoners. On the last day it rained and those who had empty tins held them outside the window slits to collect droplets of water - whereupon the German guards utilised the tins as targets for their weaponry.

Next morning we crossed the border into Germany. Welcome to the Fatherland. Blinking in the unaccustomed sunlight we emerged from that blighted train to be introduced to Stammlager IXA in the vicinity of Limburg. Here I was officially registered as a POW but most memorable of all were the hot showers and, by POW

standards, the not unreasonable food. Overcrowding and boredom were the chief sources of irritation and, for me, anger when my tiny but priceless portion of a bulk issue of Red Cross goodies was stolen. At the end of August the complement of the camp departed for a stalag situated on the Czech-Polish border, a four-day journey. Crossing the Elbe River at Dresden we were attacked by American fighters, but sustained no casualties though the Germans, in compensation, painted large red crosses on the wagon roof and added half a dozen ammunition trucks to the rear of the train.

Escape-minded at last, a few of us attempted to prise up the floorboards of the wagon, but were resisted by the majority who were fearful of the consequences. I must admit to a certain sense of relief since I hardly relished the idea of leaving a moving train by way of its floor.

Stalag VIIIB at Teschen was the HQ camp of a number of outlying working camps stretching as far as 80 miles away. Its construction was very much on the lines of the universally perceived prison camp; rows of huts and an exercise area, the whole bordered by triple curtains of barbed wire between guard towers. But, as at Limburg, the food and conditions were passable with boredom soon the main concern. I stood it for a month buoyed up by various escape plans hatching in my head and then just as I was preparing to put theory in to practice, a hundred of us were consigned to a work camp in Polish Silesia.

We were taken there by train again. It was a five hour journey and, with a guard in each compartment and others in the corridor, there seemed to me to be but one escape exit, that via the toilet. Escorted there by a soldier I straightaway assaulted the window, forced it open and, thanks to my German diet, managed to wriggle my thin body halfway out of the small aperture before I was apprehended.

Our latest journey ended at the industrial town of Zabreze which the Germans had renamed Hindenburg. Smoke-stacks and pit-head hoists filled the horizon. And it was then I learnt the nature of the work to which we were to be put. In direct contravention of the Geneva Convention we were to become slave coal miners on behalf of the German Reich, contributing to its war effort and the destruction of our own country.

Anger, frustration and determination welled within me. Not only did I detest the very idea of hacking coal out of the bowels of the earth, particularly on behalf of my enemy, but now I had every incentive to break the bonds of my captivity and effect a really worthwhile escape.

It was not simple patriotism or an eagerness to rejoin the lethal struggle going on in North-West Europe that prompted my unauthorised departure from the Silesian Zabrze coal mine in which, as a slave worker, I now found myself. Hacking coal while lying on one's back so that the stuff falls on one's face for eight or sometimes 12 hours a day on a diet of watery soup plus a seventh of a loaf of stale bread I found to be an unattractive pastime. Escape was the solution - or so it seemed to me, although the nearest Allied forces were those of the unpredictable Red Army advancing westwards across the Ukraine. In company with one Gordon (of his namesake Scottish regiment) we put into operation our first breakout from German captivity with the object of attaining the Soviet front line.

Our camp enclosure comprised two 12-foot high barbed wire fences in between which lay a pyramid of coiled barbed wire. A third fence of thick wire mesh lay the other side of the guard's cinder patrol path while every corner of the enclosure was overlooked by a watchtower equipped with a searchlight and machine gun. To breach the fences we had 'borrowed' a pair of wire-cutters, a plank of wood plus a length of cord. This last item we envisaged using to prise apart the top coil of wire from the two bottom ones by means of a pulley device (likewise 'borrowed') and inserting the plank between them giving precarious passage through this particularly prickly obstacle, once the first fence had been breached. We also had the unwitting co-operation of the Royal Air Force, the bomber fleets of which passed overhead on most nights. This had the effect of dousing the perimeter lights for the period the aircraft were in the vicinity.

The breakout went almost according to plan. Emerging from the odious latrine block in which we had hidden for the first part of the night and crawling to the nearby selected portion of the fence with our 'tools' we attacked the lower strands with our cutters, then separated the wire coils and spread-eagled ourselves in turn over the plank which we had inserted between the coils to finally attack the second fence to

emerge onto the cinder path, having twice been forced to 'freeze' as the blue-tinged beam of a searchlight swept over us. A crisis occurred when it was found that the cutters failed to sheer through the stout wire mesh of the third fence by which time the crunch of boots on the path heralded the return of the patrol. In desperation we threw ourselves at a pole forming a support for the wire mesh fence and scaled it, helping each other to attain the top.

The aircraft noise had faded to the extent that the lights came on just as we jumped down the other side into an allotment of cabbages. Crawling through these we moved off out of range of the illumination, took to our heels and ran straight into an anti-aircraft battery we had often heard thudding away when Allied planes were overhead. Panic-stricken we sheered away, taking to the darkened open countryside with guttural challenges ringing in our ears.

Our way led eastwards and for the first few days we moved on foot, walking openly through villages and towns if these could not be avoided and sleeping in woods or barns. Travelling by night we found to be fraught with difficulties. Our small stock of fodder soon gave out which left us with nothing to eat but raw potatoes gathered from clumps since we dared not light a fire. Finally we resorted to simple robbery, breaking into Silesian German farmhouses and stealing not only anything edible but items of clothing for disguise and, when available, money. I have to admit that entering a life of crime proved to be not without its attraction though Gordon was a far less conscious-stricken criminal than I and, on one occasion, had to be persuaded from nicking the family silver.

All too soon physical weakness slowed our plodding footsteps to the point where a long dormant 'train plan' was reborn. Jumping a freight train seemed the only solution; it looked so easy in the movies even if we could raise no philharmonic orchestra to provide background inspiration. Finding a location for this new project took us two whole days wherein to select a suitable section of railway track that suited our purpose. The line had to be remote, going in the right direction and bordering terrain that offered concealment. Further, we needed a gradient that would slow the train enough for us to attempt to board it and a curve in the track to foil vigilance from armed guards in the locomotive and brake van.

It took another 12 hours of dallying by the trackside before the arrival of a suitable coal train. And just you try climbing aboard a moving high-sided steel wagon as it moves by. Signal wires and stone ballast made running alongside a nightmare with those iron wheels ready to crush the legs of the unwary. Remember too that we were half-starved and weak with exhaustion. But we made it and, concealed in an empty - too empty for our liking - wagon we rumbled eastwards. Not for long though. Then came a whistle and the grinding of brakes following which the confounded train halted and moved off again but in the *opposite direction*. Moving too fast for us to bale out we were involuntarily transported back westwards for some 60 miles, out of Silesia into Germany proper. When finally the thing halted again, this time in a village freight yard, we were able to steal away under a pre-dawn sky leaving us with one final course of action to make up the lost miles and attain the city of Cracow, our initial objective. Since we had money we would use the services of a passenger train for at least we would know where we were going. Our fluency in the German language was abysmal and it was only because we found the word 'erster' (first) easier to pronounce than the equivalent for 'second' or 'third' we became first-class passengers on an oft-stopping 'personenzug' bound for that fair Polish city having tended our money and acquired tickets at the village station without raising too much suspicion. At one point our judiciously empty compartment was invaded by two German Luftwaffe officers of friendly disposition who wanted to chat - though we didn't. Presenting ourselves as Hungarian hospital workers tending poor wounded German soldiers we were cajoled into a description of Budapest, a city I had not then visited. I gave them a brief run-down on Bristol, which seemed to satisfy them in spite of Gordon, getting his wires crossed, offering a counter portrayal of Glasgow! For our troubles we were offered a bunch of grapes.

Approaching the main station of Cracow we avoided the assured presence of military police, Gestapo agents and other nasties that afflicted such establishments by jumping out of the slowing train as it wound through the suburbs. And it was just our luck that our landing place turned out to be a military transport depot in which we had to hide under a truck until midnight when we emerged onto the streets of the town. But the streets were bewilderingly empty - until we remembered the curfew which German authority inflicted on citizens of their occupied territories. The sublime smell of new-baked bread took our minds momentarily off this latest debacle to the extent that the famished Gordon took matters into his own hands by hurling a brick through the baker's shop window and grabbing a loaf - just as a three-man Wehrmacht patrol came round the corner. Never one for good timing was Gordon. Thus we found ourselves staring down the muzzles of two rifles and a schmeisser. Though they could have shot us on the spot the soldiers became exceedingly friendly and, joined by an initially-indignant baker, we all sat down to scoff vast quantities of new warm bread - which did little good to our already badly treated stomachs. The patrol sergeant, looking miserable, bade us eat all we could since he had to perform the unpleasant task of handing us over to the Gestapo. 'It's a firm order,' he explained apologetically.

So, my first glimpse of this fine old city of Polish kings came about under German escort en route to Gestapo HQ off the cloistered main square where a black-uniformed clerk signed a receipt and curtly dismissed our initial captors. There the fun came to an abrupt end.

Taken into a bare concrete-walled room we were questioned thoroughly by a vile little man wearing civilian clothes. The thrust of his questioning concerned the identity of the Poles who had helped us to get this far without capture but, as we had received no help, it was a question we were unable to answer. This resulted in a heavy beating which fractured my ribs and, after being kicked to the floor and then kicked up again, our arms were burnt by lighted cigarettes. We had, beforehand, agreed to say that we had escaped from the Stalag from which we had been sent to the coal mine since it was a far more relaxing and less taxing abode than that of Zabrze and we stuck to this through the gruelling procedures that followed.

Finally we were led to an underground and windowless cell where we remained, unfed and in considerable pain, for several days with just the concrete floor for a bed. Then one night we were hustled into the back of a truck reeking with petrol fumes. Our guard was a blonde SS youth who took the greatest pleasure in informing us that we were going to be shot. The revelation came hardly as a shock so low and ill did I feel and Gordon, seemingly, felt the same. Get it over quick, I thought to myself and since it's no good pleading for life with such people as these, I might as well die like a soldier. I asked why they didn't do the job in the cellars and was told that it made the place untidy. The man's sense of humour was then dented slightly when I was sick over his shiny jackboots.

But we were permitted to live another day to find ourselves, at the end a multi-hour journey, at what appeared to be a gigantic barracks where we were incarcerated in a kind of enlarged dog kennel containing a wooden bunk and a bucket. The whole area reeked of death and now and again people shuffled by, their faces

> **Then one night we were hustled into the back of a truck reeking with petrol fumes. Our guard was a blonde SS youth who took the greatest pleasure in informing us that we were going to be shot. The revelation came hardly as a shock so low and ill did I feel and Gordon, seemingly, felt the same.**

downcast as if our presence was not to be noticed. Their gaunt faces were almost inhuman and we wondered whether we too were beginning to look likewise.

We were to remain here for more than three weeks, perhaps a month; we had no means of telling. However, once a week we were taken under guard across an open space to an ablution block, our legs exhibiting a tendency to give way by virtue of our own physical condition, there to perceive the true horror of the place.

In the open space was a litter of half-naked men and women, their gender barely discernible, who sat, squatted or lay upon the ground. Among them, ignored, were forms mercifully concealed by their ragged shrouds that were plainly dead; a few maybe in the process of dying and others, alive, picking lice from their rags of striped pyjama-type clothing. I stared, mesmerised by their faces, looking in vain for a vestige, a flicker of human emotion, but there was nothing. The bestial treatment they had received had sucked all life out of them leaving these husks of semi-alive skeletons, their skull-like heads containing eyes, large and luminous, staring into a void; dead men still clutching to a life not worth living. On our first sighting of this horrendous scene I fought, within myself, to disbelieve what my eyes looked upon. I heard Gordon eject an obscenity and glanced at our contemptuous guard who took not the slightest notice of the hideous apparition.

The ablution chamber lay at one end of a single-storey, rectangular wooden building that formed part of an accommodation block containing rows of treble bunks that filled most of it with a narrow corridor running down the middle. Rising almost to the ceiling, each set of bunks contained not one but up to three occupants, the majority seemingly too weak to move. Here and there livid straining faces and thin emaciated arms and legs emerged from filthy blankets. All this I could only glimpse but it was enough. The stench was nauseating, all but unbearable. In Normandy I had looked upon mangled bodies lying among the debris of ruined villages and burnt, blackened corpses hanging out of destroyed tanks but the obscene spectacle of what I was seeing now was different; such images could hardly be repeated in the very depth of hell. After splashing our faces under a row of taps releasing cold water we were returned to our 'kennel'; it was akin to a transfer from a hovel to the Ritz.

Our sojourn in what we believed was the transit zone of the camp came to an end when we were taken to the administrative block and handed over to two very frightened elderly soldiers who had been ordered to collect us from a POW cage from which we had never escaped. Only as we arrived at the train station for the journey did we learn that the hell in which we had been held bore the name of Auschwitz-Birkenau. If nothing else our breakout had achieved more than a month and a half away from the dreaded coal mine which was at least one plus in the whole sorry affair. And this was extended by another fortnight of solitary confinement in a darkened cell on bread and water as punishment for our sins.

Eventually returned to Zabrze our notoriety as escapees earned us the exclusive grade of 'dangerous characters' and, back on the

Above: Christopher Portway took this photograph of the gates to Auschwitz on a visit made after the war.

coal face the bright yellow markings on our clothing singled us out for the worst jobs and the meanest of treatment. As a 21st birthday present I was given a double-shift but retaliated by sabotaging the main conveyor belt in our seam. When an epidemic of diphtheria laid me low in the camp 'hospital' I deemed it a blessing but when a crate of weak beer was discovered under my bed I was straightway consigned back to work though I could barely stand. Christmas Day was a holiday - paid for by another double shift.

A new year - 1945 - lay before us, What future did it hold? Starved of news we were not the happiest bunch of men. Yet when the camp was evacuated and we found ourselves preparing to trudge southwards in a bitter cold snowbound January this should have told us that the war was entering its final phrase. In fact, though we did not know it then, we were upon the threshold of one of the most sickening episodes of World War Two; one that was to reveal an unsurpassed savagery and known as the 'Death March'.

At least, with the end of the 1944, the strategic situation of the German and Soviet armies effected our release from the hated coal mine in which Gordon and I had been incarcerated for many months with just one interval brought about by our autumn escape and its horrific aftermath of Gestapo 'treatment' and Auschwitz sojourn. But, again, that release was no more than coming out of the frying pan and into the fire. And, again, with a vengeance.

Soon after the gloomiest Christmas I've ever known, occurred one of the most brutal episodes of the whole of World War Two as the greatest migration in history pushed ahead of the steamroller advance of the Russian armies across the eastern lands. This titanic evacuation involved, literally, millions of civilian refugees, captives like ourselves, slave labourers, concentration camp inmates and broken units of the German Wehrmacht fleeing westwards, the tide of human misery stretching from Konigsberg to Danzig and on through Pomerania, Prussia and Silesia to the banks of the River Oder. Along 250 miles of snow and icebound roads, the endless procession of desperate humanity stumbled, in enormous convoys, towards a river that was looked upon as the great divide beyond which, it was imagined, lay safety. This safety, to be sure, was threatened by incessant attacks from the air; yet what was a bomb or two compared with the fury and carnage about to descend on their homeland? But carnage was already here too, along roads strewn with the stiffened bodies of those who froze, starved or had been murdered by merciless SS troops in the coldest winter the region had experienced for decades.

The populations did not commence their flight until the Eastern Front had been shattered and retreating formations of German rear echelons came racing through the towns and villages. Panicky parties of refugees began mingling with the grey-faced beaten troops and, within days, the tragedy had engulfed everybody as a vast tide of people, including those who had been evacuated from air-raid-stricken cities in Germany, joined the enormous migration. In mid-January the front of the Second Army on the Narew River broke under the Russian assault, the inhabitants of more towns and villages thrown overnight into the path of battle, fleeing headlong. Treks formed, numbering up to 30,000 souls, of whom many vanished without trace in the maelstrom and in temperatures dropping far below zero.

Into this snowbound hell we were pitched, unprepared, unequipped and already half-starved to become one tiny unit among the endless columns. Escape would have been easy; death by freezing the certain reward, our corpses adding to the thousands that littered the roads. For day after day; sometimes night after night, we trudged on with occasional sojourns in deserted farms where we fell onto hay or floor to sleep where we lay, often too exhausted to consume the meagre items of food that our guards could scrape together.

Man-hauled carts carried those who fell ill en route but to ride these was little more than a short cut to death in the freezing temperatures. I was struck down with severe dysentery but somehow managed to keep walking. All too frequently, however, I was obliged to squat in the snow to answer the call of nature; hurrying to get nearer the front of the column to gain time before the posse of SS squads at the rear could execute by bullet or bayonet those who delayed too long.

Never, in all my life, have I experienced hunger like that which gnawed at my empty stomach during those hellish weeks on the road. I would drive myself nearly insane thinking about favourite dishes at home; my existence revolved entirely around acquiring food and staying alive in the intense cold. Occasional issues of soup allegedly made from boiled grass and rotting beet were issued when we halted at night in nearby farms and starving men fell upon the disgusting substance as if it were manna from heaven. But even these distributions came few and far between. So hungry did we become that we found ourselves searching in farmyards for fragments of turnip that long-departed pigs had spurned, rooting for them in the mud like the beasts themselves had done. It was rumoured that men were eating cats, dogs and even rats, sometimes raw, yet my only reaction was that of disappointment that I could not share their bounty.

I became aware of the deterioration of my companions into thin, wild-eyed creatures though I fooled myself into thinking that this was not happening to me. But then, while resting in a barn, I caught sight of my reflection in a piece of shiny tin forming part of the wall to find myself staring at little more than a gaunt, filthy skeleton. However, I still considered myself luckier than those of my fellows who were in even worse physical condition and suffered more painful frostbite than my own.

Sometimes too we caught up with half-alive Russians in their tattered coats with bloody bandages wrapped around festering wounds and rags tied around their frost-bitten feet. Time and time again we did our best to drag these wretched prisoners along with us to save them from execution but, one by one, were forced to leave them to their fate.

Along the way I was to witness incidents of sheer horror as desperate Russians dug up long-buried corpses in graveyards and consumed the uncooked, putrefied flesh. We saw a body being roasted on a spit like that of a wild boar and the bayoneting of a woman and child for no reason whatsoever. And, near the town of Raciborz, the execution in a small concentration camp of those inmates deemed too weak to join the exodus. In batches of about 50, lines of naked human beings, unrecognisable as man or woman, tottered like mechanical dolls before a bullet-scarred wall, there to stand in resigned silence to be mown down by SS machine-gunners. If there was any flicker of emotion in those withered frames it must have been simple relief that the suffering was at an end. The tortured eyes of these poor wretches will haunt me to my dying day.

Witnessing such scenes instilled in me a consuming hatred that I have never felt before or since and hope I never will again. Revenge and retribution was all my mind could generate - and yet this utter loathing and disgust was tempered by the sight of our German sergeant-major retching in the snow as a result of observing the actions of his own countrymen. I was not alone in my hatred. Like a forest fire, the anger of those in the column who were witnessing the massacre, spread to become virtually audible in its intensity. I have no doubt we would have got completely out of control had we not been hastily moved on by abruptly alarmed guards.

By the end of February, the worst excesses of the hideous exodus were behind us and the survivors of the columns dragged themselves onto the soil of Czechoslovakia in their countless thousands. The snows had receded and we had entered a land whose populace looked upon us with infinite compassion. Our German overseers beheld a solution to the well nigh insurmountable supply problem and permitted Czech bread and soup, in restricted quantities, to be distributed as the columns ground westwards. Overnight accommodation in the larger Czech farms with their easily guarded and spacious barns became a more regular feature than before; their hay and straw storage greatly appreciated for the warmth and snug comfort generated.

With the improvement in conditions, Gordon and I began to re-assess the practicalities of another escape. The daily marching stint of 15 to 20 kilometres remained a gruelling ordeal for our wasted bodies, its only heartening aspect being that every step was bringing us nearer to the Allied armies, now within the western frontiers of Germany. We were also aware that our route would eventually lead out of Czech territory onto that of Germany and an assured renewed deterioration in our treatment. Thus the attraction of remaining in Czechoslovakia was strong.

The execution of another escape, however, was not going to be so easy. The guards had become more watchful and in the flat open country of Bohemia, there was little hope of making a dash from the column. This left the alternative of a breakout from or self-concealment within a farm; one or other action we proposed to take as soon as the opportunity presented itself. At first the circumstances required for both projects refused to materialise; either the Germans were too skillful with the placing of their guards, or the props of concealment were too poor.

Until, one day, we arrived in a barn with its contents meeting our requirements. The hour of another escape had arrived and this one was to change the course of my life.

Within minutes, several hundred captive soldiers turned the building into a seething ant-heap of tired and irritable humanity staking claims to bed-space. Gordon and I hurriedly located ours close to the slatted walls and, with the dawn next morning, we burrowed ourselves, with the co-operation of a Durham Light Infantry corporal, deep down into the bowels of the haystack keeping close to the barn wall for air. Above us our

> **Never in my life, have I experienced hunger like that which gnawed at my empty stomach during those hellish weeks on the road. I would drive myself nearly insane thinking about favourite dishes at home; my existence revolved entirely around acquiring food and staying alive in the intense cold.**

colleague stamped wads of hay down on top of our descending bodies, so that the composition at the surface would remain uniform.

Judging our depth to be out of range of the long bayonets with which the Germans search party would probe the stack, following discovery of our absence from the reassembled column, we waited with considerable trepidation. From outside came muffled sounds of movement as our compatriots prepared for another day of trudging.

Hours later – or so it seemed – I heard a door crash open and disjointed voices percolate through to our ears. Then a pause, a prolonged pause. There came vibrations as heavy boots scaled a ladder. More voices, closer now, and distinguishable as German, and the thud of feet above our heads. A shouted warning and the scything motion of jabbing bayonets began. Obeying a reflex reaction, we squeezed into balls to make smaller targets of ourselves.

Fear had me within an ace of giving up and scrabbling to the surface but the knowledge that I would be betraying my companion became the stronger emotion. Above and around us the long knives prodded deeply and methodically.

The new vibration made by a descent of the ladder was sweet music to our ears. The barn door closed indicating the departure of the search party but we were taking no chances - the ruse by which searchers would pretend to depart but leave one of their number behind was known to us. We lay motionless, determined to stick things out for another hour, even after the sound of multiple tramping feet had faded into the distance.

As certain as we could be that nobody was laying in ambush, we fought our way to the surface, breathing heavily. All was quiet within the building as we descended to the ground and

Right: The winter of 1945 was exceptionally bad all over Europe. Here we see German refugees in Silesia desperate to escape the advancing Red Army.

205

Above: Christopher is still a frequent visitor to Prague more than six decades after his initial highly dangerous acquaintance with the city while he was an escaped POW. This is a photograph he took just a year or so ago.

tiptoed to the door. So accustomed were we to crowds that our initial sensation was of a peculiar loneliness. The farmyard, too, was deserted. Warm sunshine bathed the peaceful countryside, mottled with unmelted snow, and the hum of a tractor reminded me of home.

This time round our evasion tactics were to run a different course from that of our earlier escape attempt in Silesia the previous year, since we were on the territory of a populace which, though aware of the terrible risks it ran by offering succour to the likes of us, was sympathetic. In Silesia and Poland we had an objective; the Russian lines. Here in Bohemia, all liberating agencies were out of reach. Gordon was in favour in making for Prague with the notion that contact with the partisan movement would be easier in the city so, for once, I gave him his head, though I would have preferred to stick to more rural climes. The loneliness persisted as we set out for the Czech capital.

The two weeks that followed were, to some extent, fruitless in endeavour, but were to mark a milestone in my life. We reached the city with little difficulty, keeping away from main roads and knocking on the doors of isolated houses to request bread whenever the pangs of hunger became unbearable. What remained of our uniforms was hardly recognisable as such, though our regulation boots, stained and grubby battledress trousers, and the identity discs around our necks could, we hoped, save us from a firing squad in the event of recapture. We both wore thick pullovers, removed weeks before from bodies whose need of them had long ceased.

Usually our appearance on the doorstep of a Czech home produced consternation but seldom were we to leave without a hunk of bread or slice of cake hurriedly thrust into our hands by the occupants, even though their fright was painful to behold. Once we were invited in for a meal at a remote farm, the farmer's

> **Usually our appearance on the doorstep of a Czech home produced consternation but seldom were we to leave without a hunk of bread or a slice of cake hurriedly thrust into our hands by the occupants, even though their fright was painful to behold. Once we were invited in for a meal at a remote farm, the farmer's wife bursting into tears upon perceiving our hunger and condition.**

wife bursting into tears upon perceiving our hunger and condition.

We reached the urban spread of Prague several days later. Barns, into which we had broken for a night's sleep, were replaced by concentrated housing as we followed the course of the Vltava river into the city centre walking openly in the busy streets, fully aware that looking shifty and frightened could attract unwelcome attention. And you'd hardly believe it, but for a full day we became tourists, observing the sights of this beautiful metropolis as if we hadn't a care in the world. German soldiers passed us without a sign of curiosity or suspicion.

But having reached Prague we were not quite sure what to do. The resistance movement was not·listed in the telephone directory and one can't just knock on a door and ask for instructions. But we did just that on one occasion as dusk was falling and were taken in by the Czech couple who responded to our summons. 'Didn't you know about the curfew?' they asked, aghast. 'You'll have to stay the night with us or else you'll be arrested or even shot.' And those wonderful people risked their lives for two unkempt and filthy strangers, giving us their best bed that we found to be too soft and comfortable for proper sleep. And in the morning we were directed out of Prague to an industrial town called Kladno, some 35 kilometres distant, that was reputed to be a hotbed of resistance.

The provision of food for the next couple of days as we headed west across country was no problem since the good couple had supplied us with wads of thick cheese sandwiches. The one time we did knock on the door for a drink of water, we accidentally selected a house that contained the village policeman. No doubt he would have happily supplied our needs but we were taking no chances and departed at considerable speed.

Factory chimneys and the skeletons of mineshafts heralded Kladno but when we got there its desolate streets offered no comfort and nobody in them looked remotely like a partisan. We didn't much like the look of the place so we turned about and left, frustrated.

It began to rain about midmorning. It spat in our faces, never continuous but like bursts of misdirected cold gunfire before the wind blew it away. The sky was low with grey cloud and it seemed to me, as the two of us walked between the tall featureless houses, the whole of Kladno was closing in on us like a trap. Walking there in the rain, I felt again that extraordinary loneliness, a loneliness that exaggerated the hopelessness within me so that it was as if the wind, the cold whip of rain and the dismal streets were combining against us. Beside me Gordon cursed the weather in his expressive London Scottish brogue. The hostility of the streets merged into a single heavy nausea that was like a sickness – a sickness to be home, in England, safe, away from it all. I longed bitterly to be out of the mess we had got ourselves into, out of Czechoslovakia, out of an environment in which you never knew if a fellow human was friend or foe

By evening we were close to a village called Smecno, or so a sign indicated, and, failing to break into a barn, spent a miserable night in a damp ditch. Earlier we had cadged a glass of milk and a hunk of dry bread from a frightened householder in a lone cottage. Increasingly we hated ourselves for having to compromise these decent folk but, other than resorting to open robbery in a friendly country, there was nothing else we could do.

A road enticed us to an unnamed town and while in its outskirts a shout had us instantly on our guard. The shout was repeated and we recognised the word *Anglicky* (English). Hesitatingly we turned to behold a middle-aged bespectacled man who had emerged from the garden gate of a house and was beckoning to us. Obeying the summons in the hope that his broadcasting of our nationality would cease, we approached. 'You are English soldiers', he said, in poor German, grinning hugely, and I wasn't sure if it was a question or a statement.

The meal we received – no more than mutton and potatoes – was, to us, a feast. While we ate, we attempted to explain our situation and desire to join the partisans. Instead, we received an invitation to remain in the family home until the war's end. But we would have none of that, tempting though the offer was. It would be tantamount to signing the family's death warrant. The man's wife, a small woman with kind eyes who spoke no German, likewise seemed quite happy to risk her life to shelter a couple of British soldiers but, eventually we came to a compromise. They would find us a place of concealment outside the town, their daughter or one of them would bring us food daily and discreet enquiries would be made about us joining the partisans.

Which is how we came to be ensconced in the innermost cavity of a quarry, a couple of kilometres away near another village. Blankets were supplied and our new–found optimism soared. Given the reliability of the premises, we saw no reason for not remaining in and around our bolt-hole until eventual contact with the partisans or arrival of a liberating army – which ever materialised first – could be achieved. Highly satisfied with the turn of events, we slept easier that night, in spite of the cold hard ground.

Broad daylight opened my eyes to look upon the girl standing hesitatingly before the cavity mouth. She must have seen me stir but made no move away. She had a bicycle with her, a wicker basket clamped to its handlebars. She was dark, and her eyes, big and bright and blue, did not falter.

The conversation that followed was stilted and superficial. A combination of extreme fatigue and awareness of our vulnerability eclipsed any sparkling repartee. The girl spoke reasonable English and showed no fear.

Gordon had woken at the sound of our voices and was as surprised as I was by the apparition. 'How old are you?' was his foray into the conversation, spoken with a soldier's directness. 'I'm 18,' she replied smiling, switching her gaze from me to him. Then she delved into her basket and brought out some bread and cold meat wrapped in a cloth, together with a flask, which she passed to us. As she came close, I caught the whiff of scent and saw in her face a perplexity of pleasure and shyness. I became abruptly aware of her youth.

I found myself inviting her to visit England when the war was over; it was as if I was inviting the vicar to tea. 'I'd love that', came the reply, with surprising fervour. She changed the subject, 'My parents want you to come and have supper with us tonight. Please come to the house as soon as it's dark. I think you know where it is'. 'Will you be there?' I burst out. 'Of course'.

My mind was a turmoil of emotions. Pleasure at the prospect of seeing her again, anguish for the danger the whole family would be incurring, incredulity that she should want to continue this fragile acquaintanceship. A strange excitement coursed through me.

With the dusk, we moved out of our quarry and found our way to the house. We dined lavishly or at least as lavishly as the strict rationing in a Nazi-occupied country would allow. But the blissful couple of hours was blighted by an undercurrent of awareness of the risks involved. I found myself listening for the heavy knock on the door.

The meal over, I enquired of the girl – I knew better than to ask her name – if we would see her again at the quarry. She made a

Above and right: Christopher returned to the place of his 'adventures' after the war and took these photographs of two of the Czech families that aided his escape in 1945, and of a farmhouse where he took refuge.

tiny gesture of dismay. 'I have to go back to college tomorrow,' she explained and I felt the bottom fall out of my world. I touched her hair briefly and, with Gordon following, slipped out into the night.

Our outlaw existence continued but, for me, a new and vital element was missing. The girl's father, and sometimes mother, brought provisions daily but it wasn't the same. Nothing seemed to be forthcoming so far as joining the partisans was concerned so, more to break the monotony of life, we decided to undertake a little resistance work ourselves. On one of our sorties from the quarry, we had discovered a single-track railway line nearby which, we decided, would make a suitable target for our attention.

Putting rocks taken from the track ballast into the switchgear of the points so that they jammed and shinning up telegraph poles to cut the wires was hardly going to win the war, but it was something to do. And it well might have been one of those trailing telephone cables that finally terminated our aimless existence. The fact remains that, one morning we were visited by two apologetic members of the local constabulary who sorrowfully announced the necessity of arresting us.

A small assembly of locals watched in silence, some making surreptitious movements of encouragement with their hands, as we were escorted to the police vehicle on the road nearest to the quarry. The notion came to me that our presence among our nearest neighbours had been well known; that the two Anglicky in their cave had become an accepted part of the community. Maybe it had even been one of them who had decided we had been around long enough and were causing more trouble than we were worth.

Our brief incarceration in the town jail was not a great ordeal. We shared the cell with a sorry specimen of Russian soldiery to whom we donated most of our prison fodder; his need being greater than ours.

A few days later we were taken to the main square. Again people stared at us with more sympathy than curiosity. We stood there, by the side of the road, our police guard shuffling his feet with embarrassment, until a ragged batch of figures we recognised as yet another prisoner convoy hove into view. At its head strode a German officer and our escort sprang to attention. The officer pointed a finger towards the shuffling ranks and, aided by a push, we found ourselves back with the nomads of the road to nowhere.

It was as if the last two weeks had never happened.

For Gordon and I, our couple of weeks of evasion and the occurrences therefrom had become almost surreal. It was as if we had taken a holiday from the horrors of the great exodus across the frozen wastes of Eastern Europe. For sure the 'holiday' had not been without its defects; dismay, cold, hunger and the awareness of danger were all ever-present. But these blemishes had been eternally with us too on the terrible migration away from the westward advancing Russian armies.

Now, back on the refugee-clogged roads of central Europe, this time with a column of fresh compatriots from camps in eastern Bohemia and Moravia that had only recently been evacuated, thus having avoided the worst atrocities of the migration, I had a new, personal and enlightening experience to ponder.

There was something about the girl who had come into my life while we were taking refuge in the quarry that was intensely disturbing. Repeatedly I chided myself for being a sentimental fool, but her image would not go away – nor did I want it to. Deep down in my soul, I knew I could not leave the matter like this. If her image still persisted and I survived the war, I simply would have to find a way of finding the girl again, if only to appease my torment. In the meantime, with a heavy heart, I lamented the fact that, though every step we were taking was one nearer the Allied armies in the west, it was one step further away from the object of my infatuation.

For Gordon and I, our new compatriots were reasonably well organised. They were appalled at our disclosure of the hideous events we had witnessed and endured in the first two months of the year and plainly thankful for not having been part of them.

This new trek was markedly different from that of January and February. The air of desperation on the part of our German overseers to ensure their prisoner columns remained ahead of the advancing Russian armies was subsiding. Spring was in the offing and its promise of warmth offered renewed hope, and with the outcome of the war in Europe plain to see by even the most radical Nazi amongst our captors, the beastliness we had suffered from them had evaporated to a remarkable degree.

Yet there remained instances of this inherent brutality even at this late hour and I was to witness one such example at close

> **We watched with some glee as a multiple force of American fighter-bombers approached from the west, headed by a squadron of target marker - or pathfinder - aircraft. Our glee turned abruptly to consternation as four smoke-trailing bombs bracketed the town and its rail junction. And here was I, together with a dozen companions, staring upwards from the dead-centre of the target.**

quarters, when one Corporal Kerr (I think that was his name) was murdered in cold blood by a rifle shot through his head, administered by an irate guard incensed at some light-hearted insult directed at him. The unfortunate Corporal dropped dead at my feet, the bullet narrowly missing me.

There were instances of brutality within our own ranks too. At one of our farms, at which we spent the night, a compatriot was caught stealing food from a colleague. Having passed from a sympathetic fodder-distributing populace in Czechoslovakia, to a sullen enemy population in neighbouring Bavaria where no such benefit existed, considerable hunger was again generated. This in no way could be used as an excuse for robbing a colleague and the punishment the perpetrator received was barbarous. Beaten almost to a pulp by a team of NCOs under the eye of a warrant officer and then ostracised thereafter by all in the column, the victim paid dearly for his stolen half bar of chocolate.

On this segment of the evacuation route, the trek ended outside the town of Plattling, an important railway junction feeding Regensburg and Passau, the latter on the Austrian border, and Landshut (on the main line to Munich) as well, in the other direction, the Czech border. Our new camp was to be a glue factory, an odious place of work; the chief ingredient of glue being bone; and in the Greater Germany of 1945, this commodity was in plentiful supply.

My memory fails me concerning the details of life over the short spell we were there. I do recollect an occasion when one of the Allied aircraft of the bomber fleets incessantly passing overhead dropped a metal canister that hit the ground close – too close – to where I was standing in the wire-fenced open field, which formed part of the factory.

The sting in the tail of this daily bomber procession was to be felt with a vengeance a week or two later when a group of us, still based at the factory, were switched to track maintenance in the very heart of the four-way rail junction near the town. That we worked – leaning on our shovels and occasionally humping sleepers and fishplates when our guards turned nasty – in the very bulls eye of a potential target never occurred to us until, one day, it was too late to do anything about it.

We watched with some glee as a multiple force of, I think, Marauders and other American fighter-bombers approached from the west, headed by a squadron of target marker – or pathfinder – aircraft. Our glee turned abruptly to consternation as four smoke-trailing bombs bracketed the town and its rail junction. And here was I, together with a dozen companions, staring upwards from the dead-centre of the target.

I gazed, transfixed, as the first shower of bombs descended from the leading machines of the main force which must have been at least 100-strong. Then, the spell broken, I dashed to take cover beneath a nearby small tanker locomotive but, in mid flight, changed direction and, even as the first crescendo of explosions streaked towards me, made for a heavy freight engine offering more substantial protection. A flat truck attached to it held a multiple-barrelled light anti-aircraft gun and its youthful crew who fired an ineffective volley into the air and dived like frightened rabbits, together with me, beneath the locomotive.

Thereafter, for minutes which seemed like hours, the world around me exploded into insanity. Searing heat, great gouts of flame and a hell of sound enveloped us, while debris rattled against the sides of our cover. Through the great driving wheels I watched the tanker locomotive explode into fragments, its boiler parts lifting into the air like autumn leaves. Our own locomotive swayed and shuddered as if pounded by a hurricane but, miraculously, was not hit as the rail sidings, junction points and crossovers dissolved into an earthquake scene of tortured soil. I found myself comforting the whimpering flak crew cringing beside me as terror turned foe into friend. And then came an ethereal silence broken only by the distant drone of departing aircraft.

We emerged, a little sheepishly, from cover to behold a scene of utter devastation. Fragments of twisted rail spiralled in the air. There was nothing left of what I presumed was the intended target, but the town too was nothing but a vast ruin. Our guard was dead, his broken body lying limply across a pile of sleepers. Escape would have been easy but shock had dulled my senses. From the town, gathering noises indicated a return to life of those who had survived the onslaught, together with an occasional crash as facades still standing of blasted buildings fell to the ground in clouds of dust.

One casualty of the raid had been a Red Cross train, its wagons loaded with food parcels that were now liberally sprinkled over the whole area; chocolate bars from burst packets could be found everywhere and were being feverishly collected by civilians and soldiers alike who had not seen such luxury morsels for years. They took no notice of me doing likewise.

Back in the glue factory our return was greeted with incredulity; everyone had presumed us all dead. In fact two of our number had, sadly, lost their lives.

Next day an edict from the commandant pronounced a resumption of the evacuation trek, this time in a south-easterly direction, away from the eastwards-advancing American Third Army. The order was greeted with disbelief, but its expected consequences were lightened when it was announced that we all were to join the Red Cross provisions scavenging melée in and around the town, since no other source of food were likely to be forthcoming over the immediate future.

Thus over the subsequent days, we became part of the rabble of treasure-hunting Plattling populace, scrounging or stealing any form of transportation for our collected booty that came to hand. The best that Gordon and I could find was an ancient wheelbarrow, but it had to suffice.

Fully loaded, our stomachs queasy with chocolate, we returned, for the last time, to base. Then we were off again on the road to nowhere.

The pronouncement by the camp commandant of our impending dose of aimless trekking between the ever-advancing fronts of the Soviet armies in the east and those of the Allies in the west, had been made too soon. A higher authority temporarily rescinded the order with a counter direction that, since the Americans had destroyed Plattling then we, their British Allies, should help clear up the mess. Thus the new trek

Above: Boeing B-17s of the US Eighth Army Air Force over Europe.

was postponed and the whole complement of several hundred British prisoners was herded into the ruined town and straight into a new nightmare.

Formed into demolition squads and rescue parties together with a force of tottering skeletons in threadbare striped suits – the inmates of a nearby concentration camp – we were put to work amongst the still-smouldering wreckage.

For five days we worked unceasingly, unearthing buried victims alive and dead from collapsed buildings, which included an air-raid bunker that had received a direct hit. I was given the grisly task, in company with a couple of partly alive Ukrainians, of removing the dead. Scores of men, women and children had been jammed together in the shelter when the blow had struck; the heat had seared the closely packed bodies, peeling off clothing and turning the exposed skin black. Where the bomb had penetrated the concrete chamber, nothing recognisable as human remained. We laid out the more complete corpses in rows before, thankfully, being directed to less sickening tasks.

Though a second raid on the town seemed unlikely, the sound of an aeroplane engine was enough to send much of the surviving population streaming into the open fields and even our guards sometimes melted away for a while, on the assumption that

The wreckage at Plattling railyards pictured a matter of days after the Allied air raid that nearly killed Christopher and Gordon.

discretion was wiser than valour. The SS guards on the destroyed Red Cross train stood their ground, however, so the pilfering of provisions from the railway sidings that had followed the raid now became a dangerous game.

With the water supply no longer operative, we were unable to wash meaning that the stench of death hung over many of us on our nightly return to the factory base.

The new trek, when our release from rescue duties was finally authorised, became virtually a pleasure; a far nicer option than had been our labours in the doomed town.

Our column resembled that of a herd of civilian refugees fleeing from an advancing foe which, I suppose, we were, but in far less a disciplined manner than had been the case earlier; each man now transporting his looted Red Cross parcels and other provisions in a variety of conveyances that we had been encouraged to acquire, since the provision of food on the journey was likely to be non-existent.

For Gordon and I, our 'borrowed' wheelbarrow showed its antiquity all too soon, its solitary wheel giving ominous warning of impending collapse. The first few miles proved its uselessness, the wheel emitting constant oil-demanding squeaks as we took it in turn to lift, heave and push its parcel-loaded bulk. For five, six, eight and more kilometres we struggled on, being overtaken all the while by colleagues with more efficient transportation devices, including even a sledge. Jettisoning some of the cargo offered one solution to continued progress, but gluttony can be powerfully persuasive when the memory of starvation is so recent. Gordon must have been thinking along the same line as I, for he took the words right out of my mouth when he exclaimed, 'let's get the hell out of this!' Thus our final escape attempt was born of both greed and futility. And in its execution, we were aided by the hand of providence.

Dodging the column was, we agreed, not going to be all that difficult. We'd just have to pick the right moment. Our guards were ranged alongside us on the offside with two or more at the rear of the column; none, so far as we could see, were on the near-side since there was little space available between our ranks and the curb. And it was the curb and any ditch and shrub cover which backed it that could provide the means of concealment resulting from a dash into it. We'd need not only this set of circumstances, but also that provided by a bend in the road, so that a minimum of guards would be in sight of our act of evasion.

The route we were taking was fortuitously rural; few signs of habitation were evident and the terrain well provided with bush cover. And suddenly as we emerged from a sharp bend in the road, there before us lay a deep culvert, half-hidden by a morass of bramble bushes. This set of circumstances was too good to miss.

'Quick. Now!' I hissed at Gordon and, following a swift glance behind us, we launched ourselves into the tangle of brambles and dived into the half-hidden ditch, and through the resisting undergrowth.

Scratched and bleeding from the barbed thorns, we lay in the muddy trench with pools of stagnant water soaking through our clothes. We waited, motionless, our faces buried in the mud, our hearts thudding with excitement. But no shouts or clicking of rifle bolts followed our getaway and the crunch of booted feet on the tarmac continued uninterrupted before finally fading away into the distance. Not even the rear-positioned guards had noticed our partly hidden prostrate forms.

Wiping the sticky mud from our faces and clothing, we emerged from hiding and took to the open fields and into a landscape of thick hedgerows that reminded me of the *Bocage* of Normandy.

The first night of a new precarious freedom we spent in thick bushes encircling an isolated pond. Sleep was hard to come by, the cold saw to that, and when finally we fell into troubled slumber, we were awoken soon after dawn by a horde of curious children out on a pre-breakfast fishing expedition. Attempting to bribe them to go away with offers of Red Cross chocolate was not a good idea; as they departed but soon returned with disbelieving mothers – stolid Herrenvolk who hadn't seen chocolate for years. Hastily we evacuated our refuge, which bordered a village we hadn't seen in the darkness.

Unlike the scenario for our earlier escape attempt in Czechoslovakia, we were now on territory with a potentially hostile population, though we presumed that much of it was heartily sick of the war and aware of its inevitable outcome. So we decided upon a strategy of open progress towards the American lines.

The village became our first test of this strategy as we walked straight through without anyone taking notice of two bedraggled mud-smeared 'peasants' pushing a barrow. And the place provided a bonus. On its further outskirts, we came across a smart streamlined perambulator standing unattended outside a house, the owner having, evidently, popped back into it for a moment, since the front door was ajar. Here was another of those God-given opportunities, this one an answer to our parcel transportation problems. In a flash, we unloaded the boxes from our ailing barrow and were about to transfer them to the pram, when we discovered it to be occupied by a sleeping infant. Hesitating for only an instant, we gently transferred the swaddled bundle onto the pavement and replaced it with our cargo. Then we were off at speed. My pang of guilt was momentary but I did wonder what the good hausfrau thought when she discovered her child on the pavement and found that her nice baby-carriage had become a broken wheelbarrow.

We left the road at the first opportunity on a track leading north. I was a little doubtful as to whether the fragile-looking acquisition would stand up to the unaccustomed weight and the rough terrain. The drone of aero engines had become incessant and we were now seeing low-flying aircraft, easily distinguishable as American.

Another miserable night of hiding; a misery at least lessened by ample fodder, and we continued along our north-westerly axis, convinced it would lead eventually to the American front line. It was a hunch confirmed in a surprising if heart-stopping manner when, atop one of many small tree-clothed hills that had become a feature of the idyllic Bavarian countryside, we walked straight into a fully-armed German soldier. Too late to take avoiding action, we could only hope to brazen things out if we were stopped. And we were stopped, but the chap was most obliging.

That we were British was all too obvious but he seemed not the slightest perturbed. He spoke good English and made the most of it with a monologue upon the injustices of the Hitler regime and the futility of war. We enquired politely of the whereabouts of the Americans and received a full situation report. It appeared that he and his unit had the task of delaying their advance; he himself being part of a spotter team for an artillery battery hidden in a nearby wood. Not that they intended much resistance, we were assured, for what was the use? The other side had so much more artillery, he went on, 'can't you hear it?' And then we realised the sullen roar that we had dismissed as the sound of aircraft was, in fact, that of the guns of the American Third Army. 'The area will be overrun in the next day or two,' he opined, 'so why not hide up and await your liberators?' Why not, indeed.

We thanked our benefactor and moved off determined to locate a suitable refuge that, hopefully, would not be shared by any fanatical last-ditch defenders. The countryside was bathed in sunshine; entirely tranquil but for the distant thunder of those guns. In the hedgerows, birds chirped, while spring buds were beginning to open.

Intent upon moving nearer the German front line – if indeed a front line as such existed – we pushed on utilising in turn side roads, tracks and grassy meadows. American fighter aircraft, flying low, gave us increasing confidence that our liberation was near and we waved ineffectively at their pilots. The appearance of German soldiers in full combat kit as well as military vehicles caused us some concern; not all enemy troops were likely to be so well disposed towards marauding Britishers behind their lines, as our friend on the hill.

However, that danger could also emanate from our own side was all too dramatically demonstrated by an incident that occurred on our third afternoon of semi-freedom.

Gordon was reloading the boxes into the pram after having negotiated a fence, when out of a clear blue-sky, death hurled down upon us in the form of a Thunderbolt fighter. We had noticed it circling the valley through which we were passing, but were too engrossed in what we were doing to recognise the change of engine note as it dived in our direction.

My yell to Gordon was purely incidental, he having already spread-eagled himself in a slight indent of ground, close up against the fence where I joined him. The swathe of half-inch cannon shells streaked towards us, kicking up the turf in a dead straight line before smashing into our abruptly abandoned pram. Venturing to turn my head from the dirt, I watched our erstwhile attacker bank steeply and disappear.

The pram was done for; its left-hand wheel demolished. With Gordon muttering angrily about non-military targets, we considered our next move. Our food supply was already depleted so it was no great physical feat to carry everything to a small wood some 200 yards away.

Thus fate had designated the choice of refuge in which, if all went well, we would await final liberation.

To attain our freedom courtesy of the American Third Army, we would have initially to pass through the German front line. Admittedly this was probably fast disintegrating, but fanatical elements still existed within the ranks of the *Wehrmacht*, which could make life difficult or even lethal for the likes of escaped prisoners caught on the run. Since our third escape bid, we had already come face to face with the enemy and been close – too close – to their military vehicles and hardware, though the nearest we had come to extinction had materialised from our own side when attacked by a Thunderbolt fighter. Thus we came to the conclusion that our best option was to sit tight in the leafy refuge of a Bavarian wood, and let the forces of liberation roll over us.

Upon arrival at our chosen refuge – a choice dictated by the loss of our bullet-ridden Red Cross parcel-carrying perambulator, entailing the lugging of our remaining provisions to the nearest wood – we straightway put down roots and awaited developments. The undergrowth beneath the tree canopy was thick enough to screen us from sight so we located a convenient spot near the edge of the wood giving a view of the terrain in at least one direction. With brushwood and foliage, we constructed a rough shelter and even found a small brook that would suffice as a water supply.

Our Robinson Crusoe existence – the wood became our island – was to last for several days. We had food – even if some of the items had to be consumed in an uncooked state – and, using empty tins as cooking pots, we sometimes felt bold enough to light a small fire on which to boil the near-stagnant water and make tea. It rained for a while as if to prove the shelter was not waterproof but by lying on the cardboard boxes

Above: People of all ages were on the move in Central Europe in the closing weeks of the war. These two young girls were pictured by the American film producer George Stevens' photographic unit.

of our dwindling provisions, we were spared the dampness of the ground. We ate frugally, not knowing how long the food would have to last.

In this manner we waited for things to happen. And we didn't have to wait long. The growl of gunfire drew closer. Aircraft roared overhead and on the third day came the indistinct rattle of machine-guns blending with the thud of tank and anti-tank fire. Excitement and apprehension gripped us. The waiting became intolerable.

Our first visitation was from a couple of displaced Poles. They almost walked into our shelter before seeing us, getting the shock of their lives as we cautiously emerged. A packet of Red Cross Lucky Strikes calmed them and, in return, they recommended a nearby herd of cows as a source of fresh milk. Next morning, Gordon tried his hand at milking using a milk powder tin as a bucket, but did no more than annoy the four-legged bovine.

Things really began to liven up on the fourth day, as we perceived convoys of German lorries pouring eastwards along a distant road. Nearer, groups of infantry could be seen crossing the open country. And as if to help them on their way, salvoes of shells burst in their wake.

A loud double crash echoed by the whine of shell-splinters, sent us grovelling on the ground. Two shells had actually fallen on the furthest edge of our wood; matters were becoming distinctly serious. In the lull that followed, we moved forward to learn the reason for this unsociable attention and received a nasty surprise when we observed German infantry retreating in droves; grey-clad figures moving across the open ground, some very close. Even as

> **We dashed off with hearts pumping with effort and anticipation. And atop the rise we beheld the wonderful sight of six Sherman tanks stationary on the flank of the subsequent slope. On their sides was emblazoned the white star of the Allied Expeditionary Force.**

we watched, three mud-splashed troopers entered the forward end of the wood bearing between them a heavy spandau, mounted on a tripod. In considerable alarm, we saw them place the gun in position, its barrel nosing out from behind a tree trunk. Vivid memories of last stands by SS suicide squads in Normandy and the holocaust of fire they drew filled my mind. The additional danger of being discovered by them was not lost upon us either and who would blame them for our speedy despatch in the circumstances.

But there appeared to be something wrong with the gun. One of the men hurriedly began stripping the breech mechanism, loudly cursing the world in general. Shattering explosions in rapid succession chased each other across our immediate front, the last burst again too close to our sanctuary for comfort – and even closer to the do-or-die trio.

All this must have been too much for the spandau crew. Probably concluding that there was more to life than dying for a lost cause, they picked up their immobilised weapon, together with its ammunition clips and retired in some disorder along the border of the wood opposite ours.

Late in the afternoon, a deathly hush fell. The view from our shelter showed no movement. A hundred yards away, our herd of cows was being expertly milked by a solitary individual who plainly was not going to let a little thing like a world war interfere with his routine. We walked over and received a glass of milk for our pains. Then the elderly cowherd, recognising our nationality, raised his arm westwards and let go a stream of words in a Bavarian dialect, giving us to understand that American tanks had halted, hidden from sight behind the brow of a low hill, directly before us.

Unwilling to disbelieve this revelation, we dashed off with hearts pumping with the effort and anticipation. And atop the rise we beheld the wonderful sight of six Sherman tanks stationary on the flank of the subsequent slope. On their sides was emblazoned the white star of the Allied Expeditionary Force.

But our joy was short-lived as a burst of machine-fire had us grovelling in the dirt once again. In the pause that followed this tawdry welcome from our potential liberators, we shouted our credentials across the lethal void of a momentary no-man's-land once again, but it seemed the GIs had heard similar stories before to their cost. Eventually a ludicrous yelled exchange resulted as we were questioned on the subject of, first, baseball and then football teams currently in vogue. And it was our very lack of knowledge on the subject that broke the stalemate, our ignorance led the Americans to conclude that, so ignorant were we, that we must be 'limeys'.

With our hands high in the air we were permitted to walk slowly forwards into a multitude of levelled hardware. We were prisoners no more.

At a military headquarters, we poured out every scrap of information we could about enemy movements in the locality, though I suppose this did little to help ease the onward advance of the unit. We even managed to persuade the commander to allow us to join his outfit until the end of hostilities, instead of being sent to rear echelons to await repatriation. So, soldiers once more but wearing another nation's uniform, we became auxiliary gunners of a half-track vehicle belonging to a mechanised infantry

General Patton's Third Army's advance into western Czechoslovakia in late April 1945 was halted on General Eisenhower's orders. Territory east of Pilsen was to be occupied by the Red Army. Patton is pictured to the left.

division of the United States Third Army, under the celebrated General Patton.

Living conditions might have been primitive by American army standards but it was fine by us and the food, if only the despised K rations, was supreme luxury. A medical officer checked our physical condition and though my weight was little more than six stone, he reluctantly allowed us to remain with the unit.

Those last days of warfare were very different from the savage fighting I remembered in Normandy. Rolling ponderously forward with much noise and clatter under an umbrella of supporting aircraft we advanced in the general direction of the Czech border. Except for periodic halts while aircraft and artillery dealt with pockets of fanatical enemy rearguards, there were no pitched battles or heroics on the part of the Americans; the heroics were exclusively reserved for the enemy. And with each strongpoint eliminated by a storm of shells and rockets, the unit ground relentlessly on over the cratered ground, ruined farmsteads and the broken bodies of dead defenders. I felt no compassion for the 16-year-old boys of the Hitler Youth suicide groups, since Nazism had turned these children into no more than killing machines, but these defenders of the older generation, the elderly warriors of the Volksturm (Home Guard reservists) were a different matter. Though many despised their Nazi overlords, they fought and died for their country with extreme courage.

Now and again our Shermans would run up against a determined pocket of anti-tank gunners and, for an hour or so, a duel would ensue, the handsome landscape echoing to the rapid thumps of the German 88-millimetres and the crack of the American 75s. My particular detachment was seldom involved in these exchanges, my colleagues determined not to become casualties at the tail-end of the war. I don't think I ever fired a shot with the Browning .50 calibre machine-gun in my charge. There was literally nothing worth shooting at – and anyway if I did fire at anything, I'd have to clean the bloody thing.

And then came the cease-fire when we were within 10

kilometres of the Czech border. The unit was disengaged and ordered back for a rest and refit. In a way I was sorry; a fanciful vision persisted of liberating the Czech girl who had captured my heart when Gordon and I were in hiding in her country. I suppose I saw myself, pistol in hand, festooned with grenades, returning to free the captive princess, the lady of my secret dreams. Yet the dream was real.

Instead I accompanied my colleagues to a base near the Danube town of Straubing, where Gordon and I left them with many expressions of goodwill. They had been a cheerful and generous bunch of men.

To make our way to the city of Regensburg, the airfield of which we had heard was to be used to embark ex-prisoners of war for the flight home, we utilised a variety of transport including a lift in a military police jeep and an abandoned lorry we coaxed into life, picking up a group of Hungarian refugees en route, before coming to grief in a bomb crater. And in the battered city, we played the victor, commandeering a house in the

> " The middle of May saw us installed in a Lancaster bomber, stripped of its offensive equipment. From the disarmed mid-gun turret, I looked down upon my own country through a sheen of tears. "

town as a comfortable base, while awaiting our turn to board a home-going aircraft.

The middle of May saw us installed in a Lancaster bomber, stripped of its offensive equipment and from the disarmed mid-gun turret, I looked upon my own country through a sheen of tears.

We landed at a Buckinghamshire airfield from where, after processing by intelligence and military authorities, I set out on the final leg of the journey. And because of strict petrol rationing in Britain at the time, I had to walk the last four miles to my home.

PORTWAY POST-WAR

With the war over, Christopher continued in military service until his de-mob in 1947. Unexcited by the attractions of 'Civvy Street', he determined to return to Czechoslovakia and meet again with Anna, the girl who had stolen his heart when providing him with food and shelter whilst he was on the run. By now though the infamous 'Iron Curtain' had been drawn across Europe and getting in and out of countries ruled by hardline communist regimes was no easy matter.

With the hostilities in Europe at an end, and with much of Europe a shattered shell, my undistinguished military career resumed, but on slightly more orthodox lines. Prior to returning to it, however, I was rewarded by a spell at home recovering from the ravages to my body resulting from a year's German 'hospitality' and my not-too-successful attempts to evade it.

Back in uniform, I underwent a three-week rehabilitation course on which ex-prisoners of war were sent to supposedly become human beings once more, a task I enjoyed immensely since the establishment near High Wycombe held the aura of a holiday camp wherein one was asked - not ordered - to 'do things please' and officers didn't mind if you failed to salute them. Then came a spell at Chichester Barracks where, temporarily attached to the Royal Sussex Regiment, the holiday camp atmosphere abruptly and painfully evaporated. There followed an extended period stationed at the long-defunct Nelson Barracks at Norwich where, beyond attempting to persuade reticent, but pretty NAAFI girls to go out with me, I was given the monotonous job of looking after the weapons store.

Thereafter I was moved to Germany where my military career continued amidst the ruins of a country destroyed by war. In the British Army of the Rhine I found myself, at one time, guarding German prisoners-of-war; a task that should have given me exquisite satisfaction but didn't. The wheel of fortune may have turned full circle, but the constant sight of hungry children and begging women offered me no joy while the misery observed in my captives' eyes was but a reflection of what, earlier, had been my own.

For six months through 1946 into 1947 I lived mostly in the bare rooms of vacated flats among the ruins of Osnabruck, Hanover, Berlin and later, Munster Lager, this last a POW camp. Life was surreal with almost anything one wanted - from female companionship to expensive *objets d'art* - available for a handful of cigarettes or a bar of chocolate or soap; items worth their weight in gold to the German civilian. Military discipline was strict and the tedium of life pronounced. At first, fraternisation with German frauleins was forbidden, a stricture that simply drove such liaisons underground so that, eventually, the order was quietly rescinded.

One of our tasks, I remember, was the erasure of Belsen Concentration Camp undertaken with the aid of flame-throwers, a job - though highly unpleasant - that did give me quiet satisfaction as the stinking accommodation huts and the paraphernalia of death went up in flames. I wished it could have been Auschwitz of which the memory of my short sojourn there in 1944 would never leave me.

My final months before demobilisation were the most boring of all. As commander of a small force of German civilian staff at Munster Lager who waited on me hand and foot I had absolutely nothing to do. Which at least was a slightly better bet than everlasting blancoing and polishing of my military equipment for constant inane inspections prior to guard duties.

Thereafter, as a newly-fledged civilian, I was no more successful as a businessman than I had been as a soldier, but life at Great Maplestead, the picturesque village that was my family seat, had its compensations. The ordered, respectable existence washed away the recollection of war, but a growing tedium infiltrated the vacuum.

All too soon my thoughts had returned and focused upon the nameless girl in Czechoslovakia who had captured my heart when, as an escaped prisoner myself, she had brought me food, hope and, I liked to think, an embryo affection. The vision of the slight, but resolute figure refused to abate; indeed, it blossomed in stature as my imagination augmented the gaps in my knowledge. Time and time again I cursed myself for being a sentimental fool; allowing a dream to occupy a mind that had more prosaic matters to dwell upon. Yet the vision persisted. I decided there was nothing for it but to go back to Czechoslovakia and seek out the girl I could not forget.

My reconnaissance took the form of a train ride on a truncated portion of the Orient Express between the Bavarian city of Nuremberg in West Germany and the Czech border town of Cheb some 15 kilometres inside Czech territory. I held no Czech entry visa so did not expect to get any further into the country.

Managing to by-pass the well-meant restrictions imposed on visaless passengers at the German border village and even the search by Czech border guards for imaginary capitalist 'spies' at the physical border of their country, I arrived at Cheb only to be removed from the train and held under guard for 12 hours until I could be put aboard the subsequent westbound express. It was not a wasted exercise. I even learnt more details of the border installations from the guards themselves. And back on West German territory I simply turned straight round to approach on foot the brilliantly illuminated triple fence through which the train had passed. My proposed unauthorised entry into communist Czechoslovakia would have to be carried out the hard way.

Dodging the West German frontier installations had been no problem and, passing onto Czech soil, I reached the formidable barrier as night fell. The pinewoods made good cover and with dusk turning to darkness I lay observing the obstacles that barred my way forward. The triple fences, two of them electrified and carrying white insulators like obscene growths, the ploughed strip for registering forbidden footsteps, and the mined zone of death ran like a poisonous snake through wood, village and meadow. Before me lay a desolation of jagged stumps, all that remained after the trees had been dynamited to give a field of fire. At intervals, but unseen, watchtowers rose to brood over the satanic device. And all this now lit by the bluish glare of arc lamps atop the fence supports.

Delaying only to allow a Czech patrol to pass by, I gingerly moved forward, into the glare to reach the base of the first fence. Then, spread-eagled on my back, I removed the wire-cutters I carried with me from my small rucksack and, firmly gripping their insulated handles, attacked the cables. Fortunately none carried a current. As I struggled with the clumsy tool, the dew-laden grass soaked through my clothes to mingle with the sweat of terror. Five severed strands made adequate clearance beneath which to squirm and, turning on my stomach, I crawled to the base of the second fence, and repeated the exercise.

Clear of the second fence I turned about once more and wriggled across the furrow of the ploughed strip. Next came the deadly swathe of ground alleged to contain World War Two German Teller mines. Taking a deep breath, I inched forward again and, like a swimmer on dry land, swept the brass with outstretched hands feeling for protruding detonators. Slowly, slowly I gained the third fence, here to breach it with an ease bred from familiarity, each snip of my cutters a drumbeat of triumph. Rising to my feet on the further side I sped away from the lights and into the protection of the dark woods beyond.

I could barely believe what I had accomplished though my triumph was tempered with caution; I was still deep within a forbidden border zone and patrols could be numerous as they maintained a lookout for westbound escapees. Moving eastwards, hopefully I'd be catching them on the hop. Navigating by compass I struggled on in the knowledge that it was imperative I

The prison at Cheb where Christopher was held for entering Czechoslovakia without a visa. He took this photograph on a later visit as an authorised visitor.

> **They threw the book at me, of course. Passed from one military and security authority to another, each rising in seniority, I ended up in a grim political prison. My alleged crimes included espionage, smuggling and insulting the People's Army, all of which amounted to a total sentence of 104 years of hard labour.**

was clear of the border zone by daybreak. It was two hours later that I came to a road bridge. It traversed a shallow river that I could have easily waded. But fatigue together with the late autumn cold had dulled my senses arid the dry route forward was just too tempting. It was my undoing. On the further bank a soldier stepped from behind the parapet. His barked order *'Sufi'* (Halt!) struck me like a whiplash. I took a step towards him but four colleagues abruptly appeared from the shadows, their machine-pistols aligned on my navel. Hastily discarding the notion of heroics I came to heel and raised my hands. My lone excursion was over.

They threw the book at me, of course. Passed from one military and security authority to another, each rising in seniority, I ended up in a grim political prison. Taken before a People's Court my alleged crimes were pronounced as espionage, smuggling, an illegal border-crossing and, because I had, in my frustration, swore at the sergeant of the group that had first apprehended me on that accursed bridge, an additional five years for insulting the People's Army, all of which amounted to a total sentence of 104 years of hard labour.

In all I was incarcerated for some four months before the British Government affected my release. There were fluctuating numbers in my fourth floor cell and I shall always remember the kind-hearted Bohuslav, a schoolmaster in for 25 years. Like everyone - and no doubt it would have included me - he was eventually sent to the uranium mines at Jachymov where, like others, he died of uranium poisoning. I seldom left the cell, equipped with no more than a bucket and two treble-tier beds, except for interrogation in another building. This I looked upon as a treat since it involved a short walk in the open air. And on one occasion while the interrogating officer was yelling at me I nicked his pencil, a priceless possession in a cell with nothing to do except listen to a distant church clock striking the endless empty hours.

Upon my release I was escorted to an unauthorised border crossing point where, watched by my two accompanying guards (I like to think with envy), I walked alone into West Germany - and freedom. Well, not quite, since a squad of Bavarian frontier police promptly arrested me for illegal border crossing! You just can't win.

Released two days later I made my way home to recommence my lone war against the European communist hierarchy waged for the sole right of meeting my girl, a task made the more difficult by the fact that I was now pronounced *persona non grata* by the whole of communist East Europe.

On the third of two further visa-less 'reconnaissance' train rides onto Czech territory, during which I was permitted to meet Anna on platform 4 for seven and nine minutes respectively before the chucking-out procedure, I slipped a ring on the girl's finger when our military escort wasn't looking and we became engaged to be married. But it was another three years and a series of incidents, adventures and disasters, including me being expelled from a number of East European countries before we could finally become man and wife.

But that is another story.

*One of Christopher Portway's books, Pedal For Your Life (Lutterworth Press) recounts the full story interwoven within the narrative of a bicycle journey he undertook across eastern Europe to mark his 70th birthday.

DEEP
TROUBLE

JANUARY 1945

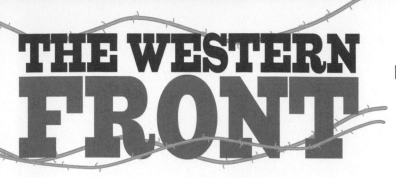

THE WESTERN FRONT

'..the Germans now found they had neglected, at their peril, to reinforce the Eastern Front as Stalin's massive armies gathered ominously on the borders of the Reich.'

On New Year's Day 1945, hundreds of Luftwaffe aircraft attacked Allied airfields in France, Holland and Belgium. The Germans claimed to have destroyed 400 aircraft on the ground and another 179 in the air. In turn, the Allies claimed to have downed 364 Nazi warplanes out of a force of 500. British newspapers later reported that the Germans had the advantage of fog clearing from their bases first and described fighters roaring in low with guns blazing at rows of parked planes.

It was clear the Germans were by no means a spent force. However, in these opening days of the year it became increasingly apparent that Hitler's dramatic gamble – the December offensive in the Ardennes - had failed completely in its aim of crossing the River Meuse to drive an armoured wedge between the US and British and Canadian armies.

German losses were estimated at 100,000 men out of a nearly half a million committed to the fight. Some 800 of the precious new panzers plus hundreds of aircraft were also lost. In bearing the brunt of the battle, the Americans sustained 81,000 casualties, including 15,000 captured and 19,000 killed. The British lost 1400. The Allies could replace the men lost and they also had an endless supply of new armour unlike the Germans who now found that they had neglected, at their peril, to reinforce the Eastern Front as Stalin's massive armies gathered ominously on the borders of the Reich.

Having halted the offensive, now was the time for the Allies to attack. But winter still had a firm grip, preventing mobile warfare. The Germans too displayed their skill in mounting stubborn defences of key towns and villages. The US retook St Vith on 23 January, a month after it was first lost. In the meantime, a considerable number of German fighting men with many of their weapons managed to withdraw back into Germany where the Allies would be forced to fight them all over again at the River Rhine.

On the River Roer front in Holland, British and Canadian forces spent January relatively inactive. They were gathering strength for a new offensive which Field-Marshal Montgomery planned for early February.

Above: This contemporary map shows the Allied advances from west and east achieved from D-Day 6 June 1944 up until 25 January 1945. The Channel Islands and several ports on the Atlantic coast of France remain firmly under German control despite their isolation from the Western Front.

Dutch Winter

I spent the last winter of the war in Holland as a Despatch Rider/Signaller in the 7th Battalion Seaforth Highlanders.

In September my unit's role was to drive the enemy out of the town of Best and open the road for the troops to reach Arnhem and relieve the British 1st Airbourne Division as part of *Operation Market Garden*. Best had, however, been fortified by the enemy with use of the railway embankment that had originally been built to enable trains to cross the Wilhemina Canal. The enemy had dug firing positions between the rails and parked wagons that they had filled with rubble over them. Neither small arms nor artillery fire had any effect on these and every movement we made could be seen from their observation post in the town's church spire.

We were suffering heavy casualties and the stalemate was only broken by the arrival of two RAF Typhoons that demolished the wagons and the church tower.

We then went on to free other towns and villages including Tilburg, a place I have returned to at the invitation of the townsfolk for anniversary celebrations in 1994, 1999 and 2004. We veterans have been shown every kindness, warmth and generosity possible during such festivities and I have made many Dutch friends, with whom I have kept in touch.

Following the liberation of Tilburg, we were sent across the Netherlands towards the River Maas to hold back a German attack on our American allies. Unfortunately, when I was riding my motorcycle behind my Commanding Officer's scout car, a shell landed in front of it and forced the driver to pull up. I also pulled up, but a three-ton truck behind me did not. The truck sandwiched my bike and me between the two vehicles, writing off my machine and trapping my right foot and ankle under a wheel of the truck. A passing Dutch civilian doctor cut my motorcycle boot off and gave me an injection of morphine.

I spent a few weeks in hospital (the first time I had slept in a bed for months) and in convalescence before returning to my unit, now lining the banks of the Maas, to spend the rest of the winter in slit trenches in heavy snow during the coldest spell for many years. We had just one blanket each and slept in all our clothes for weeks over the Christmas period and never took them off. When we got ourselves breakfast, we could not walk properly because our boots would not bend.

In the extreme cold our guns would not fire because the mineral oil froze - how we overcame that problem I am not saying, except that it was not by pouring our morning cup of tea over the mechanism - we would not have given that up for a king's ransom. We were eventually issued with vegetable oil instead.

By some miracle I survived to the end, although later in Germany I received a leg wound. I consider that I have had a bonus of 60 years on my life.

Charles Dunesby, Bournemouth, Hants

A GERMAN CHRISTMAS & NEW YEAR

Anita Birch today lives in Portsmouth, Hampshire. Here she recalls her childhood in wartime on the Baltic coast of Germany and remembers the kindness of the British POWs who shared their Red Cross parcels with her family.

Above: Anita pictured in the summer of 1944 in the North of Germany with her two brothers.

In 1944 I was a four-year-old German girl, living with my parents, auntie and two small brothers in the town of Elbing, in what was then West Prussia, way up on the Baltic Coast. Today it is part of Poland. That year for us children seemed free from danger; the sound of gunfire and the bombing was a million miles away in the western part of Germany, although like all wartime families we felt the effects of food rationing and the wartime restrictions etc.

During the summer of 1944 a small group of British POWs on a work party were billeted in our back yard, working for our landlord. The POWs had their own wooden hut, but my mother allowed the men to use the facilities of her kitchen to brew their tea and coffee or to make drinking chocolate. In return, quite often some cocoa powder would mysteriously appear on top of the kitchen cupboard, a treat we children had never known.

Red Cross parcels

As the summer wore on the relationship between the family and the POWs was maintained in a polite and friendly way. As small children, we were the bond between all. I am sure that many of the men had families and children of their own back home and they must have missed them terribly. As in all such cases language was a problem, as neither side could understand much of what was said, but a smile and a

thank you was adequate.

As Christmas 1944 approached the POWs put up a Christmas tree and decorated it with sweets and chocolates received in their Red Cross parcels. On Christmas Day we small children were invited into the hut. To our delight we were taken to the Christmas tree and allowed to pick off some of the sweets and chocolates. We put these into a colourful brocade pouch, which must have been sent to one of the POWs in a parcel from Britain. I kept that pouch well into my teenage years. In mid-January 1945, however, everything changed. The Russians were advancing swiftly from the east and our POWs were returned to their camp in Elbing. History tells us that they were joined by thousands of other POWs and forced to march to the western part of Germany. For my family, as well as other Elbing families, we were given one hour to evacuate the city. We left our home with what we could carry and made our way westwards, joining countless other people on the same trek – a journey made in deep snow which was to last for six days.

Wounded soldiers

Cold and hungry we eventually arrived at a railway station that was still operational. Many people were hoping to catch a train west. Fortunately my father knew the train driver and managed to get us on the last train. We were all huddled together at the

end of the carriage near the door. This was the only space available as it was a hospital train packed with wounded soldiers from the Russian front. Whilst the nurses tended the injured troops my mother assisted by holding candles (these were among the few items we brought with us), giving the only light available. They did not allow children to come into the compartment, but through the open door we often caught a glimpse of the soldiers. Although at the tender age of four I never knew the significance of my adventure, the sight of those wounded soldiers heavily bandaged and in pain still remain, as do the images of nurses brushing their teeth with snow.

The journey was long and arduous. Every so often the train would have to stop to avoid the bombing and on these occasions every opportunity was taken by all the able-bodied men (including my father) to search for food. After many days on the train we eventually arrived at the hospital town of Hamelin, in what was to be known as West Germany.

I spent my childhood and my teenage years in that area. Then in 1962 I married an Englishman, John, - and moved to England where I have lived ever since.

GREEK TRAGEDY

As the Germans retreat Civil War threatens to engulf Athens.

On 4 October 1944, a British airborne force helped liberate Patras in the Greek Peloponneses. A few days later, more air landings took place on and around the aerodromes at Elevsis and Megara. Then on 14 October, a mixed Greek and British naval squadron dropped anchor in Piraeus, the harbour of Athens, to disembark the British III Corps under the command of Lt-Gen Ronald Scobie. *Operation Manna* was under way.

The undertaking had two aims. Firstly, to be sure that once the Germans were chased out, Greece's borders with Albania, Yugoslavia and Bulgaria, especially, would be respected. Churchill feared that the Communist regimes now rising to power in these countries must inevitably have designs on northern Greek provinces such as Eastern Macedonia.

Secondly, General Scobie was ordered to prevent, by force if necessary, the Greek Peoples' Liberation Army (ELAS) from usurping the established political system by unconstitutional means. George Papandreou headed up the *de facto* Greek Government at this point. He struck a liberal and democratic posture and his

British troops in Athens admire the Parthenon.

appointment earlier in the year seemed enough to bring together opposing factions in the Greek political spectrum. At one time, a mutiny by pro-Communist Greek sailors on a warship in Alexandria had led to bloodshed.

But now the danger of subversion was growing daily. In answer to a call by the EAM (a left-wing Liberation Committee), units of ELAS converged on Athens, en route passing large numbers of retreating *Wehrmacht* soldiers without seeking battle.

Churchill under fire

A call by Papandreou for the demobilisation of all guerilla groups of both the Left and the Right on 1 December was refuted by the EAM. Within days fighting flared on the streets of Athens between police and rebel ELAS supporters. On 5 December, Churchill ordered Scobie to restore order. At the same time as the general declared a state of martial law, ELAS fighters moved in to seize key points in the Greek capital. The British seemed inextricably caught up in someone else's civil war.

Early successes for ELAS included the capture of the rear RAF headquarters at Kifissia where around 500 British military personnel were trapped in a wrecked hotel and taken captive.

However, it was not long before the trained and disciplined British army gained the upper hand, even though the ELAS threat could not be entirely extinguished. Over the Christmas period, Churchill himself went to Athens, basing himself aboard the cruiser *HMS Ajax* in Piraeus and meeting representatives from all sides of the conflict to a background of intermittent gunfire in the city. Shells were even lobbed at his ship, which responded in kind on the Prime Minister's orders.

Within a week of Churchill's departure, full-scale talks began to find a peaceful solution. A new Greek premier, General Plastiras, assured both sides of a role in the political future of the country and urged a return to duty for 'all who have been misled and turned their arms against their country'.

On 12 February 1945, Harold McMillan, British Minister Resident in the Mediterranean, could report to London that the Civil War in Greece was, for the time being, over.

J S Herbert of Cumbria writes:
I was a member of 107 Staging Post Transport Command stationed at RAF HQ in Kiffisia. On 18 December 1944, ELAS rebels attacked the hotel we were billeted in. Myself and around 500 other servicemen were taken prisoner and made to march over 200 miles into the Greek mountains where we were held until our release was arranged on 23 January 1945. One prisoner had a camera with which he secretly took pictures of us on the march. I have a cutting from the Daily Express which later published them.

J C Simpson of Fareham, Hants contributed the following:
My father (Wing Commander J Simpson) was in charge of the defence of the RAF HQ at Kiffisia in December 1944, an event described in Kingsley Oliver's book *Through Adversity*. The defenders had expended their ammunition when ELAS blew in the side of Air HQ hotel. The relief column did not arrive in time and the captured defenders subsequently experienced hardship, abuse and ill-treatment until the insurgents melted away.

The lesson was that the Army never had enough resources to defend the RAF on the ground, a situation that still persists to this day.

Tom Dean of Wickford, Essex, served in the 46th RTR (Royal Tank Regiment) which was sent to Greece to combat the EAM and ELAS communist rebels. He wrote this account a decade ago:
We learnt the hard way soon after our arrival in the Greek capital that tanks were not the right answer for house to house fighting. Consequently we tankmen were often used as infantry. It was a messy business, made more so because we didn't know who we could trust in this virtual civil war.

A group of us were guarding the wireless station in the hills at Pellini, some miles outside Athens. After the street fighting it seemed a cushy billet. Supplies came in via RAF parachute drops and one canister was found to contain a bazooka and ammunition.

A loyalist Greek told us that three members of our Regiment together with two infantrymen were being held captive by ELAS in a nearby village. Our officer decide on a night raid and so, at 1am, he plus one sergeant, one corporal (myself) and four troopers set off with our friendly guide.

Luck was with us and we were almost out of the village with our freed prisoners before the alarm was raised and indiscriminate firing began. At this point we split into pairs and legged it smartly back to the station.

Within a few days we learned that ELAS were planning a retaliatory raid. Sure enough, a couple nights later they opened up with machine-gun fire from three sides. Next we heard the roar of an armoured car coming up the road towards the main gate. It turned out that ELAS had acquired the vehicle in an earlier raid on an RAF aerodrome.

Fortunately for us, we had two infantrymen, armed with the bazooka, in a slit trench near the gate. They loosed off a missile and scored a

This poster from early in the war points out that there are Free Greeks fighting on against the Nazis.

direct hit on the armoured car which promptly blew up in a tremendous explosion. The enemy immediately withdrew and didn't come back. It seems that the rebels had stored a box of dynamite in the vehicle and had planned to wreck the wireless station.

As a consequence of the raid on the village, our officer was awarded the Military Cross and the sergeant got the Military Medal. What the outcome would have been for us if we hadn't had the bazooka and the two infantry lads who knew how to use it, I wouldn't like to speculate!

A leaflet from the communist rebels aimed at demoralising the British forces trying to keep the peace in Greece.

HAPPY NEW YEAR TO YOU ENGLISH FRIENDS

English Officers and Soldiers.

The New Year finds you, our ancient friends, fighting against the Greek people who have been your faithful allies in 1940, when everybody else had left you and you were alone.

The New Year finds you in war against the Greek people who have been fighting four year fascism by your side.

And the Greek people ask you now: Which is the difference between you and Germans? And where is the liberty and the democracy you promised us, when you came, as liberators in our country?

Although your gifts for the New Year to the Greek people are bombs, and musket balls, the Greek people find time in their destruction and misery, to think about you and they wish you happy New Year. Our women and children who have been murdered by your aircrafts and machine-guns whish you to, from their graves: Happy New Year.

We know that you don't agree to the jobs of general Scobie as well as all the English people disagree.

And in the New Year, we invite you to stop fighting your friends Greek people, for the civilization' sake.

Athens January 1st 1945

EAM

No. 74.
...HLEY CITIZENS'
...ICE BUREAU,
...RAND ARCADE,
...DON N.12.
...ORGANISATION OF THE BRITISH RED CROSS
AND ORDER OF ST. JOHN

ternational
Rouge

Expéditeur SENDER Absender

Foreign Relations
Department.

PAINE
MINNIE

MESSAGE Mitteilung
...ds) (25 mots au maximum) (Nicht über 25 Worte)

did not pass your Exam.
next time. So
...ran you are all well
...m.
Fondest love
...Auntie
...tum 7.3.44

Nom ...tataire ADDRESSEE Empfänger
Christian name
Vorname Prénom
Address
Adresse

BULLOCK
PATRICA
12, LANDSCAPE GROVE, 12
MONT COCHON
JERSEY
C.I.

PASSED
P.72

4184

Reply overleaf (not more than 25 words)
Réponse au verso (25 mots au maximum)
Antwort umseitig (nicht über 25 Worte)

5 AVR. 1944

No Ordinary Childhood

Mrs Patricia Foster remembers the German Occupation of Jersey.

How very strange it was to go to school in the dark to be fitted with a gas mask. Yet this is my earliest memory of how the war affected my early life on the Channel Island of Jersey. Shortly afterwards my English-born parents faced a very hard decision indeed; whether to leave their home with three young children and return to London or Bristol as evacuees, or to stay.

Father decided to join the queue for registering at the Town Hall for places on the steamers sent by the British Government, while my mother prayed for guidance and talked to neighbours, most of whom had decided to stay and face whatever the future held. Father returned home with no tickets and no desire to travel to England in an old coal boat.

Life almost returned to normal, which included visiting my grandparents. They had recently had to abandon their home in Alderney, when the authorities ordered a total evacuation of that island. Next they'd travelled to London, but then learned from another relative that we had decided to stay in Jersey. So they made a quick decision to return. As it transpired, they travelled on the very last mailboat that was to sail for Jersey for almost five years. Fortunately, a family who had lived in one of their properties in Jersey had left it empty, so they moved in.

28 June 1940 was uneventful until 6.45pm, when we were having tea with my grandparents. Suddenly all hell let loose as planes swept overhead with machine guns blazing; the thud of bombs exploding in the harbour was frightening. Grandfather ushered us into a coalhole, thinking it was the safest place if we were hit. Always a bit of a 'character', he kept running down the garden path to look up at the sky, with my mother shouting at him to come back!

White flags flown

Early in the morning of 1 July 1940, more German planes flew overhead, dropping messages for the authorities. White flags had to be flown on all buildings as a sign of surrender. Mother duly found a pillowcase, which she attached to a rose arch. A lone German pilot landed to investigate and found that the Islanders were complying with the terms of surrender. More planes arrived, including Junker 52 transport aircraft filled with soldiers, who were then billeted in hotels and houses commandeered by German officials. All forms of transport had to keep to the right of the road – just one of many imposed regulations. Clocks were put forward two hours, so my school day did not start until 10am GMT. Sterling soon disappeared and was replaced by Reichsmarks. Each Mark was worth two shillings and one penny (just over 10p). This currency was only useful while there were things to be bought in the shops, together with rationed food and fuel brought in from France.

Father's business of buying and selling commodities required by the island's 40 bakers soon came to an end. Yeast was scarce, so he resorted to collecting spent yeast, still containing the wort liquor, from a brewery. It left a none too pleasant smell in the car. Even this soon came to an end and we became accustomed to seeing him at work all day in the garden, growing vegetables and soft fruits. The house next door was empty, so he added a second garden to ours and used the back yard and outhouse to keep rabbits. These were mainly the colour of wild rabbits, but one was white and became more of a pet, called Lucy. When mother was ill and needed extra nourishment, sadly Lucy had to provide it. No mention of this was made at the table, but by then we were old enough to put two and two together!

As a family living on the edge of St Helier, we had little to barter for food, so father took to mending watches and clocks for whatever their owners could give in exchange. As foods became scarcer, substitutes took their place. Carrots and sugar beet were grated and roasted for tea, and parsnips and acorns were used for coffee. Potatoes were grated, and washed many times, then dried to give flour that could be used for thickening. The outhouse copper (when not being used for heating water) was employed to make sugar beet syrup – the only form of sweetening we had once rations of sugar or saccharin were used up. Necessity being the mother of invention, father discovered that boiling some rancid margarine (kept too long for the rainy day!) with soda and ivy leaves became a product which, when cold, could be cut into blocks and used as a passable washing soap.

Dreaded knock at the door

15 September 1942 was for me a birthday never to be forgotten. The newspaper carried a German order that stated (sic): 'All those men not born in the Channel Islands between 16 and 70 years of age who belong to the English people, and their families, will be evacuated and transferred to Germany.' Local officials protested to no avail, as this was a direct order from Hitler's HQ. Apparently the order was a reprisal for the imprisonment of German civilians in Persia (Iran). Down came the suitcases once again from the loft, to be packed in readiness for the dreaded knock at the door. Fortunately, for reasons unexplained, the deportations stopped before the Island was cleared of all the English. Father had been appointed a Food Controller by the authorities, so he was considered an essential worker, and was one of the last on their list. How my grandparents escaped I shall never know, as they were still within the eligible age range.

Life at junior school continued much the same as before, but with increasing privations, one of which was a lack of fuel for heating in the winter months. Wood was burnt in fireplaces, but only those sitting in the front could feel the warmth. Those sitting at the back used fingerless mittens, which became very fashionable. We also used stones warmed in the ash from the fire to give some comfort to hands swollen with chilblains. Footwear for children was a constant problem. Friends who kept a general store and bakery provided me with some Victorian-style boots that came halfway up the leg. It was good to have some new footwear, but oh those long laces to tie when running late for school in the morning! When they became too small, we had to make do with locally-made clog boots. These had coarse leather tops and wooden soles to which father attached strips of old car tyre to stop them wearing out too quickly.

After school activities were not all play – hopscotch, skipping and cycling – but included collecting dead wood and twigs from nearby fields for the fire. After the meagre meat rations stopped, the rabbits had to be well fed, so collecting suitable greenery became a regular occupation. At harvest time, the whole family went gleaning. A friendly farmer allowed us to gather ears of wheat from the edge of the field. Father winnowed it in a breezy private road and took it to a mill to be ground into flour for making birthday cakes.

My first experience of death was sadly the funeral of a fellow pupil, a quiet boy about three years older than me. He had picked up a hand grenade, which had exploded. On another occasion I and another pupil were asked to remove dead flowers from the graves of RAF airmen whose bodies had been washed up on the shore, and had been buried in a cemetery near the school.

Forced to learn German

When petrol was still available for the Germans, two soldiers appeared at our door, and demanded to see our car, saying it was required for essential services. However, as we could not use it, father had removed the seats and wheels, and hidden them in the empty house next door. He had then piled sacks and potato boxes on top of it, to make it look as much of a wreck as possible. The soldiers took one look at it, and walked off swearing in German. Father was greatly relieved, as he was depending on it to restart his business after the war.

Shortly after D-Day in June 1944, I changed schools, having won a scholarship to the grammar school in the town and I cycled there each day on my junior bicycle, which was rather small. Exercise paper (from France) was at a premium, and ink unobtainable, until someone discovered that soaking the 'lead' from indelible pencils in water created reasonable ink. All secondary pupils were forced to learn German and the German officers even gave prizes for the best pupils! By December 1944, life was at an all-time low, so the school staff

organised a concert for an end of term activity. The rations of coarse brown bread had ceased, and home-grown vegetables, particularly potatoes were eaten three times a day – sliced and simmered in milk for breakfast, mashed for lunch and boiled in their jackets for tea. What I disliked most was mashed potato and swede without salt! Carrageen moss gathered from rocks and boiled with milk produced a milk jelly, which we ate most evenings.

At the end of December electricity supplies ended, and afterwards, even candles became unobtainable. We then had to make do with one small light from a car battery, which was recharged by a friend who had a wind generator on his roof. The gas supply had finished even earlier in December and, after a little experimentation, we used the dining room fireplace for cooking, for which father made a trivet for the saucepans. A hay box proved to be of benefit for slow cooking and keeping food warm.

Top right: German soldiers march along a Jersey Street. They occupied the Channel Islands in June 1940 following the fall of France. Right: A scene following the Liberation of Jersey in May 1945. Patricia says that her father is in this picture, which was published in the Jersey Weekly Post Liberation Supplement. He is in the bottom righthand corner, half turned and between two men wearing hats.

The Union Jack and Jersey flag replace the Nazi flags at former Standortkommandant

In January 1945 the health authorities decided that children did not have sufficient energy to cope with a full day at school due to the lack of good food, so schooling time shrunk to just 2½ hours each morning. A bowl of watery soup was also provided before we departed for home. In this same month we began to receive Canadian Red Cross parcels, packed with the kind of goodies we simply had not seen for many years. On its second trip, the *SS Vega* came from Lisbon, bringing a much-needed supply of flour; bread once again became available.

Slave labourers

The German soldiers were now worse off than the local population. It was not uncommon to see parties of them picking limpets off the rocks. But stealing was rife both by the Germans and their slave labourers. Two of the latter came to our house with rags tied round their feet, a pitiable sight. All mother could give them were a few cold boiled potatoes. These poor people were employed in the construction of massive defence structures around the island.

Because Adolf Hitler was immensely proud of his 'British' conquest, he became obsessed with ensuring that this tiny part of the Third Reich should not be lost. After he had won the war, the Channel Islands were earmarked to be the perfect place for good Nazi families to take their holidays in a 'Strength Through Joy' camp.

When VE Day dawned, while the rest of Europe was celebrating the defeat of Nazism, the Channel Islands were still awaiting Liberation. Early in the morning, it appeared as if nothing was going to happen. I cycled to school and the day started with the usual school assembly – hymn singing and prayers. Then, much to our surprise, we were all told to go home and not return to school until further notice!

Loudspeakers were being erected so that we could listen to Churchill's speech at 3pm. I cycled to a friend's house, where her father also had a wind generator used to charge batteries for a clandestine radio. We stood in the garden and heard Churchill say '... and our dear Channel Islands will be freed today!' Ecstatic cheering followed, flags were brought out and church bells were rung.

The rest of the day was spent looking out to sea, watching and waiting for ships of the Royal Navy to appear. The evening was warm and nobody wanted to go to bed; friends lit a huge bonfire in a field overlooking St Aubyn's Bay. We joined hands and encircled the fire, singing and dancing, with flames lighting up excited faces.

Above and right: *The Red Cross ship* SS Vega *brought supplies to the Channel Islands for distribution in the first few days of 1945. The vessel returned on several more occasions. The Red Cross parcel pictured here is still in the possession of Mrs Patricia Foster.*

At last, next morning a flotilla appeared in the bay. We watched, fascinated, as out of the big ships came little ships – assault craft that brought the troops ashore. Soldiers arrived throughout the day and were given heroes' welcomes. Everyone cheered, children clamoured for autographs and soldiers and sailors showered sweets and cigarettes on us. Liberation had brought to an end nearly five years of a way of life that was all that some children had known. We could now look forward to a future bright with hope, and give thanks for those who had paid with their lives to give us our freedom once again.
Mrs Patricia A Foster

*Mrs Foster's maiden name was Bullock. Today she lives with her husband **csma** *member Doctor Roy Foster in Maidenhead, Berkshire.*

No light in the DARKNESS

Jersey seashore scene and sunset on Guernsey.

The Channel Islands today are a popular destination for holidaymakers with a wealth of hotels, bright bars and restaurants with tempting and extensive menus. It makes it hard to imagine what the privations of wartime occupation could have been like, although there are a number of very well designed museums that portray the story of the years 1940 to 1945 to great effect.

Even after the Red Cross ship *Vega* brought desperately needed food supplies to the Channel Islands around New Year 1944 - 45 and again in February, the situation on the islands remained dire. On 16 January of the last year of the war, the German Platzcommandant on Jersey published an order prohibiting the collection, cutting or gathering of any description of wood for fuel, even by owners or occupiers of land, in private gardens, farms, public parks or roads. Any person breaking the order would be liable to severe punishment. The rule deprived the misery-haunted, half-starved islanders of the chance to collect fuel to give them a few hours' warmth in what was an exceptionally cold and bitter time of year.

By 25 January even the electric light was cut off as supplies of coal and diesel were exhausted. With candles scarce and paraffin unobtainable, thousands of people had access to no artificial light whatsoever, not even matches. Seventy eight islanders died in January in St Helier alone. German soldiers were suffering too and becoming noticeably thinner. The wretched slave labourers, kept mainly out of sight of the islanders, fared worst of all.

The German garrison, though, was still capable of defending itself. Earlier in the month on 7 January, a US fighter aircraft was hit by flak and crashed on Jersey near St Brelade's Church. The pilot came down by parachute and was captured. On the next day, two American POWs on the island escaped captivity and hid out for a week before 'liberating' a small boat and sailing to France.

On the last day of January, the Jersey civilian authorities announced that there was only flour left sufficient for 10 days bread ration. The Red Cross steamer *Vega* arrived from Lisbon on 14 February but its relief cargo did not include flour though there was plenty of chocolate and jam. Islanders were dismayed at the lack of priority displayed by the British Red Cross Society who were directing the operation from London.

A BALTIC TRAGEDY

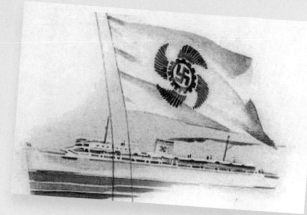

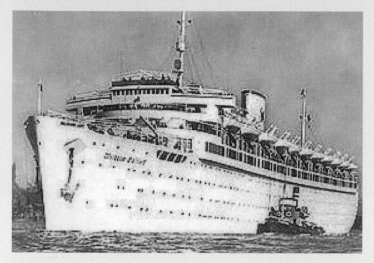

The world's largest-ever loss of life from a single ship sinking occurred early in 1945.

At approximately 9.10pm on 30 January 1945, the German liner *mv Wilhelm Gustloff* was sunk in the Baltic Sea by torpedoes fired from the Russian submarine S-13.

Nothing very remarkable about that, you might think; just another victim to add to the thousands of tons of shipping already lying on the seabed as a result of the war. But this sinking was different. Firstly, it was some years before the real scale of the tragedy became clear. Secondly, to this day, no one knows exactly how many men, women and children perished in the icy Baltic waters that night, but the most reasoned estimates suggest that it was in the region of 7700, making it the most horrific single ship sinking disaster in maritime history, far larger in scale than that of the *Titanic* or *Lusitania*.

Because the liner was grossly overcrowded with desperate refugees, wounded troops, U-Boat cadets and military personnel, no proper passenger manifest was ever recorded – hence the uncertainty over numbers.

Wilhelm Gustloff was launched in 1937 as a 'one class' cruise liner for the Nazi 'Strength through Joy' propaganda programme and was designed to accommodate 1465 passengers on cheap holidays to Mediterranean resorts. Early in the war the vessel was noted as being suitable for transporting troops for *Operation Sealion,* the German invasion of Britain that never happened. Next she went to Norway to serve as a hospital ship. Poorly maintained, by 1945 the ship's speed was diminished to around a maximum of 15 knots which added to her vulnerability when she made her fateful voyage of escape from Gotenhafen

Terrified refugees

With the Russians swarming across Poland and East Prussia, ships sailing from the Gulf of Danzig represented one of the last escape routes for tens of thousands of terrified refugees seeking to move west towards unoccupied Germany. Hundreds of thousands of frantic people were desperate to find places on the few remaining evacuation ships, some even scrambling up boarding nets after the *Wilhelm Gustloff* had cast off.

The night was icy cold with snow showers and poor visibility. The ship sailed with two small escort vessels, one of which had to return to port with a leak. The captain of the *Gustloff* decided to keep the ship fully illuminated as a protection against possible collision and this proved the undoing of the vessel. Torpedoes from the Russian submarine struck with terrible force and the liner immediately began to list to port, so much so that the starboard lifeboats were rendered

unusable. The escort vessel *Lowe* was alongside within 15 minutes and her crew soon became exhausted from pulling passengers from the freezing sea. The water was so cold that many people had died within minutes of immersion.

Hope was re-kindled with the appearance of the battle cruiser *Admiral Hipper*, herself already laden with 1500 refugees. But after assessing the situation, Captain Henigst decided that it would be too great a risk to stop his vessel and present another target to the lurking submarine. Signalling the rescue vessels 'success and good luck', the warship resumed her course and swept away at 32 knots, leaving the stranded survivors with a sense of bewilderment and betrayal.

Bout of heavy drinking

By an irony of war, the S-13's captain, Alexander Marinescu, had sailed from his base port of Hango (on Finnish territory occupied by the Russians) ahead of schedule, allegedly to escape the shore patrol who wanted to arrest him for unruly behaviour after a bout of heavy drinking. In spite of the declared aim of Stalin to utterly destroy Hitler's Third Reich, Marinescu failed to receive any sort of official recognition for his exploits in the Baltic, which included the sinking of the *General Steuben* on 10 February in the course of the same voyage with the loss of over 4000 lives. Indeed, after the war he was sent to a Gulag labour camp and later worked in a motor factory.

Today, the liner rests at the bottom of the Baltic, about 50 miles from the wreck of the *Steuben* and some 70 miles from the *Goya,* another ship crammed with refugees sunk whilst fleeing the Russian advance. The watery graves have been designated permanent war memorial sites, off limits to divers and salvage crews but, nevertheless, many artefacts have been removed from the wreck by souvenir-hunters. On Polish navigation charts, the wreck of the *Wilhelm Gustloff* is described simply as 'Obstacle No 73'.

Top left: The Wilhelm Gustloff *in peacetime.*
Top right: The ship with its pennant.
Above (clockwise from top left): Wording from the ship's menu. Two recent views of the wreckage lying on the Baltic's seabed.

The dramatic scene above depicting a British warship ramming an Axis submarine is by Marc Stone. It pre-dates 1944 and was intended for the 'Back Them Up' Ministry of Information series of posters (National Archives - Art of War). The photograph inset (reproduced much larger on page 215) was published in the German magazine Signal in 1944 with the heading 'The Big and the Small Submarine Man'. The U-Boat Commander Joachim Schepke - regarded as an Ace - was long dead; his vessel was rammed by the destroyer HMS Vanoc in the North Atlantic on 9 March 1941.

As 1945 dawned the Germans had made a number of technical advances; for example, with the 'Schnorkel' device that enabled submarines to stay submerged for much longer than before. These gave them hope that the U-Boat could once again threaten the naval lifeline of the Allies.

War Correspondence

As individual instalments of Sixty Years On were published we received numerous letters from readers. On the following pages we have collated a collection of contributions that have a nautical theme.

Battle of the Atlantic

I served in the Royal Navy during World War II as a watchkeeping officer on a frigate escorting convoys. Between December 1943 and June 1944, we were engaged in three different aspects of the Battle of the Atlantic.

Firstly, in December 1943 we were with an escort group acting as an additional support to convoys in the centre of the Atlantic. Our senior officer's ship, *HMS Hurricane*, was torpedoed on Christmas Eve. We took off the survivors on Christmas Day.

Then in February 1944 as additional escort to Russian convoy JW57, which was successful, although *HMS Mahratta* was sunk. When nearing Murmansk, our escort group was ordered to return to Scapa Flow, but we ran into such appalling weather that two of our group nearly ran out of fuel.

On 5 June of that year we escorted 20 blockships to be sunk at Omaha beach as a breakwater for the Mulberry harbour. We escorted convoys to Omaha every few days thereafter until the breakout in August 1944.

The Battle of the Atlantic was an unremitting struggle which lasted nearly six years.
W J J Whetnall, Liverpool

dot dash dot dash dot!

I volunteered for the Royal Navy and went to *HMS Royal Arthur* - Butlins Holiday Camp, Skegness - for training. After six months I passed as an Ordinary Telegraphist and was sent to Portsmouth to join *HMS Quorn*, a destroyer. The next few months were spent chasing E-Boats. We were out every night from 7pm to 7am next morning but the German torpedo boats were elusive and very fast.

Next I was drafted to *HMS Belfast* in Belfast docks. From here it was on to Scapa Flow to carry on our training. Then we were on convoy escort duty, sailing 15 miles behind the main body of ships keeping a lookout for the German pocket battleship *Scharnhorst*. We spent quite a while within the Arctic Circle operating in temperatures of 60 degrees below freezing but never saw the enemy, even though we patrolled the Denmark Strait for a week. This was the stretch of sea through which the German surface raiders had to pass in order to reach the open Atlantic.

After returning to Scapa Flow I was sent back to Portsmouth and then to Gairloch Bay in Scotland where I joined a useless old aircraft carrier. My next voyage was with *HMS Emperor*, a seaworthy carrier crammed inside and out with damaged fighter planes which we were to take across the Atlantic in convoy to Norfolk, Virginia, for repair. On the way we sailed through a tremendous whirlwind, in which the ship was hoisted to a height of 60 feet before plunging down into a flat calm and then rising again to 60 feet at the other side. U-Boats were sinking ships to the right and left of us every night but we got away with it. The speed of the convoy is the speed of the slowest ship so it took us three weeks to get there and three weeks to get back.

Next we were sent to Southampton to a tiny little boat not much bigger than a Norfolk Broads pleasure cruiser. It had a one-inch gun screwed to the bows. We sailed this vessel to Juno Beach, Normandy, on D-Day itself. Our task was to pick up any soldiers or sailors who ended up in the water but we never found anyone and spent most of our time begging the bigger ships for fuel.

Of all things, I was then transferred to the Army! New uniform, rifle, the lot. Because we were known as wireless operators someone had decided it would be a good idea if we taught our Allies how to do it. What a laugh; we couldn't speak their various languages and they couldn't speak ours. I remained in the Army for just about a year before being demobbed in 1945.

Even though all this took place 60 years or so ago I still know every dot and dash of the morse code. dot dash dot dash dot means: end of message.
R Swift (address supplied)
*HMS Belfast is pictured in the stamp at the top of this page.

The *Strathallan* story

The *mv Strathallan* is mentioned on page 109 of *Sixty Years On*. I was on this ship when she was torpedoed off the North African coast and can tell you the story.

I had joined a TA Signals company in May 1939 in Cardiff and spent the following August training in camp. The prospect of being 'stood down' at the end of four weeks became slimmer as the probability of war with Germany increased. Listening to Neville Chamberlain's speech on the wireless in camp on 3 September, I realised that my month's camp would be somewhat extended!

In December 1942 I sailed from Gourock on the Clyde estuary with over 4000 others (including 250 Queen Alexandra nurses) on board the *Strathallan* bound for ... goodness knew where. After zig-zagging across a very stormy Atlantic for 10 days we passed through the Gibraltar Straits into the calmer waters of the Med. We guessed (correctly) that our destination was Algiers but I had not appreciated that I would be expected to swim part of the remaining 200 or so miles.

At 1.30am on 21 December U-Boat 562 fired off two torpedoes at us, one of which hit our engine room. The Captain gave orders to abandon ship and we went down rope ladders and swam towards various rafts and lifeboats. I was picked up by *HMS Verity* and taken to Oran. Together with five others of my Section, I spent that Christmas in an American field hospital before going to Algiers by train to take up duties in the Mediterranean Allied Air Force HQ.

Ten months later I went to Italy and in February 1946 I headed home to Blighty to gladly hand over my khaki uniform in exchange for a new suit and trilby hat. I was a civilian once again.
Selwyn Jones (address supplied)

Force H about-turn!

Having joined up and trained as an Ordinary Telegraphist and gone round the Cape to the Med, I joined *HMS Antwerp*, an ex-cross channel steamer, fitted out as an escort vessel with one 4-inch gun forrard. However, Admiral Ramsey chose it as his headquarters ship for the Sicily invasion and we then flew an admiral's flag. Shortly before the invasion we were in Grand Harbour, Malta, tied up opposite St Angelo, the HQ of the Vice Admiral, Malta, when the famous Force H returned to the island. They came down the fairway, bugles blowing and bags of swank with their crews lined up to port ready to salute VAM. In fact, the first ship, perhaps *HMS Renown*, had already sounded off when

someone spotted our flag! Panic! All the crews had to about-turn to salute our rather more modest vessel (with its puny 4-inch gun). It quite made our day.
K V Osborne, Surrey

Torpedo attack

I spent my first war years flying as a Naval Airman and then in 1944 at the age of 27 I was appointed to an aircraft carrier, *HMS Trumpeter*. She was to spend the next 15 months attached to the Home Fleet based at Scapa Flow. The task was to attack the Germans occupying Norway, protect our Russian-bound convoys, land Commandos on the beaches and coastline of Norway and stop the German battleship *Tirpitz* from attacking the convoys.

In July 1944 *HMS Trumpeter* and a large force from the Home Fleet set out to tackle the *Tirpitz*, where she lay in a Norwegian fjord. On the way there, at about 2pm on 22 August, I was standing on the starboard side of the ship's flight deck looking out to sea and admiring the great concourse of battleships, carriers and destroyers.

Suddenly I spotted the tell-tale signs of a German torpedo directly approaching me. What in fact I saw was a stream of bubbles rising from below the surface of the sea and leaving a distinctive wake. It was an indication that a German U-Boat was close by, had taken deliberate aim at *HMS Trumpeter* and had only just ordered 'Fire'.

Fortunately I was not so petrified with fear that I forgot to shout 'Torpedo Approaching' and raise the alarm. Everyone on deck at the time expected a huge explosion and a mighty shock. But none came. The torpedo passed right underneath without detonating and continued its progress in a straight line beyond us. The trail of bubbles was clearly visible. I saw it going on its murderous journey and then smash into the next ship in the line, *HMS Nabob*, another aircraft carrier.

The expected enormous explosion followed. A mighty sheet of flame sprang into the sky followed by black smoke. There was no doubt about it, the ship had received a crippling blow. A great hole appeared in her side, the water rushed in and she seemed to be sinking.

However, due to the heroic efforts of the crew, and especially of the damage control parties, who plugged the hole and shored up the internal bulkheads, the ship stayed afloat. In the end she was down 43 feet in the water but was able to limp 800 miles back to port.

When the German U-Boat fired its torpedo at *HMS Trumpeter* there must have been less than 40 feet between them. That would have been insufficient distance in the water for the torpedo to have armed itself. Each had a magnetic device in the nose that's designed to activate itself when within the magnetic field of a steel ship. The submarine might therefore be blown up by its own torpedo if

Left: Roy Nockolds painted this Hawker Hurricane approaching an Escort Carrier. These ships were usually converted merchantmen with a rudimentary flight deck that could take a small number of aircraft.

the device did not have a 40 feet safety range. In this case the torpedo passed underneath *HMS Trumpeter*, as intended, but was not detonated by the magnetic field. It was still in a 'safe' state.

My ship was clearly the intended victim. The torpedo ran straight at her but had been fired from too close. Hapless *HMS Nabob* took the blow intended for *HMS Trumpeter*.
Paul Housden VRD, Shropshire

Cold chalets to Canada

I am writing my memoirs for my grandchildren and thought the following might be of interest. In February 1944 I started my National Service with the Royal Navy. I had opted for the Fleet Air Arm as a TAG (Telegraphist Air Gunner). As with many others I arrived for entry routine at *HMS Royal Arthur* at Butlins, Skegness. Memories of very cold chalets!

Basic training was at HMS *St Vincent* Gosport, where the recruit in the next bunk introduced himself as Don Revie, a Leicester City footballer who, of course, went on to occupy a significant place in English soccer history. Time here was spent 'square bashing' and learning the basics of seamanship, including 'pulling' a whaler round Portsmouth Harbour.

As well as seeing Doodlebugs going over, there were night time air raids. During one, when I was on fire watch duty, I witnessed an awesome fireworks display. There were batteries of anti-aircraft rockets going up and parachute flares slowly coming down, completely illuminating the whole area. The most frightening thing was the knowledge that all that 'ack-ack' going up had to come down again somewhere – not to mention the small matter of the bombs. Still, I had my tin hat on!

During my time there, I remember seeing the D-Day fleets assembling at Spithead and the bus station at Gosport Ferry being taken over for storing military vehicles.

Next came serious training under what I believe was known as the Empire Air Training Scheme. In August 1944 I arrived at *HMS Waxwing*, Dunfermline, to await transport to Canada. Experiences in Dunfermline included being able to have ice cream, permitted only in Scotland, and a one day Ship's Fire Fighting Course at Rosyth Dockyard.

We were taken by rail to Gourock and by tender out to our vessel anchored in the Firth of Clyde. The grey painted liner was the *Queen Mary*. A very comfortable five day zig-zag voyage to New York followed. My job aboard was to transport food from the cold store to the galley passing through the watertight doorway each time – stand clear when the doors were tested daily!

VIPs used these liners and on this particular voyage Lord Halifax, Britain's Ambassador to Washington was seen walking the deck every day. We had a slight mishap on docking in New York. The stern hawser broke and the stern swung out and struck the fender of a warship, producing a very loud 'boing'.

We were transferred overnight by train from Jersey City to Montreal, where we had a couple of hours before getting another train

via the south bank of the St Lawrence to Mont Joli, thence south to a transit camp at Moncton, New Brunswick, where I got involved in an all night forest fire fight.

A few days later we went to the RCAF airfield at Yarmouth, Nova Scotia, for our air training. This involved Morse code by buzzer and Aldis Lamp and Japanese aircraft recognition. The planes we used were Ansons and Swordfish; difficult to imagine air-ground signalling by lamp to and from a circling aircraft. I was in the squad chosen as Guard of Honour for a visit by the Canadian Governor General, the Earl of Athlone.

Sadly, I lost one of my mates, killed when two planes collided. Another mate, a very talented jazz pianist, Louis D G Bobb, was a 'Geordie' West Indian. I often wonder what happened to him.

As happens in war, things change suddenly, causing massive waste of resources; we were told that we were surplus to requirements, so after 42 flying hours, the training ceased before completion. We were shipped back from Halifax to Liverpool in March 1945 on the French liner *Louis Pasteur* - this ship rolled all the way across the Atlantic.

At *HMS Daedalus*, Lee-on-the-Solent, I was again involved in Guard of Honour duty, this time for the Duchess of Kent (Princess Marina) who was head of the Wrens. I was offered re-grading as a writer (clerk) or take discharge, so in August 1945 I went back to my 'civvy' job in the coal industry.

But five months later I was called up again as I hadn't done all my National Service time. I opted for the RAF and spent an uneventful two years doing clerical work.
Alf Boston, Worcestershire
PS. I did meet another footballer – Scottish international Joe Crozier.

A brother's war

My brother Arthur always had a weak chest. He was the envy of his pals when he was about 10 years old because he could fill his hanky with blood but they couldn't. So it wasn't surprising that, a few years later, when he got his call up papers, they laughed and said, 'you'll never pass the medical'. He kept quiet about his chest trouble because he desperately wanted to serve at sea. He duly joined the Royal Navy.

Not long after he became a sailor, he was detailed to the armed merchant ships. Merchant ships travelled in convoys for safety and some of these were equipped for protection with guns and depth charges. Naval and army personnel were carried to man them.

Arthur was assigned to the *MV Empire Bede*. While on this ship Arthur and a pal undertook the laundry for the crew. One day they ruined the Captain's best suit by over-soaping the trousers to the point where they couldn't get the stuff out. It was my brother's brilliant idea to tie the trousers on a rope and fling them over the side to give them a good rinse in the sea. This might have been a good idea if the rope hadn't broken! The trousers were lost for ever.

The Captain, of course, kept asking for them and the boys kept making excuses. But then in the Caribbean something happened that saved them from having to confess. The something was quite drastic. The *Empire Bede* was torpedoed by a U-Boat! With the ship listing very badly, the crew managed to get some lifeboats away. Arthur was ordered into one of the boats which eventually got away with about 20 men on board before the ship went down.

The U-Boat surfaced and came alongside their lifeboat demanding to know if the Captain or any servicemen were aboard. Some were, of course, but as the Germans would have taken them prisoner, they replied that everyone in the lifeboat was a merchant seaman. Though the Germans refused to give them a map or supplies, the U-Boat crew did wish the men in the lifeboat luck before sailing off.

Arthur and the others were lucky too, because the next day they were picked up by a British ship. On board they were reunited with more survivors from the *Empire Bede*, including the Captain, whose hair appeared to have turned white since the sinking!

The ship landed them at Santiago-de-Cuba and from there they went to Havana. As the first British survivors of a sinking to go there, they were made a lot of fuss of and their photos taken for the newspaper.

After enjoying life in Cuba for about a week, they were flown to Miami. From there the party travelled to New York by train, a very long journey which took them through Georgia, the Carolinas and Virginia. Arthur greatly enjoyed this, being fascinated by all the things he saw. When the other passengers discovered they were shipwrecked British sailors, they showered them with gifts and money. Upon arrival in New York, some of the passengers invited them to stay at their homes. This was too good an opportunity to miss, especially as they now had money to spend. When the money ran out, they thought they had better report to the Navy and face the music. There was plenty of 'music' to face too, because they had been missing for 10 days!

While Arthur was in America, it was decided to send six ferry boats and three escort ships across the Atlantic to Britain to form part of an Allied fleet for the future invasion of Europe. About 60 men were required to man each ferry. Volunteers were requested, but as the ferries were all wood, they did not have much luck. So Arthur and his fellows under barrack arrest found they had been volunteered without even raising a finger!

They joined the ferries at Baltimore. Arthur was allocated to the *Yorktown* and on this ferry in the North Atlantic he was shipwrecked for the second time. The Nazis claimed to have sunk three large troop ships. In truth they had sunk a few ferries and one of the escort ships. The *Yorktown* was struck around 1am and went down in minutes. Arthur was thrown into the sea but managed to grab onto a cabin door and was able to use it as a raft. The sea was extremely rough and he gripped the edges of the door as if his hands were glued to it. Each wave would carry him to its crest then leave him and his door in mid air as it fell to its trough; then he would follow down with a crash. To this

day he doesn't know how he managed to stay on. By dawn the sea had calmed down, so when a real raft came in sight, he was able to drift over to it and climb aboard.

After several hours, another raft was sighted which only had a few men on board, so some of the sailors left the first overcrowded raft and joined it. These wooden rafts had a bench along two sides. Beneath the seats were storage boxes for survival kits of water, biscuits and prunes, flares and torches. The food and water was rationed sparingly and every so often they were given a biscuit, a mouthful of water and a prune.

After three days adrift they saw a plane but its crew failed to spot the raft.

By the fifth day things were getting worse and rations were getting very low. A couple of the men died and their bodies were put overboard. When a survivor was caught stealing prunes, he joined them.

On the sixth day another plane was spotted. This time when they waved, the pilot signalled back before he flew off. Four hours later, after six and a half days adrift, they were picked up by a naval ship and taken to Londonderry. Arthur thought he had been very lucky because although he suffered frostbite in his feet – and still feels the effect in cold weather – he heard later that some of his companions had to have limbs amputated.

One of the survivors was his pal Joe Long. Joe later told our family that when depression set in on the raft, it was Arthur who kept everyone's spirits up by getting them all to sing. In Joe's opinion they owed their lives to Arthur for keeping them going.
Mrs J Stewart, Essex

Crossings to Canada

Like many teenagers wanting to go to sea, I joined the Merchant Navy, aged 16 in 1944. I was assigned to a Dutch ship, *ss Volendam*, which acted as a troop-carrier. My first voyage was to Malta for a stopover before taking troops to Egypt and then carrying other troops from Egypt to Sicily and Italy.

Back in England a consignment of Canadian soldiers embarked and we joined a large convoy for an Atlantic crossing. This was in April 1945 and the U-Boats were still active, evident by the distant sound of depth-charges and the presence of escort vessels between the convoy lanes.

Thankfully our part of the convoy reached Halifax, Nova Scotia, safely, with much celebration on the dockside welcoming the Canadians back home. For me, Halifax seemed a world apart from England what with no black out and clothes, fruit and chocolate readily available. Best of all, was a feeling of complete relaxation, even for a short while prior to the return voyage, taking a new batch of service personnel back to England.

Again, the journey was marked by escort ship activity, so it was with some relief that we reached Liverpool. After a short while in dock, more Canadian troops came aboard and we realised the ship was again bound for Halifax. This time the convoy seemed larger than ever, but generally the crossing was uneventful until the ship's radio

announced on 8 May 1945 that hostilities had ceased in Europe. By this time we were in the mid-Atlantic. My first thought was, 'I hope the U-Boat captains realise it's all over.'

For the Dutch members of the crew it was an emotional moment, knowing that at last they were soon to return to their homeland. For me, I was happy in the knowledge that the German defeat put an end to further development of weapons such as the V2 rockets and that my home town of London was free from any more devastation.
Harry Bridges, Crowborough, East Sussex

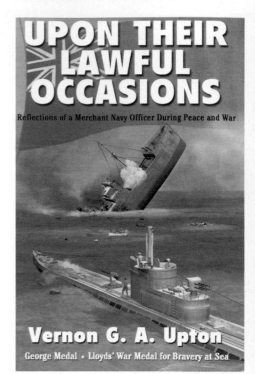

This is the cover of a fascinating and informative book published in 2004. Upon Their Lawful Occasions *is a personal account of a Merchant Navy Officer's experiences in peacetime and wartime. Vernon G A Upton begins the book by tracing his early life in Japan and Canada before detailing his 27 wartime ocean passages in nine ships.*

The Second World War claimed the lives of 30,248 British merchant seamen and over 50,000 merchant seamen of all nationalities. The fatal casualty rate was over 31% and was higher than in any other Service body in either the First or Second World War.

The book also includes a statistical record of the sinking of 1836 merchant ships and 350 U-Boats. For example, it shows that the ship Empire Bede *(referred to by Mrs Stewart in her letter 'A brother's war' on this page was sunk on 18 August 1942 by U-553. She was part of Convoy TAW13 and was carrying cotton. Of the 46 crew 44 survived.*

Vernon Upton's book (ISBN 1 904744 25 7) was published by Matador of Leicester. E-mail: **books@troubador.co.uk** *Or visit:* **www.troubador.co.uk/matador**

WAR DIARY *January 1945*

1 January: The 1948th day of the war opens with a surprise German attack along a 50-mile front between Saarbrucken and Strasbourg. *Operation North Wind* is directed against a section of the Allied frontline weakened by the redeployment of the US 6th Army to counter the earlier German offensive in the Ardennes. A further attack from the air, *Operation Bodenplatt,* is mounted by hundreds of aircraft and concentrates on Allied airfields in Holland and Belgium.

In the Pacific, American naval forces are suffering increasing losses from 'Kamikaze' aircraft. The Japanese also have a number of explosive-filled submarines with crews who have vowed to die in attempts to close in on US warships.

2 January: Admiral Sir Bertram Ramsay, naval chief of the Allied Expeditionary Force, is killed when his aircraft crashes in Paris. Ramsay was a key figure in planning the Dunkirk evacuation and the Allied invasions of North Africa and Sicily. He was also in charge of naval operations in support of the D-Day landings

In Copenhagen, resistance fighters destroy a factory making parts for V2 rockets. In the Atlantic, a new weapon of war is introduced to the Allied arsenal as the Sikorsky helicopter is used for convoy escort duties for the first time.

3 January: The strategically important Burmese port of Akyab is liberated by a single British artillery officer after the Japanese had pulled out of the town 48 hours previously.

Canadian forces are being augmented through conscription. Today the first draftees set sail for Europe from Halifax. A Nazi concentration camp is liberated at Breendonck in Holland – it is one of the first of Hitler's death camps to be revealed to the outside world.

4 January: Intense naval actions are taking place in the East China Sea, off the Philippines and in the Indian Ocean. A 'Kamikaze' pilot slams his aircraft into US carrier *Ommaney Bay* causing it to sink with the loss of 93 lives.

The US press is speculating on an alarming warning from Admiral Jonas Ingram that New York may soon be attacked by flying bombs launched from German submarines. The Kriegsmarine are thought to have at least 300 U-Boats still operational and they have been noticeably more active in the North Atlantic of late.

5 January: In Greece the new premier General Pastiras has formed a moderate cabinet in a bid to resolve the bitter civil war blighting the country. In the Ardennes, the weather again intervenes to bog down a major American offensive in the snow. Air support is denied by low cloud. On the home front construction begins on the first of Britain's 'prefab' houses.

6 January: On the Philippine island of Luzon the Japanese continue with their 'Kamikaze' air campaign. Today 150 US naval crewmen die. By the end of the day, the Japanese have less than 100 aircraft left. Meanwhile, American bombers continue their relentless raids on Tokyo.

7 January: In Burma, Japanese forces are retreating towards Mandalay whilst Royal Marine Commandos attempt to block their path. The general advance of British and Commonwealth troops is supported by naval bombardment. Heavily-armed motor launches are harrying enemy vessels in the maze of coastal inlets in this part of Burma.

Meanwhile, in Moscow, Stalin agrees to step up operations on the Eastern Front in order to relieve the pressure on the British and the Americans. Meanwhile, during a press conference, Field Marshal Montgomery upsets the Americans by apparently playing down their contribution to stemming the German advance in the Ardennes.

8 January: The US 7th army is engaged in fierce fighting to repulse a determined German attack at Rimling.

9 January: General Heinz Guderian, Chief of the General Staff, warns a disinterested Hitler that the Russians are planning a major Eastern Front offensive.

In the Philippines, the US 6th Army, supported by heavy naval bombardments has landed at Lingayen Gulf, 110 miles north of the Phillipines capital, Manila.

10 January: A Hitler decree issued in Berlin sanctions the death penalty for anyone found guilty of diverting essential supplies from the military.

In the Malacca Strait, on **11 January,** the British submarine

Left: A trio of British soldiers in a frontline town on the Dutch-German border.

Tally Ho sinks the Japanese cruiser *Kuma*. On the same day, in the Ardennes, troops of the US 3rd Army link up with men of the British XXX Corps at St Hubert. At a conference in Versailles, Allied air force commanders determine to step up attacks on Germany's dwindling sources of fuel.

General Guderian's warning to Hitler three days ago is vindicated when, on **12 January,** the Russians hurl 163 divisions at German positions in Poland and East Prussia. The Germans resist from well prepared defences, but are outnumbered by five tanks to one.

14 January: General Slim's army in Burma commences crossing the Irrawaddy in force. This day also sees the Red Army cut the important railway line south of Crakow as its headlong advance across Poland gains momentum.

15 January: More good news comes from the Far East as two Chinese armies link up and the famous 'Burma Road' is reopened under Allied control. In London, the boat train service to the Continent starts again after a five year break.

16 January: Russian troops capture Radom and move to encircle Warsaw which finally falls on **17 January** to an assault masterminded by Marshal Zhukov. It is a city largely in ruins and destined for a bleak future after a Soviet-sponsored 'puppet' government is installed on **18 January** under President Bierut. He denounces the Polish Home Army who led the uprising against the Germans last August as 'irresponsible' and 'murderers who are provoking civil strife'. It is clear he intends a purge of all those who do not follow the communist line.

In the concentration camp Auschwitz-Birkenau, the Nazis order the immediate evacuation of 20,000 inmates considered fit enough to travel.

20 January: The Germans advance to within eight miles of Strasbourg causing panic in the city. *Operation North Wind* has proved a brilliant German counter-stroke and has stretched the forces of the American/French 6th Army Group to near breaking point.

In Washington, Franklin D Roosevelt is inaugurated for a fourth term as President Harry S Truman becomes his Vice-President. In Budapest, the provisional government agrees to pay $300 million reparations to the Allies and join them in the fight against Germany.

21 January: Indian troops have landed on Ramree Island in Burma and attack Kangaw.

On **22 January** in Berlin Hitler agrees a major ship building programme utilising slave labour. It's a strange decision but typical of the air of unrealism pervading around the Führer and his Nazi acolytes.

Next day **(23 January)** Hitler appoints Heinrich Himmler as C in C of Army Group Vistula. Himmler has no experience of operational command.

24 January: French forces halt the German advance on Strasbourg at the last bridge before the city. One of the Wehrmacht's top generals – Heinz Guderian - meets von Ribbentrop, the Nazi Foreign Minister, to tell him bluntly that 'the war is lost'. Guderian's outspokenness has put him out of favour with Hitler.

25 January: The Pacific island of Iwo Jima is heavily bombarded by the US navy who are anxious to break down the Japanese defences ahead of landings planned for next month.

26 January: The Red Army closes to within 100 miles of Berlin where old men, officer cadets and young boys have been recruited into the Volkssturm defence force and ordered to defend the capital to the last man.

27 January: The world is waking up to the existence of the dreadful Nazi concentration camps. Today, four young Red Army soldiers advance into Auschwitz-Birkenau to be greeted by a host of 'living skeletons' moving slowly in a landscape of corpses sprawled in the snow.

Right: A monument to 61 British officers and men of the 13th (Lancashire) Battalion The Parachute Regiment who died in a battle for the village of Bure in the Belgian Ardennes between 3 and 5 January 1945. Below: Sherman tanks in the snow during the Ardenne fighting in January 1945. Inset: A Sherman on display in the region today.

28 January: Despite the persistence of the Arctic winter, the liberation of northern Norway – an area known as Finmark – continues. The Red Army has the largest number of men engaged in this snowy theatre of war, but now there are also Norwegian troops, sent from Britain after five years of waiting and training, keen to play a role in ending the Nazi occupation. The retreating Germans operate a 'scorched earth' policy and are destroying towns and villages. Over 40,000 civilians have been deported from Finmark in recent months; around 20,000 remain to greet their liberators.

29 January: In Burma, the Fourteenth Army continues to tighten its grip around the important city of Mandalay and is steadily pressing in on the Japanese who have little hope of reinforcement or major re-supply.

30 January: In the Baltic, Russian submarines are taking a heavy toll of German shipping and thousands of refugees are drowning in the freezing waters.

31 January: Russia's top commander, Marshal Zhukov, crosses the German frontier as Soviet forces advance to the River Oder and cut the rail link between Berlin and Danzig in East Prussia. They now pose a real threat to the city of Frankfurt, just 45 miles from Berlin.

HOME FRONT

FEBRUARY 1945

AT HOME

By the early spring of 1945 things were improving in the kitchens of British housewives. At the end of February, fresh supplies reached London greengrocers, a fact noted in the *Daily Telegraph*: '... dwarf runner beans of the French variety are in the West End shops. Grown in Cornish and Devon hot-houses, they cost 30s per lb. Grapefruits from the Middle East have also arrived. They will be distributed in the same way as oranges and lemons at a controlled price of 8d a lb.'

Even so, there was still rationing of meat and shortages encouraged alternatives. Rabbit was widely used and sausages often contained interesting substitutes for meat. A very popular film of the period, *Millions Like Us*, memorably includes a character observing: 'It's a mystery what's in these sausages... and I hope it's not solved in my time!'

Tinned meat was imported in huge quantities from the United States and in this way Spam (chopped luncheon meat) entered the national diet. Corned beef too was regularly on the menu. Whalemeat become widely available in 1945 but was generally disliked because of its fishy, oily taste.

Further strain on the food front came with the need to feed the millions of newly liberated peoples of Europe, many of them displaced or living in areas devastated by the fighting. As a consequence of the shortages most British people who had access to a garden or allotment continued to grow as many vegetables as they could.

Britain's war effort was sustained by the efforts of countless women workers, who had replaced men sent off to serve in the Forces. Women were involved in just about every light and heavy industry as well as in such occupations as ferry pilots delivering new aircraft to RAF bases. An exception was the mines. In the pits the Bevin Boys toiled to keep up with Britain's insatiable need for energy from coal to drive the manufacturing machines and heat homes.

Following an announcement by Minister of Labour, Ernest Bevin in December 1943, boys of 18 had been conscripted to work in the mines. It was a tough business. One youngster –

> **It's a mystery what's in these sausages... and I hope it's not solved in my time!**

T Buckland – working down Glapwell Colliery in Nottinghamshire told a newspaper: 'I travel five miles by bus to get there. Then I drop down the shaft in a cage at about 60mph, with the draught through the holes blowing right up our legs, and it's cold!

'It is roughly four miles from the pit bottom to the point where I work, which makes it nine miles from my home. We're making a new roadway and work in 70 degrees of heat. Halfway through my shift I have generally drunk my four pints of water and then have to go thirsty. It makes you value water.'

'We fill between 12 and 16 tubs of rock in a shift and a tub holds about one ton. 12 to 16 tubs a night isn't bad, is it?'

HARRY'S WAR

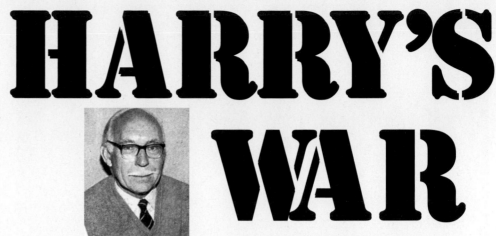

Ex-Radar boffin Harry Warren of Windscale, Cumbria, recalls landing on Omaha Beach, a meeting with Albert and an encounter with an irate Spitfire pilot a short time before VE Day.

Three things impressed me about the ship's captain. Firstly, how young he was, about my own age of 22; secondly how scruffy he was with no cap and a slept-in looking uniform with only a hint of gold-braid at the sleeves. Thirdly, his mastery of bad language. 'Go, go, go' he screamed, 'Get this effing heap of crap off my effing ship. I'm not getting effing well stranded on a lee effing shore with an effing falling tide'. Real Hornblower language.

The driver revved up the engine and let in the clutch. We dived into the sea and the windscreen turned green, but the waterproofing did its job and we slowly ground ashore through a choppy surf avoiding the mined obstacles, destroyed transport and all the other obscene detritus of war.

It was the end of June 1944 and the place was Omaha Beach, Normandy. We were some 40 or so vehicles of the 15081 Ground Control Interception Radar. Our role was to locate enemy aircraft at night and direct our night fighters in for the kill. We were very good at our job. At the end of the war we had 99 swastikas painted on the side of the Ops Wagon. Omaha was, of course, the American Sector, and we were there because the Yanks had no Radar. We lived on American rations, tinned ham and pineapple and warm white bread and coffee. There was no tea but there was certainly danger; mainly because we looked 'different' and the Yanks would shoot anything that they didn't instantly recognise.

So how did I arrive at this rather precarious situation? Only a matter of weeks earlier I had been enjoying life on a Radar Station at Kilkeel in Northern Ireland. Then they closed the station and I was posted to Yatesbury for a three week course on the new top-secret Centimetric radio. This used the Magnetron, a British invention now used in microwave cookers. It produced a very high frequency output, many times higher than the enemy could detect. Ordinary Radars (Types 15 and 11) could very accurately find the range but height finding was a bit of a guess. My Centimetric Type 13 produced a very narrow beam and elevation to give an accurate height; invaluable to our night fighters and disastrous to the enemy.

On D-Day I was at RAF Hornchurch being processed for Overseas. Medicals, innoculations, khaki uniform, issued with personal weapon, Sten Gun. Tremendous excitement as the news filtered through that we had landed in France! Tannoy announcement, Corporal Warren and two others, get down to Bournemouth top speed;

your Unit is waiting to cross to France. Eventually we found the Unit under canvas in a field, complete with Types 13 and 14 Centimetric equipment and no apparent urgency. And so we waited. On 10 June I was able to sneak home to Grays for my birthday.

For the crossing from Southampton we were part of a motley collection of RAF, Navy and Army personnel and full of smutty jokes and stories. No fear, just excitement but we sobered up when instructed 'don't hang about, the Germans are still shelling the beaches'. Then we joined our vehicles, the doors opened and we traversed a football-pitch size area of upset sea to the beach. The debris had that distinctive smell of war, instantly recognised and never forgotten.

'Send for Lofty'

Active Service consists of periods of frantic activity, sometimes sadly with casualties, and then long periods of boring inactivity. We found a convenient apple orchard, which offered some camouflage, put up our tents, dug latrines and located the nearest source of US rations. And then waited, confined to camp for fear of land mines, booby-traps and 'friendly fire'. No fraternising with the locals. About this time I found that my schoolboy French was coming in handy. Surprisingly, nobody else seemed to have rudimentary skills and 'Send for Lofty' became a familiar cry when it was necessary to converse with the locals - for example, to secure a supply of water.

Being liberated is no joke, all the houses were smashed to pieces and the fields were full of dead and bloated animals. I am quite sure that the inhabitants of Normandy would much have preferred our landing in the Pas de Calais. There had also been a lot of pointless bombing, which destroyed property and killed

civilians. Our American Allies were so randy that farm girls had to be escorted by males when they went to milk the cows. Rape and Pillage were furthest from our thoughts. At Hornchurch, we had been forced to watch some horrendous films on the effects of VD; to catch it was considered a 'self inflicted wound' and severely punished.

Strolling along a sunken lane I felt a sharp pain at the side of my head. A passing bullet makes quite a distinctive sound, a sort of 'zzzzzt' noise. Also the bullet travels faster than the sound of the shot so you don't hear the report of the gun until you have received the bullet. I hadn't been shot but a bullet had shattered a twig near my head and I had been hit by the wooden shrapnel. Then came the crack of an American carbine. Friendly fire!

In the first week or two, we moved camp a couple of times and on one occasion started to erect the equipment. A shell passed overhead and landed a couple of fields away. In another couple of minutes another came our way and landed short. The penny dropped, we were the target and we drove out of the field with the partly erected aerials flapping from side to side. A further shell landed bang in the middle of our vacated field. Amazingly we all fell about laughing.

We came across some Marine Commandos and played them at football. They had small kit bags bulging with looted watches, binoculars, cameras, Lugers, daggers and French money. It transpired that the whole unit including Officers were in a punishment camp. At that time the Port of Cherbourg had been isolated but it was ordained that the Yanks would capture it, as some sort of pay-back for the terrible losses they received on Omaha. Our Commandos had nipped in via the Port and looted the Paymaster's Office. Did the official records show this? I doubt it!

In late July we set up our equipment near Carteret and on the 28th recorded two successful 'kills'. On 5 August we moved south to Granville and into a large Chateau overlooking some cliffs. The Germans had left in a hurry leaving some personal effects

> **Our role was to locate enemy aircraft at night and direct our night fighters in for the kill. We were very good at our job. At the end of the war we had 99 swastikas painted on the side of the Ops Wagon.**

Left: A suspected collaborator has been cornered by a group of armed and angry Resistance men in Rennes in August 1944.

besides the beds. These included hairnets and we assumed that they had female companions. But the staff assured us that this was not the case and that the German airmen wore them when sleeping! We carried on with our night-time activities, swam in the sea, visited the odd café and even played table tennis with some of the locals in the Casino.

We moved near to Bayeux. Walking in the outskirts of the city with a group of the lads I passed a doorway where three bodies of men in smart suits and raincoats were lying. They were quite clearly dead and the cloth was still smouldering around the bullet-holes. On the opposite pavement were a group of the arm-banded ruffians who claimed to be Maquis. I instinctively swung my Sten Gun in their direction and one of them approached, saying 'It's OK, Johnny, Gestapo!' I replied 'You Bastards' and just received a Gallic shrug. Afterwards, when I found out what the Gestapo did I felt quite ashamed of my reaction.

This section of a 1944 map shows the route Harry Warren took to end up on the Belgian coast near Ostend.

Savage reprisals

In popular fiction the Resistance were all heroes. Trouble is that there were three types. Firstly, the Communists. Probably the best organised, their priority object was to turn France into a Marxist State rather than fight the Germans. The second group were de Gaulle's freedom fighters. There was an obscure third band led by British Officers who operated south of the Dordogne. When they succeeded in killing Germans the Germans carried out savage reprisals. Anybody with kindly thoughts about the Nazis should visit the village of Oradour sur Glane near Limoges. On 10 June 1944 soldiers of the SS Panzer Division 'Das Reich' herded the local women and children into the Church and set it alight. The men were put in barns and machine-gunned in the legs, so that they could not escape when the barns, too, were torched. The village was then destroyed. On that day 638 persons were murdered; this was the same day when, back in England, I was able to go home and celebrate my birthday. Oradour stands today as it was left after the massacre. But be warned; it is something that you will not easily forget.

In late summer we left Bayeux heading for Belgium. I was co-driver of a three ton Bedford truck, a vehicle I'd never driven before. When my companion got tired I took the wheel. As we crested a ridge in the road an MP jumped on the running board and shouted 'Don't stop and don't go slower than 30mph'. It was the River Seine, bridged by pontoons. I kept going, the pontoons sinking alarmingly as our quite heavy lorry crossed each one. Had we stopped we would have toppled over and sunk like a stone. But the whole convoy managed it and we camped the night at Gourney near Rouen.

Travelling in a convoy can be tedious. My driver and I decided to seek adventure. So we slowed down until the forward vehicles were out of sight and then sped up to lose the ones behind. We noticed a road off to the left signed Albert, a name that had vague Great War connections, so we decided to investigate. Arriving in the main square we were surprised to find ourselves surrounded by excited civilians, mainly kids and old ladies. This was real Liberation excitement and what to do? Never having been trained in the art of Liberation we decided that the decent thing to do was to hand out some of the rations stored in the back. This was going down very well, until money started coming back. Oh dear, handing out rations would have been OK but 'flogging the stores' was a quite serious offence. So we stopped operations and crossed the square to dispose of our ill-gotten gains at a Pharmacy.

Entering the shop we got quite a shock, for at the counter stood a couple of Germans clearly making a purchase. 'Just ignore them', I hissed to my companion. They were unarmed and we had our personal weapons but a crowded Pharmacy was no place to start heroics. They soon left, accompanied by a couple of arm-banded Resistance types and it was explained the Germans were waiting to surrender and the Commandant was stocking up with essentials prior to captivity. It was all too much so we gave the money to the kids and beat a retreat.

We regained the main road and then, for a bit more excitement, took the next turning to the right. Before long things started to get a bit noisy and turning a corner we arrived at an American artillery position frantically trading rounds with the enemy. An American MP jumped on the running board and putting his .45 Automatic to my driver's head shouted 'Get this goddammed effing wagon out of here or I'll blow your effing brains out'. My driver tried a frantic three-point turn and we ended up across the road with the rear wheels spinning in the ditch. Disaster, but suddenly soldiers arrived en masse and lifted the rear end back on the road. As we departed, rather red-faced, Typhoon aircraft appeared overhead and sent missiles screeching towards the enemy.

> **"On VE Day a drunken Officer came up to me and said 'I'm glad the war is over, Lofty, because now I won't have to shoot you.' He had been told that it was top priority not to let the technicians fall into enemy hands."**

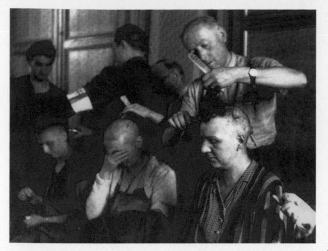
These women are having their heads shaved as punishment for consorting with German soldiers during the Occupation.

Declare undying love

We caught up with our Unit which had stopped by the roadside for the night. Thus ended a rather active, if unofficial, day. Our final destination was Den Haan in Belgium, reached by way of Lille and Ostend. An empty seaside hotel became our home and the radar was erected on the sand dunes. It turned out we were bang on top of a field of large anti-vehicle Teller mines, which had become deeply embedded in drifting sand. When exposed by the wind they could quite safely be lifted and removed.

We got down to the serious business of intercepting the Hun. As the Senior Technician for the Centimetric Radar I was very busy keeping 'on the air' with this vital equipment. Our location was interesting; to the east was the town of Blankenburg, completely evacuated. Further on, we had Zeebrugge, still occupied by the Germans. Once a day a couple of Canadian armoured cars from Ostend would pass us en route for Blankenburg where they would loose off a couple of rounds in the general direction of the enemy.

Soon after our arrival in Belgium, it was time for the locals to take revenge on the collaborators. Especially the women who had become too friendly with the Germans. And if you were one of these unfortunate women what's the solution to avoid the upcoming public humiliation? Easy, you locate the most stupid looking soldier, sailor or airman of the liberating forces and declare your undying love. Within a week of frantic courtship the mug has proposed marriage and has approached his CO for permission to marry (which is, of course, refused). This happened to one of our companions and one day he came running in shouting 'They've grabbed my fiancée and are going to torture her'. So we recruited colleagues and, mob-handed, headed towards the Marie with a view to rescuing the maiden. But there we found a large revengeful crowd; we simply stayed to watch the poor females being stripped, daubed with paint and having their heads shaved. It could have been worse; in Brussels, collaborators were being hanged from lamp posts. Such are the darker sides of Liberation.

One night there was a large explosion from the direction of Ostend. Next morning we discovered a long line of dead ATS girls washed up along the beach. It seemed such a terrible waste of young life and all we could do was pull them ashore and cover them until they were collected. But they had been discovered earlier by a local who had relieved them of their shoes. The footsteps in the sand told the story. Had we located this person he would undoubtedly been summarily executed. It appeared that a ship had been sunk by a mine upon entering the harbour. Death and destruction were never far away.

We had much of the German 'West Wall' as a playground. Pretty much destroyed, it still had masses of ammunition in underground bunkers. We vied with one another to create bigger and more dramatic explosions and having obtained German rifles and unlimited ammunition we used the beach fortifications for target practice. These wooden tripods had Teller mines on top and sometimes these would explode very dramatically but more often they just became riddled with bullets or caught fire, with a mini-explosion from the detonator. Needless to say, these antics were frowned upon by higher authority but discipline was pretty slack, as we technicians were left to our own devices so long as we kept the equipment capable of performing the requisite night-time activity. I remember our CO had liberated a German car and an Alsatian and he would often sit outside his tent with a drink in his hand and faithful dog by his side. One day he drove his Mercedes to recce Blankenburg but returned rather quickly with a bullet hole in the windscreen.

Insolent erk shifted

At Christmas 1944 it was rumoured that the Germans had broken through in the Ardennes and in true Blitzkrieg fashion were heading our way. As usual nobody knew the true situation. I recall that our Unit's only serious armament was a Browning machine-gun. Loading the gun with .303 ammunition was very sore on the fingers. We built a wall of sandbags and took it in turns to sit behind them with the gun awaiting the approach of the dreaded Tiger tanks. Fortunately they never arrived.

In March 1945 I came home on leave and can't forget my first wonderful sight of the white cliffs of Dover. On the ferry the tannoy warned: 'You will be searched by Customs at Folkestone and anybody found with contraband or illegal souvenirs will be returned to their Units'. In Dover Harbour somebody's nerve broke and a couple of hand-grenades went over the side. This provoked a rush of other 'souvenirs', anything from Schmeisser machine-guns to ornamental Nazi daggers. The harbour bed must be thick with rusting metal. Of course, when we arrived it was straight on the train to London. Being some of the first on leave we were cheered at level-crossings and as we passed

> **Our CO had liberated a German car and an Alsatian. One day he drove his Mercedes to recce Blankenburg but returned rather quickly with a bullet hole in the windscreen.**

the East End there were sheets hanging from the windows marked 'Well done Lads'. It was a very emotional time and Vera Lynn's *They'll be Bluebirds over the White Cliffs of Dover* can still bring tears to many an eye.

One day in the late spring I was sitting on top of the Type 14, sunbathing and slowly rotating. A Spitire came by and lazily circled around. I could see the pilot and gave him the usual two fingers (Victory?) salute. I continued my rotation and suddenly found myself being attacked by - so I thought - a swarm of bees. On the way down the 10 foot drop, my ears were blasted by the sound of eight machine-guns and my eyes observed the sea being churned up just off the shore. It is quite possible that out there, somewhere, an 80-something former Spitfire pilot tells the story of how he shifted an insolent erk at the end of the war.

VE Day had to be celebrated so after sending aloft all our hoarded star-shell mortar bombs, a fellow technician (Alan Potts, we still communicate at Christmas) and myself decided to set off some black powder. It was a windy night and Alan took too many chances. We ended up in hospital and were greeted with the cry 'Oh, here come the first of the VE casualties'. I was only scorched but Alan was kept in for several days. No action was taken.

Later, a drunken Officer came up to me and said, 'I'm glad the war is over, Lofty, because now I won't have to shoot you'. Apparently, when we came over to France, he had been told that it was top priority not to let the Centimetric equipment or the technicians fall into enemy hands.

PS. I write these notes in September 2004. In June I visited Normandy with my caravan and after a rather hair-raising drive through Caen, joined a couple of hundred 'odds & sods' type Veterans like myself at the Abbaye aux Dames to receive my Badge and a two-cheeked kiss from a VIP Frenchman. I must confess to having mixed feelings about this 60-year Reunion. Those men who stormed the Beaches and lost comrades in the early days deserved the honour of marching to Avranches and meeting the Queen. For myself, a confirmed Francophile who has visited France most years and has watched it transform from a smouldering disaster into a modern, highly efficient state, it seemed all a bit stage-managed and highly political. But perhaps my war was a bit unusual.

THE WESTERN FRONT

'In this, the twilight of their gods, the defenders of the Reich displayed the recklessness of fanaticism and the courage of despair...'

At 0500 hours on 8 February 1945, 1400 guns of the Canadian 1st Army opened fire on German positions along a seven-mile front between the Maas and Waal rivers close to the Dutch-German frontier. At 10.30 hours, Montgomery's XXX Corps, under the command of General Pat Crerar, moved into the attack with three divisions of British troops and two of Canadians. In reserve was the British 43rd Division and the tanks of the Guards Armoured Division.

The German position was heavily mined and included a flooded area and the thickly-wooded Reichswald Forest on one flank. Hitler and his commanders had viewed the risk of an attack in this sector as unlikely and Crerar's men had a good first day, taking in 1300 prisoners by nightfall.

On 10 February, the US Ninth Army were due to launch an offensive aimed at Dusseldorf on the Rhine but were frustrated in a landscape purposely flooded by the Germans. The flooding was also hampering the British advance and the enforced delay allowed the Germans to bring up paratrooper and panzer reinforcements.

The middle of February saw much bitter fighting. The Canadian Army official history records show the Germans seemed to have lost none of their morale: 'In this, the twilight of their gods, the defenders of the Reich displayed the recklessness of fanaticism and the courage of despair. In the contests west of the Rhine, in particular, they fought with special ferocity and resolution, rendering the battles in the Reichswald and Hochwald forests grimly memorable in the annals of this war.'

The Canadians secured the Reichswald and took the little town of Cleve before being reinforced across the Maas by the British 52nd Division and 11th Armoured. But in 11 days of fighting they had only advanced some 15 miles.

A *Daily Express* reporter recorded: 'So wet is this battle that the troops now call their commander Admiral Crerar. He often directs the fighting wearing fisherman's waders. The men mainly sing the Bing Crosby ditty, "..or would you rather be a fish?". The wounded come back from battle riding high in "ducks" across the floods.

'At any hour you are likely to meet Field-Marshal Montgomery... suddenly along the sodden road marked "Cleared of mines only to verges" comes a busy little jeep with a great red light flashing on and off by the radiator. Two grim MPs with red caps ride the bumps with stiff backs. Behind them comes the biggest car I ever saw, shining black and silver, with an outsized Union Jack fluttering at the bonnet. And inside alone sits Monty, who never misses a salute.'

Even so, the Allies were winning the war of attrition. Now the weather improved and Montgomery fixed 23 February for the start of a renewed attack (joint Operations *Veritable* and *Grenade*). In his order of the day to the men of the 21st Army Group, Monty assured them that this was to be the beginning of the last round against Germany.

The intended 'knock-out' blow was preceded by the biggest Allied air attack of the war with 10,000 bombers and fighter-bombers smashing the Third Reich's remaining communications network.

By the last day of February the Allies had broken through in a number of places. The Germans now saw that their only hope of staving off defeat in the west was to retreat behind the Rhine. Harried by the Allied air forces, thousands of men and vehicles escaped over the river. As the Allies closed up, the Germans ordered the demolition of all the Rhine bridges, to leave their enemy frustrated before this immense natural barrier. Getting across the river in strength would clearly be a daunting task.

Left: Cheerful Allied troops pictured massed for the entry to the Reichswald Forest in early February 1945. Ahead of them lay a desperate battle amongst the barrage-blasted trees, thick with German defence posts, and accessed by muddy and potholed tracks. The forest, along whose northern side ran the Siegfried Line, was cleared of the enemy by 13 February.

WAR DIARY

February 1945

The month opens with the Red Army spreading out across Poland as the German retreat continues. Fighting alongside the Russians is a considerable force of Polish soldiers who have embraced the communist doctrine, either through willingness or political expediency. On **1 February** the town of Torun falls. However, the weather does not favour the attackers and Marshal Zhukov's tanks massing along the River Oder are bogged down in a sea of mud.

1 February Far East: A massive 50,000 ton floating dry dock at Singapore is sunk by US Super-Fortresses. The dock had been constructed in Britain and towed the 8000 miles to the island prior to the outbreak of war. Ironically, it is the second time the dock has been sunk; the British scuttled it in the face of the Japanese invasion early in 1942.

2 February: The Hungarian capital Budapest remains under siege by Russian forces. Troops of the 1st French Army, together with US troops, today enter Colmar, south of Strasbourg in Alsace. This far south, Germany's Siegfried Line is on the eastern bank of the Rhine.

On **3 February** USAAF bombers drop 3000 tons of ordnance on Berlin. Five square miles of the city are set ablaze. Ecuador declares war on Germany and is soon to be joined by Venezuela, Chile and landlocked Paraguay. All these countries seek invitations to the planned post-war United Nations conference.

4 February: Stalin, Roosevelt and Churchill are meeting at Yalta on the Black Sea for a conference to discuss the post-war shape of Europe. They will agree on the division of Germany into four zones of occupation.
In Wales Rudolf Hess tries to commit suicide with a bread knife whilst under guard in a mental hospital. Hess, at one time Hitler's chosen successor, flew alone to Scotland in 1941 on a 'peace' mission clouded in secrecy.

All of the territory of Belgium is now free of the Nazi invaders.

5 February: The Red Army is crossing the River Oder and has secured a small salient on the other bank. On the same day, Greek communist insurgents give up their arms as the government agrees an amnesty. Weary diplomat Harold Macmillan is able to report to London that the civil war in Greece is over.

6 February: In the Philippines, General Douglas MacArthur announces the imminent liberation of the capital, Manila. House to house fighting continues in the downtown business area and the old city.

7 February: Russian forces continue to clear the east bank of the Oder of the relatively small numbers of Germans who still offer resistance. RAF bombers make night attacks on enemy troop concentrations around Cleve and Goch, between the Maas and Rhine rivers.

8 February: RAF Lancasters raid a synthetic oil plant at Politz near Stettin, Germany. The Nazi war machine is rapidly running out of fuel. Lancasters also drop 12,000lb bombs on concrete pens sheltering E-Boats at Ijmuiden, Holland. Two days later the RAF will return to hammer nearby U-Boat pens.

The German navy still has a considerable submarine force. The latest vessels incorporate ingenious devices to avoid detection by sea and air. The 'Schnorkel' is a tube or funnel device fitted aboard a U-Boat, enabling the latter to draw down fresh air from the surface and discharge exhaust gases from the engine. In this way, it can stay submerged for extended periods of time. Other U-Boats carry a gyro-plane in a special container on deck. The gyro-plane can lift an observer several hundred feet into the air and hover while he makes a reconnaissance for enemy warships or merchantmen. There is also the 'water donkey', a dummy U-Boat hauled behind a real submarine. The dummy boat creates a wake near the surface and attracts the attention of prowling Allied aircraft. Hit by bombs, the 'water donkey' releases oil and wreckage to convince the attackers they have destroyed a real U-Boat.

9 February: British and Canadian troops are pushing through a gap in the Siegfried Line following a bombardment by 1000 guns and a heavy bomber attack. The Canadians use amphibious vehicles to cross flooded lowlands and reach the Rhine.

Round-the-clock Allied bombing continues over German-held Europe throughout the early days of February.

10 February: The Nakajima aircraft works at Ota near Tokyo is the target of a raid by Super-Fortresses. Long range carrier-based Mustang fighters also struck at Japanese positions in the Chinese seaport of Tsingtao.

The important port of Elbing on the Vistula river is captured by Russian Marshal Rokossovsky's army, cutting the rail link between Berlin and Konigsberg in East Prussia.

11 February: Scottish troops enter the town of Cleve in Germany while Canadians occupy Millingen on the Rhine.

Burma: British and American bombers raid Rangoon today.

The 'Big Three' pictured at the Yalta Conference in February 1945, where plans for the post-war occupation of Germany and settlement of Europe's borders were discussed. Churchill, Roosevelt and Stalin and their advisers decided that British, American and Russian forces would each control a separate zone of Germany. France would also be invited to take a zone of occupation. A Central Control Commission representing the three major powers was to have its HQ in Berlin. The Nazi leaders would learn of the fate of their country only after agreeing to unconditional surrender to the Allies.

WAR DIARY
February 1945

12 February: At Yalta in the Crimea, US President Roosevelt, Russian leader Stalin and British Premier Churchill issue a statement on joint plans for the defeat of Germany of the post-war settlement of Europe. They also agree that a Conference of United Nations should be called to meet at San Francisco on 25 April 1945.

After a bloody 50-day siege, Budapest falls to the Russians on **13 February**. The Austrian capital, Vienna, is next in the Soviet sights.

14 February: The historic German city of Dresden, an important rail and communication centre for the Wehrmacht in their struggle to stem the Russian advance, is raided by around 800 Lancaster bombers who virtually obliterate the city. Over 50,000 people die in the resulting firestorm.

In New York, a pair of captured German spies - William Colepaugh and Erich Gimpel - who landed from a U-Boat last November, are sentenced to death.

15 February: Soviet forces encircle Breslau, where martial law is declared, and in Burma, Indian troops capture Pagan.

16 February: After a massive air and sea bombardment, American paratroops and seaborne forces assault on the island fortress of Corregidor that dominates the entrance to Manila Bay. The 5200 Japanese defenders, fighting from a maze of caves and tunnels, put up a fanatical defence. In early 1942, General McArthur left the doomed island garrison by fast torpedo boat in the face of overwhelming Japanese forces, vowing: 'I will return'. Now he is fulfilling his promise.

17 February: US carriers are into the second day of mounting big air raids on Tokyo and Yokohama. They will also complete the final wave of bombardments of Iwo Jima, ahead of the invasion. Four days of intensive ground fighting will follow before the Stars and Stripes are raised on Mount Suribachi, boosting the morale of the sorely tested marines.

18 February: German women are being drafted into the Volkssturm to support the armed forces – previously the call was for female volunteers. At the same time, the Soviet advance forces missile expert Wernher von Braun and other scientists to abandon the rocket establishment at Peenemunde on the Baltic coast.

On **19 February**, Heinrich Himmler meets Red Cross representative Count Folke Bernadotte to make overtures for peace talks with the western Allies.

In the Pacific US Marines land on the island of Iwo Jima in the Volcano Islands, less than 1000 miles from the Japanese mainland. Bitter fighting lies ahead.

The German garrison in cut-off Konigsberg stages a counter-attack to clear the road to Pillau.

20 February: En route from Yalta, US President Roosevelt and British Premier Winston Churchill meet for four hours in Cairo to discuss the war against Japan, in the aftermath of the certain defeat of Germany. Churchill confirms Britain is determined 'to throw everything it has against the Japanese'.

21 February: Japanese resistance ends on Luzon but fierce fighting continues on Corregidor and around Manila. Kamikaze aircraft sink the carrier *Bismarck Sea* and damage the *USS Saratoga*. The next day around 2000 Japanese soldiers die when a vast ammunition store on Corregidor blows up.

22 February: US troops cross the Saar river. Eisenhower claims that to date the Allies are holding 900,000 prisoners from the European campaign. Uruguay declares war on Germany and Japan.

23 February: The German garrison in Poznan has held out for a month against the Russians. Around 100 miles behind the front line, the survivors today surrender to the Russians. Its rail network will greatly assist him in the final assault on Berlin.

Turkey today declares war on Germany and its remaining Axis partners. The country can now claim a place at the UN Security

Conference in San Francisco in April.

24 February: Egypt's premier, Ahmed Maher Pasha is assassinated by gunmen from a pro-Axis group.

Thirty of the latest design U-Boats have been launched in German shipyards this month in the face of the tremendous Allied bombing campaign. By the end of February, the Kriegsmarine will have lost 19 submarines in action. The German navy's big problem is the attrition in experienced crew.

25 February: A raid by 172 B-29 bombers sees 450 tons of incendiaries drop on the centre of Tokyo, gutting around 28,000 buildings. At the same time, Berlin is the target for another massive 100-bomber daylight raid by the USAAF. Follow up attacks by RAF Mosquito fighter-bombers rekindle the fires as soon as they are extinguished. All over eastern Germany millions of refugees are making their way westwards, desperate to escape the advancing Russians.

28 February: In the Rhineland, on a 150 mile front from Trier in the south to Udem in the north, US, Canadian and British forces drive the Germans back towards the Rhine. The American Ninth Army is two miles from Munchen-Gladbach, the gateway to Düsseldorf. The famous city of Cologne with its distinctive cathedral is only 10 miles from the front and in range of US 150mm 'Long Tom' howitzers.

In Burma, after an 80 mile advance from the Irrawaddy, the 17th Indian Division and 255th Indian Tank Brigade encircle picturesque Meiktila. If Major General 'Punch' Cowan's column can take the town, the bulk of the Japanese army in Burma will be captured or killed.

On Iwo Jima, the Americans still face fierce pockets of resistance but have now taken the central airfield to facilitate fighter support for B-29 raids on Japan. In the Philippines, after the capture of Manila and Corregidor, the Americans land virtually unopposed on the island of Palawan, only 800 miles from the Chinese mainland and 250 miles from Japanese-held oilfields in North Borneo. Deep water anchorages will allow naval units to harass enemy shipping en route to Japan.

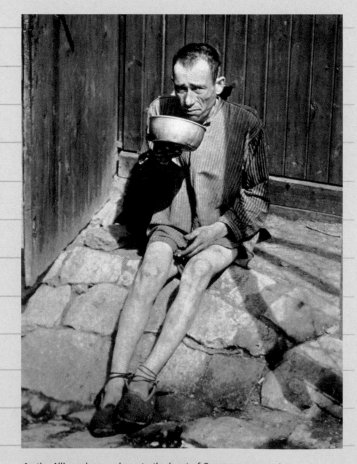

As the Allies advance closer to the heart of Germany more and more evidence of the Nazi genocide programme is uncovered with the discovery of concentration camps where millions of men, women and children - mainly of Jewish origin - have been murdered. A few inmates - such as this man - survive to bear witness to the horror.

Over the Rhine

MARCH 1945

Bax, Max and Big Ben!

A celebrated radio broadcaster but probably best-known as the most popular presenter of the BBC *Tomorrow's World* programme, Raymond Baxter was also a Spitfire pilot in World War Two. Here he recounts an unusual operation over Occupied Holland in the closing months of the conflict.

One evening in early March 1945 Squadron Leader Max Sutherland DFC, CO 602 (City of Glasgow) Squadron, gathered his four senior pilots to the bar at RAF Ludham. After the first round of drinks, his brown eyes blazing with challenge, he said, 'Listen chaps, I've got an idea'. Our minds became concentrated; we knew Max to be unpredictable, to say the least.

At that time we were flying our socks off in *Operation Big Ben* - the anti-V2 campaign. On several occasions during those ops we saw the white trail of V2 rockets arcing up at incredible speed and height towards their indiscriminate targets. It made us the more determined to strike back as hard as we could. Equipped with Spitfire XVIs we were dive-bombing every reported or suspected launch site, and dive-bombing, skip-bombing and strafing interdiction targets throughout Occupied Holland. In addition we were committed to normal Fighter Duties, Readiness, Bomber Escort (US and RAF), Air-

Sea Rescue and shipping and reconnaissance patrols. Four sorties per pilot per day were not uncommon.

'Just outside The Hague,' said Max, 'is the former HQ of Shell-Mex. It is now the HQ of V1 and V2 operations. I have worked out that the width of the building equals the total wing-span of five Spitfires in close formation'. He paused to let it sink in. 'I reckon we could take it out.'

Then he said, looking me straight in the eye, 'What do you reckon, Bax?' I took a long slow draught from my Guinness and said, 'Might be a bit dodgy, Boss.'

The concentration of heavy and lightflak from Den Helder to the Scheldt was our daily experience and later we learned that no less than 200 batteries of well-manned guns would lie in our path.

'Yeah, I know,' said Max. 'But we'll get 453 to lay on a diversion and we'll go in flat and low.'

453 were the Australian Squadron in our Wing, led by Squadron Leader Ernie Esau, another major character. They were our neighbours on the airfield, with whom we had developed a close bond both in the air and at the pub. So it was agreed and, somewhat surprisingly, approved by Group. After a disappointing abort, because cloud obscured the target on 18 March 1945, the attack was delivered precisely according to plan. We peeled off from 453 at about 8000 feet, crossing the Dutch coast, and Maxie transmitted the seldom-used codeword, 'Buster' (hill throttle), and 'Close Up'.

He then led us in a perfectly judged diving arc, in which the controls became increasingly heavy and, therefore, more demanding for

close formation. We flattened out at about 100 feet with the target dead ahead and square in our gyro-sights - range about 300 yards. We let go with our two x 20mm cannon and 0.5in machine guns and released our single 500lb and two 250lb, 11-second delay bombs 'in our own time'.

Black cockerel

Then, as I cleared the roof of the building, I looked ahead. And approaching me at eye-level, and near enough 400mph, was this black cockerel atop the weather vane on the church spire across the road! I can see it to this day.

The PRU (Photographic Reconnaissance Unit) print, which we had studied, showed the church (which we were determined not to hit), but not the height of its spire. With no space to turn, I could only tweak the stick and say, in my head, perhaps two seconds later, 'Thank You, God'.

Then the Boss damn near got his tail shot off. Our pre-attack briefing had been that the moment we cleared the target we should fan out, continuing at rooftop height. So five Spitfires swept at extremely low level across the centre of the Dutch capital. This, as was hoped, presented the anti-aircraft gunners with such a variety of fast-moving targets that the amount of flak we encountered was comparatively light. Unfortunately, however, Max Sutherland (as he had done on many occasions previously), decided to pull up to have a look back and assess the extent of the damage which we had inflicted with our 11-second delay bombs. This, of course, attracted the concentration of anti-aircraft fire

Above right: Raymond with dashing MG used to "impress an American nurse" as he relates in his book, Tales of my Time.

Opposite page: The dramatic painting by Michael Turner of the audacious raid on the Shell-Mex building near The Hague in Holland by 602 Squadron on 18 March 1945. Raymond Baxter's spitfire is the middle one.

Above: Raymond with Lt Sylvia K Johnson of the US Army Nursing Corps at her Bridport hospital on the eve of D-Day. The pair later married.

onto him. Nevertheless, he had the satisfaction of observing that the whole of the Shell-Mex building was occluded by a cloud of smoke, flame and dust.

But almost immediately, Max called us again, first using the call-sign 'Tarbrush' (as I recall) before saying, 'Proceed as planned to re-arm and re-fuel. I have been hit. Bax, please come and have a look at the damage.'

So, clear of the built-up area where the flak was, Max pulled up to about 3000 feet and, as the rest of the formation sped towards their refuelling point, I closed to him and had a careful look at his tail.

'Boss,' I said, 'you've got a big hit on your starboard elevator.'

'Is it still flyable, do you think, Bax?' he asked.

Up to you, Boss,' I said, 'but I'll keep a careful eye.'

'I will continue at bail-out height,' he replied. 'Please stay close.' So I did that, at about 3000 feet and on his starboard side, slightly behind and below, keeping a very careful eye on that severely damaged tail of my leader. We made it to the circuit at Ursahl, our planned refuelling point near Ghent in Belgium, and as Max had his airspeed indicator and flaps working I remained close and watched him make a perfect landing. Then I followed him in and we had time to

take a look at what we had achieved by comparing notes with our mates, who were all safely down and undamaged.

Bar to his DFC

Max got a Bar to his DFC for that, and the rest of us got a Collective Mention. The BBC News at 9pm that night reported, 'During the day, RAF fighter bombers continued their attacks on selected ground targets in Occupied Holland'. Just so!

Years later my friend Michael Turner, the distinguished aviation artist, read about my cockerel and said he'd like to paint a picture of it. Rummaging about in my box of goodies in which I keep my logbook, imagine his delight when I found the original PRU photograph on which our attack had been based. The resultant painting was shown in the Guild of Aviation Artists' Exhibition a few years ago.

A few months after that Michael received a letter from a total stranger in Holland requesting my address. It transpires that, totally by chance, Aad Devisser had visited an exhibition of Second World War aviation art, seen Michael's painting and realised that he too was there on 18 March 1945.

As a 16-year-old, he was doing his best to avoid deportation to a labour camp. With his parents he lived in caretaker quarters in the Shell-Mex building. As he described it, 'I heard you coming... and looked into your eyes.'

Mercifully, although we destroyed their home, he and his family survived, including the dog. My late friend, Aad Devisser, wrote of 'the admiration and gratitude he and his fellow Dutch men and women felt for the RAF pilots who were risking their lives for us.'

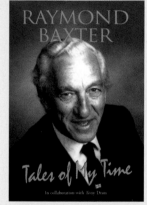

The story here appears as 'Opening Sequence' in *Tales of My Time*, the life story of Raymond Baxter as recounted to his good friend of many years, Tony Dron, himself an accomplished writer and veteran racing driver.

Raymond Baxter's life has been more action-packed than that of any comic book hero. A World War Two fighter pilot, he went on to become one of Britain's best-loved radio and TV commentators at major events from motor races to great State occasions. In his book he recalls such incidents as an amazing escape from a fiery doom at the controls of a Spitfire over Sicily in 1943 to speaking to the nation while suspended in a box near the roof of Westminster Abbey observing a Royal wedding. A spritely Octogenarian, Raymond still actively participates in the Dunkirk Little Ships organisation, making his latest commemorative return sailing in the summer of 2005 aboard *L'Orage*, a vessel which took part in the miraculous evacuation of the BEF in late May and the first days of June 1940.

Tales of My Time *was published by Grub Street in the autumn of 2005 at the bookshop price of £18. Visit: www.grubstreet.co.uk*

DIVISION KANADA

The German garrison in the Channel Islands called themselves 'Division Kanada' as they believed that country to be their eventual destination as POWs. However, in the spring of 1945 they proved that as far as they were concerned the war was far from over.

On 9 March 1945, the day that the American 9th Armoured Division famously captured the Remagen Bridge across the Rhine, Admiral Huffmeier, commander of the German forces on the Channel Islands, 500 miles behind the front, launched one of the most audacious commando raids of the war; he had sent his men to capture the French port of Granville, once Eisenhower's first HQ in France, and now a quiet backwater of the war.

Lt-Commander Sandel in the US torpedo boat PC 564 had been the first to spot the German convoy. The young naval officer had only taken over command a few days before and his crew was a scratch one, recruited mainly from US port offices in England. But he didn't hesitate. As soon as the first suspicious green blobs appeared on the radar screen, he set course for the Germans.

He saw them when they were three miles away. Immediately he ordered three flares to be shot into the air for identification purposes. But almost simultaneously, a German flare burst directly above his ship, bathing it in an icy white light. His response was immediate.

'Open fire!' he yelled to the gun crew. The 76mm cracked into action. The little ship shuddered. But the shell hit the water 200 yards away from the leading enemy ship. The crew went to fire again. Nothing happened – the brand new artillery piece had jammed after the first round!

Above: An 88mm anti-aircraft gun in Jersey with its Luftwaffe crew. The 'kills' ringed on the barrel were obtained prior to the gun coming to the island.

Complete surprise

The torpedo boat didn't get a second chance. With a roar a more powerful German 88mm gun opened up. The shell hit the bridge, killing or wounding everyone on it. Three more rounds punched into PC 564; drifting helplessly, its steering gone, its radio knocked out, the little ship disappeared into the night, leaving the Germans elated at the first success in their daring venture.

The Germans took the port by complete surprise. A French infantry company, alarmed by the noise, got out of their bunks. But their CO Captain Amand ordered them back to their quarters. Later, when asked why, the Frenchman shrugged and said, 'I thought the Americans were out on night manoeuvres and everybody knows that they do things completely different to the rest of the world.'

The Germans swarmed ashore. The US port commander ran for help but could find none.

The German engineers, working against time as they wanted to be at sea again before the dawn, blew up installations throughout the supply port, cheering every time a crane or loading device came crashing down.

Meanwhile, the infantry of Division Kanada swept through the town freeing their own men who were working for the Allies in the docks, jubilantly herding Allied officers, some still in their night clothes, out of their hotels at bayonet point and everywhere cramming anything edible down their starved throats. The audacious raid went without a hitch. The Germans took scores of prisoners, released 55 of their own men, blew up four ships and captured one British coaler complete with crew. When the first American Sherman crawled cautiously into the port just before dawn, it found the birds flown and the docks a smouldering shambles.

Besieged Dunkirk

A few days later Admiral Huffmeier held a parade at which he awarded the Iron Cross to several members of the raiding party. This he followed up with something more welcome than the piece of metal – a packet of cigarettes and a jar of looted jam for each man.

Huffmeier's example caught on. In besieged Dunkirk, Admiral Frisius headed a 12,000 strong garrison. He sent a force to attack the mainly Czech troops surrounding the port. The Germans caught the Allies completely off guard. While British tanks rolled into Lübeck in Germany, British engineers at Gravelines, 10 miles south of Dunkirk, blew the bridge across the River Aa in the face of the surprise attack. Over 89 Czech soldiers wandered into the triumphant Germans' POW cage!

All along the coastline Allied troops reported attacks by German forces, real or imaginary, and while in Germany itself the front-line Allied soldiers celebrated their imminent victory, their second-line comrades dug themselves in, fearful of further German commando attacks.

ESCAPE!

Around 2000 German POWs were housed in Island Farm Camp 98 at Bridgend, South Wales, in the opening months of 1945. A year previously, the camp had held US troops awaiting the invasion of Europe and General Eisenhower once paid a visit. Despite the fact that the war was clearly going very badly for their country, German morale was very high, although it was greatly influenced by a large number of pro-Nazi officers who held sway over the camp. Local civilians were subjected to loud singing of military songs and said the noise from the camp often resembled that of a 'bad tempered football crowd'.

On the night of 10/11 March 1945, a mass escape took place when some 70 prisoners made their way through a tunnel under the wire. For many the resulting freedom was short-lived and most were quickly rounded up. At Laleston, two miles from the camp, church bells were rung as an alarm for the first time since Churchill had ruled in 1940 that they were only to be sounded in the event of a German invasion.

However, four of the escapees – who included U-Boat commander Oswald Prior – managed to steal an Austin 10 car that belonged to Dr R Baird Milne. Intent on getting to the big airport at Croydon, they only made it as far as the Forest of Dean before running out of petrol. They next stowed away on a goods train and were finally caught near Castle Bromwich, about 110 miles from Bridgend.

Back in captivity, when one of the Germans learnt they'd taken a doctor's car, he apologised and offered to pay for the petrol!

BRIDGEWORK

The Allied crossing of the Rhine was the big story of March 1945. For the British it was going to be the last big operation of the war and Monty saw to it that the preparations were thorough, involving boats, airborne and a huge concentration of troops, tanks and artillery.

It was imagined that all the bridges over the Rhine were down. However, late in the day on 8 March the astonishing news broke that US troops had captured intact a bridge over the mighty river. The Germans had delayed blowing the Ludendorff Bridge at

Remagen, between the cities of Bonn and Coblenz, until the last moment in order to allow as many of their retreating soldiers across to the east bank as possible. Unfortunately for them , the demolition charges failed to ignite properly, leaving the bridge damaged but still standing. First Army US troops bravely rushed across to establish a first bridgehead in the German heartland.

Despite German shellfire, the bridgehead was rapidly reinforced under the cover of a powerful air 'umbrella' and US columns were soon probing deep into Germany. The Luftwaffe tried to bomb the bridge and enemy frogmen came down the river and attempted unsuccessfully to plant explosives on the structure's supports. In the middle of the month the damaged bridge collapsed into the Rhine but not before thousands of Allied men, tanks and vehicles had crossed into Germany.

It was a different story at Cologne, 35 miles to the north of Remagen. The city had long been a regular target of RAF bombers since 1941 and was the scene of the first 'thousand bomber raid' on 30 May 1942.

By March 1945 over 13,000 houses in the city had been damaged or destroyed and the Hohenzollern Bridge was down in the river (see photograph on page 243. However, Cologne's distinctive twin-spired cathedral led a charmed life; like St Paul's in London it was surrounded by rubble and broken buildings yet miraculously remained largely undamaged as can be seen in the photograph here.

Above: A painting of Cologne being bombed by the RAF (National Archives - Art of War).
Left: Cologne Cathedral still stands amidst the ruins of the city.
Right: The Ludendorff Bridge over the Rhine at Remagen.

The Rhine REMEMBERED

Above: Dennis Fox and Stan Scott. Dennis is in the top photograph.

Some British veterans of the Rhine crossing in March 1945 told their stories to Neil Barber.

Following the defeat of Hitler's last-gasp offensive in the Ardennes, bitter fighting continued for two months as the Western Allies forced the Germans back beyond the River Rhine. Being their last great natural defensive barrier all of the bridges across it had been destroyed during the retreat, apart from the Ludendorff railway bridge at Remagen, 30 miles south of Cologne, which was heroically captured by an element of the US 9th Armoured Division.

In the absence of a bridge further north, Field Marshal Montgomery devised *Operation Plunder*, a plan to secure a bridgehead on the east bank from which to break out and isolate the industrial Ruhr and to thrust into the northern plains of Germany.

The demarcation line between the two assaulting Allied formations – the British Second and the US Ninth Armies – was the important communications town of Wesel. Spearheaded by the 51st Highland and 15th Scottish Divisions, the British landings were to be carried out to the north, between Wesel and Rees, around 12 miles up river. Ferry crossings bringing reinforcements would continue until engineers were able to construct Bailey bridges.

All this would take time, so to protect the

bridgehead against counter-attack, part of the plan, *Operation Varsity*, employed the 17th US Airborne and Sixth British Airborne Divisions. Both were to land in an area several miles north of Wesel, and as far east as Hamminkeln on the River Issel, eight miles beyond the Rhine.

Operation Plunder was set to begin during the evening of the 23 March and *Varsity* the following morning.

The Highland Division's 5th Black Watch Battalion, which had been practising the crossing near Roermond on the River Maas, began its approach towards the crossing point at Rees. Supporting them were the Vickers heavy machine guns of 12 Platoon, 'C' Company, 1/7th Middlesex. Jeff Haward the platoon sergeant recalled, 'to avoid enemy identification, all markings on our vehicles were painted out and we had to wear our tunics inside out so that no badges were visible. However, the Dutch civilians were calling out, "good luck, Jocks!"'.

During the two days prior to the operation, the German positions were heavily bombed and, finally, with two hours to go, an immense barrage was begun by around 2000 heavy and medium artillery guns.

At 21.00 hours the Black Watch began its crossing, leading the way through a heavy smoke screen which had been laid to conceal the build-up and now the journey. Minutes later the Jocks wired back to say that they were safely on the east bank.

Then came the turn of the Middlesex. Jeff Haward gives this account: 'The Rhine was completely obscured by a smoke screen. Our

crossing was from the village of Honnepel near Rees, between two lines of green and orange Bofors shells. In our six Buffaloes [amphibious vehicle/troop carriers] of the 2nd Northants Yeomanry, we entered the water. Due to the strong current our progress was 'crab-wise', taking us downstream. This was to our advantage, as the German counter-fire was mainly falling where we should have crossed.

'It was the 21st birthday of one of my men, Dennis Daly. With this nasty stuff landing on either side of us, he said, "some bloody birthday this is!" Reaching the far bank, we managed to get onto a track. Enemy counter-fire was intense. I knew that if we went upstream, we would come to where we should have landed. Reaching our original landing area we were directed along a road where a guide from the Black Watch would be waiting. However, at this spot everyone was dead. Moving on, at a track junction was a Black Watch carrier upside down, its crew also all dead.

'Our officer, who had proceeded on foot, had not returned and, as we didn't know where we were to contact our infantry, I decided to halt our Carriers alongside a hedge, as there was fire coming from all directions. Of course, typically British, we had a brew up!'

Above: British and American airborne troops flew over the Rhine and landed beyond the east bank by parachute or glider. The operation cost many lives but achieved all its objectives. With the daunting physical barrier of the river now overcome, there was little to stop the Allies thrusting into the bomb-battered heart of Germany.

The 1st Commando Brigade had been given the task of capturing Wesel itself, and, at around the same time as the Black Watch, made a crossing a couple of miles north of Wesel. Half an hour later, having formed up, they waited while the RAF carried out a raid on the town. Almost before it was over the Commandos entered the smoking ruins, meeting various levels of resistance.

While heavy fighting raged in the villages to the north east, at 0200 hours, four battalions of the 15th Scottish Division began crossing at Xanten, seven miles from Wesel, and immediately became involved in fierce action.

Much of the Commando's work through the night was the clearing of pockets of enemy resistance in what was a mass of damaged buildings and rubble, but by the morning a large part of the town had been taken. Stan Scott was a member of 3 Troop, No 3 Commando. He remembers: 'I got to the top of what was left of a block of flats. There was a big empty space in front of me, tramlines in the middle and telephone poles. I was looking half-right. I thought, "is that something over there?" I had another look. It was Germans, five of them, coming this way, up the edge of the open space. All of a sudden one of them came forward. I waited, taking an aiming mark on a telephone pole.

'As he went behind the pole I squeezed the trigger and he came out the other side and met the bullet. It hit him straight through the neck, at about 300 yards – a good shot. I even missed his chin-strap! Up came Sergeant Jimmy Synnott. "What's up?," he asked. "A German. I just shot him. He had four mates over there."

'"Why didn't you wait?" he asked. "We could have got the bloody lot of them!" Although it was a good shot, I did deserve a b********g, but this was interrupted by a droning sound. It was the 17th American Airborne and the Sixth British Airborne. We were all saying "Cor! Look at that!" And Jimmy forgot my b********g!'

Their astonishment was due to the extraordinary procession of over 1500 planes and 1300 gliders. In near perfect weather, the Airborne began its assault, with the majority of paratroops managing to land on their respective Dropping Zones, although some ended up in trees of surrounding woods, making easy targets as they fought to free themselves.

Sergeant Sid Capon of the 9th Parachute Battalion was one of the fortunate ones: 'I ended up upside-down in a tree off the DZ. A Canadian Para saved my life by

climbing the tree and cutting my rigging lines. I was very dazed and walked straight across the DZ, but luckily managed to avoid all the bullets.'

The paras secured the DZs and moved off to capture their local objectives such as high ground. Groups of German paratroops dug in amongst the woods put up stiff resistance. Dennis Fox belonged to the 7th Parachute Battalion: 'We just got in this wood and there must have been a tank with an 88 up by the railway station. I was just getting down to this radio set and WHOOOFFF! "F****** hellfire, what was that ?" It blew me arse over tip.

'I got little bits of burning metal in my arm. I got up and there was Bill Bateman standing by this tree. Beside him was Major Fraser, he'd got little pieces in him. Bateman's arm was just hanging on by a piece of material. I'm giving him his morphine in the other arm, and WHOOOFFF! It hit this tree that he was leaning on... The same blast blew me down.

'So I got up and there was Bill, still standing there, but it took his head clean off. The officer was still there. The binoculars had buried in his chest. We managed to get Major Fraser to a barn on this farm where some Jerry first-aid people were.'

A little further east, glider troops of the 2nd Ox and Bucks approached their LZ beyond Hamminkeln. Johnny Johnson was in a glider containing six men and a jeep: 'We were hit twice in the air, once in the tail and then right underneath the two glider pilots. They were screaming their heads off but managed to get us down, crash-landed. We landed right on top of the German positions.

As the other gliders were landing, Jerry had machine guns trained on them and 88mm guns. I saw gliders hit in the air and jeeps and men falling out... It was terrible. Nearby were some power lines with six American paratroops, dropped wide, hanging on them, electrocuted.'

On the Rhine, although fighting continued in Rees, the follow-up battalions started crossing in other areas as further ferries came into operation. Through the morning and early afternoon the British and US Airborne troops gradually overcame their opponents, and at around 15.00 hours the first ground troops reached the Sixth Airborne.

By the end of the day three bridgeheads had been established north of Wesel; the Highland Division around Rees, 15th Scottish beyond Mehr and the Commandos in Wesel. To the south the Americans had met with similar success.

Over the next few days the bridgeheads were linked, and by 28 March had attained a depth of over 20 miles.

Varsity was a success, but an expensive one. On the 24th, the Sixth Airborne suffered 1078 men killed or wounded, with 50 aircraft and 11 gliders shot down. However, *Operation Plunder* paved the way for a rapid advance across Germany.

Neil Barber is an accomplished student of military history. His most recent book is The Day The Devils Dropped In (Pen and Sword Books Ltd) that tells the story of the British 9th Parachute Battalion's attack on the Merville Battery in Normandy on D-Day (see pages 92-93 of this book).

Right: Men of the Cheshire Regiment prepared to board LVTs (Landing Vehicles Tracked) that would ferry them over the Rhine in the afternoon of 24 March to rendezvous with the 1st Commando Assault Brigade who had secured a bridgehead the previous night.

Action Stations!

By early 1945 it was rare for any major engagements involving Allied and German surface warships to take place in the Mediterranean. A notable exception occurred on the night of 17 – 18 March when a pair of British destroyers intercepted three German warships off Cape Corse, the northern-most point of Corsica. C J Thorpe of Lincoln was a Seaman Torpedo man aboard *HMS Lookout* and participated in the action.

The British destroyers *Lookout* and *Meteor*, together with the French destroyers *Tempete* and *Basque*, were patrolling several miles apart to the westward of Cape Corse. The night was calm and by midnight the new crescent moon had long since set behind dark clouds. At 2am on the morning of 18 March information was suddenly received that three enemy warships were at sea and somewhere near Cape Corse.

After days and weeks of patrolling on the part of the Allied destroyers the news was almost too good to be true. The enemy was some 70 miles from his nearest bases at Genoa and Spezia. There was a reasonable chance that he might be intercepted before reaching the protection of his minefields and coastal batteries and without waiting for further orders, the *Meteor* and *Lookout* increased to full speed and steamed to northeastward. The Lookout, which was nearest, steered directly towards the enemy, while the *Meteor*, considerably to the westward, headed to cut him off if he retired north. The *Tempete* and *Basque*, further west still, moved to cover a convoy in the vicinity and later joined in the chase.

Glimmering wakes

One can imagine the scenes on board these ships at the prospect of action – the men in the engine and boiler rooms using every effort and artifice to obey the sudden order for full speed; the watch below tumbling out of their hammocks at the pipe 'Action Stations!'; the gun and torpedo tubes' crews mustering round their weapons and making them ready; the Captains and personnel on the bridges checking the relative positions of their own ships and the enemy and peering out through the darkness for a first glimpse of black shapes with their glimmering wakes and low waves.

The *Lookout* was alone. Her Captain, D H F Hetherington DSC, knew there were three enemy vessels and that the odds were against him. But acting in the best Service tradition he did not hesitate. He went in to attack, and his temerity was rewarded.

At two minutes past 3am the enemy was sighted – three ships in line ahead steaming at high speed for their bases and seemingly oblivious to any prospect of trouble. Sweeping down upon them the *Lookout* opened up a heavy fire at point blank range and fired torpedoes when the sights came on. The first few salvoes brought an ill-directed and confused reply from the enemy, though as the action proceeded it became accurate enough, the *Lookout* frequently passing through the spray flung up by falling shell.

Presently the second ship in the enemy line showed signs of distress. She turned out of the line and came to a standstill, with tongues of flame and dense clouds of smoke from fires between decks. Her crew abandoned ship, throwing rafts into the sea and themselves after them. The other two enemy ships, repeatedly hit by the *Lookout's* guns, made off to the northward at top speed, firing wildly back as they strove to make good their escape. In spite of the fire that had been poured upon her, the *Lookout* was entirely undamaged.

Solitary survivor

The *Meteor* made contact with the two fleeing enemy ships at 3.52pm, some 13 miles to the northward of where their consort had been sunk. Closing in the *Meteor* poured in a devastating fire and also fired torpedoes, one of which went home in a pillar of flame and smoke on the second ship in the enemy line, which finished her. The solitary survivor sought safety in flight and managed to

C J Thorpe pictured aboard HMS Lookout *late in the war. He sent us this account of the naval encounter off Cape Corse that is based on a contemporary report published in* The Times of Malta *dated 3 April 1945.*

escape into the enemy minefields and coastal batteries.

The *Meteor* rescued 120 men from her victim, all of them being Germans. When daylight came, no trace could be seen of the *Lookout's* opponent, but another 125 of her survivors were later rescued from rafts by coastal craft sent out to the scene of the action. The vessels sunk were ex-Italian warships each of about 1000 tons.

The *Meteor* and *Lookout* were both congratulated by the Commander-in-Chief, Mediterranean, Admiral Sir John Cunningham, on their most satisfactory night's work that still further reduced the small numbers of enemy warships now remaining in the ports of the Gulf of Genoa.

Captain Hetherington ended his Royal Navy career as a Rear Admiral.

Right: A painting by an unknown artist of a British warship in action (National Archives - Art of War).

WAR DIARY
march 1945

On **1 March**, US troops capture München-Gladbach and approach the town of Neuss. The Western Front now runs in almost a straight line from Holland in the north to France's border with Switzerland in the south. The River Rhine – swollen from the winter rain is the biggest obstacle in the way of the Allies.

2 March: Bucharest falls to the Red Army and the Kremlin will waste no time in installing a client communist regime. The people of Rumania have suffered ruination through the reckless gamble of their leaders when they joined Hitler in making war on their feared neighbour, Russia.

Cologne suffers an attack by 858 RAF bombers who leave much of the city in ruins. Miraculously, the 13th Century Gothic cathedral is hardly damaged and regular services continue to be held in the vestry.

3 March: The last pockets of resistance in Manila are mopped up by US forces. Over 20,000 Japanese soldiers have died defending the capital of the Philippines. Also in the Far East, Meiktila, south of Mandalay in Burma, is declared free of the enemy.

Meanwhile, in Holland over 500 civilians die in The Hague when an RAF attack on a V2 rocket site misses the target.

For the first time since June 1944, Luftwaffe piloted aircraft bomb random targets in southern and northern England. Around 70 fighter-bombers and Heinkel 188s are involved; up to eight of the raiders are believed shot down.

4 March: German bombers again target England, but in smaller numbers than last night. Luftwaffe night fighters shoot down 20 British bombers returning from a raid on the Dortmund-Ems canal.

On the same day, Finland joins the list of nations formally declaring war on Germany and American armour reaches the Rhine between Cologne and Düsseldorf.

5 March: Desperate to bolster their fighting strength, Germany is conscripting 16-year-old boys to do battle against the advancing Allies. Some have already been awarded the Iron Cross for destroying Allied tanks with *panzerfaust* (bazooka) rounds. Today US troops are entering the suburbs of Cologne on the west bank of the Rhine.

Buckingham Palace reveals that the King has granted to Her Royal Highness the Princess Elizabeth a commission with honorary rank of second subaltern in the Auxiliary Territorial Service. At present the Princess is attending a driver training course at a centre in the south of England.

6 March: Dutch resistance fighters who today ambush SS General Hans Rauter planned to execute him for 'crimes against the people of Holland'. The attempt fails and 17 Dutchmen will be executed in reprisal.

7 March: US troops are amazed to find a bridge over the Rhine intact at Remagen when demolition charges fail to explode. Soldiers make it to the eastern side of the Ludendorff Bridge and form a perimeter. General Omar Bradley tells his commanders to 'shove everything you can across it'.

In the Far East, Chinese forces capture Lashio, terminus of the Burma Road supply line from India to China.

British newspapers report that the milk ration for non-priority adult consumers is to be increased from two pints to two and half pints a week later this month.

8 March: Late tonight, and with great audacity, the Germans launch a surprise attack from the Channel Islands against the port of Granville in Normandy, around 500 miles behind the Allied armies on the Western Front.

9 March: The Red Cross supply ship *Vega* berths in Jersey, bringing more provisions for the civilian population and a small quantity of petrol for the island's ambulance.

In Indo-China, the Japanese go on the offensive against French troops who seek to re-impose colonial rule by Paris.

10 March: Tokyo suffers the single most destructive air raid of the war so far when hit by US B-29 Super-Fortresses flying from the Marianas Islands. Around 16 square miles of the industrial area of the city are destroyed and around 83,000 people die.

11 March: Nagoya in Japan is bombed by 285 Super-Fortresses.

Europe also racks up a record raid in the same 24-hour period when 1108 RAF bombers drop 4851 tons of ordnance on Dortmund. Another 1079 Allied planes shatter the vital Krupp works at Essen. U-Boat yards and oil refineries at Hamburg, Kiel and Bremen are also attacked.

In Wales, German prisoners stage their own 'Great Escape' when 66 men exit their camp via a 45ft-long tunnel under the barbed wire. By nightfall 43 have been recaptured, some by Land Girls armed with pitchforks.

12 March: The bridgehead at Remagen is now over 10 miles wide and four miles deep. The Germans have tried to bomb the bridge and have also sent frogmen down the Rhine with explosive charges, but all attacks fail.

13 March: A young girl dies of typhus in the Bergen-Belsen concentration camp. Her name is Anne Frank. Although she is just one of millions to perish without trace in the Holocaust, the diary of her wartime experiences – not found by the Nazis when they discovered her family's Amsterdam hiding place – will become an icon of how the human spirit can shine through in the midst of evil.

Anne Frank

14 March: The supply of oil from Hungary to Germany is further curtailed after Allied bombers strike refineries just 35 miles away from the advancing Russians.

15 March: *The Daily Telegraph* reports how last night RAF 617 Squadron – The Dambusters – scored a direct hit on the Bielefeld viaduct using an enormous 22,000lb Grand Slam bomb designed by Barnes Wallis. The viaduct carried the last intact double track rail line out of the armaments manufacturing Ruhr region of Germany. Though factories will continue to build tanks and aircraft, the means to transport them to the front lines in east and west has been all but destroyed.

16 March: Rudolf Hoess, former commandant of the death camp at Auschwitz, admits he had two million inmates murdered – mainly gassed – between June 1941 and the end of 1943 on the express orders of Hitler's cohort, Himmler.

The V2 offensive against England is all but over. Although some of the elusive mobile launch sites in Holland have evaded Allied air attacks, lack of fuel and the inability to transport newly-built rockets is curtailing the campaign. One of the last blasts hits Smithfield Market in London, where 110 people are killed and 123 seriously injured.

17 March: Supreme Allied Commander Dwight D Eisenhower reins in General 'Blood and Guts' Patton and orders a halt to any advance towards the Czech border, now less than 100 miles away, even though the Germans have little to stop the

Americans from reaching Prague before the Russians.

The bridge at Remagen collapses today, causing the death of 28 US soldiers.

In Tokyo, the Japanese leadership order children over the age of seven to give up school and assist in the war effort.

18 March: The Polish First Army captures Kolberg as Russian forces close in on the Baltic ports of Danzig and Gdynia.

In the Pacific, US warships bombard enemy positions on the Kurile Islands, north of the Japanese mainland.

19 March: Hitler issues the 'Nero Command,' demanding that Germans choose the utter destruction of the Fatherland over surrendering to the Allies. 'If the war is lost, the nation will also perish,' he declares.

German jet aircraft works are attacked in the south of Germany.

The British Government says that peace will signal a two-year period of frantic house-building. With 750,000 new dwellings required, hundreds of thousands of building workers will be given priority release from the services.

20 March: In Burma, the 19th Indian Division under Major General Peter Rees capture Fort Dufferin in Mandalay. The city is finally secured after 10 days of close quarter fighting, much of it with swords, bayonets and kukris.

Overshadowed by events in North West Europe, in Italy the Allies are preparing a major offensive to trap the German army in the Po Valley. Shortages of ammunition and the transfer of units to the Western Front are made up for by the arrival of new flame-throwing tanks and 400 amphibious troop carriers, ideally suited to river crossings.

21 March: General Heinz Guderian fails to persuade Himmler to accompany him to Berlin to help persuade Hitler to seek an armistice.

Denmark: RAF Mosquito aircraft bomb the Gestapo HQ in Copenhagen.

22 March: General Patton sends his Third Army troops across the Rhine at Oppenheim, south of Mainz. Montgomery is disappointed that Patton's move pre-empts his own major Rhine crossing further north, planned for tomorrow.

23 March: Monty's army of British, Canadian and US forces cross the Rhine in the Wesel Sector. The British general promises to 'chase the enemy from pillar to post,' across the North German plain.

A *Daily Telegraph* report from US war correspondent Cornelius Ryan describes the last stand of German forces on the west bank of the Rhine in the Mainz-Wurz area. The Germans are desperate to cross the river, but are caught between General Patton's Third Army and the Seventh Army of General Patch. Ryan observes: 'It is a hopeless venture for the Germans. They cannot hope to hold out very long because of the terrific weight of men and material that threatens them from either side.'

24 March: The German Ninth Army commanded by General Busse has mounted unsuccessful attacks twice in recent days in attempts to relieve the encircled defenders of Kustrin. Hitler orders Busse to prepare for another attack.

25 March: Many American generals believe they can make it to Berlin before the Russians get there. Major-General Isaac D White, commander of the Second Armoured 'Hell on Wheels' Division has detailed orders and map overlays completed today. His plan is to advance to Magdeburg on the Elbe, 80 miles away. Once across the river his men will dash up the autobahn and he believes they could make it to Berlin within 48 hours.

26 March: Carrier-based planes of the British Pacific Fleet carry out attacks on airfields on Okinawa, Formosa and neighbouring islands. Taking Okinawa will be the final step before an assault on the Japanese home islands. A vast invasion force of 1400 ships carrying 182,000 troops is *en route*.

Hitler's deputy, Martin Bormann, calls for volunteers to become 'Werewolf' guerillas who will strike at the enemy from any direction in the Fatherland.

27 March: The last V2 to fall on Britain strikes Orpington in Kent today. Since early September 1944 it is reckoned that 1050 rockets have targeted Britain, killing 2754 people and injuring another 6523.

US troops land on the island of Cebu in the Philippines.

Soviet forces break into Danzig and Gydnia in East Prussia. General Busse mounts another attempt to relieve the German forces trapped in Kustrin. Although some of his Ninth Army panzers break through to the city, the main attack is smashed by an overwhelming massive Russian artillery barrage. Busse reports he has lost 8000 men in the fruitless fighting.

28 March: Berlin is the target of wave after wave of Russian fighter planes who rake the city with machine gun fire. The German capital is just 50 miles from the Red Army's leading tank spearheads. They are meeting fierce resistance. Western forces are nearly 200 miles from the Nazi capital, but face light opposition. Churchill has advised the Americans that, 'we should shake hands with the Russians as far to the east as possible.'

29 March: Montgomery's armour reports a significant advance out of their bridgehead on the east bank of the Rhine. British and Canadian troops clear Emmerich and cross from Holland into Germany.

30 March: The famous German university town of Heidelberg falls to the US Seventh Army. General Tolbukin's Russian forces cross into Austria from Hungary. General Slim's Fourteenth Army reports the capture of the important town of Kyaukse in Burma. Grapefruit from the Middle East has been arriving in British shops recently costing 8d per lb.

31 March: Allied HQ issue a bulletin claiming the Allies are poised for the final attack on Germany. The ultimate goal of Montgomery's 21st Army Group is Germany's Baltic ports. Patton is about to link up with the US First Army at Kassel while the French First Army is over the Rhine between Mannheim and Karlsruhe and swinging south towards the Swiss border.

In Japan, US Super-Fortresses bomb airfields in Kyushu and the aircraft factories at Nagoya are hit again.

A timely warning that danger lies ahead.

BLOODY
END FOR
HITLER
AND HIS
1000 YEAR
REICH

APRIL 1945

VICTORY! THE RED ARMY RAISE THEIR FLAG OVER THE REICHSTAG BUILDING IN BERLIN

Daily Mail

NO. 15,285 ONE PENNY ★ ★ FOR KING AND EMPIRE WEDNESDAY, MAY 2, 1945

LATE WAR NEWS

HITLER DEAD, GERMAN RADIO TELLS WORLD

Admiral Doenitz is new Führer: 'The battle goes on'

ADOLF HITLER is dead. Grand Admiral Doenitz, Commander-in-Chief of the German Navy, has been appointed his successor. The German radio gave this news to the world at 10.25 last night in the following words: "It is reported from the Führer's headquarters that our Führer, Adolf Hitler, has fallen this afternoon in his command post in the Reich Chancellery fighting to his last breath against Bolshevism."

"On April 30 [Monday] the Führer appointed Grand Admiral Doenitz as his successor. The Grand Admiral will now speak to the German people."

Admiral Doenitz, who immediately came on the air, said: "My task is to save the German people from annihilation at the hands of Bolshevism. We shall have to fight on against the British and Americans so far as they hinder our aim."

The naming of the admiral as the new Führer comes as a complete surprise.

It suggests that what remains of Germany has been split into two camps—those who wish to fight on, led by Doenitz, and those who want to surrender, led by Himmler.

It is significant that no reference was made in the announcement to Himmler, who has already offered unconditional surrender to Britain and the United States, and is expected to comply with the Allied demand that capitulation must be made also to Russia.

Doenitz said: "German men and women, soldiers of the German Army, our Führer, Adolf Hitler, has fallen. The German people are bowed in sorrow and reverence.

"Our Führer had recognised very early the grim danger of Bolshevism and consecrated his life to the struggle against it.

"At the end of his struggle he met a hero's death in the capital of the German Reich.

'WE FIGHT SOVIETS'

"The Führer's life was given entirely to the

✌ DAY
The full official plans

By Daily Mail Political Correspondent

NEWS that the war in Europe is over will be given by the Prime Minister in a special B.B.C. broadcast. This may be given by Mr. Churchill at any hour of the day or night in the very near future.

It will be followed by a broadcast by the King to the Empire, which has been fixed for nine o'clock on the night of VE-Day.

The day following, as well as VE-Day, will be a Public Holiday.

The Home Office letter sent out to local authorities last night suggested the opening of churches and chapels for private prayer on VE-Day, and the ringing of church bells throughout the country.

☆

THE appointment of the Sunday following VE-Day as a Day of Prayer and Thanksgiving to be accompanied by local victory parades in which all representatives of the armed and civil forces in the district shall take part.

The King will attend St. Paul's, in London, on this day and will be represented at special services at Edinburgh, Belfast, and Cardiff.

Local authorities are urged to use such floodlighting facilities as they have, but street fighting will not be restored in full and the dim-out will be continued in coast areas.

All public buildings in London—Buckingham Palace, Whitehall, and the Houses of Parliament—will be floodlit on the night of VE-Day.

Searchlights will play a part in the illuminations.

Nazi radio kept world in suspense

Wagner build-up

By Daily Mail Reporter

BEFORE the announcement of Hitler's death, Hamburg radio held the world in suspense for more than an hour.

From 9 p.m. until 9.30 Wagner's Tannhäuser Overture and a piano concerto by Weber were played.

This was interrupted with the warning: "Please stand by for an important announcement! It will be broadcast on this wavelength."

The station went silent for a while.

At 9.40 the stand-by warning was repeated and Wagner's "Twilight of the Gods" was played.

At 9.43 the announcer shouted: "Achtung! Achtung! the German Broadcasting System is going to give an important German Government announcement for the German people."

The old phrase

It was the first time since Hitler came to power that the term "German Government" was used over the German radio. Previously all major announcements were made "by the Führer."

More music followed, this time from Wagner's "Rhinegold."

At 9.35 a woman announcer at the Bremen station, which had been

NO NEWS FROM HIMMLER, BUT
Surrender begins on three fronts

REPORTS received in London late last night indicated that, while no fresh offer of capitulation has been received from Himmler, large German forces on widely separated fronts have begun to surrender piecemeal to the Allies with or without his authority.

Here is the latest position:

DENMARK.—German occupation forces were reported from Stockholm to be evacuating the country with all speed.

NORWAY.—Negotiations are said to be going on for the German garrisons to lay down their arms at the Swedish frontier.

CZECHO-SLOVAKIA : A delegation of German and Czech industrialists was reported by Luxemburg radio to have left Prague to meet Allied representatives and hand over the territories of Bohemia and Moravia.

ITALY : Marshal Graziani and Lieut.-General Pemsel, German Chief of Staff of the Italian Fascist Ligurian Army, last night announced the surrender of that army and ordered all troops to lay down their arms.

Count Bernadotte, on arriving back in Stockholm yesterday, told a Press conference that he had not seen Himmler during his second visit to Denmark and had brought no fresh message from any German authority.

German army scurries out of Denmark

From Daily Mail Correspondent

STOCKHOLM, Tuesday.

THE "Battle of Denmark" is beginning and ending simultaneously to-day. As Montgomery sweeps through the German northern province of Schleswig Holstein towards the Kiel Canal and the Southern Jutland border, the Germans are scurrying out of most big Danish towns.

Busmen to strike to-day

LONDON busmen at Camberwell, Clapham, and Streatham garages decided late last night to go on strike to-day in protest against the summer schedules. Their decision followed an agree-

FOOD SHIPS FOR DUTCH

SHAEF announces Allied and German representatives made agreements for food supply to Dutch by air, sea, and road. Ten air-dropping zones agreed ; food ships to enter Rotterdam, and Germans to make available one main road. Supply starts to-day.

ment reached at a union conference with London Transport to work the schedules, as from to-day, pending discussion of the men's call for more buses.

DEATH OF THE DICTATORS

As April opened there was cheering news for the Allies from every theatre of war. In Burma Lord Louis Mountbatten declared that the Japanese forces in the country had been decisively defeated and no longer existed as an effective fighting force. In the Pacific the Americans were grinding down the Japanese ability to wage war. On the Chinese mainland, Nationalist and Communist forces were attacking the Japanese.

But it was events in Northern Europe that most occupied the attention of the British press and radio. On the Western Front prisoners were coming in at a rate of 25,000 a day and British, Canadian, US and French formations reported daily gains. The Red Army too was rampant, clearing Hungary of the Germans and taking the centre of Vienna on 9 April. The Russians were also inexorably closing in on Berlin. Only diehard Nazis refused to believe that utter defeat was inevitable.

Battle of Berlin

Hitler's cohorts were briefly cheered on 12 April when they heard the news of US President Roosevelt's death. Propaganda Minister Josef Goebbels congratulated his Fuhrer and assured him it was the turning point of the war, citing astrological predictions as evidence. However, when Harry Truman was sworn in as the new President and the Allies remained clearly resolute in their aim of inflicting total defeat on Germany, a cloud of depression again descended on Hitler's bunker in the heart of Berlin.

The German leader was 56 on 20 April, by which date the rumble of Russian artillery was clearly audible in Berlin. Two days later the battle for the city began, an eight day fight of apocalyptic proportions that cost the lives of hundreds of thousands of German soldiers, civilians and Red Army men and further devastated the already bomb-blasted capital.

Hitler held out hope of a last-gasp relief of Berlin by one of his few remaining cohesive forces. But when Russian forces got within a few hundred yards of his bunker, the Dictator knew his time was up. At 3.30pm on 30 April 1945, Hitler shot himself; his bride of just a few hours, Eva Braun, took poison. Both bodies were dumped in a shell hole, doused in petrol and set alight.

On the same day that Hitler died, the symbolic Reichstag building fell to the Russians. The vaunted 'Thousand Year Reich' was all but ended.

In Italy, two days earlier, another Dictator with much blood on his hands came to a gruesome end. Benito Mussolini, his mistress Clara Petacci and a dozen supporters were captured by partisans at Dongo on Lake Como as they fled towards Switzerland. Executed by firing squad, their bodies were hung upside down on a garage forecourt in Milan and reviled by a jeering crowd.

Adolf Hitler, pictured with Benito Mussolini.

MEIKTILA MEMORIES

Eric White's war saw him shooting at Doodlebugs over Kent and being shot at on a latrine in Burma. For good measure he later participated in a police raid on a Tong gang gathering in Hong Kong.

I recently looked at a map of Burma and saw Meiktila. At once, I was there again. The 17th Indian Division had cut the Japanese line of communication between Mandaly and Rangoon and all hell was let loose. General Honda had been ordered to retake Meiktila at any cost.

But I must start from the beginning. I was called up at the start of 1940 (I am now aged 85). I chose the RAF because my mother had brought home from one of her cleaning jobs copies of *War Illustrated* that told the story of the Great War (1914 to 1918). Although I was very young, I learned to read from these publications and the experience made me never want to end up in a trench; that's why it was the RAF for me!

After several gunnery courses at Douglas and Ronaldsway on the Isle of Man, I became a Ground Gunner manning all kinds of guns on various airfields. Later we became the RAF Regiment. I was promoted to Sergeant 1/c in No 3 Flight 2853 Squadron and when I marched my men on to the parade ground windows went up to watch a very smart display of drill.

When the Flying Bombs came we formed part of the 'Diver Belt' across Kent meant to prevent Hitler's rockets from reaching London. First we were based at Dungeness then at Sandgate, right in the path of their fixed course. The Flying Bombs had the unmistakable sound of a two-stroke motor bike and were coming over continually. Behind us were heavy guns. Any rocket that was hit usually came down on or near us. I was also bemused to find myself in a trench for the first time!

We were near the beach and on one occasion, when swimming amidst the barbed wire, we were strafed by a ME109. I saw the bullets ripping up the water.

Over 'The Hump'

When this was over I joined an RAF Regiment Squadron that was going overseas 'to guard the Khyber Pass.' Great I thought. We sailed from Liverpool on the *Queen of Bermuda*. In India we went by train to Agartala to do a battle course after which my CO asked me to go on a three-inch mortar course with the Army. This was a new weapon for us. I was to take four corporals

and 14 men. We also had a young officer who promptly went sick and was never seen again. I was left in full charge.

At the end of the course our depot gave me two of the latest three-inch mortars with reinforced base plate and barrel to take better bombs. The mortar is a simple weapon; the barrel has a fixed firing pin and provided you're handed the bomb right way round you drop it down the barrel and if the angle of barrel and compass bearing etc are all lined up you usually get the mortar bomb on target. 'Keep them well oiled in their wooden boxes. Being RAF you will never use them,' was the advice. Next minute we (me and my team) are sat on forms along both sides of this American aircraft with our mortars and bombs lined along the centre in front of us. We took off and flew over 'The Hump'. This was the name given to the range of hills or mountains separating India and Burma. There were lots of air pockets. Though we didn't know it at the time, Meiktila airstrip was below us and all around us puffs of smoke appeared. We were being fired upon by Japanese anti-aircraft guns. The thought occurred that we had no parachutes. The American pilot skillfully avoided getting hit and we landed.

We were still under fire and all our gear was more or less thrown off. 'Handle high explosive mortar bombs with care' didn't apply. An army major with jeep and trailer appeared (he had been expecting us) and I tried to tell him we were RAF Regiment. 'You're in the ******** 17th Indian Division now!' he exclaimed upon arriving on the perimeter.

Rock hard ground

We were ordered to dig a pair of mortar pits with a communicating trench and issued with a field telephone and a list of 16 targets. I still have the list. It includes range and compass bearings and different code names: Thorneycroft, Terraplane, Trogan, Patna, Able 3, Peter 5, Nagpur, Dodge, Morong, Lahore etc. The OP (Observation Post) would watch for any enemy in any of these places. Digging in was difficult as the ground was rock hard but we were well exposed and spurred on by enemy fire. By evening we were almost ready. The field telephone rang with the instruction to line up on Nagpur, as none of our patrols would be in the area that night. Both mortars were lined up but both were not pointing the same way. We had to sort if out. Eventually we became very good at it.

Top: Eric pictured with his wife Joan. Today the couple live near Warrington, Lancashire.

Left: A section of a map of the Meiktila area of Burma that has remained in Eric's possession since 1944.

Inset on the map is a Japanese propaganda leaflet that Eric collected in Burma. They were intended for the Burmese population and aimed to convince them that the British and Americans were their real enemy and that Japan was their friend.

In order to prevent disease we had two latrines. One for night and one for day. It was preferable to use the day one even though it was outside the wire. One day a Sgt Major asked if I was going to the day latrine. We both put a full magazine in our Sten guns and set off for the toilet, which was two oil drums dug into the ground with holes in the top to sit on and very hot with the sun. We were sat talking and suddenly – ping ping; bullets were hitting our drums! Understandably, we got away pretty smartish.

Back in relative safety, the Sgt Major got his cigarettes out. His Sten gun sling was over his shoulder as he lit his cigarette. The sling slid off his shoulder and the butt of the gun hit the floor, whereupon the bolt of the gun recoiled and fired a 9mm bullet into his person. The Sgt Major was evacuated by air. I was glad I didn't smoke.

After Meiktila we rejoined our squadron and went down to Toungo, Pegu, and Rangoon. I was told to ride a motorcycle – a Matchless, I believe, and get ahead of the convoy to check the road was clear and then wave it on. My job was then to catch up with the convoy, get past it and do the same 'wave on' procedure further down the road.

Japanese stragglers

I remember it was wonderful riding that machine. But then it rained and I stopped to put on my gas cape and was delayed. I got going again but then suddenly there were some Gurkhas by the road waving at me to stop. There were Japanese stragglers in the area so I did as they indicated but unfortunately crashed in my haste. The bike was damaged and I gashed my leg. The Gurkhas bandaged me up and gave me an anti-tetanus injection. Eventually, I got the bike going again, but in first gear only. I got as far as Pegu before the engine finally seized up.

We were in Rangoon making preparations to attack heavily-mined Japanese-held islands when the atomic bombs were dropped that ended the war.

Next stop was Hong Kong where I was attached to the police on the Kowloon side. One day we found ourselves waiting in an opium den breathing it in. Across the road was a brothel where we had been tipped off some Tong gang leaders were meeting to play Mah Jong. At a given signal we dashed across the road up the stairs and arrested them.

Upon leaving the colony I was given this reference by E Tyrer, Supt of Police, Hong Kong: '995494 Sgt White E RAF Regiment has been working in cooperation with the Hong Kong police force for the last two months. He has been employed on special preventative measures against armed robbers. He has shown himself to be a capable executive officer'.

Back in Britain I then did 30 years in the prison service.

Eric White lives in Warrington, Cheshire.

The photograph above features Eric and pals in a trench at Meiktila in the spring of 1945. It was first published in The Yorkshire Post of 11 August 1945 with the headline, 'Yorkshiremen in Burma'. When the photograph was first released by the Air Ministry on 27 April 1945 the full caption read: 'After defending the Meiktila airstrip in Central Burma in conjunction with other ground forces against the crack Japanese Imperial Guards Regiment for nearly four weeks, the men of the RAF Regiment are now having a few days rest by the side of Lake Meiktila. The Japanese suffered very heavy losses and casualties were sustained by the Regiment.

'These Regiment gunners were photographed in a Japanese foxhole and come from the Yorkshire area.

Left to right they are: Sergeant 'Chalky' White of 30 Church Lane, Crossgates, Leeds; Leading Aircraftman William Thompson of 20 Regent Place, Keighley; Leading Aircraftman Norman Wingfield of 12 North Bridge Road, Doncaster and Leading Aircraftman Walter Priestley of 185 Granville Street, Park, Sheffield.

The photograph is inset on the actual mortar target co-ordinates issued to Eric and his men at Meiktila and is one of a number of fascinating items of memorabilia he has in his possession. The reverse of the form was utilised to list casualties (reproduced in part below). Inset on the co-ordinates document is an example of a Japanese Occupation banknote.

Casualty Return–V.C.Os ; British and Indian W.Os and other ranks ; non-combatants (enrolled) ; and non-gazetted European and Indian Civilian Personnel.

All down to luck

Don Feesey recalls some cruel twists and turns of fate for air crews.

In the last years of the war I was a navigator in a four-engined Lancaster bomber, following 24 months of concentrated training in classrooms and in the air taking in astro navigation, meteorology, armaments, photography, aircraft recognition and engines. To qualify required tough study.

There were seven airmen in a Lancaster crew - pilot, engineer, bomb-aimer, navigator, wireless operator, mid-upper gunner and rear gunner. Our squadron was located in a desolate part of North Lincolnshire, where the wintry weather of 1944/45 consisted of frequent fogs, frost and snow. It all added to the strain of the constant night operations over Germany. For navigators there was a great deal of pre-flight preparation to be done, and often these efforts were wasted when a raid was 'scrubbed' at the last minute due to weather conditions locally or over Germany.

Once in the air, the navigator was constantly checking the aircraft's position, revising the wind speeds and direction and changing course and air speed in order to be at the various turning points and at the target on time. There was no visual navigation as we flew in darkness and usually in dense cloud. Oh - and it was cold. On one occasion, I poured hot tea from my thermos into my plastic cup, which split open with the temperature at minus 40°C. The tea immediately froze to my maps preventing me from plotting courses or winds and it also froze to my lap and thighs.

Our crew completed 311 operations. We were the lucky ones as enemy night fighters, searchlights and flak were terrifying and many new crews on the squadron perished due to bad luck or inexperience early on. Once, all four of our engines packed up and the pilot gave the order 'abandon aircraft'. We had been losing height for some time and now we were falling rapidly. The pilot and I were the last to leave and as I was preparing to fall through the hatch by the pilot's feet I felt him pulling at my shoulder. I guessed that he was probably caught up somewhere and needed my help to get free. I went back, fearing that we were then so low that we should both die when the plane crashed. It transpired that an engine had come back to life and he wanted me to help him fly back to England. We kept losing height and over the Channel we were only just above the waves and lower than the cliffs ahead. I had been desperately operating the throttles and petrol cocks and miraculously a second engine burst into life and we were able to clear the cliffs and make an emergency landing at Manston near Margate.

By April 1945 we had nearly completed our tour of 30 operations. So too, had our Flight Commander and his crew and they finished before us. The navigator had been at school with me in the 1930s. He was married and his pregnant wife came up to stay in the

EYE WITNESS

STORIES OF THE WAR IN THE AIR

A Lancaster flies home past an East Anglian windmill, bombing mission accomplished.

local pub to celebrate the end of the crew's tour. Within a day or two the length of a tour was raised to 32 and although the Flight Commander had officially completed he elected to do the extra two. At the briefing for the 32nd, the air gunners were warned to be particularly vigilant as the bomb aimer's wife was also pregnant and due to give birth that night. It would never do to shoot down the stork! Sadly the plane was shot down and all the crew died. The joy of the poor girl at the pub was cruelly destroyed and two new babies were to be fatherless.

Survival or death on each raid was just down to luck.

Peter J Welham remembers flying from Bombay to Britain in a bomb bay!

A week before Christmas 1943, I reported to the Air Crew Reception Centre (ACRC) at St Johns Wood, London, as a Cadet Wireless Operator. During the next two or three weeks I and my comrades were kitted out with uniform including flying kit, medical inspection, various painful innoculations and physical tests all to confirm that we were acceptable for training as Air Crew. Most of the process took place in the Lords Cricket Ground buildings which had been taken over by the RAF. Strange to say my Grandfather had been concerned with catering at Lords in the early 1900's.

On completion of the induction process, we moved to RAF Bridgenorth for 'Initial Training'. This consisted mainly of spending hours on end in a large unheated hangar practicing receiving and sending in the Morse Code. We were also introduced to the pleasures of drill (always conducted in double time)and had some weapon training. Halfway through the course we were invited to drop the wireless side of our training and re-grade as Air Gunners. Many of our intake volunteered to do this but I and the remainder opted to stay as Wireless Operators or, as we were then known, Signallers (Air). We later learned of the considerable loss of Air Gunners over the latter half of 1944.

At this point Bridgenorth became the IT Wing for Air Gunners and we Signallers were transferred to the Gunners IT Wing at Bridlington on Sea, arriving there on a cold and snow swept early morning to be met by a particularly unpleasant Flight Sergeant who frightened the life out of us 18-year-old boys. A week or so later he was posted on to Bridgenorth, no doubt to the horror of the Air Gunners who thought they had seen the last of him.

As a result of this change our Initial Training Course lasted six or seven months longer than usual and our ability to read and transmit Morse was greatly enhanced. During the summer months of 1944 the weather was pleasant but our time there was marred by an unfortunate incident when one of our Flight stepped on a mine on the cliffs to the

north of the town. It was Easter weekend and I and my friends were sitting on the beach as the column of smoke from the explosion rose in the air. He was a gentle natured 'Geordie' and a popular member of our group.

Late summer 1944 saw us posted to RAF Madley to commence the main Air Signaller's course which entailed intensive Morse practice and instruction on the radio equipment used in all bomber aircraft. The course also included the operation of radio equipment in the air and to this end monoplane single engined aircraft with 'foldback' wings known as Proctors were used. Exercises could be pretty 'hairy' at times and more than one accident occurred with fatal results. Other groups were undergoing various courses including a party of French aviators. I recall seeing a Lysander parked on the perimeter so possibly some covert flights into France originated from there.

Our group passed out as Sergeants (Signallers) in the spring of 1945 and with the end of war in Europe were posted to RAF Cranwell for training on radio equipment used in the American Liberator aircraft with a view of a posting to the Far East. The war with Japan ended and with that so did my aircrew career. After a course in aircraft traffic control I was posted to India. At that time there was a shortage of troopships so I and a collection of RAF personnel were placed on the County Class Cruiser, *HMS Devonshire*, as part-of-ship, the significance of this being that we would be part of the crew and entitled to a tot of rum each midday. As most of us were unused to strong spirits it soon became clear that this was not a good idea and this was changed to a small monetary allowance in lieu.

Our 'Passage to India' took us through the stormy Bay of Biscay. We then sailed through the Mediterranean, went down the Suez Canal and stopped at Aden to refuel before going on to Bombay. My service in India was short-lived as in 1946 I was released to continue my work with the Post Office Telephone Service, but whilst still there, was posted across India to Bengal, travelling by rail on a journey lasting several days. Two months later, it was back to Bombay, flying in a Halifax. For the flight to the UK I travelled in a Liberator converted to take passengers in the bomb bay. On this journey we stopped off in Iraq, what was then known as East Palestine and Libya. After landing in Cambridgeshire I was de-mobbed.

When war broke out I was still a 14-year-old schoolboy but by the time I reached the age of 21 I had, like many of my contemporaries, survived the conflict and in the process gained an experience that has stayed with me all my life. My father who had served in the Royal Flying Corp in the First World War was called up as a member of the RAFVR in 1939, but was discharged shortly after on health grounds. My brother later entered the Army as an Officer Cadet, but in training was seriously injured by a bomb exploding in the barrel of a mortar. This ended his military service. I count myself lucky that I was able to finish 'my war' without a scratch.

Why Len Sullivan and Lancasters were not to be

Leonard Sullivan, 'Len' to his mates, was 14 in 1939 and living in Downham, a suburb of London near Bromley, Kent. A trainee draughtsman at the local college, under the threat of German bombs Len was evacuated to Robertsbridge, near Hastings in Sussex. He stayed with a family who had the village sweet shop. Bliss! Except that after three months he and his college chums moved to Loughborough in Leicestershire to continue their course in draughtsmanship.

Len joined the Loughborough ATC 132 Squadron and in October 1943 at 18 he volunteered for the RAF. He recalls a trip to London and a stay in a posh hotel at Regents Park where they were kitted out. He then went on to Aberdeen in Scotland for his Preliminary Air Crew Training (PACT) after which he was then stationed at Cranage, Cheshire, where he had his Initial Training Wing (ITW), which he describes as 'square bashing'. Len was initially trained as a Pilot Navigation Bomb-aimer (PNB), but he re-mustered and opted for the post of Flight Engineer. This, however, was a course lasting nine months and when the war in Europe ended he was still a month away from qualifying at St Athan.

Len never received his official 'brevvy' (wing) but has somehow acquired one anyway. He remembers that he and his fellow trainees all felt as though they had missed out after all the training. They didn't even get to fly in a Lancaster and had to be content to just sit in the cockpit on the ground. He agrees with hindsight that really, given the casualty rate of bomber aircrew, he and his colleagues were definitely the lucky ones being born just those few months too late to fly missions over Germany.

With the war over, Len re-mustered and trained as a motor mechanic at Melksham in Wiltshire. He was then stationed at 4MT Unit at Kidbrook in SE London where he worked on many vehicles including huge Scammell recovery vehicles. At Kidbrook he met Winifred 'Wyn' Marshall, an electrician in the WAAF, and the pair hit it off and married in 1947 in her home town of Brighton. They enjoyed more than 50 wonderful years together and had four children. Wyn passed away in 1998. A resident of Lewes in East Sussex, Len reckons that, for him, meeting Wyn was the best thing that came out of the war.

Len and Wyn Sullivan at their wedding.

ITALY
THE FINAL PUSH

Two Spitfires pictured on patrol over Italy.

April 1945 saw the final Allied offensive in Italy.

Nine days into the month, the Eighth Army launched a powerful assault against German defences on the Senio River. Flame-throwers played a big part in the initial attack, which had been preceded by a tremendous artillery barrage.

By midday on 10 April over 1200 prisoners had been taken and the advance was going well. Allied air support dropped 350,000 fragmentation bombs on German troops and fortifications. Some Italian fascist supporters – Blackshirts – still fought alongside the Germans, but many more Italians were engaged on the Allied side, either as regular troops or partisans.

Though fierce fighting continued for several days, good progress was reported by both the Eighth and Fifth Armies. Argenta, a key defence town, was liberated on 17 April and after Bologna fell on 21 April it became clear that the enemy was close to collapse, as they hastily retreated to the River Po. Eighth Army men crossed the river on 24 April and on the same day took Ferrara. On 26 April

Verona was taken and the next day US troops entered Genoa. Popular uprisings against the Germans and Blackshirts took place in many towns and cities. At the same time Tito's Yugoslav patriots – having liberated their own country – were moving into Italian territory, determined to reclaim the city of Trieste ceded to Italy after the Great War.

In about 20 days, the remaining German armies in Italy were virtually eliminated as a fighting force opening the way for an Allied thrust northwards into Austria, always the goal since the landings on Sicily. The unconditional surrender of nearly one million German soldiers, sailors and Luftwaffe personnel in Italy and Southern Austria was signed at Caserta on 29 April, after the Allies had completed their swift advance across the North Italian plain. However, the surrender would not come into official effect until 2 May when Field-Marshal Alexander issued a declaration to the men of the Eighth and Fifth Armies: 'After nearly two years of hard and continuous fighting you stand today as victors in the Italian Campaign. You may well be proud of this great campaign, which will long live in history as one of the greatest and most successful ever waged.'

WAR DIARY
April 1945

1 April: It's the 2038th day of the war. The Red Army captures Sopron close to the Austria-Hungary frontier and threatens Vienna. In Italy, the Allies are preparing a massive assault on the German forces south of the River Po. Will this be the last big battle of the gruelling Italian Campaign? Eighth Army commander, Lt-Gen Richard McCreery, leads a force that includes British and Americans (many of Japanese origin), Brazilians, Italians, New Zealanders, Poles, Indians, Gurkhas and a Jewish Brigade. British commandos began their attack east of Lake Comacchio on the Adriatic coast tonight.

In Paris the famous landmarks of Notre Dame and the Arc de Triomphe are floodlit for the first time since the outbreak of war in 1939.

In the Pacific, the largest amphibious landing of the Pacific campaign is taking place. Over half a million US personnel are involved as troops land on the island of Okinawa.

2 April: In Berlin Hitler's favoured deputy, Martin Bormann calls for 'victory or death' from the German people. British and US troops occupy the town of Munster.

Moscow announces the capture of Hungary's oil centre at Nagy Kaniisza.

Italy: Eighth Army forces land on a spit of land separating Lake Comacchio from the Adriatic, north of Ravenna.

Germany: Men of the British 6th Guards' Tank Brigade liberate 9000 Russian POWs from Stalag 326 at Eselheide, between Munster and Hamm.

3 April: U-Boat yards at Kiel are bombed by US Flying Fortresses while RAF Lancasters attack German troop concentrations at Nordhausen, north east of Cassel.

Canadian First Army troops advance in Holland and cross the Twenthe Canal between Zutphen and Hengelo.

Far East: Super-Fortresses attack aircraft works on Japan's Honshu island.

4 April: The *Schwarze Korps*, a Nazi propaganda publication controlled by SS leader Heinrich Himmler, concedes that Germany is 'on the verge of absolute collapse'.

In Germany French forces enter Karlsruhe and the towns of Cassel, Gotha and Aschaffenburg are reported clear of the enemy by other Allied armies.

> " The Eighth Army's ranks now include British and Americans (many of Japanese origin), Brazilians, Italians, New Zealanders, Poles, Indians, Gurkhas and a Jewish Brigade. "

U-Boat yards at Kiel and Hamburg are again the target of US heavy bombers.

The Russian army led by Marshal Malinovsky takes Bratislava, capital of Slovakia, by storm. The Red Army also announces further territorial gains in Austria.

RAF Coastal Command Mosquitoes attack German shipping in the heavily defended anchorage of Sande Fjoord in Norway.

5 April: The Kremlin announces the Soviet Union's scrapping of the five year neutrality pact with Japan. Already reeling from the devastating US bombing attacks on her cities and industries, Japan now faces the certainty of a new front opening up against her along the Soviet Far East border with Manchuria and the eastern Pacific seaboard as soon as Stalin feels the time is right. Moscow's denunciation of the pact coincides with the resignation of General Koiso's cabinet in Tokyo. The new prime minister is Admiral Suzuki. Advisers at the court of the Emperor urge the premier to end the war quickly.

In Germany, the British First Commando Brigade clear Osnabruck of the enemy, while Minden is secured by men of the Sixth Airborne.

6 April: Red Army troops break into the suburbs of Vienna where street fighting takes place.

Over 100,000 prisoners are rounded up in the German industrial heartland of the Ruhr.

Minister of Labour, Ernest Bevin, says that the wartime coalition government led by Churchill will be dissolved at the earliest opportunity to pave the way for a general election.

In the Balkans, Yugoslav partisans under the command of Marshal Tito moved in to take control of the town of Sarajevo after the Germans had largely withdrawn.

Far East: Three US destroyers reported sunk by Japanese aircraft off Okinawa.

7 April: The 72,000 ton Japanese battleship *Yamato* is sunk by carrier-based US aircraft off Kyushu. With little fuel left, the ship's hopeless mission was to draw US aircraft and naval units away from the Okinawa battle and into the range of kamikaze pilots flying from the Japanese home islands. Two Japanese cruisers and three destroyers are also destroyed in the same action. US bombers attack Tokyo and Nagoya.

RAF Mosquitoes, flying from Continental bases for the first time, attack targets in Berlin. At night Allied parachutists land in Holland, east of the Zuider Zee.

A British officer in the north of Italy surveys the distant Alps and Austria. In April 1944, 10 months after marching into Rome in triumph, the Allies at last know that a German military collapse was imminent.

WAR DIARY
April 1945

In Germany, soldiers of the US First Army seize 13 rail wagons loaded with V2 rockets destined for launch sites on the Dutch coast. It is the first time any of the missiles have been captured intact. The train was held up because in all parts of the Netherlands still occupied by the Germans, the Dutch rail workforce remains on strike with many key personnel in hiding. The 30,000 rail workers first failed to turn up for duty on 18 September 1944 following an appeal broadcast by the free Dutch government after consultation with the Allied High Command. Since then the country's rail service has been greatly incapacitated. A number of the strikers have been executed and families taken hostage. Thousands of others remain in hiding. A Dutch transport official later describes the situation: 'One half of occupied Holland was in hiding – the other half kept it hidden.'

8 April: General Patton's troops discover art treasures and what appears to be the entire Reichsbank gold reserves hidden 700 yards inside a salt mine at Merkers, 30 miles south of Mulhausen. There are also millions of pounds worth of various foreign currencies.

Denmark: A flotilla of 21 small vessels crammed with Danish patriots escaping from the German occupiers of their country is heading across the Baltic for the safety of neutral Sweden.

9 April: The Third Reich's one-time 'spymaster', Admiral Canaris, is hanged for treason. The former head of the *Abwehr* (military intelligence) was suspected of involvement in the plot to assassinate Hitler in July 1944 and of making peace overtures to the Allies.

The US Ninth Army takes over the Krupp plant in Essen, a major source of German armaments. RAF bombers damage one of Kriegsmarine's two remaining pocket battleships, the *Admiral Scheer,* and inflict serious harm on the heavy cruiser *Admiral Hipper.*

In Italy, the Eighth Army reports the crossing of the River Senio after a heavy bombardment of German positions from the air.

10 April: One by one Germany's major cities are falling to the Allies. US Ninth Army troops today capture Hanover where they liberate 60,000 slave workers and 300 British POWs. The road to Bremen is now blocked and the Allies have also occupied Essen. US bombers are in action attacking jet aircraft bases in the Berlin area and claim to have destroyed 305 enemy planes. RAF bombers hit railway yards at Leipzig. These attacks are just two of 5600 Allied sorties flown today; 40 aircraft are reported lost, mainly due to German flak.

11 April: Soldiers of the US Ninth Army reach the Elbe near Magdeburg and enter Brunswick. Tomorrow US troops will cross the river, but will not advance much further east in strength; they expect to rendezvous with Red Army forces at any time.

The surviving 21,000 emaciated and disease-ridden inmates of Buchenwald Concentration Camp are liberated by the US Third Army. Over 1000 German civilians from Weimar will be marched the six miles to the camp to observe the horrors inflicted on victims of the Nazi system.

Vichy police chief and enthusiastic collaborator with the Nazis, Lucien Rottée, is sentenced to death in Paris.

In Germany, US troops capture an intact V-weapons plant at Nordhausen. They race to remove material relating to rocket science ahead of the arrival of the Red Army. The latter will have post-war control of the region. Franz Von Papen is captured in the Ruhr region.

Norway: RAF Coastal Command set on fire five German merchants ships off the coast.

Off Okinawa, the US carrier *Enterprise* is crippled and the battleship *Missouri* seriously damaged in kamikaze attacks. On shore, progress is painfully slow in the face of the fanatical Japanese defence.

12 April: The world is stunned by the sudden death of US President Franklin Delano Roosevelt. The only president ever elected four times, 63-year-old Roosevelt, a polio sufferer for 20 years, was a good friend to Churchill and a staunch supporter of the British stand against the Nazis – even when America was still neutral. Roosevelt is succeeded by Harry S Truman, the son of a Missouri farmer.

The Eighth Army are advancing in Italy and today units cross the Santerno River.

Tokyo and Koriyama aircraft works bombed by USAAF Super-Fortresses.

13 April: Seven years and one month since the *Anschluss* – when Hitler forcibly joined Austria to Germany – Vienna has a new master as Marshal Tolbukhin's men take complete control of the city, making 130,000 Germans prisoner in the process. Despite the fighting, most of the principal buildings have survived major damage.

Unimaginable scenes of death and suffering greet US troops at Ohrdruf and Buchenwald. The latter was one of Hitler's first concentration camps, created in 1938. Battle hardened commanders Bradley, Patton and Eisenhower are moved to tears at the sight of piles of rotting corpses and mass graves.

Carrier aircraft of the British Pacific Fleet attack Japanese airfields on the island of Formosa (Taiwan).

14 April: Now only 40 miles from Berlin, victorious Red Army marshals Zhukov, Koniev and Rokossovsky are poised with massed strength for the final assault on the German capital. Elsewhere the Luftwaffe reel from non-stop attacks on airfields. In a 48 hour period 1738 aircraft are destroyed on the ground and another 332 shot down in combat.

Too little, too late. German jet fighter technology produced aircraft that would have regained mastery of mainland Europe's airspace for the Luftwaffe had they entered service in numbers a year earlier. Fortunately for the Allies, vastly superior aircraft like the twin-engined ME-262 arrived too late to affect the outcome of the war. A damaged ME-262 is seen here on an airfield captured by US troops.

British troops are set to liberate Arnhem in Holland. The town with its bridge over the Rhine was the target of *Operation Market Garden* in September 1944. Just a single battalion of lightly armed British skytroops got to the bridge and held it for a few days before being over-run by superior German forces backed by panzers and artillery.

15 April: Allied attention is turning to German garrisons besieged in towns and ports on the country's Atlantic coast since the previous summer. Yesterday, 1350 US aircraft bombed German positions in the Gironde estuary, not far from Bordeaux. Over 1300 aircraft hit the same area today dropping 7000 bombs and incendiaries and 460,000 gallons of a new inflammable liquid. The liquid is held in containers that burst and splash their contents over 60 square yards. Following the air attacks, French forces mount land and sea attacks and it is reported that their Second Armoured Division has entered Royan.

Canadian units reach the North Sea coast of Holland; tomorrow they will liberate the town of Groningen. Die-hard Nazis set fire to the already badly battered centre of Arnhem as they retreat from the Dutch town. With the famous Arnhem 'Bridge Too Far' now collapsed in the Rhine, British troops cross the river in landing craft.

British troops enter the concentration camp at Belsen. They find one Englishman among the 60,000 inmates.

16 April: Burma: Rangoon is now firmly in General Slim's sights and the Japanese are in retreat throughout Burma. Taungup, the last coastal Japanese supply base in Burma's Arakan region, is captured by the Fourteenth Army. The Imperial Army in the country now has no hope of outside aid reaching them.

On Okinawa, the Americans still battle against an estimated 80,000 die-hard Japanese who are concealed in a vast maze of tunnels and caves. In two days of vicious fighting the US forces have advanced just 1800 yards.

Berlin: Hitler retreats to his bunker under the Reich Chancellery accompanied by his mistress Eva Braun. The besieged population also seek shelter in cellars and trenches and await the arrival of the Russians with dread. Deserters and 'defeatists' are hunted down and summarily executed by roving SS quads. Food supplies are dwindling and many people wish only to surrender.

A small force of RAF Lancasters with 12,000lb bombs sink the pocket battleship *Lutzow* at Swinemunde. So far in April the Allies claim to have destroyed 3599 German aircraft, 3214 of them on the ground. In one single day US bombers and fighters raided 55 airfields in Germany, Austria and Czechoslovakia.

17 April: Germany: Fierce fighting continues in the city of Nuremberg following the entry yesterday of armoured spearheads of the US Seventh Army.

Denmark: RAF Mosquitoes make a low-level attack on the Gestapo HQ at Odense. Another 832 German aircraft are reported destroyed today, most of them on the ground.

Austria: Soviet troops capture the oil centre of Zistersdorf.

In London, St Paul's Cathedral is packed with mourners headed by the King and Queen at a Memorial Service for President Roosevelt.

18 April: Field Marshal Walter Model commits suicide in a forest outside Dusseldorf. Only a few months ago he assumed command of German forces in the West and issued a ringing call to arms. Now the battle for the Ruhr has ended and there are 325,000 German prisoners in Allied hands.

In Holland, the Canadian First Army approaches the Zuider Zee in the face of stiffening opposition. Today the Germans breach dykes and cause flooding that will further delay progress. The Dutch in the north of the country have been waiting nearly 10 months for liberation after the failure of *Market Garden* and destruction of the Rhine bridges deflected the Allies into a different direction of attack.

Madrid: Hoping to appease the Allies, Generalissimo Franco prohibits all German aircraft from landing on Spanish territory. The fascist dictator kept his country neutral in the war and fears that western governments will press for 'regime change' in Spain after the defeat of Germany.

Men of the 2/6th Queens advance in the Po Valley, April 1945.

Nearly 1000 RAF bombers pound German defences and an airfield on the tiny North Sea island of Heligoland. They will return to finish the job with 12,000lb bombs tomorrow.

The Eighth Army capture Argenta in Italy.

19 April: Leipzig is captured by the US First Army. Polish troops serving with the Red Army capture the German city of Rothenburg. Russian units report the establishment of a bridgehead over the River Oder, west of Kustrin.

Long-range Mustang fighters flying the 1500 mile round trip from Iwo Jima make a first attack on Atsugi Airfield, south west of Tokyo. They report 85 Japanese aircraft destroyed.

Burma: The last of the country's main oilfields will fall into Allied hands over the next few days as the Fourteenth Army advances up to 50 miles a day.

20 April: Berlin: Hitler spends his 56th birthday listening to the rumble of Russian artillery coming ever-closer to his capital. The Fuhrer emerges from his bunker just once to decorate members of the Hitler Jugend. Tonight RAF Mosquito fighter-bombers and Red Air Force aircraft will range over the city.

All organised German resistance in Nuremberg has ended.

Italy: Fifth Army units have entered the Po Valley west of Bologna. Operating with Eighth Army assistance they will liberate that city tomorrow.

21 April: Berlin is now virtually surrounded by Russian armour, artillery and soldiers; Zhukov's men are probing into the city suburbs. Allied bombing raids on German targets continue; today railway yards in the Munich area are hit by US aircraft flying from airfields in Britain and Italy.

Patton's Third Army captures the town of Asch in Czechoslovakia.

The USSR announces the signing of a 20-year pact of mutual assistance with the Polish (Lublin) Government. The pact effectively consigns post-war Poland to the Soviet sphere of influence.

Burma: With the capture today of the major centre of production at Yenangyaung, almost all of the country's oilfields are in Allied hands.

22 April: Himmler meets Swedish Count Folke Bernadotte representing the International Red Cross in secret at the Baltic port of Lubeck and offers to cease fighting the Western Allies but not the Russian enemy in the East.

RAF Lancasters bomb the great port of Bremen in the north of Germany. French forces occupy Stuttgart and Freiburg and advance down the eastern bank of the Rhine to the Swiss frontier.

The US Seventh Army troops under General Patch capture a bridge over the Danube at Dillengen unopposed. They are heading for Munich.

French leader General de Gaulle goes in person to congratulate his troops who have cleared the Gironde pockets at Royan and Pointe de Grave of German resistance.

Russian assault troops report being less than three miles from the Unter den Linden in the centre of Berlin.

Soviet Foreign Minister Molotov arrives in Washington on his

WAR DIARY

April 1945

way to a conference in San Francisco.

23 April: Marshal Koniev's forces join in the battle for Berlin when they attack from the south. RAF Mosquitoes twice bomb Kiel and German shipping at Travemunde on the North Sea coast.

Japan: US Super-Fortresses raid an aircraft works at Tashikawa, west of Tokyo.

On the Home Front, the authorities remove lighting restrictions over most of Britain.

The Czech Government-in-Exile calls for a popular uprising.

24 April: Goering sends Hitler a telegram offering to take over command of the Reich in view of the fact the Fuhrer is trapped in Berlin. A furious Hitler promptly orders the arrest of his one-time highly favoured crony from the earliest days of National Socialism.

RAF bombers attack a rail centre near Hamburg and British troops enter the suburbs of Bremen.

Soldiers from the armies of Zhukov and Koniev link up in the southern suburbs of Berlin.

In Italy Ferrara is occupied by the Eighth Army; Modena and Spezia by the Fifth. Allied troops are across the River Po.

London: At sunset tonight the Speaker of the House of Commons switches on the lamps in the famous Clock Tower housing Big Ben, an action he describes as lighting, 'a beacon of fresh hope in a sadly torn and distracted world'.

The ferocious fighting on Okinawa continues. On the west coast of the island, the Americans re-occupy the town of Kakuzu, captured in a Japanese counter-attack two days earlier.

25 April: Churchill and President Truman discuss Himmler's offer of a German surrender on the Western Front. The pair agree that nothing less than unconditional surrender on all fronts is required to end the war in Europe.

Berlin is now completely encircled by the Red Army and there is no way out for the defenders and no way in for relief forces. In fact, the latter only exist as figments of Hitler's imagination.

The flags of 46 countries hang as a backdrop at the opening of the historic Allied Nations Conference in the Opera House, San Francisco.

Okinawa: 21,000 Japanese have been killed so far in the battle for this island, while just 400 have been captured.

26 April: US troops advancing from the west meet with Red Army soldiers from the east at Torgau on the River Elbe. The historic rendezvous is sealed with handshakes. Second Lt William D Robertson from Los Angeles is credited with being the first American to greet a soldier of Marshal Koniev's First Ukrainian Army.

A month after the last V2 rocket fell on England, the authorities release details of the very first one to crash to the ground in 1944. The explosion occurred in Chiswick, West London, at precisely 6.49pm on 8 September; three houses were destroyed, three people killed and 20 injured. The authorities add that 1050 rockets came down in total, killing 2754 people and seriously injuring another 6523.

27 April: General Sir Miles Dempsey's British Second Army announces that Bremen has been cleared of enemy resistance. In the port's Deschimag shipyards, 16 almost completed U-Boats were discovered.

Russian and American troops make contact on the River Elbe north east of Leipzig and Germany is cut in two.

A British Parliamentary deputation of two peers and eight MPs which visited Buchenwald concentration camp has issued its report detailing the horrors inflicted on thousands of prisoners.

28 April: 'Il Duce' – Benito Mussolini – deposed dictator of Italy, is discovered and detained by partisans as he and an entourage attempt to escape to Switzerland. He is executed at Dongo, Lake Como. Later his body is suspended ignominiously upside down from a garage roof in Milan. His mistress, Clara Petacci, and other Italian fascist leaders meet the same fate. All organised resistance in the Genoa area has ended. In the north east of Italy, Eighth

Army soldiers are just 30 miles from Venice. Overnight they will enter the city.

American and Russian forces link up on a 50-mile front along the Elbe, north and south of Torgau.

29 April: After three weeks of negotiations, representatives of the German army in Italy sign a document agreeing to unconditional surrender at Caserta. More than one million German and Italian fascist soldiers are preparing to lay down their arms and march off to prison camps, although the surrender will not come into effect until 2 May.

Royal Marine Commandos of the British No 1 Commando Brigade cross the River Elbe to establish a broad bridgehead and capture Lauenburg.

Netherlands: Unescorted Lancasters of RAF Bomber Command drop sackloads of food to the starving civilian population in the German-occupied cities of The Hague, Rotterdam and Leyden. Before the drop, a radio broadcast assures the Dutch, 'Allied aircraft are on their way. The next aircraft you hear overhead will be carrying food, not bombs.' The International Red Cross had previously secured agreement with the Germans not to attack the British relief effort. Elsewhere in Holland, at Amersfort, a Dutch unit of the German SS is fighting against the British 49th Division.

In San Francisco a Reuters correspondent puts out a report revealing that Himmler has made an offer of surrender to the Western Allies. Hitler is visibly shocked when he hears the news that same night.

30 April: Berlin: The ruined Reichstag is captured by the Russians, effectively signalling the end of the bloody battle for Berlin. In his bunker, Adolf Hitler takes a last lunch and then shoots himself at 3.30pm. Eva Braun, the Fuhrer's long-time mistress who became his bride just 36 hours previously, takes poison. Their bodies are taken into the grounds of the Chancellery and cremated in a shell hole. The vaunted 'Thousand Year Reich' has lasted little more than 12 years. Hitler's successor is nominated as Grand Admiral Karl Donitz, the mastermind of Germany's deadly U-Boat campaign, which accounted for the loss of 15 million tons of Allied shipping. Donitz is in the north of the country. He realises Germany faces certain defeat, but knows that his duty is to secure the most advantageous terms he can for an armistice. Some of his staff hold out hope that hostilities might cease on the Western Front allowing Germany and the Western Allies to join forces against the Soviet armies now pouring into Eastern Europe in vast numbers.

Italy: Turin is liberated and New Zealand troops cross the River Piave.

Burma: Fourteenth Army troops are at Pegu and have driven the Japanese from a defile which was their last natural defensive position before Rangoon.

This sign was erected near the spot at Torgau on the River Elbe where the first official rendezvous between soldiers of the Red Army and US troops occurred on the afternoon of 25 April 1945. The encounter – around 75 miles south of Berlin – meant that the Third Reich was split in two.

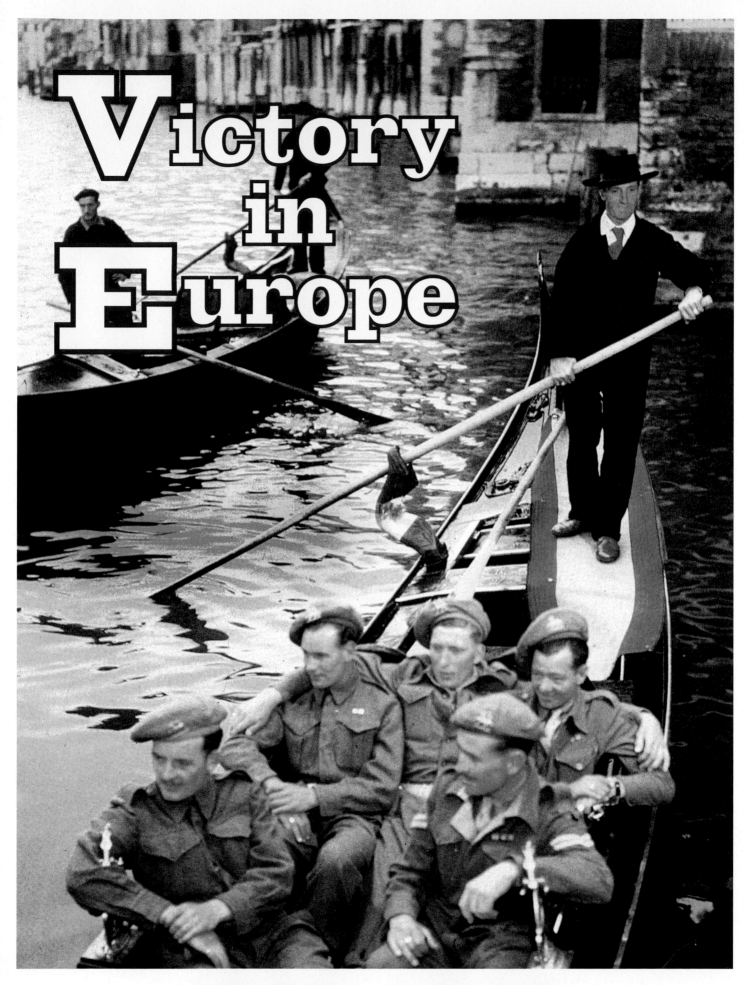

Victory in Europe

MAY 1945

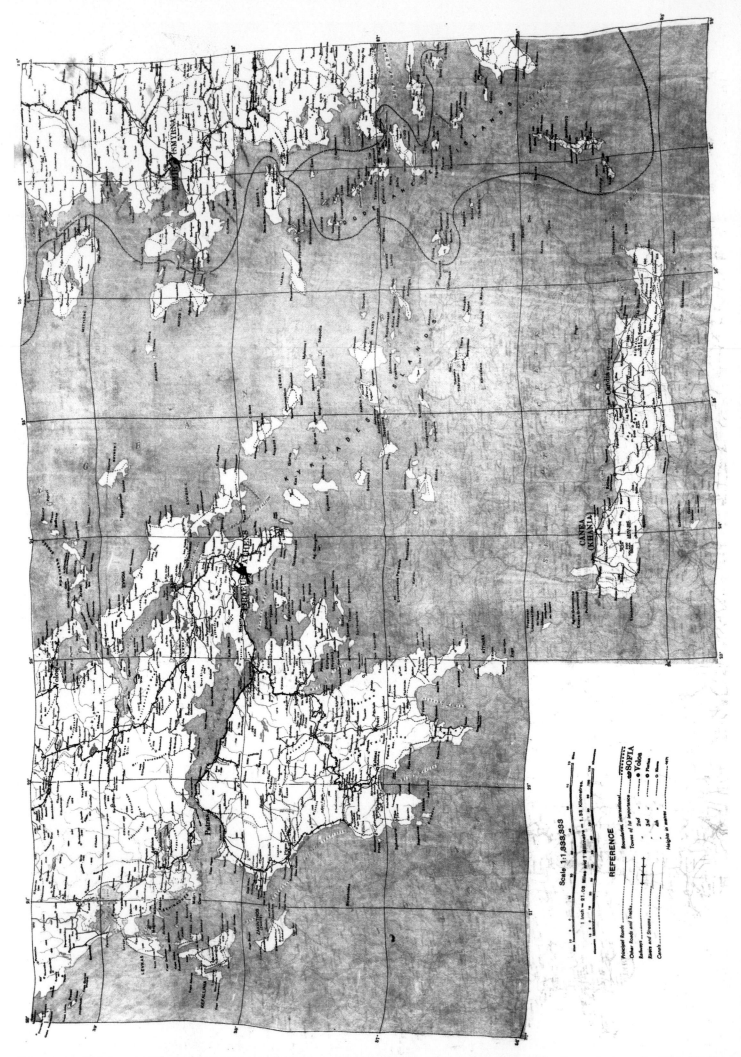

This map of southern Greece and the Aegean is printed on a silk scarf. It was issued to Alan Wilkins, a Senior Officer in the Raiding Support Regiment. The RSR had heavier weapons than the SAS and SBS and as the name implies their role was to afford back-up to special operations.

WILKINS' WAR

Alan Wilkins remembers his time with the Raiding Support Regiment in the Adriatic.

Above: Men of the Raiding Support Regiment taking advantage of the Mediterranean sun. The photo is one of a number that Alan Wilkins gave to the Editor of Sixty Years On. *Alan himself is shown on this page in a picture from the last decade.*

Over 10 years I was privileged to probe the memory banks of Alan Wilkins, one-time Commandant of the Middle East Battle School who went on to help form and lead the Raiding Support Regiment. Prising nuggets of information out of this modest man was like putting together a jigsaw - unfortunately one with lots of key components missing!

The problem was that Alan didn't keep a wartime diary and has never been tempted to write his memoirs. 'I dropped the Lt-Colonel stuff as soon as I got back to Civvy Street and went into the printing business' he explained with disarming cheerfulness, 'Over the years one tells lots of anecdotes but it has surprised me how all the events have merged in my memory so that the chronological order especially around the 1943-44 period - is muddled.'

Not helping was the fact that so very little has ever been published about the Raiding Support Regiment, an outfit set up to lend firepower to other Special Forces such as the SAS and SBS. In the summer of 2004 I asked Alan if he could put pen to paper with a few more memories and he duly obliged. I have subsequently merged the two contributions into this single account of Alan's war.

Mules and mountain guns

'In the early days in Syria we had a battery of captured Italian mountain guns on mules' recalled Alan, 'But I don't remember ever using the guns in anger. Later we used 3-inch mortars and had four 25-pounders.'

Alan told a wonderful story of his Middle East Battle School days when he put on a big show for a visiting Turkish Delegation. The mock battle greatly impressed a Turkish General. At the end of it he congratulated Alan on his 'superbly trained men' who seemed much more competent than the Germans. When Alan asked how the General had heard about the German methods an

aide de camp explained that the same Delegation had been invited to watch the Germans preparing for battle just a short time previously! Both sides were obviously keen for Turkey to join them in the war.

'I suspect our Turkish friend would also have told the Germans that they were better trained than the British' said Alan, 'But I know the fellow was visibly shocked when informed that our chaps had used live ammo for the demonstration - stray rounds had been flying all over the place!'

Waiting Wellington crew

RSR men were used in penny packets in Greece and the Balkans. Alan recalled one occasion when he and his men went ashore in Albania. 'We were padding forwards up the beach and I had a revolver in my hand. Suddenly, out of the pitch darkness came this very English voice exclaiming "And about time too. We've been waiting for you."

'I was shaken, to say the least' said Alan. 'It turned out that the chap was one of six crew from a downed Wellington bomber who had teamed up with an Italian and had been stuck in Albania for nine months. The SBS had gone ashore a few days earlier to recce things for us and they'd told the aircrew we were coming.

'The RSR had a key role in supporting Tito and his Yugoslav partisans. We were all trained parachutists and were based at Bari in the south of Italy after the Allied invasion where the bulk of the men came under my command. We went to the island of Vis, off the Dalmatian coast, about 40 miles from Split. From here we participated in raids on the other islands and on the coast of Albania.

'American aircrew flying B27 bombing missions from the south of Italy against the Ploesti oilfields in Rumania were told that if they got into trouble, the British were on Vis and they could parachute onto the island, leaving their aircraft to ditch in the sea. Quite a few were saved in this way while others were rescued from the sea.'

Mussolini's daughter

Later in Italy, Alan visited places such as Monte Cassino after the battles there. He also

went on leave to Rome where, along with some fellow officers, he was invited to lunch one day at a rather grand address. 'The meal was served by flunkeys in white gloves using silver tongs' remembered Alan, 'and we couldn't believe the opulence of it all in the middle of a war. But we didn't stay for the whole meal - most of us walked out embarrassed when we discovered that our host was actually Mussolini's daughter, the widow of Count Ciano, who had been executed as a traitor by the fascists.'

RSR men were drawn from many sources: 'We had South Africans - one of them got the Military Cross for blowing up a bridge - and even a Finn.

'Towards the end of the war at Lake Commachio I remember we were to be part of an attack mounted via DUKWs to surprise the Germans. I recall we were supporting the famous "Popski's Private Army" for this operation - or certainly for some similar operation. It was supposed to be a night attack conducted as quietly as possible. In the event there was so much commotion and general noise going on that the attack was called off.

Waiting to surrender

'Next day we discovered that the Germans had indeed been waiting for us. But not to fight. Instead they'd formed up in ranks waiting to surrender and were disappointed when we didn't show up. Such was war - we'd get a lot of things right but there was always a cock-up waiting around the corner!'

Alan supplied me with some of his 'souvenirs' from his Raiding Support Regiment days. We've reproduced part of the silk-scarf 'Escape Map' of Greece and the Greek Islands he was issued with. It's on a very large scale and one wonders how much use it would have been to an escapee in reality. Other items included ingenious shirt studs which house tiny compasses.

David Arnold

Sadly, Alan did not live to see his story published in Sixty Years On *as he died, aged 90, in November 2004 peacefully at the Hertfordshire home he had moved to from Richmond in London last summer.*

Victory in Europe: Britain goes Crackers!

From *The War Illustrated*, early summer 1945:

'It is recorded that when the young Queen Victoria returned to Buckingham Palace after all the pomp and ceremony of her coronation, the first thing she did was to put off her magnificent robes and bath her favourite dog, Dash. Another "royal" dog figured in a tailpiece (or should it be tail-wagging piece?) to the recent Victory celebrations in London.

'Again the scene was Buckingham Palace. It was just after midnight at the end of VE Day plus one. Their Majesties had acknowledged the greetings of their cheering subjects for the last time, the floodlights had been switched off, the crowds were quickly dispersing. But a few groups of public still lingered by the railings, reluctant to sever too abruptly those ties which seemed to bind the Londoner with peculiar intimacy to the persons of his King and Queen.

'They were rewarded. For presently a door opened and a servant appeared in the forecourt with a dog. It was Crackers, the Queen's Corgi, out for his nightly airing, probably somewhat impatient that it had been delayed so long. On this exceptional occasion, Crackers was introduced to the people through the railings and was held up so that his handsome proportions could be generally admired. Then he was led back to bed. "Where does he sleep?" an over-inquisitive woman asked, and was courteously rebuked with, "I wouldn't like to tell you that, madam."

'Those who took part in this informal encounter with an important member of the Royal household found it a happy little anti-climax to all the tumult and shouting.'

All pictures: Getty Images

Above: St Paul's Cathedral pictured floodlit during victory celebrations in London on 9 May 1945.
Far left: A happy group marches down a London street on 8 May.
Left: Children at a Victory Tea Party and Concert held in Wimbledon, South London.

HOME FRONT

Nearly 300,000 civilian casualties.

From 3 September 1939 to the end of February 1945 (a total of 66 months) the armed forces of the British Commonwealth and Empire suffered 1,128,315 casualties, a figure that included 307,201 deaths, stated Winston Churchill in the House of Commons on 29 May 1945.

Civilian losses caused by the enemy bombardment of Britain during the same period totalled 60,585 killed and 86,175 seriously injured. In addition it was estimated that upwards of 150,000 people had suffered slight injuries.

These armed forces casualty figures are much lower than those of the Great War when (for 52 months) there were 3,286,090 casualties and

996,230 dead. However, civilian casualties in the mainland UK in the Second World War were vastly higher than those sustained in the 1914-18 conflict when the relatively ineffective air raids were carried out by cumbersome Zeppelin airships and Gotha bombers and occasionally a German warship or U-Boat would lob shells at east coast towns. There can be no comparison to the damage and death inflicted by the Blitz of 1940-41 and subsequent intermittent bombing offensives that culminated in the indiscriminate V1 and V2 attacks of 1944-45.

The war in Europe may be over, but the fight to feed the British population goes on. Indeed, a Ministry of Food announcement on 22 May 1945 makes it seem as if it is a losing battle. The civilian rations of cooking fat reduces to one ounce and bacon to three ounces. All meat is in short supply and the soap allowance is cut by an eighth. It's all to do with the massive food shortages in the newly-liberated or Allied-occupied nations of Europe where millions of displaced persons need feeding.

German POWs build houses

In addition there is a strain on the supply chain caused by the thousands of freed POWs now returning home to Britain each day, along with large numbers of servicemen and women released from the armed forces because they are able to do specialist work, especially in the construction industry where housebuilding is a priority. German prisoners in this country are being put to work helping rebuild the strained services infrastructure. Their labour is particularly needed in London and the South East.

Famous military figures are often to be seen in Britain, particularly in the capital. Allied Supreme Commander General Dwight D Eisenhower stayed in a London hotel and attended a Victory celebration on 15 May 1945. Just over a week later it was announced that the honorary freedom of the City of London, together with a sword of honour, were to be conferred on him.

The hero status of the victorious commanders created press speculation about their future status in society. For example, the Editor of *War Illustrated*, mused: 'How many innocent babes are now destined to bear lifelong evidence of the times into which they were born, by being given the baptismal names of Montgomery, Alexander or Eisenhower, or, perhaps more subtly, names that fit the momentous initials VE? This sort of thing is liable to occur at the climax of every war.

'The years 1940 and 1941 provide a fairly excusable crop of little Winstons – not forgetting the real Winston's own grandson. I doubt if the 1918 news story about a child called Armistice Brown was ever verified. But a schoolmaster once told me of six boys in his form all with the initials D H, for Douglas Haig. Another called Verdun Smith, was in a higher form, as befitted his seniority in chronological significance. Recently I heard a broadcast by an American jazz expert with the odd Christian name of Woody. This, I gathered, was short for Woodrow, which put a date on him at once.

'People are usually more careful to avoid saddling a daughter with any name that may betray an age too exactly. Yet there must be many women, now aged either 48 or 58, who have long ago dropped from their signatures that tell-tell name of Victoria which would reveal them as the Jubilee babies of parents whose loyalty outran their discretion.'

On 22 May 1945 Londoners were treated to the astonishing sight of a German U-Boat sailing under Tower Bridge on its way to a berth at Westminster Pier, close to the Houses of Parliament. The 500-ton heavily-armed minelayer U776 had survived her only operational patrol of 54 days and fired just one torpedo (which missed) before she surrendered to a naval sloop off Weymouth. Flying the White Ensign, the submarine was commanded by Lt-Commander P B Marriott, who had previously been captain of the U-Boat U507 captured in 1941 and renamed *HMS Graph*. At times of low tide U776 heels over to port in the Thames mud.

On VE Day the streets of London were packed with joyful crowds.

BUSINESS *as usual*

Hugh Thomas tells the story of a remarkable airman who flew from start to finish of World War II and beyond.

For Spitfire test pilot Peter Ayerst DFC, the summer of 1945 was very much business as usual at the Vickers-Armstrong factory at Castle Bromwich. Then aged 25, Peter was a fighter pilot ace. Despite being shot down, hit by flak, chased by more than two squadrons of enemy aircraft and flying secret missions behind enemy lines, he had somehow survived six intense years of war.

He had joined Vickers-Armstrong with legendary Chief Test Pilot, Alex Henshaw, at the helm, in February 1945.

Castle Bromwich was then the biggest aircraft factory in the country. At the peak of production, 330 Spitfires were built each month, in addition to the completion of 30 Lancasters. The working day normally started at about 8.30am, ending at about 6pm. Thereafter, most of the flight team retired to the local in Sutton Coldfield, to relax and unwind.

The art – or science – of test flying was dramatically different from the operational variety. Squadron flying involved formation-flying towards a specific, defined objective. Test flying was, in many respects, harder; it required more discipline and restraint – the testing and analysing was down to Peter and the buck stopped with him. The workload was also greater with more objectives to test, respond to, and analyse.

There were differences with the Spitfires, too. Operational aircraft had radios and other electronic devices. There were no radios or navigational aids in factory-fresh Spitfires; test pilots had none of these luxuries when testing in bad weather.

In May 1945, Peter was flying Spitfire Mk IXs. He took his last European wartime flights at Vickers on 7 May, flying three different machines; Peter climbed into the cockpits of TD 406 (twice), TE 181 (once) and TE 232 (twice). The entries in his logbook record that the flights were routine and uneventful. And then the declaration of peace in Europe came.

Victory bells

Peter didn't fly again until 11 May. Many people know precisely where they were on 8 May – VE Day. Peter can't remember in detail how he celebrated this momentous event, but thinks he must have gone in to work as normal, only to be told by Alex Henshaw that the pilots should take a few days off. There was only one place where he wanted to celebrate – and that was with his fiancée, Betty, in her family's pub *The Three Compasses* in Canterbury. While the bells rang out across Britain, Peter was doing a 'dirty dart' to Kent!

On the eve of VJ Day, he test flew no less than five aircraft and remembers his final wartime flights as routine. Peter believes he heard the declaration of the end of the war on the eve of 14 August, on a radio in a hotel close to Lichfield, with another test pilot from an RAF Maintenance Unit, along with both of their partners. When he went into work on 15 August, Henshaw gave them five days off.

Peter and Betty (who were married by this time) left for Canterbury that morning. Peter says that in the evening of that memorable day, everyone was going bananas. The town and streets thronged with people. By the time they had arrived to join in the celebrations, it was getting dark. He recalls that as jubilation swept through the crowd, two men could be seen swinging on a lamp-post by the Westgate Towers. Sadly, the motion caused the lamp-post to snap and break, resulting in a fatality. With the streets packed solid with people, singing and drinking, most of the crowd were unaware of the tragedy.

Although wartime had ended, the constraints placed upon the test pilots were as strict as ever – 'business as usual' as Peter puts it. By 31 August, Peter had made eight flights in the Mk 22. The Spitfire 22 was his favourite flying machine because of the sheer volume of power available to the pilot. For him, it was the definitive aviation experience, the ultimate thrill.

Fighter ace

The test flying was the end of a unique flying career during the war, because Peter was not only a test pilot. As a fighter pilot ace, he had nine kills to his name. He was also the first RAF fighter pilot to have come into contact with the ME109 over France, six years earlier, in 1939. But not just one – 27!

On 6 November 1939, he was alone at an airfield in France on aerodrome defence, sitting in his Hurricane. The sun was warm and there were blue skies everywhere. At around 2.30pm Peter looked to his right, over to the little road and the early warning post. The Poilus were waving their red flags, signalling an alarm.

He looked up at the sky and saw a little dot, travelling in a westerly direction – it was the enemy aircraft he was supposed to chase. The dot decided to fly over the airfield, high up at about 20,000 feet.

The Rolls Royce Merlin engine roared into life and Peter hurtled over the grass. It took him about 10 minutes to match the enemy aircraft in height. Operationally inexperienced, Peter was intent on chasing the raider – a Dornier bomber. But what he omitted to do in all the excitement was to keep an eye on his compass. Suddenly he realised that by flying in an easterly direction for so long, he had strayed well into German airspace.

Without delay he turned back on a reciprocal heading, making for France. As the Hurricane turned, he looked down over his starboard side. Inside his turn – and below him – were nine aircraft, in line astern formation, turning in precisely the same direction. Peter tacked onto the end of the line with the other aircraft at 18,000 feet. But something didn't seem quite right. They looked unfamiliar. Were they Hurricanes? No. These aircraft had ugly black crosses painted

Peter and Betty with their wedding guests at Canterbury on 5 June 1945.

on either wing. Messerschmitts! Peter gave a quick squirt from his guns towards the tail-end Charlie and shoved the stick forward so that the Hurricane flew into a very steep dive towards some broken cloud some 4000 feet below. He kept the aircraft on a westerly course.

Nine Me-109s with black crosses peeled off and began to chase him. The Hurricane was fitted with a special booster operated by a 'tit' on the throttle. To increase speed, a tiny wire had to be broken which allowed the pilot to pull the engine booster and obtain extra thrust. Heart pulsating, throat dry, eyes wide, Peter broke the wire and pulled the booster tit.

ME-109s in pursuit

What he didn't know at that time (but was told by witnesses later) was that there were another 18 Me-109s on patrol in the area that same November day. Having seen nine of their comrades peel off after something, they, in turn, decided to investigate. So, in effect, there weren't just nine on Peter's tail, but no less than 27 enemy aircraft!

At this point Peter confesses to feeling more than a little scared, although his RAF training warded off outright panic. He tucked himself in the Hurricane seat, ducking in front of the armour plate that protected the back of his head. Darting and nipping in between the broken cloud, he kept an ever-watchful eye on the direction bearing of the compass. It still pointed west.

There were no radio or directional aids to assist Peter. He saw one of the landmarks that Allied pilots used to look for in evaluating their location; factories with window glass painted blue by the French. So now he knew he was back over France, but didn't have the foggiest as to precisely where.

At this point 27 Me-109s were still chasing one under-powered Hurricane flown by one green and very nervous pilot. Peter prefers to think of it as one Hurricane leading 27 Messerschmitts towards a group of French fighter aircraft. Never had Peter been more relieved to see a bunch of Moraine-Saunier 406s and Curtiss P-40 Hawks. Salvation had arrived. This was to be the first genuine dogfight of the Second World War, with dozens of aircraft scrapping high over the French frontier. Nine Me-109s were shot down by the French.

If the enemy aircraft weren't enough to contend with, Peter was confronted with another problem. His fuel was very low. He had to find somewhere to land – and soon. Far away to the distance he could see aircraft circling. The needle on the fuel gauge rested on the bottom. Unable to afford the luxury of flying a circuit before he landed, Peter went straight in on the grass airstrip, finished his landing and turned off, aiming to taxi to the active side of the airfield. But as he turned off the engine cut. He had run out of fuel. The airfield he touched down on, with literally a drop of petrol to spare, was Nancy.

Unwitting decoy

The following morning Peter left Nancy for the short hop to his base at Rouvres. All Peter had to do was to keep heading north, in order to make the final side of the triangle. The greeting he received from his No 73 squadron groundcrew at Rouvres was less than effusive – he hadn't noticed that bullets had damaged his tail-plane, which could easily have come adrift.

What had happened on the previous day was the largest air battle of the Second World War to date, and Peter had been right in the centre of it. For evading the 27 Messerschmitts, he was dubbed 'Decoy' by the boys in the squadron. Moreover, he had now invaluable experience of fighting with the enemy. Experience was the key for a fighter pilot; the more you had, the better your chance of survival. The magnitude of this episode was played upon by the press and one account was accompanied by a dashingly portrayed double-spread illustration by the artist, C E Turner.

War Illustrated wrote: 'A fact in which the RAF may feel justifiable pride is that the French success was the outcome of a British pilot finding himself far over the line, after pursuing a German reconnaissance machine and actually joining up with a Messerschmitt formation. The enemy pilots did not recognise the British machine at first. When they did, the

The 'Wings for Victory' poster reproduced here dates back to 1940. Alongside it is a picture of Peter Ayerst taken in the same year. Note the likeness between Peter and the pilot depicted on the poster!

pilot was able to escape and led the Germans into the arms of the French.'

The event was also featured in daily newspapers in Britain, especially *The Daily Mail* and *The Daily Mirror*. It also made the *Southend Standard*: 'Westcliff airman's busy day – Chased by 27 planes. Westcliff Officer in thrilling escape – an unwitting decoy.'

Mutton Lancers in Venice

A holiday in the Dolomites a year or so ago offered the opportunity of a day excursion to Venice. It was well over half a century since I had last been in that city and I welcomed the chance to see it again.

We set off by coach early in the morning and duly arrived in the Venice dock area, where we boarded a boat that would take us direct into the centre of the city. We were soon berthed alongside the quay adjacent to St Mark's Square. The weather had begun to deteriorate but this had deterred the crowds in the square, mostly grouped attentively around their respective guides. We made our way despite the rain toward the Rialto Bridge jostled by a mass of people. By then the rain was falling heavily so we dodged into a café for some pasta; when we came out the rain had eased so we made our way to the Academy. There it was quieter and we felt that we had found the true Venice again.

It was all very different six decades ago. As a signaller with C Company of the 2/5 Battalion of the Queen's Royal Regiment, I had marched up from the River Po wondering where and when we would make contact with the enemy. But they had retreated and we entered the docks of Venice without a shot being fired. We spent our first night aboard a liner and came into the city itself the next morning. St Mark's Square was empty as we marched into the barracks some way further out, where spit and polish soon reasserted itself. Venice gradually came back to life as cafés and shops re-opened for business.

As the first company into the city, it fell to us to provide the victory parade in St Mark's Square a couple of days later. The partisans also appeared in strength and many were reluctant to surrender their weapons. Convincing them to do so seemed to be the underlying reason for the parade. But it was all resolved quite peacefully. A few days later we moved on to a remote area north of Venice where, sadly, our battalion was disbanded.
Freddie Woodiss, Surrey

* The Queens (Royal West Surrey) Regiment was known as the 'Mutton Lancers' because its badge features a sheep (or lamb) with a lance.

HMS *Petard*

My last seagoing trip before demob was aboard the *Petard* when she was towed from Chatham to Plymouth to be broken up in June 1962. Having been mothballed she retained much of her wartime armament and fittings, albeit the armament was unusable as we had no ammunition!

Two and a half years after my demob, I managed to flannel my way into GCHQ at Cheltenham, the successor to Bletchley Park, as a Radio Technician. I finally left GCHQ on retirement as a Senior Scientific Officer in 1997. Sometime during my career there I had learnt of *Petard*'s action in recovering the German codes and the *Enigma* machine from a U-Boat but I had no idea of her other exploits with the *Uarsciek* or the I27 as

related by Eric Sellars (page 32).

My naval career was as an Asdic operator (now called Sonar) and I well appreciate the activities of those ratings involved in hunting submarines. She must have had a good Asdic crew! Bearing in mind the *Petard*'s record, it is a pity that she could not have been saved from the scrap yard.
Phil White, Tewkesbury

On her father's arm

I was four years old, living with my mother in two rooms in a house opposite the Coach and Horses pub in Caerwent. The evening of VE Day my mother stood at the living room window watching the revellers in the pub celebrating. She was standing quietly with tears trickling down her cheeks because my father was in the South Wales Borderers on active service in Burma with the Fourteenth Army and there seemed little hope that his war would finish for a long time. It is one of the memories that haunts me whenever the war in the Far East is mentioned.

I can also proudly say that my father always carried me with him. All paper work, and of course photographs, were easily damaged in the damp, humid jungle. My family called me the Jerome baby because I would never pass the photo studio in Newport without having my photograph taken and of course a copy was always sent to Dad. He took one of these with him to a tattoo artist and it was copied onto his left forearm (with colour added for the large bow

of ribbon in my hair because it was a black and white photo). I feel so proud that I travelled with him for the rest of his life.
Judy Hunter, Sleaford, Lincolnshire

Lancaster memories

I was most interested to see the mention in the May *War Diary* of the flights over the Magnetic and Geographic North Poles by the RAF Lancaster *Aries*. I helped maintain and test flight this aircraft at Shawbury. It was joined by '*Aries 2*' which flew on navigational pioneering flights to Tripoli, Iraq, India, Ceylon, Nigeria, Rhodesia, Cape Province, Transvaal, Burma and Singapore.
R Weaver, Weston-Super-Mare

Rangoon remembered

I was a Royal Navy Gunner on merchant ships during the war. Three weeks before VJ Day my ship docked in Rangoon for the third time. Our cargo was comprised of 8000 tons of bombs and shells.

Next morning I was on deck when a Colonel and a Major from the Royal Artillery came on board. I greeted the Colonel with, 'Good morning Sir, can I help you?' He replied that he and the Major had visited every ship that had docked in the Burmese port over the previous three weeks looking in vain for shells for their 25-pounder guns. Their artillery had completely run out of ammunition and they would be unable to defend themselves if attacked. He added that if the Japanese found out they would be quick to react and could recapture Rangoon.

I responded, 'Sir: We have 3000 tons of 25 pounder shells on board.' He was so delighted and relieved, he put his arms around me and picked me up and swung me around the deck. He then said: 'Please don't call me Sir or Colonel any more. My name is Fred and the Major here is Harry.'

On VJ night itself, I clearly remember putting out a large fire on the ship which, if unchecked, would undoubtedly have resulted in the vessel blowing up.
Stan Russell ISM, Kent

Bombay INTERLUDE

Malcolm Hutton of Suffolk remembers a very quiet VE Day aboard the *SS Carthage*.

I volunteered for the RAF in February 1941 and was commissioned in the RAF Regiment in December 1942. A month later I was sent on a course at the Army's 45th Division Battle School near Frinton in Essex.

It was an establishment notorious for the high casualty rate of trainees due to the use of live ammunition in exercises. Sheep's blood and entrails were thrown over participants in the exercises to simulate battle conditions.

I particularly remember our seaborne assault on the Naze Tower on the cliffs at Walton on the Naze which, in fact, housed a top secret radar station. It was protected by a gun emplacement and two pill boxes and surrounded by barbed wire. In addition, there were two rows of triple Dannert concertina barbed wire, with a third row on top of them, standing between the cliff edge and the tower. (Today, the cliff edge is some 50 yards further inland, and the pill boxes have fallen to the beach below.) On previous courses we had only tackled triple Dannert at night with wire cutters or by day with some stalwart hurling himself face down on it in full pack so that his comrades could trample through on top of him. But methods like that were useless against the massive barricade protecting the Naze Tower. However, the Battle School taught its own solution.

Crossing the beach under fire from machine guns positioned along fixed lines, we scrambled up the crumbling cliffs with two of the team carrying a long length of drainpipe. We took cover just below the cliff top while the drainpipe was edged over the top and forward under the barbed wire. It had been stuffed with explosive and primed with a detonator at one end. The long lead of fuse was lit and we clung to the cliff face. When the device exploded the shock waves and reverberations through the ground dislodged one of the team who tumbled down the cliff

to the beach. When we clambered over the cliff top to make the assault there was an awesome 12 foot wide gap in the barricade for us to charge through. That was my first experience of what is known as the Bangalore Torpedo.

Ablaze with lights

My experience of VE Day was a little unusual. I was posted to the Far East three weeks before the war in Europe ended and while the war against Japan was still very much ongoing. On 14 April 1945 I embarked at Gourock on the small P&O ship *SS Carthage* and, escorted by two corvettes, we crossed to Belfast to pick up some women and children who were being returned to Gibraltar. Later in the voyage I discovered the Ministry of Health representative accompanying them was a Waaf I had met in 1941!

We joined a convoy off the south coast of Ireland and reached Gibraltar on 23 April. It was wonderful, for the first time in years, to see a town ablaze with lights. After dropping off the civilians and no longer blacked out we continued without escort to Port Suez. There the Middle East personnel disembarked and a contingent of Waaf and Wren officers boarded. They were a refreshing sight as they strolled the deck in their lightweight tropical uniforms in the searing heat of the canal and the Red Sea, although we ourselves could no longer lie around half naked. We anchored briefly at Aden and left there with the ship blacked out again.

Nearing Bombay early on Tuesday 8 May we prepared for disembarkation, handing in emergency rations, money, library books and games. The mailbags were sealed and we expected to disembark the next day. Then, unexpectedly, at 7.30 in the evening (ship's time) the ship's radio came to life and began transmitting from London where it was just before 3pm. A few moments later we heard Churchill announce that hostilities in Europe had ceased and the war had officially ended at 02.41 that morning. His speech lasted about eight minutes, of which several minutes were devoted to the war against Japan. That fight was still on, he reminded us, and we must press on with it.

Above: Malcolm in RAF Regulation attire (Tropical gear, Top Left)

Not a happy ship

After his speech, my feelings were mixed – I was glad, of course, that the war in Europe was over, but wondering what the future held for me, especially as, back in England, my wife was expecting our second child. When we dropped anchor in the bay outside Bombay harbour on Wednesday 9 May those mixed feelings turned to dismay when we learned that the ship could not be docked because the day had been declared a public holiday. All around us were ships flying bunting, flags and streamers as their radios played music. From on shore came the noise of fireworks and sounds of merrymaking. On the *SS Carthage*, however, you could feel the weight of gloom like a wet blanket. Nothing to drink – the ship's Mess was closed – and in any case we had no money. No books to read, no games to play – everything locked away ready for landing. And not much point in writing letters because the mailbags were sealed. There was nothing to do but sit on deck listening to the distant jollity. We were not a happy ship that night.

That's my memory of VE Day. Life never turns out quite as you expect, though. The war in the Far East was ended abruptly by two atomic bombs and by then I had been repatriated. I was back in England for the birth of my second daughter and, in another twist, she was born on 8 August 1945, the day of the official end of the Japanese War. Not surprisingly, that day was an extra special cause for celebration by me!

Years later, on the way to a hotel from the airport in Gibraltar, the taxi driver asked if I had been to the Rock before. When I explained my brief glimpse of the town from the deck of *SS Carthage* in April 1945 he was quite overcome. It turned out he'd been 15 at the time and was one of the children we had landed there.

Going Home

Christopher Portway (see 'One Man's War' starting on page 197 of this book) flew home to England in a converted Lancaster bomber similar to the one pictured above, surrounded by newly-freed POWs. The picture below shows a group of delighted British soldiers just released from incarceration. They are displaying a number of trophies seized from their former guards.

Released prisoners ran a gamut of emotions from guilt at being made captive in the first place, to deep depression, to unbridled joy. For some, their liberation heralded a time when they would meet their families and friends for the first time in nearly six years. It was not unusual that some fathers would be seeing sons or daughters for the first time ever, their offspring having been conceived before they marched off to war and born when 'Dad' was overseas or already a captive of the enemy.

The first garden party to be held at Buckingham Palace since pre-war days took place on 24 May, when the King and Queen were hosts to nearly 2000 former prisoners-of-war, men who had served with the army, navy and air force. The picture (above) shows the King chatting to some RAF officers with Princess Elizabeth on the right.

A POSTCARD OF *Hope*

Vicky Chart tells the story of how her father survived the war in a POW camp near Auschwitz.

My dad, Victor Emanuel McDonald, was born on 11 November 1918 – VE Day of the Great War – hence the initials VE! He was called up at the beginning of World War II. The youngest of three sons, his elder brothers were excused conscription due to their reserved occupations in the electrical industry.

After his initial training, my dad was dispatched to France, serving with the King's Royal Rifle Corps. He was a motorcycle dispatch rider and responsible for taking messages between platoons. When they landed in France most of the soldiers were captured immediately by the Germans. My dad, however, managed to evade capture but only for a couple of weeks.

Once made prisoner, all the belongings of the men were taken. However, my dad put the ring given him by his mum for his 18th birthday under his tongue. He kept it hidden all through the war. I have that ring still.

Along with all the other POWs, he was marched from France through to Germany and on to a POW camp somewhere near the German/Poland border. My dad believes the camp was located near Auschwitz as he used to talk of the clouds of smoke rising from it. At the time, of course, the soldiers had no idea what was causing the smoke – later they learnt it was the crematorium in which thousands upon thousands of prisoners were incinerated after having been gassed.

Missing in action

The march to the camp became known as the 'Long Walk' and took many months. The postcard reproduced below was thrown to the ground by my dad during the course of the march. Someone must have picked it up and posted it for him. It represented the first contact his mum had had from him since he was declared missing in action. She had previously tearfully locked herself in her bedroom for a week. The postcard was the only time she heard anything from him at all until he returned home in 1945.

Above left: Vicky Chart. Above: A photograph taken in the POW camp. Victor is on the right in the bottom row.

During his time as a POW he worked in a coalmine for over a year, 12 hours every day. On the whole he always maintained that they were treated well, other than having very little food. My dad felt that the German guards had a respect for the British. A definite cheeky chappy, my dad survived his experience by stealing whatever he could from his captors. He also quickly picked up the German language and became an interpreter.

American soldiers liberated the POW camp at the end of the war and all the prisoners simply walked out. My dad took the opportunity to acquire a number of items from his former guards, including a ceremonial dagger to protect himself with as he tried to get home. The leather belt for the dagger has a swastika embossed on its silver buckle (see picture below left). I still have the knife and belt in my possession.

Once home, my dad – by then aged 27 – found it difficult to settle back into society and actually missed life in the POW camp. For a while he was admitted to a special home to readjust.

My dad passed away in May 1995 in very tragic circumstances – when on holiday in Turkey he was knocked down by a car. I have always thought what a sad end this was for someone who had survived so much at such a young age.

The postcard reproduced here was sent by the person who found it, to Victor McDonald's mother in London, soon after he was taken prisoner in France in May 1940. Dated 31 May, it reads:

Dear Mum and boys,

I am OK and thankful I am alive and I think you should think the same. I am a prisoner of war now in Germany – well I am not in Germany yet but soon will be. When I get in a proper camp you can send me a parcel and a letter once a week. Half the Battalion have been taken prisoners ... George Balow has been wounded - on hospital boat bound for England. Bobby and a few of my pals are with me. A lot of my friends were killed but still lucky I am alive and you should thank God ... (here the writing in pencil has rubbed away).

Love Vic xxxxx

LIBERATION OF JERSEY

Brian Jones of East Yorkshire was a sailor on *HMS Cosby* when the ship was part of Force 135 that sailed to liberate the Channel Islands on the day after Britain celebrated the end of the war in Europe

When we first heard of the job, we were not at all keen on it. The war in Europe had ended, but the Germans in the Channel Islands had not surrendered. We had three-inch guns, but it was known that the islands were heavily fortified, and as we approached we expected to get blown out of the water.

However, all went well and we (ourselves and one LST) arrived quite safely in St Aubin Bay, Jersey. We had barely anchored before we were surrounded by hosts of small boats and rafts loaded with the local population. The natives appeared friendly; in fact they cheered us and shouted 'up the Navy'. That was Wednesday.

There were thousands of Germans wandering around on the island, but they were not openly hostile. Within a very short time many of the locals clambered up the ship's side, and as 'Jack' opened his heart and pocket, out poured chocolate and cigarettes. In exchange they gave us souvenirs of the Occupation and related tales of life under German rule.

The next three days were absolutely terrific. We were the first British Forces the people of Jersey had seen for five years, and they certainly let us know it. Our first blokes ashore (motor-boat crew) didn't even touch the ground, as they were chaired and cheered round St Helier. On Thursday we had a ships' concert and some of the local girls sang too. We provided many with supper by the simple means of giving them our own. But to see the pleasure on their faces as they tucked into their first square meal for five years was well worth our slight sacrifice.

Each night we could see the fireworks and hear the sounds of revelry ashore. On Friday came leave, which was what we were waiting for. The people had had a very thin time, but looked remarkably fit, despite the fact that since the start of the year, they'd been existing on Red Cross parcels weighing nine pounds each, but which had to last a month. The canteen was nearly bought out. Believe me, you could have bought a house with a pound of tobacco, but no one took advantage.

I was 'Watch' so stayed on the ship, but spent another very pleasant evening with the islanders who came aboard. By now they had just about the run of the *Cosby*! I made some very good friends whom I met the following day, and still more suppers were given away. Indeed we crew hardly ate whilst we were there, except for breakfasts. And even then, some of the islanders were aboard.

Next day was our turn. My 'oppo' (Ken) and I were to meet Martin (one of the local lads) by a well-known hotel. Martin hoped to have his car out, but he couldn't get a battery; frustrating because petrol 'borrowed' from the Germans was plentiful.

The party we were with were all from Victoria College. There were four chaps, Hugh, Martin, Eric and Dick, and three girls (sisters) Jean, Nora and Ruth (I think their surname was Mossop).

We thoroughly enjoyed ourselves. The food parcel we got ashore was greatly welcomed and they gave us tea from their Red Cross supplies. Jean was a nurse, Ruth and Nora were teaching. All the boys had been in prison for having wireless sets and/or trying to escape. Martin had only got out of prison on our arrival, and Hugh's name was in the *Daily Express* as one of the leaders of the island's resistance movement.

Girls who had been with the Germans were called 'Jerry-bags' and they were having a pretty rough time. We had been warned not to get involved. Our friends showed us all round St Helier. We saw the houses of the 'Jerry-bags' tarred with the swastika, but the thing that really struck one was the abundance of British flags and ribbons that appeared. Many had been saved since the Coronation and had been hidden away from the Germans for five years.

Another amazing thing was the large number of Germans wandering around, though they were quite docile. I know, now, what a film star feels like – if I signed my autograph once that day, I signed it a hundred times. One of my treasured souvenirs is a Jersey note with all the autographs of all of our party of friends on the back.

The day was sweltering but that didn't stop a soccer match between the ship and the island. We lost 4-1. But considering they had about 18,000 potential players (to our 180) to choose from that's not surprising. The local scouts were very much to the fore, acting as messengers and guides to the relieving troops. They'd hidden their uniforms during the Occupation.

When it was time to go, we were very sorry to leave Jersey and its people.

SIXTY YEARS ON

I was pleasantly surprised to receive an invitation to Liberation 60 in Jersey over the weekend of 6 - 10 May 2005. We duly sailed from Weymouth for St Helier and shortly after departing an announcement was made inviting veterans of Force 135 to attend a reception.

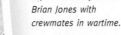

Opposite page: HMS Cosby underway.

Left: The Cosby show! Brian Jones with crewmates in wartime.

Below: Brian renews friendships with Jersey folk first forged six decades ago when he was part of the Liberation force.

AN EXTRAORDINARY TALE

Brian Jones served as a seaman from 1943 to 1946. Most of the time he was on the full commission of *HMS Cosby*, a US-built Destroyer Escort classified as a frigate in the Royal Navy and one of 78 transferred to the RN. The ships played a significant role in the war at sea but their importance has been overshadowed by more glamourous vessels. Brian says that *HMS Cosby* served mainly escorting convoys on the Atlantic, North Sea and English Channel, 'having a fairly unexciting time until participating in the Liberation of Jersey'.

In August 1945, he was witness to an extraordinary incident that led to the revealing of a sad and poignant story. It was reported at length in the William Hickey column in the *Daily Express* (reproduced in part here).

Brian was on board *HMS Cosby* in Falmouth Harbour, Cornwall, when a shipmate hooked a large fish that was promptly sent down to the galley. There the cook gutted it and, inside the fish, discovered, wrapped in tinfoil, a photograph of a lady. The *Express* carried the story on a Monday, written up in slightly tongue-in-cheek vein. By the weekend the mystery had been solved. The lady was Mrs Bianca Dault of the George Hotel, Largs, Ayrshire. Her husband was Captain Georges Dault of the French Mercantile Marine. His ship, *Villa de Tamatave,* had been torpedoed and sunk in the Atlantic en route to New York on 23 January 1943. Captain Dault was officially posted missing.

On her husband's last leave home, Mrs Dault had given him the photograph. She told the Express: 'I wrote a message in Italian on the back: "My love, I love you so much." He said he would carry it with him everywhere. I never saw him again.'

Five of us were there and were able to tell our stories for TV. I was the only one from the Navy, the others being soldiers.

Having found our hotel in St Helier we had a short reception party and more interviews, this time with the press; our photographs soon appeared in the evening editions of The Jersey Post.

The Saturday was free time until the evening so we explored the excellent Jersey Museum and a Museum of the Occupation in St Helier. Our Force 135 badges gained us many greetings and warm welcomes. I believe there were 63 veterans and their wives in our group. That evening we enjoyed a Gala Dinner in the Pomme d'Or Hotel where the entertainment was courtesy of a lady who sang the old songs of the Forties to lots of applause and much joining in.

On Sunday 8 May there was a Liberation Thanksgiving Service in the Royal Square in the presence of the Lieutenant Governor and the Bailiff of Jersey. The veterans paraded, led by the Caledonian Pipe Band. The Address was given by Terry Waite. But the most telling tribute was told in tableaux presented by local schools with various themes linked to 'Living under Occupation'.

Monday 9 May was Liberation Day. The island's main event was held in Liberation Square in St Helier. Just after 1pm we were thrilled by a display by the RAF Red Arrows. This was followed by the arrival of the parade of States Members and Members of the Royal Court, led by the band of the Island of Jersey at the head of a procession of Armed Forces youth groups and welfare organisations.

An Ecumenical service was led by the Dean of Jersey. It finished with 'Beautiful Jersey' sung by Sadie Rennard, accompanied by the Band of the Royal Welsh Regiment. The arrival of Force 135 was re-enacted by serving soldiers of the Hampshire Regiment together with sailors from *HMS Albion*.

The arrival of HRH The Queen and the Duke of Edinburgh was greeted with a 21 gun salute and followed by a presentation of music, dance and theatre celebrating the act of Liberation. The cast included children from Bad Wurzach in Germany to where 618 Jersey residents, men, women and children, were deported in 1942, the castle being their prison until the end of the war. Despite the deprivations suffered by

the deported islanders, lasting friendships were formed with the people of Bad Wurzach and the town is today twinned with St Helier. Over 2000 Islanders were uprooted from their homes and sent to internment camps in Germany. Many never returned.

During the Occupation many young Islanders tried to escape; some were successful, others were arrested, imprisoned or shot and some drowned. From an Identity Card I traced Denis Vibert who escaped on 21 September 1941 in a rowing boat. Three days later he was picked up off Portland Bill and subsequently he joined the RAF. These days he lives in the USA.

The Queen made a point of meeting many of those who had been on Jersey during the war, paying great attention to their stories. In the evening we enjoyed the Liberation 60 Gala Night at the Opera House. Six decades of music were featured, culminating in a performance of the Jersey Anthem. The night concluded with a fine *Son et Lumiere* show with spectacular fireworks.

The next day we were invited to lunch by two of the 'girls', Jean and Nora, I had met in 1945. We had all changed somewhat but were soon exchanging memories of 60 years ago. They had also invited some friends who'd also lived through the Occupation. We had a most enjoyable afternoon; this was a visit that brought back memories and renewed old friendships.

Now think about this. You live on an island threatened with occupation by the enemy. The island's defenders have been withdrawn. You have 24 hours to decide whether to leave the island with all you wish to take contained in just a single suitcase. You do not know if you will ever see your home again. The alternative is to stay and face a ruthless and cruel invader. This was the choice facing the people of the Channel Islands in June 1940. What would your decision have been?

The Daily *Express, August 1945*

WILLIAM HICKEY

But it was true

LAUGHTER is very near to tears.

A fish · story · was published in this column on Monday —how a sailor, fishing from the frigate Cosby in Falmouth harbour, caught a fish · with a snapshot inside it. On the back, in Italian, "My love, I love you so much. Your Signature illegible: looked like "Beatrice."

Frankly, I suspected it was a fo'c'sle yarn; offered a guinea for the·most ingenious story of how the portrait got into the fish.

Shoals of stories arrived by first post yesterday—tales of mystery and imagination; leg-pulls full of laughs. And the true story, which is a theme for tears.

SOMEONE snowed Mrs Bianca Dault the picture. This "Bianca" was the name I couldn't quite read; not "Beatrice." It is her portrait.

DAS BOOT!

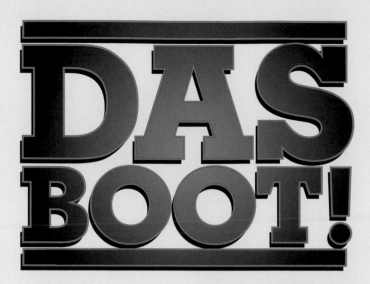

Former Royal Navy signaller Roy Holley remembers the time he saw service aboard a German U-Boat in the North Sea.

In February 1940, I turned 20 years of age and with thousands of others was 'called up'. I opted for the Royal Navy. It has never ceased to amaze me that on mobilisation, all sorts and all trades ranging from lorry drivers, bank clerks, postmen, shop assistants etc, were simply thrown together and told 'We are going to make you sailors'. It's even more amazing that by and large the 'system' worked.

I served 5½ years in various parts of the world in a variety of ships ranging from frigates to cruisers. In that time, you can imagine there was a variety of experiences covering good, bad and sometimes even hilarious. However, my strangest experience was reserved for my last ship. This was HMS Philante, a private steam yacht converted for wartime service. Before hostilities broke out it had belonged to Thomas (Tommy) Sopwith, the yachting enthusiast.

Strictly speaking, my story is not of a war time experience. The war in Europe ended in May 1945 and as a part of the surrender terms, the German U-Boat fleet was ordered to stay on the surface and fly a white flag, whereupon they would be accompanied to a UK port by a Royal Navy vessel. My ship was detailed for such a duty.

Coast of Norway

We met 'our' U-Boat somewhere off the coast of Norway and I, as a Signalman, together with a Sub-Lieutenant and four Able Seamen, comprised the escort party. I can remember trying to clamber up the seaweed-encrusted side of the U-Boat in a choppy sea. Indeed, so slippery was it that one of our men fell in the water and had

Above: Roy Holley 'then and now'.
Right: The view from a U-Boat as it closes in on a merchant ship it has already torpedoed.

to be pulled out by one of the German submariners. Upon going aboard, we did wonder what sort of reception we'd get, having had all the propaganda about this arrogant 'master race'.

In fact it was all very amicable. The U-Boat crew were for the most part young lads like ourselves, in our early 20s, who like us had been called up willy-nilly. They were soon showing us photographs of their girlfriends. We'd taken emergency food rations with us and I swapped my Spam for some salami-type sausage and all participants enjoyed the exchange.

Powerful binoculars

On the way back to the UK - destination Loch Eriboll in the far north of Scotland, we ran into a Force 10 gale. The Kapitan, who spoke very good English, wanted to submerge, explaining that in such conditions it would be much more comfortable below the surface. After a hasty confab with our 'subby', it was decided we would rough it out on top. Our thinking was perhaps influenced by the events of the First World War when the German Grand Fleet scuppered itself in Scapa Flow; we reckoned there was always the chance that the Kapitan might be one of the death or glory boys. So we stayed on top and took a pasting from the storm.

My 'loot' was a pair of very powerful binoculars, acquired on the basis of where the German crew were headed (a POW camp) they would have no need of them. I have them still.

Whenever the German U-Boat movie, Das Boot, is shown, it brings it all back to me; especially the all-pervading smell of diesel (and other substances!) in the confined spaces. From my short experience, this film seems to me far more realistic than some of the American films on the war.

Finally, on reflection, I don't suppose that many of the thousands of British lads 'called up' for the Navy ever imagined they'd end up serving on a German U-Boat!

WAR DIARY
May 1945

1 May: On the 2068th day of the war Field Marshal Gerd Von Rundstedt – one of the Wehrmacht's top commanders – is captured by US forces.

Tito's Yugoslav partisans have pushed into the port of Trieste just ahead of New Zealand troops in Britain's Eighth Army. The two forces meet at Monfalcone, west of the city. Trieste and the Istrian peninsula have been in Italian possession since the break-up of the old Austrian Empire in 1918. It will now become a focus of dispute between Tito, who says that the non-inclusion of Trieste in post-war Yugoslavia is 'unthinkable', and the Italians who want to retain it. One suggestion is for the city to become a freeport.

All of Munich, the city that played a prominent role in the rise of Hitler and the Nazis, is now in the hands of US forces.

Pacific: Australian and Dutch East Indies troops land on Tarakan Island off Borneo.

2 May: After 17 days of bitter house-to-house fighting, Berlin finally capitulates to Marshals Zhukov and Koniev. In the afternoon the garrison laid down its arms, and by evening more than 70,000 German soldiers are in captivity. British troops capture the Baltic ports of Lubeck and Wismar.

In Italy, the negotiated surrender of all Axis forces is formalised. The Wehrmacht in Trieste surrender to New Zealand troops of the Eighth Army, but other German units fight on against Tito's partisans.

3 May: Burma: Following parachute landings by Gurkha troops at the mouth of the Rangoon river two days ago, an amphibious assault is now underway. But the Japanese have already evacuated the area after destroying the oilfields and most of the city infrastructure. The Japanese retreat is confirmed by an Allied pilot who sees a message painted on

> " The Japanese retreat is confirmed by an Allied pilot who sees a message painted on the roof of the gaol: 'Japs gone. Exdigitate.' "

the roof of the gaol by POWs: 'Japs gone. Exdigitate.'

Europe: Hitler's chosen successor Admiral Donitz moves his seat of government to Denmark. Portugal observes an official day of mourning for Hitler. Irish Free State Prime Minister Eamonn de Valera calls on the German Embassy in Dublin to express his regrets at the Fuhrer's death.

Baltic Sea: Three liners carrying survivors from two concentration camps are sunk in Neustadt Bay by rocket-firing Typhoons with the loss of an estimated 8000 lives. The RAF pilots believed the vessels were German troopships. Nazi officers had forced the inmates onto the ships rather than allow the Red Cross to discover them in their camps.

British troops move in to occupy Hamburg.

4 May: Germany: Luneburg Heath is the scene of the signing of the official surrender to Monty's 21st Army Group of all German armed forces in North West Germany, the Netherlands and Denmark with effect from 8am tomorrow. More than 500,000 troops will join the 500,000 already taken prisoner in the past 24 hours. Montgomery turns down a request that German civilians fleeing the Russian advance be allowed to pass through British lines.

Japan: As the bitter battle for Okinawa goes on, the aircraft carrier *HMS Formidable* is damaged by Kamikaze attack and a further 17 US ships are sunk. Over 130 Japanese aircraft are destroyed.

By the time it ended on 2 May 1945, the Battle of Berlin is estimated to have cost the lives of at least 100,000 German civilians. Around 6000 people are believed to have committed suicide, many of them women in abject fear of rape by the vengeful men of the Red Army. German military casualties are unknown but including Volksturmm 'Home Guard' men must have equalled or surpassed the civilian figure. The Soviet command said that in the fighting in Europe in the last month of war, including the conquest of Berlin, their own dead were in excess of 150,000. It seems certain then that in the last six weeks of the war in Europe civilian and military dead will have exceeded 500,000, especially when one takes into account the fate of the hapless inmates of the Nazi death camps.

WAR DIARY
May 1945

After occupying Innsbruck and Salzburg in Austria, soldiers of the Seventh Army drove through the Brenner Pass to link up with Fifth Army troops at Vipiteno in Italy.

5 May: In Prague, Czech patriots have started an armed rising against the German garrison still occupying the city. General Patton is within reach of the capital, but the Russians insist it is their 'prize'.

Red Army units capture Swinemunde and Peenemunde on Germany's Baltic coast. The latter was the site of a key research and manufacturing plant for Germany's secret V-weapons programme. On 17 August 1943 a force of 596 RAF Lancaster bombers largely destroyed the plant.

Austria: Mauthausen concentration camp and satellite camps at Gunskirchen and Ebensee are the last such centres to be liberated. There are 110,000 survivors of whom 28,000 are Jews; 3000 emaciated inmates will die from disease and the effects of privation even after liberation. The bodies of 10,000 prisoners are discovered in a single communal grave.

Just 24 hours after Admiral Donitz ordered all remaining U-Boats at sea to return to base, five vessels are sunk by an Allied air strike in the Kattegat. The Kriegsmarine have now lost 784 of 1162 U-Boats employed in the course of the war.

Denmark: Allied troops enter Copenhagen.

Hitler's mountaintop eyrie at Berchtesgaden is captured by French Chad Territory forces. Much of the building was destroyed in an RAF raid several weeks ago.

Oregon, USA: Elsie Mitchell and five children in the town of Lakeview are killed by a bomb attached to a balloon that has floated across the Pacific from Japan.

6 May: Donitz dismisses Heinrich Himmler from all German Government offices.

Portugal severs diplomatic relations with Germany.

The important Czech arms centre of Pilsen is captured by the US Third Army as they advance on a broad front towards Prague.

7 May: In an undistinguished schoolroom in the city of Rheims, General Jodl, on behalf of Admiral Donitz signs an agreement for the unconditional surrender of all German land, sea and air forces in Europe. He states: 'With this signature, the German people and the German armed forces are, for better or for worse, delivered into the victor's hands.' General Walter Bedell Smith, Eisenhower's Chief of Staff, signs for the Allies. The surrender will come into effect at 23.01 hours tomorrow and includes German forces still fighting the Red Army. Today the garrison of Breslau capitulated to the Russians after an 82-day siege.

Troops of the Eighth Army cross the Italian frontier and enter Austria.

British and Canadian troops are moving into northern Holland and Denmark in force.

Norway: General Boehme broadcasts a 'cease fire' order to the 400,000 German service personnel occupying the country.

Firth of Forth: The last casualties of the Third Reich's war at sea are sustained when U-2336 sinks two Allied merchant ships off the coast of Scotland.

8 May: In Berlin the ratification of the surrender is signed by Chief of the German High Command, Field-Marshal Keitel, Marshal Zhukov for the Russians and Air Chief Marshal Tedder for the Western Allies. At 3pm, British Premier Winston Churchill, speaking in the House of Commons, proclaims the end of the war in Europe.

Top Nazi Herman Goering – disgraced by Hitler in the last days of the war – is arrested by US troops in Fischhorn. The last large German city yet to fall under Allied control, Dresden, is occupied by the Red Army at the end of a two day battle.

Fighting between German and Russian forces continues in parts of Czechoslovakia, although the German commander in Bohemia today ends the conflict in Prague when he surrenders the capital.

German Army Group Kurland – long cut off in this peninsula in Latvia - surrenders to the Red Army.

Croatian capital Zagreb is liberated.

Oslo: Eleven Allied officers arrive with Norwegian troops and Crown Prince Olav to declare the liberation of Norway.

Washington: President Truman warns that the war is only half won. US B-29 crews claim to have finally destroyed the last Japanese air bases on Kyushu. Aircraft from this island had helped slow the American advance on Okinawa.

9 May: The cruisers *Nurnberg* and *Prinz Eugen*, the only major German warships to survive the war intact, surrenders in Copenhagen harbour along with the last remnants of the Kriegsmarine surface fleet.

The Channel Islands are finally freed when the German occupiers sign an unconditional surrender aboard *HMS Bulldog* at 7.14am. A token force of 22 men of the Royal Artillery go ashore on Guernsey to take custody of the 10,000-strong island garrison.

Prague: Red Army troops finally secure the city after four days of hard fighting.

10 May: Norwegian patriots arrest Vidkun Quisling. The invader Nazis installed Quisling as head of a puppet administration. The name Quisling will remain synonymous with betrayal and treachery.

The first U-Boat to give itself up under the terms of the surrender arrives in Weymouth Bay, Dorset. The crew of U-249 line up on deck under the watchful eyes of a party of Polish naval ratings. Another U-Boat flying the black flag of surrender is sighted from the air off the coast of Scotland.

Field-Marshal Von Kesselring surrenders to the Americans at Hitler's Berchtesgaden retreat in Bavaria. Kesselring had led the German defence of Italy which held up the Allies for so long.

Burma: The Japanese retreat continues. It is announced that a Burma Star medal will be struck for issue to men who have fought in this campaign. On the northern coast of New Guinea Australian troops are within two miles of Wewak.

11 May: Still more German forces surrender, this time in Czechoslovakia and in the Aegean Islands.

In New Guinea, Australian forces attack Wewak where they seize the area occupied by the Japanese Eighteenth Army after a gruelling six month campaign in steamy jungle conditions. General MacArthur's 'leap-frog' policy of by-passing Japanese strongholds has left the Australians with the arduous and costly task of defeating a stubborn enemy who is more often prepared to die than surrender. MacArthur, meanwhile, has his hands full with the desperate struggle for Okinawa and the gradual liberation of the vast archipelago of the Philippines. Fresh landings of US forces on Mindanao are announced today.

Oslo: British airborne troops arrive at Gardemoen airfield. The 300 men march through the Norwegian capital's crowded streets while armed Germans remain on street duty.

12 May: Field-Marshal Montgomery is cheered by thousands of Danes lining a six-mile route in Copenhagen. Monty later lunches with King Christian and Queen Alexandrine at Amalienborg Castle where he is invested with the Grand Cross of the Order of Dannebrog with Diamond Star as a mark of the Danish people's gratitude for their liberation.

Guernsey: A convoy with 2000 tons of foodstuff is unloaded.

Crete: The unconditional surrender of the island's German garrison is signed in Heraklion.

Okinawa: Japanese reinforcements come ashore behind the American front line but are successfully repelled.

13 May: Germany: The 51st Highland Division make a ceremonial Victory Parade in the port of Bremerhaven. Kilts are in evidence along with skirling bagpipes. German civilians are confined to their homes during the period of the parade. British troops, including Scots Guards, occupy the North Sea island of Heligoland.

Suffolk: Two E-Boats put into Felixstowe Harbour bringing the German E-Boat fleet commander, Admiral Bruening, to surrender.

London: Churchill makes a broadcast to mark the Allied triumph in Europe but warns people that, 'all our toils and troubles are not yet over.' Today King George and Queen Elizabeth drive through the capital to a Thanksgiving Service at St Paul's. Elsewhere in Britain, 4407 freed POWs are flown in from the Continent by No 46 Group RAF Transport Command.

Russian troops who landed on the Danish island of Bornholm in the Baltic two days ago are in the process of rounding up the 25,000-strong German garrison which had refused to surrender. In all the operation will take five days.

14 May: On Okinawa US forces capture the important airfield at Yonabaru. In attacks on US warships the Japanese lose 21 aircraft and succeed in damaging just one vessel. In Luzon (Philippines) the Americans capture the important Balete Pass. The Allies mount constant bombing raids against Japan's home islands; today they also hit enemy airfields in China.

London: Work is about to commence on the removal of 80,000 sandbags that have successfully protected Westminster Abbey from air-raid damage for well over half a decade.

A British warship visits Gothenburg now that Sweden has declared her ports open again.

15 May: The last pockets of German resistance surrender in Yugoslavia. Nearly a million and a half Yugoslav civilians (including 55,000 Jews) and 305,000 soldiers have perished out of a pre-war population of 15 million. Partisan leader Tito is determined to keep his country united and has accepted royalists into a provisional government while making it clear that Yugoslavia will be a communist state.

Oslo: Crown Prince Olaf of Norway, wearing British battledress, arrives from exile in England aboard a Royal Navy destroyer. He is welcomed by Maj-Gen Robert Urquhart, commander of the British First Airborne Division, who are in the vanguard of the Allied liberation forces. Urquhart led the First Airborne at the ill-fated 'Bridge Too Far' battle at Arnhem in September 1944.

Okinawa: In the face of fierce resistance US troops inch their way into the island capital, Naha. The Japanese war cabinet announces the abrogation of all treaties with Germany and other European nations.

16 May: The last major surface action of the war takes place in the Mallaca Straits west of Penang in Malaya and ends with the sinking of the Japanese cruiser *Haguro* by aircraft and destroyers of the Royal Navy's East Indies Fleet.

A British naval and military expedition re-occupies Alderney, the last of the Channel Islands to be freed, and takes 3200 Germans prisoner.

17 May: In London the Minister of Fuel and Power announces a basic petrol ration for civilians as from 1 June.

Indian Ocean: Allied heavy bombers attack Japanese strongholds on the Andaman Islands.

18 May: US casualties on Okinawa approach 20,000 – more than those sustained in the conquest of Iwo Jima. Though the capital Naha was entered yesterday, the campaign has been bogged down, with average daily forward movement of just 133 yards.

Japan withdraws garrisons from the Chinese ports of Foochow, Amoy and Swatow and transfers them to Hong Kong. Chinese troops will enter the Treaty port of Foochow later today.

Trieste: Marshal Tito and his partisans refuse to leave this disputed territory and claim they have the right to make the city part of Yugoslavia.

London: In a radio broadcast, Clement Atlee MP says: 'I have just returned from San Francisco. There the delegates of nearly 50 nations have been meeting in order to try to construct the framework for the preservation of peace.'

19 May: The unceasing daily round of air strikes by US Fortresses and Super-Fortresses against Japan continue. Targets today include Hamamatsu, near Nagoya, and the island of Formosa.

Burma: Around 66,000 Japanese soldiers remain in Burma boxed into three areas. Around 40,000 are in the eastern sector and this is the only place where organised resistance goes on as the enemy seeks to keep open an escape route to Siam and Moulmein. It is estimated that Japanese casualties in Burma total 105,328 since 1 February 1945.

20 May: Okinawa: Japanese soldiers in US Marine uniforms make a desperate counter-attack, but are bloodily repulsed.

On 8 May 1945 the destroyer HMS Bulldog and escort HMS Beagle left Plymouth to rendezvous with the Germans four miles off Guernsey. After tense negotiations, the German commander of the Channel Islands finally agreed to a full surrender with effect from the next day, 9 May. This was in fact the day after VE Day was heralded in Britain and most of the rest of Europe! Indeed the last Channel Island to be freed was Alderney on 16 May. All civilians had been evacuated from this island but it was not until December that the inhabitants were able to return. The picture on the right shows German prisoners on the beach on Jersey waiting to be shipped to camps on the mainland. The pages from an autograph book reproduced here contain the signatures of soldiers and sailors of the Liberation force. The book is in the possession of Mrs Patricia Foster who was a schoolgirl on Jersey during the war. Her memories of the Occupation appear on pages 220 and 221 of this book.

WAR DIARY

May 1945

China: Rail installations along the River Yangtse near Nanking are attacked by Allied bombers.

21 May: On the orders of the British, the last hut of the infamous Belsen concentration camp is burned to the ground. Allied troops hold an outdoor dance on the site of the camp; the men's partners are Yugoslav girls held in Belsen and now awaiting repatriation

Washington announces that the US First Army under General Hodges is on its way from Europe to the Pacific via the USA.

Chief architect of the Nazi terror policy, Heinrich Himmler, is caught by the British. He was found disguised as a rural policeman. Admiral Donitz is also arrested in Denmark, along with leading members of his short-lived government.

Middle East: The Government of Syria and the Lebanon protest at the presence of French troops and call for the withdrawal of all foreign forces, 'now that the war is over'.

22 May: Copenhagen: The cruisers *Prince Eugen* and *Nurnberg* are handed over to the Senior British Naval Officer in Denmark, Rear-Admiral Reginald Holt. The German crews of the two ships will sail them to Wilhelmshaven to join four destroyers and about 130 Kriegsmarine warships in the custody of the Royal Navy.

On the 1262nd day of the war against Japan, the US War Department makes public for the first time the existence of the enemy's balloon bomb campaign that has caused casualties along the western seaboard of the USA and Canada.

A French poster celebrates the fiery death of the Nazi eagle.

23 May: British Second Army HQ, Luneburg: Despite stringent security measures, Gestapo and SS chief Himmler manages to commit suicide by biting on a cyanide capsule concealed in his mouth. Yet another top Nazi prepared to betray Hitler in the last desperate days of the Reich, Himmler chooses suicide over the ignominy of a war crimes trial by the Allies.

US troops in Germany discover 4 million in mixed currency, believed to be Himmler's personal cache.

At home, Winston Churchill visits the King to resign as Prime Minister, thus ending the wartime coalition government. He is invited to form a new administration ahead of a general election to be held on 5 July.

24 May: Australian troops have been fighting hard in the jungles of New Guinea for the first five months of this year. Cape Moem, the last enemy stronghold in Wewak, falls to the 6th Australian Division today.

Okinawa: The Japanese mount another desperate attempt to turn the tide of battle when aircraft carrying assault troops crash land on US airfields. The Americans are on permanent high alert in anticipation of surprise attacks and kill all of the enemy.

Burma: Fourteenth Army troops reach the inland port of Bassein.

25 May: More honours for Montgomery when he receives the Grand Cross of the Legion of Honour from General de Gaulle in Paris.

In Tokyo, Emperor Hirohito and his family barely escape with their lives as part of the Imperial Palace is destroyed by B-29 bombers flying from the Marianas; 464 aircraft have dropped 4000 tons of bombs on the capital in the past two days. The Japanese retaliate with even more Kamikaze attacks on Okinawa and Allied shipping; 111 Japanese aircraft and pilots are lost. The US Navy announces the sinking of the destroyer *Little* and four small vessels.

Burma: Fourteenth Army units occupy the inland port of Bassein, 88 miles west of Rangoon.

26 May: A round-the-world RAF Lancaster completes experimental flights over the Magnetic and Geographic North Poles to test radio and radar, compass and other navigational equipment. Today the aircraft, codename Aries, touched down at the Empire Air Navigation School at Shawbury, Shropshire.

Middle East: Tension between French troops and Syrian forces grows and shooting is reported in the city of Aleppo.

27 May: Okinawa: Part of the capital Naha is declared secured. Chinese troops entered Nanning, capital of Kwansi province.

The rail link between Berlin and Moscow is operating once more. Carriages and engines must change at the River Vistula due to the different rail gauges.

28 May: The seaport of Yokohama, Japan, suffers a first air raid by 500 US Super-Forts which drop 2500 tons of bombs. Earlier, Mustangs from Iwo Jima neutralised the city's fighter defences. It is estimated that 60,000 homes are destroyed and 250,000 civilians made homeless. Units of the British Pacific Fleet arrive at Apra Harbour, Guam.

Germany: The British traitor William 'Lord Haw-Haw' Joyce is captured by the British Second Army. Joyce broadcast pro-German propaganda from Berlin for most of the war.

Middle East: Syrian workers go on strike in Damascus and Aleppo. French guns shell the Syrian local administrative office at Homs and three French soldiers are killed by tribesmen at Hama.

29 May: Air Force chiefs still believe the non-stop aerial assault on Japan will prove to be the decisive factor in preventing a long drawn out infantry invasion. Thousands of civilians have abandoned urban areas and blitzed factories producing war supplies and armaments. Domestic morale has slumped profoundly. Additional B-29 aircraft have been ordered to the Far East from India to intensify the onslaught. Today the Allies announce that 51 square miles of Tokyo have been destroyed in Super-Fortress firebomb attacks.

30 May: Over 100,000 US troops went ashore on Okinawa in the landings which commenced on 1 April. Just 325 miles from the Japanese mainland, the enemy has mounted a fanatical defence of the 34-mile long island. The US claim that the Japanese death toll up to today is 61,519; just 1353 soldiers of the Emperor have been made prisoner.

Damascus: A truce has been arranged between the French and Syrian nationalists to allow the evacuation of British and US civilians caught up in the fighting in the city.

Tehran: The Persian Foreign Minister demands the withdrawal of British, US and Russian troops from oil-rich Persia.

31 May: England is gradually returning to normal life. The last air raid shelter bunks are removed from South Wimbledon Underground station. On beaches along the South and East coasts, civilian casualties still occur from incidents involving mines and unexploded ordnance. Royal Engineers and navy divers are tackling the long and dangerous task of clearing minefields on beaches identified as possible invasion routes for the Germans in the danger years 1940-41. Unfortunately, some maps identifying mine locations have been lost and coastal erosion has added to the problems of locating the mines. In cities and towns other teams work on defusing unexploded bombs discovered buried in rubble. It is a task that will go on for many years.

The Admiralty announce that between 3 September 1939 and 8 May 1945, 730 Royal Navy ships have been lost.

Levant: Intervention by the British diplomats leads to a cease-fire in Syria and the Lebanon.

Thirteen Japanese flying-boats were smashed in a heavy Royal Air Force raid on the harbour of Port Blair in the Andaman Islands.

SMASH JAPANESE AGGRESSION!

JUNE 1945

the Royal Australian First Tactical Air Force.

A Brigade of the Ninth Division also quickly occupied Labuan Island in Brunei Bay and secured the port on 10 June, seizing the airport on the same day. Surviving Japanese withdrew into a pocket where nearly all of them were to die. The capture of Brunei Town was announced on 13 June.

In mid-June, Seafires, Fireflies and Avengers from the British Pacific Fleet were in action against Japanese positions in the Caroline Islands, just north of New Guinea. No Japanese aircraft opposed them and the British lost just one plane to ground fire.

At this time it was thought that the war against Japan would go on for many months or even years to come. With this prospect in mind, it is fascinating to learn that there was a jungle warfare school established in Derbyshire, at Rowsley, midway between Chatsworth and Haddon Hall. Experts were brought back from Burma and the Far East to teach fighting techniques that had proved effective against the Japanese to men who expected to eventually go into action against the enemy in Burma and the Malayan peninsula. British soldiers wore captured Japanese uniforms to give realism to the exercises.

THE FAR EAST

The Burmese capital, Rangoon, had been captured by Slim's Fourteenth Army on 3 May and mopping up continued throughout the month. Japanese forces still in the country were in a precarious position. Then in June the monsoon rains came and the Allies found it difficult to advance.

Most of the Japanese were concentrated behind the Sittang river and from here they mounted a number of counter-attacks against a lightly-held front, at one time establishing a bridgehead on the western bank of the river that necessitated the withdrawal of a Gurkha battalion.

The rains meant that no significant Allied operations could be mounted. However, there were an estimated 10,000 Japanese troops cut off in the Pegu Yomas mountains who sought to escape. They were in very poor shape, short of food and ammunition and it was estimated by the end of June that half of them had been killed in attempts to break through the

Fourteenth Army cordon. Slim was confident that few of the remainder would get away.

Elsewhere in the region, Australian and Dutch forces were making progress. In the first half of June 1945 the Australian Ninth Division met no opposition when it landed at Brunei Bay on the island of Borneo and Labuan and Muara islands.

Brunei Bay offered the best harbour on Borneo's north west coast and the US Navy proposed it as an advanced base for the British Pacific Fleet. The British felt that it was located too far from the main theatre of operations and would take too long to make ready – possibly until the end of the year by which time Singapore might have been recaptured. Not withstanding these reservations, the Aussies went in, supported by the US Seventh Fleet and

The fierce and prolonged fight for the island of Okinawa in the spring of 1945 gives a graphic picture of the bitter cost of war in the Pacific.

Okinawa

Allied preparations began early in March with long-range air strikes against Okinawa, the Japanese home islands, air bases in China, on Formosa and on other Chinese offshore islands. Aircraft from carriers in British Task Force 57 assisted in the campaign, in the main by preventing Japanese reinforcements from flying in to Okinawa from Sakishima Island. The British had Seafires – the naval version of the Spitfire – fitted with 'drop' fuel tanks that doubled their flying range.

In the last days of March, as the vast invasion armada of 1200 ships approached the Ryukyus Islands, of which Okinawa was the largest, the Allied air strikes intensified. On 26 March, the Americans made a surprise landing in the Kerama Islands, 20 miles west of Okinawa and five days later captured Keise, an island that gave the US forces artillery positions able to cover the landings on the main island.

The Japanese were taken by surprise at these moves. The loss of Kerama was a major blow to their defence plans for they had hidden 350 motor-torpedo boats there. Loaded with high explosive and manned by volunteer suicide crews, these boats were intended to ram and sink Allied warships and transports as they gathered for the landings.

During the early hours of 1 April, the great amphibious armada approached Okinawa and commenced a massive bombardment of the eight-mile-long landing area. Marines and infantry poured ashore from 8.30am onwards and found to their astonishment and delight no enemy resistance; by the end of the day 50,000 Americans were ashore backed by artillery and tanks.

Devastating suicide weapon

Japanese commander, General Mitsuru Ushijima, was content for the US forces to land unmolested. Though he no longer had the motor-torpedo boats he could still count on another potentially devastating weapon wreaking havoc on the American fleet; hundreds of Kamikaze suicide pilots awaited the order to crash their aircraft into Allied ships. Ten of Japan's few remaining warships, including Yamato, the biggest battleship in the world, were also to sail from Japan intent on confronting the Allied navies. Confident that the combined air and sea attacks would severely disrupt the American fleet, Ushijima wanted to keep his 140,000 strong force complete in order to launch an all-out attack when he perceived the enemy had weakened.

Kamikaze attacks began in earnest on 6 April and caused much damage to the invasion fleet. Next day, however, US carrier planes spotted and sank the Yamato and five other vessels and severely damaged the remainder of the Japanese warships.

The Americans ashore found few Japanese in the north of Okinawa and by mid-April were in possession of 80% of the 64-mile-long island. A few weeks later, island-based US fighter planes were now able to intercept enemy aircraft coming south from Japan and this factor combined with improving navy tactics for dealing with Kamikaze attacks greatly reduced the threat they posed.

Mountain strongholds

Meanwhile, in the south of Okinawa, the most ferocious period of fighting began when the Americans came up against a Japanese defensive position known as the Shuri Zone that comprised a deep, interlocking complex of mountain forts extending across the island. Steep slopes, broken ridges and cliffs honeycombed with caves greatly favoured the defenders.

At dawn on 4 May, as US forces reorganised, the Japanese emerged from caves and defiles all along the frontline in a major counter-attack co-ordinated with a mass Kamikaze air attack. Combined US artillery, aircraft and rifle and machine-gun fire held the assault; after two days and 5000 soldiers killed the remaining Japanese pulled back into their mountain strongholds. There were around 1000 US casualties.

Out at sea on this same day, HMS Formidable and HMS Indomitable are both hit by single kamikaze aircraft. The armoured decks of the British Pacific Fleet carriers minimise the damage and they are both soon operational again. By contrast, many US carriers without armoured decks sustain severe damage. On 9 May, Formidable is hit a second time along with a suicide strike on HMS Victorious. Damage is again limited.

On 11 May the US commander, General Simon B Buckner Jr, launched an offensive on both flanks of the Japanese line. The battle-hardened Americans made slow and costly

Top: The US aircraft carrier Enterprise survived all the major engagements including Okinawa and was nicknamed the 'Survivor of the Pacific'.

Right: Japanese 'kamikaze' speedboats captured before they could be deployed.

Okinawa

progress in the face of fanatical Japanese resistance. Then on 21 May, Ushijima began a skillful withdrawal from the Shuri Zone to avoid the threatened encirclement. US efforts to prevent an orderly retreat were thwarted and the Japanese pulled back into a last-ditch position in the mountainous southern tip of Okinawa.

Families die rather than surrender

The Americans were not in a position to attack this last redoubt until 12 June. Again they deployed in encircling drives around the centre of the stronghold, smashing in turn each stronghold or pocket of resistance but all the while incurring heavy casualties from a determined enemy. The two spearheads met on 20 June. All organised resistance now collapsed, as Japanese troops, for the first time in the war, began surrendering in large numbers. Even so, the majority preferred death to captivity and many civilians as well committed suicide by jumping off cliffs, some taking their children with them, rather than give up to an enemy they believed would kill them anyway.

The US commander did not live to see the final victory he had planned. On 18 June he was at a forward observation post of a Marine battalion, peering at Japanese positions less than 300 yards away. One of the few remaining Imperial Army artillery pieces scored a direct hit on the post, killing General Buckner outright.

Heavier US losses than at Pearl Harbour

It is estimated that 130,000 Japanese were killed in the campaign and 7400 were made prisoner. US ground, air and naval losses totalled over 13000 dead and 36,000 wounded. The US Navy, in fact, suffered its heaviest losses of the entire war, even greater than at Pearl Harbour; 36 vessels were sunk and 368 warships, transports and smaller ships were damaged. Nearly 8000 Japanese aircraft were destroyed; the Americans lost 763.

Between 24 March and 21 June, British carrier-borne aircraft had flown 5000 sorties in the East China Sea area in support of the Okinawa invasion. No British ships were lost.

Now, with an outpost and a major base only 350 miles from Japan itself, the Allies were ready to start planning for their final invasion. Privately, senior commanders thought that the fight to subdue the Japanese home islands could cost a million Allied lives or more.

RACE TO RANGOON

The reference in the April 1945 *War Diary* to the Fourteenth Army reaching Pegu in Burma on the 30th of that month has spurred me to write. After their defeat at Kohima and Imphal it became apparent that the Japanese had become greatly disorganised. Once Meiktila was cleared the great anxiety became the need to establish a supply port before the monsoon broke and Rangoon, some 300 miles away, became the primary objective.

Except for a short pause at Toungoo we just kept going. We made 'Harbour' and dug-in each night just off the narrow main road and every morning had a regular supply drop from Dakotas. Everything we needed, from thousands of gallons of petrol to ammunition and food (US 'K' rations), came to us by parachute. We were strafed by Japanese Zero fighters on two consecutive mornings, but on the third a flight of Spitfires saw them off and we never saw an enemy aircraft again.

I heard it said that this advance might well have been the fastest in history. It was also said that the advance went against accepted military principle in that 255 Tank Brigade was out on a limb without infantry support.

Pegu lies at the junction of the main road from Mandalay and the main road round Moulmein Bay from Rangoon. The defile referred to was actually a *chaung* or dried-up river bed. In the monsoon this would become a raging torrent. Road and railway bridges across it were both demolished. The enemy objected to our arrival at the *chaung* so we withdrew about a mile and pulled into a dried-up paddy field on one side of the road. On the other side there was a pagoda from where a sniper took a personal dislike to me. I think he fired three rounds, without doing any damage, before being despatched. Shortly afterwards a flight of American fighter-bombers arrived. After circling around the first aircraft peeled off and dived towards his target. For some reason the pilot failed to pull out and went straight into the deck and exploded. The others hesitated for a few minutes and then plastered the target.

Meanwhile a patrol had crossed the *chaung* and encountered a column of British prisoners being marched from Rangoon towards Moulmein. The patrol brought the prisoners back with them; I have never seen men in such a deplorable condition. Our immediate instinct was to offer them our

rations, but this was not permitted

because in their emaciated state they would be unable to digest the food and could die. Overnight, a landing strip was prepared and next morning Dakotas landed and took them off to safety.

First into Kuala Lumpur

A few weeks later I was on board a troopship contemplating taking part in the invasion of Malaya. It was called *Operation Zipper* (because there was nothing buttoned up). The landing was delayed and we were later told of the dropping of the (second) atomic bomb and the Japanese surrender. There was some uncertainty about the reaction of local Japanese commanders, so we were ordered to land in the expectation of a fight as planned. We went ashore in landing craft on Morib Beach to the north of Port Swettenham but were thankfully unopposed.

Chinese guerillas turned up shortly after the landing and, guided by them, I was part of a small section despatched to Kuala Lumpur. Except for columns of Japanese troops marching to their surrender assembly point, the city seemed to be completely deserted – not a soul to be seen or a sound to be heard. Near the main railway station, passing the end of a back-street, there was a fleeting glimpse of a black, hooded figure. A few minutes later we were surrounded by nuns from a nearby convent. Their joy at seeing us was, for me, a high point of the war. They were mostly Irish and Belgium ladies but Mother Superior apologised for the absence of one nun – a Japanese lady who she said was too ashamed to meet us because of the conduct of her countrymen during the occupation.

A final observation; when things go wrong one man usually bears the brunt of the criticism – in Burma this would have been the Yorkshireman, General Slim. But things did not go wrong. While Slim could not have done it all himself, certainly his team did a remarkably fine job. I have never ceased to wonder at the organisation needed to deal with thousands of men, their supplies and support, not to mention the unforeseen complications which had to be – and were – dealt with. Whoever they were they should be heartily congratulated.

R T Purvis, Southsea, Hants

War Correspondence

End of the war

Winter 1944. Following three years' involvement with landing craft in various activities I found myself on draft to *HMS Cricket* (the insect not the game) as an Able Seaman in an Assault Flotilla of ALC's (Assault Landing Craft).

After a period of refit and replacements of personnel, the flotilla having lately returned from operations in the River Scheldt, the day arrived when we chugged off down the river from Bursledon and picked up our American Dock Landing Ship in the Solent. This conveyed us across to Ostend in Belgium. We then undocked and proceeded under our own steam (or rather the power from the Ford V8 petrol engines in our boats) to Antwerp. Then, oddly, each boat was loaded onto a Tank Transporter. They conveyed us to Oosthout in North Brabant, Holland, where we finally again took to the waters of the River Maas. No word of explanation as to why we were there was ever bestowed on we Ratings.

However, during the following opening months of 1945 we, together with sundry Army details, patrolled the canals and rivers of that part of Holland until the happy day in May 1945 when we heard that the Germans had packed it in.

I do remember the Officers' dinner at an inn in Oosterhout. I had been detailed to assist at their celebrations and passed the time in an alcoholic haze! I also recall the visit of us Ratings to a travelling Army Bath Unit where a luxurious hot shower was on offer. Our battledress was taken away and later returned clean and pressed; a most memorable experience!

Our appearance gave some of the locals amusement and I suspect they couldn't make out whether we were sailors or soldiers as battledress topped with naval caps somehow didn't seem to fit together. I can't recall how we got back to the UK, perhaps it was by our own efforts.

I do know that we were drafted to *HMS Lizard*, in Grand Avenue and Kingsway, Hove. We were then drafted to *HMS Braganza* in Bombay, courtesy of *HMT Monarch* of Bermuda. The intention was to take us onwards to Port Swettenham in Malaya for further amphibious operations against the Japanese. However, the war ended and the need for our services ended with it.

L C Hedge, Hassocks, West Sussex

Prisoner on Formosa

June's *Sixty Years On* (page 282 of book) carries the statement, 'Allied preparations for the invasion of Okinawa began early in March 1945 with long range air strikes against… air bases in Formosa.' I was a POW of the Japanese on Formosa for three years (one of which was spent in the notorious copper mine at Kinkaseki) and in 1944 was in a camp at Hai-To in the south of the island. I kept a diary and I first start mentioning air raids in October – presumably by American planes. We had seen B29s flying high overhead on the way to other targets and assumed the Americans were working their

way across the Pacific towards Japan. We never had any up-to-date news.

During air raids we were confined to our huts. There was a bucket at each end for bodily functions because our diet of rice meant we were constantly in need of relief fore and aft. Most of the rice on air raid days, having been cooked overnight, was sour.

During my time in this camp I mainly worked on the railway loading trucks with stones and gravel, but in early 1945 I worked in a factory about a mile away where sugar was produced from locally grown sugar cane. We were constantly having to make for the air raid shelters and on 7 February I record that the camp itself had been attacked with anti-personnel bombs, resulting in 28 prisoners killed and around 80 injured. A few days later, when we returned from the factory to the camp, we were issued with blood-stained blankets. The camp from the air would have looked like a military target as it was not marked in any way as a POW camp.

Soon after this we were moved back to the north of the island where we were employed on menial tasks. Finally, on 10 June we were taken up into the hills after being told that we would have to grow our own food. But first we had to build our own camp. Conditions were very bad. We were all suffering from starvation (and many from dysentery and malaria and other ailments) and were all sleeping directly on the ground. Those who simply could not work were put on half rations amounting to about a cup of rice twice a day with weeds as vegetables.

By the middle of August we learned that the war was over, but many of the original 100 fellow prisoners captured with me did not see that day.

Basil Baker, Croydon, Surrey

Good news from the air

The piece *Italy – the Final Push* in the April *Sixty Years On* (page 252 of book) reminded me of how I learnt of the end of the war in Italy. I was with 15 Airfield Construction Group at Treviso airfield, north of Venice. I had restored the cratered grass runway and our 'Spitbomber' wing had flown in ready for operations.

Soon afterwards a B17 Flying Fortress flew low over the runway, dropping several bundles which turned out to contain copies of the US Army's *Stars and Stripes* Mediterranean newspaper, dated Thursday 3 May 1945. The banner headline read NAZI ARMIES IN ITALY SURRENDER. I still have a copy.

D J Wakefield CB, Gillingham, Dorset

D J Wakefield (see letter on this page) learnt of the end of the war in Italy from a US military newspaper dropped from a Flying Fortress. The British equivalent of the Stars and Stripes *was the* Union Jack. *This is the front cover of the special edition issued on Thursday 3 May 1945 announcing the surrender of the German army on the previous day. Field-Marshal Sir Harold Alexander's Special Order of the Day is quoted: 'Soldiers, sailors and airmen of the Allied Forces in the Mediterranean Theatre. After two years of hard and arduous fighting, which started in Sicily in the summer of 1943, you stand today as the victors of the Italian Campaign.'*

For many of the men of the Eighth Army, the fighting had begun long before the landings in Sicily; they had been fighting the Italians and later the Germans in North and East Africa since 1940.

Sea of SECRETS

Main picture: US sailors heading for home excitedly view the skyline of New York.
Inset: A postcard showing the Queen Elizabeth in peacetime paintwork. New York was the most frequent destination of both this vessel and her sister ship the Queen Mary.

May 1945. Some incidents at sea kept secret from earlier in the war are being disclosed. One concerns a naval disaster off the coast of Donegal on 2 October 1942. The *Queen Mary* – with 15,000 US troops on board – was travelling all-out for the Clyde with an escort of two cruisers. The *Queen Mary* was steering the usual zig-zag course so as not to present an easy target for torpedoes. Travelling at 30 knots, she crashed full tilt into *HMS Curacao*, which, cut in half, sank in five minutes, taking 338 of her crew with her. *Queen Mary* sustained a huge dent in her bow and was forbidden to stop to aid survivors because of the danger posed by any lurking U-Boats.

Sister ship *Queen Elizabeth* came close to grief in April 1945 when, two days out from New York, an enormous 'rogue' wave almost overwhelmed her. Thousands of tons of water cascaded onto her decks and for a second or two the entire vessel was immersed. Fortunately, the ship righted herself; there were no casualties although the material damage was extensive.

Bombs smuggled aboard

Two years previously, *Queen Elizabeth* had been involved in a serious breach of security while berthed in New York. Despite a guard of 750 security personnel, two small bombs were somehow smuggled aboard the ship, presumably by Nazi agents or sympathisers. Upon being discovered, the devices were thrown into the harbour.

Figures released on 19 May 1945 show that the two Queens between them since the spring of 1940 had transported 1,250,000 Allied troops across 95,000 miles of the world's oceans. In fact the *Queen Mary* still holds the record for the most people on board a single ship at one time – 16,683. Hitler offered a bounty equivalent of £50,000 to any of his U-Boat crews that sank one of the Queens. But the Grey Ghosts, as they were known, remained unmolested in their high-speed zig-zag dashes across the Atlantic throughout the war even though Nazi propaganda chief Goebbels once announced to the world that the *Queen Elizabeth* had been torpedoed.

Churchill's tribute to the Queens

After VJ Day, the *Queen Mary*, while still primarily in her wartime grey, had her funnels repainted back to Cunard red and black. It was with this appearance that she made 11 more crossings to the United States and Canada on these occasions carrying British 'GI Brides.'

The *Queen Mary*'s 1001st and very last Atlantic crossing began on 31 October 1967. She was en route to Long Beach, California, where she now resides as a floating hotel and conference centre. Sister ship *Queen Elizabeth* met a much more dramatic end when, on 9 January 1972, she was gutted in a mysterious fire that left her a sunken hulk in Hong Kong harbour.

Winston Churchill crossed the Atlantic three times aboard *Queen Mary* during his wartime premiership. It is fitting then to let his eloquence pay tribute to the war service of the two great Monarchs of the Atlantic: 'Built for the arts of peace and to link the Old World and the New, the Queens challenged the fury of Hitlerism in the Battle of the Atlantic. Without their aid the day of final victory must unquestionably have been postponed.'

A Boy's Own WAR

In the last years of the war, Ron McGill was a teenager living in South West London. He left school at the age of 14 in the second half of 1944 to become a Telegraph Boy Messenger with the GPO. Here he records some of his many memories of those turbulent times, beginning with the build-up to D-Day, taking us through the V1 and V2 rocket assaults on the capital and concluding in the euphoria of the Victory summer and autumn that followed the surrenders of Germany and Japan. An accomplished artist, Ron's stories are accompanied by his own delightful pen sketches.

UNDER THE TREES

Sometimes I find it hard to believe that 60 years have passed since 1944, a year which so many people in Europe today regard as one of the most vital and momentous for our civilisation.

I was living with my family at Roehampton at that time and many items remain fresh for me to this day – even though I was just a schoolboy. Like countless other youngsters I had quickly become an expert with aircraft and military vehicle recognition. But living in the London outskirts we could never see aircraft on the ground, taking off or landing. Then one day my friend John was told by his Uncle (who worked for Vickers at Weybridge) that you could sit near the runway at Wisley airfield and get a good view of the planes.

That was it! Out came the road maps, our cycles were oiled and cleaned, parental permission obtained (reluctantly!), sandwiches were packed and one early morning on a springtime Sunday five of us set off for the 20 odd mile ride to Wisley. Cycling up and down the hills between Esher and Cobham was hard going but tired limbs were forgotten as it soon became clear by the mass of military road traffic that something was well and truly up!

We turned left off the main Portsmouth Road near Wisley and entered the long and leafy country lanes that led to Effingham Junction.

What a sight for our eager eyes for all along one side of the road and drawn up on the verges under the trees were rows of camouflaged tanks. There seemed to be miles of them and their resting crews happily cheered our little group all the way through to the edge of Wisley airfield.

We knew they were Churchill and Sherman tanks and the crews were British and Canadians who asked us where we'd cycled from and whether we had folks in the services and suchlike. The Canadians gave us gum, boiled sweets and wonderful chocolate! We were allowed to climb all over the Shermans until we finally left our new friends with our best wishes for what they said was 'another exercise!'

We sat by the airfield fence for our sandwiches and watched a succession of Wellingtons, Oxfords and Ansons doing circuits and bumps. Then it was time for the homeward ride via Cobham and Esher to Roehampton. The round trip of some 50 miles was hard on our little legs but the day was so memorable with that incredible sight of countless tanks and their super crews who had quite overwhelmed us with their kindness.

I was discussing this incident in later years with a sub-Postmaster friend who was a D-Day Landing Craft veteran. He was certain that the armoured squadrons we had stumbled upon in Surrey were part of the assault group held back until the Normandy beaches were secured.

He recalled the armoured units being landed and launched into the massive drive to the left of Caen code-named 'Goodwood'. Sadly, I subsequently found that our tank losses there were dreadfully heavy and I could but wonder how many of our friends on that sunny day under the trees had survived that battle and made it to peacetime.

A RACE FOR LIFE

As Britain's famous Jonathan Edwards came pounding down the running track for his final jump in athletic competitions a year or so ago I thought that most of us can only marvel at the speed he achieved with his superb leaps. Yet I can recall a day in the second half of 1944 when somebody ran faster than Jonathan in a frantic race for life.

The speed-star was none other than my dear Mother, then in her late 40's, about five foot in height, amply built and hampered with a shopping bag and two children of 11 and 13 years respectively hanging on her arms - yet her sprint over some 60 yards was truly something else!

Mother decided to chance the air raid warnings and travel from Roehampton to visit her sister Rose who lived in Paradise Road in Stockwell, South West London. My sister Jean and I went as well and we travelled by bus to Clapham and then on to Stockwell without incident ? but the siren's alert sounded as we stepped off the bus.

Chilling clatter

Although it was early afternoon the day was gloomy due to the low clouds and we hurried to Paradise Road with many anxious glances up at the sky ... suddenly we heard that most fearful of sounds, the chilling clatter of a V1 Flying Bomb (or Doodlebug) approaching from the Camberwell direction.

By this time in the war Londoners had learned that the V1 could just arrive and dive straight down to explode the 1000lb warhead or the motor could cut out and the missile glide down before exploding. Thankfully, this particular Doodlebug proved to be the latter and as we looked back we heard the motor cut out and saw the dreaded shape of the V1 nosing out of the clouds and gliding down towards us!

There was a brick built shelter in the roadside ahead of us with people waving their arms frantically to us - my Mother just grabbed us and literally took off in the desperate race for the shelter. I have no recollection that our feet ever touched the ground as my Mother, clearly fuelled with adrenalin in abundance, made that astonishing race for the shelter door. We were dragged in to safety as the black winged shape swished overhead to fall to the rear of my Aunt's house nearby. The explosion was deafening and most of the blast went forward to demolish the houses in the next road where there were many injured but I think no fatalities.

We were choking in a vast cloud of dust and grit and when this gradually cleared we could see the top of my Aunt's house had disappeared but the front bay window was intact (minus glass) with the begrimed figure of my Aunt Rose still sitting at the piano! As the Wardens and helpers pulled her from the debris she was fighting mad and could say nothing but 'that ******* Hitler had ruined her prize piano!'

In later years we often teased my Mother for her remarkable turn of foot in a crisis but we also knew that it was only the cut out and glide of the V1 that had saved us that day for the more usual immediate powered dive would surely have ended our lives out in the open in Paradise Road.

BLOWN UP!

That was a remarkable time for many Londoners who somehow lived and worked on throughout the massive assault on Britain from Nazi Germany's 'Vengeance' weapons. After over four years of war, for many folks this first-ever attack by unmanned missiles on a capital city was rather a last straw. People were only buoyed up to carry on by the daily news from France where, following D-Day, the Allies seemed to be winning the war and were inexorably closing in on Germany to end World War II.

I left school in the autumn and joined the GPO as a Telegraph Boy Messenger, based at Hammersmith in West London. At the age of 14 I had my blue uniform and had begun telegram delivery it was autumn and the V1 Doodlebug attacks had eased - although the devastating V2 rockets were in full flow and had became another dreaded menace to all.

Most of us were not aware of the use of radar against the V1s or radar-predicted Ack-Ack gun-laying tactics but we know now that they were quite successful. Even so, a few V1s would slip through the defences of London... particularly on days of low cloud.

Fearful clatter

I well remember one such instance. I was cycling in the Stamford Brook/ Ravenscourt Park area of West London on telegram delivery when I heard the unmistakable and fearful clatter of a V1 approaching high in the clouds and to my rear. I cycled on cautiously with constant backward glances at the sky and suddenly I heard the engine stop. This could be followed by a dive and explosion of the 1000lb warhead or the missile could glide on with eventually, the same destructive results.

Naturally scared stiff and with my heart in my mouth I just could not see the wretched thing but all of a sudden, my handlebars were twisted out of my grip and I felt myself turning up and over in the air to hit the ground with a mighty thump. There was an immediate taste of blood on my lips and I had painful hands - I was also completely winded and I could but lay there absolutely 100% certain that I had been blown up - yet I had not heard a thing and luckily, I was still alive!

Suddenly a woman's voice bellowed at me, 'Get up you fool you've flattened my roses!' I was quite shocked and bemused and as I climbed painfully to my feet I heard the distant boom towards Chiswick of the exploding V1 bomb.

The truth quickly dawned on me ? as I had been cycling along and looking skywards the road had curved and I had gone straight on and crashed into a hedge - throwing me over and into the bed of roses! I said to the lady 'I thought I had been blown up'. 'Clear off,' she said... so I did!'

Back at the delivery office at Hammersmith I had a hard job explaining my torn new uniform and my countless scratches... there was very little sympathy when I said I had survived being blown up by a Doodlebug!

BRIEF ENCOUNTER

Although very much the 'Home Front' it was a terrifying and, at times, sad period to be cycling through the streets of West London with bundles of telegrams for delivery. The peril of Hitler's missiles combined with the wretched business of delivering the frequent casualty telegrams, made it difficult to enjoy the outdoor life of a 'telegram boy' as 1945 was ushered in.

The hard work and gloom was lifted for me by a brief encounter that by its very unexpectedness still makes me laugh to this day. I had been cycling on early morning deliveries in the West Kensington streets near the Olympia Hall. The last telegram in my batch happened to be for Addison Road, on the other side of the nearby railway and to save a long ride round I decided to walk and push my cycle up and over the footbridge of the Goods Only railway Station.

Frantic waving

As I clattered down the last steps of the footbridge I saw what I thought was a passing goods train that had just come to a crunching halt at signals – leaving the rear end of a carriage just overlapping the platform. Every window was suddenly flung open and crammed with deeply tanned faces and brown uniforms...spotting my blue uniform and red cycle they all began waving frantically for me to come to them.

I ran to the very edge of the last section of the platform and saw that it was really a troop train – jammed tight with sunburnt soldiers who looked just about the fittest I had ever seen! They all shouted at once for my stock of telegram forms and I handed over my whole supply to their eager hands at the windows of the carriage – and they seemed to come back to me just as quickly...filled in with pencilled addresses and the minimum of text words such as 'Back in Blighty', 'Safely home', 'Home and writing soon' and so on. Suddenly there was bedlam as great shouts came ringing back from other carriages – Sergeants and NCOs began bellowing for their men to keep on the train and away from me on the platform.

The train began to jerk and the carriages eased away from the platform as the last of the completed telegram forms came floating down amid truly showers of silver coinage from the waving soldiers. They gave me a tremendous cheer which then turned to delighted jeers at outwitting their NCOs further along the train – which luckily for them was not a corridor train.

Troop train puzzle

The train quickly disappeared from sight and it must have been a strange scene on that deserted Goods Station as the lone Telegram Boy scrambled around picking up the telegram forms and all the coins. The latter were eventually stacked into more money than I had ever handled in my 14 years!

I rushed back to the Hammersmith Post Office and handed over the forms and money to the astonished Counter Clerk who was certain I had broken all Post Office records for reply telegrams. We all puzzled what on earth a troop train was doing at the run down Goods Station of West Kensington at that stage of the war but nobody really knew the answer.

Many years later I was reading of the impact of the surprise German offensive in the Ardennes at Christmas 1944 and the sudden need for reinforcements to contain these attacks and then mount the final thrusts to defeat Germany in 1945. It seems battle-hardened desert veterans were withdrawn from the Italian Front, shipped to Liverpool and entrained down through England to the Channel ports and thence to the Western Front.

My meeting at West Kensington must have been with some of these fine soldiers and I can now realise the anxiety of their NCOs about the breach of security I inadvertently posed. I understand many of these men were lost in the bitter fighting across the Rhine before the final surrender in May 1945 and I can recall their absolute delight in outwitting their NCOs and my accidental part in the proceedings. I also wonder what some 60 odd families thought when they suddenly received a telegram from their menfolk, serving on the Italian Front – but with a date-stamped origin of Hammersmith Post Office!

MEETING WITH A STAR

At the beginning go 1945 we were at war, but by its closing months we were at peace, with many countries throughout the world struggling to rehouse their people, rebuild their countries and restart their industries.

Those early winter weeks of that year, with snow and heavy rains, were quite unpleasant for me as a teenage Telegram Boy on outdoor delivery work in the Hammersmith and West Kensington part of London. Additionally, we continued to have the sudden bouts of death and destruction with the fearful arrival of the German V2 rockets, which maintained their attacks on London and the south east until March of 1945.

I can recall that it was taxing work, out cycling on the heavy red bicycles in all weathers... 48 hours per week for the princely sum of £1. I remember telling my father how it was hard work for such poor reward. He simply pointed out that we had free clothing/uniforms and, wonder of wonders, were guaranteed a pension on retirement - a situation that for me at that time seemed a thousand years away with no guarantee I would live that long!

A heavenly vision

Those weary weeks for me did have one quite memorable and lovely moment when, quite out of the blue, I found myself talking to a famous film star ? Anne Crawford.

At that time, towards the end of the war, the famous film Millions Like Us was constantly being shown in the cinema (and indeed, is still occasionally shown on television today).

Miss Crawford was one of the stars in this film and I had no idea I was ever going to meet this lovely lady. Then one day I called at an apartment block known as Kensington Court in West Kensington, soaking wet and as untidy as ever, to deliver a telegram addressed 'Crawford', a name that just did not register with me in any way.

What a surprise when my ring on the bell saw the door opened and a vision of loveliness in a shimmering pink gown appeared at the door to take the very damp telegram from me. I was quite speechless as I recognised her and just could not believe that this beautiful lady was standing there in front of me, reading her telegram.

She looked up and said sweetly, 'There is no reply thank you.' And with a cheek that I did not know I had, I said to her 'Could I have your photograph please?'

Without hesitation she replied, 'Of course - just a moment', and went into her apartment. She quickly returned with a large photograph, which she signed in front of me and placed in my grubby hands. 'It is nice to meet you and thank you for calling', she said graciously.

I left Kensington Court, marvelling that I had actually met and talked with a famous film star.

Popularity boost

I could not wait to rush back in the rain to our delivery office and tell the other 20 or so boys of my good fortune and then show them the autographed photograph that I had kept dry under my heavy blue coat. All were truly impressed, as were my parents that evening. My father said dryly, 'There, I have got you a job where you are meeting film stars ? what a lucky lad!'

The inevitable happened afterwards. If one of our boys delivered a telegram to any apartment in Kensington Court, they would ring her bell and also cheekily ask for a signed photograph! She was a very patient lady. For she would just laugh and hand a photograph over without a murmur, with her gracious smile that we all came to know so well. She quickly became known in the local Post Office circles as the 'messengers' pin-up!'

We all followed her subsequent film career with great interest through the post-war years and how wretched we all were to hear that she was very poorly with an illness unknown to us, leukaemia, and she sadly died, aged just 35 in 1956.

It is all such a long time ago now, but I can still recall the wintry weather of early 1945, that for me was suddenly made bearable by the kindness of a beautiful film star.

THE HAPPY TIMES

The constant delivery of Priority (casualty) telegrams, was often a wretched business for us GPO Telegram Boys. Most of us were aware that as you slowly cycled down a road looking for a specific house number, curtains would twitch and sometimes fearful faces would look out, hoping and praying you would not stop at their house. For in those days most households would have a family member away serving with the Armed Forces.

This obvious and understandable dread of our arrival was always in our minds and there was truly nothing we could do about it, other than to politely and kindly hand over the small yellow telegrams. The misery of clearly devastated families taking our telegrams was all too obvious and some of the young messenger boys were affected more than others. For myself, I always found it a harrowing experience and I was frequently close to tears with all those families to whom I had personally delivered the bad news – many of these addresses remained clear and fresh in my young mind for many years.

Flags and bunting

Then how things changed! The period arrived that we all called 'the happy times!' – the months of February, March and April of 1945, when the Allied forces began to liberate the prisoner of war camps. As the British prisoners were freed and received medical treatment, those who were fit to travel began to be airlifted back to England. Some apparently called it being 'freed and refitted for service'! For after home leave, most thought they would eventually be sent to the Pacific to fight the Japanese.

The first the messengers began to know of this factor was the arrival of Priority telegrams that simply would say, 'Home Wednesday, all well', with a signature. Suddenly, a few houses in my delivery area of Hammersmith and Fulham began to show flags and bunting, and it was truly wonderful to cycle down a road, stop and produce the telegram, then to be swamped by ladies and children quite beside themselves with relief and joy!

Kiss and hug

One example I can recall came with my delivery of such a Priority telegram to one of the small terraced roads that lay to the south of the Greyhound Road area in Fulham. I had propped my cycle against the kerb and a young woman came rushing out to me – ripped open the envelope then gave me a resounding kiss and a hug! Neighbours suddenly appeared and read the good news that her husband would be home within the week and what a party they began to plan – with me as an invited guest!

In fact I did cycle there in the following week and met the returning hero. He was a small, gaunt man, name of Reg, and he told me he had been part of the army rearguard defending Dunkirk, and as they finally retreated towards the beaches, he was caught by shrapnel in the legs as he climbed a wall to safety. Subsequently captured, he spent the rest of the war in a POW camp until released by American troops and brought home in a Dakota transport.

My new friend Reg told me that his wife had received three Priority telegrams in all, the first in 1940 to say he was missing, a second in 1941; alive but wounded and a POW. The third was the precious 'home soon' message that I had delivered, which they proposed to frame and keep for all time!

For me it was a lovely few moments of pleasure that made up in some way for the usual misery I had been delivering to so many nice people in that locality.

TALES OF THE RIVER BANK

The closing months of the War are still fresh in my mind. My job as a Telegram Boy involved long hours and cycling in all weathers and was more than taxing for youngsters at that time when the V2 rockets were still being fired at London and the Home Counties. They would arrive unexpectedly with a massive explosion, leaving death and destruction on a large scale wherever they fell.

I was eight years old when the War broke out and living at Vauxhall in South London. Naturally at that age, great sporting events did not register that much with me and this was the same later in the conflict with our group of young Boy Messengers. This came home to me one day on my delivery rounds in the area of Upper Mall, a district of historic and attractive houses that graced the bend of the River Thames between Hammersmith Bridge and Chiswick.

As I was cycling along, I noticed a knot of people at the river wall looking out on the Thames and I recognised Ray, one of our local Postman friends, in this group. Inquisitive as ever, I propped my heavy red cycle against the wall and asked Ray what was so interesting. Ray was a Great War veteran with a damaged left arm, well liked and respected by the Messengers, for he always treated us as adults and he was quite a fount of knowledge.

Sporting spectacle

It seems that Ray had been a keen oarsman in his youth and after the Great War had ended, had helped out with the running of various rowing groups and particularly, with the Oxford and Cambridge University Boat Race between the Wars. I, of course, knew very little about this sporting spectacle and Ray told me about the pre-War crowds with their rosettes and flags that had flocked to Hammersmith and Chiswick. Thousands of onlookers had lined the riverside to cheer the rowing crews on their 4 1/2 mile long race that apparently dated back to 1829 and was the longest surviving sporting challenge which raced between Putney and Mortlake.

Ray had helped out with the 91st Boat Race in 1939 and it had been his fond hope that he would be around to do the same for the 92nd event, whenever that would be resumed. He explained that the small crowd that day were all rowing fans and they had gathered to watch several crews race by in a match between oarsmen drawn from HM Forces personnel. Needless to say I stayed with him to watch the straining crews go by to our cheers of encouragement and I promised myself that perhaps one day in far-off peacetime I would come back and see the real thing with all the bustle and lively crowds.

Smokes without fire

There was a special and unexpected bonus for me that day, for as the boats raced by, their wash brought flotsam along our foreshore. What a surprise! For there, by the water's edge, was a pristine but soggy packet of 'Lucky Strike', the well known and popular American cigarettes. I managed to retrieve this

waterlogged treasure and I regret to say that on my return to our office, I carefully propped them on a radiator. They dried out beautifully and I was delighted to receive one shilling for them from one of our male Counter Clerks, who it seemed smoked anything going and who had been amazed to be offered such a quality pack!

Post-war, the Boat Race resumed in 1946 with the 92nd race. In later years, from my subsequent home near the river at Putney, I was able to see and enjoy the spectacle of the University Boat Race. I have seen it many times now and each time I recall my introduction to this sport at the Hammersmith Mall and that so welcome boost of a shilling to my modest weekly salary!

THE LONG BLUE LINE

Many readers experienced and treasure the memory of the absolute joy, relief and exultation we all felt when VE Day arrived on Tuesday 8 May 1945. At Hammersmith Post Office we were relieved as this would lead to a lessening of the constant delivery of the dreaded Priority casualty telegrams to the families in our area.

Within the universal joy of those days we knew only too well that the Pacific War was continuing and that we were not fully at peace until later in 1945. Even so, for my group of young Messengers it was the start of a peaceful era quite unknown to most of us as we had all been aged under 10 when war had broken out in 1939.

The Post Office had given us VE Day off from our duties so that we could all celebrate as our respective families thought fit. Naturally, when we resumed our delivery work on the Wednesday many of us were still excited and festive and this happy feeling was with us all the rest of that week!

It was clear that our group of lads just had to do something else to celebrate further and when one of our lads returned from delivery and mentioned that 'Grumpy Joe' was on duty then that was it! I should explain that in the 1945 period before any flyovers or motorways the traffic flow in and around Hammersmith Broadway was truly a congested nightmare and it was the Met Police system to station an experienced Sergeant there on a small pedestal in the middle of the Broadway to guide the traffic flow with suitable signals from his white gloved hands.

Personal tribute

We were the bane of the Sergeants' lives and we frequently dashed through their signals in our attempts to carry out

important deliveries as quickly as possible. Occasionally, one of the Sergeants would wait until the very last minute to signal HALT! This would mean we had to queue on our cycles in and around the buses and lorries while they belched out their suffocating diesel fumes – and indeed, one Sergeant known as 'Grumpy Joe' had this knack off to a fine art.

Naturally we all agreed with one of our senior lad's suggestion that we would provide our own personal VE Day celebration and

as many as possible, without our Overseer's knowledge, would go out on our delivery together, riding our red cycles with our right hands on the handlebars and our left arm outstretched and resting on another lad's shoulder to the left. With luck, and if the traffic allowed, we should all pass the Sergeant in a long blue line and we could give him a disciplined 'Eyes right!' as a personal tribute.

At that time it seemed a good way to celebrate the atmosphere of that week and we managed to get 10 Telegram Boys in line, some with paper Union Jacks and one with a coloured rosette. We all 'pushed' off together and we worked our way through the traffic to get to the front to wait for the Sergeant's signals. This duly came and we linked up our arms and managed to get a good (but wobbly) line of blue uniforms on red cycles as we headed for the unsuspecting Sergeant – in this case, our Grumpy Joe!

Jaw dropped

It was such a joy to see him with his arm aloft suddenly glance behind him to see 10 Messengers in a linked up line bearing down on him very fast. His jaw dropped and his face went beetroot red as we swept past him with a superb shout from our senior boy of 'Eyes right!' Once our formation was past him, we quickly broke up and hared off in different directions before he could positively identify anybody.

I have a vivid recollection of a bus driver, hanging out of his driving cab quite hysterical with glee and there were countless cheers for our display from the crowded pavements – all enjoying the sight of the frantic Sergeant trying to stay upright on his pedestal.

The next day the inevitable happened and ALL the Telegram Boys were summoned to meet a Superintendent at the nearby police station. We were lined up while Grumpy Joe read the riot act to us for the benefit of the Superintendent. When his dialogue had finished, I swear that the Superintendent's upper lip was twitching in a strangled smile.

After a pause he recovered his composure and formally warned us all to behave ourselves in the future and to obey the road users system in his area – or else! We dutifully said thank you and left the station, this time to think of other ways to continue with our personal VE Day celebrations.

In retrospect it was a daft thing to do in heavy traffic but my word, what an hilarious episode it was for all the crowds to enjoy at dear old Hammersmith Broadway in that so memorable VE Day period of 1945.

A POLITICAL MOMENT

The 98th annual art exhibition of the Post Office and BT artists took place in September 2004 at the St Sepulchre's Church in the City of London. I had organised this event and the opening ceremony had been ably carried out by Lord Roy Hattersley and his remarks about the quality of our artists work artists were very complimentary and those about current modern art were not!

We all enjoyed his visit with us and afterwards I had the pleasure of a quiet conversation with him and, in particular, his surprise that I had begun my Post Office Service six decades before. He was quite incredulous and highly amused when I told him that my Boy Messenger life had once brought me into close contact with Professor Harold Laski, the then Chairman of the Labour Party and the person credited with being the 'brains of the outfit' in gaining Clement Attlee his astonishing electoral victory for Labour in July 1945 - defeating Winston Churchill and the Conservative Party in the process.

As the European theatre of the Second World War came to a close, we were being managed by a Coalition Government. I believe that many thought it would be wise to continue with this system but no, the decision was made to seek a General Election immediately, although what was known as the Servicemans' vote would be weeks arriving and likely to delay a decision.

Not a bit of it - it was a clear landslide for the Labour Party who were returned to power with a majority of 150 seats - which was the first majority Labour Government in British history.

Giant parcel to deliver

To be frank, I was not that aware of the political turmoil of an election until my telegraph duties changed all that, once the news came of the Labour victory. We began to receive literally hundreds of telegrams for Professor Laski who, as it happened, lived at Addison Bridge in our delivery area. When our telegraph clerks saw the massive pile of messages arriving, they knew that we could not spare boys to keep delivering them as they arrived, so they were stored up until there was a giant parcel and I was told to go and deliver them!

I subsequently turned into normally quiet Addison Bridge with a stack of yellow telegrams precariously balanced on my handlebars and, what a surprise, ran into my first experience of reporters and photographers who were outside laying siege to Professor Laski's small house. Apparently, he had not yet made an appearance to comment on the Labour triumph but the media men knew he would come out for his parcel of telegrams - and sure enough, he did. This quiet and dapper man, sporting the usual small moustache of political leaders of that era, came out and posed with me for the official hand-over of his telegrams. With the crowds and flashlights going off, I was more than nervous and I know I dropped some - this had me grubbing about on his step trying to pick them all up, all the while trying to smile at the photographers! Trust me, I must have looked quite foolish at such an historic moment!

As it happened, Professor Laski was more than gracious and thanked me for the prompt delivery and sent me on my way with a firm handshake. I left, still bemused by all the fuss and only realised later that if I had waited I might have been given a large tip!

GAME OF A LIFETIME

With the long awaited celebrations of VE and VJ days behind us in 1945 many people could not wait to pick up the threads of normal life and for many, this was the welcome resumption of national sporting events, which naturally at first, were on a small scale.

Not so for professional football, some of which had continued during the later war years with servicemen/footballers playing for any team they could that was near their service location. Understandably us sports-minded Telegram Boys could not wait to see the resumption of full-time professional football. So in autumn 1945 our score of 14/15 year old boys was quickly sorted out into Brentford, Chelsea, Fulham or Queens Park Rangers supporters before the football began.

In my office there were three Chelsea fans and what excitement was afoot for us when we heard that Moscow Dynamo were coming to play Chelsea in October. Fancy that, the great Russian team would be here at Stamford Bridge for a match that so many just had to see.

In those days, we had to rely on fathers and uncles etc to go to the matches. Tickets were a distant dream and we all usually chose a regular entrance point and then stood on the invariably wet concrete terraces. Our threesome had become used to entering the grounds at what was known as the 'Bovril Gate', simply because the entrance hoardings carried this advertising slogan. Our system was to cycle to Stamford Bridge, leave our cycles under lock and key in a nearby house or garden for a small fee and make our way to the Bovril turnstiles.

Hordes of supporters

The day of the match was truly incredible, the atmosphere was electric and we all knew it would be a special day in footballing history. The roads were clogged with traffic throughout Fulham and Chelsea hours before the match was due to start. On our cycles we slowly made it through the jams and were able to leave our cycles in the usual place and begin the slow shuffle from Waltham Green to Stamford Bridge, the roads and pavements packed tight with fans edging a few paces at a time towards the stadium... and this with the kick-off two hours away!

We tried this edging along, but it was hopeless for three small lads and clearly the Bovril gate was out of the question. Sadly, we had to face the facts and we sat on a small garden wall and munched our apples etc. Suddenly our hero arrived – Jim, a Postman at Blythe Road Sorting Office in our delivery area and known to us all, came over to us, having guessed our plight. Jim had been invalided out of the Army after Dunkirk in 1940 with bad leg wounds and he was more than grateful that the GPO had given him full-time employment, despite his obvious disabilities. He was much liked by his postal colleagues and our messenger boys alike.

Jim simply said, 'If we wait out here we won't get in until after the match, so follow me,' and we did! He knew the buildings well and took us back against the crowd flow to the front gardens of a small block of residential flats. Between the ground floor flats was a tiny alleyway that led to the gardens at the rear and we found ourselves amongst garden sheds and a high fence, against an extensive grassy embankment. Jim found a few loose panels and we all scampered through, helping Jim with his weak leg at the same time.

Dream of a game

Once in and against the slopes, we scrambled up to the top and, joy of joys, found ourselves high up at the District Line end of the ground. Although the stands were full, we had enough room to see the pitch clearly. We cheered ourselves hoarse when the teams came out, then fell about laughing when the Russian Captain kissed Tommy Lawton, our deadly centre-forward, on both cheeks and presented him with flowers – then the match kicked off.

Records will show that it was truly a dream of a game that ended up 3-3, played to a crowd of between 80,000 and 90,000, many of whom, like Jim and our three lads, had gained access to the football without paying! Mind you, this probably evened out in later years as we paid in full for many games that were not really worth the entrance fee.

We were so grateful to our friend Jim for getting us in to see such a memorable game. That was not the end of things, for it seemed that other frustrated fans had seen us go through the alleyway into the flats and tried to get into the ground as well. Some even knocked at the flats and were allowed through their homes (for a donation) and over the fences and into the ground, just as we had done earlier.

The newspapers carried a famous cartoon afterwards of a scantily clad couple, sitting up in bed with the sheets around them, watching in amazement as the football fans passed through their home... swinging rattles and suchlike as they went! What a sporting day it all was and no wonder we have remained Chelsea supporters to this day.

RETURN TO VAUXHALL

Even now, looking back at that period of 1945 I can still feel the incredible joy and feelings of relief that my family had come through despite losing our home at Vauxhall in South London in April 1941 and being 'bombed out' of our second home at Roehampton in July 1944.

Now well into my 70's I still have those summer of '45 thoughts and how vivid they are to me. On a recent train journey from my home in Guildford to London the train made an unspecified stop at Vauxhall. On impulse I jumped out and spent an hour in that neighbourhood before travelling on to the City for my meeting. I walked along the Vauxhall platform and remembered how in September 1939 we schoolchildren had waved goodbye to the line of distraught and tearful parents on the opposite pavement - but most of us were excited at the

Lawn Lane School in 1936.
Ron McGill is in the second
row next to the wall.

adventure of the forthcoming journey to the countryside. We were happy with our lunch packs and enjoyed being with our classmates and kindly familiar teachers from our school.

Sense of loss

Having arrived in Berkshire and been deposited around various homes about half of us gave up by Christmas and had returned home to be with our parents once more. They were more than relieved for they had found the impact of silent streets and childless homes more than they could bear... a sense of loss that is rarely mentioned. The early part of 1940 was a school-less holiday for the returning children until that marvellous LCC (London County Council) organisation managed to restore some order to things and arranged limited half-day classes for us. This exercise was halted with the start of the Battle of Britain. At Vauxhall, we had a grandstand view being so near one of the Luftwaffe's aiming points, Waterloo Station.

On my recent return trip I walked along the side of our old school at Lawn Lane, then a Victorian structure but nowadays one with many modern additions. At Vauxhall Park nearby I listened and could hear again the laughter and cries of the WAAF Barrage Balloon girls raising and lowering their billowing charges as quickly as they could. They were all so kind and would offer us sweets and apples etc whenever they could. I turned into Vauxhall Grove and paused outside No 71, the house where we had lived in the middle flat of three during the 1930's. There used to be a small brick shelter in the roadway here and I recalled sheltering there after an air raid warning and popping my head out to see the vast formation of German bombers overhead, twinkling in the September sunlight and curving round in superb formation to follow the Thames en route to the London Docks. This was the famous raid of 7 September that destroyed much of London's dockland area.

I recalled once more the time of the Dornier that crashed on to Victoria Station and the sight of the mortally wounded pilot parachuting across the people in Harleyford Road and over the Oval Cricket Ground to land and die by the nearby Underground Station. Although he was the enemy this was a sad and wretched incident for he was attacked by some bombed-out survivors living in a nearby Community Centre.

Massive attack

Very soon we were into the Blitz period when London was attacked for 57 consecutive nights. Local damage at Vauxhall was so severe that we began to spend most of our nights as a family together in the large shelter underneath platform six at the Station.

On my walk I looked up at the top window of our old house and remembered the massive attack on the City of London by the Luftwaffe at Christmas 1940. This attack was on a Sunday night when we had chanced it and stayed at home. My father had lifted me from the safe place under the stairs and took me to the window, placing me on his shoulders to look over the rooftops to the burning City of London saying, 'Have a look, son, at a sight you will never forget'. How true, that awful sea of red flames and smoke seemed to be the end of our world in London and of course for many citizens it was.

I remembered now how life in the Vauxhall shelter changed for us with an air raid in April 1941. This was a widespread attack on London and we somehow lived through the nearby explosions, the clouds of dirt and dust, to find in the morning that the outside wall of our house had collapsed; the two floors and rooms were sagging at all angles - all this caused by blast from a parachute mine that had landed and exploded on the nearby Milk Depot.

Like so many with their homes gone we then spent two weeks in a Church Hall before further evacuation, this time as a family but minus belongings and a home, back to the Berkshire countryside on the western outskirts of Reading. We never returned to Vauxhall as we were eventually re-homed in 1943 to a small house at Roehampton, also in South London. Nazi Germany had another go at us in July 1944 with a V1 Flying Bomb that left us roofless and despatched us on the move again to Blackpool in Lancashire, until our roof was repaired and the house made habitable again.

Breaking point

From this time onwards for me it was a case of leaving school and working as a Telegram Boy for the GPO at Hammersmith. Long and tiring hours and out in all weathers for just under £1 per week. This was a difficult time for all Londoners with the V1's still arriving and exploding and then the dreaded V2 rockets with their silent approach and ear-splitting explosions that stretched so many to breaking point.

As I walked back to Vauxhall Station on my recent visit I thought again of my mates in Class 2 at Lawn Lane School. We were all evacuated together, drifted back to London, went through the day and night bombing of the Blitz, shared our boxes of bomb splinters and shrapnel and limited classes at school and were deeply saddened to hear that some children had been killed and injured.

The War had of course brought massive upheavals to millions of people in Europe with death and destruction on an extensive and unforgettable scale. Even so, and on a much lesser scale of upheaval in South London, I remember pondering in the weeks following VE Day that I had never seen or heard any news of my 1939 classmates and sadly, nothing has been known to the present day.

As I travelled away from Vauxhall Station and on to the City I said a quiet 'goodbye dear friends' to all my young classmates in Class 2 at Lawn Lane School in 1939 with the sincere hope that some had made it through to that Victory summer of 1945.

DRAWING ON EXPERIENCE

The war was a terrible time for so many people. Yet in my case, at least, something good and life-enhancing came from it. Becoming a Post Office Boy Messenger meant there were times when, after finishing a shift, I would go back to the office and enjoy a mug of cocoa. One day one of the older lady counter clerks gave me a number of pre-war copies of *Cycling* magazine. It was whilst browsing through one of these, mug in hand, that the wonderful world of art suddenly opened up. I became entranced by a series of pen-and-ink sketches that were simply signed 'Pat'. I found out later that the artist was Frank Patterson and he had been producing superb work for the previous half century!

Although only a young lad even then I was astonished how 'Pat' could achieve his super scenes with a 303 nib and a bottle of ebony stain in lieu of ink. He most certainly gave me a 'prod' to have a go at drawings and in later life, this led me on to become a professional artist in oil painting, literally painting with a fine brush in the beloved Patterson tradition.

Frank Patterson was truly a countryman who had settled in Sussex and lived in the 16th century Pear Tree Farm near Billingshurst for something like 45 years until he passed away in the summer of 1952. He seems to have followed in the tradition of William Cobbett of the early 1800s who rode around England on a horse and packed that experience into his famous Rural Rides. Patterson, a century later, had a similar affection for the countryside and exchanged the horse for a bicycle with the pen-and-ink work of a naturalist.

During the 1970s and with my role as exhibitions organiser for the Post Office and BT Art Club, I remembered my first sight of fine art work seen in the middle of a deadly war. I made contact with Ken Evans, then the Editor of *Cycling*, who kindly gave me a free hand to delve through their old files and extract a sample of the original sketches for display in the annual art exhibition of the PO/BT Art Club in the City of London.

It proved to be astonishing when we 'opened' the exhibition; there were so many elderly current and ex-cyclists riding into the City of London and they flocked to see our display of original Patterson works! The pictures were naturally yellowed with age and use, some had editorial comments scribbled on them but no matter, there was a daily group of cycling-linked visitors who just stood and gazed at these previous smudged works that had lost none of their priceless original charm.

Two examples of Frank Patterson's art appear on this page.

WAR DIARY

> " A typhoon rages around Okinawa and damages four battleships, eight aircraft carriers and 21 other US Navy Ships. Kamikaze attacks cripple the battleship *Mississippi* and the heavy cruiser *Louisville*. "

1 June: British troops begin to hand over some 40,000 Russian Cossacks who have served with the *Wehrmacht*. The soldiers – many accompanied by their families and horses – had surrendered to British forces. They claim they have been led to believe they would be allowed to settle in the west.

Repressed under Stalin's communist regime, the Cossacks know that repatriation means almost certain death in Russia. Some officers and men commit suicide rather than return.

Japan: US aircraft drop 3000 tons of incendiary bombs on Osaka.

Burma: A British attack on a bridgehead at Kama, east of the Irrawaddy, leaves over 1000 Japanese dead.

Damascus: Fighting in the city has stopped.

In Berlin, the Allied-appointed Mayor warns that 50 Nazis will be killed for every attack made on the occupying forces.

2 June: The Pope broadcasts his hope that Germany will lay aside the spectre of Nazism and start a new life.

Paris: General de Gaulle blames Britain for the crisis in the Levant and says British agents have been stirring up trouble for the French.

Britain: Clearing the beaches has been going on since August 1943 when the threat of German invasion was deemed to have passed. The Royal Engineers announce that the process has so far cost the lives of 98 officers and men with a further 26 blinded or maimed.

3 June: In Southern China, Chinese forces continue to make gains against the Japanese and today occupy Chenkiang and move within 30 miles of the border with Indo-China.

New Zealand announces that its forces sustained 36,747 casualties – including 9445 dead – from the beginning of the war until February 1945.

4 June: On Okinawa, US troops now control most of Naha airfield. The US Navy Department in Washington announces the loss, with heavy casualties, of two destroyers, *Morrison* and *Luce*, off the island.

London: Churchill warns that voting Labour will result in a 'Gestapo' type political policing to enforce a socialist system. Labour leaders accuse him of 'vile and vicious tactics'.

A Sunderland V flying-boat today carried out Coastal Command's last convoy escort for the Royal Navy. 'Z for Zebra' was patrolling some 500 miles south-west of Ireland when she received the final 'cease patrol' order.

5 June: Germany: Britain, Russia, the USA and France sign an agreement dividing the country into four zones of occupation. Berlin itself will also be divided into four zones. German frontiers are identified as those which existed on 31 December 1937.

Japan is pounded again by US B-29 bombers and tip 3000 tons of incendiaries on Kobe. A typhoon rages in the Okinawa area and damages four battleships, eight aircraft carriers, seven cruisers and 14 destroyers of the US Third Fleet. Kamikaze attacks cripple the battleship *Mississippi* and the heavy cruiser *Louisville*.

Please put your litter in the bin

Damascus: The evacuation of French soldiers and civilians is completed.

6 June: The Russians say they have found a body, believed to be that of Hitler, in the Chancellery garden.

London: 184,512 British and Canadian soldiers went missing, or were killed or wounded, between D-Day 6 June 1944 and VE-Day. Services of remembrance are held on various Normandy beaches today to mark the first anniversary of *Operation Overlord*.

7 June: King George VI and Queen Elizabeth visit the Channel Islands to a rapturous welcome. On the same day, King Haakon returns to Norway.

Germany: All citizens of the zones occupied by the Western Allies are ordered to watch films of the Belsen and Buchenwald concentration camps.

8 June: The British Air Ministry announces the discovery, near Grenoble, of the wreckage of the plane in which Air Chief Marshal Sir Trafford Leigh-Mallory lost his life last November.

Germany: Dr Karl Hoven, resident physician at Buchenwald concentration camp is captured.

9 June: The RAF reveals details of the Vampire, a jet fighter which can fly at over 500 mph.

Continued aerial pounding of Japan's mainland cities, and the imminent defeat on Okinawa, diminish hopes that the new 'moderate' Premier, Mr Suzuki, will sue for peace. To the Japanese mind, surrender would be a betrayal of their forces still in the field.

Trieste: The dispute over the status of this city is settled by the signing of an agreement between the British, US and Yugoslav governments. The region known as Venezia Giulia will be divided in half. The western part, including Trieste, will come under the control of the Supreme Allied Commander and the eastern part remains under Tito's sway. It is expressly stated that this arrangement in no way prejudices the ultimate disposal of the territory. Most of Tito's men will pull out of Trieste in two days' time, although up to 2000 soldiers will be allowed to stay on.

An awkward situation prevails in Piedmont and the Val d'Aosta between the French and Italian Governments. French language and culture have prevailed in many of the Alpine valleys for centuries but under the fascists, schools and place names were Italianised. Now the French-speaking inhabitants want their former liberties restored.

10 June: Far East: US forces on Okinawa's Oruku peninsula reduce Japanese resistance to an area of 2000 square yards. Over the next 48 hours the area will halve. Desperate defenders start to commit suicide rather than surrender. The Australian Ninth Division lands at Brooketon, Labuan and Muara on the west coast of North Borneo and immediately moves to take the oil town of Brunei. General MacArthur goes ashore with the assault troops at Labuan.

Germany: In Frankfort-on-Main (sic), Russia's Marshal Zhukov confers the platinum and diamond encrusted Order of Victory on Montgomery and Eisenhower.

Borneo: General MacArthur goes ashore with Australian assault troops at Labuan on North Borneo. There is little resistance. Later MacArthur will observe: 'Rarely is such a great strategic prize obtained at such a low cost of life.'

11 June: In Czechoslovakia the Soviet authorities commence the forcible expulsion of ethnic Germans from the Sudetenland. They are being sent to Germany.

Tokyo: Premier Suzuki is given emergency powers by the House of Representatives. He can now function as a virtual dictator. Off Okinawa, two more US destroyers and an auxiliary transport are sunk.

Chungking reports that Chinese troops are 10 miles north west of Kweilin, capital of Kwangsi province.

12 June: In London, Eisenhower is given the freedom of the City of London together with the Order of Merit.

At Trieste, the Yugoslav flag flying over the town hall is lowered and the flags of Britain and the US are hoisted.

13 June: Okinawa: Japanese resistance on Oruku is ended.

Burma HQ announces that reinforcements for SE Asia Command are now arriving by air. The journey takes five days and troops break their journey in the Middle East to help them acclimatise to the new conditions.

Northern Italy: French troops withdraw from the Val d'Aosta region and are being replaced by US soldiers.

14 June: Former German Foreign Minister Joachim von Ribbentrop is captured by British troops in Hamburg.

Brunei on Borneo is captured. RAF aircraft drop 25,000 gallons of jellied petrol on Hong Kong causeway.

15 June: In London, King George officially dissolves Parliament.

Japan: Another 3000 tons of bombs are dropped on Osaka. The British Pacific Fleet arrives off Truk in the Caroline Islands and commences a 48 hour bombardment by carrier-based Seafire and Fairey Firefly fighters and Avenger bombers supported by warships. Truk has a garrison of 40,000 and has been dubbed 'Japan's Gibraltar'.

Rangoon holds a Victory Parade to celebrate the reoccupation of Burma by the British. The Red Ensign of the Port Commissioner of Rangoon flies again over the city. It was seized by the Japanese in 1942 and later found by the Americans in Attu in the Aleutian Islands.

16 June: Dachau: It is revealed that nearly 2500 people have died – mainly from typhus – since the camp was liberated on 27 April.

Brussels: Premier Achille van Acker and his entire cabinet resign in protest against the proposed return of King Leopold. Since his release from German captivity, the King has been staying in Salzburg. The Catholic party is the only one that favours the King's return. His brother, Prince Charles, continues as Regent.

17 June: On Okinawa the end is in sight with less than 2000 of the defenders left alive. Japanese commander Admiral Minoru Ota commits ritual suicide. However, a shell fragment kills Lt-General S B Buckner, commander of the US Tenth Army, as he observes marines in action.

Over the next two days, US bombers initiate a series of raids on civilian targets in 58 smaller cities in Japan.

Britain: The armed services start demobilising at the rate of 30,000 persons per week. The figure is expected to rise to 60,000 by August, in spite of the continuing war in the Far East. Over a million British servicemen have passed through the British Transit Camp at Calais since the end of hostilities.

18 June: London: William 'Lord Haw-Haw' Joyce appears at Bow Street Police Court to answer charges of high treason in adhering to the King's enemies. He is remanded in custody for a week. The Act under which he is arraigned dates back to the year 1351.

Over 20,000 German POWs captured around the River Elbe are now arriving in Britain where they will employed as farm labourers and in the building trades.

19 June: In San Francisco, Spain is banned from joining the United Nations as long as Franco is in power.

Fire-bomb raids by 400 Super-Fortresses hit spinning mills and a rubber factory on Japan's Honshu and Kyushu islands.

20 June: In Borneo, Australian troops capture the Seria oilfields, the largest in the British Empire. Reinforcements land at Lutong in Sarawak.

New York: Four million people cheer Eisenhower as he drives 35 miles through the city in a motorcade.

21 June: After some of the bloodiest fighting of the entire Pacific campaign, Okinawa is finally secured following an 82-day battle. Some Japanese soldiers and civilians throw themselves off cliffs rather than surrender. Generals Sho and Ushijima fall on their sabres and die with their faces turned in the direction of Tokyo and the Emperor. US forces now have a base just 330 miles from the mainland of Japan. The intensity of the Japanese resistance sparks fears in America that a land invasion of Japan could cost 250,000 US lives.

22 June: B-29s continue to pound Japanese aircraft plants and the naval arsenal at Kure.

WAR DIARY

June 1945

China: Japanese troops abandon Liuchow, setting it on fire before the advancing Chinese army. Resistance is ended on Tarakan Island off the coast of Borneo.

Northern Ireland: Over 50 surrendered U-Boats are now moored at Lisnahilly, near Londonderry.

23 June: In San Francisco, the Big Four powers agree to admit Poland to the United Nations. A compromise agreement between Britain, America, the USA and Russia approves a power-sharing Government to include three 'exiles' from London, and two non-communists from within Poland. The deal has been brokered by President Truman's emissary, Harry Hopkins.

24 June: In Borneo, British and American aircraft drop 1000 tons of bombs on Japanese positions. British bombers also destroy a bridge over the River Kwai in Siam (Thailand), built at the cost of many lives of British and Commonwealth prisoners of war. British and Indian troops, fighting in country flooded by monsoon rains, continue to harass Japanese units seeking to escape on trails over the Shan Hills.

Moscow: The Soviet armed forces hold a massive Victory Parade in Red Square. Soldiers trail 200 captured German banners, including Hitler's personal standard, across the Square and hurl them at the foot of the Lenin Mausoleum.

25 June: Australian forces occupy the Miri oilfield in the Protectorate of Sarawak (Borneo).

Tokyo: The Japanese Domei news agency has broadcast a statement this week saying that the Western Allies were trying to induce Russia to enter the war, for which action, said Domei, there existed no reason or problem.

26 June: San Francisco. A momentous day as envoys from 50 countries sign the charter of the new United Nations organisation. Seven delegates sign for the USSR. The ceremony follows nine weeks of negotiation to fashion an organisation capable of maintaining world peace. President Truman tells delegates: 'The charter is a solid structure upon which we can build a better world.' He adds, 'If we had this Charter a few years ago... millions now dead would be alive. If we should falter in the future in our will to use it, millions now living will surely die.'

27 June: The burned and battered US aircraft carrier *Bunker Hill* steams into a West Coast harbour today, the astonishing survivor of a dramatic story of the sea that began six weeks ago. On 11 May off Okinawa, two Japanese planes each dropped a 500lb bomb on the carrier and then crashed their planes onto the burning deck, killing 373 Americans. For six hours the crew fought the flames to little avail. Then Captain George Seitz ordered a 70° turn which caused the burning part of the ship to plunge into the sea. Tons of seawater poured over the edge of the carrier and carried away masses of flaming petrol and oil. The vessel was saved and will now be repaired.

Right: A swarm of mighty Flying Fortresses look like tiny models on an airfield near Munich in Germany in June 1945. These are replacement aircraft that never saw action in Europe but are on standby to join in the continuing war with Japan.

Since the end of the war it is estimated that the Allied armies have uncovered over 2,500,000 displaced persons in Germany alone. Russians constitute by far the largest majority of them at around 40% with the French, at around 25%, the next largest. In fact the total is 2,000,000 less than anticipated and it is not clear why there is such a huge disparity.

28 June: Philippines: General MacArthur announces the end of operations on Luzon. Some 23,000 Japanese soldiers remain at large.

The liberator of Paris last August, General Leclerc, has been named commander of a French Far East expeditionary force.

29 June: Washington. President Truman approves a plan to invade Japan which could involve up to five million US servicemen. *Operation Olympic* calls for a landing on Kyushu on 1 November and *Operation Coronet* is the codename for a landing on the main island of Honshu on 1 March 1946. Kyushu calls for 13 divisions and Honshu 23 divisions, including the US First Army from Europe. British involvement will include a long range bomber force to assist the main assault.

Tokyo radio announces that Japan has begun to move her war factories to Manchuria to avoid the US bombing.

Europe: Czechoslovakia cedes 4781 square miles of Ruthenia to the USSR. In Warsaw the Government of National Unity is finally formed. It includes several members of the London-based Polish Government in Exile.

30 June: China: Chungchin is captured and Chinese forces advance into Indochina. In Borneo, US naval and air forces bombard Balikpapan.

Washington: Edward Stettinius resigns as Secretary of State to take up the position of ambassador to the United Nations. James F Byrnes replaces him.

JULY TO NOVEMBER 1945

THE ROAD FROM WAR TO PEACE

The picture-postcard style image above depicts British forces in action in North Africa soon after Monty's decisive victory at the Battle of El Alamein in the Western Desert. The image is partially peeled back to show the same location in a peaceful future, as an ideal tourist destination, secured by those who fought for the place against the Nazis. The tourist bus carries labels for four destinations: London - Algiers - Baghdad - Calcutta. The artist Roy Nockolds could surely not have imagined that a brand new airport and 4-Star luxury resort complex would open at El Alamein in the spring of 2005!

The Story behind a photograph

There have been many coincidences and connections that have come about because of the *Sixty Years On* series, *writes Ron McGill*. Several have happened to me personally. Perhaps the most astounding one occurred soon after the photograph above was first reproduced in June 2005. Soon afterwards I was off to a meeting of friends and colleagues from our mutual Telegraph working days in the 1948 -1970 era at the Central Telegraph Office in the City of London. Sitting with one of my friends, Fred Smith, I recalled that he had spent much of World War II in Ceylon. Knowing he was following the series I asked him whether he had noticed the photograph of a group of ATS girls lining up on the Quay in Colombo?

'Too true' he responded, 'and I've sent that photograph on to my old friends for one of those girls married my fellow Sergeant, Bob Cressy, out there in Ceylon.' He went on to explain that his friends would celebrate their Diamond Wedding Anniversary at the end of 2005 and furthermore, that they lived just a few miles from his home in Brentford, Middlesex.

Of course, I just had to follow up the story. The girl in the photograph is Jean (originally Justine Davies) who lived in Swansea in late 1941. All of her friends were enlisting to do their bit and, despite being just 15 years of age, she also joined up - passing herself off as 18. She was appointed to ATS Signals. Later in the war she volunteered for Overseas service and was posted to 3 HQ Company/ATS at Colombo and Kandy which was part of SE Asia Command.

Jean remembers quite clearly leaving their transport ship and being lined up with their luggage on the Quay at Colombo for what became the **csma** photograph. Counting along the front row of the girls, from the right, the fifth lady along was Captain Hill, their Company Commander. The lady next to her (6th) was her second in command Lieutenant (cannot recall her name!) and Jean herself is just a face, tucked in to the left of the Lieutenant's cheek and is in the second row.

My friend Fred was a Sergeant in Signals in Colombo and he and his colleagues made prompt efforts to make the girls out from England very welcome in their Sergeants' Mess. His friend Bob, also an ex-Post Office man, quickly 'fell' for Jean and proposed, was accepted and she thus became the first ATS girl out there to be married, by now just 18 years of age.

Their mutual Army friends collected enough money to pay for their wedding and quite fortunately, that prolific romantic novelist Barbara Cartland was in Ceylon at that time visiting her friend Lady Louis Mountbatten and she kindly kitted Jean out in a special wedding dress for the occasion.

Resuming civilian life after the War Jean worked with the GPO at Victoria Exchange in SW London, then was seconded to the War Office switchboards and finally to British Airways and

Above: Women of the ATS arriving in Ceylon in wartime ready to play their part in the Allied South East Asia Command.

the Coal Board. Husband Bob also resumed work with the Post Office and subsequently retired after 40 odd years of service.

Fred incidentally also had a hectic Army life before he ended up in Ceylon. Called up on 2 September 1939, he went to France with the BEF. Stationed near Arras, the subsequent speed of the German breakthrough cut them off from Dunkirk. The group managed to obtain a lorry, found a deserted petrol dump, loaded up and began a long and eventful journey to St Malo. They were fortunate to find an empty Collier and all of his group climbed aboard and settled down in the hold among piles of gritty coal dust until nightfall. They got away safely in the dark and sailed to Weymouth and safety where they climbed out black from head to foot in coal dust!

Fred's teleprinter group of Signals were eventually fitted out to travel to Singapore and left the UK in December 1941. However, with the sudden surrender of Singapore they were diverted to Batavia in Java where they also came under Japanese air attacks and they were shipped off again, this time to Colombo in Ceylon where he remained for the rest of the War. He married his WAAF girlfriend Joan in late 1945.

Isn't it simply remarkable that Fred should see that photograph of the ATS girls and remember them arriving in Colombo?

Empress Memories

The Empress of Scotland and *Empress of Australia* served as troopships during and after the war carrying many thousands of servicemen and women all over the world. Mention of their names sparked a flood of correspondence.

Air Navigator

I went to New York on the *Queen Mary* around October 1943 for air navigator training in Canada and returned on the *Empress of Scotland* in April 1944. I remember the boat drill notices were written in English and Japanese and I understood at the time that the vessel was owned by the Canadian Pacific Railway. Conditions aboard the two ships were very different. Going out with maybe 200 air crew cadets and a small party of German POWs, plenty of food, three meals a day, sleeping in bunk beds in a cabin in the large liner compared with the return trip in a smaller crowded ship, two meals a day, hammocks slung between decks.

Alan Mercer, Hampshire

Fire in New York

Empress of Scotland began her career as Canadian Pacific's *Empress of Japan* on the company's route to Japan from the west coast of Canada. She was renamed after Japan entered the war on the Axis side. After the war she was acquired by the German Hamburg-Atlantic Line, refitted (losing one of her three funnels in the process) and renamed *Hanseatic*. Under her third name she sailed a regular service from Germany to New York via Southampton. I was an Immigration Officer at Southampton in the 1960's and remember the liner as attractive and well appointed. However, she never docked, always anchoring off the Isle of Wight and being dealt with as 'a tender job'. Beck's beer - then unknown in this country - was on offer in her bars.

In the summer of 1966 the *Hanseatic* caught fire in New York shortly before she was due to sail for Europe and was damaged beyond economic repair. Her passengers were transferred to Cunard's *Queen Elizabeth*, which had also embarked many of the passengers from the American liner *United States*, which was strikebound in New York at the same time. As a result and in the dying days of the transatlantic liner traffic, the *Queen Elizabeth* arrived at Southampton with virtually her full complement of some 2000 passengers.

Incidentally, I believe my daughter-in-law's grandfather served on the *Empress of Scotland* in her wartime trooping role. He was a gunner in the Maritime Regiment, Royal Artillery.

M R Smith, Berkshire

Bound for Colombo

On 1 July 1945 my wife sailed on the *Empress of Scotland* from Liverpool bound for Colombo, Ceylon. The voyage took 16 days. My wife was in the WRNS and I believe this was the first troopship to go through Suez without escort after the end of the war in Europe. Contrary to the belief of some, the WRNS did not have first-class accommodation but six shared what was a two-berth cabin! My wife's next voyage was on *MV Devonshire* to Singapore after the surrender of the Japanese and she returned a year later on the *Athlone Castle*. There is a fine model of the *Empress of Scotland* in Glasgow Maritime Museum.

Charles Clothier, Glasgow

Gandhi assassinated

As a military married family, we returned to England from India in 1948, via the Deolali and Colaba (Bombay) transit camps. We duly received orders for embarkation aboard the *Empress of Scotland* to take place on 1 February 1948. However, on 30 January, Gandhi was assassinated resulting in much rioting throughout India, not least Bombay. As a result of this, our embarkation was brought forward by a day with a stipulation that once on board, we all had to remain there until she sailed on 1 February.

The journey was uneventful but I clearly remember the wide staircase leading down to the Dining Hall that had its own very distinctive 'porridge' type smell. We stopped at Port Said where many 'Gully-Gully' men in their small boats converged on the ship to sell their goods, making contact with the deck customers via long ropes attached to which were tin cans used to exchange goods and money. The voyage ended at Liverpool on 14 February 1948 and that's the last we saw of the ship.

Adrian Webber, Oxon

Daily rum ration

In December 1946 I was on the troopship *Empress of Australia* in the Mediterranean homeward bound/demob bound from Japan. Conditions on the ship were shocking with the mess decks inches under water and made worse by a violent storm that prevented us from picking up some hundreds of personnel from Malta. The daily rum ration was well received!

While in the Med we heard on the radio that the *Empress of Scotland*, due to sail for Japan from the Clyde, I think, was delayed by the objections of the troops to on-board conditions. Those leaving the UK were obviously less inclined to accept poor conditions! Eventually, of course, the *Empress of Scotland* set sail and I believe we passed one another at night in the area of Gibraltar round about 18 December 1946.

J C Champion, Wiltshire

Empress of Canada sunk

Early in April 1942, along with about 3000 other members of HM Forces, I boarded at Liverpool the Canadian Pacific liner *Empress of Japan* which later that year was renamed *Empress of Scotland*, apparently on the express instructions of Sir Winston Churchill. Next day we joined a large convoy of merchant ships and other troop ships in the Clyde accompanied by Royal Navy escorts. We were bound we knew not where, the only clues being the innoculations we'd received, together with the fact that we had been issued with tropical kit.

Life aboard a wartime trooper had to be experienced to be believed. Packed like sardines, sleeping in hammocks, the atmosphere - especially at night - was pretty horrendous, especially so as we neared the tropics. A pal and I spent many nights up on deck sleeping on life-rafts rather than suffocating down below. The tedium of daily life was relieved only by the lifeboat drill. Generally the food on troop ships was not too good, but on the *Empress* we had very good white bread baked daily by the Chinese crew (the officers were Canadian). We also actually had bacon and egg for breakfast on Sundays, both of which were unheard of at home in those days.

During this period of the war, the North Atlantic wasn't the safest place in which to sail, but after two weeks at sea without incident we dropped into Freetown harbour, Sierra Leone, for refuelling. During these two or three days we were entertained by the locals diving from their fruit-laden 'bumboats' for 'Glasgow Tanners' (farthings wrapped in silver paper disguised as sixpences). After a couple of days we were off again, safely negotiating the exit from Freetown where U-Boats tended to lay in wait. The *Empress of Canada*, a sister ship which was also in our convoy, was sunk entering Freetown in 1943 with heavy loss of life.

After a week or so cruising through tropical seas and watching the flying fish, our peace was shattered one afternoon by a large explosion. An old cargo boat on our starboard quarter was on fire with bows down in the water. Two hours later a naval supply ship was also in trouble after another explosion. Several years after the war I found out that the convoy had run into mines, laid by a lone German freighter running the gauntlet of the Royal Navy en route from Germany to Japan. Apparently the cargo ship sank but the naval supply ship reached port safely.

Empress of Australia

at any time. Meals were rather awful, being composed mainly of various ways to cook rice, and it took another six weeks to get to Port Tewfik in the Suez area. That was a total of 14 weeks from leaving 'Blighty' with no contact at all with our homes. No mobiles or a handy telephone in those days or news from home. One just had to put up with it.

Simon J Driver, Essex

In mid-May we docked in Durban. What bliss! Good food and drink and lovely girls. We were treated royally and spent two months there. Normally it would have been only a few days before moving on to the Middle or Far East. However, all good things come to an end; by mid-July we found ourselves on board the *Ile de France*, dashing unescorted up to Port Tewfik at the southern end of the Suez Canal, accompanied by the heat, dust, sand and flies of Egypt in late July.

I was in the RAF Middle East, on 47 MU for three years and eight months and came home on the *Empress of Scotland* in February 1947. It was fantastically comfortable compared with the standards of accommodation to which we had become accustomed. The journey from Suez to the UK took only a couple of weeks, as we came back through the Suez Canal.

It was a different story on the 14 week journey out when we all occupied hammocks in a deck below the water line, so didn't fancy our chances much should we have been torpedoed, but happily that did not happen. This was on the *Duchess of Bedford*, which had a sister ship, the *Duchess of Richmond*.

The hammocks, once we had mastered the knack of getting into them, were strung so closely together that when any one turned over it seemed as if we all turned over as well. The hold was absolutely crowded with no natural ventilation and no doors on the toilets in case they got jammed in an emergency. Rather embarrassing in certain circumstances. We were ordered not to undress or to take our boots off for the first three days. We zigzagged across the Atlantic for a couple of weeks and docked at Lagos and Freetown for water and supplies. After that we zigzagged again to miss U-Boats and after another five weeks, finished up in Capetown and were stationed at Retreat Camp. This was absolute heaven as we had proper beds and could buy large bunches of grapes for three old pence (or a 'ticky' as it was called there) as well as tobacco for 'thruppence' an ounce. Sunshine all day and the most glorious food including the best jams one could ever taste.

Of course, it was too good to last and three weeks later we boarded a Khedive Ishmael Line boat, which was much smaller and reeked of onions. Not my favourite food

Empress of France

Fifty years ago I was very privileged to sail on the *Empress of Scotland* from Liverpool to Montreal. At the time she was the flagship of the Canadian Pacific Line, and I was an 18-year-old, newly commissioned officer in the RAF, en route to Canada for pilot training. I caught the 12.37pm special Boat Train from Euston to Liverpool on Friday 6 May 1955 for sailing that evening from Gladstone Dock. Due to industrial action by the Port of Liverpool tug boat crews, the Captain (R A Leicester OBE) himself manoeuvred the ship from the berth to hold in one of the port channels to await daybreak. A brief description of this difficult feat appeared in the London evening papers, together with a night photo of the ship as it left the quayside.

At daybreak on the Saturday we set sail for Canada, missing out, as I recall, the previously scheduled stop at Greenock. Travelling First Class, seven days of luxury followed, and myself and the other 18 members of Course No 5503 were 'spoilt rotten'! I also understood at the time that we were only the fourth liner that year to sail up the St Lawrence River after the winter ice had melted. We docked at Montreal on 13 May after first calling in at Quebec.

Following our 15 months flying training and a Survival Course in the Rockies, we sailed for home on 31 July 1956 on the *Empress of France*, arriving at Liverpool on 7 August. Finally and coincidentally, 50 years ago, 6 May 1955 fell on a Friday - the same day as 6 May in 2005!

John M Davis MBE, Copthorne, Sussex

Afrika Korps POWs

I undertook a wartime voyage on the *Empress of Scotland* when I sailed from Liverpool to Canada via Norfolk, Virginia. When our draft was called and we left Heaton Park and were sent off to Liverpool for embarkation. The Canadian Pacific liner set sail on 25 June 1943, not without some trepidation for apprehension among the 2000 Afrika Korps prisoners on board was considerable. They were convinced that every ship crossing the Atlantic was a cert for being torpedoed and rumour had it that many of them refused to sleep.

Although we had scant sympathy for them, we could understand their fear as they were in accommodation below the waterline. They were allowed up on deck for an hour or two during the day but always under armed guard. These Germans were destined for work on the Mississippi levees, which was an acceptable occupation for prisoners under the Geneva Convention. The ship was escorted by aircraft for the first day and a half and there were constant changes of course as well. We discovered that we were on a southerly route, which took us down towards the tropics.

After four or five days, the sun became very strong and we saw flying fish galore. From the sixth day at sea, our general direction changed to a north-westerly one and speculations arose as to the landfall. None of us guessed correctly. We did get an escort of one of the US Navy's blimps, which gave a certain degree of assurance and then learned that we were due to dock at Norfolk, Virginia. What surprised us was the length of time it took to negotiate the entry into Chesapeake Bay and achieve the docking. When we did dock it was obvious that they had not had a ship of our size as a normal event. The wooden dock and caissons took a bit of a pounding and some of them splintered under the weight of the *Empress*.

I regret to say that we took advantage of the US Marines who were patrolling the harbour because of the prisoners we had on board. We reckoned that these 'Snow Whites' (they wore white tin hats) made good targets for our apple cores until we were told to desist from this unfriendly behaviour.

Our onward travel had been well arranged and eventually we boarded Second Class carriages that had wooden slatted seats that could be folded down to provide not very comfortable sleeping berths. It was pretty warm so we didn't need much in the way of covering. The best bit was the food. After three and a half years of austerity, we enjoyed the luxury of white bread, lashings of butter, eggs aplenty and fruit. On 4 July, we passed through New York having earlier caught a glimpse of the Capitol in Washington. It was an interesting journey all the way up the coast of the New England states. We stayed on the train for a total of three and a half days, crossed into Canada and made towards New Brunswick, finally arriving at Moncton which was to be our home for the next two weeks.

Eric Clarkson, Berkshire

Grin and bear it!

I was amazed to learn that the *Empress of Australia* had survived beyond the end of the Second World War, seemingly unscathed and was still engaged in moving troops around the world. I sailed from Liverpool on that troopship on 30 August 1941 as a member of the 1st Armoured Division, which was sailing to Egypt and the Western Desert to do battle with the Axis forces. Disembarking in Durban on 3 October 1941, we were transferred to another troopship and completed the journey to Port Tewfik in Egypt, arriving there on 14 November 1941.

I still have the allocation ticket for my accommodation on the *Empress of Australia*. It reads 'Hammock, Section 1, F Deck, Port'.

F Deck had no portholes and minimal ventilation. Had we been any lower, we would have been in either the bilges or the engine room! Needless to say, our accommodation was very cramped and the food very basic. However there was a war on, so we had to grin and bear it.
Ted Holmes, Leicestershire

Overnight to Baghdad

On my way to demob, in September 1947, I travelled on the *Empress of Australia* from Port Said to Liverpool, calling at Valletta in Malta on a lovely Mediterranean morning. The Bay of Biscay was quite wild, but not enough to stop my enjoyment of the excellent food. It was helped by my sharing a cabin with three other NCOs, one of whom was on his way home from India after 17 years.

It was a more comfortable journey than the one from Shaibah to Port Said. We travelled by train overnight to Baghdad and the following night was spent on a Nairn bus to a transit camp near Amman. The company were unable to continue to Haifa, so we stood in the back of a lorry all day, with a lunch stop at Tiberias, arriving in Haifa after dark. Next morning, we boarded a train to Cantara, preceded by a mine-clearing diesel. Another lorry trip in the dark took us to Port Fouad Transit Camp, across the canal from Port Said. We were allocated to ships on morning parade.

I was allowed home on leave for Christmas 1946 and spent over a week in Port Fouad, so you can imagine that morning parade became quite interesting. On that occasion I crossed to Toulon on the *Dunnottar Castle*, and the Med was very rough. About 300 of us were crowded in a rear hold. Those pictures of crowded slave ships remind me of the scene at night and getting out of a hammock and stepping between bodies whilst trying to reach the deck rail in time, made a hectic start to the day. We had two nights on a crowded train before crossing to Dover. I arrived home near Doncaster at 4am on 23 December 1947.

So three cheers for the *Empress*. I still have one cufflink with its picture on that I bought on board!
A H Buckley, Hereford

Height of luxury

In 1952 while serving in Malaysia, I was sent to Hong Kong for an exercise, and after six weeks there was returned to Singapore aboard the *Empress of Australia*. Due to us being a small party and there being plenty of space, we were billeted in cabins, the height of luxury for other ranks, instead of the mess decks. The cabin steward then told us that it was to be her last run as she was to be broken up.
P R Fletcher, Liverpool

RAF Tiger Force

I recall my own two trips on the *Empress of Australia*. The first was in about June 1945 when, as members of the RAF Tiger Force, we

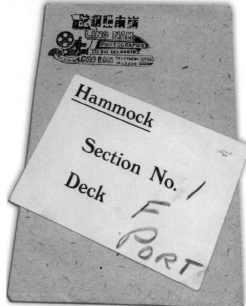

The ticket that allocated Ted Holmes the use of two metal ceiling hooks in the hold of F Deck is pictured, above right. This ticket entitled him to sling his hammock! He informs us it was a relief to disembark in Durban for a few days before continuing the journey to Egypt in another troopship. Ted participated in Operation Crusader in the Western Desert in November 1941 when the Eighth Army relieved the siege of Tobruk and temporarily drove back Rommel's Afrika Korps.

At the end of the war Ted Holmes was posted to Indo-China; behind the allocation ticket we reproduce the cover of a paper envelope that held the photograph of him, reproduced above left. The picture was taken in October 1945 in Cholon, a city near Saigon in French Indo-China (now Vietnam). By then, Ted was serving as a Lieutenant in the 20th Indian Infantry Division Signal Regiment. The troopship that transported Mr Holmes' unit from Rangoon in Burma to Saigon was the Circassia, *an Anchor Line vessel.*

The colour photograph, right, is of Ted Holmes and his wife Margaret, who, from 1944 to 1945, served with Force 136 (the Special Operations organisation responsible for maintaining and receiving intelligence from agents in Japanese-occupied territories in South East Asia). Her voyage from Liverpool to Bombay was made aboard the P&O liner Strathmore. *From Bombay Margaret endured an eight-day train journey from Meerut to the south of India before crossing to Kandy on the Indian Ocean island of Ceylon where Mountbatten had his South East Asia Command (SEAC) headquarters.*

set sail for Okinawa (though we didn't know that until later). We sailed across the Atlantic, traversed the Panama Canal and went on to Hawaii and then on to Enewetok in the Marshall Islands. We were escorted across the Pacific Ocean by six American destroyers and they made quite a sight. It was in the Marshalls that we heard of the Japanese surrender. So we sailed off to Manus in the Admiralty Islands.

We were then ordered to Hong Kong to retake possession of the British colony from the Japanese. After being caught in a typhoon in the South China Sea for four days and nights, when the *Empress* was tossed about like a cork, we arrived at Kowloon on 1 September (I believe) where we disembarked to carry out our required duties. I served in Hong Kong until October 1946 when I was detailed to return to the UK for demob. The ship which took us home was none other than the *Empress of Australia*. This time we travelled via the Suez Canal and the Mediterranean. In other words I went right around the world on the same ship.
Clifford Blackford (address supplied)

Originally named the Tirpitz, *the* Empress of Australia *was built in Germany and after the First World War was ceded to Great Britain as part of the war reparation. In 1920 she was used as a troopship under P&O management and was then sold to Canadian Pacific and renamed* Empress of China. *In 1922 she entered Canadian Pacific's transpacific service and was renamed* Empress of Australia. *In September 1923 just as she was putting to sea at Yokohama in Japan, an earthquake struck the port. The pier was shattered and the vessel swirled through the harbour. Brought under control, she aided the rescue of some 3000 Yokohama residents, earning her the gratitude of a great many Japanese. She remained on the Pacific until 1926, when she was sent to Glasgow for refitting and was then placed on the express North Atlantic service. In 1939 she was requisitioned as a troopship, which was to remain her role until 1952 when she was broken up.*

1 July: It's day 1302 of the war against Japan. In China, Chiang Kai Shek's Nationalist forces liberate Liuchow. Australian and Dutch troops go ashore at Balikpapan, an important oil-centre on the south-east coast of Borneo. Other Australians are moving forward on the island of Bougainville.

News is released of a wave of paper balloons carrying incendiary bombs launched from Japan over several weeks last month. The crew of US Navy ships off the Aleutian Islands reported seeing hundreds high in the air at the time of the San Francisco Conference. Prevailing winds in the stratosphere blew the deadly balloons 6000 miles across the Pacific to the western USA and Canada. Some damage was sustained along with minor casualties when the balloons – 33 feet in diameter – fell to earth. It's the second time in a year that Japan has tried this desperate tactic. By the end of the month, the remnants of 230 of the ineffectual weapons will have been recovered.

Germany: British forces withdraw from Magdeburg which now becomes part of the Soviet zone of occupation.

2 July: The Japanese claim that five million civilians have been killed or injured in US bombing raids. Today 600 Super-Fortresses drop 4000 tons of incendiaries on the cities of Kure, Shimonoseki, Ube and Kumamoto.

In London, Mountbatten receives orders to launch Operation Zipper, the liberation of Malaya, in August.

The *London Gazette* carries the story of the 'Tin-openers', the name given to Royal Navy experts who defuse bombs and mines in captured ports and harbours. In the Italian port of Leghorn alone, divers cleared around 19,000 teller mines and other obstacles. They also had to cut up sunken blockships. The teams sport a tin-opener on their vehicles as a badge of recognition.

3 July: Advance units of the British and US occupation troops arrive in Berlin accompanied by 200 newspaper correspondents. Edwin Tetlow of the *Daily Mail* writes: 'Cossack horsemen, cavorting in the early morning drizzle and shouting their traditional war cries, gave us a rousing welcome. They were exercising their mounts, sending great clods of earth into the air as they performed their unrivalled tricks of horsemanship.'

Japan: Over 500 Super-Fortresses bomb cities on Honshu and Shikoku islands.

4 July: Thousands of Berliners watch the arrival of the main British occupation force. Large numbers of German women are clearing the rubble brick by brick. Initially their working day was 13 hours, but this has been reduced to seven. There are long queues for food, fuel is scarce and most buildings left standing have no glass. The Black Market is rife and rumours circulate that Hitler is still alive.

In Manila, General MacArthur announces the complete liberation of the Philippines. It is known, however, that there remain large numbers of Japanese soldiers hiding in the forests and on small, isolated islands.

5 July: The US and Britain give recognition to the Provisional Government of National Unity in Poland. The Foreign Office points out that under the Yalta agreement 'free and unfettered elections' must be held as soon as possible on the basis of 'universal suffrage and secret ballot.'

In Britain, voting takes place in the General Election. A result will be delayed to allow for the collection of the votes of servicemen and women overseas.

Washington gives General Carl Spaatz command of the air offensive against Japan. Nagasaki and airfields around Tokyo are bombed today.

Isle of Man: Ancient Tynwald Hill where every year public proclamation is made of Acts passed by the *Manx* Parliament, witnesses history today when King George and Queen Elizabeth direct the traditional rite as part of a Royal Victory Tour.

6 July: Nicaragua is the first country to ratify the United Nations Charter.

In Berlin, the Allied occupation forces hold a victory parade.

In Washington, US chiefs of staff authorise a special operation known as Overcast to exploit chosen German 'rare minds'. German scientific knowledge, particularly in rocket science, is sought-after by all the victorious Allied nations. Dr Wernher von Braun and members of his team who developed the V-weapon rockets are already in US custody.

Brussels: The RAF hold a farewell parade in the Belgium capital.

7 July: French troops of occupation enter Saabruecken in Germany.

Indian Ocean: Warships of the British East Indies Fleet bombard Japanese positions on the Nicobar Islands.

8 July: US aircraft from Okinawa attack targets on the Japanese island of Kyushu and Formosa, off the coast of China. Also in the Pacific, it is announced that three British aircraft carriers have been damaged in kamikaze attacks.

London: Sappers working on bomb sites in Oxford Street put up signs pointing out that they are British and not German or Italian POW workers. More of the 185,000 Germans held in the country are being deployed on site-clearing jobs.

9 July: Chinese forces sever the last link between Japan's China Army and its garrison in Indo China. Three US air bases on the Chinese mainland, abandoned in the face of a Japanese offensive last year, have been recaptured and will soon be operational again. More than 1000 carrier-borne US bombers attack airfields near

Right: British groundcrew prepare a Catalina flying boat for a mission to Burma

Tokyo. At times over 700 American planes are in the air over the targets at the same time. The Japanese lose 342 aircraft against just 10 downed US bombers. This action follows a night attack by a large force of Super-Fortresses on four cities on Honshu.

Paris: General De Gaulle announces a referendum to decide France's system of government.

10 July: The US Third Fleet joins the attack on Japan, sending 1022 fighter-bombers to raid 70 airfields; 173 enemy aircraft are destroyed.

In Borneo, Australian progress east of Balikpapan is halted by barriers of flaming petrol ignited by the retreating Japanese.

Argentina: The German U-Boat U 530, last known to be operating off the coast of Norway in March, surfaces off Mar del Plata in Argentina. Captain Otto Wermoutt surrenders the vessel and his 54 crewmen to the authorities – nine weeks after the end of hostilities in Europe. There is speculation the submarine carried high ranking Nazis to sanctuary in South America. Newspapers carry reports of other submarines being sighted in Argentine waters and the landing of mysterious personages in rubber boats on the coast of Patagonia. Captain Wermoutt maintains that his submarine had been on patrol alone for four months. However, to do so the U-Boat must have obtained food and fuel from somewhere or have been lying concealed in a safe haven for part of the time.

Far East: British carrier aircraft bomb Japanese airfields on Sumatra.

Berlin: The Russians officially hand over the western half of the city to British and US forces.

William Mackenzie King wins the general election in Canada.

Britain: HM trawler *Kurd* hits a mine off The Lizard, Cornwall, and sinks with the loss of 15 of the 26 crew. It's the first such British casualty since another mine sank an MGB (motor gunboat) in the North Sea on 12 May.

12 July: In Paris, concentration camp survivors carry a huge cross through the city in memory of French victims of the Nazis.

Australian troops capture Maradi in the north of Borneo.

Field Marshal Montgomery invests Red Army Marshals Zhukov and Rokossovsky with the Grand Cross of the Order of the Bath in the shadow of Berlin's Brandenburg Gate.

13 July: The British garrison in Berlin stages a march-past before Allied commanders.

The Japanese are reinforcing their air forces in Manchuria and Korea in the expectation of an attack by Russia.

14 July: A fraternisation ban is lifted in the British and American zones of occupation in Germany and Austria. The Supreme Headquarters, Allied Expeditionary Force (SHAEF) will be dissolved at midnight.

The US Third Fleet closes on the coast of Japan to bombard steel works in the industrial city of Kamaisha while 1000 carrier aircraft bomb Hokkaido.

15 July: US battleships South Dakota, Indiana and Massachussetts bombard Muroran on Hokkaido.

In Brussels, King Leopold repeats his refusal to abdicate.

Full illumination is allowed again in London's West End after 2000 nights of blackout. President Truman and Churchill arrive in Potsdam, Germany, to join Stalin for another 'Big Three' conference.

16 July: In Alamogordo, New Mexico, US scientists successfully test the first

Left: A poster urges the British public to vote for a Labour Government

atomic bomb. 'The Manhattan Project' is top secret and the public know nothing of this device which explodes with a force equivalent to 20,000 tonnes of TNT. The blast sends a mushroom cloud 40,000 feet into the air and the flash is visible 125 miles away.

Chinese troops recapture part of the important Kweilin-Liuchow railway.

Japan: A British task force joins the US fleet in attacking the Tokyo area.

17 July: President Truman presides over the opening of the Potsdam Conference.

The King, Queen and Princess Elizabeth fly to Northern Ireland to continue their Royal Victory Tour.

Buenos Aires: The Argentine Government agree to hand over the U-Boat U 530 to the custody of the British and US Governments, together with the crew and all available information concerning her belated and mysterious surrender.

18 July: US and British carrier aircraft destroy the remnants of the Japanese navy at the Yokosuka naval base. This loss includes the fleet's most powerful battleship the Nagato. At the same time, the US fleet fires 2000 tons of shells on Hitachi in the space of 50 minutes.

In Potsdam, Churchill and Truman receive a coded message about the successful atomic bomb test in New Mexico. Churchill is unsure whether Stalin is aware of the test, but it seems likely that Red spies have informed him already.

19 July: Far East: Trapped Japanese forces attempting to escape east break out from Burma's Pegu Yomas mountains. Although monsoon rains and mud have so far prevented the Allies from finally crushing the enemy, more than 10,000 Japanese will die by the end of the month.

On Borneo it is reported that Australian troops have occupied the town of Marudi.

20 July: Brussels: Premier Achille Acker maintains pressure on King Leopold to abdicate because of his 'grave and unpardonable mistakes' in dealing with the Nazi occupation of Belgium.

In Potsdam, British Premier Churchill and US President Truman privately agree to drop the Atom Bomb on Japan if it fails to surrender unconditionally. The Allies select Nuremberg as the venue to try major Nazi war criminals. On the same day, Truman presides over the ceremonial hoisting of the Stars and Stripes in the heart of Berlin.

21 July: A Victory Parade of 10,000 British men, including 'Desert Rats' with their self-propelled 25-pounders, takes place before Winston Churchill in Berlin's Charlottenburger Chaussee. At Churchill's side are Field-Marshals Montgomery, Maitland-Wilson and Alexander. Guns of the Royal Horse Artillery fire a 193-round salute.

22 July: A statement issued in Tokyo declares that the government is open to peace negotiations, but not to threats. This night for the first time US destroyers will enter Tokyo Bay and torpedo enemy shipping. The massive bombing offensive against Japan continues to build. With the end of the fighting in Europe, aircraft are being directed to the Pacific; up to today 4082 US aircraft have been redeployed from the UK, France and Italy. A large number are now operating from air bases in southern China.

23 July: In Paris, Marshal Petain's trial for treason begins.

China: Japanese positions in the Shanghai area are attacked by Allied aircraft. Targets on the coast of Japan are shelled by British and American destroyers sweeping close inshore.

24 July: British Eighth Army troops entering the town of Graz in Austria receive an enthusiastic welcome from the townspeople.

Japan: 1000 US Third Fleet carrier aircraft hit numerous targets throughout the home islands.

The British Admiralty reveals that one of the most isolated places in the world, Tristan da Cunha, played a wartime role. Some 1600 miles off the coast of South Africa, the extinct volcano was commissioned as HMS Atlantic Isle on 15 January 1944. This 'Stone Frigate' served as a meteorological station forecasting weather for the Cape and the Indian Ocean.

25 July: Truman secretly gives the order for the Atom Bomb

WAR DIARY
July 1945

to be dropped on Japan as soon as possible after 3 August.

Malaya: British warships carry out mine sweeping operations off the island of Phuket and commence a bombardment of Japanese strongpoints on the country's west coast.

Over 100 Super-Forts drop 450 tons of bombs on two oil refineries (one of them is the biggest in Japan) at Kawasaki, 10 miles south of Tokyo.

Churchill, Anthony Eden and Clement Atlee fly home from Germany to London for the announcement of the general election results.

26 July: Labour wins a sensational landslide victory over Churchill and the Tories. Voters had cheered Churchill wherever he went during the war, but do not see him as a suitable peace-time leader. Britain's soldiers, sailors and airmen overwhelmingly back Labour. Churchill goes to see the King who invites 62-year-old Clement Atlee to form a new Government. Churchill accepts the verdict with grace: 'I thank the British people for many kindnesses shown towards their servants.' Atlee has acted as Churchill's deputy and is the only politician to have served in the War Cabinet continuously from its formation. Churchill held his own seat at Woodford, Essex, with 27,688 votes against the 10,488 polled by his Labour opponent.

On this same day, Britain, China and the US issue the Potsdam Declaration threatening 'prompt and utter destruction' if Japan does not surrender unconditionally.

27 July: In London, the Chiefs of Staff hold their last conference with Churchill.

US aircraft drop leaflets on 11 Japanese cities warning the inhabitants of impending fire-bombing. Six of the 11 cities will be attacked within the next three days.

28 July: The Japanese Cabinet rejects the Potsdam Declaration that demands unconditional surrender. Fundamental concerns remain about the fate of the Emperor.

With Churchill out of office, the new British Premier Atlee, with Ernest Bevin, the new Foreign Secretary, fly out to rejoin the Potsdam Conference.

Brussels: Troops of the Guards Armoured Division march through the city and are presented with plaques and standards to mark the population's gratitude for their liberation last year.

29 July: The British Eighth Army is disbanded in Europe.

In the Pacific, the US cruiser *Indianapolis* is sunk by a Japanese submarine while returning from the airbase at Tinian where it had been delivering uranium-235 needed for the assembly of the atomic bomb.

Chinese troops recapture Kweilin Airfield from the Japanese.

The village of Stedham near Midhurst in Sussex witnesses a parade and memorial service for the Glider Pilot Regiment. This body of men saw service in Sicily, Normandy, Arnhem and the Rhine crossing. Two out of three of the original 1200 recruits who first mustered at Tilshead in Wiltshire are dead or missing.

30 July: Japan: US fighter-bombers have another day of intensive activity when they bomb Kobe, Kure naval base and Honshu. More leaflets are dropped on other cities warning of intense bombing to come. The targets include Hiroshima and Nagasaki. The Japanese say that by 6pm more than 1600 aircraft have attacked the main islands.

Austria: British troops and armoured cars are warmly welcomed by the Viennese as they enter the city and prepare to take over control of the southern districts.

Eire: The latest edition of an American newsletter distributed in southern Ireland reveals secret Nazi plans, newly discovered in Brussels, for the invasion of that country earlier in the war.

31 July: Far East: In Singapore harbour, British frogmen sink the Japanese cruiser *Takao* using limpet mines. The US Third Fleet claims to have destroyed or damaged 1230 Japanese ships and 1257 aircraft during the preceding 22 days.

Pierre Laval, former Prime Minister of collaborationist Vichy France, lands in Linz, Austria, after quitting Franco's Spain. He is placed in French custody and is expected to return to Paris shortly to stand trial for treason. Elsewhere in Europe, the Allies are still faced with a vast multi-lingual mass of destitute people. When the fighting stopped, over 11 million non-German men, women and children were homeless refugees, having either fled before advancing armies, been forcibly deported by the Nazis or were released POWs. About a quarter of Germany's population is also destitute. The Red Cross and UNRRA (United Nations Relief and Rehabilitation Administration) have worked tirelessly to assuage the situation. By providing medical aid, food, clothing and money, over eight million people have been repatriated so far and around 78,500 more are helped each day.

In China, the problem is on a different scale. Here some 43 million people have fled from the Japanese in the past seven years, abandoning everything they owned in order to survive.

Britain: Two whaling-factory ships are launched today at Haverton-on-Tees, Yorkshire. They will be crewed by Norwegians for that country's whaling industry. An agreement between the Norwegian and British Governments, extends the whale-catching season from 24 November to 24 March 1946.

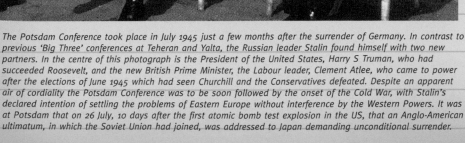

The Potsdam Conference took place in July 1945 just a few months after the surrender of Germany. In contrast to previous 'Big Three' conferences at Teheran and Yalta, the Russian leader Stalin found himself with two new partners. In the centre of this photograph is the President of the United States, Harry S Truman, who had succeeded Roosevelt, and the new British Prime Minister, the Labour leader, Clement Atlee, who came to power after the elections of June 1945 which had seen Churchill and the Conservatives defeated. Despite an apparent air of cordiality the Potsdam Conference was to be soon followed by the onset of the Cold War, with Stalin's declared intention of settling the problems of Eastern Europe without interference by the Western Powers. It was at Potsdam that on 26 July, 10 days after the first atomic bomb test explosion in the US, that an Anglo-American ultimatum, in which the Soviet Union had joined, was addressed to Japan demanding unconditional surrender.

SAVED BY THE BOMB

Ron McGill relates how a British POW held captive near Hiroshima in August 1945 survived the terrifying advent of the Atom Bomb.

In the summer of 2005 we remembered the 60th anniversary of VJ Day and the ending of the war against Japan with gratitude and thanksgiving. These thoughts were once before very evident for me when I recall a lunchtime discussion in August of 1985 when the dropping of the Atom Bomb was the topic of debate at our lunch break. I suddenly found out that there was another side to the rights and wrongs on the decision to use this devastating weapon that abruptly ended the Second World War.

This change of mind for me came during my spell as a BT business manager at the Wimbledon HQ in South West London when it had become a tradition for a few of our management team to dine briefly together in the staff restaurant.

One person had mentioned the horrors of the Atom Bomb and the massive loss of life and that humanity should have dictated against its use at a time when Japan was obviously losing the war. Many at our table seemed to be in agreement with this view when suddenly, a quiet voice said, 'I do not agree with you for it saved my life and that of many other doomed colleagues'.

We looked astonished at this obviously truthful and sincere statement which was made by one of my engineering colleagues, Ted Harker. Ted, a cheerful person, was stockily built with grey thinning hair and soon to retire on his 60th birthday. Bless him, for Ted normally kept his own counsel and rarely entered into the lunchtime discussions but we all wanted to hear him out and we pressed him for his story.

Captured at Singapore
And what a story – for Ted was one of the thousands of our soldiers captured at the fall of Singapore in February 1942. There followed for Ted and his friends much hard work on construction and railway sites for the Japanese, always hungry and suffering constant disease and malnutrition that gradually eroded their numbers as many died in captivity.

When the New Year of 1945 dawned the Japanese authorities sifted some of the hardiest of the survivors and shipped them to Japan and a city facing an extensive bay that led to the open sea. The new job (good for only as long as their poor wretched bodies would last) consisted of loading and unloading goods and engineering work of many kinds in a shipyard in a place they learnt was called Hiroshima.

Ted had about 50 soldier colleagues with him and, with the poor food and frequent beatings, they felt they could not last long in their weakened state and life looked more than bleak during those months of 1945. They did not have the luxury of huts or barracks and they were placed in deep caves in the foothills about 10 miles away that surrounded Hiroshima. Contact with Japanese citizens was almost nil for they were 'trucked in' to the dockyards and brought back to their caves at the end of the working day. They were given just enough food and drink to keep them working effectively by the Japanese guards who lived in rough quarters at the entrances to their caves.

Earth-shattering experience
That fateful morning of 6 August dawned and the B29 (*Enola Gay*) arrived high over Hiroshima and dropped the first Atom Bomb to be used in anger at 8.16am. This was equal to about 20,000 tons of TNT and we now know that 80,000 citizens were killed immediately and that four square miles of the city was turned into a burning wasteland. For Ted and his colleagues down in the caves all they could hear and feel was the earth-shattering experience of what appeared to be an earthquake, not uncommon in Japan.

Weakened as they were the prisoners remained resting in their caves waiting for the usual call to the trucks by their guards. This call never came and at noon some of the men checked the entrance and were astounded to find that their guards had gone and their quarters were abandoned. They then made a decision that probably saved their lives from the then unknown dangers of deadly radiation. They stayed resting in their caves and shared out what food and drink they could find in the deserted guards' quarters. They treated this break as a luxury rest and recovery period for by now there were only 35 of them left alive and able to walk and work.

Skeletal soldiers
After about two weeks a small group of Japanese civilians passed nearby and stopped briefly at the caves to be amazed at the sight of the almost skeletal soldiers coming slowly out into the daylight. A few of the POWs

understood the Japanese language and they told the others that a massive disaster had overcome Hiroshima and they all agreed again to stay where they were, out of the possible earthquake chaos and hopefully safer where they were – although by now their stock of food was diminishing rapidly.

The world soon knew of the Japanese surrender that was signed on 2 September and subsequently, various US military units began to arrive to study the complete devastation of Hiroshima. They in turn somehow learned of the presence of Allied prisoners somewhere in the nearby foothills and they came and searched the area and the caves and discovered some of the soldier prisoners still alive. Needless to say the surviving POWs found it all a miracle; liberation at last.

Miracle of liberation
A US officer later told my friend Ted that they had found some of their missing guards who admitted that they knew the prisoners could not last much longer. They said that the plan was to execute their captives in the next few weeks as the guards were being withdrawn to help reinforce the coastal defence of Japan against the expected Allied invasion of the mainland. Instead of that fate it was time to receive medical care and attention and proper food and drink to see them on the slow but sure recovery road after their three hard years of captivity.

After he had explained this dramatic tale some four decades on in our BT restaurant Ted would only say dryly, 'it was rather a close run thing.' Clearly, he and his colleagues were forever grateful for the Atom Bomb which gave them many extra years of life after they had come to terms with the fact that they had seemed surely doomed to die in Japan in 1945.

Happy retirement
Needless to say there was very little discussion at our lunch break after this story, for we were all quietly marvelling that our friend should have escaped such a dramatic end to his life. None of us had any prior knowledge that he had even been a prisoner of the Japanese. In what Ted used to call his 'extra years', he enjoyed following his favourite hobby of horse racing. He went on to live happily and gratefully in his retirement at his Earlsfield home in London.

Sadly, I heard later that he had passed away peacefully in the late 1990s, by then well into his seventies. For me, it was the loss of a good friend who would never be forgotten for his part in a miracle amidst the horror of Hiroshima.

ATOM BOMB AFTERMATH

It was nearly a year after the end of the war before an official report of what happened to Hiroshima and Nagasaki was published in Britain. Under the direction of the Chiefs of Staff a British Mission visited the two cities to study the damage done by the two atom bombs dropped on 6 and 9 August 1945.

Their report published in June 1946 revealed that in Hiroshima the bomb destroyed over four square miles of wooden houses, first by blast, then by fire. Buildings of reinforced concrete resisted the blast but were burnt out. Light, single-storey concrete buildings were wrecked at about a mile from the centre of damage. When the bomb fell, some 80,000 of the 320,000 people in the city were killed.

In the picture *above* a sailor from *HMIS Sutlej* (an Indian Navy vessel) surveys the devastation in Hiroshima. In the picture on the *right* a road can be seen trailing away to nothing in the rubble. The original caption says that there are signs of life returning in the form of young shoots pushing up from the base of shattered trees.

WAR DIARY
August 1945

1 August: Indo-China: In the early hours of this morning the British midget submarine *XE4* returned from a successful operation to cut the Saigon-Singapore and Saigon-Hong Kong undersea telephone cables. The three-man submersible was towed up the Japanese-controlled Saigon River by the submarine *HMS Spearhead* on the night of 30 July. After slipping her tow, *XE4* moved further upriver trailing a grapnel and chain along the bottom. Once the cables were located Sub-Lt K M Briggs, 22, and Sub-Lt A K Bergius, 20, went outside the submarine in breathing apparatus and cut the cables, returning with small sections as evidence of a job well done. The divers will be specially commended for working in much deeper and more dangerous waters than anticipated.

Allied forces seal off the Japanese at Buin on the southern tip of Bougainville in the Solomon Islands. Japanese shipping on the Yangtsze river in China is brought to a halt by mines dropped from the air.

In Paris, Pierre Laval is charged with treason. He is put under armed guard to protect him from the public.

In London, Labour MPs sing *The Red Flag* as the House of Commons elects a new speaker. Thousands of 'GI brides' are awaiting ships to take them to the US to marry American servicemen who proposed during service in England. Over 20,000 have already taken the plunge and the total is expected to reach 80,000.

2 August: Pacific: Only 316 survivors are rescued from USS Indianapolis, sunk on 29 July when returning from her top secret mission to Tinian airbase carrying nuclear material. Another 880 men are feared lost in the shark-infested Philippine Sea.

In Potsdam, the three-power conference comes to an end. Germany's disarmed, divided and deprived of the power to make war. Italy – a country that quit the Axis alliance in 1943 – is treated more leniently, and is offered a peace treaty. Spain is denied membership of the United Nations because of Franco's sympathy for the Nazi cause.

3 August: In Burma, organised Japanese resistance comes to an end as the Allies win the 'Battle of the Breakthrough'. Over 8300 Japanese are killed out of a total of 10,000 defending the Pegu Yoma mountains.

France: The battle cruiser *Strasbourg*, scuttled in Toulon in 1942, is refloated.

London: Clement Attlee appoints 19 new ministers, including Aneurin Bevan as Health Minister.

4 August: Far East: General Douglas MacArthur adds 500,000 Allied troops to the 250,000 already under his command in the Philippines. The US plans to have 650,000 men ready to invade Japan's southern island of Kyushu by 1 November. A further million, including Australian, British and Canadian troops, are scheduled to land on the main island of Honshu in March 1946. Twelve more Japanese cities receive leaflet drops warning of impending raids. US bombers continue to attack Japanese positions on Java.

5 August: Chinese troops capture Tanchuk and Hsinning from the Japanese. On the Mariana Islands, seven US B-29 aircraft take off heading for Hiroshima in Japan. One of these is the Enola Gay piloted by Colonel Paul Tibbets. It is carrying an atomic bomb.

6 August: At 8.15am the city of Hiroshima on Japan's Honshu island becomes the first victim of the dreadful power of atomic weapons. The explosion exceeds the force of 20,000 tons of TNT, and the lightweight structures of the city centre are virtually vapourised. Only a few concrete structures remain. Exact numbers of casualties are not known, but it is thought that, in a city with 290,000 inhabitants, up to 100,000 could have perished instantly. 'This is the greatest thing in history', declares President Truman upon hearing the news on his way back from Potsdam.

Canadian troopships and aircraft are arriving at the Pacific island of Guam in preparation to assist in the invasion of Japan.

A *Daily Telegraph* report tells of the discovery of an enormous stock of poison gas shells contained in four square miles of German forest: 'The deadly cargo is to be carried by ships manned entirely by Germans and thrown into the sea. There, 200 fathoms below the surface, near the Channel Islands, it may remain intact for as many years.'

7 August: In Britain, the secrets of radio direction finding, known as Radar, are revealed.

Over Japan 200 US aircraft pound Yahata, Tokyo and Kukuyama with conventional bombs.

8 August: Keeping a promise made at Yalta, Soviet leader Stalin declares war on Japan. Red Army forces will tomorrow

DOES IT ~~DOESN'T~~ MATTER: COUNTRY THE ~~FIRM~~ PAYS FOR IT

Don't waste HERE – the Fuel you save AT HOME!

WAR DIARY
August 1945

launch a massive assault into Manchuria supported by over one million troops and nearly 4000 aircraft.

9 August: In Washington, military and scientific communities are already split over the decision to use the atomic bomb. Today a second bomb is dropped on the shipbuilding port of Nagasaki in western Kyushu, with devastation equalling that at Hiroshima. The explosion is visible 250 miles away. On the same day 3,000,000 leaflets urging Japan to end the war are dropped all over the country.

10 August: By nightfall, Soviet forces have already advanced 120 miles into Manchuria. A broadcast from Tokyo offers surrender provided the 'prerogatives of the Emperor' are not prejudiced.

Burma: RAF Spitfires are in action against Japanese forces on the east bank of the Sittang river. Spitfires and Thunderbolts will also be in action tomorrow in against various other targets.

11 August: In Manila, General MacArthur says the use of the atomic bomb on Japan was 'unnecessary' since the Japanese would have surrendered anyway. A major US warship is reported to have been hit by an aerial torpedo off Okinawa.

England: The liner *Queen Elizabeth* docks at Southampton for the first time since 1939.

12 August: The Netherlands is facing up to the gargantuan task of rebuilding. No other country in Europe has been so ravaged and devastated by the Germans. Almost a third of the land area was flooded when the Nazis destroyed the dykes. Now the Dutch must repair the damage and drain the sea from their lands, which will be spoiled by the saltwater for many years to come. There is a great need for clothing; half a million pairs of shoes are on the way from the USA and three million pairs of reconditioned army boots suitable for men and women to wear are being made available. But Holland can't replace the thousands of its citizens who died in the war. Many were victims of the bombing and fighting but most died at the hands of the Nazis, either through starvation or deportation to the death camps.

Japan: Allied air forces attack shipping off Kyushu, Honshu and the northern Ryukyu islands. The Soviet Pacific Fleet lands Russian marines at the Korean ports of Yuki and Rashin.

13 August: British and US carrier aircraft attack the Tokyo area while US warships bombard Kurile Island. Outer Mongolia declares war on Japan. British Sunderland and Liberator aircraft have been attacking Japanese vessels in the Gulf of Siam region for the third day in succession. Later it will be revealed that since the beginning of 1945, 80 Allied aircrew downed in the Bay of Bengal have been rescued by Catalina flying boats.

14 August: It's been 1346 days since Japan attacked the US fleet at Pearl Harbour and declared war on Britain and her Commonwealth in December 1941. On this Tuesday the Japanese Government at last accepts the Allied terms of surrender. The Second World War is almost over after nearly six years. The news is announced simultaneously in London, Washington and Moscow. General MacArthur is authorised to accept the Japanese surrender. Emperor Hirohito prepares to broadcast to the Japanese people – the first time anyone outside court circles will hear the man they believe to have been divinely appointed.

15 August: Japan: At dawn today British-flown Avengers make what may well be this war's last British bombing raid when they attack a factory near Kamohaura. In Tokyo, military fanatics attack the royal palace to urge the Emperor to continue the war. The attempt fails and the coup leader commits suicide.

In Paris, Marshal Petain is found guilty of treason and sentenced to death. In America, the rationing of petrol and canned goods is ended. Throughout the world's capitals, celebrations commence to mark VJ-Day.

London: Field Marshal Montgomery is made a Freeman of the Borough of Lambeth before a cheering 30,000-strong crowd. Monty is hailed as a 'local boy who made good'; 50 years before, the young Monty had 'sprawled and tumbled and got into fixes' in the vicarage of St Mark's where his father was the parson. His response to the honour catches perfectly the spirit of the day: 'I like to think that my welcome is meant as a mark of gratitude to those wonderful fighting men who have won the final victory we enjoy today.'

16 August: Emperor Hirohito orders all Japanese troops to lay down their arms and a new government is formed under Prince Higashikuni. In spite of the broadcast, many Japanese troops continue to fight on, particularly in Manchuria and outlying Pacific areas where communications are poor. British warships off Tokyo are ordered to cease fire from 11.15am. But isolated Japanese aircraft continue to attack the Allied ships and five are shot down, 'in a friendly way', as instructed in the Allied rules of engagement. In Burma, the last shots are exchanged between Japanese and Fourteenth Army troops in the Sittang Bend.

Java: Indonesian nationalists led by 'President' Sukarno, with Japanese support, proclaim the 'Indonesian Republican Government', calling for workers to strike against the return of Dutch colonial rule.

London: No longer Premier, Winston Churchill, makes a speech in which he warns of a Soviet 'Iron Curtain' coming down across Europe. Plans are announced to speed up the demobilisation of a

Field Marshal Montgomery pictured in Berlin in July 1945 with a group of senior British and Red Army officers. On the left of Monty is the conqueror of Berlin, Marshal Zhukov. A favourite of Stalin, gifted with a remarkable strategic insight, the Russian was involved in all large-scale military operations on the Eastern Front, from the Battle of Moscow in 1941 onwards. This photograph was taken at the Brandenburg Gate and Montgomery has just presented Zhukov with a British decoration.

million men and 100,000 women by 31 December. An additional one million people will be released from munitions work within eight weeks.

17 August: Moscow: A recently concluded treaty of friendship between the Soviet Union and Chiang Kai-shek's Nationalist Government allows for the return of Manchuria to China within three months.

Southampton: The *Queen Mary* sails for New York carrying an entire US army division of 15,060 men.

In Paris, General de Gaulle commutes the death sentence on Marshal Petain to one of detention for life.

Argentina: The German submarine U977 arrives at Mar del Plata.

18 August: Manchuria: The Red Army claims to have captured 150,000 soldiers of Japan's Kwantung Army which was earlier reported to comprise half a million men in arms.

Canton: Chinese troops enter this important city on the country's southern mainland.

19 August: Britain: King George VI and Queen Elizabeth lead nationwide thanksgiving services to mark Victory Sunday. A fanfare of trumpeteers of the Household Cavalry, marks their arrival at St Paul's Cathedral this afternoon.

20 August: India: From New Delhi Lord Louis Mountbatten makes a broadcast in which he orders Field Marshal Terauchi, commanding the Japanese Southern Army, to send representatives to the Burmese capital, Rangoon.

Norway: The trial for treason of Norwegian Nazi Party leader, Abraham Vidkun Quisling, begins in Oslo.

21 August: In spite of agreeing a ceasefire two days ago, Russian forces continue to advance into Manchuria, completing a lightning 12-day campaign which has ended 14 years of Japanese occupation. The Russians are only one day away from Port Arthur, seized by the Japanese from Russia in 1905. Senior Allied POWs have been found safe and well in a small camp 100 miles from Mukden. They include Lt-General Arthur Percival who commanded the garrison of Singapore in 1942 before giving in to Japanese forces. The attackers were far fewer in number than the defending force, but the city's defences had been built to face the threat of a sea invasion and not an attack from mainland Malaya.

Germany: In response to a wave of lawlessness, Montgomery issues a stern warning of drastic measures against displaced persons committing crimes against the civil population.

Britain: It's announced that 24 clothing coupons per adult valid from 1 September must last until 30 April 1946.

22 August: Japan's armed forces in Southern China agree to surrender to a representative of Marshal Chiang Kai-shek. Soviet airborne troops land at Darien and Port Arthur. London: The War Office estimates the total number of Allied nationals still in Japanese hands, comprising British, Dominions, US, Netherlands, French and Indian, to be 250,000. Of these, British servicemen total 38,000 and civilians 112,003.

23 August: Britain: Innovative construction techniques employed in the building of the concrete Mulberry Harbours towed to Normandy in support of the Allied invasion in 1944 are being utilised in the great house-building initiative now underway across the nation.

Far East: A Russian Order of the Day announces the Soviet occupation of the whole of Manchuria, south Sakhalin and of Shumshu and Paramushiro in the Kurile Islands.

24 August: Freight ships are setting sail daily for America each carrying hundreds of the 35,000 US army vehicles that have been reconditioned, sprayed with rust-preventative and, in many cases, put into crates, ready for their Atlantic crossing.

London: The Charter of the United Nations is approved in Parliament. Chiang Kai-Shek will sign for China in Chungking tomorrow.

New Guinea: The Japanese commander orders his men to stop fighting.

Korea: Russian forces continue to advance southwards.

25 August: President Truman ends the lend-lease programme with Britain first introduced by President Roosevelt in 1941.

Prime Minister Attlee warns Britain to brace itself for a long period of peacetime austerity.

Burma: Japanese military chiefs prepare for a formal surrender. Fighting has virtually ceased, although there occasional clashes with isolated Japanese troops who have not heard the emperor's call to 'endure the unendurable'.

Germany: British occupying forces are re-designated as the British Army of the Rhine (BAOR).

26 August: Sir Arthur 'Bomber' Harris, architect of Britain's air campaign against Germany, resigns.

China: Nationalist troops enter Nanking and Shanghai.

Queen Elizabeth, the world's biggest and fastest liner, sets sail from Southampton heading for New York with 15,000 homeward bound US troops. RAF fighters circled overhead as she pulled out of the docks.

27 August: The free world's press speculates on whether the awesome power of the atomic bomb means the end of war. In Britain an article in *War Illustrated* says, 'there can be little doubt that they (the bombs) have saved at least one million lives of the Allied armies by bringing the Mikado and his war-mongers to their knees when confronted with their impending fate. Moreover, they have quite probably saved far more Japanese lives than they have taken. And it is pretty evident that from the first the atomic bomb was devised as an awful warning rather than a weapon to be used at large...'

Japan: US carrier-based aircraft drop supplies of food to Allied POWs in the Tokyo area.

28 August: A huge US naval force of nearly 200 vessels sails into Tokyo Bay. The Allies set foot on mainland Japan for the first time when US paratroops land at Atsugi airport near Yokohama.

Malaya: British naval forces arrive off Sabang and Penang on the east coast. In Siam (Thailand) the first airlift of POWs and civilian internees takes place when over 100 British, Australian, American and Dutch men and women fly by RAF Dakota transports from Bangkok to Rangoon.

29 August: In China, General Chiang Kai-shek and Mao Tse-tung meet in Chungking for talks to try and avert civil war between the Communists and the Nationalists. In Hong Kong, the British fleet arrives to reclaim the colony for Britain and, in Singapore, Japanese troops in SE Asia surrender to Mountbatten.

In Germany, the Nuremberg trials prepare to get under way with Hermann Goering heading the first list of 24 war criminals.

30 August: In Japan, General MacArthur arrives to organise the US occupation, and sets up HQ in Yokohama. The US cruiser *San Juan* starts to repatriate Allied POWs. Harrowing tales of cruelty, filth and malnutrition are starting to emerge as prisoners are released. An official report on the main camp in the Tokyo Bay area states: 'There has never been such a hell-hole.' In addition, details are beginning to be released of cruel experiments on live POWs carried out at a number of 'research' establishments by Japanese doctors. To date, only 1000 prisoners have been evacuated to freedom – a further 36,000 are believed to be awaiting liberation from camps across Japan.

Hong Kong: The Royal Navy enter the famous Crown Colony today with the cruiser *HMS Vanguard* leading the task force. At Picnic Bay 150 explosive 'suicide' motorboats are discovered along with their surrendering crews. The 30,000-ton aircraft carrier *HMS Indomitable* rides at anchor in Victoria Bay awaiting the arrival of the Japanese envoy. Over 2000 British internees sing *God Save The King* as the Union Jack is hoisted at Camp Stanley for the first time in almost four years.

Manchuria: Soviet troops are welcomed by the city's inhabitants as they march into Harbin.

31 August: In Manila, Japanese troops in the Philippines formally surrender. In Burma, Japanese forces based at Abya also surrender. General MacArthur becomes the first foreigner in authority over Japan in 1000 years when he establishes the Supreme Allied Command in Yokohama. The greatest and most destructive conflict that the Pacific has known is now ended, although the formal surrender will not take place for two more days.

PEACE POSTPONED

The Second World War was ending but new perils awaited British forces caught up in conflicts in Greece, Palestine and the Far East.

The sudden surrender of Japan in the summer of 1945 left a large number of occupied European colonies in the Far East without effective government. In many cases they also had burgeoning nationalist movements with leaders who were anxious to seize territory and power and resist the return of British, Dutch and French colonial rule.

Britain had made contingency plans for a swift return to Malaya, Singapore and Hong Kong and military and civilian personnel quickly moved back and assumed a governing role. However, as neither the French nor the Dutch had the necessary forces in the Far East, their colonies posed problems. The Anglo-American Joint Chiefs of Staff decided that whatever Allied troops were available should be used in these areas to disarm and repatriate the Japanese and restore civilian administration.

As a result, British and Indian forces became involved in policing the Netherlands East Indies (NEI) and the southern part of French Indochina (later known as South Vietnam). Unfortunately both territories contained strong nationalist movements and the British found themselves in the midst of bitter confrontations as the Dutch and French governments sought to re-impose their authority.

The first British landings in the NEI took place on 29 September at Batavia (now the Indonesian capital, Jakarta) on the island of Java. Early hope that the local people would accept the British presence was quickly dashed; the Indonesian nationalists, led by Ahmed Sukarno, had already formed a government and had achieved a semblance of political control over most of the island. The Japanese garrisons had encouraged the nationalist movement and even provided them with arms and training.

Inevitably there were military clashes between the British and Dutch forces and the Indonesians. Reinforcements were sent to Java and by November 1945 there were a corps of three divisions and an armoured brigade, supported by two RAF fighter squadrons and a transport squadron.

Japanese assistance

As well as dealing with the nationalist threat, the British troops also had to restore law and order in many areas where looting and murder held sway in the absence of authority. Ironically, local British commanders used armed Japanese soldiers to aid them in this task, a measure allowed in accordance with the terms of the Japanese surrender.

Even though Dutch forces were arriving, it would not be until November 1946 that the last

British and Indian troops were able to withdraw. It had been a difficult operation and one which the British had not expected to undertake. The fact that they did so in an unfamiliar country against armed opposition is very much to their credit.

British in Saigon

In September 1945, at the same time as the operations on Java were underway, British and Indian forces moved into southern Indochina. Their arrival in Saigon was part of an Allied move to clear the former French possessions of Vietnam, Laos and Cambodia.

A communist-controlled group known as the *Viet Minh* had already picked up the reins of power and set up a revolutionary government in the northern city of Hanoi. Nationalist Chinese troops who moved into the north of the country to disarm the Japanese, did not interfere with the *Viet Minh*, who presumed from this that the French were unlikely to return.

In fact the French were intent on resuming their pre-war status, using the British presence as a preliminary move. The British, on the other hand, were going in under orders that they were to merely supervise the Japanese surrender in the south of Vietnam and restore law and order up to the 16th parallel. It was another recipe for trouble.

The first British troops landed by air near Saigon on 8 September. By the middle of October all three brigades of Major General D D Gracey's 20th Indian Division were present and facing a very tense situation. Armed resistance broke out in many places, usually taking the form of attacks on individual soldiers and convoys of vehicles. Gracey quickly recognised that he had insufficient resources to secure the whole of the south. Instead he opted to concentrate his forces in and around Saigon, holding the city until the French could take over. To exert control over Saigon, Gracey had to enlist the support of the surrendered Japanese, who were re-armed and joined the British and Indian troops on the streets. It was a tough few months with the men facing raids, sabotage of utilities, bombs, sniping and a resentful population generally set against a return of the French.

Clamour for independence

The first major French military units arrived in October. They were under the command of General Leclerc, who had led the Free French liberators of Paris in August 1944. But in Saigon and Hanoi, Leclerc was not viewed as a liberator but rather was seen as an enemy of a people eager for independence.

By the end of 1945 most of the British forces had been withdrawn.

In this same period, far more serious trouble had been brewing in India, where the clamour for independence had developed during the Second World War and had been encouraged by British promises that it would be granted in the long term. In the winter of 1945 - 46 there were mutinies in the ranks of the Indian Army and British battalions were called into action to put them down. There was also bitter religious strife between the Hindu Congress Party and the Moslem League. It would be several years before Partition would see the setting up of a mainly Hindu India state and Moslem Pakistan. The last British troops withdrew from the sub-continent in February 1948.

Problems in Palestine

The British had other problem areas to look after in the immediate aftermath of the war. In Greece, there was simmering violence between monarchists and communists in which the British were caught up in offering support to the existing anti-communist government. The British were not to leave Greece until 1948 when their role was passed on to US forces.

Palestine, too, posed problems. At the end of the war the First Infantry Division was the only British formation in Palestine. It was charged with keeping the peace there and also stabilising neighbouring Lebanon and Syria. In the autumn of 1945 the Sixth Airborne Division was released from service with the British Army On the Rhine (BAOR) and sent to Palestine.

Opposition to continued British rule came mainly from the Jews, angry at official policies that restricted the flow of refugees who had survived the Holocaust in Europe only to be denied access to a Jewish homeland. During the war, Jewish units had fought for the Allies; a Jewish Brigade Group fought in Italy with the British Eighth Army. The British Officer Orde Wingate, famous as the leader of the Chindits in Burma in 1943 - 44, helped train the first Jewish fighters in the late 1930s. Unfortunately, once the war in Europe ended, many of these well-trained men enlisted in Jewish militant bands such as the *Haganah* and *Stern Gang*.

It was a very messy situation, not eased by Arab fears of an impending Jewish state likely to emerge in the near future. In September 1947 the British Government acknowledged that the Palestine issue was one they could not resolve and accordingly announced they would be relinquishing the Mandate on 15 May the following year, handing the question over to the United Nations.

By the time the British withdrew in 1948, the lives of 338 British soldiers, police and civilians had been lost.

Day by Day DIARY

September 1945

1 September: Italy: The Polish cemetery at Monte Cassino is dedicated in a ceremony attended by Field-Marshal Alexander, Allied Commander of the Italian Campaign at the time of the impasse in front of the German-held Gustav Line, in the first half of 1944.

On Penang off the coast of Malaya, aboard *HMS Nelson*, the British receive the Japanese surrender of the island.

2 September: Japan: At 8.30am, an 11 man delegation signs the formal document acknowledging the surrender of Japan to the Allies. The signing takes place on board the battleship *USS Missouri* in Tokyo Bay after General Douglas MacArthur keeps the Japanese waiting in front of Allied Officers, the world's press and thousands of watching sailors.

USSR leader Stalin announces that the Kurile Islands and the south of Sakhalin will become Soviet territory.

Indo-China: Nationalist leader Ho Chi-Minh today declares independence from France and the foundation of the Democratic Republic of Vietnam.

Press censorship in Britain is abolished from 9am today exactly six years after it began. Petrol restrictions are slightly eased.

3 September: Far East: British troops land in Hong Kong and The Royal Marines take over the island of Penang, Malaysia, following the surrender of the Japanese.

Philippines: Japanese General Yamashita, dubbed 'The Tiger of Malaya' in 1942, surrenders the remnants of his forces at Baguio on Luzon. The event is witnessed by US General Jonathan Wainwright, commander of Corregidor, and Lt-Gen A E Percival, British Commander at Singapore, who had both surrendered to Yamashita when Japan was at the height of her triumph. Other surrenders take place aboard US warships off various Pacific islands, including Truk in the Carolines.

Kent: Londoners flock to the 'Garden of England' as the hop-picking holiday season begins. With almost 100,000 acres planted, a bumper crop is predicted.

Pacific: Japanese garrisons on numerous islands by-passed by the Allies are giving up. Today Rota in the Marianas surrenders.

Red Army and Navy units have taken control of Port Arthur, seized from the Russian Tsar by the Japanese in 1905.

Berlin: The colours of the four great powers are flown in front of the Allied Control Council HQ today on the sixth anniversary of the outbreak of war in a ceremony attended by Field-Marshal Montgomery, Marshal Zhukov, General Eisenhower and the French General Koenig.

4 September: Tokyo: Occupation of the Japanese mainland begins in earnest when men of the 188th US Infantry Division arrive by transport planes at Atsugi airport near the capital. To the east, far out in the Pacific, the Japanese commander of Wake surrenders the tiny atoll back into US hands. In the second half of December 1941, following the devastating attack on Pearl Harbour which pitched the USA into World War II, a small American garrison gave the enemy a bloody nose in their initial attempt to seize this useful stepping stone to Midway Island and the strategically vital Hawaiian Islands. Overwhelmed by a second landing later in the same month, Wake has been in Japanese hands ever since, her status as an air base marginalised by the astonishing proliferation of the Allied Pacific carrier fleet.

5 September: In Singapore, British troops are warmly welcomed by the local population as they land and take control without opposition.

6 September: Singapore: A British officer survivor of the Changi POW camp - Lt P A D Jones from Smethwick, Lancs - remembers that 52,000 Indians went into captivity when the British colony fell to the Japanese on 15 February 1942. Today he believes just 15,000 of them are accounted for as still alive.

The document authorising the surrender of Japanese forces in the SW Pacific area is signed today aboard *HMS Glory*, off Rabaul, New Britain.

7 September: Australia: The House of Representatives ratify the United Nations Charter.

Germany: Red Army Marshal Zhukov takes the salute at a military parade in the German capital where he announces: 'We are celebrating today in Berlin victory over the forces of repression in the Far East.'

Britain announces it is disposing of 8000 tons of deadly Mustard Gas, part of a store held in readiness against a German threat of chemical warfare. Contained in shells and projectiles it will be shipped from Cairn Ryan, near Stranraer, and dumped in the Atlantic.

8 September: The ex-premier of Japan, Hideki Tojo, attempts suicide, but his life is saved by an American medical team. He will live to stand trial. The US-born propaganda broadcaster Iva Togori - 'Tokyo Rose' - is arrested. US troops fly to the south of Korea to balance the Soviet occupation of the north of the country.

9 September: Nanking: This ancient walled city today sees the signing of the formal surrender to the Nationalist Chinese of 1,000,000 Japanese troops in China. The country's one-time capital was the scene of a notorious massacre on a vast scale by the Japanese in 1937.

South Korea: Japanese forces surrender to US representatives.

10 September: In Oslo, Quisling is sentenced to death for treason.

More tales of suffering and privation emerge as emaciated Allied prisoners return from Japanese captivity. Thousands have died building the infamous railway from Siam to Burma.

11 September: Borneo: This is the first day of peace on the world's third largest island following the formal surrender of the Japanese to the Australian Ninth Division at Labuan yesterday. However, there are many isolated pockets of enemy troops hiding out in the jungle and it will take time for word to spread that the Emperor has declared the war over.

Indo-China: Nationalist Chinese troops today enter the city of Hanoi in the north of the country.

12 September: The Imperial Army of Japan in SE Asia formally surrenders to the British. Guards at the notorious Changi Jail in Singapore, scene of many cruelties, are obliged to bow to their erstwhile captives. The RAF ensign flies from the control tower at the airfield in Bangkok, Siam.

13 September: Tokyo: General MacArthur abolishes the Japanese Imperial Headquarters. By the end of the month there will be 500,000 US troops on Japanese soil. It is planned that 7,000,000 enemy soldiers will be disarmed, demobilised and returned to their homes by mid-October.

New Guinea: Japanese forces finally surrender at Wewak.

14 September: Exported British cars are arriving in the USA. The first include Austin four-door saloons priced at $1600 including import tax.

Malaya: A document is signed agreeing to the total surrender of all Japanese forces in the country.

15 September: SE England: On the fifth anniversary of the Battle

Life can soon return to normality seems to be the message in these peacetime scenes of life in London. However, there are several years of post-war austerity ahead, something not reflected in the paintings (National Archives - Art of War).

Day by Day DIARY

of Britain, BBC commentator Richard Dimbleby broadcasts from the famous RAF fighter station at Biggin Hill on the North Downs in Kent. The late-Victorian mansion on the Westerham Road called Towerfield housed the the Fighter Command 'Ops' Room. Dimbleby declares: 'It is one room in which you could say, 'that is where they won the war.' *War Illustrated* comments, 'The Towerfield story is part of our history, with Trafalgar and Waterloo, and this shabby and deserted building should become a national monument, preserved intact for posterity as a visible reminder of Britain's finest hour.'

On the same day 300 RAF fighters led by Group Captain Douglas Bader fly in faultless formation over St Paul's and the heart of London.

Japan: Former Foreign Minister Togo gives himself up to the Americans.

16 September: London's main attractions are jet-propelled today. In Trafalgar Square there's a 49 foot tall V2 rocket erected for Thanksgiving Savings Week. In the air spectators can see the first public outing of the distinctive twin tail of the de Havilland Vampire, claimed to be the world's fastest fighter and capable of over 500mph.

17 September: In Germany, 44 camp guards, and the commandant of Belsen Concentration Camp, are put on trial.

In London, William 'Lord Haw-Haw' Joyce begins his trial for treason.

Formosa (Taiwan): The Chinese national flag flies again on this island after 50 years of Japanese occupation.

18 September: *The London Gazette* reports awards for bravery to civilian workers who bravely tackled the accidental igniting of explosives at a factory in Kirkby, Nottinghamshire, on the evening of 15 September 1944.

Singapore: The first post-war shipment of Malaysian rubber leaves for Britain.

19 September: In London, the Government announces that India will be granted home rule 'at the earliest possible date'. This promise has been heard before, but Premier Clement Attlee seems determined to hasten the convening of a constitutional conference to allow the Indians to decide their own destiny.

At the Old Bailey Central Criminal Court, the traitor 'Lord Haw-Haw' is sentenced to hanging.

20 September: All over Germany the destruction of weapons of war continues. The RAF now have 13 Air Disarmament Wings in the British Air Forces of Occupation (formerly the Second Tactical Air Force) which comprises around 90,000 RAF pilots and crews. Large numbers of Ju 88 transport planes sit on the big airfield at Flensburg waiting to be dismantled. Cattle graze among them. Commercial river traffic has resumed on the Rhine between Duisburg and the sea.

England: A submarine commissioned when Britain was still at war is launched when the nation is at peace. The Royal Navy's *Achate* was built at Devonport.

21 September: The Indian Congress Party call for the freedom of India, Burma, Malaya and Indo-China from foreign colonial rule.

22 September: Official figures record that almost 33,000 British and Indian former POWs in SE Asia have so far sailed for home.

23 September: In London, the Government refers the issue of Jewish immigration to Palestine to the United Nations. News is also released of how in June 1944 an unexploded V2 rocket landed accidentally in Sweden and was handed over to British agents and brought to this country by air.

India: An RAF airfield three miles outside the city of Baroda is hit by flooding in the early hours of the morning. Up to five foot of water inundates the area and cuts off the camp for two days. Miraculously, there are no casualties. The British Resident in

Baroda, Lt-Col Hancock, makes part of his journey out of the flood on the back of an elephant.

Denmark becomes the first non-neutral country in Europe to be declared free of mines, 2,000,000 having been lifted.

24 September: In Tokyo, Emperor Hirohito says that he was always opposed to the war and blames Tojo for the attack on Pearl Harbour.

Germany: A temporary wooden plaque marking the site of the German surrender at Luneberg is reported to have been defaced by local Nazi supporters.

25 September: A proclamation to the German people affirms details of the rules pertaining to the individual areas of Allied control.

Post-war austerity measures are underlined by the news that ships from New Zealand and Australia carrying UK Government-ordered supplies will sail via the much longer Cape of Good Hope route in order to avoid paying Panama Canal dues in dollars.

26 September: At Luneberg in Germany, a Polish Jew breaks down in the witness box while describing his ordeal in Auschwitz.

Indo-China (Vietnam): A US officer is killed when Annamite nationalists clash with Allied forces.

27 September: Tokyo: Emperor Hirohito of Japan visits General MacArthur's HQ.

Singapore: The last batch of freed prisoners and internees, including several hundred men of the British 18th Division, leave this port aboard the Polish vessel *Sobieska*.

28 September: It is announced today that the British Mediterranean Fleet's HQ is being transferred from Caserta in Italy to the George Cross island of Malta. Among the first ships to arrive in Grand Harbour, Valetta, will be *HMS Norfolk*.

Britain: HM King George, Queen Elizabeth and Princess Margaret inspect the Home Fleet in the Firth of Forth.

29 September: Germany: The grave of Himmler at a secret location near Luneberg Heath is found decked with flowers this morning.

Java: British troops land on this pre-war Dutch colony without interference from Indonesian nationalists who do not want Dutch rule to return.

30 September: A rail tragedy claims 39 lives when an express bound for Scotland is derailed near Hemel Hempstead.

October 1945

1 October: Czechoslovakia resumes diplomatic relations with Rumania. Both countries are within the USSR sphere of influence.

2 October: Calais: Visitors celebrating the first anniversary of the French port's liberation include the Mayors of Britain's front line towns of Dover, Folkestone and Canterbury. They inspect German batteries in the Pas de Calais regions that had shelled the coast of England from 1940 through to the early autumn of 1944. London: The first travelling Post Office train for five years leaves Euston bound for Aberdeen.

The outspoken US General 'Old Blood and Guts' George S Patton speaks out once too often about the continuing need 'to uproot Nazis'. Eisenhower relieves him of his command of the eastern half of the US occupation zone.

Indo-China: A ceasefire is agreed between Annamite nationalists and French authorities.

3 October: Holland: A major gap in the dyke at Walcheren is sealed today. When the dykes are fully restored, sections of the Mulberry Harbours from off the beaches of Normandy will be used to form an outer sea-wall.

Saigon: Rebels give up rifles and revolvers in the Indo-Chinese capital to Allied forces. Elsewhere in the country, the battleship *Richelieu* covers the landing of more French forces.

4 October: In Britain, 17,000 dockers are now out on strike over a pay demand. A reporter with the London *Evening Standard* records a visit to Oxford where he views one of the 'world's biggest scrapheaps' where countless Spitfires, Hurricanes and

313

Aircraft production lines no longer need to produce fleets of military aircraft such as the Lysanders seen here and are seeking new products in late 1945 (National Archives - Art of War).

Wellington bombers are being recycled at the Ministry of Aircraft Production's No 1 Metal and Produce Recovery Depot. An even greater recovery centre is operational near Durham.

5 October: Pope Pious XII appoints Cardinal Jozsef Mindszenty as Primate of Hungary.

London: For the first time in six years, men of the Life Guards perform the Changing of the Guard ceremony, although in Service dress, a sombre contrast to previous peacetime splendour.

6 October: In Palestine there are clashes between illegal Jewish immigrants and the Transjordan Frontier Force. Orderly demonstrations of Jews protesting against British immigration policy will gather pace in days and weeks to come.

7 October: The liner *Corfu* arrives at Southampton carrying the first Far East prisoners of war to return to Britain.

8 October: The former deputy to Adolf Hitler, Rudolf Hess, is flown from Britain to Germany to stand trial.

9 October: In Paris, Pierre Laval is sentenced to death for treason without right of appeal. Two days before, Laval and his lawyers withdrew from the court as a protest against the conduct of the trial.

Greece: The Government headed by Admiral Voulgaris resigns.

Indian Ocean: British troops re-occupy the Andaman Islands.

10 October: Head of the pro-Nazi French Militia, Joseph Darnand, is executed.

Britain: Troops have been drafted in to help counter the effects of strike by dockers which today extends to include workers in London.

11 October: Far East: There is trouble brewing in a number of former colonies of the French, Dutch and British as nationalist groups seek independence.

12 October: London: Men of the Royal Signals have started work helping the GPO with their mammoth task of installing 70,000 new telephones for would-be subscribers on the waiting list.

13 October: Returning POWs who have difficulty in readjusting to civilian life are being offered places in Civil Resettlement Units which have opened all over Britain. One unit is in historic Hatfield House in Hertfordshire where around 250 men are staying and taking part in workshops aimed at reviving old skills or laying the foundations for a new career. Built in 1610, Hatfield House was once the home of King James I and is full of magnificent furnishings and works of art.

14 October: In the Dutch East Indies, nationalists declare war on the Netherlands.

Britain: As the dockers' dispute deepens, 6000 troops are drafted in to unload ships in London, Hull and Merseyside. Around 43,000 men are now refusing to work unless they receive a minimum wage of 25 shillings a day.

15 October: Pierre Laval, the Vichy leader, is executed by a French firing squad. He dies shouting *'Vive la France.'* In Oslo, the traitor Quisling is also executed.

16 October: Over 6000 soldiers are now assisting the fast turn-around of food ships in the strike-crippled British docks.

17 October: Argentina: Colonel Juan Peron is asked to take over the Government only eight days after he has been ousted by army colleagues.

18 October: Berlin: The Black Market in the Tiergarten is temporarily interrupted following a major raid by German police and British military police. Over 2000 arrests have been made and the suspects include over 100 Russian officers and men.

19 October: Java: British troops reach Samarang, third largest city on the island, where extremists have reportedly seized internment camps containing 22,000 people.

Hungary: Martial law is declared throughout the country because of increasing civil unrest at the Soviet occupation and their imposition of communist rule.

20 October: In Vienna, the Allies recognise the provisional Austrian Government of Dr Karl Renner.

21 October: Germany: Luftwaffe bombs are being used by Royal Engineers engaged in demolishing the massive concrete U-Boat pens in Hamburg. Today the Finkenwarder pens are blown up by a clutch of 500lb bombs, wired to explode simultaneously.

22 October: Germany: The death sentence is passed on the captain and two crew members of U-Boat 582 by a court of British and Greek officers convened in Hamburg. The trio were found guilty of ordering the murder of the crew of the Greek ship *Peleus* after torpedoing the vessel in the South Atlantic on 8 March 1944. Just three survivors - including a British man - were picked up by a Portuguese steamer.

23 October: In London, Chancellor of the Exchequer Hugh Dalton's budget cuts income tax from 10 shillings to nine shillings in the pound.

French communists win a narrow two-seat majority in elections for the new Assembly.

24 October: The United Nations Organisation is inaugurated. An RAF jet fighter flies at a world record speed of 540mph.

25 October: Java: Unrest continues in the capital Batavia. Dutch nationals are the target of roving mobs of Indonesians who do not want to see Dutch control reinstated.

26 October: Large numbers of displaced Germans continue to surge into the British Zone of Occupation in Germany. Many come from the former East Prussia which has been handed over to Poland. Others come from the Sudeten district of Czechoslovakia.

27 October: 'There is no peace for Britain's Lifeboats' reads a newspaper headline. As a week of gales lash the seas around the British Isles, for the volunteer crews of the RNLI it's business as usual. Since the end of the war, the RNLI have responded to over 200 calls for help and saved nearly 300 lives. Throughout the war (3 September 1939 to 8 May 1945) their big red, white and blue boats went out 3760 times to assist ships and downed aircraft. A total of 6376 lives were saved in this period, an average of 12 per week.

28 October: Prague: British troops of the 78th Division led by the Pipe Band of the Royal Irish Fusiliers take part in an Allied parade on Czechoslovakia's Independence Day. It's the first time since 1938 that the country has been able to celebrate the occasion.

29 October: Moscow: Stalin orders a secret 'crash' programme to develop Russia's own atomic bomb. He is determined to catch up with America, regardless of cost. Ruthless secret police chief, Leonid Beria, is put in charge of all the laboratories and industries which will help produce the bomb. Captured German scientists are also working on the project.

30 October: Far East: The British Commander in Surabaya, Java, is shot dead by an Indonesian mob. Brigadier A W S Mallaby was touring a naval base to ensure that the terms of the truce were being observed.

31 October: Britain: Road safety is becoming a major issue. A newspaper column comments on one new initiative: 'Even a chicken has its good reasons for crossing the road, however much the motorist may rage. The introduction of compulsory pedestrian crossings in built-up areas will deny human beings the right of a chicken by finally robbing them of the freedom of the highway, which nowadays means in effect the freedom to risk their own lives.'

UNITED NATIONS

FOR FREEDOM FROM FEAR

UNIO

51/1006

The United Nations Organisation was inaugurated on 24 October 1945. This is the original artwork for a poster encapsulating the UN's hope for the future (National Archives - Art of War).

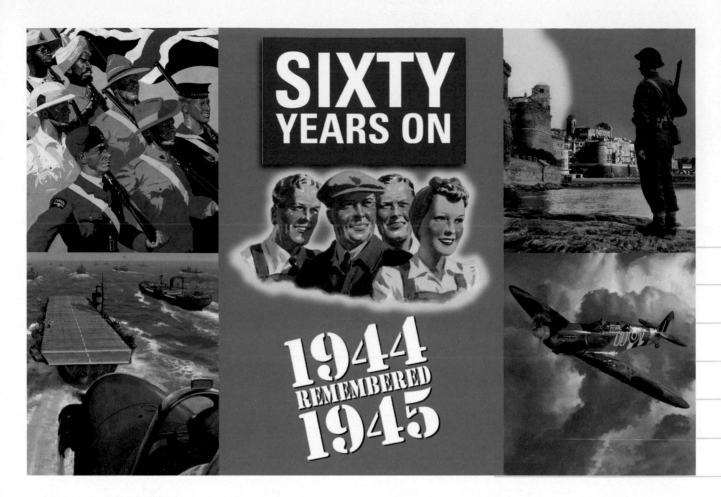

SIXTY YEARS ON

1944 REMEMBERED **1945**

1 November: A British intelligence report ends continuing speculation that Hitler is alive.

Far East: Men of the Seaforth Highlanders land at Batavia on Java and go into action at once against nationalist snipers.

Tokyo: A big demonstration takes place near the Imperial Palace to protest over food shortages.

2 November: Rioting breaks out in several Arab countries against the establishment of a Jewish homeland in Palestine. Arabs begin a general strike in Jerusalem.

3 November: In London, the Labour Government announces that all civil airlines will be state-owned and controlled.

4 November: The existence of a bomb-proof HQ for the British War Cabinet is revealed. Military campaigns in three Continents were directed from this nerve centre, situated 70 feet below Government buildings in Whitehall. Churchill often stayed here overnight and the HQ has a big mahogany desk from where, as Premier, he made most of his famous war broadcasts. When it was first built nuclear weapons did not exist. Reporters, however, who have been allowed access say that they doubt if even the blast of an atomic bomb could affect it.

5 November: Britain: The seven-week old unofficial dock strike ends and 43,000 men return to work.

The 100th flight of the England-Australia Air Service is complete today when a Lancastrian touched down at Hurn, near Bournemouth. It has flown the 11,762 miles from Sydney in just over 63 hours. The Lancastrian is a civilian version of the Lancaster bomber that has a crew of five and space for six passengers. The service is jointly operated by the British Overseas Airways Corporation (BOAC) and Qantas Empire Airways.

6 November: In Moscow, Molotov announces that Russia will go ahead and build its own atomic bomb.

7 November: A Gloucester Meteor jet fighter piloted by Group Captain H J Wilson achieves a world air record speed of 606mph off Herne Bay in Kent. The previous official record of 469.2mph was set by a German Messerschmitt 109 in April 1939.

8 November: In Java, British troops order Indonesians at the Surabaya naval base to surrender.

9 November: Germany: One of the largest floating bridges in the world has just been completed by the Royal Engineers. The Freeman Bridge (named after a major of the RE largely responsible for its construction) crosses the Rhine at Dusseldorf. The semi-permanent structure is half a mile long and can carry loads of up to 40 tons.

London: The Lord Mayor's Show brings out big crowds in the City and is observed to have regained 'much of its pre-war glory'. Prime Minister Atlee greets the new Mansion House incumbent, Sir Charles Davis.

10 November: The writer George Orwell is enjoying success with his latest novel *Animal Farm*. The left wing author fought for the Republican cause in the International Brigade in the Spanish Civil War and is a noted anti-fascist. However, *Animal Farm* is intended to expose the failures of communism. It contains the observation that, 'All animals are equal, but some animals are more equal than others.'

11 November: Berlin: In the heart of Germany's capital, in the famous Tiergarten, an impressive memorial, surmounted by a Red Army man in bronze, is unveiled by Marshal Georgi Zhukov, Stalin's most brilliant commander. The memorial commemorates Russia's victory over the Third Reich and the countless thousands of Soviet servicemen and women who perished. Other Allied troops took part in the ceremony with Britain's 2nd Battalion of the Devonshire Regiment mounting a Guard of Honour.

Britain: *HMS Strathmore* docks at Southampton to a rousing welcome. The troopship carried 3750 officers and men of the 2nd Division, Fourteenth Army, from the Far East for demobilisation.

On this same day, all over Britain at 11am many millions of people observe a silence in honour of those who have given their lives in the service of their country. Officially marking the anniversary of the 1918 Armistice that ended the First World War, the occasion is a time for remembering the more recent sacrifices of so many. Tomorrow, it will be stated in Parliament that the Government is considering, in consultation with Commonwealth Governments, the fixing of an official Day of Remembrance for both wars.

LEST WE FORGET

SCRAPBOOK!

HRH The Queen and Prince Philip acknowledge the cheering crowds at the 60th anniversary celebrations of VE and VJ Day in London in the summer of 2005. The painting is a wartime one of Princess Elizabeth (National Archives - Art of War).

Bonfire Boy's Tale

Don Short was born in Lewes, the County Town of Sussex, on 17 August 1922. Lewes is a place famous for the enthusiasm of its Guy Fawkes Night celebrations and a very large number of the townspeople are Bonfire Boys and Girls, who wear costume and join in the traditional, huge torchlight parades when thousands of people march through the streets on each 5 November.

As a young lad Don determined to join in the fun. One day he spotted a coveted Indian Chief head-dress for sale in the window of a house on the corner of St John Street and West Street. It was a boy's head-dress and at around two bob, Don simply had to have it. He then made his own Indian costume to complement the head-dress and in 1935 joined the Commercial Square Bonfire Society (CSBS), who have upheld the tradition of Bonfire since 1855. Don is the boy in the black and white picture below.

In 1938 Don joined the local Territorial Army unit and was mobilised on 1 September 1939. As a member of The Royal Engineers the war first took him from England to France where, in his words, 'we were thrown out of Dunkirk'. Next he went to the Middle East and participated in the Eighth Army victory at El Alamein, the Invasion of Sicily and the slow advance up the boot shape of the Italian mainland. Don's war concluded in Greece during the near civil war between Left and Right. He was demobbed in April 1946.

Back in Civvy Street, Don lived in Kent and then Buckinghamshire, with his wife Pat. Many years later, during a visit to Lewes to attend nearby Glyndebourne opera, Don got up early to enjoy a wander around his old home town. Knowing how much it meant to Don, Pat treated them to a longer break in Lewes which coincided with the 5 November celebrations. They made contact with the Commercial Square folk and he and Pat were made

warmly welcome, fitted out with costumes and before they knew it had joined in with what had grown, post-war, into a huge and thrilling event; Lewes Bonfire.

Don and Pat enjoyed themselves so much that they became regular attendees and even moved back to the area. Nowadays, Don is the oldest member of the CSBS still marching. The year 2005 will be remembered as a very special one for the Society. In May nearly 300 members of the CSBS undertook a torchlight parade as a highlight of the *Sixty Years On* Air Show / Concert at Glynde Place. Don and Pat participated in this amazing spectacle. It was most likely the first time that the traditional *Sussex By The Sea* was played by a 60-strong orchestra where the musicians slowly disappeared in a swirling cloud of smoke from the torches and commemorative flaming poppies!

Then on 5 November itself the Society will most certainly have marked their 150th anniversary in spectacular style. Remembering the sacrifices of so many in the two World Wars fought in the last century is a main tenet of the Bonfire tradition in Lewes. All five Societies lay wreaths at the town's War Memorial on Bonfire Night. Paying respect to the Fallen is particularly important to Don as he personally knew a number of the people whose names are carved on the Memorial.

For 2005 the CSBS will also have carried a new banner depicting the theme of this book, *Sixty Years On*, and Don will have taken his usual place in the vanguard of the procession.

Joey Clark

We Met Again

Dame Vera Lynn had a very busy 2005 but we were very pleased that she found time to come along to a very special *We'll Meet Again - Sixty Years On* event held at Glynde Place, near Lewes in East Sussex on 28 May. Organised by **csma** - publishers of *Sixty Years On* - the event featured a wonderful air show with some 30 planes from the Forties and Fifties. A Dakota aircraft made a poppy drop in memory of those who gave their lives in World War II.

There was also a splendid concert that went on into the evening, culminating in a magnificent fireworks display. Highlight of the occasion came when Dame Vera was reunited on stage with three veterans from the Burma Campaign. The trio had last seen Dame Vera at a concert in 1944 when she visited the British Forces involved in fighting the Japanese. Accompanied by the 70-strong Pendyrus Male Voice Choir, the three veterans - Leslie Sumption, John Ashby and Stanley Johnson - together with Dame Vera sang *We'll Meet Again* before an audience of around 8000 people, many of them veterans themselves. It was a most wonderful experience, never to be forgotten by anyone who was there.

The story of the three Burma pals appears on pages 158 and 159 of this book.

Dame Vera told us of another occasion in this 60th anniversary year of the end of World War II that she can never forget. Annually, for many decades now, London taxi drivers have organised an annual outing to the seaside for veterans from the Royal Star and Garter Home for Disabled Soldiers, Sailors and Airmen and Dame Vera has always been a regular on the outings.

Anyway, this year being a special anniversary one, Dame Vera and a party of veterans were invited to Clarence House by His Royal Highness Prince Charles for drinks and canapés. Next would come a taxi ride to The Tower Restaurant for lunch. This was the morning of 7 July when London fell victim to the terrorist bomb outrages. As the tragic news broke, London's major transport routes in the city centre closed or became gridlocked. The official gathering at Clarence House was delayed. While Charles and Camilla welcomed their guests as and when they arrived, it became clear that any hope of crossing the city in taxis was fast disappearing.

Dame Vera and the veterans, however, were not going to let the bombers win. The party marched over the road from Clarence House, walked through Green Park and the wartime exhibition there and, instead of lunch at The Tower Restaurant, tucked in to that traditional British favourite - Fish and Chips!

*The theme of Sixty Years On was marked at the **csma**'s Annual Family Horserace Day at Goodwood on Sunday 28 August. The Sixty Years On race was televised live on BBC TV and Dame Vera and some of the veterans whose stories appear in this book were interviewed for the television. Dame Vera can be seen presenting the award for the winner of the race, Nannina, ridden by Jimmy Fortune. In the main picture the two 'sash girls' are Helen Arnold (left) and Sam Kettle. Helen is the daughter of Sixty Years On Editor, David Arnold.*

FORCES
Sweetheart

Dame Vera Lynn in conversation with Joey Clark.

I was delighted to be invited for tea with Dame Vera just a few weeks before the 60th anniversary of D-Day. Having admired her impressive array of awards for her singing achievements (also including one for being Woman Of The Year in more modern times), I asked her to tell me about the big band characters of the wartime era.

'I had been broadcasting with Joe Loss and Charlie Kunz, and auditioned with the BBC to sing with bands such as Billy Cotton's. But he sent me home after a week and a half,' said Dame Vera, adding 'Nor did I get the job with Henry Hall.

'Finally, Ambrose was persuaded to take me on and after a tentative start, gave me more and more to do. We all called him Ammy. While we were playing at the Kilburn Empire the war started and the boys in the band all went to Uxbridge to join up. They didn't imagine they would be sent into the RAF with immediate effect so they had to negotiate a week's leave to finish their stint with Ambrose.

'George Chisholm, Tommy McQuater and my future husband - Harry Lewis - were among the musicians who got special dispensation and they eventually played together in the RAF's leading dance band, The Squadronaires.

'A lot later while visiting an army camp with Joe Loss, we did a broadcast with Glenn Miller.'

In part it was the fact that the boys joined up that influenced her decision to go solo. Ambrose had had to pull out of engagements and Dame Vera's agent kept getting enquiries about the beautiful girl with a singing voice that everybody loved.

I asked her for her memories of the variety show *Applesauce*: 'I used to drive from Barking to the theatre in my Austin 10. I drove along 'Bomb Alley', so-called because of the bombing of the East End docks. I arrived at the Holborn Empire one day soon after the show had opened, to find an unexploded bomb had dropped on the stage. It was just as well we couldn't continue with the show after that as the theatre later received another direct hit - but this time the bomb exploded! When I think about it now,

no wonder my Mum was really worried about me working in town each night.

'I signed on as everyone had to and fortunately I was allowed to continue as an entertainer, visiting hospitals and camps. I had been doing lots of radio too, *ITMA*, *Music While You Work* and *Worker's Playtime*. The Forces programme began in 1940 and the request spot got a very good response. I was delighted when they gave me half an hour and named it *Sincerely Yours*.'

I asked the inevitable question, did she choose *We'll Meet Again* for the show? She smiled and replied, 'I had sung it years before with Ambrose, but began performing it for the show because the sentiment seemed so right for the times.'

What about Dame Vera's decision to join ENSA? 'Every Night Something Awful,' she laughed, 'I knew places like the Middle East and Italy were doing well for entertainers, so I asked to go somewhere where not many performers got to. The next thing I knew I was having my injections, was fitted for a uniform and I was off to the Far East and Burma'.

Could she describe the experience? 'The intense heat and flies were constant. I never actually wore the uniform as it was far too hot, but some of the boys sorted me out the smallest pair of Khaki shorts they could find, which wrapped around me almost twice! Our band consisted of just me, a pianist and a driver most of the time. It was very basic, but I always felt safe.

'I would just turn up at my destination to sing. One of the most expensive stages I ever sang on was constructed using crates containing six Spitfire engines. It was covered with parachute silk.

'Sometimes I would watch as soldiers walked out of the jungle, sat with their rifles throughout the concert and then got up and disappeared back into the jungle at the end.'

I wondered if she knew what was happening on the battlefield while she was there? 'Not really,' replied Dame Vera. 'Although it was very strange to arrive at places where the troops had been told I'd been killed in an air raid somewhere else.

'Dimapour really affected me. There were so many wounded and what with the smell, I

Dame Vera received a letter recently with a photograph and the words, ' I am the baby you are holding in that photograph.' Dame Vera regularly receives letters from folk all over the world whose lives have been touched in big and small ways by this most remarkable lady.

am ashamed to say my tummy turned over, so I asked for a drink of water. They had no water, but somehow found some lemonade.'

I asked her if there was anything she would like to have done differently, to which she replied, 'Yes, I wish I could have kept a diary, but it was forbidden in case we were captured. When I got home I recorded a lot of what happened but it isn't the same as a day-to-day account. I still get letters, cards and photographs from people I met and I recently received a photograph with a letter explaining that the sender was the baby I am holding in the photograph!'

I asked Dame Vera if she could remember where she was on D-Day: 'Flying home from Burma, via Cairo, Djerba and Gibraltar, I was aware something big was going on. An army official was listening intently to the radio in the cockpit. Later I found out it was D-Day.'

Dame Vera shared some of her extensive and fascinating photograph collection with me. It includes pictures of her taken with groups of soldiers and also visiting one of the very basic hospital shacks in Burma. She has photos of herself with Joe Loss and Glenn Miller and another with Bob Hope.

'I received a letter this week from a lady who was in Occupied Holland,' said Dame Vera, ' She and her family would listen to *Sincerely Yours* on Sunday nights. This was very dangerous because if you were caught listening to the radio you would be shot. There was no electricity or batteries, but necessity being the mother of invention, they took the back wheel off a bicycle, and rigged it up to a generator. The one in the group with the most stamina had to pedal steadily for the duration so that they could all listen to the show. If the pedalling faltered, the music wavered!'

In the Nick of Time

How a veteran and a razor went back to El Alamein after a six decade interval.

Left: Peter Theobald at the El Alamein Museum leans on a German 88mm gun.

There has never been a shortage of stories for *Sixty Years On*. The book, after all, deals with a period of time that's within living memory still of so many people. Whilst a great deal of material was sent in unsolicited from addresses all over Britain, a number of contributors live in and around my home town of Lewes in East Sussex.

Eighth Army veteran Peter Theobald is one example. My wife and I have known him for many years (I was at school with his daughter Pauline) and we share a common interest in supporting the local non-league football team, Lewes FC. Indeed, Peter had even played for Lewes before the Second World War!

Chatting to him about the *Sixty Years On* project, Peter responded with tales of his time in the Eighth Army in North Africa. He'd made the rank of Sergeant in the Royal Army Ordnance Corps and had been in charge of mobile equipment. He'd gone out to North Africa in mid-1941 aboard the *Strathnaver*, a troopship with three funnels that set sail from Scotland.

Peter served in the Western Desert when things weren't going so well for the British and he remembers Luftwaffe raids and bad news such as the fall of Tobruk. He was lucky; the worst that happened to him was a very painful injection following contact with a suspected rabid dog.

Peter was still there when Montgomery took over and remembers how the General transformed the morale of the Eighth Army and reinforced them with masses of tanks and guns.

After the victory at El Alamein, Peter went with the British Army right along the North African shore, all the way to Tunisia, in pursuit of the Afrika Korps. With the Germans out of Africa, much of the Eighth Army went first to Sicily and then on to Italy. Peter, however, headed back the way he'd come and ended up as part of an advance unit in Haifa in Palestine. They were earmarked for occupying the Greek islands but the order to go never came. He remained in the Middle East for the rest of the war, came home for a month's leave around VJ Day time when he remembers people dancing in the streets in Lewes. He was finally back in Blighty for good in January 1946 and soon afterwards Peter and girlfriend Ethel got married.

At around Christmas 2004, I asked Peter if he'd ever wanted to go back to Egypt. Flights from Gatwick direct to a new airport at El Alamein were starting in the spring and a new luxury hotel complex was opening on the coast of the Med. He said he'd jump at the chance. Having in recent years survived a heart attack and couple of strokes, he wasn't worried about health implications and nor was his doctor. So we applied for funding to be made under the Heroes Return scheme, where Lottery money was available for veterans who wished to revisit places where they'd served in the war.

Peter, myself and my wife went to El Alamein in April 2005. It was a splendid trip. As well as visiting the well-tended and beautifully maintained battlefield cemetery and wandering around the El Alamein Museum, we were able to go to Cairo on an overnight excursion and see the awesome Pyramids. In a Coptic church in the city, Peter remembered having lit a candle there over six decades before.

All the Egyptian people we met made us very welcome; Peter had a few ice cold beers and even enjoyed an enthusiastic session with the obligatory belly dancer. It was hard to believe that a luxury hotel and resort with swimming pools had sprung up in the middle of this desert battleground. Peter told us that in his Eighth Army days, he would sometimes get just a single mug of water a day to wash and shave with and often had little more than a hole in the ground to sleep in!

Talking of close shaves, when it was time to return, we went to El Alamein Airport and checked in our baggage. When Peter put his hand luggage through the X-Ray machine, it triggered an alarm. Within seconds he was surrounded by security men, demanding to know what was in his bag.

It took around 10 minutes to sort the problem out; Peter had packed his razor in his hand luggage, contrary to the rules. But he didn't want to see the razor confiscated. He wanted to take it back home with him. Eventually, it was agreed that the razor would fly up front with the Captain and be reunited with Peter at Gatwick.

So why was this item so precious to Peter? It turned out to be the very same razor he'd had with him in the desert in 1942 and it's still today perfectly functional for close shaves!

STOP PRESS!

Just as this book was going to print, the Dripping Pan (where Lewes FC play) provided another coincidence that I knew just had to go in these pages, even if it meant shouting 'Stop Press'.

At an FA Cup game, my attention was drawn to a gentleman wearing an Airborne tie. I introduced myself and he told me he was Sid Sallis and that he was at the game with his son Tom and daughter-in-law Jane because Tom had regularly played for Lewes some 36 seasons or so before.

I asked Sid about the tie and he told me he'd been with the Sixth Airborne Division during the war and in Palestine in 1946 trying to keep the peace between the Jews and the Arabs.

I told Sid I'd get his name in *Sixty Years On* for no other reason than the sheer coincidence of meeting him. At which point he opened his wallet and gave me the photograph reproduced here. He explained that he does go to reunions and has been to Arnhem with First Airborne veterans. But he has a few mates from the Paras that he hasn't seen in 60 years and it would be amazing if he got news of them all this time later.

I also learnt that daughter-in-law Jane is a member of the Commercial Square Bonfire Society. It's a small town!

A LOST BROTHER
Remembered

Above: Arthur Gordon (left) with Peter Theobald in the Battle of El Alamein Museum

While at El Alamein we met Arthur Gordon, a sprightly 80-year-old from Dundee, who was wearing a kilt in the hotel on his first night there. Arthur had seen the mention of the hotel in the *Sixty Years On* instalment of February 2005. He had then applied to the Heroes Return scheme to ask if they would fund a visit so that he could pay his respects for his brother at the Alamein Memorial and cemetery.

Arthur's older brother, Norman, had been a Flight Sergeant in the RAF 205 Squadron and the pair had last seen each other in 1941. On 15 April 1942 Norman's aircraft was reported missing on a mission over the Mediterranean; Arthur believes he flew from a base in the Western Desert of North Africa. Six months later the family received confirmation that Norman must be presumed dead. No body was ever found and so his death on active service was marked with his name appearing in the El Alamein Memorial, together with many others having no known grave.

Being four years younger than his brother, Arthur's war began later, after spending two years in Carlisle as an evacuee from Newcastle. At the age of 17 he put his name down for the Fleet Air Arm and was called up a year later in 1943. He did his training at Arbroath and *HMS St Vincent*, Gosport and spent some time at the Anti-Submarine School in Londonderry as well as other establishments. At the Royal Naval College, Greenwich, he recalls seeing Doodlebugs overhead in June 1944.

Arthur flew as an Observer in Swordfish, Albacore and Walrus aircraft and served aboard the *MV Alexia*, a Merchant Aircraft Carrier (MAC) that was manned by the Merchant Navy, together with RNVR, Army and RAF

personnel. He describes the ship as an 'oil tanker with a lid on top'. It carried four Swordfish on deck and Arthur accompanied it as part of a convoy that assembled off the coast of Northern Ireland and made the crossing to Nova Scotia.

On his first flight from a carrier forward of the convoy, the Swordfish had to ditch in the sea some 15 miles ahead of the ships after suffering engine problems. Arthur and his two crew companions scrambled into a dinghy and were picked up by *HMCS New Glasgow* when it reached their location. Bad weather meant they had to spend several days on the Canadian warship before being returned to their vessel, *Alexia*. For ditching in the sea, Arthur qualified to join the 'Goldfish Club'. *The equivalent for airmen who had to use a parachute to escape an air crash was the 'Caterpillar Club', so-called because of the connection with the silk used to make parachutes.*

From January to March 1945 he flew in Barracuda aircraft. Later, after more training at Londonderry, he resumed anti-submarine work. Then came VE Day and he was sent on leave. He was demobbed in October 1946.

Arthur met his wife Irene when she was in the WRNS in wartime Londonderry. Post-war he took a Reconstruction Examination for the Civil Service and went on to pursue a career in HM Customs and Excise.

This poster dates from the North Africa Desert campaign days and depicts a bright future for travel and recreation after the war. Some six decades on and it's come true with an international airport and luxury holiday resorts springing up at El Alamein!

Acknowledgements

I am grateful for the support and assistance of a large number of people who have helped with this project in many different ways. Some of them are named here, in no particular order:

Sue Worsley, Anna Hyman, Tom Johnson, Sarah Harvey, Mary Kalmus, Sharon Hitchcock, Julia Holland, Joey Clark, Kate Telfer, Malcolm Ashby, Chloe Dyson, Jon Partridge, Simon Jones, John Roy, Sean McGreevy, Sue Angell, David, Rose, Rob, Tim, Nicola, Marion and all at Oliver & Graimes Design Associates, Ron McGill, Christopher Portway, Bob Mayston, Martin Barton-Smith, Steve Mosley, The National Archives (especially Jason Hargreaves, Sam Evans and Daniel Sherman), Andrew Wilson and the late Alan Wilkins. I also extend my thanks to all my colleagues at **csma** Headquarters for their encouraging words when this project began taking over my entire life. My thanks are also due to the **csma** Board of Directors for their full support in making the production of this book possible.

Whilst information on the history of World War II is widely available, this book would not exist but for the many hundreds of people who submitted their stories and photographs. I am so sorry that I could not include everyone's contribution and if your story or letter does not appear in this volume please do know that I am grateful nonetheless that you made the effort. There are many fascinating tales that remain untold so, who knows, if this book proves to be a popular success then perhaps a second volume may be forthcoming.

I also must thank my family for putting up with me over many, many months of obsession in pulling this project together. Above all, my wife Barbara has been wonderful and unstinting in her support; at times the interior of my house has been literally covered in blizzards of proofs, photographs, manuscripts and documents galore.

Finally, I dedicate this book to the memory of my brother Jimmy Arnold (1955 -1966) and the happy hours we spent playing with our army of little soldiers.

David Arnold, Editor, Sixty Years On

Links to the Past

Christina Lee looks at how the world wide web is an ally in the search for information about people who lost their lives in wartime.

'In Britain we remember those no longer serving, including those who have died for their country; for we in this nation have a deep and abiding respect for our past' - Her Majesty The Queen's Jubilee Address to the Armed Services, broadcast on BFBS 26 June 2002.

We remember the fallen, not only for our own peace of mind, but also, to show future generations the price that was paid for their freedom. As those who fought in the two World Wars are increasingly no longer with us, bringing history to life with their oral accounts, we look to monuments and graves in order to remember and understand.

It is important to note Britain's standing army was not formed until the 17th century, and prior to the 20th century mass graves were rare and the bodies of officers were usually repatriated for burial. This all changed with the First World War, when shockingly efficient weapons of mass destruction (machine guns and artillery) in the hands of both sides led to a military stalemate and static trench warfare where enormous casualties were sustained. Britain and her Empire recorded 1,104,890 fallen (between 1914 and 1918); it is almost impossible for us today to conceive of the grief and trauma of those left behind.

It was against this backdrop that the Commonwealth War Graves Commission was founded by Royal Charter in 1917. This body established the principles that: each of the dead should be commemorated individually by name on a headstone or memorial; headstones and memorials should be permanent; headstones should be uniform; and there should be no distinction made on account of military or civil rank, race or creed. These principles were extended to the dead of the Second World War. The duties of the Commission are, therefore, to mark and maintain the graves of members of the forces of the Commonwealth, to build memorials to those that have no known grave and to keep records and registers, including, after the Second World War, a record of the civilian casualties.

In total approximately 1,700,000 men and women of the Commonwealth died in the two World Wars. Of these the remains of 925,000 were found and their graves are marked by a headstone. Where the remains have not been found, the casualty's name is commemorated on a memorial. There are war graves in over 150 countries, mostly in the 2500 war cemeteries and plots constructed by the War Graves Commission.

The 'Debt of Honour Register', available online at **www.cwgc.org**, is the Commission's database listing the details of the 1.7 million who died and the 23,000 cemeteries, memorials and other locations world-wide where they are commemorated. You can search the database

Men and women of many nationalities are remembered in the cemeteries around Cassino. Here we picture the last resting place for 4267 British and Commonwealth casualties and a sign indicating the location of the German cemetery. We also reproduce a postcard that shows the Polish Military Cemetery in its dramatic setting within sight of the famous Montecassino Monastery. Around 1000 Poles died in the battles for the town and the mountain peaks that were the key to prising open the Gustav Line. Polish-born Pope John Paul II had visited the Monastery on a number of occasions.

easily by entering the casualty's surname, initials, which war they died in, the year of death, the force they served in and their nationality. It is not necessary to enter all the information; for example, if you don't know the year of death, the search engine will still send back accurate results.

I used a personal example to undertake the search. My uncle, Neil Kirkwood Devlin, died in Singapore - I did not know his year of death. The search results showed his rank, his service number, the date of death and his regiment. More importantly, particularly to my mother, his sister, they also told me where he was commemorated. From this initial information return I clicked to be forwarded to a page which confirmed his parents' names (so I knew I had the right man), and in the cemetery section I was able to view the details of the Singapore Memorial, including location and historical information. I was staggered to find that the number of identified casualties totalled 24,313.

My mother still has the telegram from King George VI telling her that her brother had died and commending his valiant effort in defending his country, she also still has his regimental staff, which I believe some of his comrades gave to her after the war. Finding the

memorial was important to her, seeing that his death and name are marked allows her to feel in some small way that his sacrifice has not been forgotten. For me, who never knew him, it provides a link to the past, and an understanding of the phrase 'Lest We Forget'.

INDEX

The Spitfire of intrepid lady pilot Carolyn Grace appeared at the Sixty Years On event at Glynde and enthralled the crowd with a wonderful flying display performed to stirring music from the orchestra. Carolyn's Spitfire actually flew in 1944 - 45 and is credited with shooting down the first enemy aircraft to be destroyed over Normandy on D-Day. In tribute to Carolyn, artist and designer Bob Mayston painted this evocative work he has simply titled Sixty Years On.

+ + + SEVERAL PAGES FOLLOW ON WHICH YOU MAY LIKE TO PLACE YOUR OWN MEMORIES OR FAMILY +
+ + + + STORIES CONCERNING WORLD WAR II TURNING SIXTY YEARS ON INTO A FAMILY MEMENTO + +